The Shaping of the American Past

VOLUME 2

Robert Kelley

University of California, Santa Barbara

The Shaping of the American Past

VOLUME 2

Third Edition

Prentice-Hall, Inc. Englewood Cliffs, New Jersey 07632

Library of Congress Cataloging in Publication Data

Kelley, Robert Lloyd, (1925)
    The shaping of the American past.

    Bibliography: p.
    Includes index.
    1. United States—History. I. Title
E178.1.K27   1982   973   81-10527
ISBN-0-13-808147-6 (pbk. : v. 1)   AACR2
ISBN 0-13-808154-9 (pbk. : v. 2)

THE SHAPING OF THE AMERICAN PAST
Third Edition
Robert Kelley
Volume 2

Printed in the United States of America
10 9 8 7 6 5 4 3 2

Editorial/production supervision by Marina Harrison
Interior and cover design by Suzanne Behnke
Picture research by Anita Duncan
Cover painting by George Luks, *Armistice Night* (1918).
    Oil on canvis. 37 × 68¾ inches. Collection of Whitney
    Museum of American Art. Anonymous gift.
Acquisition editor: Stephen Dalphin
Manufacturing buyer: Edmund W. Leone

Acknowledgments of Excerpts

p. 558, copyright Alfred A. Knopf, Inc.

p. 572, reprinted by permission of Grove Press, Inc.
Copyright © 1961 by Grove Press, Inc.

pp. 678–79, reprinted from *Russia and the United States*
by Nikolai V. Sivachev and Nikolai N. Yakovlev by permission of The University of Chicago Press. Copyright
© 1979 The University of Chicago Press.

p. 713, from *A Rising Wind* by Walter White. Copyright
© 1945 by Walter White. Reprinted by permission of
Doubleday & Company, Inc.

p. 795, from Arthur M. Schlesinger, Jr., *Imperial Presi-
dency.* Copyright © 1973 by Arthur M. Schlesinger, Jr.
Used by permission of the publisher, Houghton Mifflin
Company.

p. 802, copyright © 1972 by Newsweek, Inc. All rights reserved. Reprinted by permission.

p. 823, copyright © 1970 by Robin Morgan. Reprinted
with permission from *Sisterhood is Powerful: An Anthology of Writings from the Women's Liberation Movement,*
R. Morgan, ed. (Random House and Vintage Books, 1970).

p. 825, copyright © 1970, The Atlantic Monthly Company, Boston, Mass. Reprinted with permission of the
author.

p. 825, reprinted by permission of The Sterling Lord
Agency, Inc. Copyright © 1972.

p. 832, reprinted by permission of *The New Republic,*
© 1980 The New Republic, Inc.

Prentice-Hall International, Inc., *London*
Prentice-Hall of Australia Pty. Limited, *Sydney*
Prentice-Hall of Canada, Ltd., *Toronto*
Prentice-Hall of India Private Limited, *New Delhi*
Prentice-Hall of Japan, Inc., *Tokyo*
Prentice-Hall of Southeast Asia Pte. Ltd., *Singapore*
Whitehall Books Limited, *Wellington, New Zealand*

to Madge

CONTENTS

Preliminary Remarks to the Third Edition

Introduction: The Historian's Task

20

Reconstruction

21

Late Nineteenth-Century America: Growth and Development

CONTENTS

22

Late Nineteenth-Century America: The Nation in Crisis

23

Gilded Age Politics: Instability and Impasse

24

Emergence to World Power

25

The Progressive Era: New Ways of Thinking

26

The Progressive Era: Republicans in Charge

27

The Progressive Era: Democrats in Charge

28

America and the First World War

29

American Life and Thought Between the Wars

30

The New Era: Triumph and Disaster

31

Franklin D. Roosevelt and the New Deal

CONTENTS

32

America and the Second World War

33

The Cold War

34

Complacent Years: Truman and Eisenhower

35

The Turbulent 1960s: The Egalitarian Surge Builds Momentum

36

The Turbulent 1960s: The Flood Tide of Reform Peaks and Falls Back

37

The End of American Innocence: The Vietnam War

CONTENTS

38

Watergate and the 1970s

39

The American People and Nation: Comparisons

CONTENTS

PRELIMINARY REMARKS TO THE THIRD EDITION

History is narrative. This book has been written most of all with that in mind. On the other hand, history is not simply one thing after another, for there are patterns in it which endure over many generations. It is these continuities in history, in fact, which are the most revealing things to search for as we examine the past, since we find in them the past's links to the present. It is crucially important to learn that the basic characteristics in American life and thought which shaped us in our beginnings in the seventeenth century still shape us today. This book begins, therefore, by exploring briefly these characteristics as they existed in the homeland from which the colonials principally came, and then follows these qualities as they evolved through the succeeding generations in this country.

In this way, an interpretive framework ties the book together, from its first chapter to the last (where a retrospective look at the preceding century of American life, from the 1870s to the 1970s, ties together the narrative's main themes and provides an overall assessment). The flow of ideas is the central stream in the narrative. From its origins America was not simply a place and a human society, it was an experience in the mind, an argument—or rather, a group of arguments around a common concept. Historians in recent years have discovered that *republicanism* was the energizing political faith which impelled Americans into their Revolution, and then inspired them as their national ideology for at least a hundred years thereafter—following which it persisted just as urgently as before, save that the language and terminology were changed. The narrative in this book follows the fate of republicanism through these many generations into the 1970s. It also periodically explores the larger history of ideas, from the Puritans to the Pragmatists, from John Locke to Sigmund Freud and Herbert Marcuse.

America is a large country with many kinds of peoples who have had differing interests and hopes. Consequently, though republicanism was the broad national ideology that all shared, Americans from the beginning had differing ideas as to what it really meant. Arguments began, and people quickly lined up in opposing ranks, forming alliances against common political enemies. Out of this came two national political parties which materialized with surprising swiftness in the 1790s, the first decade after adoption of the Constitution. Under varying names, these two parties have endured with remarkable persistence for two hundred years. Through them, Americans have argued out what their country should be, and have selected the people and the ideas they wished to have govern the nation.

The central focus of American life, in fact, lies in its politics. Here, in reality, may be found our national theatre. The lights are almost never out; something is always on the boards. In the play itself we reveal ourselves as a people, proclaim our values, our animosities, our fears. Recently it was my experience to be a visiting professor of American history at Moscow University in the USSR, and while teaching undergraduate and graduate students in that setting, I observed (and aided) the historians there conducting

PREFACE

a long-range study of our national political parties since their origins. Nowhere else, they believe, do all the strands which make up American life come together so openly and interconnectedly as in our politics. From its first edition, this book has been built around that same concept. Politics is the focus of the narrative: conflict, argument, the clash of ideas, of economic motives, of cultural forces.

In history, we observe not only the shaping influence of large movements, we note the impact of the personal element as well. What if Lincoln had been a Franklin Pierce or a Calvin Coolidge, unable to inspire and to lead, bereft of a capacity for vision and good judgment and iron will? The influence of particular individuals shapes events in every setting, from the family to the nation at large. Seeing history through biography, then, is not only intriguing, it is sound historical philosophy, and the narrative in this book has taken close looks at key personalities and their role. In the present edition the biographical approach has been deepened by beginning each chapter with a brief vignette which focuses on an individual whose life illustrates a major theme within that chapter.

Together, these vignettes offer a composite portrait of a many-sided (pluralistic) society: an immigrant philosopher, an Indian woman, and an inventor; a gifted black poet, two labor leaders, a Franciscan priest and missionary, and a revolutionary; an atomic physicist, a runaway slave who became a great abolitionist leader, and two men who struggled to hold back the inflooding tide of whites upon Indian lands. There is the head of a lost cause, and a caustic Yankee senator; a brilliant conservationist, and a woman who pioneered the slum settlement house and inspired a generation of social reformers. These people, and the others chosen—such as Queen Elizabeth I, J. Pierpont Morgan, and Al Smith; Betty Friedan, Douglas MacArthur, and Denmark Vesey—tell us much of who we are, what Americans have believed in, and how things have happened.

In recent years, social history as a field of research has been exceptionally active. The historical literature on women, children, and the family, as well as upon demographics (population trends), immigration, and other social topics is now quite rich. From this book's early chapters to the end, therefore, social history has been given greatly expanded treatment. The colonial chap-

ters have been extensively recast and rewritten, and they contain much on the village, the life of labor, and race relations. Indian history, and the history of the Spanish-speaking, black Americans, Catholics, Jews, Germans, and other peoples, take up significantly more attention. Demographic patterns are explored, the process of industrialization has been carefully examined, women's history is returned to again and again, in each period of national history,* and American labor history is considerably expanded.

From fresh standpoints in recent scholarship, there are also new discussions of the nature of slavery, Reconstruction, and segregation, as well as of that formidable and always absorbing topic, the causes of the Civil War. Southern and Western populism appear in a new perspective. The social and cultural dimensions in Progressivism are closely examined, and a new way of understanding the nature of Progressivism, and its politics, is presented. At several points in the narrative on the twentieth century, links between the politics and ideas of this period and the republicanism of the nation's first century are explored. The 1920s and 1930s are extensively re-examined, in an expanded treatment. Based on what I learned while living and working in the Soviet Union, the role of the USSR in the Second World War, and the way the Soviet peoples feel about that conflict and the ensuing Cold War, have been brought into the narrative so that both sides of the question, whatever their intrinsic merits, may be better understood. "Revisionism" among American historians toward the Cold War is discussed herein at greater depth than formerly, and the Supreme Court revolution under Chief Justice Earl Warren has been taken up within larger dimensions.

I have always felt that historians miss their greatest opportunity to demonstrate to students how the past flows into and shapes the present when they give reduced attention to the years after 1945. The national scene which currently surrounds us is fascinating to observe not only for the reason that we are involved in it, but because the past so prominently (and daily) surfaces in it. For this reason, in the present edition as in its predecessors, I have worked as diligently to examine, reflect upon, and narrate the story of the last twenty years as I have concerning

---

* Refer to the extensive Time Line of Women's History in the Appendix.

PREFACE

comparable periods in earlier times. In fact, this feature of the book—its detailed narrative of the years since 1960 to tie the present to the past—has been considerably strengthened and enriched in this edition.

In this connection, the Kennedy-Johnson years have been rethought and recast, with new attention to Kennedy's role in the Second Reconstruction, the impact of the Cuban missile crisis, and—especially—the surprising results of the Immigration Reform Act of 1965, which has inaugurated a new era in America's ethnic makeup. Particularly attentive looks have been taken at Japanese-Americans, the Hispanic insurge, and Chicano culture. Richard Nixon's intriguing foray into national planning, with its historic emphasis upon environmental controls, and his creation of the "New Federalism," have been examined at some length. The terminal point in the narrative is now the presidency of Jimmy Carter, whose achievements and failures are analyzed, and at the same time an extended exploration of the revolution among women and in the family since the 1950s is presented. The concluding chapter, reflecting the great increase in social history in the narrative throughout, has been retitled "The American *People and* Nation." The entire chapter, which consists of comparisons across time and space, has been rewritten and new topics added, producing a much-expanded concluding essay. In all, approximately two-thirds of the chapters in *The Shaping of the American Past* have either been rewritten in major ways, or have had new historical information included. The result is a somewhat larger book, richer in illuminating detail, considerably wider in scope, and more broadly in touch with existing scholarship.

Looking at our national experience over its whole sweep gives us understandings of ourselves that we can acquire in no other way. For this reason, many of us who teach American history find giving the survey course our most exacting challenge. Tying it all together, giving the history of this country a framework and an inner structure of explanation, is surely our largest task as historians of the United States of America. Offering the beginning course never fails to teach the teacher a great deal. It requires staying in touch with new research in many fields, a task with its own pleasures. And it means coming to grips with the central issue: what is the essential American experience? How best to grasp it, depict it to stu-

dents? Teaching as a life work involves regularly confronting new times with new generations of students, and new problems before us as a people which must be examined historically. Also, the flow of fresh research, from historians here and abroad, provides ever deeper understandings of the past. Thus we find ourselves telling a different story, as the decades pass. Often it is not that the earlier version was wrong, but rather that that story no longer answers the questions we are now asking of the past. Of course, the main events still occur, and every historian must deal with them. The Revolution takes place, Theodore Roosevelt gets elected, and the Cold War seizes the world. But these old and accustomed topics, as well as many other aspects of our past, are being looked at in unaccustomed ways.

So it is that the political narrative in this history is presented from the vantage point of what has been called the "new political history." Politics, this new approach holds, is shaped by *cultural* forces as well as by *economic* ones. It is not just a matter of dollars and cents, or of controversies over land and tariffs. In part this new thesis springs from cultural anthropology and the depth psychology of Sigmund Freud; in part from what we have experienced since the 1930s. The Second World War revealed the appalling power of cultural hatreds. Driven by these feelings, Adolf Hitler massacred millions of Jews and millions of the Slavic peoples of the USSR. In a similar mood, the American government incarcerated Japanese residents and citizens, and far more freely bombed the peoples of Japan than it did those of Germany. Scholars now realize that cultural identities, feelings, and conflicts provide an explosively active force in public life. We see not only farmers against bankers and laborers against employers, but Scotch-Irish against the English in the Revolutionary period, Catholics against Protestants in most of American history, as well as pietists against free thinkers, blacks against whites, Chicanos against WASPs, teetotalers against drinkers, and Yankees against white Southerners—to take only a representative sampling of these conflicts. People have to make a living, and they have material ambitions: hence, economic politics. They also have to have meaning in life, and want to live in certain ways: hence, cultural politics. Sometimes one influence is dominant, and takes all our attention; sometimes the other absorbs the country. Cultural politics obsessed the 1920s, while economic issues took practically all attention in the 1930s.

Observed in this light, American political history takes on a different aspect from the one we are used to. We see it shaped in good part by a bipolar rivalry between the English-British-WASP "host culture" (identified with the Federalist party and its descendants, the Whigs of the age of Andrew Jackson and the modern Republican party, formed in the 1850s), and the many minority groups—the "outsiders" (identified with the Democratic party and its predecessor, the Jeffersonian Republicans). Tactics may change, but this line of battle has persisted with remarkable tenacity from the beginnings. (In another work, *The Cultural Pattern in American Politics: The First Century* [1979], and in "Ideology and Political Culture from Jefferson to Nixon," *The American Historical Review*, 82 [June 1977], 531–562, I have been able to explore these matters, and the origins of this way of historical thinking, in greater depth than is possible herein, with citations to appropriate sources.)

This Edition remains what former editions have been: it is a book written as if I were speaking directly, face to face, to the students who will be reading it, talking to them through the typewriter. This whole enterprise is aimed at helping them *understand* their country, and through that experience, themselves. All it takes is a time of living and working in a genuinely foreign culture to learn how true it is that to understand the peoples of that country, we must first ask, what has been their experience through time? The Chinese, the Irish, the Russians, the Germans: how could anyone comprehend them and their distinctive societies, even the particular ways in which individual persons within them behave day by day, without looking at their history? It is no different with ourselves.

My thanks go to the professors who have used this book in their classrooms in its earlier editions and have given me advice as to improving it. That *The Shaping of the American Past* has been put to use in several hundred institutions of higher learning by fellow historians, here and abroad, has been a most heartening encourage-

ment. I wish also to thank the students who, while learning from the book, have said that they have enjoyed reading it, and have been intrigued by its approach. Searching out the nature and meaning of the American past has been a rich learning experience for me at least since I began teaching American history, in the early 1950s, to undergraduate students at UC Santa Barbara. It has been a rare privilege, in this book's several editions, to be able to share the results of that search with so many colleagues, and with so many younger and older students, in practically every state of the Union and overseas.

Many reviewers in the historical profession provided detailed critiques and commentaries. For their invaluable assistance, I am grateful to Richard M. Abrams, University of California, Berkeley; Richard Beeman, University of Pennsylvania; Joseph Blackman, Tulsa Junior College; Stephen Botein, Michigan State University; John Buser, Del Mar College; Richard T. Farrell, University of Maryland; Patrick Foley, Tarrant County Junior College; John Howe, University of Minnesota; Harvey H. Jackson, Clayton Junior College; John Kushma, University of Texas at Arlington; Walter Licht, University of Pennsylvania; Howard N. Rabinowitz, University of New Mexico; and Philip R. Royal, Jefferson State Junior College.

Two colleagues at UC Santa Barbara have aided me, for which I am also grateful: Mario T. García has again considerably reviewed the pages on Chicano history and culture, and Patricia C. Cohen has read carefully through the sections on the history of women and related topics, offering me valuable suggestions. My editors at Prentice-Hall, Inc., especially Marina Harrison and Steve Dalphin, have skillfully guided the publication of the Third Edition.

From first to last, my wife Madge has once more read every line of the manuscript, serving as my valued and thoughtful first reader, and she has encouraged me at every turn in this lengthy undertaking. If the book reads clearly and makes sense, those who study it hereafter have her, most of all, to thank—as here, for them and for myself, I now do.

Robert Kelley

INTRODUCTION: THE HISTORIAN'S TASK

What is the *value* of history? Why has humanity studied its history for literally thousands of years? Tribes that lack a system of writing commonly have a "Rememberer" whose task it is to commit to memory (by learning it from an older Rememberer in the tribe) all the important things that have happened to that people. He tells the young who they are, what their tribe has suffered through, what things they have learned, who their gods are, and the values given to them that they must follow. History, in this sense, was probably one of the earliest distinctively human activities to emerge when *Homo sapiens* made their appearance many thousands of years ago. Language and recorded memory: they appear to have been born together.

This is so because human beings have a sense of time—a sense that things happen in sequence, the appearance of each laying the basis for what follows. Thus, we early sensed that we cannot understand ourselves or the world surrounding us without seeing how things have evolved, over time, into what they are. This applies to the history of civilizations; it applies to the history of a town or an industry; it applies to individual lives. No one can be understood simply as he or she stands before us, having taken some intelligence test or shown us what they like or are afraid of. Rather, we instinctively ask, Where did you come from? What has happened to you? What do you do? Why? We are historians of each other in our daily lives.

All of us are imbedded in a culture, in a larger society, that has itself evolved out of the dim past into what it is now. It shapes us, just as we, during the brief span of our individual lives, shape it. The value of history, therefore, comes from its giving to us that same strong basis for understanding the culture that rears us and makes us what we are, that we acquire when we learn about the background of someone we want to be close to and work with.

The value of history lies in more practical directions as well, as we have been discovering in recent years. The nation at large is engaged in rediscovering its *local* history. Americans are tired of being mobile; the "new" is not so exciting. They want a sense of roots, and they are turning to historians to ask, How did this community evolve? Where are the marks of its past, its earlier peoples and eras, as seen in particular buildings or neighborhoods that should be restored and preserved? In city after city "old towns" are appearing, their discovery guided by painstaking research into the surviving records and artifacts. Also, governing officials are starting to ask, What is the origin of our policies, of the issues we are dealing with, and how did they evolve over time? Where did our water rights come from (because we ae being sued over them)? Why was this flood-control system designed as it is? For what specific reasons did we take this policy toward that country, or toward wheat surpluses, or toward atomic energy?

The dimension of time: this is the historian's unique commodity, and in a country that is no longer heading into the future in such a pell-mell rush but wants to know how it came to where it is, the historian is becoming an ever more valuable person. The historical profession is no longer concerned just with teaching students in class about the past; it is also solving problems in the surrounding public scene. We are, in short, entering the era of "public history" and the "public historian." If the historical method can be brought into the public process so that policy makers consider how the issues they deal with have evolved into their present form—and not just examine the existing nature and context of these issues—that process will have been made more informed and effective.

Of course, in the classroom academic historians have long sought to do just this. As each generation has faced new problems, historical research has looked in new directions to explain them. When a depression occurs, economic history has flourished and many books on this topic have appeared. When civil rights became a great national problem, historians began searching in the past for the background to this issue and started writing books on black history and race relations. Now that we are concerned with changing the role of women, histories of women in our past, and of the family, have begun appearing from the book publishers. When Americans awakened to the fact that they were a world power, diplomatic history became an active field of study (which it remains today). So we have known for a long time that the value of history is in good part the help it gives us as we attempt to understand the present scene.

History, however, is not read simply because it is "relevant." It has purposes that reach deep into the human condition. History is valuable to the educated mind because it takes us out of the present. By steeping ourselves in the history of an older time or of different peoples, we broaden the horizons of our mind. We develop a greater sensitivity to human possibilities, are humbled by the knowledge that our present culture is not the only way, or perhaps even the best way, that human beings have lived. This helps us begin to lose the present-mindedness that makes for superficial thought. In other words, we become less provincial, less inclined to think that the whole world, all of human life, is somehow exactly like—or should be like—what we see in front of us in our daily lives. In this sense, as the English historian and statesman Thomas Babington Macaulay observed, history is like foreign travel.

History serves, in short, not only specific purposes (how was the TVA built?—for we might want to build another one), but also the large purposes of giving us fundamental understandings of humanity and society: What motivates people in politics? What have our failures been, and our successes? What is it that holds us together as a people? Is life just a repetitive round, or is it evolutionary? Can we anticipate goodness or evil in humankind? In the broadest sense, history is studied because it gives us a frame of reference.

If there are many ways in which history is used, one statement holds true of all historians as they go about their work: they are trying to find out as nearly as they can what the truth is about the past. They are attempting to answer the question of what happened and what it meant.

Thus, the historian searches for the kinds of documents that will bring him or her as close as possible to the events themselves. These are called *primary*-source materials, for they are produced by the people who participated in or observed the events. They include letters, diaries, speeches, news articles, testimonies of eyewitnesses, artifacts, and photographs. The historian will also look for all *secondary* sources that will help: books, articles, or reports prepared by someone else who has also studied the primary materials.

This search poses knotty problems: Are the letters genuine? Was the observer close to the event? Was he biased? Do other of his letters give a different picture? How soon after the events did he prepare his account? Are there other observers of the same events, and if so, do the accounts differ? If the document is old, what did the words commonly mean at the time they were written? If it is a secondary work, how thorough was the author's research, how impartial was he, and did he ask the right questions?

In short, historians test the evidence they find, using guidelines that their craft has developed over the generations. Above all, they are guided by a judicious skepticism. If the study of history teaches historians nothing else, it teaches that people usually do not fully understand or accurately report what they see. For this reason, the evidence they leave behind does not speak for itself. It usually presents a partial or conflicting story that must be sifted, analyzed, and skeptically yet sympathetically winnowed out. The person who examines historical evidence cannot just passively pile it up; he or she must penetrate it actively and search for the truth.

The problem, of course, is that all evidence is incomplete. We see everything in the past through the eyes of others, but a great deal of information is hidden even from them. Direct observation of a religious ceremony will not reveal much to the onlooker about what the ceremony means to the participants. Direct observation of a speaker will not tell us his motivations—which he may not understand himself.

Historians are hampered, too, by the fact that some activities produce documents while others do not and some societies preserve documents while others do not. A committee hearing produces documents; the dinner party held the evening before in which the committee members discussed the issue does not. The Normandy invasion produced mountains of documents; the Anglo-Saxon invasion of England, so important for all future history, was carried out by an illiterate people and is therefore almost totally beyond the reach of historians.

In short, much that is important about the past never gets written down. Historians have been compared to astronomers, who gather light on the mirror of their telescopes and try to decide what the dots and flares tell them about the universe, which they cannot visit personally. Historians, too, cannot visit the past and must search among its physical traces to elicit the story. In their case, however, many of the heavenly bodies *they* are trying to perceive never report their presence at all!

There is another problem. The American historian Carl Becker reminded us that all perception of historical facts is set in the framework of the perceiver's experience. We cannot avoid our preconceptions; they are the lenses through which we see the world. Each historian is alive to some aspects of the past, oblivious to others. Just as one person, walking into a crowded meeting, notices those individuals who are important to him or her and remains indifferent to the others, so historians who are by nature inclined to react to one class of evidence, while ignoring others will assess matters differently from their colleagues. They will "see" some evidence while being blind to other materials, not through conscious bias but simply because of the way their perceptions

work. If a historian is inclined to believe that the profit motive is the key factor in what people do, then he or she will "find" money, vested interest, and wealth-seeking behind events.

In other words, scientific history—reproducing the past exactly as it was—is not the hope of the historian. Not only is the past too huge and complex, not only is the evidence it leaves behind too incomplete, but also we are too subjective in our views, guard against this failing as we will.

For that matter, there is a vigorous tradition that the objectivity implied in the ideal of scientific history is not only impossible but undesirable. It implies blandness, purposelessness, lack of commitment. The British historian Lord Acton insisted that the historian must sit in judgment upon past men and their actions, and that the sentences passed must be terrible and harsh. To seek only to "understand" in the light of circumstances— "The Nazis set out to kill off the Jews, and from their point of view did a good job"—is to be guilty of an inhuman and destructive relativism.

Most historians feel, however, that while such terrible events as the massacring of the Jews may be easily condemned, there is a vast range of human activities that is not as easily assessed. The act of preparing oneself to be a historian does not simultaneously endow the scholar with intellect, experience, and knowledge superior to those of the presidents and premiers who actually had the job to do. Making harsh judgments of past individuals may only betray the arrogance of ignorance. An event that seems simple to someone reading about it in a university library may actually have been extremely complex and unmanageable when it took place. One must, therefore, practice the historical art with appropriate prudence, and try in most cases not to take sides. Suspension of judgment is a valuable historical virtue.

It remains true, however, that complete neutrality is impossible, and that proceeding as though it were possible is a mistake. Carl Becker's view perhaps sums up best the spirit in which most historians work: basic in their character must be a *concern* about the issues they examine, a deep involvement with the fate of the movements and ideas they describe. There cannot be, and should not be, impartial history in the sense of indifferent history.

These remarks about the subjective aspect of history should not lead to the assumption that the cumulative work of the profession is merely a collection of personal statements. Historians who are true to their craft seek always to base their work on verified facts, and they have succeeded in searching out and validating a steadily mounting quantity of factual historical data. The main point about the problem of the historians' own subjectivity and unconscious bias is that they must try to keep these dangers in mind and achieve as much honesty as they can. They are constantly searching for the facts that bear on the question they have asked of the past, and are continually making painful efforts to put the story together as truthfully as they can.

To the extent that history is factual, it is a social science. Historians now draw extensively upon the concepts and methods of the social sciences as they try to understand the past more deeply. From anthropologists we have taken the idea of "culture" as an organizing principle, and have focused on values, life styles, world views, and customs. Psychologists and sociologists have been looked to for theories about behavior, role theory, status and reference groups, and class and mobility. The application of quantitative methods to historical analysis is flourishing. Here we observe historians making *collective-biography* studies: analyses of large groups of people in the past designed to uncover common and varying characteristics. The methods used include counting the frequency of concepts and words used in speeches and writings (*content analysis*); making extensive population studies (*demography*); and analyzing voting and legislative behavior by the use of statistical methods (*correlation* and *regression*). More complex procedures appear in the use of mathematical models, in what is called the new economic history, to seek answers to such questions as whether slavery was profitable. All of this counting and the use of computers goes under the general term *Cliometrics*—Clio being the ancient muse of history.

There is much controversy about the use of these procedures. In fact, there is a spectrum of opinion and practice ranging from those historians who think of themselves as social scientists and who make rigorous efforts to be scientific in their procedures, to historians who insist that they are humanists, not scientists, and that they deal with essentially unquantifiable entities when studying and recounting the doings of human beings. The gifted historian Richard Hofstadter

perhaps said it best when he observed that the fresh perspectives provided by the social sciences add to "the speculative richness of history. The more the historian learns from the social sciences, the more variables he is likely to take into account, the more complex his task becomes."

Ultimately, however, most historians believe that their task is not to work out the laws of human behavior (the classic goal of social scientists), but to describe that behavior faithfully in its actual individuality, its actual forms, "warts and all," as Oliver Cromwell told his portraitist to paint him. We take the whole of human life as our concern, and we try to describe its multiplicity, its variety, its stubborn resistance to being shoved into any particular formula. We are essentially pluralists, in that most historians seem, with the philosopher William James, to believe that there is always something left over that does not fit whatever scheme of interpretation is being applied; that life stubbornly and persistently flows out of our ideological containers. Reality is "manyness," and it is best seen in particulars, in actual individuals doing actual things: that is, in narrative.

Therefore, historians do not seek to cast what they describe into a rational sytem. It is life's unpredictability, the uniqueness of each sequence of events, the capacity life has for presenting us with inexhaustible freshness and uniqueness that history celebrates. This means that our methods cannot be entirely rational. Historians must rely on such qualities as empathy—the capacity to feel oneself into an era, to look at life from inside the other person's situation.

Readers should not be misled by the factual character of the historical account, then, into making false analogies. The historian is not only a scientist with human perspectives but a creative artist as well. As Sir Lewis Namier has written, historians are like painters, not like photographers. They do not reproduce an exact image of the past, for they are certainly not interested just in its surface appearance. Rather, they analyze the whole, search for its essence, and paint on their canvas what is revealing and important. What matters in history, Sir Lewis observes, "is the great outline and the significant detail, what must be avoided is the deadly morass of irrelevant narrative."

It is in this sense that history is a branch of literature. The greatest practitioners call on the same resources of imaginative insight, grace and

INTRODUCTION

clarity of language, sensitivity to human experience, and concern with fundamental questions as do the great writers of fiction. It is, after all, the *human situation* that the historian seeks to describe.

So it is that some of the greatest historians have thought a great deal about the problems of narrative artistry. A brilliant producer of narrative history, Thomas Babington Macaulay, wrote that "history has its foreground and its background; and it is principally in the management of its perspective that one artist differs from another." The selection of detail by which to hint at the whole is extremely important. The portraitist does not depict every pore in the subject's skin, but rather its hue; not the eye entire, but its aspect. History, George Macaulay Trevelyan insisted, is "a tale." It must therefore be as full as life. It must flow; narrative must be its bedrock. The tale must show us past events as if they were fresh, as if we were participants. How is this achieved? By presenting the facts of the past not narrowly but in their full emotional and intellectual value. This requires that historians have "the largest grasp of intellect, the warmest human sympathy, the highest imaginative powers."

History, then, is at once science and art. This is an ambivalent and precarious condition. Perhaps the perceptive words of the great German historian Johann Gustav Droysen strike closest to the heart of the matter. For all its faults, Droysen remarked, "history is Humanity's knowledge of itself. It is not 'the light and the truth,' but a search therefore. . . ."

20

TIME LINE

1863 President Lincoln's Reconstruction plan issued

1864 Lincoln vetoes Wade-Davis bill
Black leaders form Equal Rights League

1865 Andrew Johnson becomes seventeenth president of the United States
Johnson attempts Reconstruction of the Union; Southern white governments formed; Freedmen's Bureau established
Thirteenth Amendment abolishes slavery
Ku Klux Klan formed

1866 Johnson vetoes Freedmen's Bureau extension
Civil-rights bill
Congressional elections establish large Republican majority

1867 First Reconstruction Act launches Radical Reconstruction
The French withdraw from Mexico
Alaska purchased

RECONSTRUCTION

New York Public Library

Among the Republicans, the party of anti-Southernism, the most prominent Radical was Charles Sumner of Massachusetts. Tall, lordly, learned, and eloquent, Sumner was as passionate in his hatreds as he was in his affections. Because of his Senate speeches before the Civil War, he was reviled in the South as a "serpent," a "filthy reptile," and a "leper." Yankee to the bone, in love with English ways and culture, he shared aristocratic England's view that much of American life was lawless, crude, narrow, and ignorant, and that slavery was America's greatest disgrace. In his youth Sumner was a disciple of the saintly Unitarian leader William Ellery Channing, and he took up all of Channing's causes: hostility to war, the inhumanity of the prisons, illiteracy and ignorance among the masses—and slavery.

After the passage of the Kansas-Nebraska Act, Sumner attacked the South with a slashing, caustic vituperation that made even his Republican colleagues wince, although the Northern masses were delighted with their champion and the New York *Times* lauded his "matchless eloquence and power." The May 1856 attack upon him at his Senate seat by Preston Brooks was one of the great flash points that drove South and North apart in unforgiving anger. Recovered and back in his Senate seat in 1859, he took up again his unending attack upon the "Barbarism of Slavery." During the secession crisis he stood fast against any compromises, and after war began he early announced that the seceded states had abdicated all constitutional standing, and could be dealt with as conquered territory. Thus, their internal social arrangements could—and must—be totally transformed to blot out Southern barbarism.

One simple faith moved Sumner: that all men are created equal. During the Civil War, therefore, he prodded Lincoln unceasingly to free the slaves; nothing else would justify the holocaust. Afterwards, he helped lead those Radical Republicans who wanted to secure economic and social as well as political and civil equality for black men. All of this sprang from his firm Yankee belief that governments exist not just to keep order and otherwise stand aside passively, but to be powerful instruments in reform, and in creating the conditions for a confident, prosperous, and sophisticated civilization. Alone among the intellectuals of his day, he chose an active career in the grubby, malodorous, and undignified world of politics in order to achieve his goals. In the crucial Reconstruction years, history and Charles Sumner came together in a rare fusion of vision and reality. Never able to get all that he wanted for black people, he nonetheless left a legacy for the future in the great civil-rights constitutional amendments of those years, forged in an atmosphere of ideas that he had done much to create.

Overview

The American nation ended the Civil War with a profound sense that it had in fact confirmed (as Abraham Lincoln believed it had to) the ideology of *republicanism*. This, the national creed, the justification for America since Revolutionary times, had been a precarious faith until the victory of the North. For generations after the Revolution itself, the world at large, which was still a world of monarchies and—with exceptions in western Europe—feudalism, had scoffed at the Americans and their republican experiment. The people could not govern themselves, it had been said over and over again. Put them in any sort of great crisis, and they will prove too weak, selfish, short-sighted, ignorant, and self-indulgent to meet its challenges. All peoples needed established monarchies, titled aristocracies, and the wise rule of the educated and the wealthy to give them law and order, stability, true morality, and strong government.

In an agony of suffering and death, however, the great republic in North America had saved itself. It had demonstrated that a country could be founded in a democratic system of mass voting and mass political parties and still muster the iron will to subdue a massive challenge from within to the very principle of law, order, and constitutional government, of rule by the majority. It had been a second American Revolution; it had been the confirming of American nationhood and the republican ideal. The United States was a "nation" in every constitutional sense. The federation that "We the people" had ordained in the Constitution was strong enough to survive; it was indissoluble. And the republican idea would not simply endure, it was triumphant.

Almost four million Americans who had been enslaved were freed of that condition, though no one yet understood what their new status was to be. The long supremacy of the South in the national capital, which had endured with only brief interruptions from 1800 until secession in 1860, was ended. The Southern states lay shattered and powerless, while the triumphant North was wholly in command of the federal government.

This meant that the Yankees of the Upper North, with their homeland in New England and in that broad band of territory running from western New York out into the northern Middle West, now possessed that opportunity they had long dreamed of—to shape the country in their image, to create the universal Yankee nation. Through the Federalists and the Whigs, and now through the Republican party, they had long insisted that the country should be thought of in the way they had, since the Republic's founding, thought of New England: as a cohesive, unified community rooted in mutual agreement upon the same values, devoted to common goals, and actively led by a strong and confident common government.

Their "citty on a hill" in New England had sought to provide an example to the world of an austere, classically democratic, virtuous, pious, and hard-working community in which the interests of each person were subject to the larger needs of the whole community. So it was now to be, they fondly believed, in the whole of the American nation.

Nationalism Supreme

During the war the nationalist republicanism of the Republican party had won out. (See the "Overview" of chapter 26 for an explanation of the four modes of republicanism: the Democrats' libertarian and egalitarian republicanism; the Republicans' moralistic and nationalistic republicanism.) The Republican party, holding a strong majority in Congress, had finally secured enactment in Washington of what amounted, with important modifications, to the program called for so long before by Alexander Hamilton and by Henry Clay in his American System: a strong protective tariff to encourage the growth of American industry; lavish federal aid for internal improvements that would speed transport and tie the economy together (railroads, and river and harbor improvements); a national system of currency and banking, controlled by private interests; a network of nationally endowed (via federal landgrants) state universities to produce the educated elite to direct the new economy; and a homestead law to encourage rapid development of resources by giving the nationally-owned public lands free to bona fide farmers. Thus, federal power was vastly expanded, and constitutional and economic nationalism firmly established. The war had made millions of Americans in the Northern states think in new ways: of the nation as a unified entity; of great and all-consuming joint enterprises. They learned of the power of the national government, and how effective it could be in achieving common goals. Proud of their victory, so hard won, and of the proof it gave to the world that a self-governing republic could survive the sternest of all tests, Northerners now looked around them for new challenges to master, new means of building a great and flourishing democratic nation.

The Meaning of Freedom

What did the ending of slavery mean to the former slaves? Some were alarmed, but most felt great joy. Now, one freedman is quoted in Leon Litwack's *Been in the Storm So Long* (1979) to have said, "I won't wake up some mornin' ter fin' dat my mammy or some ob de rest of my family am done sold." Separated families searched eagerly for each other. And the whipping was over! "Everybody went wild. . . . We was free. Just like that, we was free." There was a great burst of singing: "purty soon ev'ybody fo' miles around was singin' freedom songs." Some ran into the woods by themselves, saying over and over, "I'se free, I'se free!" A black man in Virginia of advanced years went to the barn, leaped wildly from straw stack to straw stack, and "screamed and screamed!"

The war had been a strange experience for them, watching the white men go off to the fighting and then feigning sorrow (or, in many cases, expressing it sincerely) when they were brought back dead or mutilated. Most slaves stayed at their work, sometimes until the last day. Indeed, in many parts of the South owners would not let them go free until officially notified that they had to. Here was the key to the future: the white South accepted the defeat, as to secession and separate nationhood, but it would try by every available means, legal and illegal, to keep black people as much as possible where they had been. Freedom did not mean equality; it did not even mean being free to go off to the cities to take up urban skills and jobs. Most black people were to be kept on the land; they were to continue as the agricultural labor force; property would remain in white hands; and the white person, by hook or by crook, would be *boss*, absolutely and completely.

There would be no voting by blacks, no equality in the courtroom, no schooling. And yet these three things were what black people and their leaders asked for over and over again. They rarely asked to be given the white man's land to make up for all the years of slavery and to provide their freedom an economic underpinning. They expected to work to get ahead (though there was a wild period right after the war when rumors rushed everywhere that the federal government was going to give each freedman forty acres and a mule).

Tremendously gratifying was the knowledge that whatever they earned thereafter would be theirs to keep. A former Arkansas slave earned his first dollar working on the railroad, and "felt like the richest man in the world!" Most felt an immediate compulsion to leave their plantations. Thousands drifted about the countryside; many tried to get by in the cities. Eventually, most black people found themselves forced to return to a farm somewhere and go to work again, though this time for wages, for the white-man boss. Working out a contract was an extremely difficult process, for neither whites nor blacks were used to the idea. Commonly, freedmen were grossly cheated. Often they were told they would be paid when the crop was in, and then at that time were fired without a penny. Very soon they also learned what it meant not to be worth anything in dollars to anyone, for now the white population, especially the part of it that was poor and with whom relations had always been bad, could maim, stab, torture, burn, and kill black people with no master to answer to. Violence in the prewar South had been primarily between whites; now it became white attacking black. In March 1865 Congress had created the Freedmen's Bureau to help freed slaves through the transition years. Many of its agents did all they could to protect black people from exploitive white employers, antiblack court systems, and violence, but no federal agency could ward off from four million black people the anger that millions of white Southerners felt toward them for their "ingratitude" and "insolence" (anything manifesting an independent spirit was so described). The white South simply could not conceive of blacks in any other relation to whites than they had been in before— economically, socially, politically, or legally. Every change in white-black relations would be stiffly resisted.

The black family, surprisingly strong even in slavery, now clasped legality about itself. Thousands of "married" slave couples went to town to be legally wed; no master could ever sell man and wife and children apart again. Black women in striking numbers manifested their concept of freedom by doing as white women did: they withdrew from field work and devoted themselves to home, children, and kitchen. To the men, this was often a matter of pride, to be insisted upon. Henceforth, black women's role was like the "Adam's-rib" status of colonial white women: performing tasks that supplemented those of the black men in an agricultural household. They raised garden crops for the kitchen, prepared food, and earned income by doing washing for nearby white homes or serving as wet nurses. Meanwhile, in the fields the black laborers, by common account, refused to work at the pace demanded in slavery times. A great slowdown occurred, much complained of by white employers. Per capita, the black work effort was down one third by 1870, according to estimates. Many blacks, restive under white bosses, worked out ways of renting land by delivering part of the crop to the landowner (sharecropping).

But being free, though every black person welcomed it, meant a day-to-day struggle to achieve individual dignity, self-respect, a livelihood, and a life without demeaning oppression by authoritative or harassing whites. Though free, blacks were expected to show deference and respect, by a host of small gestures and phrases, just as in the days of slavery. Laws soon appeared that denied them equal use of public facilities. A phenomenon known formerly only in the North made its appearance in the South: the race riot. By 1867, whites and blacks had fought each other in bloody battles in the streets of Charleston, Norfolk, Richmond, Atlanta, Memphis, and New Orleans. There were hundreds of deaths and thousands of wounded. The courts, meanwhile, refused to prosecute whites accused of crimes against blacks, which grew rapidly in frequency and violence. Nothing was more disheartening to blacks, in fact, than their total inability to receive anything like justice in the courts of the Southern states, even to bring suit or testify or sit on juries. "The idea of a *nigger* having the power of bringing a *white man* before a tribunal!" said a Georgian. "The Southern people a'n't going to stand that."

Andrew Johnson and Reconstruction

What did the North intend to do about all of this? A hint had come late in December 1863, when Abraham Lincoln had issued a presidential proclamation offering pardon to any Southern white who would swear loyalty to the United States Constitution. A former Whig, he seems to have put his hopes for the future in former Whigs in the South, most of whom had joined the Democratic party when Whiggery dissolved. He knew that they had essentially Northern principles, drawn from the New England leadership of the Whig party, and he hoped to build new state governments in the South on such men. If a number of voters equal to one tenth of those who cast ballots in the election of 1860 took such an oath, Lincoln stated, then they could form a loyal state government and, after abolishing slavery, secure presidential recognition as being back in the Union. As to the blacks in the South, Lincoln clearly relied upon the former Whig leadership to meet their needs in a principled and just fashion, but without expecting or calling for the vote and the right to hold political office to be given to blacks.

In April 1865 Lincoln was assassinated. Stunned Northerners tried to absorb the fact of his death. Mourners filed by his casket in the Capitol rotunda and massed silently by the railroad tracks to watch his funeral train take its slow way home to Springfield, Illinois. Black people in the South grieved, for to them Lincoln was the Great Emancipator. Then all eyes turned to see what manner of man was the new chief executive. Few liked Andrew Johnson personally, for he was rigid and quarrelsome, but many respected his courage, personal strength, and vigorous administrative talents. A gifted and powerful speaker, from his early twenties he had won a long succession of political victories, serving in both houses of the Tennessee legislature, and as governor, congressman, and United States senator. A Jacksonian Democrat, he had bitterly blamed the Southern aristocracy for bringing on the Civil War. For this reason, Southern blacks reassured themselves that Johnson would be their friend. The only Southern senator to remain in Congress after his state seceded, he became the military governor of Tennessee in 1862 and was chosen to be Lincoln's vice-president in 1864.

In the eight months between Lincoln's

This photograph of Richmond after the war shows the terrible devastation many Southern cities suffered.

death and the reconvening of Congress in December 1865, Johnson moved briskly to reconstruct the Union on his own authority as president. It was quickly apparent that he shared what many Republicans regarded as Lincoln's too lenient Reconstruction ideas. That is, unlike such men as Senator Charles Sumner of Massachusetts, he did not believe that the Southern states had ever actually left the Union, since secession was by definition an illegal act. Also, he clearly intended to leave race relations in the South in the hands of its white people. Blacks, it turned out, did not find an ally in him in their postslavery struggle to win a status of at least civil and political equality with whites.

Johnson accepted Reconstruction as complete in the four states that had already begun the process under Lincoln (Louisiana, Virginia, Tennessee, and Arkansas) and initiated proceedings in the other seven ex-Confederate states. He used whatever proportion of the local populations he could get to take the loyalty oath to get Reconstruction started and new governments formed. He made only three requests of them: that they declare secession null and void from the beginning, repudiate any Confederate war debts (that is, Johnson did not want the new governments to pay off the debts of the Rebel governments), and ratify the Thirteenth Amendment. At first the South was apathetic and submissive, expecting the North to make many demands for social change as its terms for readmission to the Union,

and was apparently ready to make those changes. But since Johnson demanded so little and actually urged the Southern states, by many things that he said or implied, to pay little attention to Northern opinion, they soon began to show much of their old-time prideful independence, to mounting irritation in the North. They refused to ratify the Thirteenth Amendment (as in Mississippi), or quibbled about repudiating the Confederate debts (as in South Carolina), or only "repealed" their secession ordinances. Southerners elected to their constitutional conventions and new state governments the very men who had led them into secession and war. They even sent ex-Confederate generals, colonels, and congressmen (including the former vice-president of the Confederacy, Alexander Stephens) to Washington as their elected representatives.

Worse yet, the reconstructed state governments enacted highly restrictive "black codes." Marriages between Afro-Americans were finally recognized as legal, and blacks were allowed to own property and to sue and be sued. But the black man's children could be bound out as apprentices; the terms of his labor contracts were specified, including hours and wages; and servants were prohibited from leaving their employers' premises without permission. If a black man tried to be other than an agricultural laborer, he had to get a license from a white judge. He could not enter any mechanical trade without going through a closely disciplined apprenticeship. Vagrancy laws made any black person who wandered about, engaged in "disreputable occupations," or acted in a "disorderly manner" subject to arrest, after which he could be hired out to a white employer to serve his sentence. Blacks were not allowed to testify in court unless the case involved other blacks. Segregation in schools and public facilities was commonly decreed. Sometimes black men could own only rural property, sometimes only urban. Most important, they could not bear arms or vote in elections.

The Issue of Equality

As early as 1863 Frederick Douglass had warned Northerners that emancipation was but the first step toward real freedom for black people. But the North in general was no more in favor of black equality than it had ever been. In recognition of blacks' courageous fighting record during the war, some of the worst antiblack laws in the North were repealed after 1860, but only 7 percent of the 225,000 Afro-Americans in the Northern states were allowed the vote, it being granted to them in five New England states. Blacks were segregated in public facilities, schools, prisons, hospitals, churches, and even cemeteries. Many states still had laws against the immigration of free blacks, and everywhere there were obstacles to equal employment, equal housing, and equal rights. Both political parties insisted that they were for the white man.

On the other hand, many Northerners grieved for the condition of the Southern black population. They heard stories of killings, the peonage of the black codes, callousness, cruelty, and lynchings, and by the end of 1865, when Congress was about to reassemble, there was a great deal of talk about doing something to promote black equality. Fundamentally, this was what the term *reconstruction* actually meant when it came into general use around 1862: some real and meaningful reconstruction of Southern society and politics in order to give blacks a better life. To believe in this was what it meant to be a "Radical Republican." In this cause, Radical Republicans in the Reconstruction era seized for their party the insistence upon "equality" as a key element in American republicanism that Democrats had traditionally made their political hallmark. (Democrats emphasized equality only among whites.) But the crucial question was, if the goal of Radical Reconstruction was equality for blacks, what was meant by *equality*?

Almost unanimously Republicans believed that this meant at least equality before the law—in other words, civil rights. Black people should not be subject to legal restrictions that did not apply to whites. They should be able to testify in court, sit on juries, move freely about the country-side, take up any occupation, and give up one job for another. They should have the same punishment as whites for the same crimes, and not be told some things were crimes for them but not for whites. They must be able to own land wherever they wished, not be imprisoned for debts and hired out, and not be subject to apprenticeship laws that limited their freedom. Special curfew laws and vagrancy statutes were to be condemned. All this added up to Lincoln's fundamental position: that black people, while living separately in society, should be free to secure "life, liberty, and the pursuit of happiness."

Radical Republicans also insisted that there should be equality in politics and government: the right to vote, campaign on public issues, run for and hold office, and serve in government posts. A few of the more extreme Radical Republicans believed that black Americans should be granted social equality as well: in social relationships and in schooling, housing, and public accommodations. An even smaller number of Radicals joined with some of the black leaders in calling for economic equality as well. This meant providing skills and education, and, most revolutionary of all, confiscating rebel-owned plantations to give land to freed black people and make them truly independent, truly able to "get ahead."

To all of this, Democrats in the North and South responded with bitter condemnation. White Southerners and Irish Catholics were harshly anti-black, and the party as a whole for decades had been the home of those who had opposed the abolition movement before the Civil War, condemned the Emancipation Proclamation during it, and now hurled curses at Radical Republicans for their pro-black campaign. Democrats had always demanded cultural as well as economic laissez-faire: that governments keep hands-off all moral questions, such as temperance and Catholicism and race relations, as well as the national economy. In Reconstruction years their tirades against Yankee puritanism contin-

Freedmen's Village in Arlington, Virginia. The Freedmen's Bureau struggled to carry former slaves through the difficult transition to equal citizenship.
Courtesy of the Library of Congress

ued to reverberate around the republic, holding up to scorn the righteous urge to supervise the private lives of others. (The racism of the Democratic party would not begin genuinely to fade until the advent of Franklin Roosevelt's New Deal, in the 1930s, and the coincident rise of Adolf Hitler and his virulent anti-Jewish racial theories and massacres.)

The Freedmen's Bureau

The Freedmen's Bureau, an organization within the War Department, sent hundreds of local agents into every Southern locale to aid refugees and freedmen. It provided emergency food and housing and built more than forty hospitals to afford medical aid. Searching out vacant lands (in some cases, in confiscated estates), it helped to settle some 30,000 people on the land. President Johnson severely cut back on this part of the Bureau's work, however, by insisting that all land taken from Rebels be restored after they were pardoned. The Bureau found jobs for thousands of blacks, then supervised hundreds of thousands of labor contracts to secure equitable treatment by white employers. It set up its own court system, under military law, to mediate disputes between employers and freedmen and preside over cases in criminal and civil law where one or both parties were black. Its most lasting achievement was the building of thousands of schools— 4,300 by the bureau's termination in 1872—to which hundreds of thousands of freedmen and their families flocked eagerly, usually to have in-

struction by a "teacher lady" from the Northern states. Southern whites hated the Bureau "more for what it stood for," as the historian George Bentley has written, "than for what it had done. . . . To most of them it was virtually a foreign government forced upon them and supported by an army of occupation. They resented its very existence, regardless of what it might do, for it had power over them and it was beyond their control."

What were Andrew Johnson's views on these matters? The president was a Southerner, he had been a slave owner, and he completely rejected the notion of racial equality. Black people, he believed, were inferior beings who should remain in an inferior position. He urged caution in giving votes to black men, since universal suffrage "would breed a war of races." Southern whites regarded him as standing between them and black suffrage. This, in effect, was the implication of his constant assertion that voting matters must be left to the individual states.

The Crisis Begins

Congress was deeply troubled when it assembled in December 1865. Every Confederate state save Texas had completed Johnson's Reconstruction procedure, and a large group of elected representatives awaited admission to Congress. To Northern congressmen, the fact that many of these representatives had been Confederate leaders seemed bold and mocking. Indeed, "an uneasy conviction had spread throughout most of the

North," Eric McKitrick has written, "that somehow the South had never really surrendered after all. . . . These feelings were neither focused nor organized; but they were pervasive, they seemed to ooze from everywhere and they invaded the repose of weary men who would have given much to be rid of them." It stuck in Northern throats to think of readmitting Southern representatives as though nothing had happened.

There was a deeper consideration. For many years Republicans had labored fruitlessly (as Whigs) to shape a new kind of American nation. Intermittently they had got brief periods of power, but never enough to achieve their goals. The Civil War had given them their opportunity, and they had swiftly passed the measures needed to open the new era. The Republicans were launched upon the building of a nation with a vigorously growing industrial economy fertilized and energized by the federal government working in close collaboration with the nation's leading entrepreneurs. With the emergence of efficiency and organization throughout the business world during the war and the creation of a strong federal government, the United States seemed about to become a strong and unified *nation* in place of the loose aggregation of separate states that had existed before.

It was too much to ask of human nature that the Republican majority should so quickly readmit the Southerners. They would bring in such a massive infusion of Democratic votes that, together with the Northern Democrats in Congress, they would form a majority. Considering Johnson's views, they might be able to enact a federal black code, or even force the federal government to pay off the Confederate debt. They would certainly dismantle the economic system the Republicans had built up—the tariffs, bounties, banks, and other aids to business. Whatever happened, Republicans were determined not to go back to the old states'-rights, decentralized, Southern-oriented regime that had dominated the nation since Jackson's day.

A joint committee on Reconstruction was formed with members from both houses of Congress, Thaddeus Stevens emerging as its central figure. Southern representatives were refused admission to Congress until that body decided that their states were actually back in the Union. Then a long investigation of Johnson's Reconstruction program was launched by the joint committee. In February 1866 the Republicans enacted a bill extending indefinitely the life of the Freedmen's Bureau (it was due to expire in June 1868). Its powers were greatly broadened in the hope that through military courts it could nullify the black codes and protect freedmen's civil rights. The bill provided that anyone "who should, by reason of state or local law, or regulation, custom, or prejudice, cause any other person to be deprived of any civil right was to be liable to punishment by one year's imprisonment or one thousand dollars' fine or both."

Johnson Strikes Back

President Johnson exploded with rage. He sent a ringing veto back to Congress in a dramatic step that wrenched apart and polarized the politics of the whole postwar period, as Jackson's bank veto had done in the 1830s and 1840s. Johnson condemned the Freedmen's Bureau as a monstrous intrusion on states' rights, condemned the use of military courts in peacetime as a violation of Southern civil rights, and scoffed at the notion that freedmen needed help. "They are self-sustaining," he said, "capable of selecting their own employment and their own places of abode, of insisting for themselves on a proper remuneration, and of establishing and maintaining their own asylums and schools."

Three days later he publicly attacked Thaddeus Stevens, the leading Radical Republican in the House, and Charles Sumner in the Senate, as wild revolutionaries who were trying to take over the national government and inciting others to assassinate him. "If it is blood they want," he yelled to a crowd outside the White House, "let them have courage enough to strike like men." Shortly thereafter a moderate Republican senator from Illinois, Lyman Trumball, tried to find some common legislative ground between the president and Congress that would ensure equality before the law to the Southern black. (This did not include suffrage, which he opposed.) He secured passage of a civil-rights bill to which, he thought, he had secured Johnson's approval. It established for the first time the status of "citizen of the United States" (formerly citizenship had been within a given state) and provided that the federal government could intervene within a state to ensure that citizens "of every race and color," save Indians not taxed, were given the same legal rights as white men. Agents of the Freedmen's Bureau would make arrests where civil rights were violated, but the federal civil courts, not the army's military courts, would hear the cases.

Once again Johnson struck back with a veto. In his message he scorned a measure that would denominate as "United States citizens" the Chinese on the West Coast, the Indians who were taxed, and "the people called gypsies, as well as the entire race designated as blacks, people of color, Negroes, mulattoes, and persons of African blood." This was a "grave question," he said, for the blacks had just emerged from slavery, and it had long been national policy to require people "who are strangers to and unfamiliar with our institutions [to] pass through a certain probation." Why discriminate against "intelligent, worthy, and patriotic" foreigners, he asked, who were required to wait five years for citizenship? The whole proposal, he said, was "fraught with evil," establishing "for the security of the colored race safeguards which go infinitely beyond any that the general government has ever provided for the white race. In fact, the distinction of race and color is by the bill made to operate in favor of the colored and against the white race."

Johnson's vetoes so outraged the moderates that they were driven over to join forces with the Radicals. His first veto had been upheld; his second one was overridden. From that point on, a strong and determined moderate and Radical Republican group in Congress, led by Sumner and Stevens, pushed vigorously ahead to take over Reconstruction, sweep away everything Johnson had done, and, eventually, come within a single vote of impeaching the president himself.

The Fourteenth Amendment

The joint committee on Reconstruction began drafting a constitutional amendment that would place the principle of equality before the law beyond any future tampering—or so they believed. The measure drawn up did not by any means meet Thaddeus Stevens's demands. He urged the adoption of a simple but powerful statement: that all laws, state and national, should apply equally to all persons. As Charles Sumner put this idea, "Show me . . . a legal institution, anything created or regulated by law, and I will show you

[an institution] that must be opened equally to all without distinction of color." "This was the true Radical argument," writes W. R. Brock. "It recognized that private prejudice could not be legislated out of existence, but maintained that discrimination could be prohibited in every activity touched by the law." There would always be discrimination in homes or private relations, "but they would have outlawed discrimination at the polls, in public places, on public transport, and in education."

The Republican majority, however, would not go this far with the Radicals. It was insisted that certain things were "privileges," not rights. The amendment should not apply, moderates said, to voting, or segregation in schools and public facilities. Its only reference to voting was to provide that a state's representation would be reduced in proportion to the number of its citizens denied the vote (this has never been applied). The amendment worked a powerful change, however, by making everyone born or naturalized in the American nation a citizen of the United States and forbidding all efforts by states to interfere with each citizen's fundamental civil rights. By conscious design, the amendment was broadened to make equal civil rights national in scope, protecting the rights of "any person" and not just those of blacks. (In the mid-1900s decades, its sweeping and powerful phrases would be enormously important weapons in social reform and in giving legitimacy to the aspirations of minority groups.)

Amendment XIV, The Constitution of the United States (ratified July 28, 1868). Section 1. All persons born or naturalized in the United States, and subject to the jurisdiction thereof, are citizens of the United States and of the State wherein they reside. No State shall make or enforce any law which shall abridge the privileges or immunities of citizens of the United States; nor shall any State deprive any person of life, liberty, or property, without due process of law; nor deny to any person within its jurisdiction the equal protection of the laws. . . . Section 5. The Congress shall have power to enforce, by appropriate legislation, the provisions of this article.

The proposed amendment was adopted by both houses of Congress in June 1866 and sent on to the states. Johnson protested against it, and recommended against ratification. The Southern states defeated this first attempt at ratification, for all the former states of the Confederacy, save

Tennessee (where ratification was highly equivocal) rejected it, plus Kentucky and Delaware. This drove even deeper into the Northern mind the belief that the Southern states, as reconstructed by President Johnson, were arrogant and unregenerate. In the congressional elections held in the autumn of 1866, the South's refusal to accept equality before the law became the major issue. Just as grave in the opinion of Northerners were race riots in Memphis and New Orleans in May and June 1866, in which policemen and whites murdered scores of blacks, shooting and knifing indiscriminately to "kill every damn nigger" they could find. No prosecutions were launched, and Johnson blamed it all on northern Radicals. Then he made an intemperate "swing around the circle" in August and September, speaking in many Northern cities. This in itself was shockingly indiscreet. In the nineteenth century, presidents simply did not do this. They did not even campaign when they were presidential candidates. To do so, in the viewpoint of the time, would be demeaning—and Johnson was demeaned. Furthermore, he lost his temper, bandied words with hostile crowds, and destroyed whatever credibility he had left. The Republicans won a landslide victory, gaining a two-thirds majority in both houses of Congress.

Radical Reconstruction

Now the triumphant Radical Republicans could begin a genuine *reconstruction* of Southern life. They undertook this task as leaders of a victorious Yankee culture at its most self-confident. "It is intended," said Thaddeus Stevens of Pennsylvania, New England–born and –educated, "to revolutionize . . . Southern institutions, habits, and manners." The ruling constitutional theory under which this was to be done was Stevens's: that the Southern states had in fact seceded and were no more than conquered provinces with which Congress could deal as it saw fit. In the language of the First Reconstruction Act, which it enacted over Johnson's veto on March 2, 1867, "no legal State governments or adequate protection for life or property now exist in the rebel States . . . and it is necessary that peace and good order should be enforced in said States until loyal and republican State governments can be legally established." The ten states still unreconstructed (Tennessee, having ratified the Fourteenth Amendment, was admitted in July 1866) were grouped into five military districts, each under a federal military commander whose powers were superior to those of the state governments. The states were to call elections for the writing of new state constitutions, all male citizens "of whatever race, color, or previous condition" being enfranchised to vote; those whites who had been federal officials and later supported the rebellion were disenfranchised. The new constitutions were to guarantee black suffrage. After ratification, and after the new state governments had ratified the Fourteenth Amendment and that amendment had become part of the federal Constitution (as it did in July 1868), then the states were entitled to be represented in Congress, though readmission would still require congressional enactment in each case.

Was Radical Reconstruction designed to help black people or to help the Republican party? The question is still debated. For many years historians took the latter view. Hungry for the graft and corruption that office holding allowed, and eager to maintain their protective tariffs and land bounties—so this version ran—greedy and vindictive Republicans incited Southern blacks to an "unnatural" hatred of whites, gave them the vote, then enrolled them in the Republican party so as to keep themselves in power. (This assessment was exactly that of Democrats when these events were going on.) In recent years historians have accepted that many Republicans sincerely wanted to help black people; that others simply wanted to make the blacks happy where they were, so they would not flood the Northern states; and that the desire to keep their own party in power, when that was the dominating motive, was not so discreditable as it has been depicted. The Republicans, after all, had a different vision of what America should be. They had been frustrated by what they regarded as a "Southern conspiracy" in the antebellum years, and now they aimed at protecting the possibility that their Yankee, nationalist republican goal for the nation might be realized. It is clear, however, that Republican concern to help black people was limited. Thaddeus Stevens tried to get his colleagues to establish an economic foundation for black equality by allowing the confiscation of Rebel estates and the redistribution of land. He was turned down. And there were no efforts to ensure social equality for black people. The dominant Republican view was that, given the vote and equality before the law, black persons were then to rise by their own initiative.

To ensure its absolute control of the Reconstruction process, Congress enacted legislation requiring the president to give orders to the army only through the general-in-chief, who was Ulysses S. Grant. Fearing that Johnson might remove Edwin Stanton, the secretary of war (who, like Grant, was sympathetic to Radical goals), Congress passed the Tenure of Office Act, which took away the president's authority to remove cabinet members without the Senate's consent. Another enactment limited the Supreme Court's authority so as to keep it from ruling on the legality of any Reconstruction legislation. Subsequent Reconstruction acts elaborated the powers of the military commanders so that any state official who should "hinder, delay, prevent or obstruct the due and proper administration" of the Reconstruction acts could be removed.

In August 1867 President Johnson tried to remove Secretary of War Stanton, primarily for failure to accept the president's directions but also in order to test the constitutionality of the Tenure of Office Act. In January 1868 the Senate refused to accept Stanton's suspension or to recognize another man whom Johnson had appointed in his place. In late February the House impeached the president for violating the Tenure of Office Act and a host of other vaguely worded "high crimes and misdemeanors." For more than two months, until the middle of May, an intensely dramatic trial proceeded before the Senate. (The president was represented by legal counsel and spared the indignity of being present.) When the votes were taken, conviction fell one vote shy of the necessary two-thirds majority because seven Republicans—at great cost to their political careers—concluded that no case had been made. A public outcry arose against them as traitors to the nation.

Black Reconstruction

Meanwhile, "black Reconstruction" was under way in the South. The first thing to be said of the freed slaves was that the fears that had apparently driven South Carolina and the rest of the South into secession in 1860–61 were without foundation. The freedmen did *not* immediately rise in bloody violence against their former masters, dealing out the massacre and rapine that had hysterically been warned against for generations. The horrors of Santo Domingo and Haiti did not reenact themselves. Few more striking instances in history exist of a mass delusion leading millions of people into a needless, disastrous war. So, too, race war did not break out when the freedmen were given the vote. Indeed, massive and violent assaults against the white community and its institutions were not ever to be mounted by black Americans in the South, either in the Reconstruction years or in later generations. The massacring was instead to be in the other direction. When black Americans did in fact join in destructive outbreaks, it was to be almost a century later, and in Northern cities.

Some 700,000 black men were enfranchised in the Southern states as a result of the Radical Reconstruction program, while 150,000 whites lost the vote for having supported the rebellion after having held federal office. In every state except Virginia, Republicans took control. In June 1868 six states were readmitted to the Union: Arkansas, North and South Carolina, Florida, Alabama, and Louisiana. The rest were readmitted in early 1870. Republican regimes did not last long: one year in Georgia, two in North Carolina, four in Texas, six in Alabama, Arkansas, and Mississippi, and nine in Florida, Louisiana, and South Carolina. When Republicans lost out, the Southern "Redeemers," who aimed at firmly reestablishing white control, took over.

The years of Radical Reconstruction have traditionally been described as a carnival of corruption that left the South crippled by enormous debts. Hordes of ignorant and greedy blacks were pictured as taking over the legislatures, rolling drunkenly in the aisles and shouting approval for huge appropriations that went into the pockets of their carpetbagger leaders (Northerners come South to fish in troubled waters) or those of the scalawags (Southern whites who joined the plunder).

This picture is now largely discredited. There was corruption, some of it spectacular, but corruption was a national phenomenon in these years. Nothing in the South compared, for example, with the luxuriant graft then going on in New York City under "Boss" William M. Tweed. In only one state, South Carolina, was there a black

RECONSTRUCTION

majority in the legislature, and there only in the lower house. No blacks were elected governor; few were judges; and only seventeen served in Congress. Those who held official positions served admirably in most cases. Blacks were not vindictive, and often supported appeals that disenfranchised whites be given the vote and allowed to hold office. There were no attempts to overturn social relationships. Indeed, Reconstruction governments did little for the black person specifically. Heavy expenditures were made because the South had to be rebuilt after the war and because emancipation doubled the civil population. Millions of blacks formerly given nothing by state governments now were citizens needing services in schools, courts, and welfare agencies.

Reconstruction Reforms

The Reconstruction governments enacted major reforms. They gave the South its first system of public schools. Manhood suffrage free of property qualifications was enacted, and imprisonment for debts was terminated. Homestead laws guaran-

teed poor men a minimum amount of property safe from attachment for debts. Popular election of county officials replaced the former oligarchical system of appointment. Salaries were provided to public officials so that someone other than a rich planter could serve. The number of crimes punishable by death was reduced. Taxes were rearranged so as to bear on plantation owners rather than just on landless individuals.

The thousands of Northerners who came south after the Civil War, the "carpetbaggers," were not the depraved and dissolute adventurers they have been described to be. Many brought needed capital and entrepreneurial skills; others were serious reformers who sought to democratize the South and teach the poor—white and black. The "scalawags" (Southern whites who joined the Republican party, who amounted to perhaps a quarter of the white population) were often new men from poor counties, with little former reputation in government. They were angry at the "bombastic, high falutin, aristocratic fools" who had dragged the South into a disastrous war, and who had been "driving negroes and poor helpless white people until they think they can

RECONSTRUCTION OF THE SOUTH, 1865–1877

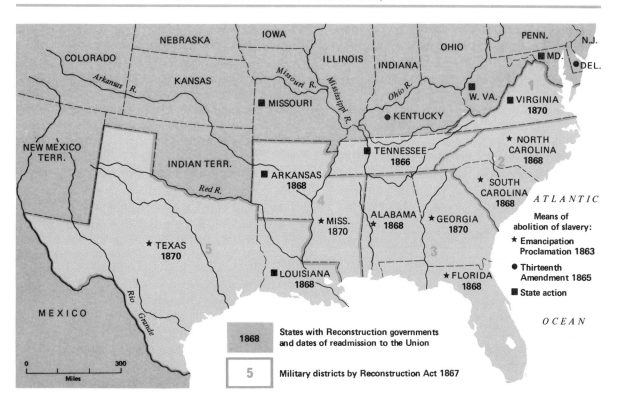

control the world of mankind." They liked Republican policies of economic development, for they promised jobs where at present there was poverty, and called for social reforms.

Indeed, the "other South" still survived strong and healthy. The Whig party had died completely in the South in the 1850s, when the whole region swung to the Democratic party, but former Whigs bulked large in the Confederate congresses. For that matter, after the first elections, which gave Democrats dominance, the Confederate congress in subsequent ballotings began to swing strongly toward the former Whigs. As the war went badly, Democrats were stigmatized by many as "radicals," and Jefferson Davis had to turn more and more to ex-Whigs—who seemed to know more about running industries and organizing things—to help him marshal the South's strength. At the end of the war former Whigs either joined the Republican party or formed parties like the Conservative party in Virginia, which sought to do for the South what the Republicans were doing for the North: develop its economy, foster industrialization, build railroads, and encourage urbanization.

It must be understood that within what became the borders of the Confederacy, 49 percent of those casting ballots in the 1860 presidential election had voted either for Bell or Douglas, thus indicating that they did not favor secession. Thousands of white Southerners served in the Union army during the war, forming almost ninety regiments. Appalachia was a hotbed of Unionism. And the white South's return so easily to the Union after the war can be understood only by taking into account that its fundamental loyalty to that Union was always strong, being overborne only in hysterical circumstances by fear of what never occurred—a black uprising.

Economic Reconstruction in the South

Radical Republicans wanted not only to reconstruct the blacks, they wanted to reconstruct Southern white society as well. Yankees had said for many years that if slavery were only eliminated, then Southern whites would stop being lazy, thriftless people who shunned physical labor, and would start taking up the hard-working ways of Yankees. Now, Radical Republicans urged Southern whites to take the road to industrialization and urbanization—and were delighted with the response. The business community of the South, composed largely of ex-Whigs who had always been irritated at the languid, unprogressive rule of the plantation owners, "burst into effusions of assent and hosannas of delivery." Thousands in the South had always admired Northern ways and had tried vainly to take their section in Yankee directions.

Virginia "Conservatives"—who took that name in politics to distinguish themselves from both the Democrats and the Republicans—worked consciously to regenerate Virginia's economy along Northern capitalist lines. The task they took on was admittedly great and forbidding. The war had left widespread devastation. Thus, to break out of the depressed conditions they were in, state governments eagerly pushed the building of railroads in the South. Project was piled on project with feverish haste, and almost every state invested huge sums in private companies. The railroad system was rebuilt, and a good deal of mileage added. Also, new industries were encouraged by state grants of funds and tax privileges. Immigration was encouraged, and this produced a heavy influx of white settlement and Northern capital. Textile mills appeared in the Carolinas and in Georgia. The Richmond ironworks were rebuilt, and flourished more than ever. Northern Alabama's iron and coal resources were opened, and the city of Birmingham, soon to be the Pittsburgh of the South, made its appearance. A movement of population to the cities occurred, since textile mills and other urban industries offered jobs (to whites only).

Almost nine of ten black Southerners lived in the countryside. Here, sharecropping became the basis of the new postslavery farm economy. Produced primarily by the black man's determination to gain at least a semblance of independence, and not to work in gangs, as in slave times, sharecropping allowed black farmers to till rented farms without white supervision. The former plantations, where everyone, black and white, lived in a tightly clustered grouping of cabins and the "Big House," now were divided into many small units to which the former slaves scattered, there to live on their own in cabins of their construction. White landlords provided not only the land, but seed, fertilizer, tools, food, and advice —necessities since very few ex-slaves had even minimal skills, and all lacked managerial experience and capital. In return, sharecropping farmers delivered half to two thirds of their crop to the landowner. A halfway house in which most black farmers would remain suspended, sharecropping at least produced more income for them than they had gotten under slavery, and it removed the indignity of gang labor and immediate white management. Many were able under the system to accumulate savings: by 1910, almost one third of the land tilled by black farmers was owned by them.

For many black sharecroppers, something resembling peonage developed. (Peons, such as those who existed in Mexico in the nineteenth century, are held on their land in compulsory servitude to a master for the working out of a debt.) To buy supplies in local white-owned stores, blacks had to contract annual loans, which, if not completely paid off by the crop receipts, forced them to stay where they were to keep making payments. However, black farmers still retained considerable mobility. Furthermore, the productivity of the sharecropping system was considerable. The Southern cotton crop had dropped from 5.3 million bales annually before the war to 2.0 million in 1865, but it was back to 3.0 million bales by 1870 and 5.7 million bales by 1880. Other crops surged also, tobacco production rising rapidly, rice and sugar more slowly.

Unfortunately, the world demand for cotton began falling off. The slow market for cotton, together with falling prices, caused Southern per-capita income to drop from 72 percent of the national average in 1860 to only 51 percent in 1880, where it remained until the twentieth century. The postwar South, shattered by the war and wedded essentially to a one-crop system suffering from sluggish demand, remained poor while the North boomed.

The Question of Segregation

The cities of the South had been thought of as white man's country before the war, though the black population in Southern cities ranged from 20 percent in Atlanta to slightly over 50 percent in Montgomery, Alabama. After 1865, city whites complained angrily that they were being inun-

dated by footloose blacks fleeing the plantations, and in fact by 1870 almost all the South's leading cities had populations that were half white and half black.

What was to be done with these people? whites asked. Must they be schooled when young, taken care of in hospitals when ill, cared for in old-folks' homes when elderly, just like the whites? Would they live scattered about, as had the prewar black population that served as household help to white people? What kind of jobs would they be allowed to hold? Surely, it was said, no jobs currently assigned to white workers? How about crime and punishment, the police, the courts? One response is familiar: with regard to criminal justice, jobs, housing, and such public facilities as streetcars, hotels, and restaurants, the principle quickly laid down was *segregation*. But concerning public services, such as hospitals, schools, almshouses, asylums, and institutions for the physically handicapped, the response is not so familiar: it was *exclusion*. The cities were poor, it was hard for them to perform services even for their white citizens, and they simply refused to take on this great load—previously borne by masters—suddenly descending upon them with the ending of slavery.

The Freedmen's Bureau moved in to fill the gap at first, providing needed services for black people by building schools and erecting hospitals. Meanwhile, urban whites kept reiterating that black people belonged in the countryside, that town life was unhealthy for them. Clinics set up by Southern cities for indigent people limited their services to whites. After Radical Reconstruction began, Republican city administrations started providing facilities for black people and opening existing institutions to them for the first time—but on a segregated basis. This, in short, was to be the answer: it seemed to officials of the Freedmen's Bureau and to Radical Republicans that the great goal they should struggle for had to be to end the system of total exclusion. The simple provision of services was regarded as a victory. That they were on a segregated basis seemed, until many more years were to pass, a relatively small price to pay. At least there was equal access, which, Republicans presumed, would involve equal, if separate, facilities. Equal but segregated access was at best a partial victory, for many facilities remained open only to whites, especially after the ending of Radical Reconstruction.

The very idea that there should be publicly supported schools was one of the great achievements won by Radical Republicans in the South. Both whites and blacks benefited from this campaign. However, from the beginning schooling was provided on a strictly segregated basis. City blacks got much better schooling than Southern blacks who lived on farms, which had much to do with stimulating black people to move to the city. The best blacks could hope for in the Reconstruction years after educational reform was put in place was for separate but equal treatment—a hope that in future years, after Southern white "Redeemers" took control of local government, was to be seriously frustrated. Separate eventually meant unequal. Richmond, Virginia, in 1890 spent roughly ten dollars apiece for the schooling of both black and white children, but in Montgomery the figures were approximately $5.50 and $3.50. Black schools were old and crowded; white schools were new and, for the times, reasonably well equipped. When high schools were built, they were usually only for white children, and salaries for black and white teachers were wide apart.

Grant's Administration

Meanwhile, national politics continued to make headlines and absorb the country's voters. The readmission of the first group of reconstructed Southern states in June 1868 was in time for them to vote in the presidential election of that year. Horatio Seymour, Democratic governor of New York during the Civil War and a strong opponent of racial equality, ran on the Democratic ticket. The Republicans chose the military hero Ulysses S. Grant, whose victory was assured by the margin of Republican votes in the electoral college won in the Republican-controlled Southern states.

Samuel J. Tilden was chairman of the Democratic party in New York during the 1868 campaign. He expressed pungently the Democratic viewpoint on Radical Reconstruction. If the Republicans had been "magnanimous" toward the Southern whites, he said, they could have built a lasting Republican party in the Southern states. But the Republican party, "which boasts its great moral ideas and its philanthropy," could not resist striking its adversary when it was down. "It totally abandoned all relations to the white race of the ten states. It resolved to make the black race the governing power in those states, and by means of them to bring into Congress twenty senators and fifty representatives —practically appointed by itself in Washington." The Republican party had no interest in the internal affairs of the Southern states; it neglected them entirely. It wanted only "to strengthen its hold on the federal government against the people of the North," so as to continue its corrupt career of handing out favors to vested interests. Southern blacks "have been disassociated from their natural relations to the intelligence, humanity, virtue, and piety of the white race, set up in complete antagonism to the whole white race, for the purpose of being put over the white race, and of being fitted to act with unity and become completely impervious to the influence of superior intellect and superior moral and social power." The 3 million blacks "will have ten times as much power [through their] twenty senators and fifty representatives . . . as the 4 million whites in the state of New York. . . . One freedman will counterbalance thirteen white citizens of the Empire State," and will count ten times as much as the whites of Pennsylvania, Ohio, Illinois, or Indiana. "These 3 million blacks will have twice the representation in the Senate which will be possessed by the five great commonwealths—New York, Pennsylvania, Ohio, Indiana, and Illinois—embracing 13,500,000 of our people."

Congress was taking control of the suffrage away from the states and was "systematically breaking down" division of powers in the federal government. It was becoming an "elective despotism." It must "pass into imperialism [and] the destruction of all local self-government. . . . The grim Puritan of New England . . . stretches his hand down along the Atlantic coast to the receding and decaying African, and says: 'Come, let us rule this continent together!'" (John Bigelow, ed., *The Writings and Speeches of Samuel J. Tilden* [1885])

Thus began an eight-year administration that has little to commend it to history save distasteful scandals. Grant was unqualified for the presidency, and he chose many subordinates who subsequently made free use of their opportunities. He allowed two noted stock-market manipulators, Jay Gould and James Fisk, to be intimate with him until their disgraceful activities in rigging the stock market became too blatant. Companies received monopoly contracts from the New York Customs House and made hundreds of thousands of dollars in graft. During Grant's administration the massive speculations of the Crédit Mobilier, the company formed to construct the Union Pacific Railroad, came to light. Con-

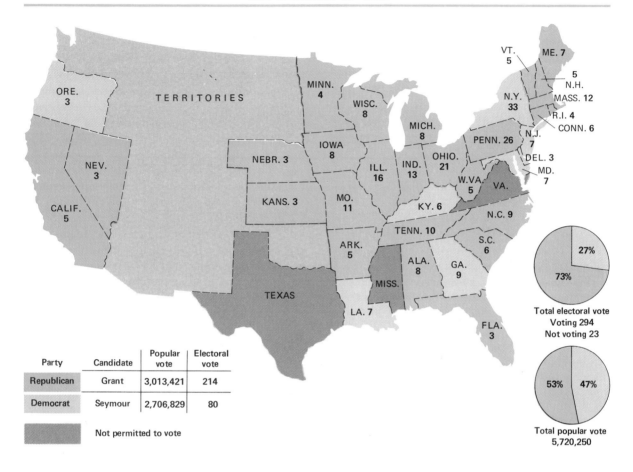

Party	Candidate	Popular vote	Electoral vote
Republican	Grant	3,013,421	214
Democrat	Seymour	2,706,829	80

Not permitted to vote

Total electoral vote
Voting 294
Not voting 23

Total popular vote
5,720,250

gressmen were caught profiting from the scheme, and the scandal reached upward to involve Vice-President Schuyler Colfax. Secretary of the Treasury Ben Butler was found aiding an arrangement whereby hundreds of railroads were forced to pay delinquent taxes, half of which, to the amount of hundreds of thousands of dollars, went to a henchman—and then, perhaps, to Butler himself.

These activities were mirrored at every level of American government. In city councils, in boards of supervisors, in state legislatures—wherever profitable deals could be made, grafters were there, and compliant legislators assisted them, for a consideration. Much of the history of the period, wherever it is touched, consists of little but damaged reputations. Ice-house franchises, street-construction contracts, railroad land grants, bank subsidies, tax rebates, purchased jurors, judges, and sheriffs—the list is endless.

All this produced a new and consuming national concern that went far to dwarf everything else in the minds of many voters. No obsession was more central to the Democrats than the problem of corruption in the economy and in government. They believed it to be simply inherent in the way that Republicans ruled. Handing out land grants, protective tariffs, bank charters, immunities from taxation, railroad contracts, and every other kind of profitable privilege inevitably produced corruption. It was the very means, they insisted, by which the Republicans rooted themselves in power—buying up supporters by creating vested interests.

Many Republicans shared these worries. After all, for generations republicanism had been criticized in Europe as certain to lead to widespread dishonesty and graft as "the people," unchecked, took over power. It was not long before Republicans of traditional Yankee puritan views were disillusioned with the Grant regime. It seemed cheap, opportunist, low in tone, and greedy. Grant was not interested in civil-service reform, as they had assumed, and the spoils system flourished. Well-educated "independent" Republicans, such as E. L. Godkin of the *Nation* and Charles Francis Adams, broke away from the "regulars" of the Republican party in 1872 and resolved to run their own candidate for the presidency in place of Grant, who was nominated for a second term. Calling themselves Liberal Republicans, they chose Horace Greeley, editor of the New York *Tribune*, to oppose Grant. The Democrats swung in with them, nominating Greeley as their presidential candidate as well.

The result was a disastrous campaign. An eager and aggressive candidate who condemned Grant's policies, Greeley also championed such unpopular causes as women's rights, labor unions, vegetarianism, and social-reform movements such as Fourierism, a form of communalism. He was ridiculed as a crank, and Grant secured a massive 750,000-vote majority. Exhausted, brokenhearted and grieved by the recent death of his wife, Greeley died three weeks after the election.

Foreign Affairs: Seward and Fish

Two gifted secretaries of state, William Seward and Hamilton Fish, directed the nation's foreign relations with notable success during the administrations of Andrew Johnson and Ulysses Grant, respectively. Seward dealt successfully with a bold adventure that Napoleon III of France undertook in Mexico while the United States was involved in the Civil War. The French emperor installed an Austrian nobleman, Maximilian, on the Mexican "throne" in 1864. But as soon as the Civil War ended, Seward placed troops on the Mexican border and informed Napoleon that the United States would never recognize Maximilian's regime. By patient diplomacy he got the French to withdraw all their troops in 1867. Maximilian, who foolishly refused to leave with them, was executed by the Mexicans.

Seward also responded eagerly to a Russian offer to sell Alaska. He agreed to purchase it for $7.2 million and, in the face of much amused comment about "Seward's Ice Box," secured the Senate's ratification of the treaty in April 1867. Looking to the Far East, Seward sent a gifted diplomatist, Anson Burlingame, to China to open

that country to American trade. Hoping to fend off European partitioning of China, the United States formally recognized China's territorial integrity and promised no interference in Chinese affairs. In return, by the Burlingame Treaty (1868) American citizens were accorded the right of travel and residence in China and the right of freely exercising their religion there. This opened the way for an extensive involvement of American missionaries and traders in Chinese life over the next several generations.

The most explosive issue in Seward's hands after the war was the negotiation of claims against Great Britain arising from the activities during the Civil War of a group of Confederate commerce raiders—the *Alabama* chief among them—that the British had allowed to be built in their shipyards and taken to sea. These raiders sank or captured many Union merchant ships, causing huge losses to northern merchants. The issue was still unsettled when Grant entered office. Hamilton Fish transferred the negotiations from London to Washington.

A joint high commission composed equally of Britons and Americans began discussions of the *Alabama* and other outstanding issues in Washington in 1871. A long dispute over who owned the San Juan Islands between Seattle and Vancouver Island was referred to the German emperor for settlement (he gave them to the United States). The Americans secured extensive privileges to fish in Canadian waters, and Canadian seamen were allowed to fish as far south as Delaware Bay. The *Alabama* claims were referred to a tribunal of arbitration in Geneva, with the result that the United States received fifteen and a half million dollars, the "indirect" claims being ignored. A counterclaim arising from attacks on Canada by Irish-Americans in the Fenian organization, who sought in this way to free Ireland from British rule, gave almost two million dollars to the British. The crowning achievement of Grant's administration, the complete restoration of good relations with Great Britian was successfully completed.

The Fifteenth Amendment

After Grant's first election in 1868, the Republicans took up once more the problem of the black man in the South. They moved carefully, for the Northern states were still hostile to black enfranchisement. This had been shown in the first local elections held after passage of the First Reconstruction Act in March 1867. In state after state, the Democrats won handily on anti–black suffrage platforms. The journal *Independent* cynically remarked that "it ought to bring a blush to every white cheek in the loyal North to reflect that the political equality of American citizens is likely to be sooner achieved in Mississippi than in Illinois—sooner on the plantation of Jefferson Davis than around the grave of Abraham Lincoln!" In Ohio a proposal to establish black suffrage went down by 40,000 votes in the autumn. "Thousands have turned against us," observed Horace Greeley in November 1867, "because we purpose to enfranchise the Blacks."

Southerners had good reason to scoff, therefore, at the stated goals of Radical Republicanism. What hypocrisy it was, they said, for Republicans to protest moral sincerity! Northerners clearly had no interest in the black man. All they wanted was to get his votes behind the Republican ticket to keep the party in power in Washington. The charge of hypocrisy was the stock reply of Southern whites to everything the Republicans attempted. An editor in Raleigh, North Carolina, ridiculed Republicans in 1867 when members of their party voted two to one in the Pennsylvania legislature against giving the vote to black men. "This is a direct confession, by Northern Radicals, that they refuse to grant in Pennsylvania the *'justice'* they would enforce on the South. . . . And this is Radical meanness and hypocrisy— this their love for the negro." Even the Republican platform of 1868 perpetuated the dual standard, insisting that "every consideration of public safety, of gratitude, and of suffrage in all the loyal [i.e., Northern] States properly belongs to the people of those States."

When congressional Republicans decided after Grant's election to aid black suffrage, they had to move with care lest they offend Northern sensibilities. Moderates and conservatives, not Radicals, dominated the writing of the Fifteenth Amendment. Even Wendell Phillips, a dyed-in-the-wool reformer since his days as a leading abolitionist, urged his followers, "For the first time in our lives we beseech them to be a little more politicians and a little less reformers." Radicals wanted a positive national guarantee that the vote would be permanently granted to blacks; moderates wanted only a negative statement that would deny taking the vote away simply on the ground of race or previous condition of servitude. As Oliver P. Morton put the matter, the intent was not to nationalize suffrage, but to leave it in state hands subject only to this one federal limitation. He went on to add, "They may, perhaps, require property or educational tests." Even a clause that would prohibit denial of officeholding on the ground of race was rejected.

Passed by Congress in February 1869, the Fifteenth Amendment went to the states and was ratified in March 1870 (Virginia, Mississippi, and Georgia were required to ratify as conditions of readmission, and they did so in early 1870). Then, and only then, did black Americans finally secure the vote in the Northern states.

Counter-Reconstruction

Since 1865 an organization called the Ku Klux Klan, or the Invisible Empire of the South, had existed for the purpose of frightening blacks, usually by nonviolent means. In 1869 it was officially disbanded by Nathan Forrest, the Confederate general who, with others of the Southern elite, had provided its leadership, because it was rapidly veering toward violence. Thereafter the Klan multiplied informally through local "dens," which began indiscriminately shooting, hanging, whipping, torturing, burning, and drowning blacks, carpetbaggers, and scalawags. Mobs took proceedings into their own hands, and private feuds were launched that soon became simple campaigns of plunder. Congress investigated and found that in only one county of South Carolina, 11 murders and over 600 whippings had taken place. Several federal laws—the "force bills"— were enacted in 1870, which reinforced the army in the South, reserved to the federal courts exclusive jurisdiction in suffrage cases, and provided troops to enforce court orders. These laws only temporarily checked terrorism.

In 1875 the state of Mississippi demonstrated what terrorist tactics used extensively and systematically could achieve. Whites began taking pledges and forming organizations to revitalize the Democratic party around the principle, as the *Democrat*, a Mississippi newspaper, put it, "that white men shall govern . . . that niggers are not rightly entitled to vote, and that when [the Democratic party] gets into power, niggers will be placed upon the same footing with white minors who do not vote or hold office. . . . Nigger voting, holding office and sitting in the jury box, are all wrong, and against the sentiment of the country." Lists of independent-minded blacks were printed in newspapers to encourage private terrorism directed toward them. Thousands of young white men and boys took it on their own to discipline the blacks. They formed militia companies, and openly practiced target shooting.

With the state elections of 1875 approaching, the unorganized, unarmed, frightened blacks of Mississippi watched as companies drilled and paraded and cannon practice produced rolling thunder. Black Republicans found their names prominently displayed in "dead books" and were warned that any further public speaking would lead to their murder. When attempts were made to register Republican voters, armed men prevented anyone from doing so.

The "election riot" was the most useful device. It simply amounted to a sudden outbreak of pistol firing and armed attack wherever Republicans gathered, sending black families and white Republicans fleeing. Many of these took place throughout the state in 1874 and 1875, when white Southerners took advantage of any pretext to begin assaults. A Republican meeting in Yazoo City was invaded by Democrats, one of whom prominently carried a rope. A native white Republican was killed, the white sheriff fled the county, and then a general lynching of black leaders in every supervisor's district occurred. Riots like this were frequently followed by days of terror, armed bands scouring the countryside and shooting at will.

When the election came, "it was a very quiet day in Jackson," an observer remarked, "fearfully quiet." In Yazoo City, "hardly anybody spoke aloud." At Okolona an armed mob took over the town, the Republican sheriff locked himself in his jail, and the Democrats picked up the ballot box and stuffed it. Such fraud, however, was hardly necessary and was little used. The Democrats simply swept the state. Merciless, overwhelming, and absolutely relentless force had turned the trick.

The North's Reaction

What was the North to do? The only appropriate response, if it genuinely wished to reestablish interracial government in such states, was to renew Radical Reconstruction in all its array and vigor. Huge sums of money must be spent for troops, the South must be flooded with agents of a revived Freedmen's Bureau, and military courts, where juries were not required, would have to be used extensively. In effect, the North would have to reopen the whole case of the white versus the black South. It was a solution that Northerners could not bring themselves to undertake. Their will, their sense of crusading—such as it had been—was dying. The North was ready to let the Southern black man and woman fend for themselves. Indeed, the passage of the Fifteenth Amendment in 1870 had seemed to most Northerners to close the account. Thereafter, blacks were to be on their own, like every other American—or so the whites conceived the situation to be.

Mississippi was in fact a special case, as it always was to be in later American history. In the rest of the South blacks continued for another twenty years to vote by the hundreds of thousands, schools were provided by white-dominated governments, a modicum of civil rights were guaranteed, and blacks even held office and sat on juries. It was not even necessary, in most cases, for Democrats to resort to violence in order to win elections; they had only to turn out and vote. Thousands of white Southerners in the old Whig regions—in North Carolina and throughout Appalachia—continued voting Republican until well into the twentieth century. The two-party system disappeared slowly and reluctantly in the South.

"Scientific" Racism

Northern commitment to racial equality had been, in the best of circumstances, only marginal. Indeed, in the Northern educated classes, where a moral concern for the welfare of black Americans had been strongest, a new climate of opinion was forming. Science and rationalism were flooding in. Charles Darwin's *Origin of Species* (1859) acquired enormous popularity. It described nature as a system in which "natural selection" doomed the less prolific and reproductive species to extinction. Count Arthur Gobineau's *Essay on the Inequality of Races* (translated 1860) classified humankind into many separate races (French, German, Welsh, Irish, etc.), each supposedly carrying irremovable characteristics in its bloodstream. Blending races always produced, he said, offspring that took on the characteristics of the "lower" race. One alleged quality of "lower" peoples was their passionate sexuality, which made them breed prolifically, whereas the more intelligent races had few children. Many educated Northerners of British (Anglo-Saxon) origin took from such "science" a grim lesson— that the Anglo-Saxon race stood in grave peril. Though alleged to be intelligent and gifted, it could be overwhelmed by swarming inferior races if it did not take steps to guard its superior position. Genteel Northerners recoiled in distaste from the grimy, illiterate, strange-looking immigrants who with their huge families were crowding into the northeastern ports. Alarmed, they began to feel a new sympathy for their counterparts in the South who detested blacks.

Another line of reasoning emerged in this setting. Black people were not the equal of whites: this was accepted. But they might *potentially* be equal. Darwinian concepts of natural selection and survival of the fittest seemed for such people to point toward long-range improvement. However, such progress would certainly be very long range indeed (so this line of thought ran). In the present circumstances, blacks were not ready for the full responsibilities of the ballot, of the professions, of social leadership. A new paternalist attitude emerged among Southern whites: the task for enlightened white leadership lay in taking the vote away from blacks (as essential to making government honest and efficient, it was said, as eliminating "boss rule" in the corrupt politics of Northern cities), and then beginning slowly and carefully to train them for eventual full citizenship. This would call for schools that offered instruction in practical, humble arts rather than schools that offered the liberal arts, the traditional training for future elites. It would call for complete social and sexual segregation while generations of educational effort had its slow effect. By this means social conflict would be ended, for each race would have its separate sphere.

In short, the new paternalism was not the harsh racial laissez faire that many racists called for in the 1870s and 1880s: standing back and letting whites obliterate blacks, as seemed promised in the race riots, lynching, and other acts of violence seen most starkly in Mississippi but appearing elsewhere in the South as well. However,

many whites were influenced by the British social scientist Herbert Spencer's early book *First Principles* (1862), which was widely read in America. It was Spencer who devised from Darwin's theories the concept of survival of the fittest. Though he later made a place for education, in *First Principles* he held that the "social order is fixed by laws of nature precisely analogous to those of the physical order." Therefore, "the most that man can do . . . by his ignorance and conceit is to mar the operation of social laws." In short, people should leave social problems entirely alone. Avoid public-health measures, so that diseases will sweep away the unfit. Avoid even the building of lighthouses, for dangerous reefs will kill off the unfit seamen. Let the "laws of nature" operate. Strong government is a curse, for it will always be misinformed and will make mistakes, thus disorganizing nature's wise plans.

The lessons were plain. What people thought to be science seemed to demonstrate conclusively that the black race could never be equal to the white. Whatever took place without government interference was best, even though it might seem oppressive. All things must be looked at coolly, dispassionately, rationally. Moral arguments were irrelevant because they were "unscientific." Let the Southern whites have their way, for that was best for the Anglo-Saxon race. Government intervention would in any case be harmful.

The Election of 1876

The stage was now set for the official termination of Reconstruction. Only three states were still Republican in the South: South Carolina, Louisiana, and Florida, their governments shored up by federal troops. In the election of 1876 the Republicans turned to a completely honest man whose public reputation was blameless, Rutherford B. Hayes, a former general in the Union army who was presently governor of Ohio. The Democrats turned to the wizened little man who was governor of New York, Samuel J. Tilden. He had led in destroying the Tweed Ring, which had taken millions from the government of New York City, and the Canal Ring, which had taken similarly huge sums from the state-run Erie Canal. Known to be "sound" on the racial-equality question—he described black men as "an element of disease and death" in the body politic, to be expelled when possible—he had the priceless political advantage of being known as a successful battler against corruption. "It is not necessary for me to attempt to paint the state of political corruption to which we have been reduced," the reformer Henry George said in California as he called for Tilden's election. "It is the dark background to our national [centennial] rejoicing, the skeleton which has stood by us at the feast. Our Fourth of July orators do not proclaim it; our newspapers do not announce it; we hardly whisper it to one an-

In the election of 1876 Democrats attacked Republicans for forcing blacks to vote the Republican ticket.
Culver Pictures

RECONSTRUCTION

other, but we all know, for we all feel, that beneath all our centennial rejoicing there exists in the public mind to-day a greater doubt of the success of Republican institutions than has existed before within the memory of our oldest man."

Tilden got a popular-vote majority of about 250,000 in the election of 1876, but the presidency went to Rutherford B. Hayes. When it appeared that Tilden was one electoral vote shy of election if he did not get the three states in the South still in Republican hands, those states were "delivered" to Hayes. Congress was thrown into turmoil. Should it accept the Republican votes from these disputed states, or agree with the Democrats that returns were fraudulent? Weeks of public and private negotiation took place in an atmosphere of near hysteria, many in the South and North warning of direct military action if the "steal" were successful. Not until early March 1877 was the "Compromise of 1877" reached. The South agreed to allow Florida, Louisiana, and

South Carolina to be counted in the Republican column as long as all federal troops were withdrawn from the South.

This was the "public" agreement. Some Southerners may have thought that the South would actually get more economic aid from the Republicans than from the Northern Democrats. Samuel J. Tilden was too good a Jeffersonian not to practice what he preached—that no government aid should be given to private business. As governor in New York he had heavily slashed all spending on internal improvements—canals, roads, and bridges. The South desperately needed its ports, rivers, bridges, and railroads rebuilt; it had not been able to get nearly enough done on its own; and the Republicans were clearly more friendly to providing federal aid to such enterprises than were the Democrats. They had constructed internal improvements all over the Northern states; perhaps they would do the same in the South if given the presidency once

THE ELECTION OF 1876

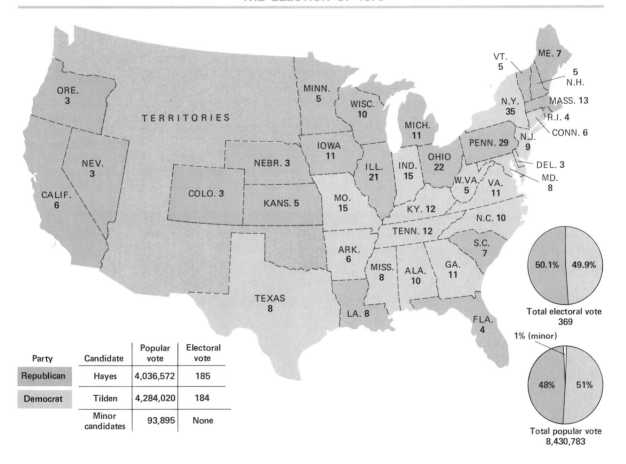

Party	Candidate	Popular vote	Electoral vote
Republican	Hayes	4,036,572	185
Democrat	Tilden	4,284,020	184
	Minor candidates	93,895	None

50.1% 49.9%
Total electoral vote 369

1% (minor)

48% 51%
Total popular vote 8,430,783

again. "The jobbers and monopolists of the North," said the disgruntled Montgomery Blair, "made common cause with the Southern oligarchy." Enough Southern votes in Congress were given to Hayes's cause to allow him to become president. Reconstruction was over.

Bibliography

Books that were especially valuable to me in writing this chapter: Eric L. McKitrick's *Andrew Johnson and Reconstruction** (1960) remains a penetrating account; Carl Degler's brilliant *The Other South: Southern Dissenters in the Nineteenth Century** (1974) opened up for me the whole non-Democratic South and its continuing role in that region's political life. Jack P. Maddex, Jr., *The Virginia Conservatives, 1867–1879: A Study in Reconstruction Politics* (1970) is an absorbing case study that buttresses Degler's position. Howard Rabinowitz, *Race Relations in the Urban South 1865–1890* (1978) aided me greatly in understanding a complex scene, especially the role of exclusion and segregation. All historians of this era, and of race relations in America, are in debt to Leon Litwack's beautifully written (and Pulitzer Prizewinning) study of the immediate aftermath of slavery for black Americans in the South, *Been in the Storm So Long** (1979). W. Elliot Brownlee's *Dynamics of Ascent: A History of the American Economy* (1978) guided me on postwar Southern economics. Robert Bannister's *Social Darwinism: Science and Myth in Anglo-American Social Thought* (1979) has given us quite a fresh understanding of an ideology whose actual role in these years we have misunderstood.

How Have Historians Looked at the Topic?

Reconstruction is rich field in historiography, one which has attracted myth-makers and propagandists as well as careful scholars. The first major American film, *The Birth of a Nation* (1915), depicted Ku Klux Klansmen as the heroes of the postbellum South, a highly distorted and blatantly racist interpretation that nevertheless influenced countless millions of viewers. After a private showing in the White House, historian and president Woodrow Wilson said the film medium was "like writing history with lightning."

Unfortunately the film did not convey history. Its characters and message only vaguely resembled the actualities of Reconstruction. However, its highly sympathetic view of the South's victimization is portrayed with scholarly conviction in W. A. Dunning's *Reconstruction, Political and Economic, 1865–1877** (1907). Standing in direct opposition to this interpretation is W. E. B. Du Bois's pioneering, militantly problack account *Black Reconstruction in America, 1860–1880** (1935).

The complexities of Reconstruction are perceived from a sharply different angle in Charles and Mary Beard's classic *The Rise of American Civilization* (1927). Rejecting the idea that the main actors in the Reconstruction drama were unscrupulous carpetbaggers and misled or courageous blacks, the Beards interpreted the struggles of the period as basically economic ones, motivated primarily by ambitious northern businessmen who were determined to keep the advantages they had gained during the war years. Robert P. Sharkey's *Money, Class, and Party: An Economic Study of Civil War and Reconstruction** (1959) brilliantly expands and criticizes the Beards' thesis, eliminating their bloc approach and emphasizing that northern businessmen took many positions, often mutually opposed. C. Vann Woodward's classic work *Origins of the New South, 1877–1913* (1951) illustrates the affinity between northern and southern businessmen and discredits the picture of hostility.

Several significant reassessments of the Reconstruction era appeared during the 1960s. John Hope Franklin's *Reconstruction: After the Civil War** (1961) offers a host of new insights and concludes that Reconstruction was a genuine search for social justice for the Afro-American. Robert Cruden's *The Negro in Reconstruction* (1969) elaborates on black attempts to exercise power during the period, and *After Slavery: The Negro in South Carolina During Reconstruction, 1861–1877* (1965) by Joel Williamson is a case study that stresses the initiative and progress of blacks in one state. James M. McPherson's *The Struggle for Equality: Abolitionists and the Negro in the Civil War and Reconstruction** (1964) explodes the theory of the abolitionists' abandonment of the black following the Civil War. A major study

RECONSTRUCTION

that examines the development of Reconstruction policy from the beginning of the Civil War is Herman Belz's *Reconstructing the Union: Theory and Policy During the Civil War* (1969). G. R. Bentley's *A History of the Freedmen's Bureau* (1970) reports the political maneuverings that led to the demise of the bureau in 1872.

Kenneth M. Stampp's *The Era of Reconstruction, 1865–1877** (1965) is a richly provocative analysis in which the Radical Republicans emerge as avant-garde thinkers rather than as fanatics. H. L. Trefousse's *The Radical Republicans: Lincoln's Vanguard for Racial Justice* (1969) supports and extends Stampp's interpretation. See also David Donald's massive recent work *Charles Sumner and the Rights of Man* (1970).

The first year of Andrew Johnson's administration is probed with care in LaWanda Cox and John H. Cox's *Politics, Principle, and Prejudice, 1865–1866* (1963). A British historian, William R. Brock, offers an important perspective on presidential-congressional relations during Johnson's time in office in *An American Crisis: Congress and Reconstruction, 1865–1867** (1963). William Gil-

lette's *The Right to Vote: Politics and the Passage of the Fifteenth Amendment* (1965) argues that this amendment was written with northern rather than southern blacks in mind.

An excellent one-volume guide to the perplexities of Reconstruction is James G. Randall and David Donald's *The Civil War and Reconstruction* (1961).

The controversial election of 1876 and the compromise of the following year are provocatively assessed in C. Vann Woodward's classic, *Reunion and Reaction: The Compromise of 1877 and the End of Reconstruction** (1966). For a scholarly recent analysis, see Keith Ian Polakoff, *The Politics of Inertia: The Election of 1876 and the End of Reconstruction* (1973). The interpretation presented in this chapter is developed at greater depth in Robert Kelley, *The Cultural Pattern in American Politics: The First Century** (1979), and *The Transatlantic Persuasion: The Liberal-Democratic Mind in the Age of Gladstone* (1969).

---

* Available in paperback.

21

TIME LINE

1851	Laramie Peace Conference
1860–78	Indian wars; Great Plains Treaty (1868)
1861	Kansas admitted to the Union
1863	West Virginia admitted to the Union
1864	Nevada admitted to the Union
1865–85	Cattle industry grows on the western plains
1867	Nebraska admitted to the Union; Alaska purchased
1873	Panic begins depression of 1870s In the *Slaughter House Cases* the Supreme Court rules that government may regulate business
1876	Colorado admitted to the Union; Battle of the Little Big Horn
1877	In *Munn* v. *Illinois* the Court rules that states may regulate rates charged by grain warehouses and railroads
1879	Standard Oil trust formed

LATE NINETEENTH CENTURY AMERICA: GROWTH AND DEVELOPMENT

New York Public Library

The historic Treaty of 1868 assigned a vast region in the northern Great Plains to the Indians. "No white person or persons shall be permitted to settle upon or occupy any portion of the territory," it said, "or without the consent of the Indians to pass through the same." But it was now the 1870s, and gold was being found in Sioux lands, in the beautiful *Paha Sapa*—the Black Hills. To the Indians, they were the center of the world, the place of gods and holy mountains. Warriors went there to commune with the Great Spirit, to have visions. When the white government offered $7 million for them, the gesture was rejected as ludicrous. "We want no white men here," said Tatanka Yotanka (Sitting Bull), the chief of the Hunkpapa Sioux. He hated whites as liars and thieves, and would never accept them or agree to their "treaties." "If the whites try to take [the Black Hills], I will fight."

So the fighting began. Thousands of pony soldiers and Bluecoats (infantrymen) under Long Hair (General George A. Custer), Three Stars (General George Crook), and other ex–Civil War commanders hungry for glory invaded the Indians' lands. After a three-day dance, Sitting Bull had a vision of soldiers falling like grasshoppers: the Great Spirit, he announced, had willed Indian victory. In 1876 he helped lead a successful attack upon a column of invading Bluecoats, then became the most honored chief at an enormous gathering of the Sioux tribes, comprising perhaps 12,000 Indians—the largest such community ever gathered together—in an encampment on the Little Big Horn. Here, on June 25, Long Hair led his men in a foolish attack against this great host. Custer's men attacked Sitting Bull's own tepees, and after a furious battle, Long Hair and his soldiers—save for a smaller isolated detachment—lay dead.

Now the white nation to the east exploded in rage. The Army ravaged the Indian lands mercilessly, seeking out peaceful villages and launching sudden attacks. "What have we done that the white people want us to stop?" asked Sitting Bull. "We have been running up and down this country, but they follow us from one place to another." In despair, he led his band to Canada in 1877. Meanwhile, the killing went on, the Indians ran out of ammunition and food, and in 1878 they had no choice but to accept settlement in reservations. Denied aid by the Canadians, after four years the great chief and his band of about 200 followers returned to America and surrendered.

Sitting Bull was now the most famous Indian of his time. Newsmen regularly interviewed him, for he continued to spit out his hatred of whites, and was great copy. He even toured the States with Buffalo Bill Cody's Wild West Show, returning amused by what he had seen. But on December 15, 1890, a party of police arrived to arrest him, alleging vague conspiracies against the peace, and in the succeeding scuffle Sitting Bull fell dead, shot through the head. Two weeks later the Massacre of Wounded Knee, the last butchery of Indians by the Bluecoats, capped the tragedy of the Plains Indians. The Long Death was over.

The years from 1860 to 1900, during which the American population grew from thirty-one to seventy-six million, present a paradoxical picture of booming growth streaked with crisis and ruined hopes. Ambitious and imaginative enterprisers ranged the continent looking for new opportunities. Inventions poured into the economy at an unbelievable rate. In the 1850s the U.S. Patent Office issued four times more patents than in the 1840s: 23,000. From 1882 on, in each *year* it issued about that many. Thomas Alva Edison (1847–1931) was the admired symbol of the era. In the 1870s—self-taught, self-made—he began turning out the more than one thousand inventions of his lifetime, among them the printing telegraph, mimeograph, microphone, phonograph, incandescent electric lamp, alkaline storage battery, and motion picture. Although business conditions lurched erratically from upswings to slumps, the country's industrial base grew rapidly and the railroads expanded quickly from the skeletal system that existed in 1865 to an intricate mesh of lines linking all parts of the nation. Out of this grew a powerful conviction of unending national progress.

Galloping cavalry and thudding .44-40 rifles swept the Great Plains brutally clean of Indian tribes and buffalo so that this tragically empty land could become a spreading empire of cattle ranches and wheat farms. The vast continental sweep between Kansas and California filled in with new states: Colorado in 1876; the Dakotas, Washington, and Montana in 1889; Idaho and Wyoming in 1890; Utah in 1896. Only Oklahoma, Arizona, and New Mexico remained territories (the first was admitted as a state in 1907 and the latter two in 1912). Watching the map in these years, Americans were filled with pride as they observed the appearance of a new, truly transcontinental United States.

But the country was also torn by crisis. Rapid changes made people feel anxious and unsettled. Hundreds of towns were swept out of their quiet isolation when railroad tracks appeared in their streets. Powerful corporations reached into every community, and prices and wages began rising and falling chaotically. Men who had worked eagerly to get railroads into their towns soon became angry critics of the "railroad monopoly." Factory owners paid low wages and worked their employees up to fourteen hours a day, thus setting off tremendous labor strikes that sent violence and disorder ripping through many communities. The cities, meanwhile, grew so fast that they could not dispose of their sewage or provide clean water. Thousands of people died annually in epidemics. So many officeholders took graft that they made a mockery of democratic government. Farmers formed the Granger movement in the 1870s to fight back against the railroads, and in the 1880s this protest spread into the Great Plains and down into the South. By this decade so grave were the nation's troubles that politicians, ministers, and writers everywhere were worriedly talking about the "social question." Grover Cleveland warned somberly that selfishness and baseness had blighted the nation's promise. When the worst depression of the century began in 1893, the sense of crisis deepened.

Yet much that was creative and solid occurred in the new industrial age. Jobs were provided for a booming population; most people lived better, as the standard of living rose significantly; isolation and rustic crudity gave way to more varied and challenging patterns of life. Many things eased and enriched the lives of ordinary people, among them electric lights, streetcars, steel plows, mail-order houses, refrigerators, and inexpensive homes. America mistreated its immigrants, but gave them great opportunities as well. Imaginative educators built vigorous private and state universities from which came confident young men and women who took up the renovation and reorganization of American society. In the countryside, farmers gladly adopted many new conveniences and welcomed the breakdown of their country-bound isolation. They eagerly raised crops to sell in the markets that railroads opened up, and used the money earned to gain a better life.

Both of these aspects of late nineteenth-century America, one ugly and the other encouraging, must be considered when assessing this complicated era. Optimism and gloom lived side by side. Generally, Republicans were the optimists, as had been their predecessors, the Whigs, while the Democrats, led by Grover Cleveland, warned of greed and corruption and looked yearningly to the past, as they had been doing since Jackson's day.

The Railroad Explosion
and the Transformed Economy

Railroad expansion fueled the booming economic growth of these years. There were 35,000 miles of trackage at the end of the Civil War, composed of local lines that used different track gauge (widths). By 1910 there were some 240,000 interconnected standard-gauge miles. In some years more than 10,000 miles of track were laid, the most spectacular undertakings being the transcontinental lines that reached westward to various points on the Pacific Coast in the 1880s. As early as 1890, the United States contained one third of the world's total railroad mileage.

Now there was one vast marketplace that extended across the continent. Industrialists and farmers piled on more productive capacity in order to profit from the new nationwide opportunities. This led to glutted markets, overproduction, and the beginning of a long price decline that lasted until the late 1890s. The railroads overbuilt badly, for to grab off each other's trade they built parallel lines and handed out rebates and special favors. This produced loud complaints from people who lived where there was only one railroad, since such companies often jacked up their rates to compensate for losses elsewhere. Small

The solitary figure of a man standing on newly laid sleepers of the transcontinental railroad at the 100th meridian, October 1866, with the road-bed dwindling off into the western distance, expresses the lonely flat expanses of the high plains country.

Courtesy of the Library of Congress

producers also protested bitterly because the railroads refused to give them rebates while handing them out liberally to large corporations whose business they coveted. Hundreds of local railroad companies suffered because their builders borrowed more money than needed during the construction phase in order to skim off funds into their own pockets. With large financial debts, railroads were forced to charge high rates to meet interest payments or to build additional mileage to compete the other roads and take away their traffic.

By the late 1870s, therefore, railroad owners began looking for some way to bring order out of chaos. They saw that if they could agree on rates and split up the traffic in some equitable way, their problems would be eased. This would also quiet the complaints of small shippers by eliminating the problem of unequal rates. It would rely, however, on the adoption of a new technique: counting everything—cars, amount of freight, distances traveled, costs, wages, and every other business expense. This, in turn, required that central business offices be established where statistics concerning freight and passenger movements could be gathered, analyzed, and used to figure costs and fair rates. In this new technique lay the embryo of modern business with its reliance on centralized, analytical, bureaucratic methods.

Such "pools," were adopted with varying degrees of success in the 1880s, and they caused much resentment. Large shippers like the Pillsburys of Minnesota did not like pools because they wanted to keep receiving rebates. Others insisted that the pools exploited the public. In the late 1860s and 1870s many midwestern and other states had tried to control railroad rates by creating commissions that were charged with regulating them. Now these commissions turned to do battle with the pools. In 1886, however, the United States Supreme Court ruled that state commissions could not regulate commercial activities that extended beyond their borders.

Formation of the Interstate
Commerce Commission

This made federal regulation mandatory, for only Washington had constitutional authority over interstate commerce. In January 1887 President

LATE NINETEENTH-CENTURY AMERICA: GROWTH AND DEVELOPMENT

Grover Cleveland signed legislation that prohibited rebates, declared pools illegal, and established the Interstate Commerce Commission (ICC) with power to ensure that railroad rates were "reasonable and just." Thus began a new era in American history. For the first time the government of the United States established a new kind of public agency: an independent commission given broad and unspecified powers to regulate a crucially important part of the national economy—with the proviso that its decisions could be appealed to the courts. Drawn partly from the British example, the ICC was a step in the direction of the kind of centralized control by high officials that has become an increasingly major feature of modern government. It was widely criticized at the time of its creation as an aristocratic, elitist, essentially Federalist idea.

As the first such agency, the ICC went through difficult times in its early years. Conducting investigations, gathering information, making rulings and publicizing them widely, the ICC helped stabilize railroading. The new techniques of statistical analysis and centralized management were widely adopted by the railroads, for they had to justify their rates and become efficient. Step by step, the new commission began teaching the owners of great railroads that they had public responsibilities as well as private rights. In the mid 1890s, however, the Supreme Court cut down drastically on the ICC's powers, and the old order of cutthroat competition and special favors—including rebates to large producers—returned.

Meanwhile the railroads continued making their operations more efficient. They adopted a standard gauge of 56.5 inches in 1886. Then they built connecting links between their systems of tracks so that cars carrying passengers and freight could pass uninterruptedly from one road to another. Then came standard freight classifications, following which railroads divided the coun-

THE UNITED STATES, 1861–1912

try into four time zones in 1883 to replace the bewildering variety of local times that had formerly existed.

In other words, it was in the effort to manage effectively the continental railroad system that modern bureaucracy, both industrial and governmental, began in the United States. Regularity of operation, efficiency, the use of trained experts, evenhanded treatment of people in widely varying situations, standardized regulations and rates, centralized planning and control, predictability, and promptness—all these qualities, which are the central characteristics of large-scale bureaucratic organizations, started here. It was impossible to run the system over such a huge expanse of territory in any other way.

The Rise of Big Business

The national market, created by the railroad system, transformed business life. By the early 1900s the economy was no longer composed of thousands of small producers who sold to local markets. Rather, it was dominated by a small number of large firms that sold nationwide and to the world at large—Standard Oil, American Tobacco, National Biscuit, United Fruit, United States Steel, General Electric, International Harvester, and others. Clearly, the era of big business had arrived.

A big business appeared when many small businesses came together or when a gifted entrepreneur discovered a product that would sell in the national market and organized his operation on a continental scale. Gustavus Swift took the latter road. A skillful meat salesman from New England, he went west in the 1870s and observed the huge herds of cattle spreading over the interior plains. The practice at that time was to bring large numbers of the animals to Chicago, place them on trains to eastern cities, and butcher them after their arrival. Swift saw the waste in this process, for the animals had to be fed en route, they lost a good deal of weight, and much that was unsalable in them had to be transported east only to be thrown away at butchering. He successfully built an industry that butchered the cattle in the West, used the new technology of refrigeration to preserve the salable meat, and transported only that part of the animal for sale in the East.

The lure of the national market or the ex-

RAILROADS, 1850–1900

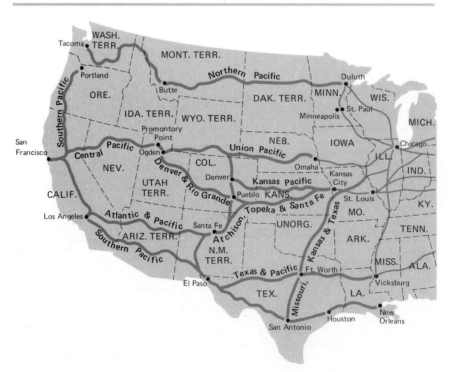

LATE NINETEENTH-CENTURY AMERICA: GROWTH AND DEVELOPMENT

citement of periodic booms would often inflate a manufacturer's confidence in the future. As all his mills or distilleries or stamping plants roared along in full production he would add more productive capacity, only to be met by a slump and dropping prices. It was common for factories to stand empty much of the time or for whole industries to operate at only 50 percent of capacity. The initial response was to mechanize operations more intensively, thus increasing efficiency and raising output. But this led in turn to oversupply and a renewed drop in prices. "It is a chronic case," said one producer in 1888, "of too many stoves, and not enough people to buy them."

The solution was for a group of manufacturers to form a pool, divide the market, and establish agreed-upon prices. But such arrangements constantly broke down. The final recourse was to place the stock of many competitors in the hands of a group of trustees. By this step the manufacturers created centralized management, though not centralized ownership. The first of these trusts was the Standard Oil Company, which was formed in Cleveland in 1879 when a group of small refineries joined forces. Its success led to the creation of many other trusts, involving such items as leather, sugar, salt, biscuits, fertilizer, rubber boots, and gloves.

David A. Wells, a nineteenth-century inventor and economist, was an early observer of the way small businesses were wiped out by mechanization: "About [1874] the new and so-called roller process for crushing and separating wheat was discovered and brought into use. Its advantages over the old method of grinding by millstones were that it separated the flour more perfectly from the hull or bran of the berry of the wheat, gave more flour to a bushel of wheat, and raised both its color and strength (nutriment). . . . The cost of building mills to operate by the roller process is, however, much greater than that of the old stone mills. . . . The consequence of requiring so much more capital to participate in the flour business now than formerly is that the smaller flour mills in the United States are being crushed, or forced into consolidation with the larger companies, the latter being able, from dealing in such immense quantities, to buy their wheat more economically, obtain lower rates of freight, and, by contracting ahead, keep constantly running. At the same time, there is a tendency to drive the milling industry from points in the country to the larger cities, and central grain and flour markets where cheap freights and large supplies of wheat are available.

"Thirty or forty years ago the tinman, whose occupation was mainly one of handicraft, was recognized as one of the leading and most skillful mechanics in every village, town, and city. His occupation has, however, now well-nigh passed away. For example, a townsman and a farmer desires a supply of milk cans. He never thinks of going to his corner tinman, because he knows that in . . . other large towns and cities there is a special establishment fitted up with special machinery which will make his can better and 50 percent cheaper than he can have it made by hand in his own town. . . . And what has been thus affirmed of tinplate might be equally affirmed of a great variety of other leading commodities. The blacksmith . . . no longer making but buying his horseshoes, nails, nuts, and bolts; the carpenter, his doors, sash, blinds, and moldings; the wheelwright, his spokes, hubs, and felloes; the harness maker, his straps, girths, and collars; the painter, his paints, ground and mixed. . . . " (David A. Wells, *Recent Economic Changes* [1889])

The Standard Oil Company was the model for all who aspired to "vertical" integration of an entire industry (that is, the owning or controlling of a complete operation, from the raw material to the finished product, by one firm). The company owned its own forests for lumber, made its own barrels, manufactured its refinery chemicals, bought up oil-terminal facilities, possessed fleets of vessels and oil cars, and carried on its own retail marketing. In the 1880s it even acquired its own wells. Soon Standard Oil agents were competing actively with Russian oil producers in the markets of central Europe and teaching Orientals the value of the kerosene lamp. The five-gallon kerosene tin from Standard became a worldwide institution.

The Antitrust Movement

The word "trust," however, rapidly became a stench in the public nostrils. Even though prices drifted downward, the notion of monopoly, which the trusts certainly seemed to threaten, was too much for people to bear. Both Republicans and Democrats joined in condemning such combinations as a flagrant violation of all the laws of the marketplace. In 1888 a Republican senator from Ohio, John Sherman, proposed the first version of what became in 1890 the Sherman Anti-Trust Act. It declared illegal "every contract, combination in the form of trust or otherwise, or conspiracy, in restraint of trade or commerce among the

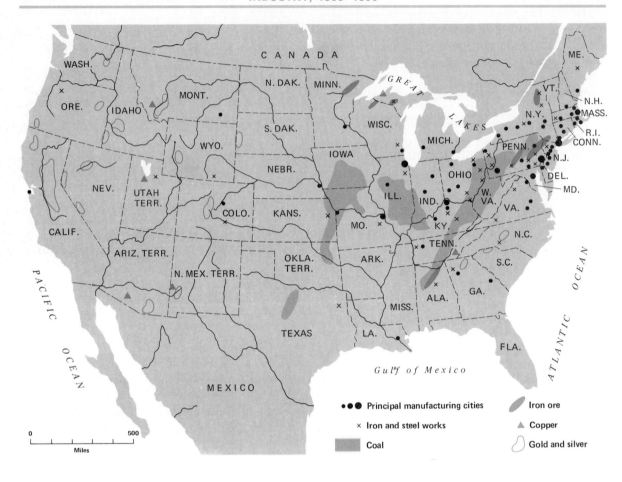

Principal manufacturing cities • • ●
Iron and steel works ×
Coal
Iron ore
Copper ▲
Gold and silver

several States, or with foreign nations." Anyone who made such agreements or who "monopolize[d] or attempts to monopolize" some aspect of the nation's business could be fined $1,000 and jailed for one year. Also, anyone injured by the monopolizer's activities could sue for triple damages.

Whatever Congress's intentions, the law had little effect on big business for many years after its passage. John D. Rockefeller simply converted his Standard Oil trust into a single corporation, headquartered in New Jersey and directed from his offices in New York City. Furthermore, the courts were hostile to the new law. In 1895 the Supreme Court went so far as to rule that manufacturing could not be considered part of interstate commerce and was therefore exempt from antitrust action.

Comparison of American and European Industry

Europeans were astonished at the swift growth of American industry, which soon surpassed their own industries in size and wealth. Why was this so? Was it simply because the country was large and had huge resources? Clearly this was a major factor, but there were other influences as well. From the beginning, American manufacturers had had to compensate for the small number of laborers available (since most were on the farms) by mechanizing operations to a far greater degree than abroad. When immigrants came pouring in after 1840 to provide labor, manufacturers were already used to machines. Even the most intricate processes were carried out by machines that could be tended by unskilled workers.

Businessmen in the United States were also surrounded by a friendly environment. In Europe, ancient governments dominated by landowning aristocracies with strong powers scorned businessmen. Furthermore, restrictive laws hampered business operations, and governments favored stability rather than change. In comparison with Europe, government hardly existed at all in the United States. A county or a state would have only a few employees whereas corporations hired thousands. Businessmen were praised and admired; young boys were trained in getting ahead; everything was assessed on strictly practical standards. At the same time, the expanse of the country and the opportunities for a huge continental market opened by the railroads encouraged a risk-taking mentality far more adventurous in the United States than elsewhere. People were convinced that if they leaped forward the future would catch them. This attitude made business efforts more wasteful but also more buoyant and productive.

Funkville on Oil Creek, in western Pennsylvania, was one of the river towns from which flowed the raw crude to distant distilleries, setting off the explosion of the petroleum industry.

The Granger Collection, New York

Northern Industry Triumphant

So matters stood in the 1880s and 1890s. Northern industry dominated the nation's life. It had scattered the country with great cities: steel cities like Pittsburgh and Philadelphia; oil cities like Cleveland; Chicago with its huge stockyards, slaughterhouses, grain elevators, and spreading train yards; Peoria with its whiskey; Waltham, Massachusetts, with its watches; and Minneapolis—St. Paul with its flour.

Industrialists prided themselves on the notion that their success was good and proper. Andrew Carnegie insisted that "the millionaires who are in active control started as poor boys and were trained in the sternest but most efficient of all schools—poverty." His father had been a poor Scottish weaver, Swift's a farmer, and Rockefeller's a traveling salesman of patent medicines. Although the proportion of rich men who came from poor beginnings increased only slightly during this period (most, as is usually the case, sprang from comfortable backgrounds), the opposite view was widely believed. It was their hard work, special talents, and the American system of unfettered individualism, rich men told themselves, that explained their eminence. Without an ancient landed aristocracy around to take the limelight, American millionaires could bask all alone in public adulation. "*We* have made the country rich," said the unprincipled speculator Jay Gould. "We have developed the country." Rockefeller, devout Baptist that he was, had the simplest answer: "The good Lord gave me my money."

The Supreme Court Protects Capitalism

The United States Supreme Court swung its massive weight behind businessmen in the post–Civil War years, although at first it moved cautiously. The American system of law, inherited from England, is rooted in the principle of *stare decisis*, or decision by precedent. Justices rarely plant their feet very far ahead of where the law is at that moment. They may edge ahead, but always retain the option to veer off in a different direction. The issue of governmental regulation of business first came before the Court in 1873, when in the *Slaughter-House Cases* a bold defense lawyer insisted that the Fourteenth Amendment protected his clients, the owners of the slaughterhouses, from such regulation. The key passage of that amendment runs as follows:

No State shall make or enforce any law which shall abridge the privileges or immunities of citizens of the United States; nor shall a State deprive any person of life, liberty, or property, without due process of law; nor deny to any person within its jurisdiction the equal protection of the laws.

The Court ruled that the amendment applied only to civil and political rights. It did not accept the lawyer's assertion that corporations were "persons" in law, and that governmental regulation amounted to taking property without due process—that is, without going through a court proceeding. In 1877 in the case of *Munn* v. *Illinois*, the Court ruled that it was constitutional for the state of Illinois to regulate the prices charged by railroads, grain warehouses, and grain elevators. Such institutions, it said, were "clothed with a public interest when used in a manner to [be] of public consequence, and affect the community at large."

One justice, Stephen J. Field, trumpeted his dissent. A self-proclaimed conservative who proudly quoted Alexander Hamilton and attacked the Illinois laws as wildly socialistic, he insisted that the judgment was "subversive of the rights of private property," which under the Constitution were placed "under the same protection as life and liberty. Except by due process of law no State can deprive any person of either."

Field lost this case but won the future, for the Court began swinging in his direction. Increasingly alarmed over attacks on business, it accepted the idea that a corporation was a "person" in law, and that property must be protected against governmental regulation. Until well after 1900, the Court consistently threw out state attempts to regulate any business with interstate operations. Such matters, it said, could be regulated only by Congress. Then, when the ICC was created, the Court turned around and ruled in 1896, in *Cincinnati, New Orleans, and Texas Pacific Railway Company* v. *ICC*, that even the federal government lacked the power to fix railroad rates. The commission could only make reports and issue protests. Following the same course in *United States* v. *E. C. Knight Company*, the Court ruled that the Sherman Anti-Trust Act did not give the government power to forbid monopolies in manufacturing, since that activity was only indirectly a part of interstate commerce.

In those instances where the Court accepted the regulation of railroad rates by state commissions, it assumed the prerogative of deciding whether the regulation was carried out in an unjust or arbitrary fashion. In the 1890s it repeatedly insisted that railroad rates would have to be high enough to allow the companies involved to earn a "reasonable" profit, which the Court would define in each case. In 1895, in *Pollock* v. *Farmer's Loan and Trust Company*, it invalidated a federal income tax enacted under Grover Cleveland of 2 percent on incomes above $4,000 a year on the ground that the income tax was a direct tax and had to be equal and bear on everyone alike in the most literal sense. Despite criticism—much of it heated and bitterly prolonged—the Supreme Court pushed ahead confidently in this "activist" mode for many years after the 1890s. It was obsessed with the idea that its task was to protect capitalist interests and preserve what it regarded as the best philosophy for the nation—laissez-faire.

The Agricultural Transformation

The impact of the Industrial Revolution struck American agriculture with full force after the Civil War. Markets expanded enormously, both because of the appearance of an integrated national market and because city populations in Europe were growing rapidly and demanding American grains, meat, and cotton. Huge sums were invested in farm machinery to increase output, from expensive steel plows to the most intricate equipment for harvesting. Whether the task was planting trees, caring for livestock, or raising flowers, a flood of inventions revolutionized operations. Mechanical refrigeration and assembly-line slaughtering transformed the meat-packing industry. In the 1870s agricultural chemists began persuading farmers to use fertilizers on a wider scale than before. Inquiries into plant diseases initiated the use of pesticides in the 1880s, which vastly increased production and saved whole industries.

While the center of farm production continued to move westward, agricultural growth flourished even in the increasingly urbanized and industrialized northeastern states. Corn, wheat,

LATE NINETEENTH-CENTURY AMERICA: GROWTH AND DEVELOPMENT

potatoes, dairy products, cattle, vegetables, fruits—all mounted in production. Since their transportation costs were low, farmers in the East could invest so much in fertilizers and equipment that the yield per acre in the Northeast was higher than elsewhere in the nation, even though New Englanders were still tilling the stony soils that had plagued the Puritans.

In the Southern states, as early as 1875 the cotton crop was more abundant than it had been in 1859, when 4.5 million bales were produced. By the 1890s, the output had reached more than 7 million bales. The use of fertilizers opened up older sections thought to be farmed-out and, by shortening the period necessary for the growth of mature cotton bolls, allowed farmers to raise their crops at higher elevations and in more northerly latitudes. Tobacco culture slowly revived. Similarly, the postwar years witnessed a vigorous revival of rice growing along the coastal regions of Georgia, South Carolina, and particularly Louisiana.

From Ohio to the rich plains of Iowa and the Dakotas stretches one of the richest growing regions of the world, matched only by the pampas of the Argentine and the vast Ukrainian plains in Russia. In the Great Plains an enormous agricultural empire grew and proliferated in the nineteenth century. The fertility of its soils was incredible. Great volumes of wheat and corn, especially in the huge and productive "bonanza" farms in the northern plains—some of them encompassing tens of thousands of acres—were harvested year after year. Thousands of migratory workers, using heavy machinery, followed the crops, producing on one North Dakota farm some 600,000 bushels of wheat in 1881. In the early 1880s, wheat prices were excellent and produced large profits. Where grasslands were abundant, as in Kansas, livestock increased rapidly.

AGRICULTURE, 1860–1890

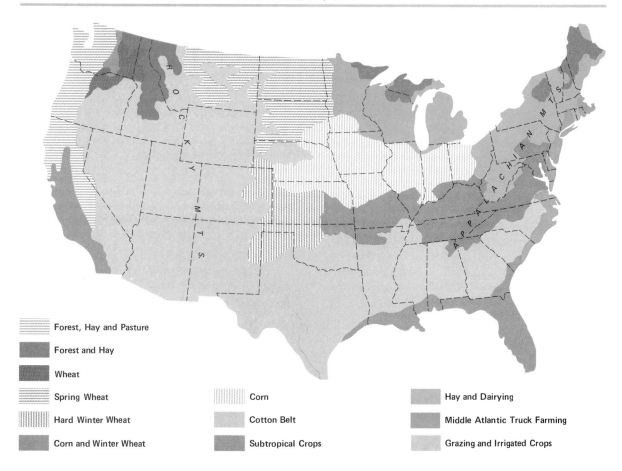

Forest, Hay and Pasture

Forest and Hay

Wheat

Spring Wheat

Hard Winter Wheat

Corn and Winter Wheat

Corn

Cotton Belt

Subtropical Crops

Hay and Dairying

Middle Atlantic Truck Farming

Grazing and Irrigated Crops

The abundance of cheap corn for hog feed produced an increase in hog production in that state from 432,000 in 1877 to 3.2 million in 1891. In the latter year, Illinois grazed 1.7 million beef cattle, there were 1.3 million dairy cattle in Iowa, and 4.5 million sheep were raised in Ohio.

Beyond the Rockies and the deserts, California became a booming agricultural state. Hundreds of vessels called annually at San Francisco to carry off to Europe the prized hard wheat of California's Central Valley, where bonanza farms stretching beyond the horizon produced millions of bushels of grain. More than in any other region, California's farmers invested heavily in large equipment and pioneered in the use of steam-driven harvesting combines that could thresh and bag as much as 450 pounds of grain a minute. At the same time, farming entrepreneurs poured large sums of money into irrigation and reclamation works and began raising fruits, nuts, and grapes for wine. In the 1880s refrigerated cars began carrying such products to eastern states.

The Mining West

Miners were early on the scene in the vast region from the Missouri frontier to the Pacific coast. Between 1858 and 1875 they explored every nook and cranny of the mountain country and the desert basins, populating a region formerly inhabited only by Indians and fur traders. After the gold rush to California, miners spread eastward and northward, discovering gold and silver in what are now Nevada, Idaho, Montana, and British Columbia. Other gold seekers rushed to Colorado in 1858 when they heard wild tales of fabulous deposits in the Pikes Peak country. Steamboats ascending the Missouri River were jammed to the rails, and a parade of covered wagons headed westward over the plains, "Pikes Peak or Bust" scrawled on their sides. Scattering out all over the eastern Colorado Rockies, they created such towns as Denver, Pueblo, Canon City, and Boulder. In 1859 large gold deposits were found near Central City, followed by others elsewhere, and a permanent population settled down in Colorado to make it a major mining state.

By the 1890s, corporation mining had entered the picture. Hired laborers and eastern-trained engineers took the place of the romantic prospector with his battered hat and sluice box.

Millions of dollars were invested in opening up California's large hydraulic gold mines—where jets of water under heavy pressure washed down whole hillsides—and the deep rock mines of the Sierra Nevada, the ranges of Nevada, and the Rocky Mountains. In time the violence of the West no longer involved the exploits of Wild Bill Hickok, but instead conflicts between capital and labor.

The Indian

Miners in the mountain and desert country encountered Indians everywhere. Those of California's Sierra Nevada were peaceable and were soon brutally exterminated. The Snake and Bannock Indians of Oregon and southern Idaho fought back bravely, as did the Ute, who occupied much of Utah and Nevada. But intermittent warfare between 1850 and 1855 broke them down, and they were eventually placed on small reservations.

The southwestern Indians (those in what are now New Mexico and Arizona) were much more difficult to subdue. Apache and Navaho Indians kept the miners out until the army was sent in during the 1850s to provide protection. In 1860 major warfare erupted. For the next four years the Apache and Navaho, riding swiftly over the high deserts on ponies, fought so skillfully that they almost won. But in the campaigns of 1863 and 1864, hundreds of them were killed and thousands captured. By 1865 they were forced to submit and were placed on reservations, which some refused to accept until hunted down in another decade of southwestern fighting.

The Great Plains Indians were another matter entirely. Here the powerful and expanding Sioux were dominant. In 1851, Washington, D.C., had tried to come to terms with the Plains Indians by convening a great peace conference at Fort Laramie, in what is now Wyoming. Behind this gathering lay major historic events. Winning the Mexican cession in the Mexican War and the Pacific Northwest by treaty with the British, in the 1840s, had changed all the elements shaping national Indian policy. With immense new possessions on the Pacific Coast, citizens of the United States came to think of the continental interior beyond the Missouri frontier not as a great western open space for Indian tribes, but as part of the internal geography of the United States of America. American settlement was swiftly rising on the Pacific Coast, especially after the gold rush to California began in 1849. Passage through the Great Plains to get to the Far West with its immense resources, and to link the two widely separated regions settled by American citizens, was essential.

In 1849 the Department of the Interior had been created to concern itself with this tremendous region. The new department assumed control of the Indian Office (later the Bureau of Indian Affairs), which had been under the army's jurisdiction. It quickly got to work developing concepts for managing the Indian country. Soon the idea of establishing distinct territorial reservations for the Indians within that region was developed, their purpose being to protect Indian hunting and residential areas while allowing travel and settlement by whites. Those Indians agreeing to live on such reservations would receive annual cash payments, food, and supplies (in place of lost game). In short, for the first time the federal government would establish a direct and continuing link to individual tribes. An Indian Agent would live on each reservation to manage federal-Indian relations.

Then the controversy among American citizens over slavery in the new territories erupted, and the Compromise of 1850 established governments to rule over the territories of Kansas and Nebraska (which ran all the way to the Canadian border), Utah, and New Mexico—all without asking the Indians resident in this great region, of course. Potentially half a million square miles of land, or one sixth of the area of the United States, was thereby opened to white settlement. Some protested that this violated earlier treaties made with the Indians, but the protests were ineffective. In the Far West, the process proceeded of negotiating treaties and establishing reservations.

This was the context for the 1851 Laramie Peace Conference. In that gathering the Sioux tribes controlled the Indian side of the negotiation, to the point of frightening away tribes they wished not to be present. Thus, the resulting treaty effectively recognized Sioux dominance on the plains, for it established borders for an immense Sioux holding on the northern plains, as dictated by the Sioux. When efforts were made to assign certain lands to other tribes, the Sioux successfully protested: "These lands once belonged

to the Kiowas and the Crows," the Sioux observed, "but we whipped those nations out of them, and in this we did what the white men do when they want the lands of the Indians."

Until this point the Sioux and the people of the United States had not come into much direct conflict, but henceforth both recognized the other as their greatest potential rival. Thereafter, the Sioux tribes joined in prohibiting all further land cessions to the Americans and sternly closing their hunting grounds to American intrusions. Soon warfare erupted, the Sioux winning a number of encounters in the 1850s. Meanwhile, they continued to expand their hunting grounds at the expense of the Crows, the Pawnees, and other tribes. (For this reason, many Indians from these tribes helped the American troops in their battles with the Sioux.)

Warfare on the Plains Swells in Intensity

The Americans who trekked across the Plains on their way to the Far West created havoc for many tribes. An unending line of wagons, stretching practically from one horizon to the other, drove away buffalo, littered trails with discarded equipment, destroyed grass, and spread disease. Cholera that raged like wildfire in the wagon trains swiftly spread to the Indians and decimated whole tribes. Indian survivors were convinced that the affliction had been purposely introduced to destroy them.

In 1859 came the Pikes Peak gold rush and the settlement of Colorado, which established more permanent wagon roads across the central plains. The government decided to clear Colorado of Indians, assigning them to large reservations in what are now Oklahoma and the Dakotas. Treaties to this effect were made in 1861, but the Indians resisted. Desperate for food, weakened by disease, Indians in the eastern-Colorado region began raiding wagon trains and driving off herds of cattle. Army detachments soon appeared, officered by combative young men eager for the glory their colleagues were acquiring in the Civil War. In 1864 warfare broke out over wide areas of the plains.

As soon as the Civil War was over, General William Tecumseh Sherman was assigned the task of bringing peace to the Great Plains. His favorite word was "extermination." Always an autocrat, he was determined that the Indians were either going to obey or be wiped out. By the spring of 1868, his winter campaigning and relentless pursuit, combined with the indiscriminate slaughter of peaceful villages (for which, to do him justice, he was not responsible), had brought Sherman apparent success. Chiefs of all the tribes signed the historic Treaty of 1868, by which they accepted residence on one of two large reservations, that far to the north or that to the south.

Many young Indians, however, could not accept this indignity. By the fall of 1868 warfare was raging on the plains; it lasted for ten years. Its most spectacular event occurred in 1876, when the direct invasion of Sioux lands to gain the Black Hills and their gold set off the triumphant counterattacks of the Sioux chief Sitting Bull and finally Custer's famous "last stand" on the Little Big Horn. The army hurled itself thereafter at the Sioux, inflicting final defeat, though sporadic outbreaks continued for years as small groups of Indians broke away from their reservations for brief raids. Indeed, they might be fighting still were it not for the fact that by the 1880s the enormous buffalo herds of the plains, which had given life and independence to the Plains Indians, were practically wiped out.

The slaughtering of the buffalo had begun long before, by the Sioux and other, smaller tribes, who sold hides, tongues, and pemmican to the whites and received guns and other trade goods in return. It was the headlong pursuit of the buffalo, in fact (as we saw in Chapter 14) that had fueled the powerful outward expansion of the Sioux to take over practically all of the northern plains. It had been white hunters, however, who had killed the most buffalo, even in the years before 1850. In the 1860s there were still perhaps thirteen million buffalo roaming the grasslands in huge herds. Then in 1871 a Pennsylvania tannery discovered that buffalo hides could be made into commercially valuable leather. Professional hunters swarmed over the plains and began killing buffalo at a steady rate. Some of the hunters were deafened for life by the detonations of their heavy rifles. Millions of buffalo were killed every year. By 1878 the southern herds were gone; by 1883 the buffalo on the northern plains had disappeared. A museum expedition sent out to search for specimens in 1883 could find only 200 buffalo in the entire West.

The New Indian Policy: Severalty and Acculturation

Without buffalo the Indians were now virtually helpless. What was to be done with them? Eastern reformers who in the 1870s began clamoring for more humane treatment of the Indians insisted that the only hope for them was to become "civilized." There was no realization that the Indians could live more fruitfully within their tribes than as scattered individuals in American society. Lewis Henry Morgan, a pioneer anthropologist, believed that the only way to solve the "Indian problem" was to teach the tribesmen the white man's ways. Another noted scientific observer who was widely familiar with Indian culture, Major John Wesley Powell, urged in 1874 that the Indians be made to settle as farmers, learn English, and adopt white values. "A reservation should be a school of industry," he said. Even Helen Hunt Jackson, whose two books in behalf of the Indians, *A Century of Dishonor* (1881) and the novel *Ramona* (1884), caused a national sensation, agreed with the idea of acculturation. This would require fixed settlement, instruction by resident Indian agents, breaking up the reservations, dividing tribal lands into individually owned plots (severalty), and learning the arts of agriculture. The land left over, surplus to the Indians' "needs," would be sold to whites, a plan eagerly approved by western whites.

In the Dawes Act of 1887 these policies were combined in permanent form, not to be changed until the 1920s. The Indians were forced to choose 160-acre allotments for heads of families, 80 acres for single persons, and 40 acres for minor children (except where the land was clearly valueless for agriculture, as in the desert Southwest). Title to each person's allotment was to be held in trust by the government for twenty-five years, so as to ward off white speculators. It could be leased, however, and this opened the door to unscrupulous whites who secured the land from unsuspecting Indians at a pittance. Altogether, most of the 135 million acres remaining in Indian hands in the 1880s was later taken from them as a result of the severalty policy. The remaining land was mostly in the mountains or deserts. So that the tribes and their authority over individuals would be broken up, the Indians taking lands in severalty were to become citizens of the United States, and subject to its laws and those of the states. Washington had already stopped dealing with Indian tribes as separate nations. Their laws were no longer recognized. As Theodore Roosevelt later said, the Dawes Act was "a mighty pulverizing engine to break up the tribal mass."

The attempt to provide agents to train the Indians broke down quickly, for the Indian agencies, ill paid and isolated, usually went to political hacks who used every opportunity for graft. At the same time, off-reservation schools were established to provide education, which was hopefully regarded as the ultimate solution to the Indian problem. The schools, however, divided the Indian world further, for those who responded positively to white education met rejection by their tribes when they returned or became a culturally disruptive influence. For the Indians in late nineteenth-century America, there was little that promised continued identity in their own culture and on their own land.

In 1869, when this photograph was taken of Heap Wolves, the Comanche—noted warriors and raiders—were confined to reservations below the Arkansas River.

History Division, Los Angeles County Museum of Natural History

Carl Schurz, a Liberal Republican (also an immigrant German, an intellectual, and an active reformer), was secretary of the interior under President Hayes. He discussed the Indian problem in the *North American Review* in July 1881. The government, he said, could continue trying to maintain vast reservations containing millions of unused acres. "But will those who are hungry for the Indian lands sit still? It will be easy for the rough and reckless frontiersmen to pick quarrels with the Indians. The speculators, who have their eyes upon every opportunity for gain, will urge them on. The watchfulness of the government will, in the long run, be unavailing to prevent collisions. The Indians will retaliate . . . and in spite of all its good intentions and its sense of justice, the forces of the government will find themselves engaged on the side of the white man. The Indians will be hunted down at whatever cost. It will simply be a repetition of the old story, and that old story will be eventually repeated whenever there is a large and valuable Indian reservation surrounded by white settlements. Unjust, disgraceful as this may be, it is not only probable but almost inevitable. The extension of our railroad system will only accelerate the catastrophe. . . .

"What does, under such circumstances, wise and humane statesmanship demand? . . . I am profoundly convinced that a stubborn maintenance of the system of large Indian reservations must eventually result in the destruction of the redmen [for land-hungry frontiersmen will obliterate the reservations]. What we can and should do is . . . to fit the Indians . . . for the habits and occupations of civilized life by work and education; to individualize them in the possession and appreciation of prop-

erty by alloting to them lands in severalty, giving them a fee simple title individually to the parcels of land they cultivate, inalienable for a certain period, and to obtain their consent to a disposition of that part of their lands which they cannot use, for a fair compensation, in such a manner that they no longer stand in the way of the development of the country as an obstacle, but form part of it and are benefited by it."

Opening the Great Plains

Pushing the Indians onto reservations opened the way for the occupation of the Great Plains from 1870 to 1890. The most important characteristic of the plains is low rainfall. An average fifteen inches of rain falls each year, and much of that during the hot summer when it quickly evaporates into the atmosphere. Only grass could grow in this climate, not forests. Such an environment could be put to use either by introducing an industry that was naturally adapted to its peculiarities, such as cattle raising, or by developing new

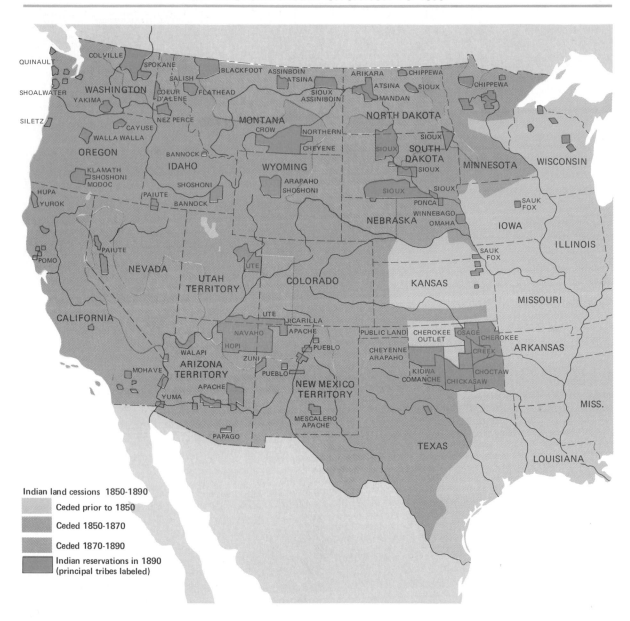

Indian land cessions 1850-1890

Ceded prior to 1850

Ceded 1850-1870

Ceded 1870-1890

Indian reservations in 1890
(principal tribes labeled)

devices and methods that would allow farmers to till the land productively.

The Cattle Kingdom

The cattle industry was the first to invade the Great Plains. It began in southern Texas, where Spaniards brought cattle and horses in the eighteenth century, and their herds multiplied rapidly. When Americans arrived in Texas in the 1830s, the Nueces Valley was a great unfenced cattle range where thousands of steers roamed freely. Dairy cattle brought in by American farmers and interbred with the range beasts produced heavier animals whose meat was more suitable for the American market. Roaming wild, cattle drifted northward in search of more grazing land as their numbers swelled. They eventually blanketed west Texas from the Rio Grande to the upper Panhandle. Some 5 million animals roamed the western high plains of Texas in 1865. Ten years later the cattle kingdom had spread northward over the Great Plains clear to Montana, a swiftness of expansion unparalleled in American economic history. In effect, cattle replaced the buffalo, and in roughly equal numbers.

This process began when Texans learned at the end of the Civil War that Northerners were willing to pay up to forty dollars a head for cattle in order to restore their war-depleted herds. The result was the beginning of the "long drive," in which a group of cattlemen gathered up a thousand or so cattle and took them to Sedalia, Missouri, then the nearest railhead. Soon a better location was found in Abilene, Kansas, a town far enough out on the plains to let the cattle drivers avoid wooded and settled areas. Huge stockyards were built there in 1867, riders headed south to intercept the trail herds, and thousands of beasts began to be loaded onto the cattle cars at Abilene —some 1.5 million by 1871. As farm settlement continued to push westward, the stockyards were moved to Ellsworth, Kansas, and then on to Newton, where cattle were received from 1872 to 1875. In that year the final move was made to Dodge City, Kansas, from where 1 million steers were shipped eastward in the next four years.

But the long drive was coming to an end. The cattle lost too much weight in their long walk, and Kansas farmers, fearing Texas cattle diseases, enacted quarantine laws against them. The only recourse was to raise the cattle near the railroads, or bring the railroads to the cattle. In Texas many lines were built, and the western part of the state was carved into huge ranches, some of them 100 miles across. Northward, railroad lines building into Colorado, Wyoming, and Montana opened that region to stock raising. By 1869, 1 million cattle were grazing in the Colorado territory.

A veritable "gold rush" set in for western ranch land. The road to wealth seemed ridiculously easy. A man had only to buy some animals, wait a few years while they multiplied on free government grazing land, and he was rich. By the mid 1880s, this mad rush had created a highly unstable situation. The dry Great Plains could support only so many cattle, and then when conditions were just right. Each year the pastures grew thinner. The winter of 1885 struck the industry a crippling blow, and that of 1886 completed the devastation. When spring came, cattlemen rode out over their ranches to find almost every ravine

filled with bodies of steers. Heaps of dead animals were piled up against fences. Company after company went bankrupt. The open-range phase of the cattle industry ended. In Wyoming alone, the number of cattle declined from 9 million in 1886 to 3 million in 1895.

A massive readjustment followed in which grass and cattle were brought back into balance. The whole of the West was divided into huge fenced pastures, and winter feed was grown in special lots. Thereafter the cattle industry was characterized by cautious investment, careful breeding, and close attention to such things as cattlemen's associations and scientific husbandry.

Farmers Invade the Great Plains

Meanwhile, the Industrial Revolution was opening the Great Plains to the grain farmer. Lack of trees made fencing prohibitively expensive, but in the mid 1870s barbed wire was invented, and practical fencing at a reasonable price was available. The lack of running streams was met by the invention of well-drilling machines that drove pipes far down into the ground. Utilizing the one perpetual source of energy on the plains, a farmer could then raise water with a windmill. This apparatus, however, was too expensive for most farmers until the 1890s.

Some other method of adjusting to the dry climate had to be found. What was needed was a system of plowing what would preserve the small amount of water that fell. The answer was "dry farming." Agricultural scientists instructed farmers to dig deep furrows (twelve to fourteen inches) that would create a deep and absorbent blotter to hold the scanty rains that fell on the plains and then would pull up subsurface water to the root zone by capillary action. The technique gave erratic results, but it did open up huge areas of the plains to agriculture.

Since farms were so large, the invention of a gang plow that opened several furrows at once was a great benefit. The grain drill, developed by the mid 1870s, sped up planting. Checkrowers put down corn seeds at equal distances. Then in 1880 came the lister, which dug a deep furrow, planted a seed, and then covered it, all in one operation. The first hay baler was invented in 1866, about the time a mowing machine became available. After this came a wide variety of harvesting machinery.

By such means huge yields resulted. Where a farmer had formerly been able to work only 7.5 acres by himself, in the 1890s he was able to put 135 acres of land to wheat. Where an acre of wheat had formerly required over sixty hours of hand labor, now it required three. The result was the greatest movement of people in the history of the United States. Millions of farmers who had been held back for a generation in their westward movement by the barrier of the Great Plains now moved out into the open country and filled up Kansas and Nebraska, the Dakotas, Wyoming, and Montana, and finally the Indians' last sanctuary, Oklahoma, after it was opened to white settlement in 1889.

Sources of Population

Where did the settlers come from? They streamed in either from the older states of the central Mississippi Valley or from Europe. So great was the exodus from the older states that most of them bordering the Mississippi lost population in the 1870s. In the following decade, more than one million people left the Middle West for the Great Plains. In the 1890s, the tide reversed because of grave economic problems encountered by the Great Plains farmers (to be discussed in the next chapter), but by then the great work of this migration had been completed: a region half the size of Europe had been brought into settlement.

Living conditions were wretched. No timber meant sod houses, which were dusty in summer and damp all winter. There was no running water and no fuel; summers blazed and winters were bitterly cold. The unending wind was a constant torment to men and women used to living in sheltered woods. Grasshopper invasions were periodical, as were prairie fires. But prices for wheat were excellent in the 1870s, and the inflow of new migrants continued heavy year after year. The American market for grain grew rapidly as its cities swelled, and the overseas market was huge. After 1875 a series of crop failures in Europe made American wheat much in demand. Then came the Russo-Turkish war of the late 1870s, when the wheat ports of Russia were closed, pushing the price of American wheat even higher.

Meanwhile, the rapid invention of new processes and new machines raised productivity rapidly, and an unusually wet cycle of rainfall produced abundant crops. The average amount of wheat acreage in the United States, which ran at about twenty million acres from 1865 to 1875, suddenly soared to almost thirty-five million acres in the ten years after 1875.

The Boomers' Spirit

In all sections of the nation the boomers' spirit captured the minds of millions. While the Great Plains were emerging as a region of huge cattle ranches and abundant wheat farms, the first great migrations to southern California filled that region with farms, towns, and land speculators' waving banners. A hundred towns were laid out—many of them soon to disappear—in the year 1887, when the Santa Fe Railroad entered Los Angeles and promptly began a rate war with the Southern Pacific, in which ticket prices from Chicago plummeted to one dollar.

In 1886, Henry W. Grady, a young and burstingly hopeful editor from the Atlanta *Constitution*, appeared before a New York audience to proclaim the existence of a New South, risen phoenixlike from the ashes of total defeat. Rejecting its ancient ways, he said, the New South was turning toward industrial development, Northern habits of industry, town building, and an abundant future in which there would no longer be a division between the North and the South. Caught up instantly, Grady's message became the widely trumpeted cry of publicists, politicians, and educators throughout the South. "Never doubting the vitality of the human resources," writes Paul M. Gaston, "and convinced of the superiority of natural ones, the New South spokesmen believed that by adopting the ways of the industrial age in the same way other Americans had done their dream would be realized."

The voices of hope and optimism, however, were joined by voices of doom. The United States entered a time of grave troubles in the 1880s. In the cities, the factories, the farms of the plains, the cotton plantations of the South—wherever one looked—there were festering sores, apparently incurable, and growing ills. Along with its productivity and its enormous creative power, the new industrial order had also brought a massive social blight. The New South turned out to be largely rhetoric; thousands of defeated farmers left the Great Plains states as their dreams collapsed; each year brought more violent convulsions to the cities as labor rebelled against the industrialists; and a generation of young people turned to reform as they entered national life and found its promises illusory.

Bibliography

Historical studies that were especially valuable to me in writing this chapter: Dee Brown's powerful book, *Bury My Heart at Wounded Knee: An Indian History of the American West** (1970); Richard White's pathbreaking article, "The Winning of the West: The Expansion of the Western Sioux in the Eighteenth and Nineteenth Centuries," *Journal of American History*, 65 (September 1978), 319–343; Wilcomb E. Washburn, *The Indian in America** [The New American Nation Series] (1975); Gilbert C. Fite, *The Farmer's Frontier, 1865–1900* (1966); Thomas C. Cochran and William Miller, *The Age of Enterprise: A Social History of Industrial America* (1961); and Walter Prescott Webb's classic, now half a century old but still valuable, *The Great Plains: A Study in Institutions and Environment** (1931).

How Have Historians Looked at the Topic?

During the past twenty years American economic history has undergone profound changes. Its special impact has contributed to a substantially different view of the booming industrial growth following the Civil War. In his *Growth and Welfare in the American Past: A New Economic History** (1966), Douglass C. North summarizes the distinctive concerns of economic history and presents an interpretation based on new quantitative knowledge. Another fine survey with insightful comments on the post–Civil War era is Louis M.

Hacker's *The Course of American Economic Growth and Development** (1970).

The importance of railroads in transforming the American economy is disputed in an intriguing study by Robert Fogel, *Railroads in American Economic Growth* (1964). John F. Stover's *American Railroads* (1961) ably presents the more traditional view. Thomas C. Cochran's *Railroad Leaders, 1845–1890: The Business Mind in Action* (1966) is a fascinating analysis of railroad leaders' letters, revealing pressures for honesty and thrift within their community. Gabriel Kolko sees the railroad magnates themselves as the instigators of federal regulation in his controversial book *Railroads and Regulation, 1877–1916* (1965).

C. Vann Woodward's classic interpretation *The Origins of the New South* (1951) highlights the triumph of northern business values. Raymond B. Nixon's *Henry W. Grady* (1969) explores the role of this influential Southern spokesman. *The Industrial Revolution in the South* (1968) by Broadus Mitchell and G. S. Mitchell ably examines, among other things, the cotton-textile industry.

The deeper meanings of industrialization—the breakdown of a personal, community-oriented system and the beginning of a bureaucratized society geared to planning, control, and efficiency—are explored in an excellent brief book by Samuel P. Hays, *The Response to Industrialism 1885–1914** (1957), and in a more comprehensive and compelling work by Robert H. Wiebe, *The Search for Order, 1877–1920** (1968). Bastions of conservatism are analyzed in Robert G. McClosky's *American Conservatism in the Age of Enterprise** (1951), a stimulating examination of the ideas of men like Justice Stephen Field.

Fite's *The Farmer's Frontier* is a fine survey of settlement in the Far West, emphasizing the stabilizing role of the farmer. Rodman W. Paul explores mining technology in his *Mining Frontiers of the Far West, 1848–1880** (1963).

* Available in paperback.

22

TIME LINE

1860–90	Ten million immigrants arrive in the United States
1867	National Grange of the Patrons of Husbandry formed; Illinois Warehouse Act
1870s	States create railroad-rate–control commissions
1873	Panic begins depression of 1870s; silver demonetized
1876	Greenback party formed
1877	Nationwide railway strike
1878	Knights of Labor formed; Socialist Labor party formed; Bland-Allison Silver Purchase Act
1879	Specie resumption
1880s	Mood of national crisis; thousands of strikes; rise of big business and trusts; wheat boom
1881	American Federation of Labor formed; Samuel Gompers elected president

1883–96	Farm prices steadily decline
1885–86	Formation of Southern Alliance, Northwestern Alliance, and Colored Farmers' National Alliance and Cooperative Union
mid 1880s	Farm rush to Great Plains; Farmers Alliance movement spreading; nativist organizations formed
1886	Haymarket labor riot in Chicago; public feeling turns against the Knights of Labor
1890–1920	Fifteen million immigrants arrive in the United States; "new immigration" from central, eastern, and southern Europe
1890	Sherman Silver Purchase Act
1892	Populist party formed, nominates presidential candidate
1893–97	Depression and major collapse of economy
1894	American Protective Association reaches 500,000 members
1910	Nearly half of population lives in towns and cities

LATE NINETEENTH CENTURY AMERICA: THE NATION IN CRISIS

New York Public Library

"What shall the workers do? Sit idly by and see the vast resources of nature and the human mind be utilized and monopolized for the benefits of the comparative few? No. The laborers must learn to think . . . that only by the power of organization and common concert of action can either their manhood be maintained, their rights to life (work to sustain it) be recognized, and liberty and rights secured." So wrote Samuel Gompers, president of the American Federation of Labor, in 1894. Join together, hang together, do not trust government, that instrument of the wealthy and of the patronizing middle class, to do the job. Form strong unions and fight for simple, realizable goals: better pay, better hours, better working conditions. Let the capitalists do their thing, we'll do ours. Don't let the "intellectuals" and their airy theories do our think-

ing for us; don't expect middle-class "reformers" ever to understand what workers do, how they have to live, or what they need. Organize.

And above all, don't radicalize. Gompers fought bitterly and in the end successfully to keep the socialists, especially those of a revolutionary, Marxist temper, from getting control of the labor movement. Having the government take over all means of production and distribution was, to him, industrial nonsense. It couldn't work. Furthermore, violence was nonsense: it couldn't work. The organized enemy was too powerful, had too much control of the police, the militia, the army, and private armies of spies and guards. Furthermore, violence simply inflamed the American public at large, and this was fatal, for industrial workers were a small minority; they needed the respect and support of the people at large.

In 1881 he was chosen first president of the newly formed American Federation of Labor, and with the exception of one year in the 1890s, so he remained until his death at the age of 74 in 1924. Short, stocky, blunt, persistent, outspoken, constantly orating and constantly writing, Gompers was a genius at pulling together jealous craftworkers (usually divided by ethnic hostilities) to form and build a strong AFL. By 1900 it held a million workers; unlike its predecessors, it would survive and grow powerful.

Most Americans did not appreciate the "conservatism" of Samuel Gompers, that antirevolutionary man. He seemed nothing but a radical. They reviled the very idea of a union as un-American, subversive, alien. Individuals should get ahead on their own; each worker should bargain individually with employers for their job, wages, and working conditions—even if that employer was a remote and powerful millionaire. The collective ideal: ultimate value to Samuel Gompers, it was ultimate evil to WASP America. That Gompers was an immigrant Jew created distrust; that most workmen were aliens, ethnic minorities, excited nativist hostility. But eventually employers would *have* to recognize the representatives of their workers, bargain with them, accept their power. In this, Gompers was in fact a revolutionary, in American terms, and, though not in his lifetime, his principle won out.

Overview

Since 1865 the nation had been swept along by a mood of confidence in the future, even during the difficult depression years of the 1870s. But the mood cracked in the mid 1880s as the economy slumped repeatedly and a mounting clamor of social protest rose on every side. "Our era . . . of happy immunity from those social diseases which are the danger and the humiliation of Europe is passing away," observed a writer in the *Atlantic Monthly* in 1882. Hundreds of strikes broke out every year as angry workers left their factories and miners with blackened faces streamed from the pitheads to protest wage cuts and layoffs. Farm prices plummeted, and from the cotton lands of the South to the sweeping high prairies of the Dakotas, farmers crowded into Grange halls to cheer attacks on the "money trust," railroads, and commodity speculators. While the wealthy continued to parade their riches, bitter anarchists, eager to destroy the capitalist system, preached revolution and issued detailed instructions on bomb making. Industrial monopolies grew everywhere; graft and corruption mocked democracy; and the smelly slums of the cities grew more densely packed as immigration soared. Old-stock Americans recoiled from the flood of immigrants, who seemed to them degraded and dangerous to the American social order.

Booming Cities and Immigration

Over 100 American cities doubled or more than doubled in population during the 1880s, making this decade second only to the 1840s as the most rapidly "urbanizing" period in American history. In 1890, more than a third of the American people lived in communities of more than 2,500 people. (By 1920, this proportion would reach 51 percent.) Most of this growth was fed by one source—American farmers who had found that farm life entailed drudgery, numbing isolation, primitive living conditions, and low income. They flocked to the cities, which to them meant neighbors, bustling streets, newspapers, theaters and saloons, and jobs with what seemed like good pay. City growth was also fueled by huge masses of immigrants from abroad.

In the 1880s the United States was receiving the second of three great waves of immigration that entered the nation in the century after 1820. The first, from 1820 to 1860, brought in five million immigrants. The second, from 1860 to 1890, brought in ten million. The third and greatest, from 1890 to 1920, comprised fifteen million people. These migrations to the United States, which have become legendary, were actually part of a larger movement in which fifty-five million Europeans emigrated overseas, only three out of five of whom went to America. Of these overseas emigrants, perhaps 30 percent reemigrated elsewhere, usually back to their countries of origin. In brief, there was not simply a great migration across the Atlantic to America, but an enormous shifting about of European peoples throughout the Western Hemisphere.

Because America's native-born population grew rapidly, the proportion of foreign-born in the United States was no higher in 1910 than it had been in 1860 (about 15 percent), even though twenty-five million immigrants had arrived since the Civil War. They concentrated in northern cities. Less than half the native American population lived in urban areas in 1910, but three out of four immigrants did so. Slum dwellers were almost wholly foreign-born. A survey made in 1910 found hardly a single native American living in a tenement.

Ethnic Enclaves

Thus was created a new phenomenon in American city life, the segregated ethnic living area. Whereas the young people who poured into the cities from the American countryside melted into the urban population, the European immigrants stood out. This was especially true of those who came in growing numbers after 1890 from eastern, central, and southern Europe, bringing in strange faces and styles of life. Almost every northern city had its German quarter with its beer gardens, German newspapers, Lutheran and Catholic churches, and *turnvereins* (men's social clubs). New York's Lower East Side was the classic Jewish quarter with its thousands of sweatshops producing clothing. Grim rows of mud-flat housing, "Hunkeyvilles," in Gary or East St. Louis contained Hungarian and Slavic workers who labored twelve hours a day, sometimes seven days a week, in huge factories. The prime example of the Polish section was Hamtramck in Detroit, with its large Catholic churches and neat, small homes. Noisy Italian enclaves and Bohemian quarters were prominent features of the "new cities." Meanwhile the electric interurban streetcar, invented in the 1880s, allowed the middle class to move to suburbs ringing the inner urban core of factories and business districts. By 1910 the foreign-born were segregated in their living areas in the same way that the northern black population had been all along.

Jews in great numbers now came to America. In 1870 there were about 250,000 Jews in the United States; by 1920 there were 3.5 million. The Jewish population present in 1870 had been predominantly German in background, religiously liberal (Reform Judaism), and widely dispersed in the population. But then came hundreds of thousands of strongly conservative (Orthodox) Jews, mainly from eastern Europe, Poland, and Russia. Their ways of life set them off sharply from the general American scene. Usually a people who for generations had lived in ghettos and worked in small shops, they formed rigidly separated urban enclaves in American cities where they could maintain their religious customs, dress, and dietary restrictions. Like those Jews already in America, they were intensely devoted to education and self-improvement. Although the first generation might labor in a cigar shop or sew coats and shifts in a loft, the carefully educated second generation frequently entered the professions. Already an urban people, the Jews brought with them—unlike the peasant immigrants from the European countryside—a richly complex and urbanized way of life.

The Catholics Emerge

From 1850 to 1900, the number of Catholics in America rose from 1.6 to over 12 million people. Before 1850, they had been overwhelmingly Irish and German, with smaller populations of French in Louisiana and Spanish-speaking in the Southwest and California. The Irish were most prominent in the Catholic hierarchy and lay leadership, a fact that gives to American Catholicism the Irish cast that strongly colors it even today (though the immense swelling of Hispanic America in the twentieth century introduces a major new element). After about 1880, American Catholicism became a church as well of Italians, Hungarians, Poles, and Lithuanians, though Catholic Irish and Germans continued to pour into the country in great numbers. Catholics strikingly shunned the countryside, probably because establishing a farm was by this time costly (it required at least $1,000 in capital) and most Catholics were poor immigrants.

Having become far and away the largest single religious denomination in the country, Catholicism was regarded with alarm by the much-divided Protestants. Burstingly vigorous, the Catholic church in the United States built thousands of churches, monasteries, and schools, a huge undertaking that gave Catholics a common enterprise and a strong sense of morale and identity. More than anything else, indeed, it was the great campaign to build parochial schools that created Protestant hostility. Part of each parish and supported by it, the Catholic school was supremely a cultural instrument designed to hold Catholics together. It provided free education, both religious and secular. After 1870, Catholic leaders even launched periodic crusades to get public funds for their schools, which led to angry counterattacks by Protestants.

To traditional Republicans (as well as thousands of Democrats) Catholicism was hated because it seemed to them boldly at war with American republicanism: its individualism, freedom of thought, and its "get ahead" attitudes. Catholics were seen as unambitious, and slavishly obedient to a distant (and historically feared) pope in Rome and his hierarchy of church officials down to the parish priest. Even Mark Twain, who was hardly a devout and moralistic Protestant, snarled at everything Catholic as he toured Europe in 1867, finally admitting (in his report of these travels, *The Innocents Abroad* [1869]) that "I have been educated to enmity toward everything that is Catholic, and sometimes, in consequence of this, I find it easier to discover Catholic faults than Catholic merits."

That the papacy in most of the nineteenth century harshly condemned all forms of political and social liberalism, and did in fact present itself in Italian life as an enemy of democratic republicanism, accentuated the feeling that a force hostile to the American way of life had entered into the United States. This anti-Catholicism, in turn, built into the Catholic community the fortress mentality characteristic of beleaguered social groups everywhere. Catholics rallied around the leadership of their priests and bishops ever more tightly, clung more determinedly to their faith, condemned "heresy," built their own separate world of schools, universities, hospitals, and newspapers—and looked en masse to the Democratic party as their political protector. There were conflicts in this growing Catholic America, for each of the new immigrant ethnic groups had their own distinctive style of worship and language. Catholicism was torn by demands for separate churches, which eventually forced the church to establish ethnic parishes within the boundaries of regular parishes. Nonetheless, to outsiders, Catholicism appeared to be a unified host with strange and un-American ways.

What it was in reality was a minority group which, to survive in America, had to fight endlessly for two of republicanism's most cherished values: liberty and equality. The growing millions of Catholics had to battle for the concept of religious toleration; that is, that principle of *cultural laissez-faire* for which Democrats had always argued, which meant liberty for all peoples to live and worship in the fashion they chose. They also needed, and argued for, political and social equality for all (white) Americans. They were not ready, as Democrats in general would not be ready for decades, to extend these ideals to black Americans. Since long before the Civil War, Catholic America had been anti-black, just as (following the pope's teachings) it had been opposed to the idea of using government to achieve social reforms. On this ground, Catholics in the northern states could form a solid and enduring alliance, within the Democratic party, with white Southerners.

In the long run, however, it would be Catholic Americans who, in search of equal social justice, would in the Progressive years initiate at the state level (as in New York) the social welfare reforms upon which the later New Deal would draw, and from which black Americans, by that time admitted into Democratic ranks, would benefit. The very cohesiveness and clannishness of the Catholics, once they got the idea that they could get control of government and improve the life of the poor and needy (among whom the Catholics bulked disproportionately), would have the effect of turning the Democratic party tradition strongly toward collectivism and community feeling. As had been true in American history from its begin-

nings, it would be in the struggle of minorities for liberty and equality—in this case, the Catholics—that republicanism as conceived of by Thomas Jefferson and his followers would be kept alive and flourishing.

City Problems

Huge problems faced the cities. City authorities had to build miles of streets, find and distribute clean water, drain off sewage, and clear away reeking mounds of garbage that blocked passages everywhere. To house the influx of people, a uniquely American dwelling was relied upon: the so-called balloon frame house. Made of light, cheap lumber, inexpensive, and quickly built, it gave ordinary Americans a standard of housing far above that of the average European. But in the most crowded cities, tenement buildings that housed thousands of people on each square block became standard. Erected by speculators, tenements crowded together back to back and lacked light, air, water, heat, or sanitation. Most apartments had only two rooms, which often sheltered five to seven persons. In the 1870s New York City contained 100,000 slum dwellers, 20,000 of whom lived in cellars. This produced a congestion greater than that of any large city in Western civilization.

Disease ravaged the slums. Typhoid, smallpox, scarlet fever, and typhus continually claimed victims. Since the medical profession was as yet hardly worthy of that name, survival was simply a case of sturdier bodies throwing off disease. The only recourse was a long, laborious campaign of cleaning up every source of contagion. Major improvements in gathering pure public water enormously reduced the death rate and also allowed a flow of water to carry off wastes. By painstaking efforts, workers cleaned up the garbage that choked the streets. In the 1880s the germ theory of disease gathered advocates. City hospitals were built, and a medical profession with a new sense of responsibility began to give attention to the poor.

Jacob A. Riis, a Denmark-born social reformer in New York City, described the city's slums: "To-day three-fourths of [New York's] people live in the tenements, and the nineteenth century drift of the population to the cities is sending ever-increasing mul-

Two pictures of Fifth Street in New York City in the 1890s show what the city looked like before a campaign was launched to get garbage off the streets, and after. By these simple public measures, health in cities was vastly improved.
Photograph by Jacob A. Riis Jacob A. Riis Collection, Museum of The City of New York

EUROPEAN IMMIGRATION PATTERNS, 1910

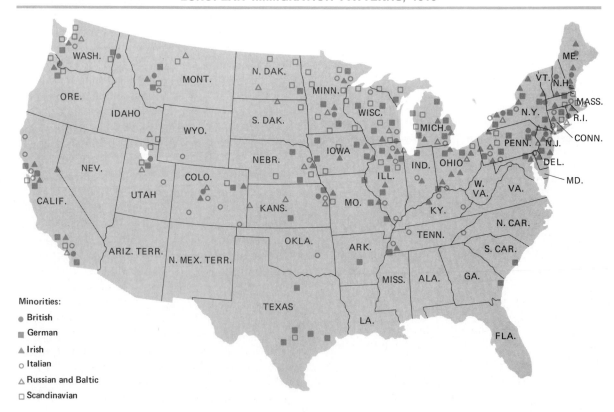

Minorities:
- • British
- ■ German
- ▲ Irish
- ○ Italian
- △ Russian and Baltic
- □ Scandinavian

titudes to crowd them. The fifteen thousand tenement houses that were the despair of the sanitarian in the past generation have swelled into thirty-seven thousand, and more than twelve hundred thousand persons call them home. . . . In the tenements all the influences make for evil; because they are the hot-beds of the epidemics that carry death to rich and poor alike; the nurseries of pauperism and crime that fill our jails and police courts; that throw off a scum of forty thousand human wrecks to the island asylums and workhouses year by year; that turned out in the last eight years a round half million beggars to prey upon our charities; that maintain a standing army of ten thousand tramps with all that that implies; because, above all, they touch the family life with deadly moral contagion [produced by overcrowding and windowless bedrooms]. This is their worst crime, inseparable from the system."

Without money for transportation the poor had to live close to their jobs. For cheap housing, the rooms of old mansions were cut up into smaller ones and multi-storied "rear houses" were put up on the backs of lots. This was done "without regard to light or ventilation, the rate of rent being lower in proportion to space or height from the street; and they soon became filled from cellar to garret with a class of tenantry living from hand to mouth, loose in morals, improvident in habits, degraded, and squalid as beggary itself. . . . Neatness, order, cleanliness were never dreamed of . . . while reckless slovenliness, discontent, privation, and ignorance were left to work out their invariable results, until the entire premises reached the level of tenement-house dilapidation, containing, but sheltering not, the miserable hordes that crowded beneath smouldering, water-rotted roofs or burrowed among the rats of clammy cellars." (How the Other Half Lives [1890])

By 1910 the cities were no longer more deadly to live in than the countryside, for they had largely caught up with the problem of sanitation. Municipal health codes required the selling of food under hygienic circumstances, the pasteurizing of milk, the wrapping of bread, and the use of refrigeration. In 1906 came the passage of federal pure-food and drug laws. Housing laws improved tenements somewhat, and the cost of food fell as the western plains were opened and railroads brought in larger supplies at lower costs. Streetcar fares dropped, so that many city workers could move their families to the better housing of the suburbs. In sum, though the urban poor were still exploited, they at least survived, ate better, and lived in housing more suited to human needs.

Labor Struggles for Social Justice

In the late nineteenth century, industrial warfare erupted. American labor struggled desperately and without much success to organize and to gain influence over the workers' situation. Even so, surprisingly, we now know that workers' real income rose markedly in these years. By 1890, real wages and earnings in manufacturing were half again higher than they had been in 1860, and by 1914 workers' income would rise another 37 percent. At the same time, the workweek shortened: in 1890 it was sixty hours, a considerable improvement over 1860, and by 1914 it would be down to just over fifty-five hours. Thus, the free-enterprise market economy worked well for American workers, though by comparison with the mid twentieth century they were overworked and underpaid. In fact, during the sixty years from 1860 to 1920, wages increased at a rate very close to the rise in workers' productivity, most of which was created by heavy investments by employers in machines that increased output. Railroads made the cost of transport much lower, and both factory owners and farmers hastened to increase production to tap the huge new market thus opened up to them. On the one hand, this meant that workers were usually in demand; on the other, rapidly mounting output in time led to overproduction, so that from 1865 to 1890 there was a long-term downward drift in the price of food and manufactured goods. Thus, the cost of living dropped as wages rose. All of this took place in a largely unrestrained free-market setting, for labor unions were as yet few and weak. In the depression-ridden 1890s, only 1 percent of American workers belonged to unions; by 1914 the figure would rise to only 6 percent.

These facts about worker income are known to us now through sophisticated economic research undertaken long after the period itself; they were little understood then. If workers' income improved proportionately, it was nonetheless very low. Hours of work were long, employers were demanding and autocratic bosses, conditions of labor were often appalling, and a great social revolution involving massive changes in life style was under way. People who had had a preindustrial existence, who had lived in traditional ways on farms and in peasant villages— mindful only of the seasons, mixing play and work, moving slowly, having long slack periods—

were being made into disciplined factory workers who were required to work steadily hour after hour, under close supervision and by the clock. This created powerful tensions and hostilities, for this new work force bitterly feared and resisted the prospect of being "proletarianized": reduced to permanent status as "slaves of capital."

Besides, while workers lived their simple lives capitalists seemed bent not simply on making enormous fortunes but on displaying them ostentatiously. A revolution of rising expectations was in motion in America. What was America all about, if it was not a life of prosperity and ease? Workers watched the wealthy few building their luxurious mansions, and observed the flight of the middle class to spacious suburban homes. In the face of this affluence, workers' gains appeared pitifully small, especially since many still labored twelve hours a day for six or seven days a week.

Great waves of protest passed through the laboring classes from the 1870s onward. Employers pressed by the steady decline in prices took every possible step to cut labor costs. Whenever business slackened there were immediate and drastic wage cuts and abrupt layoffs. Employers acquired the same habit of authority that British life had bred into its middle and upper classes. Every worker's protest, however mild, was regarded as monstrous insubordination. Obedience was desired above all else. Workers, said one employer, must "submit to our orders, otherwise their places would be vacant." Unions were seen as fundamental challenges to the employer's authority, so that labor-management disputes involved much more than the issue of wages or hours. The question often became, Who was master? "Yellow-dog contracts," which required workers to agree at the time of employment that they would not join a union, were common. Blacklists of "disloyal" laborers were circulated. "Experience with laboring men," a shoe manufacturer once said, "has convinced me that nothing saves men from debauchery and crime so much as labor—and that, till one is tired and ready to return to the domestic joys and duties of home."

To make these hostilities more intense, employers were usually native-born Americans, British in descent, Republican, and Protestant, whereas the workers were often immigrants from Ireland or the Continent, Catholic, and, when not socialists or outright anarchists, at least Democrats (save for many of the skilled workers, generally British or old-stock American, who voted Republican). Worker protests were seen, therefore, as by definition un-American and disloyal. Giving in to their demands was widely seen as a defeat of Yankees by dirty aliens.

The Problem of Tactics

What were workers to do? Many argued for "pure and simple" unionism: concentrating on getting better wages and hours through bargaining with employers and utilizing the strike as an ultimate weapon. Others called instead for broad programs of social reform on the ground that only a more humane social order would create lasting improvement. This meant agitating for land reforms, new banking and currency systems, and even governmental ownership of major segments of the economy. A small minority of workmen demanded a violent war against capitalism, looking toward the creation of anarchy, in which all forms of power, including government itself, would disappear.

In the mid 1870s, a predominantly Irish organization of coal miners called the Molly Maguires adopted a startling new tactic: terrorism. By sabotage, arson, pillage, assault, robbery, and even murder, they tried to force employers to pay desired wages. Soon a number of workers were arrested, tried for terrorism, convicted, and executed. The Molly Maguires disappeared, but the nation was left with the firm belief that the Irish, and miners as a class, were criminally inclined.

Following this came the most enormous labor upheaval of the nineteenth century, the railway strike of 1877. Smoldering labor discontent burst into open rebellion when a number of eastern railroads abruptly cut wages. Beginning in western Pennsylvania, workers went on strike in July and began blocking trains, burning buildings, and battling openly with police and militia sent to quell them. Popular hatred of the railroads spread the disorder until it involved practically the whole nation. There were hundreds killed and uncounted injured. Property damage was estimated to have run to ten million dollars.

The overwhelmingly native-born American and British-descended middle and upper classes were terrified. Not since plantation owners in the antebellum South had been frightened by fears of slave revolt were so many alarmed by the prospect of mass social upheaval. Aghast at the "enemy" in their midst, many cities hurriedly built large armories and staffed them with a disciplined militia. But strikes and disorders continued to flare up across the industrial scene, for workers were thoroughly aroused. Even in such a relatively prosperous year as 1881, there were almost 500 strikes, involving 130,000 workers. In 1886 over 600,000 workers participated in more than 1,500 strikes, and from then on there were at least 1,000 strikes a year, culminating in massive outbreaks in the depression-ridden 1890s. A conflict of cultures as well as of economic classes seemed to be tearing the country apart.

Labor Tries the Tactic of Social Reform

In 1878 American labor began a decade of experimenting with the tactic of reforming the whole society in order to improve the worker's lot. A secret organization, the Knights of Labor, was formed in that year. Led by an exciting Irishman, Terence Powderly, who had the conviction—bred into the Irish people by their long struggle with England—that everyone must hang together in the face of the common enemy, the Knights welcomed all workers into their ranks, whatever their ethnic background, whether skilled or unskilled, male or female, white or black. The Knights believed that the ultimate solution to the laboring person's problem was to end the wage system, establish cooperative factories where no one was employer and no one employee, and share the wealth equitably. In the interim, before such a sweeping goal could be achieved, trusts and monopolies should be closely regulated, the currency reformed, land made available to all, and both child labor and drunkenness swept away. Organized labor, in short, should become a great force for social reform.

The Knights, however, got nowhere with their program, since to most Americans they looked like wild-eyed radicals. The coincident rise of an anarchist socialist movement, derived mainly from German immigrants, intensified national anxiety. In 1884 the socialists formed the Central Labor Union, which aimed at "emancipation of mankind" through "the open rebellion of the robbed classes." Meanwhile, a depression in 1883 brought huge numbers of unskilled workers

into the Knights of Labor, for, whatever the value of the Knights' idealistic reform philosophy, the union had begun to demonstrate that organized workers could win strikes. The organization mushroomed, and by 1886 it contained 700,000 members. Hundreds of strikes were launched, culminating in an immense labor stoppage on May 1, 1886, in a demand for an eight-hour day. On the fourth of May, a bomb was thrown at policemen who were trying to break up an anarchist rally at Haymarket Square in Chicago. When the ensuing gunfire died down, ten persons lay dead and fifty more were injured.

The Haymarket riot electrified the country. A tidal wave of labor repression swept across the United States. In Chicago, eight radicals were jailed and blamed for the bombing simply because of speeches they had given. Four of them were executed; one committed suicide; the rest were imprisoned until pardoned in 1893. State after state hurriedly passed laws restricting workers' freedom to organize, and scores of union members were tried for conspiracy, intimidation, and rioting. Employers, emboldened by public support, turned massively against the Knights; the disheartened unskilled workers began leaving the organization; and during the 1890s the much-reduced Knights of Labor finally expired.

The American Federation of Labor

The American Federation of Labor (AFL) rose to take the place of the Knights of Labor. Its president, Samuel Gompers, was an immigrant Jewish cigar maker in New York City, who had headed a union composed of skilled Jewish workers in his craft. The experience of the Jewish people through generations had taught them tactics different from those adopted by the Irish. Living in small, scattered communities surrounded by Christian majorities, they had come to value tight organization and limited objectives, not mass campaigns inspired by soaring ideologies. Gompers believed that the working person's best hope was to build strong organizations of skilled craftsmen that would concentrate on pure and simple unionism. In 1881, the cigar makers' union joined with seven other skilled trade unions to form the American Federation of Labor.

When the Knights collapsed, the AFL bur-

This *Puck* cartoon, in its attack upon Cardinal Gibbons's 1887 statement to the Vatican in support of the Knights of Labor, reflects middle-class hatred of unions. They were seen as composed of strong-armed thugs who prevented honest men from practicing their trade unless they joined up.

Culver Pictures, Inc.

geoned. Several influences aided this growth. The skilled workers were frightened of the unskilled. They felt demeaned by having to work in the same organization with them, as in the Knights of Labor, and they were alarmed at the unskilled workers' militance. Most of all, however, they were frightened because new machines were being invented that could be tended by unskilled and semiskilled workmen. Unless the craftsmen banded together to gain job security as well as higher wages and better hours, disaster seemed inevitable. Furthermore, many trades were monopolized by particular ethnic groups who wanted to keep exclusive control over the craft. The Irish worked in transportation, Jews in the needle trades, Italians in stone masonry, Englishmen in brick laying, Germans in heavy framing, and Frenchmen in artistic trades. To each of them, the principle of autonomy for each craft union was practically sacred.

The 1890s, a time of widespread labor disorder aggravated by the severe depression that began after 1893, was a time of testing for the AFL. Union after union was crushed by management, for corporations had grown far more powerful than they had been in the past. They were larger, had learned better how to use the courts against unions, principally in the securing of injunctions, and how to band together to break strikes. Gompers steered the AFL clear of involvement in disastrous strikes, and when the depression began lifting in 1897 and factories afterward resumed full production, the organization was ready to expand. Winning a series of spectacular victories in the coal fields through one of its member organizations, the United Mine Workers, the AFL swelled to a membership of 1,675,000 in 1904. Nonetheless, as earlier observed, as late as 1914 only 6 percent of American workers would be in a union.

Nativism

The Haymarket riot of 1886 fixed a specter in the American mind—the bearded, bomb-throwing, foreign radical. In its time of grave troubles, the nation was looking for scapegoats, and many Americans found them in the flood of immigrants debarking at Boston, New York, and Philadelphia and crowding into the already jammed cities.

When nativism—hostility to aliens—erupted in the mid 1880s, it did so because practically every problem afflicting the United States seemed linked to the immigrant. Growing cities, municipal corruption, urban filth and disease, low wages, the rising "threat" of Catholicism, alcoholism, social and political disorder and radicalism—each seemed to derive from the "strangers in the land." They were "an invasion of venomous reptiles . . . long-haired, wild-eyed, bad-smelling, atheistic, reckless foreign wretches, who never did an honest hour's work in their lives . . . crush such snakes . . . before they have time to bite . . . a danger that threatens the destruction of our national edifice by the erosion of its moral foundations." Josiah Strong, a Congregational clergyman, warned in his popular book *Our Country* (1885) that the immigrants were criminal, immoral, socialistic, and corrupt. Temperance workers were alarmed by heavy-drinking foreigners. Women's-rights advocates found peasants from European villages hostile to their ideas.

Aliens did in fact feed political corruption. The Irish, who dominated city government by the 1880s, freely used graft to hand out favors to their immigrant friends, especially those of Catholic faith. The ordinary European peasant, after all, had been denied any experience of democracy and the concept of the "citizen." Government to him had always been a highly personal affair, chiefly concentrating in the local landowner or nobleman. The important thing was to get on his good side, give him loyalty, and receive in return such patronage as he could bestow. Irish political bosses in the United States played this same role. The immigrant could see that they were clearly men of power in the confusing cities of America and that they had jobs, food, legal services, and other aids to give those who voted their way. Corruption, to the poor European immigrant, functioned like social welfare, delivering jobs and food when most needed.

Immigrants were also accused of being politically radical, and in fact the revolutionary and anarchist movements were largely foreign-born. The Socialist Labor party, founded in 1878, was mainly German in membership, and its twentieth-century descendant, the Socialist party of America (which won more than 900,000 votes in the presidential election of 1912), drew support primarily from the foreign-born. In truth, however, the radicals formed a tiny minority of the alien influx. Most immigrants were frightened, divided among themselves by their diverse languages and customs, illiterate, and quite bewildered by public affairs. Their main concerns were getting and holding jobs, and they took such wages as were offered.

Nativist Movements

Joined to the nativist fear of bombs and revolution was alarm at the huge upsurge in Catholicism. The swift rise of Catholic parochial schools in these years seemed to many people a direct attack on the heart of the American system, the public schools. Huge crowds cheered such men as the Reverend Justin D. Fulton when he shouted that the Pope was plotting to destroy American education and that James Cardinal Gibbons, bishop of Baltimore and American Catholicism's leading figure, was already the ruler of the United States. A further irritant was the growing Irish stranglehold on municipal government. To zealous Protestants this was indisputable proof that the Roman Catholic Church was getting hold of the country. Many secret anti-Catholic societies appeared, such as the American League, founded in Chicago in 1886, which demanded that employers discharge all Catholics.

In the 1890s nativism grew more hysterical. The nation's troubles worsened after a severe depression began in 1893. Labor battled capital with unmatched ferocity, and governor after governor called out troops to quell strikers. Farm radicalism reached new heights in the Populist crusade of 1892 and in William Jennings Bryan's free-silver campaign of 1896. In these circumstances, "fear of the stranger accumulated on all sides," the historian John Higham has written, "mounting into hatred, bursting into violence, and intruding into politics." Vast campaigns exhorting "Americanism" swept the country.

Schools instituted daily flag salutes, American history became a required subject for students, and prestigious organizations such as the Sons of the American Revolution (1889) were formed. Anti-Catholicism became a giant movement. The Iowa-born American Protective Association soared to perhaps a half-million members in 1894. It announced the electrifying "news" that the panic of 1893 had begun because the Pope, in preparation for taking over the country, had instructed Catholics to begin runs on all the banks.

The "New Immigration"

Americans became aware that in the 1880s a "new immigration" had begun: Jews, Italians, Slavs, Poles, and Sicilians were entering the country in huge numbers. Settling in slums, they lived apart from others and aroused repugnance by their strange dress, hair styles, and swarthy appearance. When Slavic coal miners in Pennsylvania went on strike, newspapers spoke of the "wild Huns." Vigilante attacks in 1897 culminated in the massacre of twenty-one Polish and Hungarian strikers by Pennsylvania deputies. Italians were thought particularly inclined to crimes with knives. Lynching parties hunted them down in mining communities and in the Deep South. Jewish businessmen and landlords had their property burned in the South, or were stoned in northern cities.

Now there emerged a racial theme in nativist ideology. Aristocratic Anglo-Saxon intellectuals in the northeastern states alleged that the new immigration was bringing in inferior blood stocks that would dilute and debase the racial purity of the predominantly Anglo-Saxon American nation. Senator Henry Cabot Lodge of Massachusetts was the leading spokesman for this point of view. Morbidly sensitive to anything that threatened to cause social change, in 1888 he began calling for the end of immigration. In the 1890s his ideas spread. The issue around which he and other nativists gathered their forces was the establishment of a literacy test for all immigrants, for it would strike most severely at the new immigration.

After 1894, when the Republican party won a huge victory in the congressional elections, the literacy campaign intensified. Lodge introduced a literacy bill after making a violent speech warning that the racial foundations of America were in danger of destruction. Whooped through Congress, it was vetoed by President Grover Cleveland on the ground that it clearly violated the nation's democratic values. Congress, he remarked, should avoid the sham of a literacy test if its real intention was to exclude the allegedly inferior races of the new immigration. To the rage of men like Theodore Roosevelt, who considered Cleveland's action a disaster to the nation, Congress was unable to override the veto. Literacy advocates confidently looked forward to a Republican presidential victory in 1896, which they believed would lead to prompt passage of the restriction. As it happened, however returning prosperity in 1897 lifted the nation's anxious mood, and nativism's strength wilted. More than twenty years passed before the American government finally enacted stringent restrictions on immigration.

Women and the Family

One trend that alarmed nativists was the continuing decline in the rate at which native-born American white women had children. Overall, the birth rate fell from 7.04 per woman in 1800 to 3.56 in 1900. Counteracting this development was a steady drop in the death rate, through public-health measures and better food, so that the population continued growing at about 2 percent a year (immigration helped too, accounting for about a third of the population increase). But from far back in the early years of the century, as we have seen, American women had been reducing the size of their families. We have noted that a powerful motive for this trend was women's desire to secure more independence for themselves within the family. There were also, of course, economic motives. Jobs outside the home were opening up, and the income was valuable to the family. Often, women put off marrying for some years in order first to work for a while. Whatever the reasons, delaying marriage reduced childbearing. By 1910, four out of five single women and one out of ten married women worked outside of the home, amounting to a fifth of the nation's work force.

Working outside the home, however, was for women a complex and often cruel business. For single women it was not so bad: they were often encouraged to work for a time, learning of the world before marriage and helping the family support itself. But married women were not supposed to work, and few did so systematically enough to be counted in the census. Their place was in the home, raising children and caring for the husband. Schools would not hire married women as teachers, nor would businesses use them as stenographers. If they simply had to work to live, therefore, they had to take the jobs no one else wanted: scrubwoman, janitor, laundress, being a maid or a servant. Or they worked at home, secretly, doing piecework sewing. The important thing was to stay inside: it was shameful for a married woman to have to work, especially a woman of the middle class.

Even single women found a highly restricted range of employments: being store clerks, saleswomen, typists (an explosively growing women's occupation from the 1880s on), or bookkeepers and cashiers. Positions of authority, of course, were always reserved to males. Teaching had become a woman's occupation by the Civil War, as had nursing. Both were thought of as appropriate for women, since they were extensions of home activities. In some industries—textiles, shoemaking, food and tobacco products—women worked in great numbers. However, they still thought of themselves essentially as homemakers, or heading for that life. Thus, their ambitions in their outside jobs were not high. Work was secondary to the home: it was undertaken not for self-realization but as a means of helping the family. (On women's history, consult the "time line" in the Appendix.)

American Farms: Eden in Distress

America was a *farming* country. This is what the people of the United States had always stressed, and with a proud emphasis. Farming was described as the occupation most loved by God, the most natural, healthy, and morally elevated of all human activities. The American republic was supposed from the beginning to draw its inner strength and virtue from its citizens being workers in the soil, independent of feudal overlords and subject only to the great challenges of the natural order: drought and flood and the diseases of plants and animals. The "yeoman farmer" was the personage who was regarded as at the heart of the great American experiment in self-govern-

ment: a self-sufficient, sturdy, courageous man who, with his strong and fruitful wife and their large brood of children, met each rising sun in the fields and lived simple but bountiful lives of secure independence.

The post–Civil War decades saw this dream shattered. Eden in distress, the Garden of America turned into a fiefdom by financial capital: these were the themes that obsessed major segments of rural America from the 1870s onward. It was not simply that America became an urban country in the sixty years from 1860 to 1920 (Americans living in cities rising from 19 percent in the former year to 51 percent in the latter). The emerging new structure of national economic life simply turned against most farmers. By the middle of the 1880s hardly a farm in the Middle West was out of earshot of a train whistle. The result was mounting overproduction, for nearly everyone rushed to produce for the newly opened national and international markets. Farm prices fell more or less steadily from 1865 to the mid 1870s, then moved upward for a few years until 1883, when they resumed their downward fall until the mid 1890s.

The farmer's immediate enemy was the railroad. Heavy debts and erratic patterns of competition led railroads to charge glaringly inequitable freight rates. When a freight war between competing roads went on between such widely separated points as Omaha and Chicago, farmers at all intermediate points would have their rates jacked up sky high to compensate. Farmers unloading at Minneapolis were forced to pay the full rate to the Great Lakes. Dakota producers learned that it cost more to ship their grain to Chicago than from that point to Liverpool, England. Short hauls were commonly more costly than long hauls, for short haulage was notoriously noncompetitive. Grain elevators were controlled by the railroads, which charged high storage prices. Where there was competition a road would charge perhaps one cent a mile for a ton of wheat; where there was none, upwards of five cents.

The first protests came in the states surrounding the Great Lakes, where the National Grange of the Patrons of Husbandry was formed in 1867. Aimed initially at relieving the isolation of farmers by providing social and cultural activities, it soon became a militant antirailroad movement. By 1875 it contained more than 850,000 members, who gathered in local Granges from

LATE NINETEENTH-CENTURY AMERICA: THE NATION IN CRISIS

Texas to Ohio, from Minnesota to Georgia. Its greatest political strength, however, lay in the states on the upper Mississippi River. In 1867, Illinois farmers secured passage of a Warehouse Act requiring railroads to pick up grain at independent elevators. In 1871, regulation of railroad rates began in Illinois, followed by similar actions in Minnesota, Iowa, and Wisconsin. Railroads fought back in the courts, evaded compliance, and even reduced service in entire states to force repeal, sometimes successfully. In 1876, the United States Supreme Court, which had not yet swung behind the railroads, ruled that state regulation was constitutional (*Munn* v. *Illinois*).

The Money Question

The farmer had many enemies to hate, but his greatest anger was directed at bankers and the "money conspiracy." Ever since the Civil War, Americans had argued constantly over the money system. No other issue so fascinated the age or was regarded as so crucial to every other problem.

The crux of the matter may be simply stated, but its implications were enormously complicated. Briefly, producers who got their income in the open market, such as farmers, favored an expanding money supply because more money in circulation seemed to produce rising prices and make it easier to pay off mortgages. Furthermore, those who needed to borrow money to start new factories, such as iron producers and enterprising businessmen in general, also liked an expanding money supply because bankers would then have plenty of money to loan them and interest rates would be low. However, those whose income was set by someone else—such as working people, the salaried, and consumers in general—favored a stable or perhaps contracting money supply because this seemed to keep the cost of food and other necessities stable, or even cause it to drop, a critically important matter to people living close to the poverty level. Those who had lent money also tended to favor stability or deflation, since this would ensure that the money paid back to them would be worth as much as what they had lent in the first place, or perhaps even more.

There was another aspect to the question.

Rawding family sod home in Custer County, Nebraska, about 1886, shows the bleak conditions of life on the treeless Great Plains, where wood for homes was not available save from great distances at high cost.
Solomon D. Butcher Collection, Nebraska State Historical Society

Those heavily engaged in foreign trade, such as textile manufacturers and exporters of raw materials, wanted to keep American prices low and thus competitive in the world market. They therefore favored stability or deflation. But those who sold primarily at home and worried about competing goods coming in from abroad took the opposite view. Inflated American currency would be able to buy fewer foreign goods, so people would tend to buy from domestic manufacturers. Protective tariffs and money inflation tended to be parallel policies; free trade and money stability or deflation also went together. Republicans, as the party of the producers of manufactured goods, tended to favor the former; Democrats, as the party of the city masses, the consumers, tended to favor the latter.

The nation ended the Civil War with several kinds of money. There were gold and silver coins as well as "United States Notes"—paper "greenbacks" not backed by gold—which the government had printed during the Civil War out of the pressing need to pay its debts. Over $400 million in face value, they were worth considerably less in gold on the open market. "National Banknotes" were another form of paper currency. They were issued by nationally chartered private banks and backed by the federal bonds owned by each such institution. This privately issued currency was limited in volume to $300 million until 1875, when all limitations were taken off. In practice, therefore, a large part of the nation's money supply was controlled by private banking corporations.

The Greenbackers

For a dozen years after the Civil War, the money argument was concerned with the question, What should be done with the greenbacks? Practically everyone in authority wanted to achieve resumption of specie payments—that is, get enough gold in the Treasury to support the greenbacks. Then anyone could get gold coin (specie) in return for his greenback if he wished. But one group of reformers strongly condemned this idea, saying that the greenbacks actually gave the country a chance to establish a permanent inflationist monetary system in which the government would simply print paper money as the economy needed it. To nearly everyone, this was a radical notion. Do

away with gold and silver and rely just on paper money? It seemed monstrous. But the Greenbackers went even further: they said it was wrong to allow private banks to issue National Banknotes and thus control the amount of money in circulation. The currency system is so crucial, they said, that the people should control it wholly and directly through their elected government. In brief, the currency system should be nationalized, not left largely in the hands of private enterprise.

Greenbackers like Henry C. Carey, long one of the Republican party's chief economic theorists, said that relying on gold and silver to form the basis for money was absurd. The economy grows; therefore, the money supply should grow. Let it rise abundantly, for the more money, the more productivity, and productivity was the proper objective. An abundant money supply, he said, would keep interest rates low and make debts easy to repay. In the early 1870s both the National Labor Union and the iron and steel makers of Pennsylvania joined in warmly supporting the greenback idea. Later in that decade farmers in the Granger states pitched in as well. In 1876 the Greenback party was formed to agitate the question nationwide, running presidential candidates in that year and in 1880 and electing a number of congressmen. Prosperity for farmers in the late 1870s reduced their interest, however, and in 1879, when the federal government achieved resumption of specie payments—so that greenbacks were fully backed by gold—Greenbackism died away. Remarkably modern in its basic assumptions (the present philosophy of a "managed" currency supply is mainly what Greenbackism called for), it was an idea whose time had not yet come.

The Rise of Silver

But the money controversy was far from over. By the late 1870s new discoveries of silver changed the whole picture with regard to the metallic base of the currency system. The nation had supposedly been on a bimetallic standard from its beginnings; that is, its currency was based on both gold and silver, their relative value being legally set at a ratio of sixteen ounces of silver equaling one ounce of gold. Since the 1830s, however, silver had been scarce and was more valuable than sixteen to one on the world market. Therefore, it was little used in the nation's coinage.

At the same time, major shifts in the international monetary situation were taking place. Most of the western European nations decided to use only gold as the basis of their money systems. This held out great hopes for an internationally unified money system to be used by all the advanced trading nations. Relying on a common stock of gold that would move back and forth from nation to nation to pay for purchases of goods, the world's traders would, so the theory ran, share a common level of prices. If inflation began in one country, gold would flee from it because it would be more valuable elsewhere; that nation's money supply would have to be contracted; and deflation would bring prices back down to the world level. If deflation began, the opposite would occur. Both international trade and price stability would benefit.

To join this unified international trading system, the American government took important steps. Since silver coins were practically nonexistent anyway, "gold-standard" supporters in the Treasury persuaded Congress in 1873 to demonetize silver—that is, to make gold the only basis for American currency. They were further encouraged to do this by the knowledge that silver was beginning to pour out of the western mines and that soon it would probably be back in circulation. At the time no one paid much attention to the shift to the gold standard, but it soon became nationally notorious as the "crime of '73." Inflationists now demanded free coinage of the white metal at the old ratio of sixteen to one, since—because it was so plentiful—its price on the open market was lower than that, and people would be glad to sell it to the Treasury and have it stamped into currency.

Under immense pressure from farmers, a Republican-dominated Congress partially agreed in 1878, enacting the Bland-Allison Silver Purchase Act. It did not remonetize silver—the gold standard remained—but it allowed the Treasury to purchase up to four million dollars monthly in silver and to coin it. It was, in effect, silver paper. The purchased silver did not itself provide a legal basis for the government to print paper currency, but was used to replace greenbacks, which were then taken out of circulation in proportion. Inflationists were thus frustrated.

The return of prosperity and good farm prices after 1879 temporarily took the issue out of national politics. But by the mid 1880s hard times had returned and farmers began agitating the issue again. In response, Congress enacted another measure designed to meet inflationist demands, the Sherman Silver Purchase Act of 1890 (passed by the overwhelmingly Republican Congress of that year). In effect, it required the government to buy practically the whole output of American silver mines and store it as uncoined metal (bullion) in the Treasury (about 4.5 million ounces monthly). A new paper currency—'Silver Certificates"—was printed to pay for the silver and to circulate as money. By the mid 1890s these measures had added about $500 million to the money supply in the country.

For many years, however, the dollars available to the growing national economy had been shrinking proportionate to the production of farm and industrial goods. The government was paying off its national debt, and this resulted in a contraction of the currency that had been based on it (the National Banknotes issued by federally chartered banks). Also, the world's supply of gold, and that in the United States Treasury, grew slowly, which meant that the United States Notes issued by the federal government could not expand rapidly. The largest counteracting force to this shrinking money supply lay in the remarkable appetite Americans had for saving their money, which gave banks in the industrializing areas large sums to lend out to entrepreneurs so that they could expand their factories.

The Impact of that Money Upon Farmers

The long-range contraction of the money supply that ensued after 1865 hit farmers with shattering force. A smaller amount of available money meant that the price of their crops in the market had to drop, beyond even the lower prices resulting from the overproduction induced by the availability of railroads. It also meant that interest rates would be high, since bankers could demand it. Yet farmers constantly required credit: to buy the expensive equipment they needed to keep production rising, which they had to do because of falling prices; to buy land; and, in regions where nonedible crops were raised (for example, the cotton of the South), to buy food in order to survive through the year. The squeeze was made sharper by the fact that the availability of money and of banks themselves was highly lopsided in the United States, being overwhelmingly concentrated in the northeastern states. This was shockingly visible in the South. When in Rhode Island after the Civil War there was $77.16 per capita available in local banks, Arkansas had only thirteen cents. The entire South had only a fifth of the national-bank circulation contained in the single state of Massachusetts. The farm crisis was also severe on the Great Plains, where a vast westward sweep of pioneer farmers after the Civil War had turned Kansas, Nebraska, and the Dakotas into an enormous wheat and corn region by the mid 1880s. Here too the crucial issue was debt, for the Plains being newly settled, were heavily burdened with mortgages. In the boom times of the late 1870s and mid 1880s debt had been a manageable problem, but overproduction, dropping wheat prices, and then terrible drought brought disaster. Some thirty-one million bushels of wheat had been raised in Kansas in 1882; in 1887 the figure was down to ten million. In the ensuing four years, half the population of western Kansas cleared out. In some counties, 90 percent of the land was lost to mortgage companies.

The Southern Farm Crisis

The South's situation was the cruelest. Since there was practically no money in the region, a peculiar financial structure had been created. Merchants got necessary goods (clothing, tools, equipment) on credit from northern manufacturers, as well as food stocks, and then sold it on credit to local farmers, but at very high mark-ups (cash customers paid the usual price). How did the farmer get this credit? By giving the "furnishing merchant" a lien on his cotton crop (that is, the legal right to acquire the crop in case of nonpayment). But since by the 1880s the price of cotton was dropping, this often meant that the crop would not fetch enough to pay the bill. In fact, only at the time of selling his cotton would the farmer learn how much he was going to make that year. Failing to "pay out" meant that part of the bill was carried over, so that the farmer, white or black, was still in debt to the merchant. As the years passed and the carry-over mounted, merchants would finally foreclose their lien, take over

ownership, and the farmer would become a tenant on land formerly his own. Thousands upon thousands of Southern cotton farmers slid over the line into tenancy as the years passed, and "furnishing merchants" became larger and larger landowners.

To escape this cycle, something like 100,000 Southern farmers headed out in the 1870s for the Texan part of the Great Plains, where they would again take up land and start over. In 1878, they formed a "Farmers' Alliance" and set out to break the power of the crop-lien and two-price systems through cooperative buying and selling among themselves. It was extremely difficult going. Merchants and bankers, firmly committed to existing arrangements, ridiculed the cooperatives and denied them credit. But by the mid 1880s the Alliance movement was spreading far and wide in Texas. It preached the new idea of cooperation, condemned by its enemies as against the American idea of competition. As some successes slowly accumulated, so did a sense of self-confidence within a population that had been demoralized and passive. Soon the Alliance was talking of actually beginning to manufacture its own farm equipment, to be sold at the lower prices cooperative methods made possible. The "hayseeds," so long ridiculed, were beginning to fight back. Alliance meetings were like vast religious encampments, the long trains of wagons coming to them, festooned with banners, stretching for miles. As many as twenty thousand men and women would gather to listen to lectures and speechmaking, to talk of their common problems, and to develop ideas. A new mood was emerging, a culture of protest that became self-feeding and self-respecting. It was the kind of mass movement, identifying itself as "the people," that arises only at rare intervals in American history.

The farmers' movement in Texas quickly learned that the crop-lien system was but one element in the larger economic arrangements of the nation. Soon it was attacking such enemies as the "money trust," the gold standard, and the private national banking system. The essential ideas of the greenback movement were revived. The money supply should be made flexible and expansive by breaking it loose from the gold standard, Alliance leaders said, and simply printing currency as needed by the growing economy. At the same time, control of this crucial matter should be taken out of the hands of private bankers. The currency supply should be entirely a public matter, resting in the hands of the people, and their democratically elected government. By the late 1880s the Farmers' Alliance, now spreading to other Southern states and northward through the Great Plains to Kansas, was calling for a subtreasury system by which government banks would be stationed out in the farming regions to meet their needs. At the same time, Alliance leaders such as William Lamb were trying to form a national partnership with the labor-union movement, saying that farmers were also laboring people, not capitalists. This meant working with the Knights of Labor, which in the mid 1880s was rapidly growing and, under the visionary Terence Powderly, was ready to join farmers in calling for sweeping reorganizations of the national economic system. As the increasingly aggressive Farmers' Alliance declared at its 1886 state convention in Cleburne, Texas, it sought "such legislation as shall secure to our people freedom from the onerous and shameful abuses that the industrial classes are now suffering at the hands of arrogant capitalists and powerful corporations."

Soon the "most massive organizing drive by any citizen institution of nineteenth-century America," as the historian Lawrence Goodwyn writes, was under way. A drive toward national organization by the Alliance in the years 1887–91 sent "lecturers" into forty-three states and territories and established contact with two million American farm families. It had become ever clearer to the Alliance men of Texas that a cooperative system and a new economic structure for the nation could not be won in one state. There was too massive a complex of enemies: furnishing merchants, wholesale houses, cotton buyers, bankers, grain-elevator companies, railroads, land companies, and government agencies. The Alliance had a sweeping change in mind for America, and it necessarily encountered stern opposition.

It did not require a "culture of protest" built around the cooperative movement for an agrarian uprising to occur, though in Texas the energy this gave to the protest organizations was powerful. In the grain states of Nebraska and Kansas, where such a cooperative movement was only thinly developed, a vigorous farmers' protest uprising also occurred. Indeed, the cooperative ideal was not widely shared outside of Texas, nor did it seize a commanding position in the farm movement nationally. Grain producers in Kansas and Nebraska were ready to join the cotton farmers of the South in the populist uprising simply because of economic suffering. Year after year, grain prices were falling, from one dollar a bushel in 1870 to eighty cents in 1885 and sixty cents in the 1890s. In the Dakotas, harvest prices were often thirty-five cents a bushel. Corn too was dropping, from forty-five cents a bushel to below thirty cents in the 1890s. In the plains, the weight of debt was very heavy, since grain farming (unlike cotton agriculture in these years) depended heavily upon machines. Poverty was a daily fact of life over vast stretches of the flat, featureless plains. Men and children habitually went barefoot in summer, and relied on rags wrapped around their feet in the winter. Railroads charged high rates, grain elevators did the same, interest rates were exorbitant, and grain and stock buyers and traders in faraway centers such as Chicago seemed to possess an incredible power over the farmers' daily life. The vaunted "independence" of the American yeoman farmer was as absent in the wheat states as it was in the regions raising cotton.

The Populist Party Arises

The farmers' movement had to enter politics to achieve its goals, and it had to create a "third party," for not only were the laws governing the nation's economy made in Washington, the Democrats and Republicans were hostile to the new proposals. The obstacles to third-party success, however, were of immense—indeed, practically continental—dimensions. The Civil War was a fresh and bloody memory to many Americans, and they were too firmly seated in the partisan allegiances that that conflict had burned into place to be ready to throw over their political identities and take on a new one. The Republican party even in the Plains states had a powerful hold on the consciousness of rural and small-town America (cities, with their ethnic-minority populations, leaned Democratic). Also, the free-enterprise system, with its individualist values, elicited a powerful loyalty from most Americans. Since Thomas Jefferson's day Democrats had consistently demanded that government keep its hands off the economy, and the radical shift to government activity that the Alliance movement called for ran against the entire Democratic tradition. In the South, furthermore, the Democratic party was the party of the "Lost Cause" and the white man's interest. How could masses of white Southerners suddenly leave it behind, and thereby split the white man's voting strength and perhaps open the door to a renewed rise of black Republicanism? Finally, it was plain that what was hurting the farmer—dropping prices for grain, corn, and cotton—was helping the city consumer, and especially the working family. Lower food costs were a vital element in the urban standard of living. Therefore, city workers had no motive for swinging behind a farmer's party.

The farm protest, however, was much too alive and dynamic, too filled with millennial zeal, to believe that its cause would not sweep the nation. Cotton and grain farmers began to call for a "People's party." In Kansas, candidates on a People's party ticket began winning local elections in 1890. In 1891, the nine congressmen elected by Alliance and People's-party campaigns organized a People's-party caucus in Washington. In early 1892, almost 900 delegates met in St. Louis to form a national People's, or Populist, party. Containing more than 80 representatives of the Knights of Labor (the AFL held aloof from political action), the Populists looked eagerly to a national coalition of laboring and farming men. On July 4, 1892, a nominating convention met in Omaha, Nebraska, and in an atmosphere of intense evangelical zeal chose a presidential candidate, James B. Weaver of Iowa, and issued a clear call to the nation for a fundamental reform of its government and economy.

The Omaha platform of 1892 was the basic document of populism. The delegates met, it declared, "in the midst of a nation brought to the verge of moral, political, and material ruin. Corruption dominates the ballot-box, the legislatures, the Congress, and touches even the ermine of the bench. The people are demoralized; most of the States have been compelled to isolate the voters at the polling-places [using the secret ballot] to prevent universal intimidation or bribery. The newspapers are largely subsidized or muzzled; public opinion silenced; business prostrated; our homes covered with mortgages; labor impoverished; and the land concentrating in the hands of the capitalists. The urban workmen are denied the right of organization for self-protection; imported pauperized labor beats down their wages; a hireling standing army [hired groups of private Pinkerton detectives], unrecognized by our laws, is established to shoot

them down, and they are rapidly degenerating into European conditions. The fruits of the toil of millions are boldly stolen to build up colossal fortunes for a few, unprecedented in the history of mankind; and the possessors of these, in turn, despise the republic and endanger liberty. From the same prolific womb of governmental injustice we breed the two great classes—tramps and millionaires.

"The national power to create money is appropriated to enrich bondholders; a vast public debt, payable in legal currency, has been funded into gold-bearing bonds, thereby adding millions to the burdens of the people. Silver, which has been accepted as coin since the dawn of history, has been demonetized to add to the purchasing power of gold by decreasing the value of all forms of property as well as human labor; and the supply of currency is purposely abridged to fatten usurers, bankrupt enterprise, and enslave industry. A vast conspiracy against mankind has been organized on two continents, and it is rapidly taking possession of the world. If not met and overthrown at once, it forebodes terrible social convulsions, the destruction of civilization, or the establishment of an absolute despotism." (Norman Pollack, ed., The Populist Mind [1967])

What did the Populists call for in their desire to save the nation from its corrupted state? The secret ballot everywhere, to guarantee electoral freedom and protect voters from intimidation; a graduated income tax, to strike at huge fortunes; restriction of "undesirable immigration," to protect American wage earners from the competition of "the pauper and criminal classes of the world"; shorter hours for labor and an eight-hour day for government workers; abolition of hired armies ("the Pinkerton system . . . the hired assassins of plutocracy"); the initiative and referendum; direct election of senators; a one-term presidency; and an end to all subsidies or national aid to private corporations. In addition, the Populists believed that "the time has come when the railroad corporations will either own the people or the people must own the railroads," and that therefore "the government should own and operate the railroads in the interest of the people." Similarly, the telegraph and telephone systems should be nationalized. Land monopoly should be ended and alien ownership prohibited. The Populists demanded, too, a sound and flexible national currency. They maintained that silver and gold must be freely coined at the ratio of sixteen to one and that the money supply must be rapidly increased to not less than fifty dollars per capita. The government should place a special system of subtreasuries in the countryside, allowing them to make direct loans to farmers, who were always in need of capital at reasonable rates. Private banks should no longer print currency; this should be left to the federal government.

For the first time a major political party had appeared that called for positive rather than passive government and for what amounted to a sharp turn leftward in the direction of socialism. Its fate (to be discussed in the next chapter) was not encouraging. The Populists' presidential candidate carried one grain state (Kansas) and three silver states (Colorado, Idaho, and Nevada) in the election of 1892, while gaining enough votes in other Great Plains and mountain states to amass slightly more than a million popular votes. But that was as far as the nation's politics allowed Populism to go as an independent third party.

Bibliography

Books that were especially valuable to me in writing this chapter: I continue to be in debt to Robert H. Wiebe's landmark study, *The Search for Order, 1877–1929** (1968), and to John Higham's brilliant classic on nativism, beautifully argued and written, *Strangers in the Land** (1955), to which now must be added his recent *Send These to Me: Jews and Other Immigrants in Urban America** (1970). The Catholic Irish may be studied in a number of works, as in Joseph M. Hernon, Jr., *Celts, Catholics, and Copperheads: Ireland Views the American Civil War* (1968); William V. Shannon, *The American Irish* (1963); and Thomas N. Brown's important work, *Irish-American Nationalism, 1870–1890* (1966). Again, W. Elliot Brownlee's *Dynamics of Ascent: A History of the American Economy* (1978) proved valuable in understanding trends in workers income, hours of labor, and related topics. Herbert Gutman's *Work, Culture and Society in Industrializing America, 1815–1920* (1976) has given us surprisingly fresh ways of seeing labor in this period. Concerning women and the family, I have drawn heavily upon Sheila M. Rothman, *Woman's Proper Place: A History of Changing Ideals and Practices, 1870 to the Present* (1978) and Carl N. Degler, *At Odds: Women and the Family in America from the Revolution to the Present* (1980). Richard Hofstadter's *The Age of Reform: From Bryan to F. D. R.** (1955) has a brilliant section on

"The Agrarian Myth and Commercial Realities." Irwin Unger's *The Greenback Era: A Social and Political History of American Finance, 1865–1879* (1964) is basic on this whole question. On the Populists, I have found Lawrence Goodwyn's shorter study, *The Populist Moment: A Short History of the Agrarian Revolt in America** (1978) most illuminating, and less given to pushing his thesis overfar than his longer work, *Democratic Promise: The Populist Moment in America* (1976). Clearly, his perspectives have greatly influenced this chapter. Walter T. K. Nugent's *The Tolerant Populists** (1963) remains perhaps the most judicious account in a field crowded with controversy, and in which there are many new historical studies available. See especially Stanley B. Parsons, *The Populist Context: Rural versus Urban Power on a Great Plains Frontier* (1973).

How Have Historians Looked at the Topic?

During the latter half of the nineteenth century, the nation born in the American wilderness moved to the city. Urban machinery, whether sewers or city hall, creaked and sometimes collapsed under the massive influx of foreign immigrants and people from "down on the farm." The impact of urbanization, uniquely coupled in the United States with rampant industrialization, has been until recently a lost dimension in American history. Lewis Mumford's classic works on urban life and culture spoke out early for urban planning and reform: *The Brown Decades: A Study of the Arts in America, 1865–1895** (1931); *The Culture of the Cities* (1938); and *The City in History: Origins, Its Transformation and Its Prospects* (1961). Arthur M. Schlesinger was one of the first historians to underscore the importance of cities in shaping American life in *The Rise of the City, 1878–1898* (1933).

Some historians have taken the city as the major focus of their work, illuminating very significant facts of urbanization. Richard C. Wade's article "Urbanization" in C. Vann Woodward, ed., *The Comparative Approach to American History* (1968), offers a perceptive overall view of the urban genre. Excellent excerpts that give one a sense of what urban historians have accomplished are found in Alexander B. Callow, Jr.'s *American Urban History** (1969). See also his fascinating book *The Tweed Ring** (1966). Blake McKelvey interprets the period between the Civil War and World War I in *The Urbanization of America* (1962). Two special studies are particularly noteworthy: Sam B. Warner elucidates the critical connection between transportation and urban growth in *Streetcar Suburbs: The Process of Growth in Boston, 1870–1900* (1962), and Stephan Thernstrom analyzes the question of mobility and presents some startling conclusions in *Poverty and Progress: Social Mobility in the Nineteenth-Century City* (1964). Valuable too is a fine group of essays edited by Thernstrom and Richard Sennett, *Nineteenth-Century Cities: Essays in the New Urban History** (1969).

Herbert G. Gutman reveals the city as the stronghold of antagonism toward the unionizing laborer in a provocative article, "Industrial Workers Struggle for Power," in H. Wayne Morgan's collection *The Gilded Age* (1970). Gerald N. Grob explores the philosophy behind the labor movement in *Workers and Utopia: A Study of Ideological Conflict in the American Labor Movement, 1865–1900** (1961). Philip Taft's *The A. F. of L. in the Time of Gompers* (1970) admires Gompers as a realistic, nonpolitical moderate, and William M. Dick studies American trade unions' rejection of socialism in favor of "Gompersism" in *Labor and Socialism in America: The Gompers Era* (1972). W. G. Broehl, Jr.'s *The Molly Maguires** (1964) is a thorough account, and John Laslett fills an important gap in labor history with *Labor and the Left: A Study of Socialist and Radical Influences in the American Labor Movement, 1881–1924* (1970).

Ethnic enclaves are highlighted in an outstanding collection of readings edited by Leonard Dinnerstein and Frederic C. Jaher, *The Aliens: A History of Ethnic Minorities in America* (1970). Two excellent studies in this vein are Moses Rischin's *The Promised City: New York's Jews* (1962) and T. N. Brown's *Irish-American Nationalism* (1966). Barbara Solomon explores the emergence of nativism among New England's Protestant elite in *Ancestors and Immigrants* (1956). John Higham's brilliant work on nativism is cited above.

* Available in paperback.

23

GILDED AGE POLITICS: INSTABILITY AND IMPASSE

New York Public Library

The world had never seen before so huge a women's movement. Several hundred thousand American women belonged to it; a million were members in the world at large. The Women's Christian Temperance Union: said another way, it meant simply "Frances Willard." Soon after her death in 1898, legends sprang up around her; her statue appeared in the Capitol in Washington (she was the first woman so honored); bridges, streets, schools, and hospitals were named for her; and by 1915, four states had made her birthday a school holiday. Until the 1930s, when prohibition finally collapsed, thousands regularly called up her name in praise—and blame.

Willard grew up the child of stern puritan Yankee parents in Wisconsin. She liked to be called "Frank," hated housework, and enjoyed hunting and shooting. An omnivorous reader and college-educated, she early became a teacher. Her ideal was to have an independent life. But in her time this meant remaining single, and so she did. In the mid 1870s the temperance crusade exploded into national prominence. Peculiarly a "woman's cause" because of alcohol's direct impact on the family, Willard threw herself into it, soon becoming the WCTU's moving spirit. Willard was a beautiful woman—small, erect, graceful—and a gifted politician. She drew women followers like a magnet, and they idolized her. As dramatic in temperament as any actress, she spoke with commanding brilliance. A canny tactician, for twenty years she held the tumultuous WCTU in the palm of her hand—even though husbands, fathers, brothers, sons, and practically every other male person railed at her followers' devoting their lives to the cause. Simply to be active in public was a striking liberation for American women. For doing so, they were condemned and ridiculed. But Willard pushed on, earning her well-known title "the Uncrowned Queen of America."

Joining the WCTU meant throwing off the housebound restrictions of women's life. Under Willard the WCTU struck out not just at drinking, but eventually for women's suffrage, the labor movement, and socialism. Above all, Willard trusted in women, and in their potential for transforming and civilizing society. She made the national conventions of the WCTU front-page news everywhere in America. Her followers, meanwhile, were liberated in spirit. They demanded equality in their churches, worked for civic reform, and showed their political strength in working for the Prohibition party. In response, the Republican party, which was the traditional home of moralistic Yankee crusades, began opening its ranks to them. Having an important role in American politics was an experience for women that began with Willard.

The charismatic symbol of the women's movement in the Gilded Age and in the Progressive Era that followed: that was Frances Willard. She made middle-class women conscious of the power that, together, they had. She got them out of the home and into public speaking, taught them how to organize, and provided a new model of what it meant to be an American woman. By 1900, the year when Carrie Chapman Catt was elected as president of the National American Suffrage Association, the women's movement had become a national force.

Overview

For more than fifty years, American history books have described late nineteenth-century politics in just the terms implied in Mark Twain and Charles Dudley Warner's choice of the name *Gilded Age* for their novel of the era of Ulysses Grant. It has been seen as a time of hypocrisy, shallow glitter, dollar chasing, and political irresponsibility. The nation's leaders were mercenary, crafty, and indifferent to the public welfare. They trumped up bogus controversies over the tariff, political corruption, and the money system to divert the people's attentions from the "real" issues: the exploitation of labor and farmers, and profiteering. By this means they fended off what was actually needed: strong government intervention to reform the country's corrupt capitalist system. Gilded Age politics, in short, were little but noise and confusion, signifying nothing. Partisan divisions were meaningless, for both Democrats and Republicans were tools of the wealthy.

We are now beginning to see that this picture is fundamentally miscast. The politics of the Gilded Age, like that of every other period, have their own inner validity and reality. It is of little use, as Geoffrey Blodgett has written, to be impatient with Gilded Age leaders "for having not yet discovered the Welfare State." There were huge changes swiftly transforming American life in these decades; the people were deeply worried about them; and they argued endlessly about the tariff, money, and civil-service questions because this pre-1900 generation believed that somewhere within their intricacies lay the answers to the nation's ills.

Probably no other generation has been so knowledgeable about such complex public issues. Huge crowds turned out year after year to listen closely to long, detailed speeches on the tariff and the currency system; to cheer when key points of extraordinary technical subtlety were made; and to carry away and distribute tens of thousands of leaflets, which were handed eagerly from hand to hand. It is ironically true that, as economic historians have now established, the protective tariff probably had little effect one way or the other in stimulating industrialization, but people believed that it did, and this is what matters in understanding public affairs. The currency question was, however, one of great importance, for the volume of the money supply is a crucial element in economic affairs. The civil-service issue was also fundamental, for nothing significant could be done by governments about any national or local problem until their employees were honest, relatively free of political intervention, and professional. Upon this foundation, when it was finally established, were to rest all of the reforms of later years.

Certainly, at no time in American history was the national electorate more thoroughly mobilized, more directly involved in governing the country. Turnouts at the polls regularly soared over 80 percent. There were almost continual rallies, speeches, torchlight parades, and mass demonstrations in the elections, which could occur as frequently as every six months. Meticulously staffed political organizations reached into every ward and precinct. From the time the Democratic South returned to national politics in the mid 1870s, the two parties were so evenly balanced that national and state victories were won by whisker-thin margins. Thus, each party relied heavily upon "army-style" politics. The objective was to keep everyone's spirits high by constant stimulation; to arouse intense feelings against the common enemy; and to get every possible voter from one's own party to the polls at each election. To be an "independent" was scorned.

It was the most politically active grassroots-voting generation in American history. There was, of course, a pressing reason for all this. With a hundred thousand patronage jobs in the federal service to be handed out to the victors, and thousands more in state and local governments, each election was treated like a battle, for the rewards were enormous. In profusely corrupt cities like New York, where contracts totaling millions of dollars were regularly given out to political favorites, poor men could become millionaires in short order.

Cultural Politics

Most of all, however, Americans turned out in such huge numbers because these were years of intense cultural conflict. We have seen that at least since Jacksonian times the hatred that Protestant English and Scots—the British—felt toward Catholic Irish, bred into them by centuries of hostility and warfare in the homeland, was at the core of American politics. From Jefferson's time, indeed, the Democrats had been the party of the Catholics, as they were in general the party of all the outgroups who did not fit the classic New England, Protestant model (save for black Americans): Southern whites, German and Irish immigrants, French-Canadians, Jews; the irreligious; the free-living and the skeptical; those of Jeffersonian temper who strongly believed that people's morals should be their own affair, and that churches should stay out of politics. Republicans, on their part, were the party of that huge ethnic group that, widely distributed in the northern states, thought of themselves as uniquely the American people: Protestants of British descent, their homeland lying in Yankee New England and the territories to the west of it into which they migrated—western New York and the upper Middle West. They dreamed of a unified, hard-working, pious America cast in their own image. They still carried with them their ancient Yankee notion that the moral life of the community was properly the concern of government, which should be actively used to promote purity and godliness.

Since immigration was huge in these years, the Democratic party grew rapidly in numbers. Then the spectacular upsurge of Republican-backed nativism in the 1880s welded the Democrats into a fighting host. The Republicans, too, kept alive the nation's oldest cultural antipathy by constantly "waving the bloody shirt" and accusing the Democrats of being the party of Southern disloyalty. From the mid 1880s on, Republican-oriented anti-Catholic societies demanded that employers discharge Catholics, attacked their parochial schools as an assault on Americanism, and bewailed the growing power of Catholics in the governments of such great cities as New York, Boston, and Chicago. In 1887 the Iowa-born American Protective Association appeared to lead the campaign against Catholics, alleging papal conspiracies against American independence. The Republican attack against labor unionism was also, in effect, an attack upon immigrants and their growing power in American life. German Lutherans, though a Protestant group, veered strongly Democratic as a result of these Republican campaigns for cultural uniformity, not only because they were non-Yankees who spoke a foreign language and clustered to themselves, but because they feared for their parochial schools. Such institutions, they felt, were crucially important in keeping their children in the old ways and maintaining their identity as a people. This meant that they swung strongly behind the notion of absolute religious freedom, and in Jeffersonian terms criticized those zealous "clerics in politics" who would presume to use the power of government to change other people's morals.

Prohibitionism

Of all the issues dividing these two broad masses of people, the most explosive was prohibitionism. As a general rule, Yankee Americans in the nineteenth century did not drink alcohol. Whiskey was known as the drink of the Scotch-Irish and the Catholic Irish; beer consumption was a German habit; and wine was what Italians and Spaniards drank. In the Southern states, with their strong infusion of Scotch-Irish people, bourbon had always been an important beverage. But Yankees, especially those of a strongly religious cast, frowned upon alcoholic consumption as the core evil that led to all the other moral impurities of the age. In the 1850s, they had worked hard to end its use.

Now, in the 1880s, with the burgeoning of great cities, the flooding of young people into them from the countryside, and the streaming influx of immigrants, prohibitionism quickened. On every side, threats to true morality flaunted themselves in city streets: theaters, dance halls, houses of prostitution, and saloons. The latter seemed simultaneously connected with crime, political corruption, vice, and personal degradation. This was not a total misconception. Alcohol was in fact the comforter of the working poor; alcoholism was a terrible scourge. Corrupt interests did in reality cluster around the liquor trade, and the saloons that were everywhere in the working-class districts could be both a convivial blessing for overworked men and a social curse. Republicans, as the party of Yankee puritanism, called for prohibition with the same passion with which they had earlier condemned slavery, and for similar reasons. Prohibitionists firmly believed that if the saloon were crushed, American life would be regenerated in the Yankee mold. Thrift, industry, and piety would reign. Like the abolitionists, they prided themselves on their radicalism. Some became violent people who smashed saloon interiors with axes, blew them up and burned them down,

Interior of a New York dive in the 1890s, classic symbol to millions
of WASP Americans of the degradation of drink and the saloon.
In fact, the saloon often was a center of crime, corruption,
and vice.

Photograph by Jacob A. Riis Jacob A. Riis Collection,
Museum of the City of New York

and proudly received violence in return. Democrats, as the party of personal liberty and the immigrant outgroups, fought back with comparable bitterness. Prohibitionism symbolized to them the ancient habit of "minding other people's business" that they had always condemned in the Yankee Republicans (and in their Whig forebears).

Year after year Republicans launched drives to secure prohibition laws in the northern states, and thereby drive away the beer-drinking Germans, now an enormous part of the American population. (Prohibitionism was strong in the South, but not until after 1900 would people there begin using legislation to achieve it, until then relying upon churches to control their members.) Then in 1889 they escalated their assault against cultural divergence by enacting, in Wisconsin, a law that directly attacked parochial schools. It stated that a school would be regarded as such only if it taught the core subjects in the English language. Under compulsory-education laws, Lutheran and Catholic children might have to be sent to the public schools, where Yankee Protestantism was openly taught in the form of "moral

instruction." The result was a sweeping upsurge of Democratic victories nationally, fueled by the anger of Catholics and Lutherans, that threatened to put the Democrats permanently in charge of American government.

Women in Public Affairs

With Frances Willard's Women's Christian Temperance Union leading the way, the campaign against drink was peculiarly a women's crusade —which was one reason Democrats condemned it. Immigrants of both sexes recoiled from activist middle-class Yankee women, preferring that women stay out of public affairs. Among these Yankee women, however, a great social revolution was under way. The swift technological changes of the late nineteenth century transformed city and town women's lives. Hot and cold running water dramatically reduced one large task for women: the weekly wash. It had taken up to a third of the housewife's time to pump water from the well, carry bucket after bucket to the kitchen, and lift and lower heavy washtubs from the stove, where they had sat slowly heating. The washing machine was a miracle of labor saving, possible with indoor plumbing and the flowing tap.

Electricity made each day longer with artificial lighting, and began providing instant aid to housewives, especially in the form of refrigeration. The telephone eliminated hours of travel by horsecar and buggy. Electric elevators made the apartment house possible, with its piped gas to the kitchen stoves, hot-water heaters, tile (and easily cleanable) floors and walls, central heating, disposal of garbage, repair men at hand to fix the plumbing or electrical connections, and elevator men to help with heavy packages. In these compact, efficient, technological dwellings, servants could be dispensed with and a large and continuing claim upon the housewife's time disappeared. After 1870 the commercial canning of fruits and vegetables produced a rich variety of readily available foods, eliminating another annual task, and refrigerated railway cars made fresh meat, cut to convenient sizes, a simple matter to find. Also, the emergence of large commercial bakeries meant that women no longer had to devote a day a week to preparing bread and cakes. Commercial laundries were another convenience: by 1900, two out of three city families sent out at least some laundry. To shop in, spend the day in, meet friends in, there was another great innovation: the department store. Goods were cheaper being sold on a high-volume, cash-only basis, bargain sales were frequent, and almost everything imaginable was available in such grand, stately establishments as R. H. Macy's or John Wanamaker's or Marshall Field's. They delivered packages, repaired small items, stored furs, and were built as "cast-iron palaces"—indeed, almost as cathedrals.

Middle-class women in the cities had, therefore, a great deal of leisure time. They could not use that time to make careers for themselves: that was out of the question. In fact, very few women wanted them. They preferred their own sphere. Women were to care for people, nurture them, and provide a shining model: the virtuous woman. Pursuing the new ideal in child rearing that spread rapidly after the Civil War, they were to raise their children with affection and love. Their husbands, being men, were described as essentially animals who needed taming, and that too was the virtuous woman's task. And they were to tame society as well. Women, it was said, were pure in thought and heart, they loved beauty, and they expressed unselfish devotion. All of these qualities, social critics wrote, were desperately needed in the rough-and-tumble boom-and-bust of late nineteenth-century America.

Paradoxically, however, women were also said to be unsuited to work in the world at large because of physical weakness. Authorities held that women were highly nervous and sensitive, especially during the menstrual cycle, which was regarded as a time of near hysteria and insanity when women would do things irrationally. Women themselves took all of this with the greatest seriousness. The new women's colleges, such as Vassar, were built around careful programs of physical exercise designed to make the students strong enough to handle the strain of academic schooling. Pregnant middle-class women were advised to rest as much as possible—preferably to stay in bed for long periods. In other words, the normal bodily functions of women were defined as disease and infirmity. The historian Sheila M. Rothman, commenting on these conflicting images, writes that women were "at once incompetent and competent, broken and whole, to be pitied and to be emulated."

Many middle-class women wanted to do something important in the world at large, given their leisure and their education (through high school, usually, and sometimes through college), in order to civilize American life and make the home safe. The great medium for doing this was the women's-club movement, which expanded to major dimensions in the post–Civil War years. Formed first for educational purposes—discussing books and listening to lecturers—and for female fellowship during the long hours now freed from household labors, the clubs soon took up campaigns to attack social ills that threatened the family. The "Social Purity" crusades found their greatest outlet through Willard's Women's Christian Temperance Union. Founded in 1873, by 1890 it had 160,000 members. The WCTU's chief goal was to build virtuous, feminine qualities into American life to balance the brutal, animal values that came from men. "Woman will bless and brighten every place she enters," said the WCTU's motto, "and she will enter every place."

The liquor trade was of course the WCTU's main target, among the many reforms it sought. Through the elimination of the saloon and drinking, it hoped to strike at the drunkenness that was such a scourge to families, and also at prostitution, a curse to women and an immediate danger both to loving marriages and to health. The WCTU clearly believed that in assaulting these twin evils it was striking at the most bestial and uncontrolled of male appetites. Prostitution in particular, with its close links to the saloon, expressed a form of "animal appetite" that the concept of virtuous womanhood warred against. Respectable women were in fact not supposed to enjoy sex, according to the widely held code. Sexual activity was to mean only one thing: being a mother, not being, in terms of mutual physical enjoyment, a wife. Indeed, Willard liked to speak of WCTU members as "Protestant nuns." From the 1870s through the 1920s, even the sale of contraceptives in any form was almost universally against the law, and they seem generally to have been thought deeply immoral.

Women's Sexuality in the Nineteenth Century

This image of female frigidity in the Victorian years, so prominent in discussions of women in the nineteenth century, requires further exploration. Historians have traditionally held over the years that women in the mid-nineteenth century decades regarded sex as an unpleasant marital duty. Certainly the entire subject was under a taboo before the 1880s, so that it was not even talked about. However, new research hints at a marked shift in attitudes from the 1880s onward; what amounts, in fact, to a reawakening of earlier behavior.

A look backward in time will be helpful. The traditional opinion about women and sexuality in Europe had for centuries been that women, if anything, were more sexually passionate than men, and had more difficulty controlling their impulses. The Bible, of course, locates the origin of sexual evil with Eve, and churchly condemnations of the allegedly insatiable sexual appetites of women ring down through the ages. Seventeenth and eighteenth-century marriage manuals were written with a full knowledge of female sex-

ual anatomy and how sexual excitement occurs. This frank recognition of female sexuality endured at least until the middle of the nineteenth century.

At this point a campaign to teach a new sexual ideology to Americans began. Some medical and other authorities began asserting that women had little interest in sex—in fact urging this as a good thing. Society in general grew more prudish, and began circulating the notion that women should regard intercourse as distasteful. The origin of this impulse appears not to have come from men in general, who had little personal interest in seeing their wives grow colder, but in the long-term trend (which we have earlier observed) among women to want more personal freedom within the family. Reduction in the number of pregnancies was the single most effectual means of enhancing this personal freedom. As the historian Nancy Cott has recently observed, projecting an image of sexual disinterest may also have helped women gain a sense of moral superiority over men.

In actuality, what was being pressed upon American society in these years was not the absolute denial of sex, but control of it. Nineteenth-century medical and popular literature about women did not totally deny women's sexuality, or their pleasure in it. Women were simply said to be different in this regard from men, in that they desired intercourse less frequently. Recently, the records of a lengthy survey conducted at Stanford University from the 1890s to 1920 on the sex lives of a sizable group of middle-class women, some of them born before the Civil War, have been recovered, and in them it becomes clear that whatever the prudery and frigidity which mid-nineteenth century American women may have manifested, in the 1890s it was clear that those women who only tolerated sexual relations with their husbands were a distinct minority.

What, then, was the real target of the new sexual ethic which was preached in the mid-nineteenth century years? It was the sexual impulses of men. Reformers wanted the family to be built upon affection, not simply upon sexual satisfaction, and they wanted also to improve the position of women within marriage. Since birth-control measures (that is, the use of physical devices for this purpose) were regarded as immoral and because their most common substitutes—coitus interruptus, the "safe period," and abortion—were either unreliable, difficult to achieve, or dangerous, a simple reduction in sexual encounter was the most effective means of reducing the number of children women had to bear. And this, by thousands of women, was regarded as a great liberation. A popular writer, John Cowan, observed in 1874 (in his widely read *Science of a New Life*): "The pains, the troubles, the heart burnings, the sickness, the danger of premature death, that woman has to experience through man's lust is beyond all comprehension. If there is one direction more than another in which 'Woman's Rights' should assert itself, it is in this choice of time for sexual congress."

The Meaning of the Social Purity Movement

When the Social Purity movement attacked prostitution, its objective was to moderate male sexuality. A common sexual morality, in which men, like women, had sex only with their spouse, and then at the frequency that the wife desired: this was what Victorian sexual morality meant, not a simple and stern demand that women repress their sexuality entirely. Ida Craddock was explicit in connecting the new ideology of sexual restraint with fewer children: "To create a few, a very few children who shall be an expression of the noblest thoughts of yourself and your husband and to give those children all possible advantages of education, travel, and society, is not this doing your duty as a wife and mother better than if you create children at haphazard and wholesale. . . ?" That such "high-quality" children were also demanded by the increasingly complex and competitive economy provided another strong motivation for family limitation.

Though the Social Purity campaigns sent women actively out into public life to agitate, it should be understood that this was not an attack on the doctrine of the two spheres within the family (women focusing upon the home and children, and men working in the world and directing the government). Campaigners limited themselves strictly to causes aimed at protecting the family and improving women's position within their sphere. In fact, Social Purity workers opposed the women's-suffrage movement, for it called openly and unquestionably for a breaking down of the two spheres by opening general politics to women. Frances Willard came to support women's suffrage only tentatively, and late. Much more important to her, in addition to the fight against the saloon, was the assault against legalized, regulated prostitution.

The crusade for Social Purity brought a new openness in talking about sex into American public life. Education on sexual issues began to make its first appearance in the schools. And the movement quite destroyed the idea of licensed prostitution in the United States: the red-light districts were effectively gone by the 1920s. With their disappearance there may also have appeared (although the evidence on this issue is indistinct) a new ethic of male self-restraint. Sexual activity for men was now to take place only within the marriage relationship, and, if the continued fall in the birth rate may be taken as a firm indication, it seems ever more to have been regulated in accordance with women's desires. We shall later observe new shifts in the relationships between married people after about 1910.

Confusion in National Politics

In the Gilded Age, meanwhile, local, state, and national politics remained supremely a part of male culture. And in that world, after the election of 1876, there was instability and confusion. With the return of the South to national politics the two major parties were so closely balanced that only in the years 1889–91 and 1893–95 did one of the two parties control both Congress and the presidency. Also, Congress lacked any center of authority, almost anyone could block the flow of legislation, and many congressmen were openly corrupt. The result was that hardly anything got done.

Five men served as Republican presidents from 1877 to 1901, all but one from the Middle West: Rutherford B. Hayes (1877–81) of Ohio; James A. Garfield from the same state, who was shot within four months of becoming president in 1881 and died two months later, to be succeeded by his vice-president from New York, Chester A. Arthur (1881–85); Benjamin Harrison (1889–93) of Indiana; and William McKinley (1897–1901) of Ohio. These men brought traditionally Whiggish and Republican ideas about the chief executive with them to the White House. If Congress passed laws, they would administer them. However, it was not their place, they believed, to provide vigorous executive leadership, to be tribunes of the people in the style of Andrew Jackson. They were, instead, quiet chairmen of the board. Even Abraham Lincoln, usually described as a "strong" president, made no attempt to guide Congress toward a legislative program. He used his powers as commander in chief vigorously, but otherwise held back.

Much more important than these men were such Republican senators as James G. Blaine of Maine, Orville H. Platt of Connecticut, and Nelson W. Aldrich of Rhode Island. The Republicans consistently chose their presidential candidates from the Middle West, so as to tap the strength of the huge transplanted Yankee community in that region, but their party was run by its congressional leaders from New England. Elected to Congress year in and year out from heavily Republican constituencies, dominating that body because their seniority gave them control of its key committees, and accustomed to watching presidents come and go, they set the tone of Republicanism. Such men instinctively thought sympathetically of the well-to-do middle and upper classes, who were overwhelmingly British and old-stock American in ethnic composition and ways of life, for such peoples made up the core of their party. New England, furthermore, was by this time solidly industrial, which made its Republican legislators ardent disciples of Alexander Hamilton and Henry Clay. Governments, in their view, should work closely with the capitalists of the country to develop its resources. This meant high protective tariffs, a moderately expansive money supply, and government aid in the form of internal improvements, land grants, and timber rights.

By these devices, they firmly believed that they were doing the best for all Americans: creating jobs, making the nation prosperous, and providing opportunities for hard-working folk to get ahead. "I am entirely sick of this idea," said Senator Platt, "that the lower the prices are the better for the country. . . ." Competition was ruinous, not helpful. Businessmen should be free to set their prices at whatever level would return them a fair profit. What lay behind the constant antibusiness attacks that came from Democrats, Populists, socialists, and the working classes (they asked)? Sour envy: little else. Republican senators warmly adopted the form of social Darwinism that insisted that the rich got their wealth because they were more able and talented, that nothing should be done to help the poor because nature intended, by the rule of survival of the fittest, to keep them in that condition. Social classes, said their favorite philosopher, William Graham Sumner of Yale, owed nothing to each other. Each must look out for itself.

The Rise of Grover Cleveland

By the 1880s this philosophy of government aids to business development had begun to produce a powerful counterattack. On every hand, critics said—with abundant evidence—this simply produced massive corruption. Legislators and public officials regularly sold their votes and influence. American public life stank of graft from top to bottom. Democratic leaders traditionally distrusted the profit motive, and regarded the booming industrialization of the country with alarm. Carried upward by this kind of public sentiment, the Democrat Grover Cleveland rocketed out of total obscurity in the early 1880s. A reforming mayor of Buffalo, New York, and then governor of the state (1882–84), he consistently vetoed proposals that would have granted funds, special privileges, and immunities to banks, railroad and subway companies, electric-power corporations, and even icehouses. In 1885, he was inaugurated as president of the United States, the first Democrat to hold that post in almost twenty-five years. No one in American history had ever risen so swiftly.

The Liberal Republicans

His victory came in part because Liberal Republicans, whom contemptuous Republican regulars called Mugwumps, had swung behind him en masse. For years they had been alarmed at the close ties that were growing between their party and business interests. In 1872 they had actually broken loose to form a separate "Liberal Republican" party. With the agreement of the Democrats, they ran Horace Greeley for president against Ulysses Grant, only to suffer a humiliating defeat. Since then they had drifted uncomfortably back to their party, hoping vainly for its rejuvenation along less capitalistic lines. The nomination of James G. Blaine for the presidency in 1884 was too much for them, because he was too openly linked to businessmen. Cleveland, on the other hand, was an honest and courageous man whose values seemed very much like their own. For as long as he was in the presidency they were among his warmest supporters, teaching him much about the need for lower tariffs and a reformed civil service, and bringing with them the nation's intellectual classes. Primarily from the northeastern states, they were men of high moral concerns, many of them veterans of the fight against slavery.

The Transatlantic Liberal-Democratic Community

The Liberal Republicans looked to British liberalism for their name and ideas. Indeed, for America in general the half-century from the Civil War to the First World War was the great Anglo-American age. For many reasons, Great Britain was the most prominent object on the American horizon. It was perhaps the most powerful nation in world affairs; its empire circled the globe; its industries were everywhere admired and copied; its Parliament was the "mother of parliaments"; and its wealth was an immense force in the world economy. The Bank of England was then the towering financial bastion of world capitalism that Wall Street became later on. For decades the American economy had been fueled by British investments. This created a rampant anti-British feeling in the western states, whose mines, cattle ranches, and lumbering operations were often controlled from London. The American middle and upper classes, British in descent, liked things British as they had in colonial days. The Irish hated Great Britain, and made the air ring with attacks on English misrule in Ireland.

The Cleveland Democrats and the Liberal Republicans admired the great leader of the British Liberal party, William Gladstone, and relied on the economic ideas of John Stuart Mill, the party's principal philosopher and economist. Mill's *Principles of Political Economy* (1848), together with Adam Smith's revered *Wealth of Nations* (1776), provided weighty authority for the low tariff–sound money outlook. Gladstone's legendary victory in converting Britain to free trade in the 1840s, and his foreign policy, which con-

demned militarism and power politics in international relations, made him a world figure. At Princeton in the 1870s, a young student named Woodrow Wilson hung Gladstone's picture over his desk and practiced the great man's ideas and style.

At the same time, American reformers read Charles Dickens and other British novelists who attacked oppression of the poor; traveled through British cities to see how their municipal authorities solved the problems that made American cities so ugly, corrupt, and filthy; and learned that a strong central government was needed to grapple successfully with social ills. Americans, in brief, continued to live and work within the orbit of British culture.

Cleveland as President

Grover Cleveland was a Jacksonian Democrat and a Presbyterian. He had been reared in western New York during the 1840s, and the ideals of Jacksonian democracy were dinned into his ears. From this training he derived a conviction that society is always in danger of being exploited by the wealthy and powerful, whether they tried to control the currency in their interest, as in Jackson's day, or to build protective tariffs, as in his own. His Presbyterianism, received from his father, a devotedly orthodox minister, gave him a brooding outlook on human affairs that carried a strong Calvinist color. What he saw, through these lenses, was a scene of grab and scramble, each person trying to get advantages over the rest. Greed, privilege, self-indulgence, petty graft— these were the forces that to him seemed to dominate American life. He was obsessed with the notion that the apparatus of privilege and special advantage, which in his view the Republicans had built, was bringing on national decay. The "spirit of selfishness is abroad in the land," he would say; unreasonable profits came from exploiting the masses. The key words that studded his speeches and writings were *selfish* and *sordid*. He lived in a corrupt age, and it revolted him.

His Presbyterianism gave him a strong sense of duty, and of right principles that cannot be violated without grave harm to society. Also, Presbyterian theology asserted that God is an active, intervening, vigorous sovereign, and so was Cleveland as president. He assumed that the

Grover Cleveland, first Democratic president since the Civil War. His stolid determination to cleanse politics, reduce the tariff to aid consumers and attack privilege, and introduce civil service made him admired by millions.

Courtesy of the Library of Congress

chief executive should use his powers forthrightly, and he did so. Senators overshadowed Republican presidents, but not Cleveland. He worked fully within the Democratic tradition of a strong presidency. He had been abruptly plucked from obscurity and sent swiftly to the White House, and he derived from this an unshakable conviction that the people were on his side.

Cleveland and the Economy

Cleveland's main concern was to cleanse the nation's economic system. He was more worried about the plundering of the West than about any other problem in his first administration. He stopped all land-office activity to investigate fraudulent claims, and harshly condemned the great robberies that had taken place. Cattle kings, land syndicates, railroad companies, and lumber barons had created a huge system of land

monopoly. Attacking the "colossal greed" of the culprits, he forced them to return more than eighty million acres. In his second administration (1893–97) he continued his assault upon speculators and began the process of setting aside great timbered regions as national forests.

In 1886, when the decisions of the United States Supreme Court took away the power of the states to regulate the rates of railroads, Cleveland gave his support to congressmen who wanted to establish some form of federal control. As mayor and governor, he had warned strongly against the harmful power of unchecked corporations. Now he agreed with those who wanted to follow British practice and establish a strong, independent commission. When the Interstate Commerce Commission bill came before him in February 1887, he ignored attacks on its constitutionality and signed it. Though unprecedented in American practice, and the first step by a Democratic president to move away from a pure Jeffersonian laissez-faire, it was quite in line with his belief that the sovereign power of the national government should be actively used to protect the community at large from exploitation by corporate power. In other words, the ICC would enhance *egalitarianism*, that traditional concern in Democratic republicanism, by helping to create more equality between the powerful owners of railroads and the farmers who used them. Cleveland was thus ready to begin some limitations on economic *liberty*, the other pole in Democratic thought.

Cleveland and the Civil Service

His first task as president, however, was to make civil-service reform a reality. This involved him in seemingly endless labors. The Pendleton Civil Service Act, established the beginnings of the system whereby government employees were appointed on the basis of demonstrated ability and were not removable save for incompetence. It had been enacted in 1883 following Garfield's tragic assassination by a disgruntled party worker. However, President Arthur had been unable to make the new law very effective, and the situation continued in which the president spent months deciding on literally thousands of individual appointments. The White House halls were clogged with applicants and their politician friends. Constant pressure from all directions was applied on the president. Cleveland struggled his way doggedly through all of this, working toward the goal of a professional civil service, though often sliding backwards as he responded to party needs. The extent of his contribution is shown in the fact that whereas at the beginning of his first term in 1885 it was a specific exception for an office to be under civil-service regulations, by the end of his second term in 1897 it required a specific exception for such a post not to be.

The Irish fought Cleveland bitterly in this cause. Civil-service reform would remove their ability to make party appointments, keep the organization strong, and, as they put it, continue to open government employment to the poor. To them, civil service reform was a direct assault upon equality. The Mugwumps, on the other hand, were absolutely obsessed by the cause. This, to them, was the nation's most important single undertaking. An efficient, educated, orderly civil service, removed from partisan control, would, as in the British example, be the chief instrument of executive action in a modernized, rationally organized state. This kept the Mugwumps in constant combat with the Irish. No cause, indeed, more sharply highlighted the conflict between ethnic politics, with its essentially inward-turning concern with local affairs—getting "our boys" a job—and the national outlook of a reforming, university-trained elite. The Irish believed government should be personal and direct, built upon networks of mutual obligation and relationship; the Mugwumps believed, instead, that it should be impersonal, efficient, and directed by general rules and national needs. In this controversy, as so often in public affairs, the conflict is to be understood not primarily as a partisan one, but as part of the long social transformation that has occurred, in every compartment of national and international life, from traditional to modernized forms of government and culture.

Cleveland and the Tariff

It was the tariff question that became the great cause of Cleveland's presidencies. Since the Civil War it had become an accepted fact of American life, added to again and again. To Liberal-Democrats the tariff question was one of the most crucial issues of the nineteenth century, and they never lost interest in it. They regarded low tariffs as essential to social justice, a healthy international economy, and peace itself. How could the world become an open and free trading community, they asked, if protective tariffs chopped it up into mutually exclusive segments? Genuine prosperity would arrive only if the world were thought of as a single trading community and if there were an international division of labor. Each country would make the product for which it was best suited, and no industry would gain unfair advantages. Consumers would not have to pay higher prices to protected home industries. Economic rivalries would give way to cooperation, and world peace would be assured. If tariffs were lowered, special privilege would be reduced, and economic egalitarianism would be enhanced.

In 1887 Cleveland startled the nation by devoting his entire annual message to Congress to an attack on the protective tariff. Thus dramatically inaugurated, the boiling national controversy over the tariff that ensued was reminiscent of Andrew Jackson's Bank War. Mugwumps were delighted. New York and New England intellectuals threw themselves into the campaign—one in which, happily for them, they were no longer in conflict with the Catholic Irish and the city bosses. Cleveland lost the battle for a lower tariff in 1888, but he was thoroughly aroused to his cause. It was part of his belief that the nation had become sick to its core with special economic privilege and materialism. Just before he left the White House at the end of his first term—Benjamin Harrison defeated him in the electoral college, if not in popular votes, in the election of 1888—in his fourth annual message to Congress he blasted the power of great corporations and the race for money and profit. Fortunes were no longer made by hard work, he said, or by enlightened foresight or sturdy enterprise; instead, they were made by arrangements in which the government discriminated in favor of the manufacturers. Unreasonable profits came largely from exploiting the masses. Trusts, combinations, and monopolies ruled the land "while the citizen is struggling far in the rear or is trampled to death beneath an iron heel."

The Republican Interlude

Benjamin Harrison's election began the Republican interlude between Cleveland's first and second administrations. The new president was thoroughly Republican. "Cheaper coats," he said in defending the wool tariff, would "necessarily [involve] a cheaper man and woman under the coat." He warned that the Democrats represented the South and its disloyalty and were responsible for the horrors of the Civil War. Bitterly hostile toward the British, as were many Republicans, strong nationalists that they were, and resentful of London's preeminence, he delighted in attacking the English, referring to the "grasping avarice" of their diplomacy.

In control of both houses of Congress and the presidency for the first time since 1875, the Republicans moved ahead quickly. They admitted a large group of new states, which promptly sent Republican representatives and senators to Congress: North Dakota, South Dakota, Montana, and Washington in 1889; Wyoming and Idaho in 1890. To dissipate the growing surplus in the Treasury, which was withholding too much capital from the national economy, and at the same time to give expression to their belief that the national government should be actively used to develop the country and its industries, the Republicans advanced on two fronts: internal improvements and an increased tariff. So costly was their program of public works that the session in which they were enacted was called the Billion-Dollar Congress. They advanced an ingenious argument that the way to reduce the revenues created by the tariff was to raise them so high as absolutely to exclude imports from abroad. The McKinley Tariff, named for Congressman William McKinley of Ohio, did more: it gave protection to industries that hardly even existed as yet, such as tin plating (thus bringing disaster to the Welsh tin-plating industry), in order to stimulate their creation, and it raised the general level of rates to a new record of 49 percent.

Thomas B. Reed, Speaker of the House, imposed rules on that body that speeded up its deliberations by giving far more authority to the Speaker to prevent delaying tactics. Loudly criticized, "Czar" Reed blandly held firm. Responding to national demands from both parties, the Republicans in 1890 enacted the Sherman Anti-Trust Act. There were few who could stomach the idea of outright monopoly. Furthermore, they reacted to western currency appeals by passing the Sherman Silver Purchase Act.

The Democrats responded to this forthright Republican program with a spectacular nationwide campaign against the tariff. Meanwhile, the prohibition controversy and the parochial-school battles worked their explosive political medicine in local and state elections. The result, in the congressional election of 1890, was a national Democratic landslide: 236 Democrats sat in the new House of Representatives, compared with only 88 Republicans.

The Return of Cleveland

Now Grover Cleveland took to the hustings again, going back and forth across the northern states to hammer again and again against materialism and special privilege. The spirit of selfishness, he said, filled the air with demands for special advantages from the government. The McKinley Tariff seemed to him the highest expression of greed. "Vile, unsavory forms," he said in Boston, "rise to the surface of our agitated political waters, and gleefully anticipate, in the anxiety of selfish interest, their opportunity to fatten upon corruption and debauched suffrage." Nominated again by his party in 1892, he achieved a landslide victory. He won 277 votes in the electoral college against Harrison's 145, a popular plurality of nearly 400,000 votes, and Democratic majorities in both houses of Congress for the first time since the 1850s.

Now, however, an economic crisis of earthquake proportions swept in to transform national politics. The great depression of the 1890s, which began in a stock-market crash in May and June 1893, within two months of Cleveland's inauguration for his second term, destroyed his hopes, his Democratic coalition, and the third-party system, founded in the Civil War era. Urban peoples suffered as never before, and they were joined in their distress by southern and western farmers.

The Populists, and western and southern Democrats with their farming constituencies to worry about, sent up a loud cry for inflation of the money supply to raise prices. Specifically, they demanded the free and unlimited coinage of silver at the former (prior to 1873) legal ratio of sixteen to one. In the mid 1890s, silver in the open world market was valued far cheaper than that: at a ratio of thirty-two to one with gold. Thus, if the United States said it would give out an ounce of gold for every sixteen ounces of silver, an avalanche of that precious metal would pour in upon the Treasury from all over the world to be exchanged for gold and, under free coinage, turned into currency. This would not only inflate the currency, it would destroy the gold standard in America, for the gold in the federal vaults would simply disappear.

Cleveland's own position was clear and unshaken. All the voices he trusted, whether those of Jacksonian democracy or of British Liberalism, instructed him in classic sound-money principles. From the beginning of his first term to the end of his second, Cleveland never questioned them. He persistently held that the United States could not maintain a bimetallic currency alone in the world. The two metals would part company entirely as gold was drained from the Treasury. This would be disastrous, he said in 1886, for gold was "still the standard of value and necessary in our dealings with other countries." Furthermore, bankers and speculators would inevitably get richer if the free-silver experiment were tried, for clever, powerful men could always profit from price rises and declines while "the laboring men and women of the land, most defenseless of all, will find that the dollar received for the wage of their toil has sadly shrunk in its purchasing power."

James Laughlin, a University of Chicago economist, attacked the free-silver idea: "As free coinage of silver would inevitably result in a rise of prices, it would immediately result in the fall of wages. Its first effect would be to diminish the purchasing power of all our wages. The man who gets $500 or $1,000 a year as a fixed rate of wages or salary will find he could buy just half as much as now. Yes, but someone will say, the employer will raise his wages. Now, will he? But the facts on that point are clear and indisputable. It has been one of the undisputed facts of history that, when prices rise, the wages of labor are the last to advance; and when prices fall, the wages of labor are the first to decline. Free coinage of silver would make all the articles of the laborer's consumption cost him 100 percent more unless he can get a rise in his wages by dint of strikes and quarrels and all the consequent dissatisfaction arising from friction between the employer and employee.

"The damage runs in other directions, [wiping out savings laid aside] for old age, for sickness, for death, for widows and orphans, or by insurance. . . . No invasion of hostile armies, burning and destroying as they advance, could by any possibility equal the desolation and ruin which would thus be forced upon the great mass of the American people. [Meanwhile] the shrewd ones, the bankers, etc., will be easily able to take care of themselves; while we plain people will be robbed of our hard-won earnings without any hope of compensation.

"In conclusion . . . extraordinary as is the proposal for free coinage, it is in truth only a huge deceit. It was born in the private offices of the silver kings, nursed at the hands of speculators, clothed in economic error, fed on boodle, exercised in the lobby of Congress, and as sure as there is honesty and truth in the American heart it will die young. . . ." (*Facts about Money* [1895])

Repeal of the Sherman Silver Purchase Act

The Treasury's gold reserve was dropping rapidly below the $100 million level, which traditionally was regarded as essential to maintain confidence in the nation's credit and currency. Cleveland decided that his most imperative duty, even before moving on the tariff question, was to obtain repeal of the Sherman Silver Purchase Act. What followed was a long and bitter struggle stretching out over many months in which he exerted every ounce of his executive power over Congress, freely brandishing the patronage axe to force men to vote his way. Eventually he won. The Sherman Silver Purchase Act was repealed and the gold standard was saved. But prosilver Democrats from the South and West revolted. In effect, two Democratic parties came into being. Cleveland had insisted that the depression would end once silver purchase was repealed and people regained confidence in the currency, but this did not happen. The nation sank deeper into depression, and more and more Democrats turned away from the hapless Cleveland. Lonely, abused on all sides, he grew bitter and depressed while remaining doggedly convinced that he was right. When the young congressman William Jennings Bryan of Nebraska rose to take leadership of the silver Democrats and stump the country as the Democratic presidential candidate in 1896, Cleveland morosely described Bryanism as a "sort of disease in the body politic." The silverites had "burglarized and befouled the Democratic home."

Tariff Failure

The president's fight over repeal of silver purchase destroyed any hopes for tariff reform, for he had made far too many enemies. He was able to force a tariff reduction bill through the House, but the Senate transformed it. The Wilson-Gorman Tariff emerged almost as protectionist as the McKinley Tariff it replaced (an average of 41 percent on dutiable goods, compared with the earlier 49 percent). Cleveland condemned it as "party perfidy and party dishonor," but let it become law without his signature.

Except for saving the gold standard and greatly widening the civil service, he had failed in his major domestic objectives. Cleveland's administration now entered the endless dog days that made the rest of his term a nightmare. He knew that he had powerful interests in the business world principally to thank for his tariff failure. "The trusts and combinations—the communism of pelf—whose machinations have prevented us from reaching the success we deserved," he wrote a friend, "should not be forgotten nor forgiven." Meanwhile, the country remained sunk deep in economic collapse.

The Depression of the 1890s

Millions of men were out of work in the mid-1890s. City police stations and government buildings were jammed every night with men sleeping in corridors and stairways. The resources of private charity were soon gone. Some cities dispensed aid, but the states and federal government refused. New York's governor rejected a plan of work relief, saying, "In America, the people support the government; it is not the province of the government to support the people."

Desperate men organized marches on Washington. Jacob S. Coxey's "army" of about 500 men from Ohio was the most famous of seventeen such groups in the spring of 1894. All they got was sympathy and a strengthened determination on the part of the established authorities not to yield to "mob rule." Some 1,400 strikes were called in that frightful year, affecting almost 700,000 people, but few won restoration of wage cuts.

The most spectacular strike was that of the American Railway Union against the Pullman Company of Chicago. Some 60,000 men eventually struck, expanding nationwide a boycott against Pullman's cars. Richard Olney, Cleveland's attorney general and a former railroad law-

yer, was determined to crush the strike. Using the excuse of protecting the mails, he authorized the swearing in of 3,600 deputies to "preserve order" in Chicago, though as yet no violence had occurred. Then he secured an injunction calling on the American Railway Union to end the strike. On the day it was served, a mob ditched a mail train in Blue Island, Illinois. Thereafter the controversy escalated. Cleveland, always determined to enforce what he regarded as rightful authority, decided to end the "reign of terror" in Chicago. Without waiting, as the Constitution requires, for the state of Illinois to request federal aid, he sent 2,000 troops to Chicago on the fourth of July, 1894. In response, mobs took over the railroad yards, burning and destroying cars and stealing property. The leader of the American Railway Union, Eugene V. Debs, was imprisoned, tried for contempt of court, and sentenced to six months in jail.

In the congressional elections of 1894, which took place soon afterward, the Democrats suffered one of the gravest defeats in American political history. The Republicans won large majorities in both houses of Congress.

The Election of 1896

As the depression worsened, the silver issue rose to overshadow all others. As against free silver, the Republicans now firmly supported the gold standard. Their inflationism had always been relatively moderate. At the same time, they urged high tariffs and nominated William McKinley, governor of Ohio, for the presidency. The Democrats were wholly at sea. Most Democrats detested Cleveland, but who was to replace him? When the party's national convention gathered in Chicago in July 1896, it was suddenly electrified by an exciting speech given by a young ex-congressman from Nebraska, William Jennings Bryan. "Upon which side will the Democratic party fight," he cried out, "upon the side of 'the idle holders of idle capital,' or upon the side of 'the struggling masses'? [The gold Democrats] come to us and tell us that the great cities are in favor of the gold standard; we reply that the great cities rest upon our broad and fertile prairies. . . . Having behind us the producing masses of this nation and the world, supported by the commercial interests, the laboring interests and the toilers everywhere, we will answer their demand for a gold standard by saying to them: You shall not press down upon the brow of labor this crown of thorns, you shall not crucify mankind upon a cross of gold." Pandemonium broke loose. Delegates cheered wildly, leapt on chairs, and wept with joy. After preliminary maneuvering, the thirty-six-year-old Bryan was chosen as the Democratic nominee for president. Then the convention adopted a platform condemning Cleveland's policies, especially on the gold standard and the crushing of the railway strikers. It also called for a low tariff, an income tax, the abolition of National Banknotes (those issued by private banks), and—now wholly won to the cause —free coinage of silver.

Gold Democrats were shocked. Some withdrew to form the National Democratic party, which nominated Senator John M. Palmer of Illi-

nois. The Populists were equally nonplused. Their issue had been taken from them. Should they fuse with the Democrats? If they did not, their votes for a different candidate might ruin the hopes of free silver. In their national convention they hit on the compromise of nominating Bryan while choosing their own vice-presidential nominee, Thomas E. Watson of Georgia.

Thereafter, the Populists simply faded away by merging with the Democrats. Many Populists held back, however. They had hoped that their party would persevere in the South by providing a genuine workingman's party that, in opposition to the Democrats, would unify both white and black labor. In the North, they had hoped that Populism would flourish as a broad reform movement, unifying both city and farm. Now all their goals seemed swept away in the interests of one cause alone—free silver.

THE ELECTION OF 1896

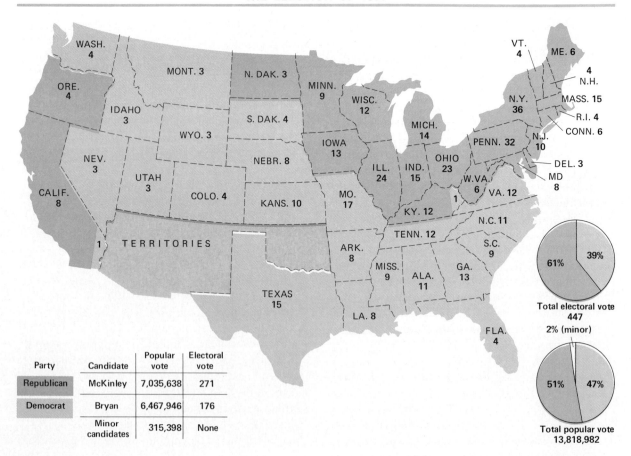

Party	Candidate	Popular vote	Electoral vote
Republican	McKinley	7,035,638	271
Democrat	Bryan	6,467,946	176
Minor candidates		315,398	None

Total electoral vote 447

2% (minor)

Total popular vote 13,818,982

William Jennings Bryan: Christian Democrat

Bryan was hated by many Republicans. Theodore Roosevelt said he and his silver Democrats were "plotting a social revolution and the subversion of the American Republic." But William Jennings Bryan was no wild-eyed radical. A deeply Christian man, he was also a Jeffersonian trying to apply the Virginian's creed in modern conditions. "The Democratic party, if I understand its position," he said, "denies the economic as well as the political advantage of private monopoly and promises to oppose it wherever it manifests itself. It offers as an alternative competition where competition is possible, and public monopoly [as in public ownership of railroads] wherever circumstances are such as to prevent competition."

He had wanted to be a minister; now he was an evangelist in politics. Bryan campaigned like no one ever had before: 18,000 miles and 600 speeches in three months, before five million people. His campaign funds were small whereas those of the Republicans were enormous. From Standard Oil alone the Republicans received a donation of $250,000, which was almost as large as Bryan's entire war chest. Newspapers and magazines were against him almost unanimously, but his obvious sincerity and his courage in taking on apparently insurmountable odds won him widespread respect.

Bryan won only the Solid South, some of the Great Plains states, and the mountain West. With 7.1 million votes, McKinley was 600,000 votes ahead of Bryan and won an electoral margin of 271 to 176. It was the largest total popular vote in American history and a landmark victory: the oscillation that for twenty years had taken place in Washington—first one party and then the other winning majorities in an evenly matched struggle—suddenly ended.

Analysis

Why was this so? In the mid 1890s, the fires of cultural conflict died down. Republican leaders, recognizing the harm that the antiimmigrant crusade was doing them, pulled back, talking far less about drink and parochial schools and far more about developing the economy and providing jobs for everyone. William McKinley led the way toward the new Republican tactic of cultural pluralism. Then the massive depression that struck the country in 1893 caused tens of thousands of Democrats, in every ethnic and religious group, in country or city, in the middle and upper classes as well as the lower, to swing Republican. People looking for jobs began thinking of themselves in economic, rather than cultural, terms. The Republicans had always called for using the national government actively to stimulate the economy and create jobs. This was just what multitudes of Americans wanted.

When Bryan and his western and Southern inflationists took over the Democratic party in 1896, millions in the Middle West and Northeast turned away. New England had never trusted the West: its burgeoning growth had always seemed a threat to the Northeast. Neither Middle West nor Northeast was comfortable with the idea of Southern domination in the national government, as it seemed would occur if Bryan won. Further-

The Republican press satirized William Jennings Bryan, whose open piety and many references to biblical texts to support his cause laid him open to the charge of desecrating the Bible while really —his critics said—being an anarchist.

Culver Pictures, Inc.

more, the city masses accepted the Republican argument that the silverites' campaign for currency inflation would raise the cost of living. Conversely, they agreed that higher tariffs would start industries going again and provide jobs. In addition, Bryan's strongly Christian style of oratory and appeal repelled many immigrants, who began to fear that a Bryan victory would lead to a renewed Protestant crusade. The result was that Republicans won the cities, long the Democratic stronghold, and with that victory secured a lasting predominance.

The Fourth Party System Appears

The third, or Civil War, party system which had taken shape in the party realignments of the 1850s, was now dead. A new party system now came into being: the fourth, or Progressive Era, party system. It would endure until the next great depression, which began in 1929. The Democratic party, which until Bryan's time had been strong in the Northeast and Middle West, shriveled to a fraction of its former strength in those regions. It became a Southern and partially a western party. The Irish in northern cities never left the Democratic party, a fact that made them thereafter even more powerful than ever within their party outside of the South. But the other non-British ethnic groups shifted to the Republican side. German Lutherans decamped in huge numbers. Since the Scandinavians, a firmly pietistic and temperance-oriented Protestant group from Norway, Sweden, and Denmark, had always been strongly Republican, what emerged within the Republican party after 1896 as its ethnic core was a WASP coalition (white, Anglo-Saxon—the term refers generally to persons of northern European origin—and Protestant). It contained the English, Scots, and Welsh from Britain; the great numbers of British Canadians who had been emigrating into the country, bringing their strong anti-Catholicism with them (induced by the continuing battle within Canada between French speakers and English speakers); German and Scandinavian Protestants; and those who were, or thought of themselves as, part of the old-stock Yankee tradition.

The years of the fourth party system were to be preeminently the years of Northern WASP America, in politics, law, and government, in the arts and the world of learning, in the national economy, and in the values that made up the predominant national creed. Certainly Anglo-Saxonism as an almost tribal mood flourished in Republican foreign policy. Meanwhile, the Northeast and Middle West became almost as solidly Republican as the South was Democratic.

After the election of 1896, Republicans had the extraordinary good fortune to be the party in power when prosperity returned, on account of the influx of enormous new supplies of gold bullion from discoveries in South Africa, Colorado, and the Yukon. Free silver disappeared as an issue, for the currency supply was expanding again and market prices rose buoyantly. At the same time, the Republicans' vigorous ideas about using national power to develop the economy and —after the rise of the progressive Republicans— to enact major reforms, helped to consolidate for them a strong and continuing hold on the loyalties of a majority of the nation's voters in most elections.

The New President: William McKinley

The new president, William McKinley, was a gentle and kindly man, through and through a politician, and sincerely and devotedly a Republican. He was a composite expression of practically everything that his side of American politics had always represented and believed in: its moralism, devotion to upright ways of life and organized religion, preference for the military, dislike of "Southernism," and advocacy of a high-tariff—economic-nationalist outlook. He was a zealous Methodist and was deeply concerned with personal morality. A courageous soldier during the Civil War, he had seemed prudish to his compatriots with his prayer meetings in camp, his avoidance of alcohol, and his chaste life. Always neatly dressed, wearing his rather formal clothes with a certain erect style, he proudly used his title of "Major" all his life, it becoming his political trademark. Believing the government should be used to regulate conduct, as a congressman he submitted floods of antiliquor petitions from his constituents, supported temperance work, and while the anti-Mormon outcry was at its height (when Utah was seeking statehood) opposed polygamy. He and his wife, though never anti-Catholic nativists, actively supported Protestant missionary activity. He had hated slavery, fought willingly in the war, detested and condemned Southern power, and supported voting rights for blacks.

William McKinley was a strong nationalist who admired Henry Clay's Whig party and built his whole career out of appeals for a new American System like the one Clay had espoused. The passion of his life was the tariff. Springing from a long line of iron makers, as a child he had heard his father complain that foreign competition made honest men close their forges. "With me," he said, "[the high tariff] position is a deep conviction, not a theory. I believe in it and thus warmly advocate it because enveloped in it are my country's highest development and greatest prosperity; out of it come the greatest gains to the people, the greatest comforts to the masses, the widest encouragement for manly aspirations, with the largest rewards, dignifying and elevating our citizenship, upon which the safety and purity and permanency of our political system depend." He was impatient with those who called for free international trade. The markets of the world, he said, "in our present condition are a snare and delusion. We will reach them whenever we can undersell competing nations, and no sooner." By closing off the domestic market to foreigners, American factories would grow to the point where they could compete in the world. Meanwhile, rising prices within the national market would lead to higher wages. "Cheap goods," he said, "meant hard times. When prices were the lowest, did you not have the least money to buy with?" Academic free-trade doctrines exasperated him as idle philosophy, and he was constantly irritated at the fact that "every college in the country seemed to produce tariff reformers."

McKinley came from northwestern Ohio, where a growing network of metal industries and their workers gave strong support to his policies. It was not that he was linked directly with any particular industry; he simply believed that an American System would create a prosperous and happy republic. Indeed, he was widely noted as the Republican with the closest ties with labor. Practically his first act as a congressman was to submit petitions from steelworkers in his district against the reduction of tariffs. As governor of Ohio he worked for safety devices in industry to protect workers, an arbitration system to require employers to negotiate meaningfully with their employees, and laws establishing fines and jail sentences for employers who refused to permit employees to join unions. He was always firmly against violence in labor disputes, and freely used troops to restore order, but sought to be "firm and kind."

McKinley as President

The new president broke sharply with Cleveland's haughty distance from congressmen, throwing open his doors to legislators, treating them warmly, and establishing good relations with Congress that survived throughout his administration. Noting his kindliness and sincerity, people held him in affectionate esteem. True to his Whiggish traditions, he did not threaten compulsion to get his way, and he gave his cabinet members freedom to run their own departments. He was always slow in making crucial decisions, but rock-firm thereafter.

When inaugurated in March 1897, he called for an upward revision of the tariff, an international conference to explore establishing silver coinage worldwide while maintaining the gold standard in the interim, and reciprocal trade agreements with other nations. Happily for him, prosperity was returning and the raging class conflicts of the depression years were dying away. A new day of content and plenty seemed dawning, when people could again enjoy long summer afternoons, dreaming days on the river, quiet canters through the woods. McKinley was everybody's friend, the spokesman of national unity, a genial president who refused to stir up enemies. His cabinet was made up of older conservative men with solid fortunes. Reform was clearly a topic to be shunned; the country was tired of theatrics.

McKinley now sent negotiators abroad, for he intended to pursue the notion of getting an international agreement to make both silver and gold the basis for national currencies. The British and French were solidly opposed, however, and the project died. Much more important to the president, in any event, was the tariff, and he called a special session of Congress to raise it almost as soon as he was inaugurated. The Dingley Tariff, which Congress thereupon produced, sent rates soaring to their highest level (52 percent), though it included some limited arrangements for reciprocal lowering of tariffs with other nations. President McKinley then began vigorous efforts to secure such agreements, for "good trade insures good will," he told the Cincinnati Commercial Club in 1897. American industries, he said, had now been built up to the point where they needed the markets of the world.

With returning prosperity, Congress passed the Gold Standard Act of 1900. The gold dollar was declared to be henceforth the sole standard of currency, and all other forms of money were to be maintained at a parity with gold. The law also made it easier for banks to be established in small towns, thus partially meeting the longstanding complaint of farmers of the unavailability of local loan capital. Following this, banks were allowed to issue more currency on the federal bonds they held, and taxes on issued banknotes were reduced. As a result, the volume of bank notes doubled by 1904. Over 500 new banks were organized in rural areas. For more than a decade these two measures, the Dingley Tariff and the Gold Standard Act, held firm and introduced some stability into the nation's taxing and fiscal arrangements.

But domestic issues were not to be the dominating features of the McKinley presidency. Just a year after his inauguration in 1897, the nation went to war for the first time in more than thirty years. What led up to this fateful event? This is the question that will next take our attention.

Bibliography

Books that were especially valuable to me in writing this chapter: Geoffrey Blodgett, author of a subtle and revealing study, *The Gentle Reformers: Massachusetts Democrats in the Cleveland Era* (1966), skillfully explains the shifts in the ways historians now look at the Gilded Age in an essay in Daniel Walker Howe, ed., *Victorian America* (1976). Richard Jensen's *The Winning of the Midwest: Social and Political Conflict, 1888–1896* (1971), a fascinating book to read, is superb on the era's "army style" politics, prohibitionism, the sophistication of its voters on complex issues, and high voter turnout. On Grover Cleveland and the concept of the transatlantic Liberal-Democratic community, my own thinking is presented in depth in Robert Kelley, *The Transatlantic Persuasion: The Liberal-Democratic Mind in the Age*

of *Gladstone* (1969). The dimension of cultural politics, in this chapter extensively explored, is derived also from: Paul Kleppner, *The Cross of Culture: A Social Analysis of Midwestern Politics 1850–1900* (1970), a work of formidable power in the use of quantitative analysis, and Samuel T. McSeveney's superb study, similarly based in quantitative studies (like Jensen's, cited above). On women, I have again drawn extensively on Sheila Rothman, *Woman's Proper Place: A History of Changing Ideals and Practices, 1870 to the Present* (1978), and Carl Degler, *At Odds: Women and the Family in America from the Revolution to the Present* (1980). On William Jennings Bryan, Paolo E. Coletta's brilliant multi-volume biography (3 vols., 1964, 1969) aided me greatly, and H. Wayne Morgan's *William McKinley and His America* (1963) was equally important to my understandings. Walter Dean Burnham's *Critical Elections and the Mainsprings of American Politics* (1970) is essential reading on the "party systems" concept.

How Have Historians Looked at the Topic?

The older way of looking at Gilded Age politics— as a time of unique irresponsibility in politics, the two parties being absolutely devoid of principle, and capitalists calling all the tunes—runs through practically all of the older writing on the period, and persists in some of the new. Charles Beard's great textbook, used year in and year out in college classrooms, is a classic case: *The Rise of American Civilization*, four vols. (1927–42). Matthew Josephson's *The Politicos, 1865–1896** (1938) is another. More recent books of this persuasion are Ray Ginger, *Age of Excess: The United States from 1877 to 1914** (1966); John G. Sproat's *"The Best Men": Liberal Reformers in the Gilded Age* (1968); and H. S. Merrill's *Bourbon Leader: Grover Cleveland and the Democratic Party** (1957), which is diametrically opposite in treatment to the account given in these pages.

A work of great power and depth for all of the period of the third party system is the most recent study by Paul Kleppner, *The Third Electoral System, 1853–1892: Parties, Voters, and Political Cultures* (1979). Other new perspectives will be found in Gerald W. McFarland, *Mugwumps, Morals and Politics, 1884–1920* (1975); Tom E.

Terrill, *The Tariff, Politics, and American Foreign Policy, 1874–1901* (1973); Edward P. Crapol, *America for Americans: Economic Nationalism and Anglophobia in the Late Nineteenth Century* (1973); Robert D. Marcus, *Grand Old Party: Political Structure in the Gilded Age 1880–1896* (1971); Frederick C. Luebke, *Immigrants and Politics: The Germans of Nebraska, 1880–1900* (1969).

Many other studies are of value. They include Rowland Tappan Berthoff, *British Immigrants in Industrial America 1790–1950* (1953); Arthur Mann, *Yankee Reformers In the Urban Age: Social Reform in Boston, 1880–1900* (1954);

Ari Hoogenboom, *Outlawing the Spoils: A History of the Civil Service Reform Movement 1865–1883* (1961).

John A. Garraty's *The New Commonwealth, 1877–1890** (1968) provides a fresh look at this period and avoids stereotypes. A solid and sympathetic account of party politics between 1877 and 1896 is H. Wayne Morgan's *From Hayes to McKinley* (1969). The upper house of Congress receives a crucially important reassessment in David J. Rothman's *Politics and Power: The United States Senate, 1869–1901* (1966).

* Available in paperback.

24

TIME LINE

EMERGENCE TO WORLD POWER

New York Public Library

Descendant of Federalists, possessor of a proud Boston name, Yankee to the core and proud of his Puritan heritage, Henry Cabot Lodge was fated to be a senator. Indeed, the seat he held in the Senate from 1893 to his death in 1924 had been earlier held by Daniel Webster and Charles Sumner, both of whom his mother had known.

But he was not a reforming senator, like the Mugwumps he grew up with, save for a brief affair with civil-service reform. He was instead a passionately partisan, true team-spirit Republican, a supporter of the status quo. To the horror of the Mugwumps, in the 1880s he cozened up to James G. Blaine, the symbol of political corruption, and got into Congress with his help. Then he turned around and bitterly attacked the "independent Republicans" he had left behind, and they henceforth treated him as a traitor. Lodge was a vindictive man, a mean-spirited person whose manner was woundingly harsh and patronizing to all who differed with him. People detested him or admired him; few were known to love him.

Lodge was a scholar in politics, one of America's first Ph.D.'s (in history, from Harvard), and a lawyer—powerful intellectual credentials in an undereducated country. He was proud of this distinction, and was convinced that he and other politician-intellectuals, such as Theodore Roosevelt, an intimate friend, should instruct the country as well as run it. And he was serious about this: books and articles on all the great public issues of the day poured from his busy pen. Foreign policy, immigration, the tariff: it was all grist for his hardworking mill, and he was clear, forceful, and informed. He condemned the "new immigration" as racially inferior, and tried to exclude it; the protective tariff always had a champion in him, fervent and powerful.

But he was obsessed with world affairs. Constantly, he preached that America must have a strong navy, that the "fighting virtues" were admirable, and that the United States should adopt a "large policy": control of the Caribbean, Cuba, and a canal through the Isthmus of Panama; possession of the Hawaiian Islands to gain dominance in the central Pacific; and a strong thrust to supremacy in world trade (the "basis of real power"), England being the great rival and enemy. Indeed, to Lodge every nation was a rival and a potential enemy; he had no sense of the community of nations. It was "America First" with him, as it was with Theodore Roosevelt, whom he closely advised in the White House. In his histories he lauded Alexander Hamilton, and like Hamilton he desired national glory. Ultimately, Lodge, the supreme nationalist, would destroy Woodrow Wilson's League of Nations and his internationalist vision. America should go it alone, dominating where it could and balancing its power against its great rivals where it could not.

A nation's foreign policy is the product of two influences—its internal condition and the world situation. When a country is remote and agricultural, it pays little heed to the outside world, especially if international conditions are not threatening. So it was with the United States for seventy years after the peace of 1815. It was concerned primarily with affairs on the North American continent, and the world was in a condition of relative stability. America was regarded by the nations of Europe as a minor power, rather on the level of Chile or Sweden today. The large navy it had built during the Civil War was allowed to crumble away, and the nation clung to its traditional policy of noninvolvement in world politics.

All this changed in the 1880s. The notion grew that the United States must leave behind its minor-power status and acquire the pride and dignity that comes with having an important say in world affairs. Influential voices called for an active foreign policy. In the 1890s the United States reacted startlingly to a series of incidents it would formerly have ignored: it almost went to war with Germany over a dispute concerning Samoa in 1889 and 1890; it nearly annexed Hawaii in 1893 after a rebellion by local Americans against the Hawaiian queen; it talked seriously of war with Italy and Chile over minor crises; it rattled the sword at Britain over a controversy in Venezuela in 1895; in a frenzy of national excitement it finally went to war with Spain in 1898, emerging after a brief conflict with an empire consisting of Puerto Rico, Guam, and the Philippine Islands, together with a protectorate over Cuba; and in 1898 it annexed Hawaii.

Now the United States was an audacious, ambitious, aggressive, even a covetous nation in its foreign relations. It put down a bloody insurrection in the Philippines; made the Caribbean an American lake by helping create the Republic of Panama, building a canal, and establishing protectorates over Haiti, Nicaragua, the Dominican Republic, and Honduras. President Theodore Roosevelt proclaimed America's right to intervene anywhere in the Western Hemisphere whenever it detected "chronic wrongdoing." Meanwhile, the United States sought footholds in Chinese markets by announcing its support of an Open Door policy in that country and by coming to agreements with Japan that tacitly recognized mutual spheres of influence. With unparalleled swiftness, a nation that had been of little importance in international politics became a world power.

The Changed World

This came about, to begin with, because the world had changed. After 1870 Britain was no longer the dominant world power. Other nations, such as Germany, Japan, Russia, and France, were challenging that supremacy. These emerging new powers equipped themselves with armies, navies, industry, and vigorous commerce. A global outburst of imperialism chopped up the map. Most of all, the rise of a united German Empire transfixed everyone. Its brilliant universities and advanced social-welfare programs attracted the admiration of intellectuals and reformers, but its militarism and autocracy, together with the belligerent pronouncements of its "blood-and-iron" rulers, were frightening. Many in America and Britain were convinced that sometime in the future an armed conflict with Germany was inevitable. In the United States rumors went about in the 1890s that the European imperialists planned to invade Latin America. In 1895 Senator Henry Cabot Lodge electrified the Senate with a dramatic oration in which he pointed to a map showing British "encirclement" of the United States, from Canada down to Latin America and out to the islands of the Pacific. He warned that France and Germany would not be far behind if the British went unchallenged in their "plans."

Many felt demeaned by the fact that America was remaining inactive while others were gobbling up huge empires. What glory was America winning? Progress was on the advance everywhere, it seemed, barbarism being replaced by European law and order. How could the United States hold up its head when other nations were carrying the "white man's burden"?

The Antiimperialist Tradition

In the post–Civil War years, however, the antimilitarist, antiimperialist tradition remained strong. Widely shared among politicians of the transatlantic Liberal-Democratic community, its international spokesman was William Gladstone, long-time British Liberal premier, and in America its leading advocate was President Grover Cleveland. Fundamentally, these men were internationalists. They believed that each country should be thought of as equal to every other, no nation overawing its neighbors. Protecting the small nations was especially important, for they were testing points of the idea of the equality and safety of all nations. Moral values of freedom and the right of all peoples to independence would govern world relations, not force. Eventually, a system of international law would emerge that would protect everyone from oppression.

When Grover Cleveland became president in 1885, he signaled his loyalty to these ideals by withdrawing from the Senate a pending treaty giving the United States canal rights through Nicaragua. It was a coercive and expansionist document, he said. Since 1850, when America had made the Clayton-Bulwer Treaty with the British, the established policy had been that any canal constructed through the isthmus of Central America should be under international control. This idea, Cleveland insisted, should be retained. Then such a canal would "be removed from the chance of domination by any single power." In 1893, at the beginning of his second term, he withdrew another treaty from Senate consideration that would have annexed Hawaii to the United States. A group of Americans in Hawaii had recently led a rebellion, with American aid, against Queen Liliuokalani, and had negotiated the treaty. Cleveland thought the whole business of the rebellion and the introduction of American force disgraceful. All nations, whether weak or strong, he said to Congress, have the same rights. There is an international morality that governs and condemns such arrogant plundering.

The Quandary: Why Imperialism?

Why was it that Cleveland and his antiimperialist followers failed to prevent America's turn to imperialism? The fact is, we really do not know. No method of historical inquiry can yield the final answer to so complex a question. We have a number of theories. Walter Millis in *The Martial Spirit* (1931) said the empire sprang from irrational militarism. Charles Beard and Mary Beard's influen-

tial *Rise of American Civilization* (1927–42) described it as an outgrowth of capitalism. J. W. Pratt's *Expansionists of 1898* (1936) pointed to broad influences in the American population— racism, the missionary impulse, "yellow" (sensationalist) journalism, and a belief in Anglo-Saxon destiny to rule the world. After the Second World War, historians such as H. K. Beale and Ernest R. May, newly sensitized to the threat of aggression and the need for security, described imperialism as part of a larger process: America's rise to world power after 1890 was in response to real threats from the outside world. In more recent years new emphasis has been given to economic motives. For example, Walter LaFeber's *The New Empire: An Interpretation of American Expansion, 1860–1898* (1963) links imperialism to a search for markets. In brief, there were many roots of imperialism, each of which has its own advocates among historians.

Roots of Imperialism: The Foreign-Policy Elite

The making of American foreign policy, unlike domestic policy, is largely in the hands of one man—the president. As the war in Vietnam has demonstrated, he has enormous powers to act on his own. His advice on foreign policy comes not only from his secretary of state but also from many public groups, the most important among which is a body of men constituting what has been called the foreign-policy community. This group consists of those in the general population who take foreign affairs as their central concern and seek by writings and speeches to bring the president (and the general public) to its point of view. Its members include politicians, intellectuals, newspaper editors and publishers, heads of major corporations, foundation officials, international bankers, and military figures.

In its modern form this foreign-policy elite took shape in the 1880s and 1890s. Most prominent among its members were Senator Henry Cabot Lodge, Theodore Roosevelt, John Hay, Senator Albert J. Beveridge, Whitelaw Reid (editor of the New York *Tribune*), and the naval historian Alfred Thayer Mahan. Most of them were Republicans. Intellectual descendants of Alexander Hamilton, they were fond of talking about "the nation," "national power," and "national destiny." Democrats tended to be localists who paid little attention to the outside world, or Gladstonian internationalists who deplored power politics in world affairs. The men of the Republican foreign-policy elite, however, usually had traveled much abroad, maintained transatlantic contacts, read constantly about world affairs, and as proud nationalists were dismayed that their country had so little military and naval power and carried so little weight in world politics. Elitist in their points of view, Anglo-Saxon in their lineage, they generally regarded dollar chasing with distaste and had little interest in big business.

Great Britain played a special role in their thinking, just as it did among the Democrats. But instead of looking to William Gladstone, American Republicans looked in admiration to his great rival, Benjamin Disraeli, for many years leader of the Conservative (Tory) party. Lodge, Roosevelt, Beveridge, and others of the foreign-policy elite shared Disraeli's idea that imperialism could be a great and ennobling mission for the "enlightened nations" to carry out. They certainly agreed with his basic notion, so different from Gladstone's, that the big powers of the world should run things, that a strong foreign policy based on the active use and display of a large navy would do the most to keep peace in the world and protect the nation's interests.

But these men were nationalists, and they tended to regard Britain as America's potential rival. They bristled at every indication that Britain might be encircling the United States. They also, paradoxically, possessed that same attitude toward Great Britain that had distinguished Alexander Hamilton—a respectful admiration. Britain, after all, was successfully doing in the world what they wished the United States would do—playing the role of a great nation with immense industrial and financial resources and a readiness, especially when Conservatives were in control of the British government, to take a strong hand. Americans like Lodge and Roosevelt were given to talking of "Mother England." Certainly they admired the British aristocracy and thought of themselves as its counterpart in the United States.

The foreign-policy elite began talking in the 1880s of the need for a new American foreign policy. They observed that the world had changed.

The rivalry with England that many felt in the 1880s is shown in this depiction of American industry threatened by foreign imports.
The New York Public Library Picture Collection

Growing empires and national rivalries made it a place of apparent danger. Large navies, swelling armies, threatened wars, hidden plans—to them, these all added up to one lesson: the United States must protect itself by building national power. How to do this? Alfred Thayer Mahan showed the way in his internationally acclaimed *The Influence of Sea Power Upon History* (1890). National power, he said, lies in foreign trade and in the wealth it creates. An expanding foreign commerce is the key to strength and prosperity. Security lies in having that trade carried in American ships protected by a strong American navy. Taken together, these elements constituted sea power—the final arbiter, at that time, of world affairs.

The "large policy" that Lodge, Roosevelt,

451

Mahan, and other such men began to call for would have the United States achieve these goals by a series of specific steps. American vessels, East Coast–based, should break out of the limited Atlantic basin; the construction of an American-controlled canal through Central America would enable this. Such a canal would breach the wall lying between American traders and the enticing markets of the Far East. To protect such a canal, some form of American control should be established over Cuba and the other Caribbean islands to prevent their becoming bases for hostile powers. As stepping-stones across the vast Pacific to Asia, coaling stations and naval bases were to be acquired in Hawaii, Guam, Wake Island, and the Philippines. The American government, meanwhile, should build a sizable merchant marine—the existing one had been largely defunct since the 1860s, when British steamships seized supremacy over American sailing vessels —and above all, a strong navy.

Senator Henry Cabot Lodge of Massachusetts, a proexpansionist, in 1895 condemned American foreign policy on the ground that it was timid and was dominated by the ideas of English Liberals, who opposed imperialism. "The tendency of modern times is toward consolidation. It is apparent in capital and labor alike, and it is also true of nations. Small states are of the past and have no future. The modern movement is all toward the concentration of people and territory into great nations and large dominions. The great nations are rapidly absorbing for their future expansion and their present defense all the waste places of the earth. It is a movement which makes for civilization and the advancement of the race. As one of the great nations of the world, the United States must not fall out of the line of march.

"In the interests of our commerce . . . we should build the Nicaragua Canal, and for the sake of our commercial supremacy in the Pacific we should control the Hawaiian Islands and maintain our influence in Samoa. England has studded the West Indies with strong places which are a standing menace to our Atlantic seaboard. We should have among those islands at least one strong naval station, and . . . the island of Cuba, still sparsely settled and of almost unbounded fertility, will become to us a necessity. Commerce follows the flag, and we should build up a navy strong enough to give protection to Americans in every quarter of the globe and sufficiently powerful to put our coasts beyond the possibility of successful attack.

"[These] vast interests which lie just outside our borders . . . ought to be neglected no longer. . . . They appeal to our national honor and dignity and to the pride of country and of race. . . . [They are] something that rouses and appeals to the patriotism and the Americanism of which we can never have too much. . . . ("Our Blundering Foreign Policy," *Forum* [March 1895])

Roots of Imperialism: The Sense of Mission

Could this program be achieved in an antiimperialist nation traditionally opposed to a strong foreign policy? Public attitudes were, in fact, changing. Americans were beginning to share with Europeans the idea that Western civilization had a mission to uplift the human sea of "barbarism" that encircled them. In a certain sense Europe's outburst of imperialism was a kind of nineteenth-century Peace Corps movement. Men were proud to call themselves imperialists, for they saw their work as the spreading of civilization: law and order; sanitation; technical skills; decent standards of living; an end to slavery; evenhanded court systems; and the outlawing of wife burning, ritual mutilation, polygamy, bride purchase, and the constant scourge of native wars.

By the 1880s racist ideas were being applied to human affairs. One of the results was the notion that the world was divided into many distinct races carrying irremovable characteristics in their bloodstreams. Northern Europeans were thought to be inherently tall and fair and blessed with minds that equipped them to think large thoughts and exert leadership. Inhabitants of southern Europe were described as inherently short and squat, made for heavy tasks and following orders. By definition, non-Europeans were even more inferior and in need of guidance and uplift.

Linked to such racism was the belief that Britain and America, the Anglo-Saxon nations, had a unique mission in the world. As Josiah Strong put it in 1885, "The Anglo-Saxon is the representative of two great ideas . . . civil liberty [and] a pure *spiritual* Christianity." Since these two ideas, he said, had done the most to elevate the human race, then "the Anglo-Saxon

EMERGENCE TO WORLD POWER

. . . is divinely commissioned to be, in a peculiar sense, his brother's keeper. . . ." Christian missionaries played a key role in spreading these attitudes. The Student Volunteer Movement for Foreign Missions was intensely active on American college campuses in the 1890s, and hundreds of volunteers went overseas to "carry out the Lord's tasks." They naturally assumed that they should spread the institutions of Western civilization as well as the gospel.

Roots of Imperialism: The Drive for Markets

As early as the 1880s some American businessmen were claiming that American industry was producing too much for the American market to absorb. The nation needed "an intelligent and spirited foreign policy" in which Washington would "see to it" that industrialists had enough foreign markets. Benjamin Harrison, with James G. Blaine leading the way as his secretary of state, made expansion of foreign trade his principal objective. As Blaine said in 1890, "Our great demand is expansion . . . of trade with countries where we can find profitable exchanges." Under Blaine's leadership in 1889, the first Pan-American Conference, including all the Western Hemisphere nations save Canada, convened in Washington and laid the groundwork for new commercial ties.

Crises in the 1890s

Then came the earthquakes of the 1890s. Calamity after calamity seemed to strike the nation: radicalism among farmers, free-silver campaigns, labor violence, and then the most stunning blow of all—the massive depression that began in 1893. Everything converged to make people believe the nation was overripe and ready for collapse. This had two results: one was a great upsurge in sentiment for humanitarian reforms; the other was the adoption of a fierce new combativeness in foreign policy. Faced with internal weakness, many Americans seemed to feel a burning

need to be reassured that their country had not lost its power and vitality. If we did not expand our energies abroad, said a Columbia sociologist, Franklin H. Giddings, our inherently active and warlike temper might "discharge itself in anarchistic, socialistic, and other destructive modes that are likely to work incalculable mischief." In this sense, imperialism was to be a lightning rod for social tensions.

The Venezuela Explosion

It was in these circumstances that President Grover Cleveland unwittingly heated the fires of jingoism by setting off a controversy with Britain over Venezuela. The background to the conflict was an increasing prickliness in the United States over Britain's apparently growing role in the Western Hemisphere. Suspicions of encirclement and commercial rivalries heightened the tension. In 1895, the Conservative government of Lord Salisbury, then prime minister and a former close associate of Benjamin Disraeli, decided in typical big-power fashion that it would settle a longstanding border dispute with Venezuela over the location of the boundary between that country and British Guiana by simply declaring that it was taking control of the disputed region.

Cleveland was aroused. After all, this was just the kind of action that the Gladstonian, Liberal-Democratic tradition had condemned—a big country bullying a small one. As a Democrat, moreover, he had little sympathy for a Tory government. Furthermore, a storm of protest built up against Britain, traditionally hated as it was by ethnic groups such as the Irish Catholics. At Cleveland's suggestion, Congress in February 1895 announced its opposition to British claims in Venezuela. Then Cleveland prepared and sent a private message to the British government. It condemned Britain's actions and demanded that the controversy be submitted to arbitration. Also, the message boldly restated the Monroe Doctrine: "To-day the United States is practically sovereign on this continent, and its fiat is law upon the subjects to which it confines its interposition."

Five months later the British reply found its leisurely way to Washington. It declared that the

Monroe Doctrine had no standing in British eyes and certainly did not apply to Venezuela. Arbitration was out of the question. In response, Cleveland and Richard Olney (who was now secretary of state) prepared and issued an ultimatum that seemed to threaten war. If Britain did not submit to arbitration, the message said, the United States was prepared to resist Britain's continued retention of the disputed territory "by every means in its power." "Many still living," wrote an Englishman in 1934, "remember like yesterday with what stupefaction the Venezuelan ultimatum was received." From all over the United Kingdom shocked messages poured into the Foreign Office pleading with Salisbury to prevent war. A flood of private and governmental messages crossed the Atlantic seeking to assure Cleveland by every possible means that war was not necessary. Arbitration on a modified basis was agreed to, and in the ensuing months the crisis faded.

In the meantime, Americans were as startled as the British. The immediate response to Cleveland's ultimatum had been an explosion of jingoistic delight. Congress broke into almost unprecedented applause, and newspapers from coast to coast praised Cleveland. But Anglophobia was not the force it used to be. A reaction soon set in. Clergymen, university professors, businessmen, and international-law specialists condemned the saber rattling and jingoistic trumpeting. A great network of ties had been built between Britain and the United States. There were commercial interests, banking houses, clergymen, eminent families that had begun intermarrying with the British aristocracy, intellectuals who traveled back and forth across the Atlantic, and politicians of all camps who admired the British example.

The result of the Anglo-American crisis over Venezuela was to inaugurate a new and much firmer relationship of friendship and cooperation. Almost overnight, the shock of the experience revealed to the two nations their mutual dependence. The British swung over to a policy of friendly cooperation, in effect recognizing American political supremacy in Latin America under the Monroe Doctrine. A form of diplomatic partnership in world affairs began to emerge, which, as it grew and strengthened in the succeeding decades, was to have great significance in the twentieth century.

The Cuban Revolution

In early 1895 a rebellion against Spanish rule broke out on the island of Cuba. Just ninety miles from the Florida coast, Cuba was intimately linked with American life. Engaged primarily in sugar culture, it sold practically all its crop in the United States. Americans, with investments of about forty million dollars in the island, had long sympathized with Cuban sentiments for independence, which had flickered and flared for decades. Americans had been reared on historical memories in which Spain represented all that was destructive and oppressive about European rule. The revolt, which sprang primarily from the ordinary people of the countryside, seemed a reenactment of the American Revolution.

Rebel bands soon were roaming the countryside, and a Cuban junta set up headquarters in New York to gather funds and release a stream of news stories to the American press. Cuban Leagues emerged in the United States to aid the cause, and the AFL formally called for support of the Cuban revolutionaries. In late 1895 the insurgents formed an independent Cuban government. Meanwhile, Spain poured a force of 120,000 troops into the island and mounted an increasingly desperate campaign against the guerrillas, and the Spanish military gained de facto control over policy. As the United States has learned to its sorrow, guerrilla warfare with widespread support in the countryside is almost impossible to crush. Locked in combat with an elusive, skillful, and often savage enemy, the Spanish military officials chose ever more extreme methods. Finally, they resorted to a virtual depopulation of the countryside by forcing rural folk to live in concentration camps so that they could no longer aid the guerrillas. The result was an appalling loss of life due to disease and starvation.

In the United States, a new form of journalism seized on the Cuban Revolution. Young William Randolph Hearst, the son of a California mining millionaire, purchased the New York *Journal* in 1895 and began a sensationalistic race for circulation against Joseph Pulitzer's New York *World*. Every Cuban event was expanded into screaming, vivid headlines. The Spanish commander in Cuba, General Valeriano Weyler y Nicolau, was called a "human hyena" and a "mad dog." His soldiers were accused of murdering prisoners, shooting the sick, and molesting young women.

The Cuban Revolution was an ideal humanitarian crusade in which to vent the anxieties and frustrations built up in the United States by the crises of the 1890s. Generous moral passions provided most of the motivation for the Cuban frenzy; the charitable concern was certainly real. In early 1896 Congress passed a resolution proposing that the belligerency of the Cuban rebels be recognized, an action that set off anti-American riots in Spain. Newspapers all over the United States spread the same stories that appeared in more passionate style in the Hearst and Pulitzer presses. Populists viewed the Cuban issue as an example of the heartless avarice of Wall Street, for the business community, generally opposed to so disruptive an event as war, had yet to come forth in favor of intervention.

Grover Cleveland refused military intercession, however, and sought genuinely to remain neutral. He is reported bluntly to have told irate congressmen that he would not mobilize the army if Congress declared war. He did, nevertheless, grow increasingly concerned over the butchery. Secretary Olney formally offered mediation to Spain, but his initiative was rebuffed indignantly. Spanish liberals called on their government to grant reforms in Cuba, but the Spanish foreign minister responded by saying that it was American aid to the rebels that prolonged the fighting, not Spanish misrule.

McKinley Takes Command

William McKinley became president in March 1897. In his party was that hard core of the activist foreign-policy elite that had been leading the *Cuba libre* cry and calling for American intervention. But McKinley was no jingo; he sincerely hoped to find some peaceful settlement. The new president, renewing Cleveland's warnings to Spain, offered to mediate. In the fall of 1897 a more liberal Spanish government came to power, the concentration-camp policy was modified, and a limited form of Cuban autonomy was granted. But the rebels rejected it. The Cuban loyalists, on their side, rioted against even the possibility of limited autonomy. The Spanish army simply brushed aside compromise, for it was determined to crush the insurgents at all costs. McKinley, discouraged now by the failure of his diplomatic efforts to pacify the island, began thinking of direct intervention.

The Road to War

The American armored cruiser *Maine* was dispatched to Havana harbor in January 1898 to protect Americans still in the Cuban capital. On February 15, 1898, a terrific explosion sank the *Maine* and killed over 250 officers and men. Jingoes now split the air with demands for war. "I would give anything," wrote Theodore Roosevelt, now assistant secretary of the navy, "if President McKinley would order the fleet to Havana tomorrow. . . . The *Maine* was sunk by an act of dirty treachery on the part of the Spaniards." Congress unanimously voted fifty million dollars for military preparedness. Spain was reported to be "simply stunned." But McKinley would not be hurried to war. He awaited the results of an American investigation of the disaster, which reported only that the explosion had come from outside the vessel, set off by unknown persons.

At this time one of the most important speeches ever made in the Senate was delivered. Senator Redfield Proctor of Vermont, a peace advocate who was known to be skeptical of the sensationalist reports of the yellow press, had gone to Cuba to make a personal tour. He returned to describe horrifying conditions in the concentration camps: "Torn from their homes, with foul earth, foul air, foul water, and foul food or none, what wonder that one-half have died and that one-quarter of the living are so diseased that they can not be saved? . . . Little children are still walking about with arms and chest terribly emaciated, eyes swollen, and abdomens bloated to three times their natural size." Shocked by these disclosures from so unimpeachable a source, the nation waited gravely for McKinley's response. The president tried diplomacy again, seeking to bring peace by armistice and an end to the concentration-camp system. Although the Spanish yielded in April, McKinley was under enormous pressure to declare war. Groups all over the country began offering their services. A Maine congressman said that every legislator "had two or three newspapers in his district—most of them printed in

"Spanish 'Justice and Honor' be darned!"—Uncle Sam's image in the Hearst press, 1898, which pressed wildly for war.

Culver Pictures, Inc.

being spent to strengthen the armed forces, which, together with a recently built battleship navy, gave McKinley confidence that a military confrontation would go well. Some had feared Spanish bombardment of the East Coast, but Winthrop Chandler wrote jocularly to Lodge that if Spanish troops invaded New York "they would all be absorbed in the population . . . and engaged in selling oranges before they got as far as 14th Street." In this spirit, so strange now as to seem incredible, the nation waited confidently for war.

On April 11, 1898, two days after the Spanish had largely given in to his demands, McKinley asked Congress for authority to end hostilities in Cuba by direct intervention. Following a week of debate, Congress agreed by passing resolutions that declared Cuba free; demanded the withdrawal of Spain; directed the use of armed force to achieve these ends; and, in the Teller Amendment, announced in advance that the United States would not annex Cuba. The latter, passed unanimously, indicates the spirit of altruism and self-denial in which the crusade was begun. No one, save a few at the centers of power, had any notion that by going to war in Cuba the United States would suddenly acquire a far-flung empire.

The Spanish-American War

The war with Spain lasted only three months, but events of enormous significance occurred during that brief period. The foreign-policy activists could now move boldly to secure the goals they had long sought. Theodore Roosevelt had earlier sent orders to Admiral George Dewey, commander of the Asiatic squadron, to attack the Spanish fleet in Manila Bay in the Philippines as soon as war began. Dewey was soon under way. His fleet of seven vessels entered the bay and steamed back and forth in front of a Spanish force of equal size for hours on end while the two fleets rained a torrent of shells at each other. When the battle was over, the Spanish ships were all sunk and the Americans had lost neither a ship nor a sailor. The stunning victory electrified the United States. Many said that it was evidence that God Himself desired America to win, a sentiment that Dewey echoed in his official dispatches. The American people had been practically ignorant of the Philippines' existence before now. Suddenly

red ink . . . and shouting for blood." A Presbyterian journal cried, "And if it be the will of Almighty God, that by war the last trace of this inhumanity of man to man shall be swept away from the Western hemisphere, let it come!"

The Cuban revolutionaries, meanwhile, were now so encouraged by American support that they would accept nothing less than full independence, a demand the Spanish government would never accept. Word came to the president from Wall Street that financial interests that had long opposed military action as too disruptive to the just-recovering economy were finally swinging over to support intervention. In February a petition from businessmen suffering heavily from damage to their factories and other investments in Cuba had pleaded for action. The British Foreign Office informed McKinley that he need not worry that European powers might prevent American action. Last, Congress's appropriation of fifty million dollars for armaments was rapidly

THE SPANISH-AMERICAN WAR: PACIFIC THEATER

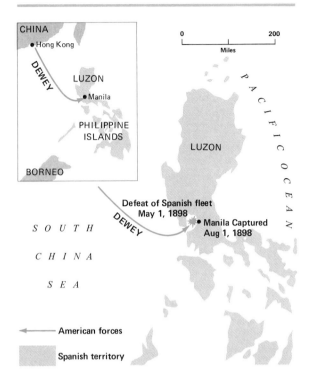

CHINA
Hong Kong
DEWEY
LUZON
Manila
PHILIPPINE ISLANDS
BORNEO

0   200
Miles

PACIFIC OCEAN

LUZON

SOUTH CHINA SEA

DEWEY

Defeat of Spanish fleet
May 1, 1898

Manila Captured
Aug 1, 1898

→ American forces

Spanish territory

no one talked of anything else. A babble of newspaper debate broke out. Should Dewey simply sail out of the bay and leave the Philippines behind? McKinley was later to remark ironically that this would have saved a lot of trouble. However, the president was strongly urged to send ground troops to protect the fleet, and in the most critical decision of the war he agreed to do so on May 16, 1898. Senator Lodge exultantly wrote Roosevelt, "The Administration is now fully committed to the large policy that we both desire." Shortly afterward, Manila was taken by American troops.

Meanwhile, a small and badly equipped army under General William R. Shafter had landed in Cuba, where it fought some brief, bloody battles. Roosevelt, then a lieutenant colonel leading the volunteer Rough Riders, secured spectacular news coverage for his exploits at San Juan Hill. The Spanish fleet hid for a time in Santiago Harbor, then came out to be completely destroyed by the United States Atlantic fleet, under Admiral William T. Sampson and Commodore W. S. Schley. Just before the war ended, American troops led by Nelson A. Miles, the command-

THE SPANISH-AMERICAN WAR: CARIBBEAN THEATER

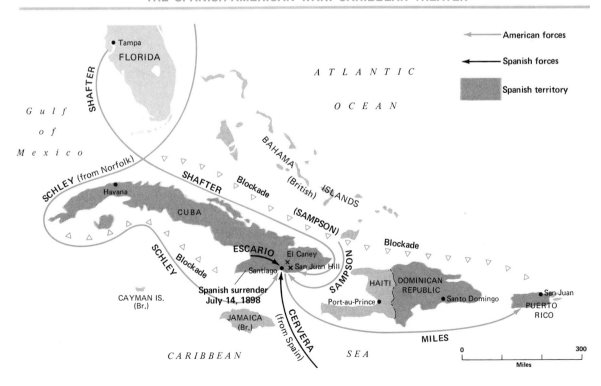

← American forces

← Spanish forces

Spanish territory

Tampa
FLORIDA

ATLANTIC OCEAN

Gulf of Mexico

SHAFTER

SCHLEY (from Norfolk)

Havana

CUBA

SHAFTER

Blockade

BAHAMA (British) ISLANDS

(SAMPSON)

SCHLEY

Blockade

ESCARIO

El Caney
San Juan Hill

Santiago

Blockade

SAMPSON

Blockade

Spanish surrender
July 14, 1898

CERVERA (from Spain)

HAITI

DOMINICAN REPUBLIC

Port-au-Prince

Santo Domingo

San Juan

PUERTO RICO

CAYMAN IS.
(Br.)

JAMAICA
(Br.)

MILES

CARIBBEAN SEA

0   300
Miles

ing general of the army, landed on Puerto Rico, Spain's other Caribbean possession, to take control of the island. Also, the flotilla taking troops to Manila Bay stopped by the island of Guam, fired a few shells at the surprised garrison—it was ignorant of the fact that war was under way—and left an occupying force. On August 12, 1898, the Spanish agreed to end hostilities by freeing Cuba and ceding Puerto Rico and Guam to the United States. The question of the Philippines was left to be settled by American and Spanish peace commissioners, who were to meet in Paris on October 1, 1898.

What should the American government try to secure in the Philippines? McKinley seems to have begun with the simple notion of acquiring a naval base at Manila, leaving the rest to Spain. Even Roosevelt and Mahan were at first undecided as to how far the United States should go. Securing a naval base was one thing; acquiring the whole archipelago was another. Should the islands be given back to Spain, allowed to become independent, sold to Britain or Germany, or kept by the United States? In the early autumn McKinley traveled about the country making speeches carefully designed to test public sentiment. He returned to Washington convinced that the American people wished annexation. A poll of newspaper editors showed strong support for it. The president walked the floor of the White House night after night, according to his own account, pondering a decision and praying for divine guidance.

And one night late it came to me this way—I don't know how it was but it came: (1) that we could not give them back to Spain—that would be cowardly and dishonorable; (2) that we could not turn them over to France or Germany—our commercial rivals in the Orient—that would be bad business and discreditable; (3) that we could not leave them to themselves—they were unfit for self-government—and they would soon have anarchy and misrule over there worse than Spain's was; and (4) that there was nothing left for us to do but to take them all, and to educate the Filipinos, and uplift and civilize and Christianize them, and by God's grace do the very best we could by them, as our fellow-men for whom Christ also died. And then I went to bed, and went to sleep and slept soundly. . . . (*Christian Advocate* [January 22, 1903])

So it was that the American peace commissioners in Paris were instructed to demand acquisition of the entire Philippine archipelago. Spain's negotiators resisted strenuously. After all, they said, American troops had not taken Manila until after an armistice had been formally signed. The islands could not be claimed as legitimate spoils of war. In response, the United States offered a payment of twenty million dollars—the act is reminiscent of the way in which the Mexican cession was acquired in 1848—and Spain accepted. Now the American people faced a fateful decision: should the treaty be ratified and a colonial empire acquired?

The Antiimperialist Argument

The debate over the issue went on for two years, from 1898 through the election of 1900. Hundreds of America's most eminent leaders argued loud and long against imperialism. In newspapers, magazines, pamphlets, and countless speeches, they begged Americans not to go down that fateful road. The antiimperialists were led by ex-presidents Grover Cleveland and Benjamin Harrison. With William Jennings Bryan on their side, the bulk of the Democratic party, most reformers, the leading liberal Republicans, labor leaders such as Samuel Gompers, industrialists such as Andrew Carnegie, former abolitionists, prominent professors and university presidents, and a host of novelists, they condemned the annexation of the Philippines as a gross violation of American principles that was certain to destroy the nation's institutions.

American antiimperialists argued that no one should be governed without their consent, and that the fight that Philippine rebels under Emilio Aguinaldo soon began against American rule—the so-called Philippine Insurrection, 1899–1902—demonstrated how strongly the Philippines wished independence. Some antiimperialists scoffed at the notion that America's rule would be uniquely benevolent; others insisted that the whole idea of colonial possessions was unconstitutional. The Constitution would have to follow the flag; the Filipinos would have to be given full American citizenship (which alarmed racists). Providence had blessed the American nation, antiimperialists said, when it had held to its traditions of liberty and self-rule; disaster would doubtless follow the abandonment of these

EMERGENCE TO WORLD POWER

sacred ideals. It was ridiculous to take on an expensive, remote colony just to acquire trade. The laws of commerce would create profits, not the law of imperialism.

The American Anti-Imperialist League, at its meeting in Chicago in October 1899, proclaimed that "the policy known as imperialism is hostile to liberty and tends toward militarism, an evil from which it has been our glory to be free. . . . We maintain that governments derive their just powers from the consent of the governed. We insist that the subjugation of any people is 'criminal aggression' and open disloyalty to the distinctive principles of our Government. We earnestly condemn the policy of the present National Administration in the Philippines. It seeks to extinguish the spirit of 1776 in those islands. We deplore the sacrifice of our soldiers and sailors, whose bravery deserves admiration even in an unjust war. We denounce the slaughter of the Filipinos as a needless horror. We protest against the extension of American sovereignty by Spanish methods.

"We demand the immediate cessation of the war against liberty, begun by Spain and continued by us. We urge that Congress be promptly convened to announce to the Filipinos our purpose to concede to them the independence for which they have so long fought and which of right is theirs. . . . The United States cannot act upon the ancient heresy that might makes right.

"We deny that the obligation of all citizens to support their Government in times of grave National peril applies to the present situation. If an Administration may with impunity ignore the issues upon which it was chosen, deliberately create a condition of war anywhere on the face of the globe, debauch the civil service for spoils to promote the adventure, organize a truth-suppressing censorship and demand of all citizens a suspension of judgment and their unanimous support while it chooses to continue the fighting, representative government itself is imperiled." (quoted in Carl Schurz, *Speeches, Correspondence, and Political Speeches* [1913])

The antiimperialists insisted that it was simply wrong for the United States to impose its rule on another people. If the Filipinos wanted independence, they must be given it, not be shot down like cattle. The savage fighting during the Philippine Insurrection gave heavy ammunition to the antiimperialist cause. More than 120,000 Americans had to be sent to put down the uprising, and the barbarities practiced by both sides were horrifying. How monstrous it was, antiimperialists said, for a war begun to free Cuba to end up as a bloody oppression of the Philippines. No republican government, they insisted, could be imperialistic and remain republican for long. Freedom was indivisible. Denying it to others would mean denying it at home. By taking colonial possessions, the United States was robbing itself of its very reason for being—to serve as an example to all the world of how a free nation could live in liberty and concern for the rights of others.

The Proimperialist Answer

It was a losing argument. The antiimperialists were generally older men who thought of an older America; their opponents were younger, more confident, more able to hold out alluring visions to a nation eager to dispel the specters of depression and national weakness. The proimperialists relied essentially on the theme that America had both a duty and a destiny that it could not avoid. Its uninterrupted success in battle was pointed to as proof that God had great plans for the American nation. Dewey's victory, said a religious newspaper, "read almost like the stories of the ancient battles of the Lord in the times of Joshua, David, and Jehoshaphat." "God has not been preparing the English-speaking and Teutonic peoples for a thousand years for nothing but vain and idle self-contemplation and self-admiration," Senator Beveridge observed. "No! He has made us the master organizers of the world to establish system where chaos reigns. He has made us adept in government that we may administer government among savages and senile peoples."

Many Protestant clergymen advocated annexation because they had great dreams of missionary work. Those of a Darwinist outlook argued that since life is a struggle, the United States had better gain strength while it could. Looming over all discussions was the reality that the United States was already in the Philippines. Administrative actions taken without prior congressional authorization had presented the nation with an accomplished fact. To leave would be to pull down the American flag, a thought repugnant to Americans in their existing state of mind. In the background was a widely stated concern that if the United States did not take the Philippines, the European powers would become embroiled in war in the subsequent scramble to get them. Ex-

Burning the palace of Aguinaldo, leader of the Philippine Insurrection, during the three-year war in which an estimated 600,000 Filipinos died.
Courtesy of the Library of Congress

aggerated alarms concerning German intentions swept the country. And most Americans doubted sincerely that Filipinos could govern themselves after three centuries of autocratic Spanish rule. Besides, it was said, they were colored people and "backward."

To some people, the great attraction of imperialism was that it would divert America's attentions from its internal problems. The nation, such people insisted, was sick with introspection; outside challenges would once again give it new goals and new dreams. The result, they believed, would be the reemergence of national unity. Henry Watterson, nationally known editor of the Louisville *Courier-Journal*, expressed this viewpoint in 1899:

From a nation of shopkeepers we become a nation of warriors. We escape the menace and peril of socialism and agrarianism, as England has escaped them, by a policy of colonization and conquest. From a provincial huddle of petty sovereignties held together by a rope of sand we rise to the dignity and prowess of an imperial republic incomparably greater than Rome. It is true that we exchange domestic dangers for foreign dangers; but in every direction we multiply the opportunities of the people. We risk Caesarism, certainly; but even Caesarism is preferable to anarchism. We risk wars; but a man has but one time to die, and either in peace or war, he is not likely to die until his time comes. . . . In short, anything is better than the pace we were going before these present forces were started into life. Already the young manhood of the country is as a goodly brand snatched from the burning, and given a perspective replete with noble deeds and elevating ideas.

Equally important was the reversal of opinion in the business community. In general, its leaders had opposed war with Spain until the last moment. But soon they had found that the war was a vigorous stimulant to business activity. Then talk began of the Philippines' providing a base from which American enterprise could finally break into the supposedly huge markets of the Far East. The beginnings of prosperity in 1897 had as yet done little to wipe away the memory of depression and overproduction. To many businessmen, the prospect of expanded overseas trade seemed the only permanent solution to the problem of glut. This opinion, communicated to legislators, doubtless persuaded many to vote for annexation.

The antiimperialists nearly won. When the treaty came to a Senate vote in February 1899, they secured almost enough votes to prevent the necessary two-thirds approval. But then William Jennings Bryan concluded that the best way to secure the freedom of the Philippines was for the United States to annex them, and that after ratification America could turn around and grant them independence. He hoped, too, to make antiimperialism the rallying cry of the Democratic presidential campaign in 1900. In Washington, he secured enough votes for ratification to carry the day for the treaty. But in the election, he found that the nation had quickly lost interest in the imperialism question. McKinley went to the people with the golden outpouring of booming prosperity behind him. A buoyant faith in the future was identified with the Republican party. Bryan was once again the Democratic presidential nominee, but he went down to complete defeat in 1900. The United States had become an imperial power.

The Pacific Adventure Expands

During the excitement of the Spanish-American War, the administration reintroduced a treaty for the annexation of Hawaii. It could now argue, following Dewey's breathtaking victory, that the islands would provide essential bases for the support of the nation's new Far Eastern adventure. "Bridge the Pacific," appealed the Philadelphia *Press* to Congress. A joint resolution was hurried through Congress, and the islands were formally annexed on August 12, 1898.

Meanwhile, the expansionist American government was looking to China, whose trade was the ultimate objective of all this activity. That nation had recently been humiliated in the Sino-Japanese War (1894–95), and in the aftermath European powers began to carve up what now appeared to be the weak and backward Chinese Empire. Great Britain, meanwhile, became alarmed, for over the decades its trade with China had grown tremendously.

London turned to its new partner, the United States, for aid, suggesting a cooperative effort to keep China open to traders of all nations. John Hay, McKinley's secretary of state, was quite ready to take a strong role in world politics, but on his own. Deeply committed to the expansion of American business as a beneficent force in the world, and a devout believer in Anglo-Saxon supremacy, in September 1899 he sent out the first Open Door note to the great powers. In it he stated America's loyalty to the principle of commercial equality and asked all nations to respect that principle in their own spheres of influence in China. Although he received evasive replies, he brashly announced in March 1900 that all the powers had given final and definitive approval to the principle. It was bold action, but everyone knew that it had little substance.

The occasion for confirming the Open Door policy was a violent outbreak against foreigners in North China in June 1900 by a society of fanatical Chinese patriots called the Boxers. The vast uprising resulted in many deaths and a flight by terror-stricken Europeans to the protection of foreign missions in Peking. Besieged there for weeks, they were finally freed by an international military force numbering 20,000 men—of whom 2,500 were Americans. Hay, meanwhile, moved swiftly to ensure that the Boxer Rebellion would not be used by any great power to expand its grasp on China. On July 3, 1900, he sent out another circular note declaring that it was American policy to "preserve Chinese territorial and administrative integrity," as well as to maintain an open commercial door.

This declaration was of great importance, for in it the United States, traditionally a minor figure in Far Eastern affairs, suddenly came forward as the guarantor of the vast nation of China. Hay's motives were hardly unselfish for he had American trade interests primarily in mind. Of course, the American government had no intention of backing up its Open Door policy with military force, a fact that made its Far Eastern policy an insecure one for decades. Nonetheless, the Open Door was now fixed as one of the most sacred principles in American foreign policy.

Theodore Roosevelt Takes Command

On September 6, 1901, William McKinley smiled his genial way through the crowds thronging the colorfully decorated grounds of the Pan-American Exposition in Buffalo, New York. Arriving in the Temple of Music, he sent word out that he would greet the public individually. A warm and considerate man, he enjoyed nothing more than to shake hands and talk with the people. In the line was Leon F. Czolgosz, an anarchist who was obsessed with a desire to kill the president. Learning that McKinley was in the city, he obtained a gun, awaited his opportunity, and, draping his weapon with a handkerchief, stepped forward slowly as the line approached the president. McKinley smiled, reached out his hand, and was shot twice in the abdomen. For eight days horrified Americans hung on every word of his condition, for they genuinely loved and respected the president. They recognized in him a man of sincere warmth and honest conviction. Prosperity and world renown, it was widely felt, had come to the nation with his presidency. But on September 14, 1901, he died, saying quietly to his physician, "Good-bye, all. Good-bye. It is God's way. His will be done."

McKinley's death brought to the White House a spectacular man, Theodore Roosevelt. He loved the glory of war. Like Alexander Hamilton, he hungered for a heroic life and hoped for the same for his beloved nation. An unabashed nationalist, he thought such men as Thomas Jefferson, with their pacifist ideas on foreign policy, to be near traitors. At the least, he was contemptuous of men who did not like power or rejoice in its use. To large-policy advocates, Roosevelt was crucially important. No one came to symbolize the new adventure of imperialism more than he.

In his foreign policy Roosevelt dispensed with the careful ways of his predecessor and moved vigorously to assert America's power in the world. He has been called a foreign-policy "realist" in the sense that he regarded the real forces in international life to be those of power and the consequent scramble for security. Democrats like Grover Cleveland might preach the message of international brotherhood and morality—indeed, Cleveland was shocked at Roosevelt's foreign policy and at the national enthusiasm it engendered—but Roosevelt preached instead the need to regard the world "realistically." This meant accepting the view that all nations are out to get as much power as they can and to take from others whatever they can get. He often talked as if he expected attacks momentarily from all directions, particularly from Germany. For this reason he firmly advocated—and built—a stronger navy and a well-organized and efficient army.

An aristocrat, he believed in leadership by the great and the talented. Similarly, in world affairs he believed that the great nations of the world should govern international relations. Each great power should supervise that part of the world in which it was supreme. Where the interests of the great powers intermixed, as in the Far East, then the principle of "balance of powers" should be maintained; that is, America should support whatever side looked weakest so as to maintain an equilibrium.

Acquiring an Isthmian Canal

The large policy was only partially completed by 1901. The Philippines were in hand, and the United States possessed Guam and Hawaii. Wake Island was occupied in 1898 to provide another coaling station for the navy. The protectorate over Samoa, which the United States had shared with Germany and Great Britain since 1889, was changed in 1899 so that the three nations divided up the little group of islands. In this step, the United States secured the island of Tutuila, with its harbor of Pago Pago. In the Caribbean, American dominance was embodied in the possession of Puerto Rico. In March 1901 Cuba's status was regularized through the Platt Amendment to the army-appropriation bill of that year, which made the island a protectorate. Its key provisions were:

Cuba was not to allow a foreign power to secure partial or complete control of the island; it was not to build up too large a foreign debt, which might lead to intervention; the United States was to have the right to intervene in Cuban affairs to preserve order and maintain Cuban independence; and Cuba was to agree to sell or lease to the United States appropriate sites for naval and coaling stations (which led to a large naval base at Guantanamo Bay still in American hands). Cubans were forced to include these provisions in their constitution, and when American troops withdrew from Cuba in 1903, the principles were made the subject of a formal treaty between the two nations.

However, the keystone of the large policy—an isthmian canal under American control—was not yet in place. McKinley had reminded Congress of this in 1898. Negotiations then began with Great Britain to replace the existing Clayton-Bulwer Treaty, which since 1850 had provided that an isthmian canal would be jointly controlled and unfortified. In November 1901, with Theodore Roosevelt urging on negotiations from the White House, an agreement was made. The Hay-Pauncefote Treaty guaranteed equal treatment to British ships but allowed the canal to be built and controlled by the United States alone. Two years later the British signaled their acceptance of American hegemony in the Caribbean by closing down their naval stations in the West Indies.

There were two possible canal locations, one through Nicaragua, the other through Panama, then a province of Colombia. A French company had tried to build a canal through Panama in the 1880s, sinking nearly $300 million in a failing effort. The concession of the firm remained alive, however, and when Roosevelt became president the concession—including the physical works the company had built—was actively being peddled to the American government for about $40 million. Meanwhile, advocates of a Panamanian canal carried on a nationwide campaign extolling the virtues of the Isthmus and publishing scare stories about Nicaragua's volcanoes. In June 1902, two months after a terrific volcanic eruption on the Caribbean island of Martinique, Congress settled on the Panamanian route. The United States proposed to buy the assets of the New Panama Canal Company and give Colombia $10 million and an annual indemnity of $250,000 for con-

trol of the canal and a three-mile strip of land on either side.

Panama Becomes Independent

Colombian leaders were unhappy. The concession of the French company was due to expire soon, and they felt the $40 million for its assets should properly come to the Colombian government. They requested either a delay or an immediate payment to Colombia of one fourth of the sum to be given the New Panama Canal Company. Roosevelt was angry, regarding the Colombians as a bunch of grasping bandits. Besides, he wanted his way at once. He now hit on a technicality that opened a new line of action. An old treaty made with Colombia in 1846 gave the United States a guarantee of "the right of way or transit across the Isthmus of Panama." Under this agreement, the United States had seven times landed troops on the Isthmus to protect "free transit," though always with the prior approval of the government of Colombia. Roosevelt concluded that the treaty actually gave the United States the right to build a canal, and he decided to push ahead on this basis.

Then, a Frenchman named Philippe Bunau-Varilla, the American representative of the New Panama Canal Company, informed Roosevelt about a revolutionary movement in Panama that hoped to make the Isthmus an independent nation. If it succeeded, Roosevelt's plans might be quickly consummated. The president gave no open commitment, but there were implications in his reactions, apparently, that were unmistakable. Bunau-Varilla proceeded on the assumption that the revolutionary movement would have American support. He began working with the rebels, providing funds, a proposed new constitution, and even a code for communications. Some 500 soldiers in the Colombian army in Panama were persuaded to take up the rebel cause.

On November 2, 1903, an American naval vessel, the U.S.S. *Nashville*, arrived off the city of Colón. The next day a practically bloodless rebellion took place in Panama. By the time Colombia sent troops to put it down, it was too late. Two hours after notice of the rebellion reached Washington, the American government recognized the

Panamanian rebel government and received Philippe Bunau-Varilla as its ambassador. Four days later it concluded a treaty with the Panamanian government, giving it $10 million for the right to build a canal and an annual sum of $250,000 for control (not sovereignty) over a canal zone ten miles wide. Meanwhile, $40 million was paid to the New Panama Canal Company for its assets.

This agreement aroused shock and dismay in the United States. It was "piracy," "scandal, disgrace, and dishonor," said many news editors. Most of the press approved, however, and a delighted Theodore Roosevelt proceeded with his typical vigor to get the dirt flying. Construction of the canal began in 1904 and was completed in 1914. By that time a Democratic administration was in power, and it negotiated a treaty with Colombia formally expressing American regret for the role of the United States in the Panamanian rebellion and paying Colombia $25 million indemnity. (The treaty was held up in the Senate until 1921, when interest in Colombian oil properties led to its finally being ratified.)

Roosevelt and the "Big Stick"

Roosevelt began a major expansion of the navy, building so many ships that by the end of his presidency the United States had become the second naval power in the world. And he proceeded to implement the principle he had expressed in 1900: "I have always been fond of the West African proverb, 'Speak softly and carry a big stick, you will go far.'" When Britain and Germany blocked Venezuela's ports and bombarded her forts in 1902 to enforce payment of debts, Roosevelt mustered a sizable naval and military force in the Caribbean in an implied warning against more serious intervention. In 1903 he used both diplomacy and covert threats to settle a dispute with Canada over the boundary of the "panhandle" of Alaska in a way favorable to the United States.

Then, in 1904, in order to make clear the new American role he had assumed, he announced the so-called Roosevelt Corollary to the Monroe Doctrine: "Chronic wrongdoing . . . may in America, as elsewhere, ultimately require intervention by some civilized nation, and in the Western Hemisphere the adherence of the United States to the Monroe Doctrine may force the United States, however reluctantly, in flagrant cases of such wrongdoing or impotence, to the exercise of an international police power." In brief, the United States from then on would be the Western Hemisphere's policeman, appropriating the right to judge when the nations to the south were running their affairs badly. In 1904 and 1905 Roosevelt worked out an executive agreement with the Dominican Republic under which the American government took control of the Dominican customs so as to ensure that American and European investors would be repaid by the then-bankrupt republic. The Senate grumbled that such actions were unconstitutional, requiring a treaty to make them legal, but Roosevelt brushed aside the criticism.

Roosevelt also looked to the world at large, firmly believing that the United States, as an emergent great power, should take up its proper role as one of the guarantors of world peace. This meant that for the first time American diplomats regularly attended international conferences and played an active role in them. This dramatic change caused much comment and protest at home, which Roosevelt characteristically ignored. In 1906 he sent negotiators to help settle a crisis between Germany and France over trade concessions in Morocco. The results of the conference, held in Algeciras, Spain, were widely taken as a rebuff to Germany.

In the Russo-Japanese War, which broke out in 1904, Roosevelt favored the Japanese on the ground that Russia had grown "grossly overbearing" to every other nation in the Far East; that is, Russia was threatening to upset the balance of power. He later said that he even informed Germany and France "in the most polite and discreet fashion that in the event of a combination against Japan . . . I should promptly side with Japan and proceed to whatever length was necessary on her behalf." The Japanese won a quick series of stunning victories, and Roosevelt publicly announced that he would be happy to act as mediator to settle the conflict (though in truth he was reluctant to take on this task and did so only under great pressure). The peace conference was held in Portsmouth, New Hampshire, in August 1905, and a settlement favorable to Japan was worked out. (The Japanese people, however,

had expected more, and were angry at the United States for allegedly frustrating their desires.) Roosevelt received worldwide praise for his role in settling the war, and in 1905 he was awarded the Nobel Peace Prize.

Agreements with Japan

Roosevelt was now worried that in encouraging Japan he might, in fact, have upset the balance of power in the other direction. He shared the alarm that many Americans felt as they watched the swift Japanese victories over huge Russia. At the time of the Portsmouth negotiations he worked out a secret agreement with the Japanese, the Taft-Katsura Memorandum. According to this agreement, the United States recognized Japanese control of Korea, which it had recently taken over, while Japan bound itself to keep its hands off the Philippines.

In 1906 a crisis erupted in California over the growing immigration of Japanese laborers. Excited over the "yellow peril," the San Francisco Board of Education ordered that the Japanese children—all ninety of them—be placed in a separate school. The proud Japanese, carried to a new pitch of national enthusiasm by their victory over Russia, protested violently at this slap in the face. By persuasive personal negotiation, Roosevelt got the order nullified, but in return he had to agree to get Japanese immigration greatly reduced. In 1907 the Japanese agreed to halt the issuing of passports to Japanese workers and farmers, thus fending off in a "Gentlemen's Agreement" the indignity of seeing legislation passed by Congress preventing their entry.

Roosevelt decided now on a bold step designed to quiet both American fears of Japan and what he took to be an inflated Japanese sense of power. "I am exceedingly anxious to impress upon the Japanese," he said in a private letter, "that I have nothing but the friendliest possible intentions toward them, but I am nonetheless anxious that they should realize that I am not afraid of them and that the United States will no more submit to bullying than it will bully." In 1907–9 he sent the "Great White Fleet," America's new battleship array, around the world. In the course of its voyage it visited Japan. Meanwhile, cautious negotiations were under way in Washington, where in November 1908 the

Root-Takahira Agreement was concluded. Another of Roosevelt's executive agreements, which bypassed the often uncooperative Senate, it provided that in the "region of the Pacific Ocean" each nation would maintain the status quo and respect each other's territorial possessions. The two nations stated, furthermore, that they would uphold the Open Door in China, and "by all pacific means at their disposal the independence and integrity of China."

The most important implication in this agreement was the unvoiced recognition by the United States that the Japanese held economic ascendancy in Manchuria, which was taken as being in the "region of the Pacific Ocean." Roosevelt, now preparing to leave the White House, had settled America's Far Eastern policy on the basis of accommodation with Japan. The Chinese might watch in surprised anger, but it was clear that the United States had pulled back from its earlier militancy on the Open Door and was ready to accept as a reality Japanese dominance in the northern regions of China. Its "big stick" would be waved in the Western Hemisphere, but not in the Far East.

Bibliography

Books that were especially valuable to me in writing this chapter: Walter LaFeber's provocative *The New Empire: An Interpretation of American Expansion, 1860–1898** (1963), probably the most successful book, and certainly one widely influential, which stresses the economic origins of foreign policy in this period. What seems to me the wisest and most balanced study of this complicated transformation is David Healy's *U.S. Expansionism* (1970). and essential too is Robert L. Beisner's study of those who opposed imperialism, *Twelve against Empire: The Anti-Imperialists, 1898–1900** (1968). As to Grover Cleveland and the Liberal-Democratic, Gladstonian view of the world, see Robert Kelley, *The Transatlantic Persuasion: The Liberal-Democratic Mind in the Age of Gladstone* (1969). Ernest R. May's *Imperial Democracy: The Emergence of America as a Great Power* (1961) allowed me to see the Spanish-American War in a multinational context. H. Wayne Morgan's two books, *William McKinley and His America* (1963) and *America's Road to Empire: The War with Spain and Overseas Expan-*

sion (1965) are essential in understanding McKinley's motivations. In Richard Hofstadter's *The Paranoid Style in American Politics and Other Essays* (1965) may be found his landmark essay on the mood-crisis of the 1890s in America. Julius Pratt's *Expansionists of 1898* (1936), a seminal work, was still valuable to me on the ideology lying behind these events. Concerning the post-1900 scene, Howard K. Beale's landmark study, *Theodore Roosevelt and the Rise of America to World Power* (1956) is fundamental.

How Have Historians Looked at the Topic?

A decade of war in Vietnam has accustomed Americans to the term *imperialist* and revived the quarrel over expansionist foreign policy that began three quarters of a century ago. In *The Forging of the American Empire from the Revolution to Vietnam: A History of American Imperialism* (1971), Sidney Lens draws a parallel between the Spanish-American War—the first American war for empire—and Vietnam. For a provocative and controversial critique of America's "noncolonial imperial expansion" by the distinguished founder of the modern school of historians who interpret American foreign policy as shaped by the imperatives of American capitalism, read William A. Williams's *The Tragedy of American Diplomacy* (1962), *The Roots of the Modern American Empire* (1969), and *Empire as a Way of Life* (1979).

In an earlier era in which anti-war sentiment was strong, Walter Millis emphasized both industrialists' profit hunger and newspaper induced hysteria as reasons for war with Spain in *The Martial Spirit* (1931). In *The Correspondent's War* (1967) Charles H. Brown showed that the yellow press acted as though it had created the war, regardless of its authentic role. Frank Freidel's small volume, *The Splendid Little War* (1958) makes it clear that the war was not splendid for those who fought it. The sordid history of the pacification of the Philippine rebels is described in Leon Wolff's *Little Brown Brother* (1961). A recent study which considers many influences to have been involved in expansionism is Milton Plesur's *America's Outward Thrust: Approaches to Foreign Affairs, 1865–1890* (1971). On the crucial shift in the Anglo-American relationship in these

EMERGENCE TO WORLD POWER

years, see R. G. Neale, *Great Britain and United States Expansion, 1898–1900* (1966); Bradford Perkins, *The Great Rapprochement: England and the United States, 1895–1914* (1968); and Charles S. Campbell, Jr., *Anglo-American Understanding, 1898–1903* (1957). A work of major new insights into the broad trends in American foreign policy is Robert L. Beisner's *From the Old Diplomacy to the New, 1865–1900* (1975). On a major figure, see Kenton J. Clymer's *John Hay: The Gentleman as Diplomat* (1975). Raymond A.

Esthus's *Theodore Roosevelt and the International Rivalries* (1970) and William H. Harbaugh's *Power and Responsibility: The Life and Times of Theodore Roosevelt* (1961) are valuable on the great president. A judicious, skilled study is Russell F. Weigley's *The American Way of War: A History of United States Military Strategy and Policy** (1973).

* Available in paperback.

25

TIME LINE

THE PROGRESSIVE ERA: NEW WAYS OF THINKING

New York Public Library

At twenty-nine, affluent Jane Addams finally began her life's work. She had wanted to serve society, but how, as a woman? She rejected being a missionary. Medicine was emerging as a socially conscious profession, and daring women were beginning to enter it, but in medical studies her health broke. Then in England in the 1880s she found her inspiration: the settlement house. A colony of the educated placed in the slums, it helped the working poor understand their problems by schooling them; reduced disease by training them in cleanliness; gave violent youth an outlet in athletics, arts, and crafts; and provided clinics, training in craft skills, day nurseries for working women, literacy, the excitement of the arts, and playgrounds for healthy exercise and the learning of teamwork.

Inspired by this example, in 1889 Jane Addams founded Hull House in Chicago, the first and most famous American settlement house, the model for scores more across the country. So, too, gifted Jane Addams in her active writing and busy career became an inspiration for young women and men of her type and generation. To combat conservative Social Darwinism, she evolved a counter-philosophy. People must not be isolated competing atoms, cut off from each other, she said. Rather, the hope for America lay in reviving the sense of community, of collective responsibility, of human warmth and interaction and love. The real curse of industrialism lay in its shattering of the net of associations that had formerly bound humanity together. Women especially, she insisted, should not care only for their individual families: they should launch out into the community and help build a better, more humane human family.

The great pioneer in social psychology Charles H. Cooley constantly cited her work and ideas as providing support for his thesis that the healthy self grows not in isolation, but in reality is created by interrelations with others. The movement for "progressive education" received a powerful boost from Addams, who wrote abundantly on the theme that the school can reshape society by immersing the student in a direct understanding of cooperative daily living. Then she demonstrated this at Hull House by fostering the practical arts in its school and emphasizing creativity in place of rote learning. In the Progressive years Addams was a national influence, the close counselor of reformers everywhere and the exciting symbol of the emerging new profession of social worker.

During the First World War she fought for the cause of pacifism, continuing her crusade in the 1920s. Ultrapatriots condemned her internationalism; the Daughters of the American Revolution expelled her; but in 1931 the Nobel Peace Prize was awarded to Jane Addams. Now ill and weakened, she warmly applauded Franklin Roosevelt's New Deal (her disciple Frances Perkins became, as secretary of labor, the first woman cabinet member). Death came to Addams in 1936, but her imprint on America was deep and lasting.

Overview

Somewhere in the 1890s, a new era of revolutionary change in American life began stirring. It is important to understand how deep this ran, how fundamental it was. The Progressive Era constitutes so massive a marshaling of reform energies from all over the nation, from the smallest community to Washington, that comparisons can be made only with the era of the Revolution a century before. Clearly the Civil War was an earthquake in American life. Nothing can compare in human importance to the freeing of four million Americans from slavery. And in the Congress during that conflict, milestone legislation inaugurated the rule of Yankee America—industrializing, modernizing, centralizing—after sixty years of Jeffersonian America. But the freeing of the slaves was a wartime creation, and the complex of American institutions, from top to bottom, was otherwise left essentially untouched by the conflict, save for the establishment of a protective tariff and the national currency and banking system.

The Progressive Era, however, reached into every community and changed it. American life after 1916 operated in sharply different ways. Americans created a new framework for their national life, involving a new relationship between government and the economy, new forms of government, and a new ideology with a new name. In the era of the Revolution, the ideology that had seized the American mind and given Americans their national purpose was *republicanism*. Now, however, America no longer stood in lonely eminence in the world as the exemplar of democracy and republicanism. Parliamentary reforms had made Britain democratic, France was now a great republic and a democracy, and similar advances seemed to be spreading across western Europe, and even to other regions abroad. Instead, the overwhelming fact about America, as its industrial system mushroomed into the most productive in the world, was its swift transformation into a new way of living. The word that pressed itself upon Americans now was *progress*. Whatever was happening in their country—and there were, as we shall see, grave and terrible ills that also obsessed the country—it was going somewhere new, hopefully better, but in any event strikingly new. On every side after 1900 there was talk of the New Woman, the New Journalism, the New

Literature, the New School, and then Theodore Roosevelt's New Nationalism and Woodrow Wilson's New Freedom. Just the flood of inventions itself produced startling improvements in daily life that in their volume and total effect made people wonder at the marvels to come.

In 1900 a historian of invention, Edward W. Byrn, fantasized what it would be like to travel backwards in time for a century, leaving the era of the "luxurious palace car behind a magnificent locomotive, traveling on steel rails, at sixty miles an hour," and approaching the time of the "rickety, rumbling, dusty stagecoach." Looking outward upon the passing scene as the century regressed to 1800, there would be the milestones of the progress achieved: the telephone, phonograph, camera, electric railways, electric lights, the telegraph, sewing machine, grain reaper, thresher, and India-rubber goods. There would be more: the steam-powered printing press, woodworking machinery, gas engines, elevators, barbed wire, time locks, oil and gas wells, and refrigeration. Byrn wrote on: "We lose air engines, stem-winding watches, cash-registers and cash-carriers, the great suspension bridges, and tunnels, the Suez Canal, iron frame buildings, monitors and heavy ironclads, revolvers, torpedoes, magazine guns and Gatling guns, linotype machines, all practical typewriters, all pasteurizing, knowledge of microbes or disease germs, and sanitary plumbing, water-gas, soda water fountains, air brakes, coal-tar dyes and medicines, nitro-glycerine, dynamite and guncotton, dynamo electric machines, aluminum ware, electric locomotives, Bessemer steel with its wonderful developments, ocean cables, enameled iron ware, Welsbach gas burners, electric storage batteries, the cigarette machine, hydraulic dredges, the roller mills, middlings purifiers and patent-process flour, tin can machines, car couplings, compressed air drills, sleeping cars, the dynamite gun, the McKay shoe machine, the circular knitting machine, the Jacquard loom, wood pulp for paper, fire alarms, the use of anesthetics in surgery, oleomargarine, street sweepers, Artesian wells, friction matches, steam hammers, electroplating, nail machines, false teeth, artificial limbs and eyes, the spectroscope, the Kinetescope or moving pictures, acetylene gas, X-ray apparatus, horseless carriages, and —but enough! (*The Progress of Invention in the Nineteenth Century* [1900])

It was a stunning experience, passing through all this swift change, this hurtling pellmell movement toward modernization. It was also an appalling experience, especially in the presence of the great depression of the 1890s, an earthquake event in American history not to be matched again until the depression of the 1930s.

And there were deeper problems: social exploitation, degradation in city slums, autocratic economic power, industrial warfare, and political corruption. Somehow, a new national ideology had to emerge that would allow Americans to take hold of this paradoxical scene of progress and poverty, render it orderly and fruitful, and make it fulfill its high promise.

In all of this change there seemed clearly, to American thinkers, to be a powerful process at work that was progressive, improving, and intelligent. The important thing was to find the secret of that process, to make social and economic policy as progressive as the technical revolution that was rushing the nation toward some strange future. In London reformers looked out upon their vast, swarming, gravely afflicted city and created, locally, what they called the Progressive party to clean up the metropolis and make it orderly, healthy, and humane, a city with a well-housed, properly educated citizenry not permanently weakened by disease and social oppression. In America after 1900, the same impulse to create the progressive society, to introduce progressive reforms, to build a progressive America took hold. *Progressivism:* this was the new ideology, based upon fresh visions of what the just American society should be.

Progressivism a Worldwide Movement

Once again, as in the Revolutionary era, American reformers looked outward to the Old World to gather ideas. Just as they had seized upon the radical republicanism of mid-eighteenth-century reformers in Britain and made that ideology their own, now they trotted the globe to study the ways Europeans were dealing with the problems that the new economic order was creating in their countries. Indeed, a democratic revitalization was sweeping much of the globe. This was the era, after 1900, of the historic Liberal governments in Great Britain, whose dramatic reforms turned that nation decisively toward social welfare. Even Germany and Austria, in the heart of traditionally autocratic central Europe, were shaken by waves of democracy and liberalism and a bold drive for reforms. Russia witnessed the emergence of parliamentary institutions in 1905,

followed by major social improvements. American progressives watched all this in fascination.

British reforms, as always, exerted a special appeal. Britons and Americans read the same reformist books and exchanged them eagerly across the Atlantic. Hardly would a new idea crop up in London before young Americans were trumpeting it in their own country. Was the subject city reform? Americans prepared long bibliographies of British books on the subject. Was it slum reform? Young Americans spent arduous years working in settlement houses in London, then returned to Chicago and New York to build similar institutions.

Perhaps as important as British reforms was the example of Germany. There the principle of a welfare state seemed to have reached its fullest development. Thousands of young Americans studied in German universities, bringing socialist views back with them. Simon N. Patten, who trained a generation of public figures at the University of Pennsylvania's Wharton School of Commerce, spoke for many of his contemporaries when he said he wanted to "help in the transformation of American civilization from an English to a German basis." Chambers of commerce urged German methods of industrial efficiency on businessmen; city planners drew notions of urban beautification from German cities; and advocates of vocational and technical training pointed insistently to the German example.

There was a note of fear running through these years. It was not only a world of reforming nations but a world of rearming nations as well. Countries regarded each other with suspicion as navies and armies grew and empires expanded. Much of the drive toward collectivism in Britain sprang from deep fears that the nation must pull together to protect itself from foreign threats. American and German industries were outpacing those of Britain, so industrial efficiency was needed. American and German fleets were growing, making imperial and naval efficiency essential. The British Fabians, advocates of collectivism, spread the word *efficiency* throughout the Anglo-American world. Soon after Sidney Webb first publicized the term in London in 1902, a young Princeton professor, Woodrow Wilson, began writing articles on the theme in the United States. Men like Theodore Roosevelt and Albert J. Beveridge were greatly alarmed at the

THE PROGRESSIVE ERA: NEW WAYS OF THINKING

"threats" from abroad and were eager to make America a strong and efficiently organized nation.

The New University

The wellsprings of the progressive consciousness lay in the American middle class. It was acquiring new ideas and new ways of doing things in the "new universities" that had taken form in the latter decades of the nineteenth century. Here, more than anywhere else, were the spawning grounds of the progressive movement. Higher education had been rapidly growing in American life since 1850. In that mid-century year there were about 550 institutions of higher learning, with 5,500 faculty members and some 50,000 students. In 1900 there were almost a thousand colleges and universities, with 24,000 professors and 240,000 students. Clearly, the college and university had moved into a major role in American life such as they had never occupied before. In 1850 only 1 out of 60 young men between the ages of eighteen and twenty-one was receiving higher education; in 1900 the figure was 1 out of 25. (By 1940 it would be 1 out of 6.5.) Increasingly, Americans appreciated the value of academic training for social and political leadership, and for "getting ahead" in income and standing.

Before the 1850s the United States had simply had a number of small colleges, most of them dating from colonial days. They were small, church-connected institutions whose primary concern was to shape the moral character of their students. The content of their courses had been fixed for generations as the proper study for gentlemen. The faculty were clergymen, as were the trustees and presidents. Each young man took the same courses as every other; all students were drilled to learn by memory; and they were kept under close discipline. The college stood in place of the parent (*in loco parentis*), and its rule was heavy. There were many riots against strict living rules.

In Germany a different kind of institution had developed. Bearing the ancient name of *university*, which means a collection of colleges and schools under some form of common administration, it was concerned primarily with creating and spreading knowledge, not morals. Between mid-century and the end of the 1800s, more than nine thousand young Americans, dissatisfied with their training at home, went to Germany for advanced study. Some of them returned to become presidents of venerable colleges—Harvard, Yale, Columbia—and transform them into modern universities. Others headed up new institutions (Johns Hopkins University, the University of Chi-

The University of Wisconsin in Madison, in the 1880s. It was one of the pioneering "new universities," which combined the search for knowledge (research), teaching, and professional training.
State Historical Society of Wisconsin

cago) or fledgling state-chartered universities (Michigan, Cornell, California, and Wisconsin). The new presidents, such as Charles Eliot of Harvard (president from 1869 to 1909) and Andrew Dickson White of Cornell (1868–85), broke all ties with churches and brought in a new kind of faculty. Professors were hired for their knowledge of a subject, not because they were of the proper faith and had a strong arm for disciplining boys. The new principle was that a university was to create knowledge as well as pass it on, and this called for a faculty composed of teacher-scholars. They were to participate in the international conversation of scholars and scientists by leading creative intellectual lives outside as well as inside the classroom. Drilling and learning by rote were replaced by the German method of lecturing, where the professor brought into class the results of his own research. Graduate training leading to the Ph.D., an ancient German degree signifying the highest level of advanced scholarly attainment, was introduced. With the establishment of the seminar system, graduate students learned to question, analyze, and conduct their own research.

At the same time, the new university greatly expanded in size and course offerings, breaking completely out of the old constricted curriculum of mathematics, classics, rhetoric, and music. President Eliot at Harvard pioneered the elective system, by which students were able to choose their own courses of study. The notion of major fields of study emerged, made possible by the wide array of programs. The new universities tried at least partially to pull back from the close supervision over students' private lives that was implied by the traditional *in loco parentis* role of the American college. Many decades passed, however, before American higher education allowed students the same freedom outside the classroom that continental European schools provided. Though the new universities were no longer church-dominated, the American people continued to think of college as a place in which the character, as well as the mind, of the student was molded.

The new goal was to make the university relevant to the real pursuits of the world. Paying close heed to the practical needs of society, universities trained men and women to work at its tasks. Especially in the state universities, the atmosphere was strongly practical, with engineering students being the most characteristic expressions of the new regime. Industrialists began making large gifts to universities, even endowing them: Rockefeller the University of Chicago; Vanderbilt and Stanford the universities bearing their names; and Ezra Cornell helping by his gifts to create a state university for New York.

The old colleges had admitted students only from certain faiths, families, or social classes. The new university was open to everyone as long as he or she had ability and the willingness to work hard. (Minority groups were excluded, however, by poverty, language difficulties, and social prejudice.) In the long run this meant that the universities became meritocratic instead of aristocratic: they divided people according to competence, interest, and achievement rather than according to their origin. Tending to be much alike in their philosophies and curricula, since they were staffed by faculty members who interchanged ideas and moved from institution to institution, the new universities stripped away locally inherited habits and customs and made their students members of a national elite with shared life styles and outlooks. Lawyers and doctors, who had formerly been locally trained, began to go instead to the universities, where they were schooled in relatively similar curricula and urged to adopt an ethic of social service. Going out into the world with them were graduates in new, university-trained professions: economists, architects, biologists, scientifically trained agriculturists, chemists, public-health specialists, social-welfare workers, and teachers of all sorts.

Not only did the new university cultivate in its students the same values of hard work and getting ahead that the business community admired, it also sent out a growing number of middle-class graduates and trained professionals who became social reformers. They were self-aware, idealistic, and equipped with a strong sense of mission. This was to have a momentous impact in the years after 1890, when the number of such graduates was sufficiently large to have an influence on national affairs.

Higher education did not change all at once. Each institution struggled through these transformations in different ways; many hardly passed through them at all. Some colleges, especially in rural areas, were alarmed by the new sciences, philosophy, and history being taught at places like Harvard and the University of Michigan. In conservative schools, the old ways were clung to with a determined sense of righteous justification.

The Revolt Against Conservative Social Darwinism

American thought after the Civil War had absorbed in complicated ways the evolutionary concepts expressed by Charles Darwin in his *Origin of Species* (1859). Some people simply accepted the broad idea that evolution is the natural pattern of life, for it flowed in with the general opinion that America was the land of progress. The difficult part of Darwinian evolution to accept, however—it bothered Darwin himself a great deal—was that central concept which said that a mindless process, *natural selection*, is what governs evolution. For reasons still not clear, species periodically have offspring whose characteristics are changed from those of the parents. Mutations like this simply happen, apparently by chance. They involve a change in what we now call the gene material—DNA. The organism so modified may be better equipped in the struggle for survival and procreation, and if so the new forms crowd out the old ones. Change by chance? Few could accept that. Where is God in such a process? Surely the changes are planned by Him? Surely there is guiding intelligence?

What other people concluded from Darwin was simply that *struggle* is the basic fact of life, and that out of the struggle of species comes progress. This harsh, pitiless version of evolution came to be called social Darwinism; it has since been termed conservative social Darwinism, since it appeared to justify rule by the powerful races and, within societies, by the wealthy and privileged. Summed up in Herbert Spencer's phrase, "survival of the fittest," it taught the doctrine of doing nothing whatever to help the unfortunate, the exploited. Reform, from this viewpoint, was softheaded sentimentalism.

To compassionate young people, this negativism was terribly discouraging. They wished to serve society, to help other people, but how could they do so in the face of these ideas? Many of them turned to the new professions being taught at the universities as a way of living unselfish lives—medicine, social work, teaching, and government service. The building of hospitals and the discovery of anesthesia and antisepsis allowed medicine in particular to emerge in the 1880s as an important field for their charitable efforts.

But the young social reformers needed and searched for a new philosophy that would justify reform. They received it from one of the most prodigious scholars and creative thinkers in American history, Lester Frank Ward, who made his living as a civil servant in Washington. He wrote a massive work aimed at destroying conservative social Darwinism, published in 1883 under the title *Dynamic Sociology*. It proclaimed that people had forgotten humanity's unique possession—its mind. Whereas plants and animals might evolve, as Darwin had said, without conscious action, humanity had been given a reasoning brain with which to consciously improve its situation. Natural evolution, he said, was aimless, without goals. Social movement must be planned, not left to haphazard influences.

All across the country professors at the new universities picked up Ward's ideas and began teaching them to their students. Search for the life of service, they urged. One outgrowth of this mood was the emergence of social work as a medium through which young reformers could serve society directly. Jane Addams of Chicago's Hull House became the most persuasive symbol of this new breed. At this famous slum settlement house her work taught her to turn away from the narrow, almost secretive isolation of conservative Darwinism. She saw that people were stronger and more able to deal with adversity if they immersed themselves in the life of the group and built a web of outward-reaching relationships.

By these and other means there emerged an outlook that may be called reform Darwinism. Society certainly evolves, said Lester Frank Ward and his followers, but only if it uses its collective intelligence to work out social goals and achieves them through its collective arms and legs, the government. The welfare of the people must be ministered to by massive infusions of public services—education, regulation of minimum wages and maximum hours, and many other social reforms. There should be a minimum standard of living for everyone; there should be *positive* liberty—liberty from ignorance and exploitation—rather than the simple *negative* liberty of traditional laissez-faire, which asked only that the government keep hands-off the economy and the society.

Lester Frank Ward disputed the implication in conservative social Darwinism that people cannot change things. "It is commonly supposed that the highest wisdom of man is to learn and then to follow the ways of nature. Those dissatisfied people who would improve upon the natural course of events are rebuked as meddlers with the unalterable. Their systems are declared utopian, their laws [vain threats]. All efforts in this direction are held to be trifling and are stigmatized as so many ignorant attempts to nullify the immutable laws of nature. This general mode of reasoning is carried into all departments of human life.

"In government, every attempt to improve the condition of the state is condemned and denounced. . . . In commerce and trade, absolute freedom is insisted upon. . . . To dilute, adulterate, or even poison food and medicine for personal gain is not objectionable, since the destruction thereby of a few unwary consumers only proves their unfitness to survive in society. . . . All schemes of social reform are unscientific.

"[This] laissez-faire doctrine fails to recognize that, in the development of mind, a virtually *new power* was introduced into the world. . . . The great fact [is that man] *has,* from the very dawn of his intelligence, been transforming the entire surface of the planet he inhabits [by his power of] *invention.*

"Glancing now at the ensemble of human achievement, which may be collectively called civilization, we readily see that it is all the result of this inventive process. . . . When a well-clothed philosopher on a bitter winter's night sits in a warm room well lighted for his purpose and writes on paper with pen and ink, in the arbitrary characters of a highly developed language, the statement that civilization is the result of natural laws and that man's duty is to let nature alone so that untrammeled it may work a higher civilization, he simply ignores every circumstance of his existence and deliberately closes his eyes to every fact within the range of faculties. If man had acted upon his theory, there would have been no civilization and our philosopher would have remained a troglodyte [cave dweller]." (*Mind* [October 1884])

Popular Prophets of Social Action

The men who preached the need for collective action and were most listened to by the general public, however, were not scholars, but popular writers such as Henry George, a California newspaperman who had witnessed labor riots in San Francisco and farm radicalism in the Sacramento and San Joaquin valleys in the 1870s. He was appalled that rich land and productive factories existed in the midst of starvation and unemployment. George concluded that it was the system, not the nature of humankind, that produced this suffering. In his book *Progress and Poverty* (1879) he noted that when civilization pushed ahead, poverty increased. There was one fundamental cause, he said, for this baffling paradox—land monopoly. Clever men had got hold of the best and most valuable city lots and farmland, then skimmed off the cream of society's advancing wealth by demanding high rents and prices. And yet the landowner himself did nothing: it was the hard work of everyone else—of society at large— that made his land valuable. Businessmen had to pay high rents for their land, and they squeezed workmen's wages to compensate. Farmers were strapped by high mortgages and could not live on the price they got for their grain. The solution: replacing all forms of taxation with a single tax that landowners would have to pay on the increased value of their land, the "unearned increment." The burden of taxation would thus be dramatically lowered, and the economy would be able to grow abundantly.

George's single tax idea was too simplistic: it could never work so powerful a change. But the enormous appeal of his book was in its convincing demonstration that it was the system that was at fault and that poverty was not inevitable. *Progress and Poverty* went through a hundred editions and by the twentieth century had been read by at least six million men and women. In Britain, Australia, and New Zealand, George was "the prophet for whom [the people] had been searching for years, the Columbus of political economy and social science." Farmers were uncomfortable with George's emphasis on land taxation, and businessmen disliked the aura of confiscation in his book, but the working class, especially the ethnic minorities in the cities, was warmly enthusiastic.

In 1887 Edward Bellamy published a utopian romantic novel called *Looking Backward.* This work described what the world would be like a century later if proper social principles were followed. At present, Bellamy said, society was like a stagecoach, with wealthy plutocrats sitting on the box above and whipping the toiling masses below as they struggled to pull the heavy vehicle. The answer was to reorganize society until it resembled a well-arranged army. The principle of individualistic competition would be scrapped, for it led to selfishness. Combination would be the secret of the new order. Industry would be nationalized, for the brotherhood of all men required that no one should have the power of ruling over others irresponsibly. Relying on the survival of the fittest, he said, simply enthroned brutality and exploitation. There should be a strong central government to plan everything carefully and do away with waste. There would be large department stores instead of many small shops, for instance, and credit cards in place of money! Serving in the state industrial army until the age of forty-five, people would then retire to follow their own desires. Bellamy's book was a best seller in the United States and abroad. His proposals seemed to appeal mostly to the Yankee middle class, where in many circles the vision of such a regulated society directed by trained intelligence was highly attractive.

Many other such books were widely read, each of them proposing some variety of collectivism. In 1894 Henry Demarest Lloyd's *Wealth Against Commonwealth* appeared, showing how Standard Oil used the laws to become a great exploitive monopoly and proposing strong governmental regulations. There was also Robert Blatchford's *Merrie England* (1894), which explained the reasons for poverty, described socialism, and advocated its adoption. In ten years, two million copies of this book were sold in England and the United States.

The Churches and Social Action

A new consciousness stirred in the churches as well. American Protestantism was severely challenged by the new age and its problems. In the midcentury decades the response of most clergymen was to preach stern messages drawn from the Calvinism that was widespread in Protestant churches. The general thesis was that godliness was in league with riches. The wealthy acquired their money by hard work, and God smiled upon them. The poor earned their sufferings by their own failings. But in the 1880s a small group of young clergymen who worked in the cities and were shocked by the suffering they saw began appealing to the churches to take up social action. Charles Loring Brace pointed out that in fact the working classes were ignored almost entirely by

Protestantism. Most of its churches were rural, and those in the cities turned up their noses at the dirty, stinking, teeming slums. Their stern sermons seemed to link Protestant ministers with exploitive capitalism.

One response to these appeals was the invasion of the slums by city missions and by such new agencies as the Salvation Army, a British organization that came to America in 1880. Another response was to transform the churches in the poorer districts into "institutional" churches. Like Jane Addams's settlement houses, the institutional church was designed to minister to the whole person, rather than simply to preach a sermon at him on Sunday. The basic thesis was that a man ground down by poverty, unemployment, illiteracy, and lack of skills would be too desperate to listen to sermons or practice a religious faith. The new churches provided reading rooms and classes to attack illiteracy and ignorance; day nurseries to help working women; sewing and manual-training instruction to provide skills; social clubs and gymnasiums to bring people together and build physical health; and personal counseling that went beyond theological matters. The reaction was startling. A church in New York that had only 75 members in 1882 acquired more than 4,000 in fifteen years after it became institutional. These experiences, repeated elsewhere, spread the institutional-church idea throughout urban America.

The Theological Challenge of Darwinism

The churches were also in turmoil because of Darwinism's implications for biblical interpretation. If the theory of evolution was valid, what happened to the Garden of Eden? Were humans simply animals, like monkeys or cats, whose present form was arranged not by God's loving hands but by the eons-old process of evolution? The Darwinian idea seemed a monstrous assault against everything that the churches had ever preached concerning man's status in creation and his relation to God. Why pray anymore to God if everything operates according to natural laws? Common people in the churches could not understand it. What had happened to the faith of their parents? For that matter, all of modern science seemed a threatening influence. In the 1870s clergymen and laymen began a long struggle to turn back modern science, inaugurating an argument that was to create half a century of destructive controversy.

Many clergymen, however, followed the teachings of what was called liberal Protestantism. Darwinism, so the liberal Protestant view ran, simply told us in new ways how God works His wonders to perform. Evolution was the divine means of achieving divine purposes. Rural churches held fast to the old faith, but the liberal teaching spread in urban churches. Science and religion were not enemies, said such prominent clerics as Lyman Abbot, but were complementary sources of divine truth. This meant that the Bible was not to be interpreted literally, but according to its spirit.

Having turned away from orthodox biblical interpretation, such clergymen were inclined to turn away from orthodox social teachings as well. They were encouraged in this by what was going on in many northern seminaries. Influenced by German scholarship and the new universities, seminaries like Andover in Massachusetts and Union in New York City brought young professors of sociology into their faculties who taught that the church must concern itself with solving social problems. Fundamentalist clergymen regarded such seminaries as seats of the devil, for they also taught the new ways of interpreting the Bible. But liberals regarded them as sources of strength for their cause.

Rise of the Social Gospel

Thus the ground was prepared for the rise of what came to be called the social gospel. Washington Gladden, a Congregational clergyman, began a widely influential career as a social-gospel leader when he published *Applied Christianity* in 1886. He thought of Christianity as a fellowship of love and saw the church as having a social mission. We must reach out to one another, he insisted, assist one another, and not stand back in cold impersonality while the alleged principle of survival of the fittest operated. Since capital was waging war on working people, labor should have the right to organize. There should be profit sharing so that workers would receive a portion of the profits their toil produced. Gladden went on in

succeeding years to endorse a long list of social reforms: public control of money; regulation of corporations; the right of black people to equal educational and economic opportunities; and all the reforms of the Progressive Era.

Walter Rauschenbusch, a Baptist of German origins, was dismayed by the grim life of slum dwellers in the 1880s. He responded by publishing his own newspaper, *For the Right*, in which he advocated Christian socialism. It was possible, he said, in this new era of progress to build the Kingdom of God here on earth. In the 1890s he supported the Populists; after 1900 he worked eagerly for the socialist Eugene V. Debs. In 1907, in his *Christianity and the Social Crisis*, a landmark in social-gospel history, he condemned capitalism as essentially un-Christian: it destroyed people's moral growth and made them corrupt. The time had come, he said, to revive the communalism of the early Christians, who had shared all things.

Though reforming Protestants were usually not as radical as Rauschenbusch, they still insisted that their denominations take up social reform. Church after church in the 1880s began setting aside doctrinal questions and coming to grips with the "social question." The Episcopalians were the first to do so, having been inspired by social-reform movements within the Anglican Church in England. In 1887 they formed the first social-gospel organization, the Church Association for the Advancement of the Interests of Labor. It immediately began working to eliminate child labor, sweatshops, and slums, and to help labor unions get just settlements in disputes with employers. The Congregationalists soon followed, bringing in their diverse and very influential newspapers and periodicals. The Presbyterians, strongly identified with the business and corporate leadership of the country, held back, as did the Methodists and the Baptists, whose primarily rural parishioners wanted no truck with radicals. But by the turn of the century strong movements toward social action within even these denominations were under way. By that time, to demonstrate the scope of the movement, the Methodist Federation for Social Service, organized in 1907, was one of the most active of such organizations.

The social-gospel movement by no means converted the great mass of churchgoers. Conservative churchmen, led by the Fundamentalists, continued to preach that their work should be directed only at saving individual souls. The social gospel was detested as simply another branch of modernism. But the movement did grow to powerful proportions during the Progressive Era, especially in the cities.

William James: The Progressive Era's Philosopher

What the reformers of the Progressive Era needed most of all was a new image of humanity and its potentialities. In this sense, the central figure in American thought from the 1890s to the First World War was the Harvard psychologist and philosopher William James. An agile, quick-witted, wonderfully tolerant man, James had served on the Harvard faculty since the 1870s. By the turn of the century his writings and lectures were reaching out to ever wider circles of Americans, making him a kind of national sage in the manner of Ralph Waldo Emerson before the Civil War. Intellectuals in Europe and the United States were deeply influenced by him, as were ordinary people in the educated public who bought and read his more popular works by the thousands. No American intellectual was so cosmopolitan, none before him so widely known and read in the transatlantic community since, perhaps, Benjamin Franklin.

Early in his career, James had struggled hard with the determinism that flourished as a result of Charles Darwin's work. He was appalled at the deterministic notion that everything is caused by physical influences, that the laws of biology, and not of the free human spirit, dominate what we are and how we think. James chose instead to believe in humanity's free will. In 1890, after years of research and writing, he summed up his vision of human nature in his first major work, *Principles of Psychology*. Gracefully written, daring in concept, it became the dominant work in the teaching of psychology. James rejected outright the idea that people are like little machines, shaped wholly by their environment. What fascinated him most of all was human creativity. There is a self at the core of each human being's personality, James wrote, and that self has a will of its own. Clearly influenced by the external environment, the conscious self at the same time acts *upon* that environment. People live in constant interaction with their surroundings. They

The philosopher William James (with his novelist brother Henry James on the left), in the turn-of-the-century period when he was becoming one of the shapers of American thought. He urged the need to ground ideas in actual experience, and to test them by it (pragmatism).

The Bettman Archive

are not passive creatures pushed this way and that by external forces.

In 1907 James published *Pragmatism*, a short work that went through edition after edition. In it he made a famous distinction between the "tender-minded" and the "tough-minded." The former, he said, are unable to face the fact that reality is enormously complicated, often confusing, and perhaps lacking any encompassing structure that one can see. Tender-minded people therefore put their faith in abstract, logical theories. Determined to fit themselves and their world into some kind of intellectual structure that they can hang onto, the tender-minded form an exaggerated faith in the ability of the mind to know all things by the use of reason and logic. By contrast, James said, tough-minded people are comfortable with the indeterminacy of life, content to work away in the midst of booming confusion, and interested most of all in coming to grips with how things really are in some limited area of examination. Skeptical, rather materialistic, they go by facts (empiricism) and not by theories (rationalism). "The tough," observed James, "think of the tender as sentimentalist and soft-heads. The tender feel the tough to be unrefined, callous, or brutal."

Most people, he went on, were mixtures of both, but in his belief the tough-minded empiricist seemed to be growing in dominance. This was all to the good, James remarked, for it meant that the pragmatic method was rising to ascendancy. What was pragmatism? It was "to try to interpret each notion by tracing its practical consequences." This put ideas in their proper place: they were only tools, not reality itself. The tough-minded observer considers facts, puts together an idea as a possible explanation for the facts, tests it, and tosses it aside willingly if it does not work. If a theory works satisfactorily, James said, then it is true. Experience, not logic, is the proper test. This approach, James said, "unstiffens" all opinion and opens up new possibilities. It lets individuals be creative, by which they actually add to what the universe contains.

Such was the message the Progressive Era received from its central thinker: examine reality directly, be quick to toss aside theories, and test everything by results. Take a kind of joyous delight in the complexity and indeterminacy of life: ride the waves, laugh at the tumbling, avoid the closed-in calms. Gather huge amounts of facts, think carefully, and then be ready to risk. Pragmatism was taken up eagerly by an age that was confident, hopeful, breaking barriers, and ready to run roughshod over people and traditions if "results" could be achieved.

Realism in Scholarship: Economics

Throughout the world of scholarship born in the new university was the kind of search for fresh understandings of "reality" that James had called for. Each field had its set of constrictive established dogmas to revolt against. In economics, the reigning concept preached a formal, logical, and highly moralistic view of the business world. The men who taught it were usually philosophers or ministers. The objective was to demonstrate that competition was the iron law. If it was allowed to operate untouched by governmental interference, everyone would benefit as far as he should benefit.

Younger, college-trained economists began disagreeing with all this in the 1880s. Richard T. Ely at Johns Hopkins University and later at the University of Wisconsin said: "We regard the state as an educational and ethical agency, whose positive aid is an indispensable condition of human progress." What should economists do to make their emergent "science" a useful discipline helping to solve actual problems, instead of

simply justifying in grand language what businessmen were doing? The answer was to stay away from methods of analysis that work downward from grand theories and begin studying the "actual conditions of economic life." Following this injunction, students of economics began examining institutions such as the corporation and the banking system or studying the ways in which prices were set. This meant leaving the library and plunging into real situations—observing markets, financial operations, and labor negotiations.

Thorstein Veblen dispensed with the classical "economic man" of the orthodox economists in his *Theory of the Leisure Class* (1899). People simply did not operate in business life according to logical calculations of profit and loss, he said. Rather, they were driven by instinctual urges inherited from the dim past of human history. As barbarians, they had fought one another with fists and weapons. They did this for emotional reasons, so as to feel superior and powerful. Evolution had changed the form, but not the spirit, of all this. Now, Veblen said, people use business life to gain their sense of power and dominance. They drain off profits so as to be able to engage in "conspicuous consumption"—the building of great mansions that flaunt their riches and, by implication, their power and social status. The economy is not an ideal mechanism, self-balancing and beneficent. It is, rather, a product of long evolution, bearing pieces and traces of the barbaric past, and it must undergo still more changes before it can become humane.

Realism in Scholarship: History

One of the features of the new university was the establishment within it of the formerly ignored field of modern history. It was a provocative field, founded on the teachings of the great German historian Leopold von Ranke. His followers began tossing aside the venerable old books that provided stylized accounts of the ancient past and, instead, went directly to the sources, to the traces of the past left to us in the form of original documents, tablets, and the like to uncover the truth. Discover what things are really like, said von Ranke; do not be content with what the old historians said. Doing so, the investigator will find a fresh story that tells him unsuspected things. Be skeptical, analytical, take nothing for granted; build from facts, not from theories.

THE PROGRESSIVE ERA: NEW WAYS OF THINKING

The result was a complete rewriting of ancient history in the nineteenth century. By the end of the century historians were beginning to apply the same methods to the examination of modern history. Scholars uncovered the largely forgotten history of their individual nations, thus giving great impetus to the soaring nationalism that captured the modern mind. In the United States a young historian at the University of Wisconsin, Frederick Jackson Turner, issued an exciting challenge in 1893: stop explaining American history, he said, by means of grand panoramas that depict the United States simply as an outgrowth of Europe. Investigate instead the actual setting in which American democracy emerged, for the United States, he insisted, was a unique phenomenon in the world. Looking for what forces really operated to shape nations, he arrived at the notion that they were environmental and economic in nature. At first he pointed to the frontier, saying that out of this experience emerged American individualism, initiative, impatience with formalism, equality, and creative drive. Later he developed the concept that the nation is naturally divided into great physiographic sections, each of them based on different economic systems, and that United States history is a record of the conflict of these sections as they struggled for dominance in Washington.

The fundamental note in Turner's form of history, however, remained: history was a story that concentrated on lively, eruptive, conflicting forces. Struggle—this was the theme that dominated the work of the men of whom Richard Hofstadter wrote in his book *The Progressive Historians: Turner, Parrington, Beard* (1968). Older historians, as Hofstadter pointed out, had sought to present uplifting stories of Washington and Jefferson that were idealistic and unifying. Progressive historians concentrated instead on change and social conflict leading ever onward toward democracy. It was a story that inevitably led to partisanship, to tales of good guys and bad guys. The essential history of the United States, as progressive historians showed it, was a struggle against privilege, usually economic privilege. As Turner said in 1910, "We may trace the contest between the capitalist and the democratic pioneer from the earliest colonial days."

Realism in Scholarship: Political Science

Keenly concerned with the public implications of their work, the progressive historians thus left their quiet studies and plunged into public controversy. The same was true with political scientists, who were also engaged in establishing their field of study as a separate and distinct discipline. They, too, had to combat established dogmas and formalistic ways of thinking. The books on gov-

Realism in art also emerged in the Progressive Era, forecast by the work of such painters as Thomas Eakins. His *Agnew Clinic* (1889) portrayed unflinchingly a grim subject and painted in every detail, even the blood on the surgeon's hands.

University of Pennsylvania, School of Medicine

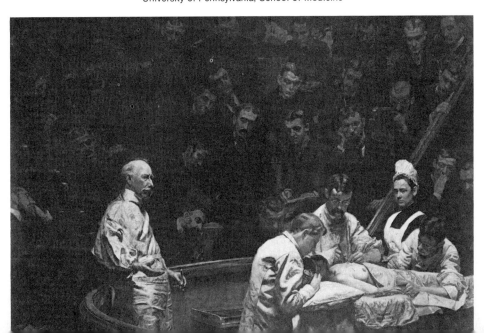

ernment that fed the nineteenth-century mind were overwhelmingly abstract and philosophical. They were, as Henry Steele Commager has commented, "vastly concerned with Sovereignty, or States' Rights, or the distinctions between People, Nation, and Government, with the Judicial Function or the Executive Power, with theories of Territorial Authority or of Reconstruction. They drew up admirable definitions of the Political Party whose resemblance to any actual political party was purely coincidental; they indulged in learned analyses of the nature of Law without bothering to trace the law in its actual operation; they made sweeping assumptions about federalism, the separation of powers, or judicial review which had little perceptible relation to their functioning." (*The American Mind* [1951])

As early as the 1880s, Woodrow Wilson, then just beginning his career as a professor of political science, inaugurated a realistic way of examining political institutions. His doctoral dissertation, *Congressional Government: A Study in American Politics* (1885), firmly rejected the old mechanical interpretation of the Constitution and how it works. He showed how it functioned in real life, demonstrating that in its actual operation all its energies were so dispersed that little could get done. What was needed, he said, was a reorganized Congress that gave real power to leadership, so that the legislative system could begin solving problems instead of evading them. Four years later, in his book *The State* (1889), he again depicted government as "not a machine, but a living thing. . . . It is modified by its environment, necessitated by its tasks, shaped to its functions by the sheer pressure of life. No living thing can have its organs offset against each other as checks and live. On the contrary its life is dependent upon their quick cooperation, their ready response to the commands of instinct or intelligence, their amicable community of purpose. Government is not a body of blind forces; it is a body of men."

Political scientists now began applying these same approaches to all other aspects of public life. They studied lobbying as well as the formal procedures for passing laws; the way laws are administered as well as enacted; the relations between banks and government; the nature of political parties as social institutions; spoils systems, political bosses, pressure groups, and a host of other groupings in public life. Instead of relying on moral laws and philosophical absolutes, they based their work on huge masses of statistics drawn from census figures, and on floods of facts drawn from state and federal agencies. Political theory was little discussed: what progressive political scientists concentrated on most of all was the impact of interest groups on public policy.

Realism in Scholarship: The Law

American legal theory had long been set in the same fixed, mechanical modes of thinking that had characterized other fields of thought. From about the middle of the nineteenth century legal scholars had settled on the notion that law was a science, a self-contained storehouse of rational, philosophical rules that needed not be changed, but simply carefully applied. Finding precedents in earlier court decisions became almost the sole concern of the careful legal scholar who decided everything by looking in books—the "black-letter" lawyer. Such men believed that there was nothing tentative in the law, nothing growing or changing. Books were put together that carefully reduced whole areas of the law to a symmetrical pattern of legal principles, all derived most logically from two to three general philosophical beliefs.

By the 1880s a few perceptive men realized that this could not be true. Life was too various and changing to fit into a series of neat pigeonholes derived from ancient decisions. In 1881 the brilliant Oliver Wendell Holmes, Jr., who later served twenty years on the Massachusetts Supreme Court and then thirty years (1902–32) as one of Theodore Roosevelt's appointees to the United States Supreme Court, thrust at the heart of these formalistic beliefs. In an epochal book, *The Common Law* (1881), he said that "the life of the law has not been logic; it has been experience. The felt necessities of the time, the prevalent moral and political theories, intuitions of public policy, avowed or unconscious, even the prejudices which judges share with their fellowmen, have had a good deal more to do than the syllogism in determining the rules by which men should be governed."

This was pragmatism in the law (or, as it was called, legal realism), uttered by a man who was a close friend of William James. Legal realism was argued and debated and shouted over for decades. Holmes's words by no means settled the matter. After he joined the Court he usually wrote dissents, for the majority of the Court disagreed with him. Realists were accused of having no principles at all, of rejecting the whole idea of trying to form general principles from particular cases. Judges were offended by the view, often stated by legal realists, that court decisions that quoted precedent and philosophical rules were nothing more than after-the-fact rationalizations. Realists replied that they never wished to dispense with general principles but only to give far greater weight to practical facts in everyday life than had formerly been the case. When Louis Brandeis argued before the Supreme Court that state laws limiting the hours of labor were constitutional, in the case of *Muller* v. *Oregon* (1908), he included in his argument a careful description of sociological conditions created by long hours of labor as well as citations to legal precedent. Law, realists said, was a tool for social action, a crucial instrument in a society rapidly changing. Jurists must not quote ancient principle and stand in reform's way.

The Intellectual as Expert

These transformations in the world of thought were important, for the time had finally arrived in America when intellectuals were gaining the public ear. The United States had always been an intensely practical nation, and Americans had regarded academics as ineffectual dreamers. But a great change had occurred by 1900. The universities formed or reorganized around 1870 had by this time been engaged for thirty years in graduating professionals in many fields. These individuals constituted, in effect, a new middle class. In business, labor, and agriculture; in social work, education, and law; in journalism, architecture, and public administration—in all these areas and more a steady influx of university-trained young people had been arriving on the scene and, by their work, gaining public respect. A cultural system that was national in scope had emerged, replacing the decentralized little social worlds—the small towns and villages—where men and women had formerly received all their training.

Professional organizations, trade associations, agricultural cooperatives, chambers of commerce, leagues of small businessmen, national labor unions, manufacturers' organizations, and other such institutions provided a nationalized structure within which the new middle class worked. Essentially urban in character, the new middle class was proud of its cities, cosmopolitan in outlook, proud of its new skills, and hopeful of a shining future for the United States. Worshiping a new phenonemon called science, they were so effective in solving problems that the public formed a new notion of college graduates and academic intellectuals: they were not sterile dreamers, but experts—and therefore men of power.

Their first arena of action lay in the states, where in the 1890s the initial attempts at regulation of business enterprise took place. Especially in Madison, the capital of Wisconsin, the use of a group of experts who provided trained advice to the government attracted nationwide attention. The "Wisconsin idea" was for the state government to call on the professors at the state university to serve as impartial advisers on such issues as taxation, railroad problems, and the like. The young economist Richard T. Ely set up a special school at the University of Wisconsin designed to promote social science in the training of public servants. When Robert M. La Follette was elected a progressive governor in 1900, he began making extensive use of the professors, forming a kind of brain trust. Soon progressive scholars were being consulted in many states and on the national level as well.

The Progressive Era was for them an exciting and exuberant time filled with challenges and opportunities. Everything seemed open to fresh examination: industrial methods, banking systems, railway franchises, the use of political power, the nature of education, social relations, and even human sex life. Everywhere the chasm that had formerly separated the men of theory from the men of practice seemed to be bridged. The progressive political elite listened closely to the expert. Henry Cabot Lodge, Woodrow Wilson, Albert J. Beveridge, Robert M. La Follette, and Theodore Roosevelt nourished themselves on ideas and surrounded themselves with intellectuals. Perhaps no other characteristic set off progressives from their contemporaries more distinctively than their passion for ideas. They sat in their studies and laboriously wrote long analyses and critiques of long-established concepts, principles, and institutions. It seemed uniquely their challenge to rethink all the old ideas that had served America for so long and had grown outworn, rigid, and useless. They responded enthusiastically to the new realism in scholarship, for it seemed to them that it was coming to grips with all that was vital and moving in American life.

Realism in Popular Literature

Well before the turn of the century, a new kind of literature emerged that was arrestingly realistic. The common Victorian novel had been flagrantly escapist, providing cozy tales of proper citizens who struggled high-mindedly with simple problems and went on to happy endings. But now writers turned to expose whatever was shabby, false, and shocking. Mark Twain led the way, culminating a long career as a humorist writer with *Huckleberry Finn* (1885). Twain's Mississippi Valley was a cynical, uproarious, but not happy place. There was too much casual death, meanness, selfishness, and crudity for that. It was a sly, jeering world of little men who puffed themselves up with false stories and scrambled around looking for success.

William Dean Howells, a contemporary of Twain's, was another realistic novelist. A simple man from the West who lived in New York City—in good part realism was a revolt against the eastern genteel tradition in literature—in the mid 1880s he began writing jarringly realistic stories. He chose New York, with its grim poor, as his setting and human suffering as his theme. His novels, such as *A Hazard of New Fortunes* (1890), focused on greedy capitalism, the confused life of great cities, the suffering caused by industrialism, and the collapse of morality under the pressures of modern life.

Other writers, younger than Howells, spoke in harsher tongues. They depicted a world in which natural passions had run riot. For these novelists, violence became the leading theme. Stephen Crane in *Maggie: A Girl of the Streets* (1893) described how city life could destroy a young woman, leading her through seduction and moral collapse to eventual suicide. Jack London's *The Call of the Wild* (1903), *The Sea Wolf* (1904), and *White Fang* (1906) described a crude, Darwinian vision of nature. He glorified physical power and spoke of civilization as just "a veneer over the surface of the soft-shelled animal known as man." Throughout his writings ran an implicit appeal that the social injustice of his day be swept away by violent revolution.

Frank Norris, like Jack London a Californian, came from the journalistic career that spawned so many realistic novelists. In his books *McTeague* (1899), *A Man's Woman* (1900), *The Octopus* (1901), and *The Pit* (1903) he saw his task as combating "false views of life, false characters, false sentiment, false morality, false history, false philosophy, false emotions, false heroism." Sadism, gore, and rampant sexuality stalked through his fiction. In *The Octopus* a great railroad, the Southern Pacific in California, laid waste countless lives and corrupted the entire state.

Theodore Dreiser wrote similar novels. Seeing people as poor fools tossed about by forces they seemed unable to control, Dreiser centered on the theme of power exploiting weakness. The characters of his novels, beginning with *Sister Carrie* (1900), discover that "life was nothing save dark forces moving aimlessly." Powerful men learn that life is a struggle for survival and push their way to the top of some social pyramid, only to spend their lives exploiting those below by any corrupt means they can find. "He had no consciousness of what is currently known as sin," Dreiser wrote of the chief character in *The Titan* (1914). "He never gave a thought to the vast palaver concerning evil which is constantly going on. There were just two faces to the shield of life—strength and weakness."

Realism in Journalism

For some time before the turn of the century, a revolution had been going on in journalism, as well as in fiction. Responding to the huge new audiences of the cities, both the number and the circulation of newspapers rose spectacularly. In 1870 there were 600 daily newspapers; in 1909, more than 2,500. In 1870, 3 million papers were sold each day; in 1909, 24 million. The revenues produced by this huge sale meant that newspapers no longer needed to rely on the financial support of particular political parties. With their own sources of income, they could drop their obsessive concern with politics and turn instead to the kinds of subjects that appealed to their teeming readership. They launched sensationalist

Cliff Dwellers (1913) the painting by the American artist George Wesley Bellows (1882–1925), fulfilled the inherent tendencies of artistic realism by concentrating on a teeming, grimy scene from ordinary tenement life.

Los Angeles County Museum of Art, Los Angeles County Funds

projects to build circulation—campaigns against vice, sniffing or stamping out corruption in city hall, or clean-up-the-city drives.

Most important, newspaper publishers found that readers were absorbed by stories that concentrated on sufferers in the slums, whether they were young girls or unfortunate families. "Sob-sister" journalism released latent humanitarian sentiments that the impersonality of urban life usually kept locked up. Thus, the middle class began to grow interested in the lives of the unfortunate, an interest that was to have major consequences in the Progressive Era. Similar discoveries were made by a new kind of magazine typified by *Munsey's*, *The Saturday Evening Post*, and *McClure's*, which, unlike the genteel and sedate *Harper's* and *Century*, built large circulations on the appeal of stories that pitilessly exposed corruption and malpractice.

These changes in the press created a demand for vivid writing. A new career emerged, that of the reporter or magazine writer. Someone who was brash, moved easily in the jumbled human world of the city, and could write color-

fully could claim a good salary. College graduates who went into the new profession brought the sophistication of the emerging social sciences. Journalism benefited from these new writers' high ideals, particularly their sense of responsibility to the public welfare. And what they found was arresting enough—the "real" story, behind the closed doors or inside the smoke-filled rooms. Cultivating their contacts, they uncovered payoffs, false politicians, and the betrayal of public trusts.

These were the muckrakers, as Theodore Roosevelt dubbed them in a moment of irritation. There was Upton Sinclair exposing the meatpacking industry, Ida Tarbell on Standard Oil, and Lincoln Steffens on civic corruption, followed by a host of other bold writers whose exposés met with spectacular success. Muckraking articles were particularly suitable, in their length and time of preparation, for the magazines. The writers had no great scheme for how American life should be reorganized; they simply concentrated on exposure. Again and again they appealed to the American conscience, insisting that the real

Jack London, most flamboyant of the literary realists, poured harsh Darwinian images of violence and human brutality into novels such as *The Call of the Wild* (1903). His own life was a tragic blend of sudden wealth from his writings and egoistic self-indulgence.

The Bettman Archive

cause for the malodorous goings-on they uncovered lay in the complacency of the American people. They eagerly described all sorts of machines and systems for corruption, but only an aroused citizenry, they insisted, could genuinely revitalize the nation.

Lincoln Steffens, a leading muckraker, wrote of political corruption: "And it's all a moral weakness; a weakness right where we think we are strongest. Oh, we are good—on Sunday, and we are 'fearfully patriotic' on the Fourth of July. But the bribe we pay to the janitor to prefer our interests to the landlord's is the little brother of the bribe passed to the alderman to sell a city street, and the father of the airbrake stock assigned to the president of a railroad to have this life-saving invention adopted on his road. And as for graft, railroad passes, saloon and bawdy-house blackmail, and watered stock, all these belong to the same family. We are . . . a free and sovereign people, we govern ourselves and the government is ours. But that is the point. We are responsible, not our leaders, since we follow them. We *let* them divert our loyalty from the United States to some 'party'; we *let* them boss the party

and turn our municipal democracies into autocracies and our republican nation into a plutocracy. We cheat our government and we let our leaders loot it, and we let them wheedle and bribe our sovereignty from us. True, they pass for us strict laws, but we are content to let them pass also bad laws, giving away public property in exchange, and our good, and often impossible, laws we allow to be used for oppression and blackmail. And what can we say? We break our own laws and rob our own government, the lady at the custom-house, the lyncher with his rope, and the captain of industry with his bribe and rebate. The spirit of graft and lawlessness is the American spirit. . . . (*The Shame of the Cities* [1904])

The detailed studies the muckrakers produced presented the American public with a fresh social drama, one that everyone could recognize, for it was right at their own front door. As Robert Cantwell has observed, the muckrakers "wrote . . . an intimate, anecdotal, behind-the-scenes history of their own times. They traced the intricate relationship of the police, the underworld, the local political bosses, the secret connections between the new corporations . . . and the legislatures and the courts. . . . At the same time, the muckrakers pictured stage settings that everybody recognized but that nobody had written about—oil refineries, slums, the red-light districts, the hotel rooms where political deals were made—the familiar, unadorned, homely stages where the teeming day-to-day dramas of American life were enacted." ("Journalism—the Magazines," in Harold E. Stearns, ed., *America Now* [1938])

This, then, was the new reality. Whatever was behind the scenes, sordid, illegal—this, the muckrakers told the public, was what America was truly like. This, the scholars told the new middle class, was what institutions were actually like. In books, magazines, and newspapers; in university extension courses, testimony before congressional committees, and public lectures; in the gatherings of professional, business, and farm associations—wherever public attention could be captured, the message of social decay was unceasingly sounded. With this image of American life before them, it is understandable that by the opening of the twentieth century the people of the United States were ready, in unprecedented numbers, to vote for men who called themselves progressives.

THE PROGRESSIVE ERA: NEW WAYS OF THINKING

Bibliography

Books that were especially valuable to me in writing this chapter: Henry Steele Commager's *The American Mind: An Interpretation of American Thought and Character Since the 1880s** (1950) put all intellectual historians in his debt when it appeared, and it is still valuable. So too is Morton G. White's *Social Thought in America: The Revolt Against Formalism* (1949), which explores the breaking out into new ways of thinking of the Progressive Era thinkers. William James's brilliance is best explored in his own works, such as *Pragmatism** (1907), *Psychology: The Briefer Course** (1892), and *The Varieties of Religious Experience** (1902). It will be noted that his books are still in print, testifying to their enduring appeal and value. Ralph B. Perry's two-volume biography, *The Thought and Character of William James* (1935) remains fundamental.

Everyone seeking to understand the Progressive mind must begin with Richard Hofstadter's superb study, *The Age of Reform** (1955), a work of major impact among historians that has helped me understand the period from the 1870s to the 1930s. Essential too is his *Anti-Intellectualism in American Life** (1963), which focuses upon the intellectual community with great insight. Hofstadter's *The Progressive Historians: Turner, Parrington, Beard** (1968) takes us deep inside the thinking of three great scholars.

Laurence R. Veysey's *The Emergence of the American University** (1965) gives us a sophisticated understanding of this fundamental transformation in the setting for American intellectual life. Burton J. Bledstein's *The Culture of Professionalism: The Middle Class and the Development of Higher Education in America** (1976) is an absorbing book which breaks quite new ground, and Christopher Jencks and David Riesman's *The Academic Revolution* (1968) is also important. I found John F. Kasson's *Civilizing the Machine: Technology and Republican Values in America, 1776–1900** (1976) essential in grasping the technological influence upon the country's ways of thinking. Once more, Robert Bannister's recent work, *Social Darwinism: Science and Myth in Anglo-American Social Thought* (1979) provided a subtle guide through the complexities of this usually misunderstood phenomenon. On the world of Jane Addams, see Christopher Lasch, *The New Radicalism in America* (1965) and Jill Conway's essay in Robert Jay Lifton, ed., *The Woman in America** (1965). Eric Goldman's *Rendezvous with Destiny: A History of Modern American Reform* (1952) provided us with the distinction between reform and conservative Darwinism. I also found Donald Fleming's sensitive essay "Social Darwinism" in Arthur M. Schlesinger, Jr., and Morton White, eds., *Paths of American Thought* (1963) an acute guide to the mind of young people in the 1890s. In John Higham's *Writing American History* (1970) will be found a brilliant exploration of the national mood in that turning-point decade. Lester Frank Ward is best studied in his own works (a fine collection from those works has been edited by Henry Steele Commager).

Henry May's *The Protestant Churches and Industrial America* (1949) gave us our first insight into this crucial confrontation; for two recent books of great importance, see also Martin E. Marty's *The Righteous Empire: The Protestant Experience in America** (1970) and Cushing Strout's *The New Heavens and New Earth: Political Religion in America** (1974).

Other Works on the Progressive Mind

Sidney Fine, *Laissez-Faire and the General Welfare State: A Study of Conflict in American Thought, 1865–1901* (1956); Allen F. Davis, *Spearheads for Reform: The Social Settlements and the Progressive Movement, 1890–1914* (1967); Richard Hofstadter and Walter P. Metzger, *The Development of Academic Freedom in the United States*, Vol. 2 (1955); Alfred Kazin, *On Native Grounds* (1942); Jay Martin, *Harvest of Change: American Literature, 1865–1914* (1967); David Chalmers, *The Social and Political Ideas of the Muckrakers** (1964); David W. Noble, *The Paradox of Progressive Thought** (1958); Robert H. Bremner, *From the Depths: The Discovery of Poverty in the United States* (1956).

* Available in paperback.

26

TIME LINE

Union; financial panic in Wall Street; Roosevelt becomes more radical, calls for many social reforms

1908   Roosevelt convenes Conservation Congress; William Howard Taft elected twenty-seventh president of the United States

1909   Payne-Aldrich Tariff

1910   Insurgents reduce powers of Speaker of the House; Pinchot fired as chief forester; Mann-Elkins Act gives ICC powers over telephone and telegraph; many antitrust suits begun; Roosevelt gives New Nationalism speech at Osawatomie, Kansas; Woodrow Wilson elected governor of New Jersey

1911   Weeks Act empowers government to acquire forest lands in eastern states

1912   Republican party splits; Roosevelt forms Progressive party; Woodrow Wilson elected twenty-eighth president of the United States; New Mexico and Arizona admitted to the Union

1913   Sixteenth Amendment authorizing income tax ratified; Seventeenth Amendment providing for direct election of United States senators ratified

1917   Flood Control Act inaugurates federal flood-control programs

THE PROGRESSIVE ERA: REPUBLICANS IN CHARGE

This was in good measure Pinchot's achievement. The first trained forester in America, Pinchot caught attention for his work with private and state lands, and from 1896 on he was a major voice in shaping the country's emerging forestry policies. Rapacious lumbering and unrestricted grazing would utterly destroy the dwindling forest lands, he said. They must be put into national forests, governed by a forest service of trained professionals, and protected, above all, from uncontrolled fire. In 1898 he was appointed the first Forester, in the Department of Agriculture.

A gifted publicist, Pinchot was soon spreading his doctrines by speaking, writing, and sending out reams of information on profitable forest management. His long-time friend, President Theodore Roosevelt, made him a close adviser, for the cause of the forests and the waterways was the most dramatic conservationist crusade that TR could seize upon. Enthusiastically proclaiming Pinchot's doctrines, he increased the national forests from 46 million to over 100 million acres, then to 200 million. In 1905 the United States Forest Service was formed, and the forests were finally placed in the hands of a regulatory agency and under a vigorous administrator, Gifford Pinchot.

His controls on stock grazing, lumbering, and waterpower use soon had private interests howling "Pinchotism." They detested this aristocratic, foreign-trained "expert" as a symbol of arbitrary, even un-American governmental meddling. Congress continually launched shots at him; it took TR's prestige to protect him and keep the cause moving. But "Czar Pinchot and His Cossack Rangers" were never forgiven. His passion for administrative efficiency and his role as high priest of conservation (not of "preservation," John Muir's ideal), kept him in the public eye. Stockmen, lumbermen, and miners hungered to destroy his alleged plan of a federal empire controlling all of the West. After William Howard Taft became president, Pinchot's enemies seemed to gain the upper hand, and the die was cast. In January 1910, in the midst of great national controversy, Taft dismissed Pinchot. The Chief Forester was gone from the federal service, but the monument he had created—the vast edifice of the national forests—had taken permanent form as his legacy to the nation.

The Bettmann Archive, Inc.

In 1890 a wealthy young New Englander of French Huguenot (Protestant) ancestry, Gifford Pinchot (pin-*show*), returned from forest-management studies in Europe. He found a United States without a single acre of forest land, public or private, that was under any form of management. At his death in 1946 at the age of eighty-one, hundreds of millions of acres of public land were protected in national forests and their use regulated. Large state forests also existed, and private forests—which hold three fourths of commercially useful timberlands—were moving toward "tree farming." Making forests an ever renewable national resource: such was the national policy.

Overview

The years from 1900 to 1916 saw the new modes of thinking about America sweep into and transform politics, launching that remaking of national life that ever since has been called the Progressive Era. Progressivism, like its predecessor of the previous century, republicanism, was a broad political consciousness characteristic of an entire generation in rebellion against what it conceived of as an older, oppressive, mindless regime and culture. The republicans of the Revolutionary era had a Tory enemy to combat, which they identified with corrupt feudal monarchism. The progressives had a similar enemy. The "Tories" of the post-1900 era (they were often called that) were the advocates of unrestrained capitalist power, elitism in government, and rule by the wealthy and privileged few. Ranged against this "Old Guard" were the progressives of both political parties, for progressivism was not the monopoly of either Republicans or Democrats.

The parallel with the older ideology of republicanism is instructive, and it bears a few words more. Whatever a person's actual political affiliation in the nation's beginnings, whether Federalist or Jeffersonian Republican (and later, in the second party system, Whig or Democratic), everyone said that they were "republicans." However, they disagreed on how best to build a great democratic republic, for they had different images of what a republic should be. The Jeffersonian Republicans and their Democratic descendants called for a *libertarian* and *egalitarian* republic. Individuals would be free to live as they wished (government would be small and inactive), capitalists would be given no assistance in legislation (laissez-faire would rule), and all white peoples would have equal standing, whatever their rank in society, ethnicity, religion, or style of life (cultural pluralism). Though widespread in American life, these attitudes had their strongest base among white Southerners and the non-British ethnic outgroups in the North, their political patron saint being Thomas Jefferson. Until the Civil War, the Democratic form of republicanism was dominant. The Federalists, and their descendants in the Whig and modern (post-1854) Republican parties, called instead for a *morally unified* and firmly *centralized* republic. Governments would guide citizens' moral behavior

(usually at the state level), thus assuring a Protestant and virtuous nation, and a strong and industrious economy would be created by active governmental aid to business enterprise. This, in turn, would open out opportunity, Republicans insisted, for the vigorous and enterprising—America's special concern—to get ahead. The guiding spirits in this tradition were Alexander Hamilton and Charles Sumner. During and after the Civil War, the Republican form of "republicanism" was dominant. Though widespread throughout the country, the Republican tradition had its homeland in New England, and among Yankees wherever they congregated in the northern states.

Democrats were distrustful of centralized power as being too often the tool of the wealthy, the powerful, and the self-righteous Yankee who wished to supervise other people's lives and establish Protestant supremacy. Thus, Democrats called for a decentralized republic of free individuals in which communities such as white Southerners or Irish Catholics would be let alone. Republicans, who admired the "self-made man," and who were oriented toward leadership by the educated and the successful (as Yankees, by comparison with the other ethnic groups in America, tended usually to be), did not look on powerful corporations, which operated across state lines and through countless small jurisdictions, as threatening giants, but as nationalizing agents of order, efficiency, and productivity. The campaign to control drinking, through legislation by state governments, or to establish different morals as to race relations, through the power of the federal government, usually seemed to Republicans a proper use of government, though how eagerly they would press these matters varied according to circumstance. In any event, government was to them a divinely instituted authority in human affairs whose purpose was to create the virtuous and industrious society—and therefore the enduring, healthy republic.

The point to these comments is this: the Republicans and Democrats in the Progressive Era divided between them its ideology of progressivism as their political ancestors had divided up republicanism—moralistic and nationalistic on the one side, libertarian and equalitarian on the other. Progressive Republicans were in power first, not simply because the political events of the 1890s had delivered national political supremacy to their party, but because the whole thrust of progressivism as a way of thinking about the nation seemed to move in their direction. Republicans had always advocated strong government, vigorous centralization, a kind of Yankee attitude that the whole nation was really one community that should be carefully supervised and guided by a common authority. The sense of "team spirit," of working together according to common guideposts, was instinctive in a party that wanted America to be essentially a homogeneous country modeled in the WASP image. That Republican foreign policy breathed this kind of assertive nationalism has already been made clear. In 1901 the progressive sociologist Edward A. Ross had published a book whose title immediately caught on as one of the catch phrases of the era: *Social Control*. The concept of social control by enlightened authority became the common currency of progressive reform in Theodore Roosevelt's era (he extravagantly admired the book).

Eventually, and by accident, the Democrats won the White House in 1912, and it was then their turn. Woodrow Wilson brought in traditional Democratic ideas, especially libertarian concepts opposed to the kind of strong government that Theodore Roosevelt had advocated, but in time Wilson too swung in that direction. The new ideology had struck too deeply; the nation's problems could not be adequately handled with the older ideas. Indeed, during the long years that the Democrats were in the wilderness, watching William McKinley, Theodore Roosevelt, and William Howard Taft run the country (1897–1913), their own ways of thinking, under the leadership and tutelage of William Jennings Bryan, underwent profound change. They created their own variety of progressivism, which expressed their traditional libertarianism and egalitarianism, but in new forms. But of this, there will be more later.

Opinion Mobilizes

The muckrakers of the new journalism did not fictionalize. The United States they so vividly described, though in a great surge of progress, was also gravely ill. It was this realization that seized the nation's consciousness in the 1890s and inspired the Progressive Era. Now the many different reform movements that for years had tried to get the public ear—the eight-hour day, votes for women, trust busting, honest government, controlling railroads—could finally get together and sweep ahead jointly to exciting victories. The Progressive Era responded to a vastly quickening sense that democracy itself, in all its meanings and aspects, was being revitalized; that "the People" (a term in constant use in these years) were seizing control of their government again. The catalyst lay in the massive depression of the 1890s. It created so great a sense of crisis that people who had formerly avoided each other were driven together to work in close partnership.

Furthermore, the new generation of young people were eager for action. In politics, literature, and scholarship they led the urban leagues, staffed the settlement houses, wrote the slashing journalism, and won the elections. Theodore Roosevelt in the White House, Robert M. La Follette in the Senate, Jane Addams at Hull House, Woodrow Wilson taking over the presidency of Princeton, Ida Tarbell exposing Standard Oil, William Randolph Hearst inaugurating yellow journalism, and Louis Brandeis arguing his brilliant briefs before the United States Supreme Court—these were the young leaders, university-trained and hungry for leadership, who led the new era of reform.

The Setting

In the cities, a social revolution seemed imminent. The lower classes in America were on the edge of starvation. Social workers who roamed the slums wrote searing accounts of degradation and disease, which the middle classes feared would spread to them. William McKinley's prosperity meant rising prices; few laborers were organized; and wages lagged far behind the cost of living. Labor–management warfare raged and flared. The Socialist party, led by Eugene V. Debs, was organized in 1901 and grew steadily in vote-gathering power. Factory workers suffered horrifying injuries, but employers refused to install expensive safety equipment or to compensate the maimed. Hours of labor were long, hitting especially hard the millions of children who labored in the mills and industries and the women who worked so many hours each day that their children saw them only late at night.

City and state governments were corrupt. Every kind of special interest paid graft to get charters, franchises, and other privileges. Immigrants flooding the inner city were desperate for work, and they voted for the bosses who gave them jobs—who in turn sold their political power to whomever was willing to pay money to receive a service. Wealthy men flagrantly refused to pay taxes, made it impossible for assessors to examine their holdings, and forced reduced tax rates through compliant city councils. The politics of entire states were taken over by powerful railroad, mining, steel, lumber, and petroleum corporations.

At the same time, there were dramatic happenings in the national economy. The great depression of 1893–96 produced a shambles in the American business community, and large financial houses such as the House of Morgan and Kuhn, Loeb and Company, swept in to restore order. Offering brilliant managerial skills, men such as J. Pierpont Morgan effectively took command of the American industrial system, pushing aside the rough entrepreneurs of the earlier period who had begun great industries but had not managed them well. The masters of the new "finance capitalism" formed centrally directed supercorporations that integrated many formerly competing units. This "organizational revolution" saw in the years from 1897 to 1904 a sudden and startling acceleration in the formation of huge industrial combines, and gave them what amounted to a stranglehold over major areas of the national economy. In 1897 there were only 12 large combinations; by 1904 there were more than 300, of which the formation of the billion-dollar United States Steel Corporation in 1901 was the most striking. Forty percent of American industry was in the hands of such giants.

The merger movement fell off rapidly after 1904, mainly because every kind of enterprise that could profitably be combined had been taken up. But these sensational events, watched closely by the alarmed nation, left a permanent mark on the national mind. If republicanism in the Revolutionary period was primarily a reaction against a swift centralization of imperial government in London, progressivism after 1900 was in large part a kind of spontaneous effort to get control of this new centralization of economic power, or to break it up. A few powerful men, so it seemed, had gotten decisive control of the nation's daily life, and in the process had closed off opportunities, so it seemed, to everyone else. Having

gained vast powers through their control over prices, they could squeeze the purses of millions of Americans and skim off huge fortunes. Some 2 percent of the population held 60 percent of the nation's money. Could these powerful men be trusted to use their great power, to which no one had elected them, rightly and wisely? Few believed so. The very structure of the country seemed gravely imperiled by the existence of gigantic corporate power.

The new middle class—the college-trained lawyers, engineers, economists, corporate executives, bankers—wanted to reach out and get all this national confusion under control. Their inclination was to think in terms of efficiency, management, planning, time-and-motion studies to increase production, and central direction. Confident that their "scientific" methods and new bodies of knowledge equipped them to take on the largest tasks, they launched bold undertakings. Physicians, confronted by slum disease, demanded nothing less than the reorganization of entire cities in order to establish effective programs of public health. Whether it was the creation of centralized systems of city government to combat urban corruption, rationalized control over natural resources to protect the forests, commissions to oversee competitive practices in business, or government regulation of the giant railroads, the predominating urge among such people was to establish national order.

Antipartyism

Out of this came a powerful Republican attack on the political party itself. The "army-style" politics of the previous generation were looked upon as a major source of the corruption that so stained and weakened democratic government. This sentiment was especially strong in the countryside and in small and medium cities, where traditional WASP America still predominated. Because state legislatures were badly tilted so as to overrepresent the rural areas and keep the multi-ethnic cities from growing in (Democratic) power as they grew in (alien) population, in state after state reforms that aimed at breaking the power of party bosses were enacted. All of them were justified in the name of bringing government directly into the hands of "the People." The Australian (secret) ballot was widespread by 1900, so that party

THE PROGRESSIVE ERA: REPUBLICANS IN CHARGE

agents could not keep control over voters. Ballots were printed by public authority rather than by the parties, so that voters could pick and choose between candidates rather than simply turning in the party ticket. The huge number of elective offices was reduced sharply, so that voters could have a reasonable opportunity of knowing the candidates' qualifications, and not be forced simply to rely upon party recommendations. Civil-service reform at the level of local government cut back sharply upon the patronage that parties could control, and upon the funds they could raise from officeholders, who, if they did not contribute, could be fired. To fight ballot-box stuffing, the law required voters to register a considerable period before elections so that their names could be checked off at the polls; strict residence requirements were also established.

The direct-primary system, which some states adopted during the Progressive Era, badly weakened parties. In those states the voters at large now had the power of selecting between possible party nominees. This made conventions, which were controlled by the politicians and provided party organizations with a powerful unifying agency, much less important. Furthermore, primary elections took away the decisive meaning of general elections. Opposition could now arise *within* parties. It was no longer necessary for the populace to rely upon the existence of a strong second party to provide this vital balancing force.

Parties were weakened in other ways. City-wide election of councilmen, instead of by wards, cut down on bloc voting and the scratching of backs within council chambers to get construction contracts, and other plums, for the people in particular legislators' districts. Middle-class candidates tended now to win more often, for they were better known throughout the city. School systems were taken out from under council control and placed under specially elected school boards, which in turn hired professional educators. Relief of the poor was taken over by city and state bureaucracies. Professionally directed street and highway departments and city-owned garbage collection took away from local politicians the staffing of these offices and the granting of lucrative contracts. More and more, the parties found themselves with less and less to do. They functioned primarily to get out the vote, in local elections frequently made nonpartisan.

The popular alarm over the trusts, which grew rapidly in numbers around 1900, is shown in this *Puck* cartoon calling for stronger antitrust action.

The Granger Collection, New York

George Washington Plunkitt, veteran ward boss for the Tammany Hall political machine in New York City, talked of graft in a 1905 interview. "Everybody is talkin' these days about Tammany men growin' rich on graft, but nobody thinks of drawin' the distinction between honest graft and dishonest graft. There's all the difference in the world between the two. Yes, many of our men have grown rich in politics. I have myself. I've made a big fortune out of the game, and I'm gettin' richer every day, but I've not gone in for dishonest graft—blackmailin' gamblers, saloonkeepers, disorderly people, etc.—and neither has any of the men who have made big fortunes in politics.

"There's an honest graft, and I'm an example of how it works. I might sum up the whole thing by sayin': 'I seen my opportunities and I took 'em.'

"Just let me explain by examples. My party's in power in the city, and it's goin' to undertake a lot of public improvements. Well, I'm tipped off, say, that they're going to lay out a new park at a certain place.

"I see my opportunity and I take it. I go to that place and I buy up all the land I can in the neighborhood. Then the board of this or that makes its plan public, and there is a rush to get my land, which nobody cared particular for before.

"Ain't it perfectly honest to charge a good price and make a profit on my investment and foresight? Of course, it is. Well, that's honest graft. . . . The books are always all right. The money in the city treasury is all right. Everything is all right. All they can show is that the Tammany heads of depart-

In order to break down further the power of parties and to make government directly responsible to the people at large, legislatures gave voters many new powers (though the pattern varied widely from state to state). They could remove from office judges and other officials; elect senators directly, thus taking this task out of the hands of party-dominated state legislatures; enact laws directly, by the initiative procedure; and nullify laws passed by legislative bodies, by putting them on the ballot and voting them down in the referendum process. In many states, reformers fought for and won the right for cities to govern themselves (home rule), through their own locally adopted charters and elected governments. Cities could thus take control over their daily life out of the hands of distant state capitals, where corruption was often a heavy influence.

Voter Drop-Off and One-Partyism

The Progressive Era was first and foremost, then, a nationwide campaign to take government out of the hands of politicians and put it directly into the hands of the poeple. Democracy, progressives trumpeted (and for decades afterward historians of the period proclaimed), was being triumphantly revived. The initiative, the referendum, and the recall; the direct primary; the direct election of senators; short, publicly printed ballots, city-wide elections, secret voting, registration of voters: all of these were proud victories won in this broad resuscitation of honest, democratic government.

Ironically, as historians now know, as these reforms took effect and parties withered—and therefore the role of professional politicians and ethnic political machines—so did voter participation. The massive turnouts of the Gilded Age, and the keen and almost continuous attention voters then paid to public issues, faded. In most of the larger industrial states, and especially in the larger cities, presidential voting dropped perhaps a fifth after 1896. About 70 percent of the South's eligible voters voted in the 1880s; by 1900, only

about 40 percent; and by 1920, voting was down to 25 percent. In non-Southern states the comparable figures were 85 percent, 84 percent, and 60 percent. (The South's figures were especially low because of the removal of the vote from black Americans around 1900, a process much advanced by the direct-primary system, which, by being an internal party process, could be flatly limited to white voters.) About two thirds of the national electorate in the late nineteenth century could be termed "core" voters, individuals who turned out regularly; a tenth were peripheral voters, casting ballots occasionally; and a quarter were entirely outside the political system. In the 1920s the comparable figures were a third and a sixth, with half of the electorate being outside the political process altogether.

At the same time, huge one-party regions appeared. The South, of course, was solidly Democratic. The Northeast and Middle West were almost as solidly Republican, and so was much of the West. Some 85 percent of the total electoral-college vote that went to Democratic presidential candidates from 1896 to 1928 was cast in former slave states. In Pennsylvania and other states, conversely, Democratic candidates for governor were almost never elected. The upper Middle West—Wisconsin, Iowa, Minnesota, the Dakotas, Nebraska, and Kansas—made up a kind of Solid North, for these states were overwhelmingly Republican. Since two-party competition had largely died away in large parts of the country, general elections were formalities, and they further reduced voter participation. Indeed, the rise of one-party local dominance may have been the most powerful single influence in this direction. When there is not much contest, and little point in voting, people tend to stay home rather than go to the polls.

Progressivism in the Cities

These changes profoundly transformed the way American communities governed themselves. Breaking the close control of party, and professionalizing government, meant drawing centers of control away from local neighborhoods and placing them in city-wide offices. The folkish, intensely personal politics of the ethnic minorities was now challenged by WASP, middle-class notions of a formal and legal social order relying upon strong, centralized administration. The role of the local ward heeler, who sat in the ethnic kitchen and offered his services, was in many cities challenged by that of the impartial, trained city worker ministering in regulation-bound and standardized ways to individual needs. The depersonalizing of government and its services meant, to many, its dehumanization.

On the other hand, a more honest and efficient government was potentially a much more powerful weapon to use in social reform. Stronger city governments could exert controls over such utilities as gas, water, and street-transportation companies, forcing them to charge just rates. Tax assessments, which had been highly unbalanced in favor of wealthy individuals and grafting corporations, were the subject of massive public campaigns of reform. Nonpartisan tax-equalization commissions were created, and the post of tax assessor made elective. Many cities began building municipally owned water, gas, and electricity plants. New controls over housing extended further the idea that government should involve itself deeply in social conditions. Death rates were slashed dramatically when water supplies were cleaned up, garbage regularly collected, and inoculation programs established. The Progressive Era was especially concerned about the health of the family, and of the nation's children. Now, with these new agencies of government and their planned budgets, audited expenditures, and logical distributions of powers, there could be new schools, free milk, public-health programs, parks, libraries, laws to limit hours of work, industrial-safety measures (and enforcement), and workmen's compensation.

Progressivism in the States

The reform wave rose up from the cities to the states, in part because the cities learned that their problems could not be completely solved until the state governments were cleaned up. Particularly in the Midwest, the South, and the Far West, a chain reaction of progressivism seemed to begin when Robert M. La Follette became governor of Wisconsin in 1901. Under La Follette's determined urgings, Wisconsin enacted a direct-primary law, created a railroad-rate commission that had real powers, curbed lobbying, began to conserve natural resources, established regula-

tions over banks in the state, raised taxes on railroads and corporations, and created state civil service. Wisconsin even went so far as to enact a state-income-tax law.

By this time the state was being called "the laboratory of democracy," and its achievements were closely followed and copied in many other states. Governors were given more power to act on their own, which helped them to centralize authority. Commissions were formed to deal with flood control, banking systems, transportation, and industrial conditions. Corrupt-practices acts were passed to cut down the influence of corporations on elections, and initiative, referendum, recall, and direct-primary arrangements were enacted. The surge for direct popular election of United States senators achieved national victory when the Seventeenth Amendment was ratified in 1913.

As in the cities, the states showed a keen concern for the welfare of children, millions of whom were employed in cotton mills and on farms. After 1901 child-labor laws were enacted, and by 1914 every state save one had established fourteen as the minimum age for legal employment. Beginning in Illinois in 1893, women's hours of work were also limited, in good part to give them more time with their children.

Progressivism in the Nation: Theodore Roosevelt

Reformers had to turn to Washington, D.C., however, to assault the nation's larger problems. The railroad system, the power of great corporations, the banking system, the protective tariff, and the problem of natural resources—all were national in scope. Above all, the reform cause needed a dynamic national spokesman. Progressives found that person in Theodore Roosevelt.

There is no way to summarize Roosevelt's character. A diplomat observed that his temperament was that of a small boy, always excitable, enthusiastic, impulsive. Certainly he loved the outdoors and glorified what he called the strenuous life. He could be an impossible clown, for, as one of his muckraking friends, Lincoln Steffens, remarked, "the gift of the gods to Theodore Roosevelt was joy, joy in life." A cultivated man —he wrote many books of still-valuable history— he was eager and able to learn quickly. As an offi-

The "man of the decade," Theodore Roosevelt, said "I had a great time as president," and in his whirlwind seven and a half years at the post (1901–9) he catapulted the nation into the Progressive Era.

Brown Brothers

cial in New York City, he had been horrified at slum conditions and had begun then to listen to social reformers. After his spectacular exploits in the Spanish-American War he was elected governor of New York (1898–1900), where he battled the utility corporations and forced them to accept important public controls. He never liked people whose only concern was in making money, and he habitually spoke of them in terms of contempt and derision. His door was open to intellectuals, poets, prizefighters, cowboys, artists, and brash young reporters.

Theodore Roosevelt, in short, fitted no one's pattern. But he *was* a Republican, and a devoted one. Why? Partly from his inherent style of life. He was an aristocrat, the Republicans were the party of "the best men in society," and that was that. He grieved over declining birth rates among Anglo-Saxons. A firm nativist in the 1890s, he had supported immigration restriction. Besides, he genuinely detested dishonesty in public office. The Irish Catholic–controlled Tammany machine of New York City, with its timeless corruption, made it impossible for him to even think of being a Democrat.

But there was much more to his party preference than this. For one thing, Republican ideology was not concerned only with elitism and aristocracy. Millions voted Republican because they agreed with its emphasis on hard work, getting ahead, and living moral and upright lives. Republicans insisted that they were the true individualists, providing opportunity through industrialization for ordinary men of talent and enterprise to become wealthy, or at least to be comfortable and independent. Roosevelt gave voice to these ideas. And then, there was patriotism. Theodore Roosevelt was a deep-dyed nationalist, and Republicans were "America First" nationalists. He liked intellectuals, but only if they were not, in his eyes, too critical of America. The novels of Frank Norris made him fume. It was Roosevelt, after all, who in distaste coined the term *muckraker*. He thought big businessmen had gone too far in their selfishness and firmly believed the poor had a right to decent wages and living conditions, but socialists and Populists made him purple with rage.

His political impulses were classically Hamiltonian: he wanted to build a vigorous America by erecting a strong and active central government that would lead the nation confidently. Like so many in his time in Britain and America, he talked constantly of the need to solve the nation's ills by making it "efficient." The way to do this, he firmly believed, was to give real authority, real power, to strong men of good character. Roosevelt never trusted the legislative process. State legislatures and Congress seemed always to come out wrong, largely because, in his view, they were confused, leaderless, and petty. Whenever he could, he directed foreign and domestic affairs in ways that circumvented the need for congressional approval.

Roosevelt, more than anyone else, talked the nation into the idea of creating strong independent commissions, staffed by experts, that would regulate large areas of national life without congressional interference. Again and again Roosevelt sought in strong administration the solution to the nation's ills, in this mirroring what the new middle class was doing at the same time in city and state governments, farm organizations, the professions, and in commerce and industry.

It must be clearly understood, however, that the strong independent commission, though widely praised as democratic and on the side of the people, is not necessarily a democratic idea at all. It represents a great concentration of public power in a few hands, presumably for good purposes, but how that power is actually put to use remains the question. Theodore Roosevelt was not concerned, for he had a simple answer: always make certain that men of good character are appointed to the commissions. Thus did the fundamental elitism of Theodore Roosevelt—his optimistic faith in strong leadership by the best men —create a new institutional pattern for the American government.

Roosevelt's First Administration: The Conservation Crusade

Roosevelt had little room for maneuver when he became president. He inherited a McKinley administration, Congress was dominated by conservatives, and the Republican organization was firmly in orthodox hands. But he was restless. He immediately launched a vigorous foreign policy, as we saw in Chapter 24. Turning to domestic affairs, he took up conservation, and it became one of his favorite causes. The notion of husbanding the nation's resources appealed to him. As he said to the Conservation Congress that he called to meet in Washington in 1908, "Let us remember that the conservation of natural resources . . . is yet but part of another and greater problem . . . the problem of national efficiency, the patriotic duty of insuring the safety and continuance of the Nation."

Conservation, as a problem and a cause, sprang directly out of the condition of the West, where forests had been swept away, creating national alarm. Beginning in Grover Cleveland's administration, millions of acres of forested lands had been withdrawn from public entry; that is, they could not thereafter become private property. At the same time, farmers in such states as California were struggling with flood problems while others in semiarid regions such as Nevada were trying to build irrigation systems.

Conservation was another issue in which centralization was competing with local control, the experts with the common people. It was an elite movement, staffed by scientists, civil servants, engineers, and far-sighted politicians, usually from the eastern states. They spoke of the planned use of resources and deplored uncontrolled exploitation. Gifford Pinchot, trained in French and German forestry practices and inspired by the possibilities of "sustained yield," pursued these goals with almost utopian zeal. But many westerners, anxious for jobs and profits, wanted to see natural resources exploited. Lumbermen, cattle and sheep ranchers, miners, men eager for farm land—all heatedly condemned the foresters, hydraulic engineers, and lawyers who urged the federal government to take control of natural resources.

Also clamoring for public attention was the preservationist movement, whose most dramatic leader was John Muir. Inspired by Henry David Thoreau's famous dictum "In Wildness is the preservation of the World," Muir had spent years living in Yosemite Valley and hiking through the Sierra Nevada, his "range of light." Nature, Muir said, was a "window opening into heaven, a mirror reflecting the Creator." It should be preserved as a restorative to jaded modern humanity. With the help of others he won an important victory in 1890 when Congress created Yosemite National Park specifically to protect a beautiful wilderness. In 1892 he helped to form the Sierra Club in San Francisco to advance the preservation idea.

For a time Muir and Pinchot were eager allies. But their aims were sharply divergent— preservation versus planned use. Muir was appalled by what happened to flowers and grasses when sheep were allowed to graze in the forests; Pinchot thought this a wise use of forested land, as long as it was controlled, for it provided essential food. In the late 1890s Muir and Pinchot contended briefly over what principle would govern administration of the new forest reserves that were being set aside. In 1897, when the Forest Management Act was passed, it was clear that Pinchot had won. Muir was an attractive figure, but he had captured the nation's mind only marginally.

Although Roosevelt loved the wilderness, he firmly agreed with Pinchot. Strong administration, centralized planning, making resources fruitful for society—these appealed to the president. With his encouragement Pinchot transformed the Forest Service from a small office that provided information to lumbermen into a vigorous corps of determined foresters who struggled to protect the forests from destructive overuse. Roosevelt expanded the area of national forests from 46 million acres to more than 150 million, despite clamors of protest from westerners, who got Congress in 1907 to take away the president's authority to establish reserves in six western states. Meanwhile, Roosevelt and Pinchot urged that the national forest idea be extended to the eastern states. This eventually led to passage of the Weeks Act in 1911, which allowed national acquisition of huge tracts of eastern forested land. The Forest Service program was thus expanded to the entire country. In the process, Roosevelt greatly broadened the concept of conservation to apply to mineral resources and power sites. He even had Pinchot withdraw 2,500 hydroelectric sites on the nation's rivers, stating that he intended to place ranger stations at these locations.

Planned Use of Water Resources

Meanwhile, new ideas concerning water use were forming. The Constitution gives the federal government control of all navigable streams, and in a hit-and-miss way there had been occasional efforts to use the army's Corps of Engineers to maintain navigability. In the 1890s it began to be urged that the government treat the rivers as a multiple-use resource—for irrigation, flood control, reclamation, and other purposes. Congress resisted the appeals for a long time, for the implications were enormous and extremely costly. It was one thing to remove snags so steamboats could use rivers; it was another to build levee systems, dams, and all the other apparatus of a system of controlled water use. Flooding was a severe problem, especially in the lower Mississippi and in California's Sacramento Valley. In both areas college-trained landowners joined forces with hydraulic engineers to draw up detailed plans for flood control. After years of intensive lobbying and the marshaling of public support, Congress in 1917 finally made flood control one of the federal government's responsibilities. From that beginning grew the continent-wide program in which the Corps of Engineers plans and builds flood-control works in practically every watercourse in the nation.

Before 1900 many western states experimented extensively with irrigation projects, most of which ended in financial disaster. Congressman Francis G. Newlands of Nevada proposed that the federal government establish a Reclamation Bureau to set up a fund derived from the sale of lands that would be improved by irriga-

tion, which would be used to finance such projects. To keep the program for the small farmer, a limit of 160 acres per family was to be established, greater holdings not being allowed to benefit from federal aid for irrigation. Roosevelt gave the scheme his eager support, and in June 1902 the Newlands Act became law.

The Problem of Business Concentration

From the beginning of his presidency, Roosevelt pondered how he might approach what to him was the country's gravest problem—business concentration. He was not in principle opposed to big corporations. On the contrary, he regarded them as an inevitable and fruitful part of the evolutionary process. They seemed much more efficient, since they could bring large supplies of capital to the development of the nation's resources, coordinate operations, and eliminate "wasteful" competition. Roosevelt always admired powerful men and was disposed to stand back and leave them alone. But the fact remained that some of these men were using their power badly, and the time had come, he believed, for the sovereign—the people's national government—to step in and act.

Accordingly, the president revived the Sherman Anti-Trust Act and began prosecutions. His first target was the Northern Securities Company, a railroad monopoly formed by the financier J. P. Morgan in 1901 that dominated the northwestern part of the United States. In February 1902 Roosevelt startled the business community and delighted the rest of the nation by beginning a suit to have the company dissolved. Within a year he won his case and opened the way for the federal government to undertake a program of breaking up the largest and most damaging combines.

Under Roosevelt more than forty corporations were brought to court, and his successor, William Howard Taft, began suits against an even larger number. In 1911 a major victory was achieved in two cases, concerning Standard Oil and American Tobacco, that had been begun under Roosevelt. This established conclusively that the federal government did in fact possess the constitutional power to break up monopolies where in the judgment of the Supreme Court the company involved had placed an unreasonable restraint on the free flow of trade.

Cultural Progressivism: Educated Motherhood and the Child

Progressivism was far more than an assault on corrupt government and autocratic corporate capitalism. It was also a cultural revolution. For many progressives, indeed, this was the real scene of the action: creating a new way of life in America. The magazines of the period were filled with excited discussions of the New Literature, the New Art, the New Woman, the New School. All of them assaulted the older genteel culture.

Nothing so captured the passions of progressive reformers as the campaign to transform the life of the child, who, in the new order, seemed both the source of a potentially healthy America and peculiarly vulnerable. In the cities, working-class children, especially those of immigrant families, paid a heavy price for industrialization. They not only labored in the mills and factories, they were denied the care of mothers, now drawn off increasingly into work outside the home. They were forced to live in cheerless slum streets, given a form of schooling that seemed of little practical value, and subjected to bad diet, crime, and disease.

In this setting, there grew among progressives a new ideal: educated motherhood. Society, they said, was too complex to rely simply upon the instincts of ordinary women, thrust from village life, perhaps, into the ugly, unwholesome city. Indeed, even middle-class women needed new training in child rearing, since that task had become so sophisticated, given the demanding lives that would be faced when children left home for young adulthood. The situation called, too, for new kinds of schools, new laws concerning children at work, and new local social institutions.

A German idea, the kindergarten, now grew rapidly in national acceptance. In 1880 there were only about 350 of them, but in 1910 there were more than 5,000. By 1920, one tenth of the nation's children attended them. The very young were no longer to be simply left in the streets to play without supervision. Instead, they were to be acculturated to working in groups (cooperation), to the clock and the calendar, to good manners and habits, and to self-discipline. All of this was to be achieved through carefully designed play. If nothing else, the kindergarten would make children better students when they entered first grade—and school administrators were alarmed at the hordes of immigrant children coming to America who did not appear to have these Yankee characteristics. Through the kindergarten progressives also hoped to reach mothers, and to help them plan a better environment in the home. Mothers clubs were organized (which eventually became the Parents and Teachers Association) and hygiene and proper habits were taught. One of the leading educators in the nation, E. P. Cubberley, expressed concisely the broad "Americanizing" objectives of school reform in relation to immigrants when he said: "Our task is to break up their groups or settlements, to assimilate and amalgamate these people as a part of our American race, to implant in their children the Anglo-Saxon conception of righteousness, law and order, and popular government, and to awaken in them reverence for our democratic institutions and for those things in our natural life which we as a people hold to be of abiding worth."

Women's Colleges and the Settlement Houses

College education, increasingly important for women, was modified. (In 1900 17 percent of college graduates were women; by 1920, 40 percent. This did not reflect itself in professional and graduate education, however, where in 1920 women made up only about 8 percent of the enrollment.) Child-study and homemaking courses were introduced, as well as instruction—in such fields as economics, social conditions, and charity work— that looked toward broader social reform. A new generation of women reformers were being trained to concentrate not simply on issues of moral degradation but also on problems created by industrialization, urbanization, and immigration. Moralism alone was not enough. Women needed to be skilled investigators, and socially conscious activists who worked with labor unions and the working class.

These impulses flowered in the settlement-house movement. By 1900 nearly a hundred of them existed in America, modeled on Jane Addams's pioneering Hull House in Chicago. They offered women college graduates the exciting experience of living in the slums, college-dormitory fashion, and participating in a whirl of lectures, discussions, good talk, and hearty fellowship. Testing the theories they were learning in their new social-science courses, they sought to teach the principles of healthy, civilized living to the poor. Unlike their mothers, who visited the poor with a market basket of food and then went back to their homes in the comfortable suburbs, settlement-house workers lived among them, offering classes in child development, hygiene, citizenship, American history, English literature, and arts and crafts, and stressing the importance of physical exercise, regular habits, fresh milk, regular medical examinations for children, and clean homes and streets. Cooperative loan funds were established to teach the values of saving and responsibility. Settlement houses also established direct aids for mothers: kindergartens, supervised playgrounds, medical clinics, legal advice, and information bureaus to aid them in dealing with city offices. They also lobbied hard for laws limiting the hours of labor for children and for women, and laws establishing compulsory attendance in school.

The Progressive School

The school itself, however, had to be revolutionized if it would meet the needs of children in the new age. The philosopher John Dewey inspired a generation of innovation in the public schools with his theories of progressive education. The school should not simply teach literacy and numbers; it should prepare the child for life. It should teach nutrition, look after the child's health, and provide carefully designed exercise. The school, indeed, became a small settlement house in each neighborhood, offering evening classes for mothers and providing manual training and work-place skills to its students. Dewey argued against merely academic book-training, which he said helped only the elite. Rather, the progressive school must democratize schooling, and thus society itself, by making the program of study more practical.

This called for making the school into a small functioning democracy, with children learning all the arts of democratic self-government, speechmaking, and voting. There should be a school newspaper and regular elections. In classwork the emphasis should be on "learning by doing." Manual-arts training would aim at teaching skills, good character, imaginative planning, and creative accomplishment. Fathers were employed at distant factories now, and could not teach their children the ancient arts of working with hand tools; the school had to fill that gap.

The playground was to foster the idea that exercise was important to a growing child, and to provide an alternative to the moral dangers of the street.

Growing directly out of the new concern for educated womanhood and the child was the campaign for "women's pensions": monthly payments for women who were the sole support of their children, so that instead of working in a factory they could remain in the home to rear them properly. The vast public-health movements of these years to clean up the water, provide proper sewage, and insure healthful food (such as by wrapping bread and inspecting establishments selling food) drew much of their strength from the concern with establishing the healthy neighborhood and healthy families. Theodore Roosevelt, like many progressive Republicans, was keenly interested in the fate of the American family, and gave his strong support to all such programs.

Cultural Progressivism: Prohibition

Another great campaign for cultural reform in the Progressive Era was a renewed assault upon alcohol and the saloon, for generations pointed to by thousands of Americans as the root cause of social corruption and human misery. By 1900, one out of four Americans lived in saloonless territory. The prohibition crusade, which had seemed for a considerable period at a standstill, took fire again in the national climate of reform that ensued in the Progressive Era.

As usual, the greatest efforts took place first in Yankee America: in New England and in the Yankee-settled regions of New York State and the Middle West. The progressive spirit, however, was strongly invading the Southern states (though, ironically, these were the years when black Southerners were thrust deepest into Jim Crow segregation, as we will see in the next chapter). Southern progressivism was strongly flavored by evangelical religious zeal. Baptists and other large Protestant churches in the South had always been opposed to drink, but their antigovernment bias had led them to insist that prohibition was to be achieved by voluntary agencies: namely, by church congregations themselves disciplining their members. In the Progressive Era, however, when the idea of using government for great social reforms seized people's minds, the prohibition movement in the South began swiftly to make use of state legislation to end the liquor trade, primarily by allowing counties to vote themselves dry. By 1907, two thirds of the counties in the South had done so. "Local option," now the new national cry, grew wider outside the South as well. Half a dozen years into the twentieth century, thirty-five million Americans (almost half the national population) lived in saloonless territory.

The crusade became an assault by rural and small-town WASPs against the life style of alien immigrants in the cities. The ethnic minorities and the liquor industry resisted angrily, but the disproportionate representation held by rural areas in state legislatures put them in a strong position to pass antiliquor legislation. Thus, whereas prohibition in the solid Democratic South was necessarily a Democratic measure, in the rest of the nation it was firmly Republican. Prohibitionism made the Irish and Germans and other ethnic minorities in cities like Chicago and New York implacably hostile to good-government people—the "goo-goos," as their enemies called them. Progressive Republicans in Congress were also strong temperance advocates.

Experts Take Over Treatment of Social Deviants

The Progressive Era saw sweeping changes in another ancient field of social policy: the treatment of deviants—that is, the criminal, the delinquent, and the mentally ill. This movement had a long history in America. In the 1820s, one of the milestone shifts in national policy had been to begin building penitentiaries for criminals, asylums for the insane, almshouses for the poor, orphanages for the homeless child, and reformatories for delinquents. Earlier, in colonial times, the poor, insane, or homeless young had been cared for either at home or in the neighborhood; whereas lawbreakers had been whipped, put in stocks, or hung. In the age of Andrew Jackson, however, growing cities and industrialization produced far greater numbers of the deviant and the homeless than these localistic methods could handle, and Americans turned to the use of institutions for this purpose. They were to be artificial, carefully supervised, walled-off communities. Believing strongly that social deviance was caused by poverty, ignorance, and harmful social influences—

drink and immorality—Jacksonians optimistically held that in such closely directed settings criminals could be schooled, purged of their vices, given useful skills, and therefore, reformed.

However, by the opening of the twentieth century the prisons, insane asylums, and other such institutions had degenerated shockingly. Those who administered them were overwhelmed by numbers; the problem of keeping order and discipline led to savage punishments; and corruption was everywhere. Horror stories filled newspapers and legislative hearings in the late 1800s. Progressives responded characteristically. Believing in the power of trained intelligence and expertise, they argued that skilled professionals should be given authority to tailor punishments and treatment to each individual case. No more fixed sentences; no more treatment of prisoners and the mentally ill en masse; and far less reliance simply upon institutions as places of incarceration.

Progressives developed the concepts of probation (freedom to stay in the community, rather than go to prison, but under the close supervision of a court-appointed probation officer), parole (an early release from prison in response to evidence of reform in the prisoner's attitudes and habits, again followed by probation officer supervision), and the indeterminate sentence (which allowed for such paroles after individual examination by boards of experts). For young people, the Progressive Era developed the juvenile court, the judge in such courts being given wide latitude to fit treatment or punishment to the individual case, and acting in a parental role. For the mentally disturbed, outpatient clinics were established to which such people were required to come for regular treatment by skilled professionals.

In each case, the new social science principle of careful investigation to gain command of the facts in each person's case was to be applied. Deviants, it was insisted, were not of a single type, and no single program of en masse treatment or reform could help them. Commitment to large institutions with standardized programs of training and supervision was wrong. The world, as William James had said, was pluralistic. Each individual was different and individualization of treatment was the only pragmatic form of humanitarianism. At the same time, the "expert" was to be in charge, with wide authority. This meant greatly expanding the power of the state and its officials to do what was felt to be necessary.

These principles, established in the Progressive Era, would shape American policy toward social deviance until well into the 1960s. Not until then did it become clear that, once more, major reforms believed confidently to be the solution to the problem were not working well. In the age of John Kennedy and Lyndon Johnson, a new time of questioning would arise, and fundamental changes would be put in motion.

Roosevelt's Second Administration: The Vigorous Progressive

In 1904 Roosevelt swept to a second-term victory, overwhelming Alton B. Parker, a conservative lawyer nominated by the Democrats. The president was now free to become a progressive leader in his own right.

He immediately zeroed in on national control of the railroads. The time had come, he said in his railroad message to Congress in December 1905, "to assert the sovereignty of the National Government by affirmative action." He demanded unprecedented powers for the Interstate Commerce Commission, which had become practically useless because of adverse court decisions. The ICC should be allowed, he said, to establish fair rates when shippers complained and to inspect the railroad's books in doing so in order to be certain what rates the railroad actually needed to stay profitable. A storm of abuse erupted, for Roosevelt was challenging two of private business's most sacred rights—to set its own prices and to keep its books secret. But he got his law. The Hepburn Act of 1906 made what for many years had been only a possibility become a reality. Railroad-rate making was no longer left to private enterprise but brought under the oversight of public experts and a powerful independent commission.

For many years scientists in the Department of Agriculture had urged Congress to pass laws cleaning up the food and meat-packing industry and forbidding the sale of fraudulent and poisonous drugs. The conditions of meat packing were revolting to all who inspected them. From state food and dairy departments came similar pleas, as well as from women's clubs and young doctors of the American Medical Association.

Many food and drug businessmen wanted regulation too—as long as it was in a form they approved. Large companies were gravely endangered by the operations of fly-by-night drug houses and malodorous packing houses that gave the industry a bad name. Foreign markets for American meats were being severely reduced as a result of European complaints. In 1906 Upton Sinclair's *The Jungle* laid out in disgusting detail the filthy meat-packing conditions in Chicago. This put the fat in the fire, and the congressmen who for years had blocked legislation as an infringement on private freedoms began to fall silent. Roosevelt, shocked by Sinclair's book, sent off his own investigators, while writing to Sinclair, "I agree with you that energetic, and, as I believe, in the long run radical, action must be taken to do away with the effects of arrogant and selfish greed on the part of the capitalist."

The big companies now swung into action, working assiduously with congressional committees to get regulation made palatable. A federal stamp of purity on their meats would restore their markets, so they approved the establishment of a corps of federal inspectors. However, they refused to provide the costs of such a service, thus ensuring that a cost-paring Congress would always limit its scope. At the same time, fines against drug manufacturers selling fraudulent merchandise were set ridiculously low, reaching only $300. When millions could be made selling a ballyhooed product, the fine simply became a license. Genuine regulation of useless and often harmful substances in drugs had to wait for many years—and has not yet been fully achieved.

Roosevelt and Labor

Roosevelt had a complicated relationship with the labor movement. Fundamentally, he was on the side of the employer, who was, after all, the man on the top. But as a compassionate person, the president had long been disturbed by the conditions in which workers, especially women and children, labored. Furthermore, he looked on big unions as he did on big business—as a natural and valuable evolutionary growth that brought order and efficiency to the system. Workers had economic interests: they should be allowed to organize to achieve them.

In 1902 Roosevelt intervened spectacularly in a crucial labor–management dispute. The coal miners in Pennsylvania's anthracite region, under the leadership of the United Mine Workers and its chieftain, John Mitchell, a careful and cautious tactician, went on strike. The miners' hours were long, a rising cost of living pressed them cruelly, and their work was extremely dangerous. But the owners, primarily controllers of the six railroads that crossed the region, arrogantly refused even to talk to the workers.

During the 1902 anthracite coal strike, the leader of the coal operators, George F. Baer of the Reading Railway, wrote a classic letter expressing a capitalist's view of his prerogatives: "I do not know who you are [he wrote to a Mr. Clark]. I see that you are a religious man; but you are evidently biased in favor of the right of the working man to control a business in which he has no other interest than to secure fair wages for the work he does.

"I beg of you not to be discouraged. The rights and interests of the laboring man will be protected and cared for—not by the labor agitators, but by the Christian men to whom God in His infinite wisdom has given the control of the property interests of the country, and upon the successful Management of which so much depends.

"Do not be discouraged. Pray earnestly that right may triumph, always remembering that the Lord God Omnipotent still reigns, and that His reign is one of law and order, and not of violence and crime." (quoted in Mark Sullivan, *Our Times: The United States, 1900–1925* [1927])

As the months passed, Roosevelt fumed. Always frightened of the possibility of social revolution, he regarded the coal operators as the kind of businessmen who, by their selfishness, would destroy the country. Panic buying pushed the cost of coal sky-high; in the fall of 1902 schools began closing for lack of fuel. Finally, in October the president, who lacked any legal powers whatever to intervene in the strike, succeeded in bringing both the operators and the union men to the White House for a conference. The operators protested against being made to "deal with outlaws" and elaborately pretended that John Mitchell was not even present. A public commission of investigation was finally agreed to, production began again, and eventually the miners were given approximately a 10-percent increase in pay. Organized labor looked in gratitude to the president, for he was the first chief executive ever to have taken their side.

Even so, labor regarded "marvelous Teddy" warily. Sometimes they gave him warm and enthusiastic support as their first friend in the White House. But they never felt wholly comfortable with him, for his attitudes were still those of an upper-class patrician. Besides, he was a Republican, and in these tumultuous years of constant labor–management disputes, it seemed to workers that the employer was always a Republican. Roosevelt might warm their hearts, but when it came to elections they often turned to the Democrats. Whatever Roosevelt did, the core of the labor movement was still composed of ethnic minorities, and most of them found the Republicans still too much the party of nativism and Anglo-Saxon Protestantism for them to support it.

Bryan and Taft

In 1908 the Democrats turned for the third time to William Jennings Bryan as their presidential nominee, and he went about the country crying out, not illogically, that he was the legitimate heir to the reforming Theodore Roosevelt. In fact, since the 1900 presidential election Bryan had gone far beyond the free-silver issue. In 1905 he had traveled around the world, visiting the deeply religious and socialist Russian writer Leo Tolstoy. He returned to an enormous welcome in New York City and began running hard for a third presidential nomination. Thomas Jefferson, Bryan's idol, had always attacked wealth as inherently exploitive, and Bryan's revived crusade focused on the power of capital. The Populist tradition had also developed a sweeping ideological attack on laissez-faire capitalism, calling for extensive controls over corporations and even for public ownership, and he drew freely upon that inspiration as well as upon what he had learned in Europe.

Bryan, in short, was calling for "positive liberty." He advocated public ownership of utilities ("gas and water socialism," as the Fabian socialists in Britain called it) and an end to speculation in the stock market. He would abolish child labor, enact stringent pure-food-and-drug laws, and transform the money system so that currency could be issued on the basis of productive assets, not simply on the possession of gold stocks in the Treasury's vaults. Openly supporting Theodore Roosevelt, Bryan began to receive ever more support from a growing progressive faction within the Democratic party that was ready to leave behind the party's traditional distrust of strong government. Reaching out to Samuel Gompers's AFL and to the struggling labor movement, Bryan in 1908 was the first major American political figure to demand that the courts not be allowed to issue injunctions (as they freely did) against workers' strikes.

Bryan's progressivism steadily broadened: he would democratize the rules of the House of Representatives, lower the tariff, and establish guarantees of private deposits in banks to protect workers' savings. He advocated controls upon the trusts, the direct election of senators to remove them from domination by corporations, and even the prohibition of corporations from contributing to campaign funds. Direct primaries and the initiative and referendum also received strong Bryan support.

Nonetheless, Theodore Roosevelt had chosen William Howard Taft as his successor, and the Northeast, Middle West, and West accepted that judgment. The predominant attitude toward Bryan outside the South must be borne in mind. Bryan was scorned, looked down upon, regarded by the respectable as both a comic and a contemptuous figure. To them he was simply a ranting rural radical. He might as well have been, in British terms, a ranting Irish Catholic radical calling for an end to English rule over that island, or, in czarist Russian terms, a ranting Jewish radical calling for the overthrow of oppressive anti-Semitic autocracy. Bryan, in short, was an outsider, he was a member of a despised minority, and he was the *Southern* candidate (he rarely won any non-Southern states in his three presidential campaigns), and in these years that was damning. The triumphant Republican North and West ran the country with unchallenged supremacy. "The South [is] as effectually cut off from all influence in the management of the United States Government as it would be if it was a British Crown colony," said a Georgia senator. In addition, Bryan's Christian evangelism, his continual preaching of the message of love and pacifism, made him ridiculed in sophisticated circles. He was regarded as an unlearned man, an ignorant man, a *mouth*. And Bryan reciprocated these feelings. For many years he had felt a burning grievance against the northeastern states, and not simply against its powerful corporations and banking establishments. He knew that Yankees regarded him with amused disdain, and in his campaigning he simply ignored those parts of the nation outside the West and the South, save for the urban working classes in the North, themselves politically weakened. He spoke, he believed firmly, for the underdog in American life.

William Howard Taft: The Unhappy President

William Howard Taft of Ohio—as was traditional, the Republicans had chosen their presidential candidate once more from the Middle West; TR had got in by accident—had been a federal judge, governor of the Philippines (1901–4), and for four years TR's secretary of war. A thoughtful man of progressive conservative opinions, he had always supported Roosevelt's policies.

Unfortunately, he was ill suited to the presidency. Huge and slow-moving, he could hardly provide a suitable successor to the lively Roosevelt. Furthermore, when on his own he proved deeply loyal to the belief that the Establishment should rule. Reformers set his teeth on edge, and he was soon locked in hostile combat with the "insurgents" in his party. Drawn from the "Solid North"—the upper Middle West—these Republican senators and congressmen loved Roosevelt, despised the "interests," and wanted to keep the reform movement sweeping ahead. In 1909 they set off a terrific fight in the Senate to win reductions in the Payne-Aldrich tariff bill then being considered. When they failed, they regarded Taft as responsible, for he had indeed given the protectionists his tacit support even though their bill was exposed as a blatant giveaway to eastern industrial combines.

In conservation, Taft appeared to swing toward the side of those crying out, "Throw open the public domain!" He appointed Richard A. Ballinger, nationally known as a fighter against conservation, as his secretary of the interior, and sided with him when Gifford Pinchot leveled charges—later shown to be untrue—that Ballinger was corruptly linked to certain coal-field owners. At this the angry Taft fired Pinchot, an act that convinced thousands that "the interests" were back in control, and that infuriated Theodore Roosevelt.

Taft actually had reform tendencies of his own. Ballinger's goal had been for the national government to cede its public lands to the states, but Taft refused. He even considerably expanded forest reserves. At his urging, in 1910 the Mann-Elkins Act was passed. It strengthened the ICC by giving it regulatory powers over telephone and telegraph companies and allowing it to revise railroad rates without waiting for complaints, after which it would be up to the railroad company to prove that the new rate was inequitable. Taft also played a role in one of the most fateful changes ever made in the structure of American institutions—the income-tax amendment, which in the long run was almost by itself to transform the whole nature of government in the United States. (It became the Sixteenth Amendment when ratified in 1913.) Taft was also a determined trust-buster. In 1910 his administration began suits that eventually totaled sixty-five in number, as against forty-four under Roosevelt.

Taft and the Progressives

Taft, however, became convinced that the progressive insurgents in his party were endangering the country. He and his Old Guard followers firmly believed that the people at large could not be relied upon to provide effective government. When progressives called for democratizing government, he recoiled. The initiative, referendum, and recall seemed to conservative Republicans dangerously socialistic. They feared such reforms would deliver social policy into the hands of those jealous of the rich. Especially after progressives began calling for the right of recalling judicial decisions (overturning them in referendum ballots by the people at large), conservative Republicans were horrified. Taft reverenced the law (he was to serve as Chief Justice of the United States from 1921 to 1930), and was appalled at such ideas. He publicly said that they would destroy freedom and order, making everything subject to the fitful gusts of public opinion.

In August 1910, in Osawatomie, Kansas, Theodore Roosevelt dramatically reentered national politics by calling for a new social order in America based upon true social justice. It would be achieved by a "New Nationalism," which would see a much bigger and more powerful national government battling with the interests and making of the presidency the "steward of the public welfare." Soon thereafter, angered at Taft, he let politicians know that if the people wanted

him as president again, he would run. Taft, meanwhile, had already decided that he had to be the champion of a true and conservative American philosophy of government, that Roosevelt's wild ideas—especially his support for the recall of judges and judicial decisions—gravely threatened the health and stability of the nation.

Taft and Roosevelt now went about the country shouting angry words about each other to wildly partisan audiences. Wherever there was a direct-primary system Roosevelt won, for he was popular with the rank and file in progressive Republican states; wherever the convention system existed Taft swept the delegates. When the Republicans gathered at their national convention in Chicago in June 1912, a huge crowd was on the scene, excited by the knowledge that over 250 seats in the convention were being contested for by rival delegations, each claiming the other was illegally chosen. Whoever got these contested seats would get the nomination.

Roosevelt debarked from his train into a roaring crowd, teeth agleam, wearing an enormous sombrero and a Rough Rider uniform. He was practically crushed, but he bellowed to reporters "I feel like a bull moose!" Wherever he went, shouting his cries for social justice, he was surrounded by an almost religious hysteria. His followers frequently burst out singing the hymn "Onward, Christian Soldiers." Indeed, the mounting reform campaign was saturated with powerful religious imagery. *Uplift, redemption, conversion, battles for the Lord, forces of evil, crusades*—these were the sonorous, powerful trumpet calls that stirred progressive Republican audiences in the hinterland. A progressive political campaign was like a religious revival, tongues of flame lighting prairie fires of political evangelism. It was Yankee republicanism come alive again: religious, moralistic, puritanical, and determined to cleanse the nation of rule by an evil, corrupt oligarchy. In the 1850s it was the slaveholding oligarchy; now it was corporate power.

In Chicago progressive arguments were expressed in biblical quotations. The *Chicago Tribune*, which backed Roosevelt, put a banner headline on the issue that was read while the Republican National Committee pondered which delegations to seat: "THOU SHALT NOT STEAL." Roosevelt responded with a roaring speech to a packed crowd on the night preceding the opening of the convention. His crusade, he said, was directed against the "leadership of men whose souls are seared and whose eyes are blinded, men of cold heart and narrow mind, who believe we can find safety in dull timidity and dull inaction. . . . We fight in honorable fashion," he concluded in a dramatic climax, "for the good of mankind; fearless of the future, unheeding of our individual fates, with unflinching hearts and undimmed eyes; we stand at Armageddon, and we battle for the Lord!"

Roosevelt was beaten before he began. The National Committee, appointed four years before by Taft, was firmly in the president's hands. The committee seated Taft delegates, and Taft's supporters took firm control of the convention. Roosevelt delegates finally stopped voting. While Taft was being nominated, they pleaded with Roosevelt to form a new political party. Now at white heat, Roosevelt agreed, and in August 1912 the Progressive Party (nicknamed the Bull Moose party) met to nominate Theodore Roosevelt for the presidency.

The Democrats were delighted. With the Republicans irretrievably shattered, their votes in the presidential election would be divided in two, and a Democrat would finally have a good chance to win. Democratic progressives determined to nominate one of their own. They concluded that the best such figure was Woodrow Wilson, the former president of Princeton University who was then compiling a stunning record of reform as progressive Democratic governor of New Jersey. When the delegates gathered in Baltimore, the progressive Democrats won the nomination for Wilson.

The Surging Democrats

The Democrats were, in fact, beginning a renewed national surge of political strength. The labor movement was still relatively small, for it had only 5.5 percent of the industrial labor force unionized in 1910 and only 15 to 20 percent of the skilled, but it was swinging strongly Democratic and helping to win key elections. Furthermore, the "new-stock" immigrants from eastern and southern Europe who had been arriving in the country by the millions since 1890 were turning to their traditional friends, the Democrats. Cleveland, with its large immigrant population of industrial workers, sent only Democrats to the state senate between 1911 and 1921, and, with rare exceptions, only Democrats to the national Con-

gress. In New York City, new-stock voters helped the Democrats win all thirty-five seats that city had in the state assembly, and all of its twelve senate positions as well. In Boston, where Democrats had formerly won half of the fifty legislators from that city who sat in the state legislature, after 1909 they began winning four fifths of them, for they were now reaping heavy Italian and Jewish as well as Irish votes.

A powerful new urban liberalism with a profoundly egalitarian influence emerged in this setting. It concentrated upon enacting major programs of social—not simply political—reform in order to equalize the conditions of life in America. In the state of New York in the years 1911–13, a strong ethnic coalition led by the Irishman Alfred E. Smith and the German Robert Wagner enacted the most sweeping such program in American history: regulating inhuman conditions of labor; protecting women and children in factories; limiting hours of labor; creating new state agencies to enforce laws concerning industrial safety; insuring one day's rest in seven; establishing minimum wages on the state canals; and creating pension funds for widows and children and for retired public employees. In Ohio, Illinois, Massachusetts, and other industrial states with large ethnic populations, similar programs were enacted.

After Taft and Roosevelt had lost the 1912 presidential campaign to Wilson, during which they had bitterly assailed each other as the nominees, respectively, of the Republican and Progressive parties, a cartoonist depicted them as saying exhaustedly to each other, "Cheer up! I might have won."

Library of Congress

THE PROGRESSIVE ERA: REPUBLICANS IN CHARGE

The progressive movement, in short, was becoming Democratic, and it was taking on a strong egalitarian cast. It had never succeeded in capturing the heart of the Republican party. Though progressive Republicans had had considerable success at the state level, especially in the upper Middle West and in California, at the national level the party remained firmly conservative. Progressive Republicans had fought against the Payne-Aldrich tariff and lost; had defended Pinchot, and he was dismissed; had tried to get TR nominated in 1912 as a Republican, and lost that battle too. For years William Jennings Bryan had been preaching advanced progressivism, insisting that the Democrats were TR's real political heirs; the solid Democratic South was burning with anger at northern financial and corporate interests; and now Democrats in many middle western and northeastern states began capturing governor's mansions. In the 1920s, the shift toward the Democrats that was now beginning in northern cities would become a landslide—and a cru-

cial question would have to be fought out within their party: were they a Southern, rural, Protestant party, or one that was Northern, urban, and non-WASP immigrant?

The Election of 1912

The Progressive Party labored manfully in the 1912 election, but Roosevelt himself had practically no hopes. "I would have had a sporting chance," he said, "if the Democrats had put up a reactionary candidate." He could have pulled out and perhaps helped Taft to win, but his passion to destroy Taft was too overwhelming. He jibed at Wilson's distaste for big government (to be explored in the next chapter), insisting, "We propose to use the whole power of the government to protect all those who, under Mr. Wilson's laissez-faire system, are trodden down in the ferocious, scrambling rush of an unregulated and purely individualistic industrialism." Wilson, however,

THE ELECTION OF 1912

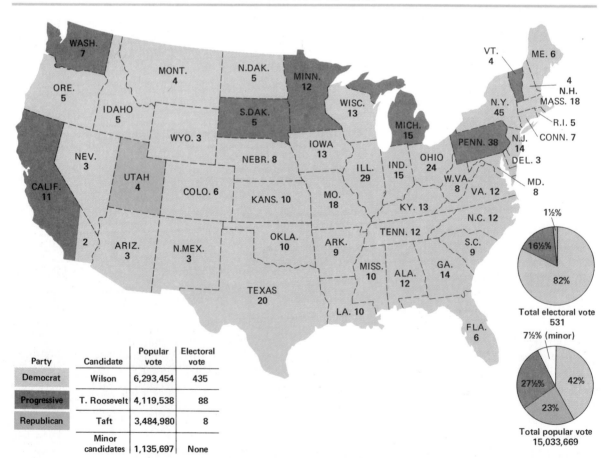

Party	Candidate	Popular vote	Electoral vote
Democrat	Wilson	6,293,454	435
Progressive	T. Roosevelt	4,119,538	88
Republican	Taft	3,484,980	8
	Minor candidates	1,135,697	None

Total electoral vote 531

1½%
16½%
82%

Total popular vote 15,033,669

7½% (minor)
42%
23%
27½%

won in an electoral landslide with 435 votes. He did not have a popular majority behind him—he secured 6.3 million votes to Roosevelt's 4.1 million and Taft's 3.5 million—but he had a large plurality. In the same balloting almost a million votes went to Eugene V. Debs, the Socialist candidate. By any reckoning, the nation wanted reform.

Bibliography

Books that were especially valuable to me in writing this chapter: Otis L. Graham, Jr.'s *The Great Campaigns: Reform and War in America, 1900–1928* (1971), a sophisticated analysis that brilliantly interweaves ideas and institutional realities; Walter Dean Burnham's *Critical Elections and the Mainsprings of American Politics* (1970), which is essential on the changed political system after 1900; and John D. Buenker's *Urban Liberalism and Progressive Reform* (1973), which has made us understand how powerful was the role of the new stock ethnic voters. The interpretation I have given here of the nature of Progressivism may be read in a broader setting, with references to key historical works, in Robert Kelley, "Ideology and Political Culture from Jefferson to Nixon," *The American Historical Review*, 82 (June 1977), 531–62. James L. Holt's *Congressional Insurgents and the Party System, 1909–1916* (1967) skillfully traces the Yankee impulse as it emanated from its Middle Western precincts, and much the same spirit appears in David P. Thelen's *The New Citizenship: Origins of Progressivism in Wisconsin, 1885–1900* (1972). Norman M. Wilensky, *Conservatives in the Progressive Era: The Taft Republicans of 1912* (1965) seems to me an exceptionally valuable exploration of the conservative Republican mind. There is a growing literature on prohibitionism in this period, as in James H. Timberlake's *Prohibition and the Progressive Movement 1900–1920* (1963).

For progressivism's nationalistic mode, see Robert H. Wiebe, *The Search for Order, 1877–1920** (1967); Samuel Haber, *Efficiency and Uplift: Scientific Management in the Progressive Era** (1964); and Samuel P. Hays, *Conservation and the Gospel of Efficiency: The Progressive Conservation Movement, 1890–1920* (1959). The literature on Theodore Roosevelt makes abundantly clear his Hamiltonianism and nationalist Progressivism in domestic and foreign affairs. Paolo E. Coletta's several volumes on William Jennings Bryan—especially volume 2, *William Jennings Bryan: Progressive Politician and Moral Statesman, 1909–1915* (1969)—as well as Merrill Peterson's comments in his *The Jefferson Image in the American Mind** (1960) reveal how powerfully Bryan revived Jeffersonian ideology and swung his party toward social reform. J. Joseph Huthmacher's *Senator Robert F. Wagner and the Rise of Urban Liberalism* (1968) is essential on the great German-American reformer, and the shifts taking place at the state level, in Democratic ideology and practice, after 1910. A ground-breaking work, *History of Public Works in the United States 1776–1976*, edited by Ellis L. Armstrong, Michael C. Robinson, and Suellen M. Hoy (1976) provides us a broad and deep understanding of the history not only of flood control, but of many other similar major programs in civil engineering: irrigation, light and power, highways, railroads, waterways, and the like. On the South in the Progressive Era, C. Vann Woodward's *Origins of the New South, 1877–1913* (1951) remains a brilliant, essential study, and it is being followed by a number of more recent works, such as Sheldon Hackney's *Populism to Progressivism in Alabama* (1969).

On organized labor and Progressivism, see Irwin Yellowitz, *Labor and the Progressive Movement in New York State, 1897–1916* (1965) and Melbyn Dubofsky, *When Workers Organize: New York City in the Progressive Era* (1968). A close look at a major ethnic group moving toward the social welfare ideology is provided in Philip Gleason, *The Conservative Reformers: German-American Catholics and the Social Order* (1968).

David J. Rothman and Sheila M. Rothman form a brilliant husband-and-wife team in social and women's history, providing powerful works in (the former's) *The Discovery of the Asylum: Social Order and Disorder in the New Republic** (1971) and *Conscience and Convenience: The Asylum and its Alternatives in Progressive America** (1980), and (the latter's) *Woman's Proper Place: A History of Changing Ideals and Practices, 1870 to the Present* (1978). Paula S. Fass's *The Damned and the Beautiful: American Youth in the 1920's** (1977) has valuable preliminary information on the Progressive Era.

* Available in paperback.

27

1906	President Roosevelt discharges black troops, charging complicity in Brownsville, Texas riots; Atlanta race riot
1910	National Association for the Advancement of Colored People formed; state of Washington enfranchises women
1912	Woodrow Wilson elected twenty-eighth president of the United States
1913	Underwood Tariff; Federal Reserve System created; Wilson greatly broadens segregation in civil service
1914	Louis D. Brandeis, *Other People's Money;* Federal Trade Commission created; Clayton Anti-Trust Act
1915	Supreme Court rules Oklahoma's "grandfather clause" unconstitutional
1916	Wilson turns in New Nationalist directions; Brandeis appointed to Supreme Court; child-labor legislation passed (later ruled unconstitutional); Tariff Commission created; Adamson Act
1917	Jeanette Rankin becomes first congresswoman
1920	Nineteenth Amendment granting women's suffrage ratified

THE PROGRESSIVE ERA: DEMOCRATS IN CHARGE

New York Public Library

In the same weeks that Woodrow Wilson was being inaugurated as president, in Rome a seventy-five-year-old man died. A towering international figure, it was his life work that the new administration set out to dismantle. As Gifford Pinchot had created the national forests, so J. Pierpont Morgan had done more than any other single person to create the complex and powerful financial network centered in New York City's Wall Street.

Morgan: for generations, it had been a name to conjure with in world finance. The Morgans were Connecticut Yankees of the purest sort, except that they were devout Episcopalians, not Congregationalists. Busy, enterprising Joseph Morgan had built a fortune in Andrew Jackson's time; his son Junius had built that stake into a major international banking house; and John Pierpont, born in 1837, far sur-

passed father and grandfather. He had a talent for mathematics, a fascination with numbers, and a passion for precision and organized harmony. He also had a genius for seeing how to bring order out of the unbelievably complicated and confused tangle of post–Civil War railroading in the United States. The wildest and most unscrupulous competition had created tangles between warring railroad lines, enormous losses, dizzying instability in rates, and angry investors. In the 1880s Morgan emerged as the banker who could painstakingly get people together, not only in banking but in coal mining and other activities where agreements to restrict production and raise prices (clearly monopolistic, but not then illegal) skyrocketed profits and exploited consumers.

British investors turned to Morgan, and he became the channel for immense inflows of British funds into American industry. In 1895, he showed his immense power by rescuing the national Treasury itself in a time of gold-buying panic. By 1900 he controlled much of American railroading, and also, by financing and organizing their formation, most of the large manufacturing trusts that appeared in the years 1898–1902. United States Steel and International Harvester only began the list. After the Panic of 1907 even more firms came under the control of his banking houses, for he had saved them. When in 1913 the Pujo Committee of the House of Representatives examined his operations, it found that the "money trust" was huge, interlinking 34 banks and trust companies, 10 insurance companies, 32 in transportation, 24 in producing and trading, and 12 in public utilities—that is, 112 corporations capitalized at $22 billion, a staggering sum.

Was Morgan troubled by all of this? Not at all. The tall, aged, powerfully built man with his great moustache and his abrupt, sometimes alarming manner, was confident: men of good character, he said, would use this massive network of power well, and he was convinced of his own goodness of character. Cooperation was the important thing, people working together, moderating ruinous competition. Big business? To J. Pierpont Morgan, that meant only efficient, rational, well-organized business. Should government regulate it? Politicians, Morgan believed, were low, contemptible men. The answer? Let the men of good character run the country. They will save it from itself.

In early March 1913 Woodrow Wilson arrived in Washington, D.C., for his inauguration as president of the United States. A cheering mob of Princeton students escorted him from the train, and a huge crowd filled the Capitol square to hear his moving inaugural address summoning the country to national restoration. The public was fascinated by this extraordinary man, the first intellectual in the White House since Thomas Jefferson and James Madison. He was a Southerner, born and reared in Virginia, but a most extraordinary one. He was clearly top-drawer, of the elite. A brilliant professor of political science and history at Princeton in the 1890s, he had become president of the university in 1902 and gained national attention as an educational reformer. In 1910 he burst into politics with an amazing performance as governor of New Jersey, where he overturned boss rule, created strict controls over utilities, and established the initiative and the referendum. Sweeping to the presidency, he seemed the man of the hour. Behind him the Democrats gained a majority of both houses of Congress for the first time in twenty years, and they welcomed their exciting new leader with gratitude and admiration.

In appearance Wilson was somewhat forbidding. Erect, precise in manner, long-jawed, his slim, neat form contrasted markedly with that of the huge, jovial Taft. Everything about him was rigidly self-controlled. A forceful man of remarkable intellectual powers, he was contemptuous of stupidity, confident of his moral righteousness, and eager for power and authority. Wilson's passionate nature found full release when he spoke to large groups of people. His massive intellect would play eagerly over his topic, words would pour from him with fiery intensity, and his usually somber face would come eagerly alive. At Princeton his students had often broken into spontaneous applause; cynical politicians were transfixed when they listened to him; and audiences of common citizens were ignited into frenzies of cheering. Theodore Roosevelt had called the White House a "bully pulpit," and the office of the presidency was for Wilson a solemn and divine obligation. He entered the presidency firmly convinced that God had chosen him for a great mission. This conviction was to be his greatest strength and perhaps his gravest weakness.

The new president was a Democrat by inheritance. Also, he was deeply rooted in the transatlantic Liberal-Democratic community. His mother was born to a Scottish family in Britain, and his paternal grandfather was a Scotch-Irishman who had immigrated from Northern Ireland first to Pennsylvania and then to Ohio. Wilson frequently went to Scotland and England for extended visits. His political ideal was that legendary Scotsman and leader of British Liberalism, William Gladstone, whom Wilson described as "the greatest statesman who ever lived." While studying at Princeton in the 1870s, Wilson pored over parliamentary debates and made British public life his model. He was a confirmed, doctrinaire free trader who regarded Adam Smith as the high prophet of political economy; a convinced supporter of sound money and the gold standard; an unbending opponent of political corruption; and a political scientist who believed that strong governments were necessarily tools of the rich and powerful.

In addition, Wilson was a romantic and a moralist. His imagination constantly seized on great epics of the human spirit. History fascinated him as a story of brave men struggling doggedly and courageously for grand ideals. Whatever he loved, he loved deeply. And whatever he despised, he despised thoroughly. His family was like a Scottish clan, bringing to America the combative, competitive life of the old country. It was infused with a feisty and almost primitive tribal loyalty in which the men seemed always to be fighting some external enemy, usually a religious one. He was more than a Democrat, he was a *fervent* Democrat. If someone opposed him on any issue, Wilson, combative Scot that he was, immediately made the opponent a personal enemy.

Shaping Wilson's whole personality was his powerful religious faith. Like Grover Cleveland, he was a Presbyterian who emphasized duty, strong government, decisive rule, moral principles, and the supreme need for law and order. God has His purposes for the world, Wilson believed, and humanity's task is to be His agent. Such a faith could make one dogmatic and conservative, and through much of his life Wilson was both of these. But it could also make one radical. The God of the Presbyterians was a stern,

THE PROGRESSIVE ERA: DEMOCRATS IN CHARGE

Old Testament Jehovah who was angry at evil and corruption in human life. When Wilson, like Cleveland before him, was seized by this same anger, he became an inspired reformer.

Wilson's New Freedom

Wilson had hungered for power all his life. Now that he had it, what was he going to do with it? In the 1912 campaign, he traveled about the country giving a series of ringing addresses that set forth what he called, in contrast with Roosevelt's New Nationalism, the New Freedom. In recent years, Wilson said, a new form of social organization had taken over American life—the great corporation. Impersonal, inherently amoral, great corporations had created an almost conspiratorial network of power that enabled them to exploit the

President-elect Woodrow Wilson, a lean and intense scholar bent upon major national reforms, stands on Inauguration Day, 1913, in sharp physical contrast with the jovial, rotund President Taft, a man who believed the nation already essentially sound.

The Granger Collection, New York

whole country. Hiding behind the protective tariff and insisting that all their affairs be conducted in secret, corporations corrupted the government into providing them with special privileges— bounties, land grants, hydroelectric-power sites, legal immunities, and the aid of the courts in putting down labor strikes.

The Republican administrations, Wilson said, had listened only to the men who ran the great banks, the big industrial corporations, and the railroads. They did so because they subscribed to the ruinous philosophy of Alexander Hamilton, which was that the nation should be run by the wealthy and the powerful because they knew what was best for everyone. This idea was monstrous, Wilson insisted, for it violated the sturdy independence and manhood of the ordinary American. The whole philosophy of "government by trustee" must be thrown aside and the people allowed to take over their own government once again. Representatives of special interests could never understand the general interest.

The tariff, he said, was a strangling monster that spawned trusts and monopolies. Take away its protective features, and the whole economy would begin to multiply and diversify. Then the federal government must make a direct assault on the trusts. It was wrong, Wilson believed, to regard trusts as inevitable, as did Roosevelt, and to propose simply that the government regulate them in the public interest. This would mean a continuation of "government by trustee." Powerful bankers would sit down with powerful government officials and settle things privately, while the public waited outside. The New Freedom would strengthen the antitrust laws so that existing combinations could be broken up; transform the money trust to remove its stranglehold on credit; and specifically outlaw the ways in which trusts unfairly destroyed competition. Interlocking boards of directors, run from the powerful banks, linked railroads, factories, mines, and utilities in a spreading network that constricted the entire nation. However benevolent the corporations' autocracy might be, it must be broken up. The United States must experience a new flowering of individualism; the people's vital energies must be liberated.

Louis D. Brandeis, brilliant reform lawyer and adviser to Woodrow Wilson, issued a famous attack on the banking system: "The practice of interlocking directorates is the root of many evils. It offends laws human and divine. Applied to rival corporations, it tends to the suppression of competition and to violation of the Sherman law. Applied to corporations which deal with each other, it tends to disloyalty and to violation of the fundamental law that no man can serve two masters. In either event it tends to inefficiency; for it removes incentive and destroys soundness of judgment. . . . It is the most potent instrument of the Money Trust. Break the control so exercised by the investment bankers over railroads, public service and industrial corporations, over banks, life insurance and trust companies, and a long step will have been taken toward attainment of the New Freedom.

"A single example will illustrate the vicious circle of control—the endless chain—through which our financial oligarchy now operates: J. P. Morgan (or a partner), a director of the New York, New Haven & Hartford Railroad, causes that company to sell to J. P. Morgan & Co. an issue of bonds. J. P. Morgan & Co. borrow the money with which to pay for the bonds from the Guaranty Trust Company, of which Mr. Morgan (or a partner) is director. J. P. Morgan & Co. sell the bonds to the Penn Mutual Life Insurance Company, of which Mr. Morgan (or a partner) is a director. The New Haven spends the proceeds of the bonds in purchasing steel rails from the United States Steel Corporation, of which Mr. Morgan (or a partner) is a director. [And so on, through a long circular trail of transactions involving firms of which Morgan or a partner was a director: General Electric Company, Western Union, American Telephone and Telegraph, the Pullman Company, Baldwin Locomotive Company.] Each and every one of the companies last named markets its securities through J. P. Morgan & Co.; each deposits its funds with J. P. Morgan & Co.; and with these funds of each, the firm enters upon further operations." (*Other People's Money* [1914])

In these orations we hear clearly the voice of the older Democratic tradition, especially its venerable insistence upon liberty (now from the oppressions of organized capital) and equality (no special privileges for anyone). Wilson, like all his predecessors in the White House save Theodore Roosevelt, had never lived in big cities or near great factories; had never directly experienced their festering social ills. As a traditional Democrat, he was concerned primarily that the economy be kept open, dynamic, and fair, so that the small men could get ahead. Roosevelt's New Nationalism called for the government not only to regulate the trusts, but for it to give direct assistance to the disadvantaged: to labor, women, children, and the unemployed. Wilson, true to his Southern Democratic inheritance, distrusted big government, and drew back from those who would use government to intervene directly and positively in the economy. He certainly did not

want a "smug lot of experts" running the country from the center. He felt the whole enterprise would degenerate into more government by trustee, where the wealthy and the government formed a corrupt alliance. Therefore, he turned away from social reforms. No one, he believed, really needed help if opportunities were open.

Wilson and the Strong Presidency

Woodrow Wilson was determined to inaugurate a new kind of presidency. He had long believed that the American president should be a kind of British prime minister. Instead of sitting at the White House and waiting to carry out such laws as Congress might in its wisdom enact, he should closely direct the work of his party members in Congress and drive legislation through by teamwork. Accordingly, Wilson's telephone line to the Capitol was constantly busy; party leaders trooped in and out of the White House for frequent meetings with the president; and a stream of handwritten messages went off from Wilson to legislators that flattered, cajoled, and sometimes discreetly threatened them to support his causes.

This was, of course, in the tradition of a governing style long characteristic of the Democratic party—the strong presidency. On the Republican side only Theodore Roosevelt had been a vigorous executive who got Congress to pass major reforms and acted as a tribune of the people. In significant measure it was on this ground that he lost the loyalty of Republican regulars and had to break with his party. On the Democratic side the list of strong presidents was noteworthy, stretching back through Grover Cleveland to James Polk and Andrew Jackson. Wilson ran things directly, and like a Scottish laird demanded personal loyalty to himself in all his policies. Time and again he "went to the people." When clouds of lobbyists swarmed around Congress during the tariff battle, he issued an appeal to the public that aroused so enormous a flood of mail to legislators that tariff reform finally had its day.

Wilson and the Tariff

After taking office Wilson electrified the nation by boldly calling Congress immediately into special session to reform the tariff. Going personally to Congress to deliver his message, he became the first president since John Adams to appear before that body. The Underwood Tariff that was enacted tumbled the rates down and down, back below those of the long Republican years, reaching levels that the nation had not seen since before the Civil War. The new tariff average was set at 29 percent. All products produced by monopolies were placed on the free list, and the new income-tax provision was put into effect—the tax being set at a 7-percent maximum—in order to make up for the loss of tariff revenues.

Reform of the Banking System

In the summer and autumn of 1913, Wilson forced Congress to remain in sweltering Washington, D.C., and tackle another huge issue—the reform of the banking system. Here at the heart of the economy was private control uninhibited and triumphant. No public agency had any voice in settling such critical issues as the volume of money in circulation (the money supply), discount rates (how freely credit would be given), the location of banking facilities, and what kinds of links banks should have with business corporations. Farmers complained that all the money was locked up in eastern banks, resulting in exorbitant interest rates in western regions. Progressives insisted that the money supply should be taken out of private hands and put in those of a public agency. Bankers themselves were alarmed at the condition of their institutions, for there was no central bank that could pool reserves and shift them about as needed to meet unusual demands. Perhaps most important, the supply of money was relatively static. The economy could grow, but there was rarely enough money to meet its needs.

Woodrow Wilson had no intention of destroying private banking. His primary goal was to establish some form of public supervision over limited aspects of the financial world. Going before Congress in June 1913 for another address to the two houses, he called for the creation of the Federal Reserve Board to supervise the banking system. Its membership would be appointed by the president and confirmed by the Senate, and bankers would be ineligible for such appointment. The nation would be divided into twelve Federal Reserve regions, in each of which would be placed a Federal Reserve bank. These institutions would be governed by boards elected primarily by the private banks in the region that had affiliated themselves with the system.

The Federal Reserve System would provide a means of shifting currency reserves about the country to meet demands. Also, it would take over the issuing of paper currency. From the Federal Reserve banks would come a new form of currency, Federal Reserve notes. These would be issued wholly as an obligation of the national government, in this fashion: when a private bank authorized a loan to, say, a local factory, it would receive a mortgage or other form of legal indebtedness (*commercial paper* is the term usually used) from that business; with this in hand, it could go to the regional Federal Reserve bank, deposit the mortgage as security, and receive Federal Reserve notes, which it would then issue to the borrower.

An important step in this process was that the Federal Reserve bank would not issue currency up to the full value of the mortgage. In effect, it would charge some interest by "discounting" the commercial paper—issuing the money in an amount slightly less than the full value of the indebtedness. By charging the borrowing bank a certain percentage of the transaction, the Federal Reserve bank could make loans easier or harder to obtain by raising or lowering the discount rate. This gave the system the potential power of controlling the total money supply and thereby damping inflations or easing deflations.

For the first time, currency was being based not entirely on gold or some form of federal bonds, but on *assets:* that is, on the value of the business and industrial system itself. This would let the currency supply grow and contract in volume in proportion to business activity. Furthermore the decentralized nature of the system—the establishment of reserve banks in every part of the country, helped to ease the Wall Street monopoly.

The nation's private bankers sent up a storm of protest. For generations they had serenely carried on their affairs with the feeling that the banking system was their private property. Now those rascals down in Washington, led by the unpredictable Woodrow Wilson, were proposing to take over, a monstrously offensive prospect to men long habituated to being in control of the nation's economic life. The New York *Sun*, voice of Wall Street, could hardly contain its outrage. "It is difficult to discuss with any degree of patience," it snorted, "this preposterous offspring of ignorance and unreason, but it cannot be passed over with the contempt it deserves." The proposal was "covered all over with the slime of Bryanism."

Nevertheless, the bill went through largely as Wilson had presented it. An overwhelming number of the nation's businessmen favored it as a major improvement of the existing situation. They too, like the farmers, resented the tight control that Wall Street had always exerted, and applauded the spreading of financial resources throughout the nation. Progressives were also pleased. "It is a communistic idea," protested a San Antonio banker, but his outburst was futile. The crowning achievement of Woodrow Wilson's domestic reforms, the Federal Reserve System was enacted in December 1913.

It was a characteristically Wilsonian reform. When all was said and done, his critics maintained, Wilson's actions did not match his rhetoric. Nothing was done about the money trust: interlocking directorates were not outlawed. Private bankers still largely controlled the supply and availability of money. The New York Federal Reserve Bank dominated the system. The Federal Reserve Board was not strong enough to serve as a central bank, or really to control the nation's bankers. It used its influence over discount rates only tentatively until after the crash of 1929. But a new and flexible currency had been created, and a system of public supervision with a large potential had come into being. The start had been made, and in the existing situation so fundamental a change was a very great achievement.

Wilson and the Trusts

The trust problem was the next item on Wilson's agenda. His attorney general, James C. McReynolds, searched out a major target in the American Telephone and Telegraph Company. Threatening the company with a long court suit, the attorney general forced it to give up ownership of Western Union Telegraph. He thus established a new procedure that became important in the Wilson administration, the *consent decree*. In this procedure, an agreement was worked out by the government and the monopoly concerned, which was then formalized in a court decree to which the company had already given its assent.

Meanwhile, new legislation was being prepared in Congress. The Clayton antitrust bill, which Wilson supported, enumerated and outlawed a list of unfair trade practices. Soon a storm of controversy erupted. Labor unions found that the legislation did not exempt them from antitrust prosecution. Some weak provisions to that effect were inserted, but they had little impact in later years. More significant, labor unions were still wide open to court injunctions during strikes.

More damaging to the bill was the fact that legislators were realizing how impossible it was to enumerate specifically what actually constituted unfair business practices. The list could be practically infinite, for the techniques unscrupulous businessmen could adopt were endlessly varied. Louis D. Brandeis, progressives in Congress, authorities on the trust problem—all urged Wilson to take a new tack. He should instead, they said, take up the New Nationalism idea of an independent commission with broad powers to investigate business activities and issue "cease-and-desist" orders when it concluded that unfair practices were being used. He should move more, in other words, toward "positive liberty": using government to liberate society from abuses by the powerful.

After considerable haggling and protracted thought—for the proposal required a major shift in his New Freedom philosophy—Wilson accepted this change. The result was the creation in 1914 of the Federal Trade Commission, which was charged with preventing the appearance of new monopolies by ensuring that businessmen competed fairly and openly (but did not specify in detail what this meant). An independent commission modeled on the ICC, it was composed of five members appointed by the president with the Senate's consent, who would hold office for seven years. Meanwhile, the Clayton antitrust bill was mostly ignored. By the time of its passage a disgusted Missouri senator said that it had been transformed from "a raging lion with a mouth full of teeth . . . to a tabby cat with soft gums, a plaintive mew, and an anemic appearance."

Wilson now announced that the program of the New Freedom was complete. No more major reforms needed to be enacted. In truth, Wilson seemed genuinely uninterested in going any further. He was implacably opposed to special-interest legislation, which meant not only that manufacturers and bankers should get no aid from the government, but also that laborers, farmers, and children were to be similarly ignored. This was, in fact, traditional Democratic libertarianism. As much as possible, government should keep hands off, giving no favor to anyone. Laissez-faire: this was the ancient Adam Smith position, the creed of Thomas Jefferson. When proposals came forward to aid exploited groups, Wilson quashed them. He refused to support the establishment of rural banks that would provide farmers with the long-term loans on low interest that they needed. When progressives appealed for a national child-labor bill he also resisted, saying that "domestic arrangements" were for the states, not the federal government, to supervise—a position not surprising in a Southerner.

Wilson Turns Toward New Nationalism

In 1916, however, Woodrow Wilson surprised the nation by suddenly launching out even stronger in New Nationalist directions, making the national government an agency of social reform. Why did he do this? First, in the elections of 1914 the Republicans won a series of stunning victories. TR had abandoned his fledgling Progressive Party (upon which it promptly expired) to return to the Republican fold. War had broken out in Europe in August 1914, and he wanted to bring the United States into it against the "beastly Hun." Where would the leaderless Progressives go—back to the Republicans with Roosevelt, or over to the Democrats? Wilson now had a straight-out two-party contest ahead of him in the coming presidential election of 1916, and he needed to win the Progressives over to gain an absolute majority in the electoral college. So, too, he needed to take positive action to hold onto the emergent ethnic Democrats in the northern states, and they demanded social reforms of the newer kind.

Being an inactive president was not, in any event, Wilson's style. Power was his meat and drink, and to sit back placidly after his program was "complete" was impossible. He had learned, too, that the nation had evils that only a vigorous government could assault. Wilson, indeed, was fundamentally devoted to the belief that government must grow and change to meet society's actual needs.

So now, in 1916, he led Congress in new directions, stimulating it to enact "the most sweeping and significant progressive legislation in the history of the country up to that time," as Arthur S. Link has written. He startled the business community by proposing the reformer Brandeis for a seat on the Supreme Court. This led to a stiff fight in the Senate over his confirmation, for the action was like waving a red flag at the Wall Street bull. (There were also those who reacted against a Jew being on the Supreme Court.) Then he began pushing a bill he had earlier opposed that established twelve farm-loan banks, each of them with $500,000 provided by the federal government, in rural regions of the nation. Conservatives angrily cried "socialism," but the measure went through.

A workmen's-compensation law for federal employees that had been languishing in Congress suddenly came alive when Wilson became its advocate. Following its enactment, he put strong pressure behind passage of a child-labor bill, going to the Capitol personally to make his plea. (The law, later declared unconstitutional, prohibited interstate trade in goods made by children under fourteen or by children under sixteen who worked more than eight hours a day.) In this landmark legislation the federal government made its first effort ever to supervise the way private employers ran their businesses. Here lay the germ of all the social-reform measures that later transformed the relationship of the national government to social conditions.

Following this, Wilson secured the creation of a new independent commission, the Tariff Commission, that would provide a continuing expert study of trade conditions. Its task was to propose "scientific" tariff changes designed to equalize the cost of production domestically with that abroad, a procedure that Wilson had specifically condemned in his original New Freedom speeches. By thus providing "rational protection," Wilson had shifted startlingly away from traditional Democratic principles, and he brought along most Democrats in Congress with him.

Practically every important proposal that the Progressives had made in 1912 had now become law, with Wilson's blessing. This allowed him in the campaign of 1916 to claim that the Democratic party was also the progressive party, that social justice would now come from his side of politics and not from the Republicans. In June 1916 a massive railroad strike gave him another opportunity to demonstrate his new loyalties. The railroad workers were fighting for the eight-hour day with no reduction in wages. Wilson supported them and pressured the railroad owners to grant their demand. When they refused, he quickly got Congress to pass the Adamson Act, which imposed an eight-hour day on the railroads and made higher wages possible.

Businessmen were now furious with Woodrow Wilson. In the 1916 campaign they threw their support wholeheartedly behind the Republican nominee for the presidency, Charles Evans Hughes, a progressive governor of New York. Once again, as was traditional, the Democratic candidate was widely depicted as antibusiness. Meanwhile, Wilson moved vigorously about the country reminding people of what he had done for labor, farmers, and the nation's children. Progressives flocked behind Wilson's banner. Labor, delighted with its new champion, pressed hard for his victory. Progressive journalists and writers applauded Wilson's transformation of the Democratic party into an agency of social reform. Many thousands of urban, ethnic voters who had cast their ballots in 1912 for Eugene V. Debs, the Socialist candidate, now swung over to the president.

Furthermore, the peace movement was in Wilson's camp, for its leaders feared that a Republican victory would mean a rapid entry into the war then raging in Europe. Theodore Roosevelt went from city to city proclaiming that Wilson was a weak-kneed coward for not immediately going to war on the British side, and every such attack gave more strength to the Wilson following. The election itself was a cliff-hanger, for the eastern states went heavily for Hughes. But when the western returns came in, Wilson was reelected with a total of 9.1 million popular votes to 8.5 million for Hughes. For the first time since Andrew Jackson, a Democrat had won reelection for a second consecutive term.

The Women's-Suffrage Crusade

One of the great victories for social justice that was finally achieved in the Wilson years was the Nineteenth Amendment, which gave women the right to vote. In 1890 the National American Woman Suffrage Association appeared, formed by the merger of two smaller and older movements. The association concentrated on converting individual states to women's suffrage, but by 1896 after incredible labors there were only four victories: in Colorado, Utah, Idaho, and Wyoming.

Why did women's suffrage lag so far behind that for men? For one thing, powerful interests opposed it: the liquor industry; textile manufacturers (opposed to laws limiting child labor); ethnic city machines, male-run, where traditional ideas of male domination in government were strong; and cultural conservatism as a general mood. Also, until after 1900 most women were either indifferent to, or actively opposed, the cause. This was the only public campaign involving women that proposed a direct assault upon the doctrine of the two spheres in sex roles. If women had been massively for it, they could probably have gotten men to pass the necessary legislation, for they had secured over the years a wide variety of other reforms, concerning women's property rights, legal status in marriage, ability to engage in business, and control over their children, to take only a few such achievements. Indeed, women's influence in politics, though exerted without the vote, had been considerable, as in the abolition crusade. In the Populist movement, women orators were spectacularly prominent. But in fact thousands of women in the Social Purity movement, and even many prominent progressive reformers, such as Ida Tarbell, openly opposed the suffrage demand. It aroused anxiety and fear that the traditional family might be ended. "The women don't want the vote," said one suffrage worker privately to another in the 1890s; "[that] is the 'stunner' that we friends of the cause have to meet at every hand." In Massachusetts, where women had had the vote in school affairs for forty years, only one in twenty women bothered to cast their ballot. When allowed to vote for or against women's suffrage in that state in 1895, four times as many men voted for it as women. Indeed, the national campaign against women's suffrage was organized, staffed, and run primarily by women.

What, then, turned this situation around? There was the large and well-organized campaign run by its advocates after 1900; there was the mood of the Progressive Era; there were now many thousands of college-educated women (8,500 received baccalaureate degrees in 1910, as against 29,000 men); and there was the obvious fact that women were increasingly involved, through work and social reform, in public life.

Also, the fear that the suffrage would begin changes that would eventually endanger women's role in the family faded as the experience of those states that did allow women to vote demonstrated that no such changes occurred. Most of all, the role of government itself changed in the Progressive Era. From this period on, it became ever more a social-welfare agency concerned with the kinds of things that women thought crucial: schools; child labor; sanitation in the cities; pure water; pure food; protection for women at work; pensions for women enabling them to remain at home (if the husband was missing) to care for the children rather than work; workmen's compensation, to prevent financial disaster to the family if its wage earner suffered disabling injury; and other issues that were child- and family-connected. Politics and voting were now clearly connected to the home. The rise of women in the labor force had another role to play in this transformation. Where some 3.75 million women had been gainfully employed in 1870, by 1910 the figure had reached 8 million. In sweatshops and textile factories, it was clear that women had a direct interest in influencing legislation that concerned them. Thus, they moved to get the vote.

The Crusade Quickens

The suffrage movement was led by Carrie Chapman Catt and Anna Howard Shaw, both college-trained. The former was the leading figure in the International Woman Suffrage Alliance, founded in Germany in 1904, and the latter was president of the National American Woman Suffrage Association from 1904 to 1915. A transatlantic connection with Great Britain was maintained by the American women, and it provided a vital spark of stimulus and example. In 1903 the Englishwoman Emmeline Pankhurst began a regular program of interrupting government speakers to ask their views on woman suffrage. Soon there were uproars leading to spectacular arrests, widesplashing newspaper publicity, and intense national interest. The women's cause had broken out of polite and subdued gatherings to which no one paid any attention, and it was never to be the same again.

The Women's Political Union was formed in the United States also with the objective of holding public gatherings and launching active campaigns against male politicians who opposed the vote for women. Parades became a distinctive tactic of the new women's organizations. Hundreds of women began traveling through the countryside in the Northeast, speaking to audiences of ordinary men and women wherever they could find hearers, who, in truth, were eager to gather for so remarkable a sight as a woman politician. At the same time, under Catt's leadership members of the National American Woman Suffrage Association began a carefully detailed and executed plan of precinct organization in order to bring direct pressure on every legislator.

Then, after fourteen dry years in which no state could be induced to grant suffrage, the state of Washington in 1910 electrified women across the country by approving it by a two-to-one margin. A whirlwind of organized publicity workers then launched an incredibly varied campaign in California featuring an effort at each polling booth to ward off the influences of liquor salesmen and barkeepers. The result was a narrow victory in 1911. Three more states were won in 1912—Arizona, Kansas, and Oregon.

But the state-by-state tactic was costly and wearing, and defeats in Ohio, Wisconsin, and Michigan were deeply discouraging. The women began to look toward Washington, D.C., encouraged by the fact that Theodore Roosevelt's Progressive party had made woman suffrage one of its electoral planks. Alice Paul, fresh from a jail term in Britain as a militant woman-suffrage worker and the ordeal of a hunger strike, emerged to provide fresh leadership. With the aid of a small group of vigorous co-workers, she succeeded in organizing a parade of thousands of women in Washington on the day before Woodrow Wilson's first inauguration. They practically had to fight their way to the Capitol building, for hostile observers jeered at them and broke up their line of march. But with this flood of publicity behind them, they succeeded in getting Congress to pay attention and hold hearings on a constitutional amendment. A petition bearing 200,000 signatures was presented, and President Wilson began to receive visiting delegations of women. A new organization, the militant Congressional Union, began a program of nationwide activities, organizing campaigns to defeat Democrats—whom the women chose as their adversaries on the simple ground that the Democrats were in power in Washington, and therefore responsible if a women's-suffrage amendment was not passed. In truth, on women's issues Democrats were traditionally opposed to change. Their numerous urban immigrant supporters preferred old-time sex roles, such as existed in the villages in their European homelands, and Southern whites shared this perspective. The women's movement had always been a Yankee Republican phenomenon.

A long siege against a reluctant Congress ensued. The women organized spectacular national pilgrimages beginning in San Francisco and arriving in Washington, D.C., with petitions bearing hundreds of thousands of signatures. Votes were forced in key committees and on the floors of both houses of Congress, usually meeting with the moral victory of narrow defeat. The White House was picketed, and hunger strikes were begun. Immense efforts were poured into referenda in four key eastern states—New York, Massachusetts, Pennsylvania, and New Jersey—where, again, defeat was the result. But Catt,

who became president of the National American Woman Suffrage Association in 1915, never relented, and the national campaign grew, if anything, more active. Money was raised, conferences held, schools established to train organizers, and every state organization given specific tasks. Woodrow Wilson was diligently wooed in his reelection campaign in 1916. On one occasion, when he appeared to speak at the national convention of the National American Woman Suffrage Association, Anna Howard Shaw said to him, "We have waited so long, Mr. President, for the vote—we had hoped it might come in your administration," at which point the immense audience of women rose silently and stood quietly looking at the president. Within a year, he came out formally on the side of the women's cause and called on Congress to act.

In 1917 the first woman ever to sit in Congress took her seat—Jeanette Rankin of Montana (who, after a long and honorable career in public life, principally as an opponent of both world

WOMAN SUFFRAGE BEFORE THE NINETEENTH AMENDMENT

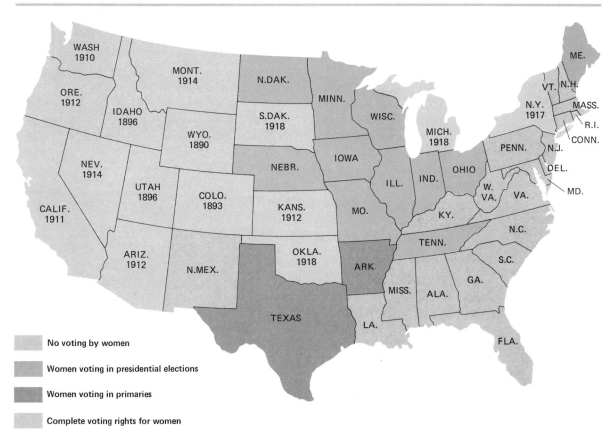

Legend:
- No voting by women
- Women voting in presidential elections
- Women voting in primaries
- Complete voting rights for women

wars, died in 1972). Enormous numbers of women, meanwhile, were pouring into the job market as war work made unprecedented demands on them to support the military forces. Indeed, the great wars in American history—the Civil War and the two world wars—worked lasting transformations in the status of women in America. Furthermore, when women took up outside jobs during the First World War, they did so in an atmosphere in which democratic values of equality and individual dignity were being trumpeted around the world by the White House. Clearly, the principles being thus invoked had a great field for application in the women's cause. State after state began to give the vote in presidential elections to women. Then in January 1918, after a massive lobbying campaign, the House of Representatives passed the women's-suffrage constitutional amendment, primarily because of heavy Republican majorities in its favor. In 1919 the Senate followed, and in August 1920 the ratification process was completed and the Nineteenth Amendment became a reality. Twenty-six million women of voting age could go to the polls and share responsibility with male Americans for the government of the country.

Blacks in the Progressive Era

In Wilson's movement toward social justice one note is harshly out of tune. Woodrow Wilson was a Southerner, and so were most of his cabinet members and Congressional leaders. As soon as he became president, his administration began to practice segregation in government departments. Black and white workers were separated "to reduce friction," it was said, and so as not to enforce "unwelcome" closeness on white workers. There was a particular touchiness about black civil servants supervising white women. Wilson, when appealed to, insisted that segregation was actually a humanitarian policy, for it would give black workers job areas of their own in which they need not fear white encroachment.

Black leaders generally believed the president was a sincere man, but nevertheless his defense of segregation rang hollow. Wilson's father had ardently supported slavery; his wife was strongly segregationist; and Wilson seemed to do nothing but cover over the Jim Crow practices with high-flown words. More disturbing, supervi-

sors in government offices seemed bent on discharging as many black employees as possible by putting them into specially organized offices that were then closed down.

This was not, however, entirely a Democratic matter. During the Progressive Era both parties were indifferent to the needs of Afro-Americans. Roosevelt and Taft had been so markedly antiblack that for the first time since black Americans began voting, significant numbers of them had actually switched to the Democratic ticket in 1912. Wilson, the intellectual, had seemed the man of the future, and he had issued encouraging statements. The aftermath, therefore, was very discouraging to blacks. Progressives everywhere had boasted that they were the spokesmen of the forgotten man, but they turned away from the race question. What could one do, they seemed to feel, about a problem that was so overwhelmingly difficult to solve, and a Southern one besides? (Some 90 percent of black Americans still lived in the South.)

Theodore Roosevelt gave much thought to the whole issue and finally gave up, telling blacks that they had to rely on the goodwill of the whites. Then, as if in violent reaction to a problem he could not solve, he took steps deeply offensive to the black community. In 1906 he arbitrarily discharged three companies of black soldiers for having allegedly been involved with rioting in nearby Brownsville, Texas. He even informed Congress that lynchings were brought about because black men were raping white women. The Republican party became ever more "lily white" in its policies, giving few positions to blacks any longer. Wilson's segregation policies were actually preceded by some similar arrangements under Taft.

Black America in the North Since Reconstruction

Indeed, none of this was new. Since the end of Reconstruction in 1877, northern whites had increasingly ignored black interests. The dominant concern in the northern mind was knitting the nation back together. This seemed to require leaving the race issue in the hands of Southern whites, in return for which they would finally and irrevocably give up their dreams for separate nationhood. The Supreme Court confirmed these views, gutting the federal civil-rights legislation of the Reconstruction era in the *Civil Rights* cases (1883). The philosophy adopted by the Court was that individuals were free to do what they wished in race relations. In 1890 in the case of *Louisville, New Orleans and Texas Railroad* v. *Mississippi* it ruled that a state could require, not simply allow, segregation in railroad transportation. Then in *Plessy* v. *Ferguson* (1896), the Court established the separate-but-equal doctrine in public facilities (and by implication in public schools). The court's view was that it was useless to try to change "racial instincts" by law. In practice, Southern state legislatures provided less money for black schools than they did for white schools, which led inherently to inequality. Then in 1898 steps taken by Mississippi to withdraw the vote from black men (to be explained later in this chapter) were ruled constitutional in *Williams* v. *Mississippi*.

Blacks in the North retained their political and civil rights but still suffered from social and economic discrimination. They usually studied in separate schools and held only the most menial occupations. Northern labor unions were strongly antiblack, especially the AFL. (The United Mine Workers was a notable exception: two thirds of its membership was black.) The notion of racial equality was almost universally condemned. If black people fell behind, it was their own doing, said white Americans.

Black America in the South Since Reconstruction

In the South, for a generation after the Civil War, two philosophies of race relations struggled for supremacy. One was that of outright race hatred, which resulted in the mass violence and intimidation described in Chapter 20. The other, held generally by the white upper class, was the concerned and paternalistic creed that existed in pre–Civil War days. Neither side, of course, even considered racial equality, but the paternalistic view taught that whites should carry out their responsibilities as trustees for blacks carefully and thoughtfully. The northern states had left the problem to the South, paternalists pointed out, and Southern whites should take up this task in a responsible and civilized way. Black men continued to vote in large numbers after 1877, and some

Life for most American blacks was little changed in the Progressive Era from the 1880s scene here presented of farm laborers picking cotton in the South. With little education and a web of Jim Crow laws enacted from the 1890s onward, the situation was, if anything, worse than at any time since the Civil War.

Courtesy of the Library of Congress

held public office, served as jurymen—even as judges—and sat in city, state, and national legislatures. In most public facilities, however, segregation was the usual pattern.

As late as 1900 three fourths of the black farmers in the South were living on someone else's land as sharecroppers or tenant farmers. At the same time, blacks were traditionally imprisoned for petty crimes that went overlooked when committed by whites. Blacks in jail were then "farmed out" to labor on white-owned farms, on the railroads, or in the frightful conditions of the Georgia turpentine farms. Meanwhile, lynch law rode the land. In the 1880s and 1890s more than a hundred black men were strung up by lynch mobs every year, often after the most barbarous torture.

Populism and Black Southerners

The uprush of Southern Populism in the 1890s introduced new ideas on race. As a class movement, Populism took up the cause of the poor farmer, black or white, against the banks, railroads, and other businesses of wealth and power. Populists welcomed blacks into their movement, stressing the equalitarianism of the poor. "They are in the ditch," said a Texan Populist, "just like we are." This was brave doctrine, for the mass of the white population was not ready to accept any form of racial equality. This was especially true among the poor whites, who seemed the most rabidly bigoted, and yet they were the group to whom the Populists directed most of their appeals. Acts of great courage marked Populism in its heyday. Populist sheriffs put black men on juries, and the party's newspaper editors took pains to laud black achievements.

The Populist campaign was doomed before it began. "Whites must stick together!" was the overwhelmingly powerful cry in the Southern states. To pull whites back into the Democratic party, race agitators began preaching black hatred. Then, by all sorts of legal devices, the vote was taken away from black men—literacy tests, property requirements, "understanding" tests, poll taxes, and even that sacred "democratic" reform of the Progressive Era, the primary election. Being purely a party proceeding, primaries could be restricted only to whites. The situation in Louisiana alone tells the story: in 1896, 130,000 black men could vote; in 1904, only 1,300. The black man had been effectively disenfranchised.

All this took place in a hysteria of race baiting that featured an explosion of racist novels, endless allegations that black men were raping white women, and loud attacks on black "uppitiness." Having lost the vote and been rendered powerless, blacks began to suffer periodic mass violence. In Wilmington, North Carolina, in 1898, 400 white men streamed into a black residential area and burned homes, killed and wounded the frantic inhabitants, and sent hundreds fleeing. The whole city of New Orleans was taken over in 1900 by uncontrolled mobs that killed and terrorized blacks. In Atlanta in 1906, after Governor Hoke Smith had won a white-supremacy victory, the city rocked to days of white rioting.

Then came a flood of "Jim Crow" laws. Railway cars and waiting stations, streetcars, theater entrances, boardinghouses, toilets, water fountains, ticket windows, parks, circus shows, halls, auditoriums, ball parks, residential areas, textbooks, schools, even prostitutes were segregated. Atlanta courtrooms had separate Bibles for blacks and for whites; public buildings had separate elevators. The result was a massive crystallization of race relations that was worse than anything blacks had endured for decades. Once the Jim Crow era began, all relations were transformed. Every black person, whether intelligent or stupid, well dressed or in tatters, cultivated or ignorant, was legally the inferior of every white person, no matter how crude or brutish.

Changes in the North

Discrimination against blacks in the North grew harsher from the 1890s onward. Almost none were elected to legislative seats any longer or held appointive office. Hotels, restaurants, and theaters frequently discriminated against blacks, and separate schools existed in many states. White customers stopped buying from black businessmen, and white unions and businesses refused to employ black laborers. Most trade unions excluded them, and the huge influx of immigrants took away much of their domestic, hotel, and restaurant work.

The background to the more severe discrimination was the impact of America's imperialism. In the late 1890s the United States took under its tutelage millions of Filipinos whom it had no intention of admitting to equal citizenship. The North, therefore, had a huge stake in racism. Theories that described white people as superior and pigmented races as inferior were widely preached. The *New York Times* observed in 1900 that "Northern men . . . no longer denounce the suppression of the Negro vote [in the South] as it used to be denounced in the reconstruction days. The necessity of it under the supreme law of self-preservation is candidly recognized."

Blacks Turn Inward

In these circumstances, the black community turned in on itself. If segregation was the order of the day, Afro-Americans seemed to say, so be it: black people would stress that they too wanted segregation and the pride of having their own spheres. The dominant message now passed around the black world was that of self-help. This was, indeed, an old idea. As early as the 1870s black leaders had stressed the need for industrial education, by which black men could acquire the jobs needed to help themselves, rise in the community, and demonstrate that they were worthy of respect—and equality. Southern states had even established industrial schools for this purpose. Hampton Institute and Tuskegee Institute became symbols of this philosophy.

Booker T. Washington, head of Tuskegee, became in the 1890s the prophet of self-help. At the Atlanta Exposition in 1895 he captured national attention by calling on black people to accept the white man's philosophy of hard work and getting ahead in the community by material advancement. Remember, he said, most black people must live by manual labor. The overwhelming majority of them were unskilled and therefore imprisoned on the farm. The best hope for them lay in acquiring skills and working faithfully, not in agitating for racial equality and demanding positions of leadership. "In all things that are purely social," he said, "[the white and black races] can be as separate as the five fingers, yet one as the hand in all things essential to mutual progress." Cooperate with white men, he urged Afro-Americans. Be "patient, faithful, law-abiding and unresentful." It is vitally important, he maintained, "that all privileges of the law be ours; but it is vastly more important that we be prepared for the exercise of these privileges."

By this utterance Washington immediately became, in white eyes, the towering figure in the world of black America. His was a philosophy that whites could thoroughly approve of. Though potentially explosive—what would happen when blacks *did* get ahead and expected the privileges that they earned?—its immediate significance was attractive, for it promised to keep away all radicalism. Philanthropic institutions hastened to fund Washington's programs and to get his advice on all the other projects that were proposed for the aid of American blacks. Theodore Roosevelt called him to the White House for consultation.

After this the White House appointed no black men to the government without clearing them first with Booker T. Washington, a fact that gave him great power in the black community. A staunch Republican, he worked hard to get out the black vote in the northern states, though he never publicly criticized the massive disenfranchisement then taking place in the South.

Great numbers of black Americans agreed with Booker T. Washington that individual effort and striving to get ahead were the answers to their situation. Jobs and a respectable standard of living: these were what they wanted. In spite of all difficulties, there was, in fact, a small and growing black middle class in both the North and the South. Self-made, proud of their success, they approved of Washington's message. Rocking the boat was not their desire. They hoped instead that some kind of peaceful and modestly comfortable life in twentieth-century America could be allowed to them. Such ideals were taught in black schools, in conventions of black farmers, and at meetings of black businessmen's organizations. Self-sufficiency was stressed. The ideal was an all-black town where black physicians, lawyers, bankers, merchants, and teachers would minister to the needs of black workers and farmers. Out of Hampton and Tuskegee went a stream of teachers schooled in the philosophy of self-help to work with black children throughout the South. As always, the black church was the heart of Afro-American life, and from its pulpits ministers preached the same message of self-help and racial pride and solidarity.

Emergence of Black Radicalism

It was increasingly difficult, however, for this viewpoint to be maintained without challenge. Southern blacks were surrounded by a rising storm of frenzied racism. The advent of Jim Crow took place to the accompaniment of screaming oratory praising white supremacy and describing blacks as plundering beasts. The black middle class, it seemed to many, was on an island of sand being eaten away by the tide. Appropriations for black schoolchildren were dropping rapidly as blacks lost the vote; race riots broke out; and in a revealing episode, the homes of the comfortable black middle class were singled out for especially savage attacks in the Atlanta riot of 1906. It was one thing for blacks to talk of hard work and patience; it was another when they actually got ahead. Whites began violently attacking the homes and property that blacks had worked hard to obtain.

In this situation, some leading black Americans began to call for a new philosophy. All around them, after all, was the progressive movement, which preached high moral values of equality and social justice. After 1900 an increasingly outspoken opposition to Booker T. Washington developed, especially among northern blacks. The new dissidents were usually college-educated professionals and intellectuals who were peculiarly subject to that cruel dilemma traditionally facing black Americans who do not remain encapsulated in the world of blackness: choosing between their two identities—being an American like everyone else, and being a black. It is a dilemma, indeed, that minority groups in every country must face. As W. E. B. Du Bois, then a professor at Atlanta University, explained in 1897:

One feels his two-ness—an American, a Negro, two souls, two thoughts, two unreconciled strivings, two warring ideals in one dark body. . . . The history of the American Negro is the history of this strife—this longing to attain self-conscious manhood, to merge his double self into a better and truer self. . . . He would not Africanize America for America has too much to teach the world and Africa. He would not bleach the Negro soul in a flood of white Americanism, for he knows that Negro blood has a message for the world. He simply wishes to make it possible for a man to be both a Negro and an American, without being cursed and spit upon. . . .

Such men rejected the implicit segregation in Booker T. Washington's philosophy. Integration, which meant full acceptance on an equal basis as a human being, was their goal. Patience and submissiveness in a caste system were unacceptable. The new dissidents insisted on their civil rights, particularly the vote. They demanded that young blacks be given not only industrial education but also training for leadership, which meant schooling in the liberal arts and sciences.

W. E. B. Du Bois

The Afro-American's "two-ness" was eloquently symbolized in the career of William Edward Burghardt Du Bois. Born in 1868 in western Massachusetts, he studied at all-black Fisk University in Nashville, Tennessee, in the 1880s. Here he imbibed a sense of racial pride, induced in him, as he said, by association with a "closed racial group with rites and loyalties, with a history and a corporate future, with an art and a philosophy." Taking a Ph.D. at Harvard in 1895, he began his career as a professor at Atlanta University. In these years he echoed much of Booker T. Washington's philosophy. Blacks, he would say, had themselves to blame for much of their treatment. "We must remember," he observed, "that a good many of our people . . . are not fit for the responsibility of republican government." The black man's real struggle, in his view, was to improve himself morally, to become a better and more responsible American, more hard-working, self-denying, and ambitious. After that, white society would open its doors.

Already, however, he was deploring the fact that young blacks were not being given liberal-arts education. Even as a student at Harvard he had begun talking about what he called the "talented tenth": those blacks with inherent leadership abilities who should be trained for the role. He remained at Atlanta University until 1910, when he moved to the University of Pennsylvania. In these years he urged that black America adopt a policy of racial solidarity—living and working among themselves, buying from each other, and turning to black lawyers and doctors for their professional services. This would lead to a United States characterized by "cultural pluralism," in which Afro-Americans could be Americans and at the same time active members of the black community. As a race, he said in 1897, "we must strive by race organizations, by race solidarity, by race unity to the realization of the broader humanity which freely recognizes differences in men, but sternly deprecates inequalities in their opportunity of development." Separation, pride in their distinctness, yet equality—these were the touchstones. Du Bois looked to Africa as a homeland and advocated "pan-Negroism."

Gradually he began to veer more sharply from Booker T. Washington's leadership. In 1901 he demanded that blacks protest ceaselessly against the Jim Crow system. In 1903 he published his famous *Souls of Black Folk,* which contained an essay openly attacking Washington. His policies, Du Bois said, "practically accepted the inferiority of the Negro," ignored cultivating the mind while concentrating only on skills for the hands, and taught blacks to accept prejudiced

W. E. B. DuBois and Booker T. Washington, the two leaders of black America whose contrasting philosophies vied for support within the black community. White Americans disliked DuBois as a radical, approved Washington for his pragmatism.

Courtesy of the Library of Congress

treatment. It was not true, said Du Bois, that the backwardness and bad habits of the black people justified their treatment, as Washington seemed to say. The time now had come to adopt the tactic that Washington had deplored—open public protest. What good did it do to work hard and become prosperous, Du Bois asked, when it was precisely the middle-class black person who received the bitterest attacks during rioting? Not separation, but integration and the full rights of citizenship should be the new objective. Black men must have the best education available, adopt the most challenging goals, and reject segregation as an insult to their manhood. "Separate schools for whites and blacks are not equal, can not be made equal, and . . . are not intended to be equal." The real result was not separation but subordination, which was what the white Southerners, he said, had been after all along.

After 1904 Du Bois began to look sympathetically toward socialism. By 1911 he was a devoted member of the Socialist party and was writing Marxist analyses of the ways in which both white and black laborers were commonly being ex-

ploited by white capitalists. Exploitation usually took the form of stirring up race animosities, he said, which kept the two groups from joining hands. He dreamed of a future in which white and black workers would jointly create a society based on economic and racial justice.

The Niagara Movement and the NAACP

Most Afro-Americans refused to follow Du Bois. All of his long life—he lived into his nineties—he was in the unhappy position of having to work against the mainstream of black American life, for the overwhelming majority of Afro-Americans rejected agitation and accepted the Washington values of accommodation, hard work and training, and the hope for a slow rise in status. Besides, Du Bois's essential following, which lay primarily among black professionals, was very small. Only 1 percent of employed Afro-Americans were professionals in 1900, and ten years later this figure had reached but 3 percent in the northern states and 2.5 percent in the South. Of these, many were without formal training, being self-taught ministers or teachers without college educations.

Even so, a small nucleus of reformist blacks responded to Du Bois. In 1905 a group composed primarily of northern blacks joined him in a meeting held in Niagara Falls, Canada, at which they formed a national organization, the Niagara Movement. They issued a call to American blacks to protest continuously against any loss of political and civil rights and to agitate against unequal economic opportunities. Liberal arts as well as vocational training, they insisted, must be a part of black education. Above all, blacks should wipe away the national impression that "the Negro-American assents to inferiority, is submissive under oppression and apologetic before insult."

W. E. B. Du Bois spoke for the Niagara Movement: "Stripped of verbiage and subterfuge and in its naked nastiness, the new American creed says: fear to let black men even try to rise lest they become the equals of the white. And this is the land that professes to follow Jesus Christ. . . . First, we would vote; with the right to vote goes everything: freedom, manhood, the honor of your wives, the chastity of your daughters, the right to work, and the chance to rise, and let no man listen to those who deny this. . . .

"We want discrimination in public accommodation to cease. . . . We claim the right of freedom to walk, talk, and be with them that wish to be with us. . . . We want the laws enforced against rich as well as poor; against Capitalist as well as Laborer; against white as well as black. We are not more lawless than the white race, [but] we are more often arrested, convicted and mobbed. . . . We want our children educated. The school system in the country districts of the South is a disgrace and in few towns and cities are the Negro schools what they ought to be. . . . We want our children trained as intelligent human beings should be, and we will fight for all time against any proposal to educate black boys and girls simply as servants and underlings, or simply for the use of other people. They have a right to know, to think, to aspire. . . .

"We do not believe in violence, neither in the despised violence of the raid nor the lauded violence of the soldier, nor the barbarous violence of the mob; but we do believe in John Brown, in that incarnate spirit of justice, that hatred of a lie, that willingness to sacrifice money, reputation, and life itself on the altar of right." (W. E. B. Du Bois, *Dusk of Dawn* [1940])

An open rupture now took place between pro- and anti-Washington men that agitated black American life for more than ten years. A small group of white liberals was attracted to black rad-icalism and gave it crucially important support. Their leading figure was Oswald Garrison Villard. He had warmly assisted Booker T. Washington, but now he began turning to the Du Bois movement. In 1910 a group of white liberals under Villard's leadership joined with Du Bois to create the National Association for the Advancement of Colored People (NAACP), to which the members of the now-expiring Niagara Movement flocked en masse. Its chief concern was to fight through the courts to win legal rights for black Americans. The first victory for the NAACP came in 1915, when it won from the Supreme Court a ruling that the grandfather clause (a provision that illiterates could vote only if their grandfather had been voting before 1867) in use in Oklahoma was unconstitutional. Another critically important organization, the National Urban League, was formed in 1911 to help blacks find jobs in the cities and adjust to urban life.

By the time of Washington's death in 1915, the split between radicals and conservatives was healing over. All shades of active black opinion agreed, in effect, with the spirit of the Niagara Movement. Accommodation, in the Washington manner, might continue to be the dominating practical philosophy in Afro-American life, but now there lay always in the future the goal of an integrated society in which black and white lived on equal terms and had equal opportunities. By this time, too, the First World War was making a great impact on the life of black America. Now more than 300,000 Southern blacks began a great exodus for war-related jobs in northern cities. This northward movement did not cease until the 1970s. In its train have come deep and profound changes in life in the United States, which will take our attention at a later point in the narrative.

Progressivism in Retrospect

Looking back on the Progressive Era from a vantage point just before American entrance into the First World War, a summing up of main trends will be useful. From the depression of the 1890s, the seedbed of progressivism, there ensued a dramatic coming together of several currents of national life that had been evolving separately in the prior decades. Essentially, there was a nationwide groping to bring order out of a disorganized, fragmented, confusing, and alarming social order. This led in the business world to what historians have called an "organizational revolution" aimed at eliminating what was regarded as destructive competition and economic chaos. Among reformers, there was a similar convergence of formerly hostile and mutually obstructive campaigns into an increasingly powerful coalition of progressive political movements within cities, states, and the nation. These reform movements led to the most sweeping reorganization of American public life and its institutions since the Revolution itself.

At the same time a cultural revitalization aimed at releasing human potentialities occurred among the nation's children and within the world of women, a movement mocked by the contemporary fastening upon black America of Jim Crowism and violent racism. Nonetheless, black America responded to the essential ideology of progressivism by developing for itself the (hopefully) liberating values to which it would return again and again in the twentieth century as black people made their way slowly to the Second Reconstruction of the 1960s. In the background, among intellectuals, there was a revolt against the genteel formalism of the nineteenth century, a revolt urging that ideas be used imaginatively, experimentally; that old formulas be cast aside; that "scientific" methods of inquiry into every human problem uncover the true reality of American life, uniting the intellectual as expert with the power of government.

The organizational revolution in business grew out of the collapse of the 1890s. Great investment banks such as the House of Morgan gathered the scattered pieces of American enterprise together, regrouped the railroads, and, by means of interlocking directorates and immense new consolidated corporations that dominated entire industries, built a massive and powerful capitalist structure. Within the corporations emerged a managerial elite composed of experts in engineering, time-and-motion studies, and efficiency. And among businessmen, a complex mesh of business associations came into being to exchange information and organize self-protection against unions and reformers. Even farmers learned the arts of cooperative organization, becoming more businesslike in their operations and in their self-image.

In the midst of this national revitalization and reorganization, progressivism emerged as a political phenomenon. The last three chapters have presented progressivism as the successor to the nation's dominant ideology in its first century, republicanism. That national creed, shared by both major political parties, had been not a single set of ideas, but rather a complex of them, different aspects of which were taken over and emphasized by Democrats and Republicans. All agreed that a republic was a country built upon individual liberty, the concept of equality, a virtuous and disciplined people whose power and wisdom were rooted in their moral wholeness, and a strong and prosperous economy. Democrats, however, put their greatest emphasis upon the first two of these four republican characteristics, whereas Republicans were most concerned with the latter two. Generally, Democrats found their strongest base in the South and among the non-British ethnic outgroups, and Republicans in Yankee, WASP America.

Progressivism on the Republican side was first of all a holy crusade to purify American government and revive democracy by ending boss rule, its enemy in this particular crusade being the ethnic political machine. Yankee moralistic progressivism also fought the "impurity" of ethnic ways of living, especially in the prohibition crusade but also in the broad effort to "Americanize" ethnic work habits and family values through the settlement house and the progressive school. Long rooted in Yankee republicanism had been a distaste for riches and for selfish exploitation of the community, and in the Progressive Era Yankee Republicans, as insurgents against the power in their party of organized capital, fought to take away economic privilege. From its Yankee roots moralistic progressivism derived a profound sense of community and team spirit, which led both to its campaigns for cultural uniformity, in the Yankee image, and to its issuing a moral condemnation of exploitive corporate capitalism. Theodore Roosevelt's New Nationalism, and the Progressive Party that sprang to life at his bidding, singing full-throated hymns at its Chicago convention, expressed moralistic progressivism most faithfully.

The other and closely related strand within the Republican party's ideological tradition, one that reaches back to Alexander Hamilton, was nationalist in its economic attitudes and its appetites in government. A strong and proud nation in the world; the use of elite, expert authority employing "scientific" methods; encouragement of the powerful, imaginative, and enterprising capitalist building great corporations and efficiency and national strength: these were focal points of nationalist progressivism as a political mood. Intellectually cosmopolitan and not particularly religious, nationalist progressivism was led by the new university-trained WASP middle class. It was in essence a modernizing crusade seeking rationality and productivity. J. Pierpont Morgan was in this sense a nationalist progressive in economics, for he was a genius at organizing and centralizing the capitalist system. Being a nationalist progressive in politics, however, meant maintaining a complicated and ambivalent attitude toward such men. Theodore Roosevelt admired the great enterprisers, but he sought at least to discipline those abusing their power. In forest management, in natural-resource development, and in other areas of the economy, nationalistic progressivism led to the exertion of the sovereign's authority over individual enterprise in the interest of the whole community. The organizational revolution extended into government as well. At the local level the characteristic figure of nationalist progressivism, in its bureaucratic, centralizing, efficiency-oriented mood, was the university-trained engineer functioning as city manager. In foreign policy, nationalist progressivism emphasized the building of military power and efficient organization by strengthening the navy and creating a general staff (a central body of planners and centralized command) for the army, as well as by "speaking softly and carrying a big stick."

Progressivism in its Democratic mold, however, was ultimately an effort not simply to discipline and regulate the increasingly constrictive system of trusts and big corporations, but to break it apart, render its reestablishment impossible, and revive an older, individualistic way of life. In this libertarian dimension, progressivism was primarily Southern Democratic and Jeffersonian, though libertarian progressivism of this sort was widespread in the country at large. It drew upon venerable Jacksonian cries against financial power and economic privilege, and called for a decentralized society and for an open field before the small enterpriser. It also condemned the moralistic crusades of Yankee Republicans. After prohibitionism became successful nationally, the great ethnic communities in such cities as Chicago and New York began massive public violations of the law on grounds of personal liberty. The classic statement of libertarian progressivism lay in Woodrow Wilson's New Freedom, and the

Federal Trade Commission and the Federal Reserve Board were its principal offspring.

In its egalitarian dimension, Democratic progressivism echoed to Bryan's endless cannonading against the powerful financial oligarchies, and to Wilson's rhetoric about the small man in economics. Most of all, however, it sprang from the emerging urban liberalism of the ethnic minorities. This first attempt to use government positively to assure some minimal equalizing of American life by means of extensive social reforms came principally from the Irish and Germans of the cities. It leaned toward collectivism by drawing upon European models of social welfare—an especially strong habit of mind among German Catholics like New York City's Robert Wagner. As a search for ways in which people could share more equally in the promise of American life, egalitarian progressivism expressed itself in urban social programs designed to improve labor conditions, housing, education, and life for the old, the helpless, and the fatherless. Northern intellectuals and urban ethnic political machines began enacting such programs at the state and local level from 1910 onward.

In 1916 the labor-oriented leftward swing of Woodrow Wilson in the national capital was the first movement at that level, on the part of a Democratic president, toward the social-welfare liberalism that would later burgeon dramatically under Franklin Roosevelt and the New Deal. Thus, the link between the urban working-class ethnic minorities and the Democratic party, which had broken down badly in the depression of the 1890s, was beginning to revive as America's entry into the First World War drew nearer.

Bibliography

Books that were especially valuable to me in writing this chapter: Arthur S. Link's numerous writings on Woodrow Wilson and his era, such as *Woodrow Wilson and the Progressive Era, 1910–1917** (1954) provide a deep encounter with this remarkable man. My general interpretation of Wilson and of Progressivism, seen in the longer historical trend, is provided in Robert Kelley, "Ideology and Political Culture from Jefferson to Nixon," *The American Historical Review*, 82 (June 1977), 531-62. I continued to rely strongly upon Otis L. Graham, Jr.'s *The Great Campaigns:*

Reform and War in America, 1900–1928 (1971), a major interpretation of this entire era. (See also the Bibliography for Chapter 26.) Concerning the women suffrage movement, I drew from Carl N. Degler's At Odds: Women and the Family in America from the Revolution to the Present (1980); Eleanor Flexner, Century of Struggle: The Woman's Rights Movement in the United States* (1959); and William O'Neill, Everyone Was Brave: The Rise and Fall of Feminism in America* (1969).

On black America, August Meier's brilliant study, Negro Thought in America, 1880–1915: Racial Ideologies in the Age of Booker T. Washington* (1963) was my principal guide, as well as C. Vann Woodward's milestone work, The Strange Career of Jim Crow* (1974).

How Have Historians Looked at the Topic?

Arthur S. Link's monumental multivolume biography is the indispensable source on Wilson; Volume 2, Wilson: The New Freedom* (1956), and Volume 5, Wilson: Campaigns for Progressivism and Peace, 1916–1917 (1965), are particularly important for the president's first administration. John Blum's Woodrow Wilson and the Politics of Morality* (1956) is a short, interpretive work that expertly captures the complexities of Wilson's personality and portrays the sense of poignancy surrounding him. Biographies of Wilson's allies and opponents include J. M. Blum, Joe Tumulty and the Wilson Era (1951); R. M. Lowitt, George W. Norris (1963); A. T. Mason, Brandeis (1946); and M. J. Pusey, Charles Evans Hughes (1951).

Debby Woodroofe's pamphlet, Sisters in Struggle, 1848–1920* (1971) has a sympathetic analysis. Although somewhat dated, Inez Haynes Irwin's Up Hill With Banners Flying (1964)—first published as The Story of the Woman's Party (1921)—graphically depicts the tactics and commitment of Alice Paul and other members of the women's movement. The monumental History of Woman Suffrage, six vols. (1881–1922) is a grab-bag of source material put together over the years by Elizabeth Cady Stanton, Susan B. Anthony, Mathilda Gage, and Ida Husted Harper, all major figures in the suffrage movement.

On black America in the Progressive Era, the background to the progressive period—aptly called the nadir in the black American's status in Rayford W. Logan's The Negro in American Life and Thought: The Nadir, 1877–1901 (1954)—is provided in several perceptive studies. Louis D. Rubin, Jr., ed., Teach the Freeman: The Correspondence of Rutherford B. Hayes and the Slater Fund for Negro Education, 1881–1887, two vols. (1959), draws a connection between the actions of Hayes and other northern philanthropists and the vogue of industrial education for Afro-Americans so often credited to Booker T. Washington's leadership.

One of the most important books published on the segregation question, The Strange Career of Jim Crow* by C. Vann Woodward (1974), offers an insightful analysis of the development of institutional patterns separating the races. Woodward's conclusion as to the recency of southern segregation is supported in a case study by Charles E. Wynes, Race Relations in Virginia, 1870–1902 (1961). In addition to Meier's book, black reaction can be studied in Samuel R. Spencer, Jr.'s critical biography Booker T. Washington and the Negro's Place in American Life (1955) and in Hugh Hawkins, ed., Booker T. Washington and His Critics (1962), a thoughtful selection of writings by and about the black leader.

The rise of black radicalism is best tasted in the works of W. E. B. Du Bois, most notably The Souls of Black Folk* (1903). Two meritorious biographies of Du Bois are now available: Francis L. Broderick's W. E. B. Du Bois: Negro Leader in a Time of Crisis (1959), which treats Du Bois's career as a student and professor as well as his years of leadership with the NAACP, and Elliott M. Rudwick's W. E. B. Du Bois: Propagandist of the Negro Protest (1960), which incorporates findings from the papers of Booker T. Washington.

The NAACP receives thorough treatment in Charles F. Kellogg's fine study NAACP: A History of the National Association for the Advancement of Colored People (1967) and an older work by Robert L. Jack, History of the National Association for the Advancement of Colored People (1943).

* Available in paperback.

28

TIME LINE

1909 President Taft inaugurated Dollar Diplomacy in China and Latin America; United States intervenes in Haitian and Nicaraguan finances

1911 Sun Yat-sen leads creation of Republic of China; Francisco Madero leads revolt in Mexico against Porfirio Diaz

1913 President Wilson terminates Dollar Diplomacy; Victoriano Huerta overthrows Madero and establishes dictatorship in Mexico

1914 First World War begins; President Wilson orders occupation of Veracruz, Mexico

1915 American troops sent to occupy Haiti; Wilson recognizes Carranza government in Mexico; Germany declares unrestricted submarine warfare, sinks *Lusitania;* United States begins preparedness campaign; Shipping Board created to expand merchant marine; House-Grey Memorandum

1916 Germans sink *Sussex,* agree to warn before sinking merchant ves-

1917   sels; Wilson intensifies mediation efforts; American troops occupy Dominican Republic; Francisco Villa raids American town, and American troops chase him into Mexico

1917 Wilson gives ''Peace Without Victory'' address; Germans announce resumption of unrestricted submarine warfare; Russian Revolution; United States enters First World War; Espionage Act

1918 Wilson gives ''Fourteen Points'' address, takes near dictatorial powers over economy, utilizes central direction and planning; Treaty of Brest-Litovsk; Sedition Act; defeat of Germany

1919 In *Schenck* v. *United States* Supreme Court confirms federal powers over freedom of speech during national emergencies; Eighteenth Amendment prohibits alcoholic beverages; Treaty of Versailles; defeat of treaty by Senate; Wilson incapacitated by stroke

1920 Nineteenth Amendment gives vote to women; Warren G. Harding elected twenty-ninth president of the United States

AMERICA AND THE FIRST WORLD WAR

HISTORY IN AN INDIVIDUAL LIFE

UPI

They made an extraordinary pair, walking under the soft green Russian birches: venerable Leo Tolstoy, in his seventy-fifth year, world-renowned, a near saint who preached selfless living for others, and the American Democrat William Jennings Bryan, in his forty-third year, twice a presidential nominee. For days on end at Tolstoy's estate south of Moscow in 1905, they talked of pacifism, God, love as the supreme human force, the toiling poor, militarism, and imperialism. Both condemned warfare as the ultimate curse.

Ten years later Bryan was Woodrow Wilson's secretary of state, a pacifist making foreign policy. His dream was to establish a world of "universal brotherhood" in which America would be "the su-

preme moral factor in the world's progress." Eternal optimist, he believed the world could settle its disputes by investigation, reason, and mediated agreements. True morality and altruism, he said, flourished on earth as never before. He plunged immediately into negotiating bilateral-arbitration treaties with thirty nations, in which they pledged that in any dispute they would hold off from warfare for a year while mediation and arbitration were pursued. Bryan's treaties assumed, he said, "that we have now reached a point in civilization's progress when nations cannot afford to wage war." He insisted that the Republicans' overbearing policies toward Latin America, an expression of the imperialism that he always thunderously condemned, would be dismantled. Latin Americans should be able "to work out their own destiny along lines consistent with popular government." "Dollar diplomacy" was out the window.

America under Wilson and Bryan, however, was soon intervening in the internal affairs of Caribbean islands to end violence and insure elective government. Moreover, Bryan insisted that Mexico's tyrannical, exploitative leadership, which violated his belief in moral, democratic government, must give way to a popular, progressive regime. This meant the withholding of recognition from the dictatorial Victoriano Huerta government, an unprecedented action, and finally the military occupation of the large Mexican coastal city of Veracruz. Missionary diplomacy, moral in its purposes, had produced bald, unblinking intervention on a scale TR had never attempted.

The First World War appalled Bryan. It was a "causeless war" to him, a battle of militarists and munitions manufactures, not a conflict between democracy and autocracy. America *must* stay out of it: no vital interest of the American people, he insisted, was involved. It was barbaric, savage, un-Christian, unjustified. He opposed allowing American arms to be sent to either side, even in foreign vessels. This would mean taking sides, and America must be free to mediate for peace. But Wilson disagreed, and in June 1915 the "Great Commoner" resigned. A pacifist as secretary of state: the two roles had ultimately proved to be incompatible.

Overview

Theodore Roosevelt made the United States a world power. By 1908, the last year of his administration, the nation was deeply involved in Asian politics, thrusting southward into Latin American affairs, and playing a significant role in European diplomacy. Equipped with a large and growing navy, the great Republic became a force to be reckoned with in the ministries of state in Europe. Following Roosevelt, William Howard Taft adopted programs designed to expand American investments, and therefore influence, in Latin America and Asia. Woodrow Wilson then took the nation far down the road toward world leadership. By the end of his time in office, American troops had established protectorates in the Caribbean region, made a major foray into the interior of Mexico, and by the millions had gone abroad to fight in the First World War. No other president in American history was so activist in his foreign policy, which is certainly one of the ironies of history, for Wilson came to the presidency devoted to Liberal-Democratic notions of nonintervention and peaceful foreign relations.

Taft and Dollar Diplomacy

President Taft, a peaceful and legalistic man, turned away from Roosevelt's power politics. He believed that the United States should use its economic strength rather than military power to spread its influence throughout the world. Commerce and the interdependence of nations directed from America's Wall Street was his prescription for world order. If dollars were put in place of guns and the country were to work cooperatively with foreign regimes to allow American businessmen favorable investment opportunities, common interests would replace the rivalries that threatened world peace.

In the Far East, Taft exercised his new Dollar Diplomacy by encouraging American investments in China, especially in railroad building. This, he believed, would halt Japanese expansion of influence there and also hold back the encroachment of European powers. E. H. Harriman, the railroad monopolist, pushed the project vigorously, for he had conceived the grand vision of a worldwide network of steamships and railroads under his direction. At Taft's urging in 1911, a group of American bankers joined a four-power partnership to loan money to the Chinese government for railroad construction. Then in that same year, a Chinese revolutionary named Sun Yat-sen led a rebellion in south China that eventually threw off the Manchu dynasty and established the Republic of China. This triumphantly nationalist movement was hostile to foreign influence, and American bankers withdrew from the railroad partnership.

Meanwhile, dollar diplomacy was actively pushed forward in the Caribbean. The basic notion was that stability in the Central American republics was vital to the safety of the Panama Canal, and that this stability would be best achieved if the United States took over their finances. Vain efforts along these lines were launched in Guatemala and Honduras. Greater success was achieved in Haiti, where a group of American bankers took control of the Haitian National Bank. Nicaragua attracted the greatest American attention because it was near the Panama Canal and contained another potential canal route. An anti-American dictator named José Santos Zelaya was overthrown in 1909 by what amounted to direct American intervention. Soon American marines landed in Nicaragua, and the United States took control of its finances. A small detachment of marines remained in the country until the 1920s to ensure the safety of American lives, property, and investments.

Wilsonian Foreign Policy

Woodrow Wilson came to the White House with a firm grounding in the foreign-policy tradition of British Liberalism, just as his secretary of state William Jennings Bryan drew upon the ideals of Christian pacifism. These traditions involved a fundamental distrust of power politics, a dislike of great empires, and a feeling that international relations should be based on moral rather than materialistic considerations. William Gladstone's ideas, which Wilson had taken up as a Princeton undergraduate, constituted a passionately religious world view stressing the family of humankind in an interdependent, global community where each country should be concerned about the welfare of all others. Wilson, like Gladstone, hated war and armaments and believed that every nation should be free from intervention by outside powers. Ultimately, some form of world parliament should provide a rule of law and order for all, in which every nation, large or small, would be equally treated. Dominating all considerations should be the moral values of the Judeo-Christian tradition. Wilson, Gladstone, and Bryan were all fervently religious men who saw everything in life as being linked to God and His purposes.

This was far removed in ideology from the nationalist power politics of Theodore Roosevelt. He and Wilson, therefore, were bitterly opposed to each other in foreign-policy matters. Roosevelt thought Wilson spineless, unmanly, a canting Presbyterian preacher who did not understand the realities of life. But the paradox was that the noninterventionist Wilson intervened far more in world affairs than Roosevelt ever did as president. A moralistic, self-denying foreign policy contains strong interventionist potentialities. Perhaps the chief difference is that a president like Wilson does with agonizing reluctance things that a president like Roosevelt does with relish and confidence.

Woodrow Wilson and William Jennings Bryan dreamed of a better world. They were devoted to a foreign policy of "movement"; that is, they wanted to do everything they could to foster the spread of a better way of life for the world's peoples. They were missionaries in diplomacy who felt impelled, for example, to teach the Latin American republics how to establish law and order, as Wilson put it. What could conceivably be better for their citizenry? he would ask. The best thing for everyone, Mexicans and Americans alike, was to help encourage, directly if necessary, the growth of democracy and the defeat of dictators. In this, Wilson has been revealingly compared with the Communist leader V. I. Lenin, who also conceived of foreign policy as an opportunity to spread what he regarded as a better way of life. Both men would have denied that their actions were meant just to benefit their own nations; both would have insisted that they were agents of an ennobling world mission. But to the nations in whose politics they intervened, it was difficult to tell the difference between world reformers and nationalists who grabbed as much power and influence as they could.

The central difficulty in a foreign policy of movement is that to those nations being "improved," the policy often looks like hypocrisy. Woodrow Wilson received perhaps more abuse on this score than on any other. To the Latin American nations that bore the brunt of his missionary diplomacy he seemed to be looking out for America's power ambitions while covering his tracks with high-flown words. His constant habit of preaching made the situation worse, for Wilson treated Latin American governments with a paternalism that could easily pass for arrogance. His democratic faith and his religious convictions, moreover, convinced him that he was absolutely right. European prime ministers were to be just as offended by Wilson's righteous ways as were the Latin Americans.

Wilson in Action

As soon as Wilson entered the White House he denounced dollar diplomacy as shameless financial intervention in the affairs of weaker nations. He withdrew American support for investments in China, relying instead on his hopes for a sweeping worldwide program of tariff reductions and freer trade to help every nation achieve prosperity. Part of his foreign-policy tradition was to applaud the rise of self-government in other nations, and he warmly supported the Chinese revolution of Sun Yat-sen. Wilson continued American support of the Open Door policy and deplored the actions of European imperialists in China.

The president also announced a fatefully important policy toward Latin America. It was his desire, he said, to help Latin American peoples by giving American support only to "the orderly processes of just government based upon law, [and] not upon arbitrary or irregular force." The result was that he and Bryan were soon deeply entangled in the internal affairs of Haiti and the Dominican Republic, where a series of bloody revolutions took place from 1913 to 1915. Faced by outright anarchy and widespread suffering in Haiti, in 1915 Wilson sent American troops to occupy the country and establish a government that he believed would be more reflective of the people's wishes. A year later, an identical course was followed in the Dominican Republic. The two countries were then made American protectorates. Meanwhile, a treaty to the same effect was negotiated with Nicaragua. What had happened to the policy of nonintervention? It had given way to what Woodrow Wilson clearly regarded as a higher and more pressing requirement—the best welfare of the people, as he understood it, who lived in these countries.

Wilson and Huerta

Much graver events were under way in Mexico. A dictator named Porfirio Diaz had ruled the country since the 1870s. An ironfisted executive who kept relative peace and good order, he welcomed American investors. Such men supported Diaz, for he created the conditions in which more than a billion American dollars were invested in Mexico by 1910, and some 40,000 American citizens could live there in safety and profit. In 1911, however, a liberal revolution led by Francisco Madero took over the country, calling for genuine representative government, widespread social reforms, and a curbing of foreign investment. American businessmen were hostile to Madero, and the American ambassador, Henry Lane Wilson, shared their sentiments. With his aid, one of the victorious generals in the rebellion, Victoriano Huerta, was able to overthrow Madero, who was then promptly murdered, apparently at Huerta's instigation.

This was the situation when Woodrow Wilson took office. Huerta had seized power only weeks before Wilson's inauguration. The contrast between the two regimes could hardly be more dramatic. Wilson was immediately besieged with advice from businessmen and bankers, including his own ambassador in Mexico City, that he extend diplomatic recognition to Huerta. This, after all, was standard practice. Nations did not then sit in judgment on each other, at least in the daily conduct of foreign relations. If a new government had de facto power—if it was in reality the effective government of a country—then it would be recognized: ambassadors would be exchanged; consuls established in various cities to ease trade relations; and all commercial interactions regularized.

But Wilson broke with this practice. He was deeply offended by the bloody-handed Huerta, and hardly allowed the man's name to be uttered in the White House. The Mexican regime, in Wilson's words, was a "government of butchers," and he would have nothing to do with it that even remotely implied moral acceptance. The State Department was staffed with people of the old diplomacy, and they were shocked at Wilson's new approach. They could understand the use of high-handed diplomacy in order to open markets and protect American property, but the same tactics adopted to reform the government of another nation were inconceivable.

As far as historians are aware, most of the Mexican people despised Huerta, but they reacted angrily to Wilson's efforts to change their government. Whatever their problems, they wished to settle them among themselves, without the indignity of intervention by a moralistic preaching *Norteamericano* (the term preferred in Latin America for citizens of the United States, *American* carrying the implication that only those living north of the Rio Grande can be so named). Whatever the "Colossus of the North" does in Latin America is necessarily regarded with distrust, just as Scots distrust their larger neighbor England and Poles react against everything Russian.

Wilson Decides on Direct Intervention

Wilson informed European governments that he intended to see Huerta removed. At first he relied on diplomatic pressure and sought to get the cooperation of the Constitutionalists in Mexico, who under the headship of First Chief Venustiano Carranza were struggling to overthrow Huerta. Following this, the upper classes of Mexico, joined by the Roman Catholic Church, rallied around Huerta so that by the spring of 1914 Huerta was, if anything, more strongly in control of the heart of the country than ever. In this circumstance Wilson felt forced either to give up entirely in his determined effort to remove Huerta and establish democratic government, or take up arms himself.

It was inconceivable, given Wilson's character and his beliefs, that he should back down. He believed the Mexican cause to be vital to the rise of democracy and constitutional government throughout Latin America. But he blundered terribly in the steps he then took. He seized on a ridiculously meaningless incident in the Mexican part of Tampico, in which Huerta's soldiers and officials had apparently treated American sailors and the American flag with studied contempt. Going before Congress in April 1914, he talked

AMERICA AND THE FIRST WORLD WAR

grandly of American honor, inflated the importance of the Tampico and other "similar" events, and asked for authority to use American forces in whatever way might be necessary to force General Huerta to treat Americans with due respect. His real objective, however, was to cut Huerta off from the sea, dry up his source of funds (import revenues from Veracruz), and topple him from power.

Wilson badly misled himself. He confidently believed that the Mexican people so detested Huerta that they would welcome his aid. He anticipated a bloodless occupation of Veracruz, followed by the peaceful downfall of Huerta. After this, American forces, having done their deed for democracy, would withdraw. He got authority from Congress to intervene, but as soon as he landed troops to take over Veracruz, an enormous uproar broke out in the United States and throughout Latin America and Europe. The Mexican people were deeply offended at this high-handed action, and a short battle ensued in which 126 Mexicans and 19 Americans died. Mexican newspapers screamed patriotic appeals. Huertista and Constitutionalist forces joined in condemning Wilson. Mobs roaming the streets of Mexican cities destroyed American property and threatened American citizens. Riots broke out all over Latin America, Europeans furiously condemned the action, and a flood of messages poured in on Wilson from outraged Americans. Few could understand so shocking an event on so puny a justification.

These events—especially the news of the casualties at Veracruz—left Wilson shaken and ashen-faced. He was shocked that his decisions had led to such a disaster. Thereafter Wilson tried to walk a narrow line. Military leaders and bellicose Americans demanded a full-scale war, but Wilson would not budge beyond Veracruz. He quickly agreed to proferred mediation by the "ABC" powers (Argentina, Brazil, and Chile), during which he insisted that the way must be cleared for the Constitutionalists to assume the government of Mexico. The Constitutionalists, however, continued proudly to spurn any diplomatic help whatsoever from the United States. But while the mediation conference was ending on an inconclusive note, Huerta finally had to give up the presidency in response to Constitutionalist victories, and Carranza's regime triumphantly took over the government of Mexico. Wilson received a flood of congratulations. A Constitutionalist regime was finally established in Mexico. The Congress installed Carranza as president, adopted a new constitution, and set in motion Latin America's first twentieth-century socioeconomic revolution.

The crisis, unhappily, was not yet over. Francisco Villa, one of the Constitutionalist generals, wished to be president and soon revolted against Carranza. Once more, Mexico was plunged into bloody civil war. Eventually, it became clear to Wilson that Carranza represented the hope of genuine social reform, whereas Villa would reinstitute the old corrupt regime of wealthy landowners and American investors. Having withdrawn American troops from Veracruz in November 1914, thus allowing Carranza forces to take the city and secure its revenues, he extended recognition to the regime in October 1915.

U.S. Troops lined up in Veracruz, Mexico, after American forces in 1914 had attacked and occupied the city. Wilson by this means hoped to bring down the dictator, General Victoriano Huerta, who had recently seized power in Mexico.

Wide World Photos

Villa then began murdering Americans in an outright attempt to force American military intervention. In March 1916 he invaded New Mexico to sack the town of Columbus. In response Wilson sent General John J. Pershing into Mexico to search out Villa. By April 1916, American troops had traveled 300 miles into Mexico and were fighting at Parral with the Mexican government's troops. But Pershing never caught Villa, and President Carranza angrily demanded that American troops withdraw. Wilson finally pulled Pershing's expedition out of Mexico in February 1917 only because affairs in Europe were so threatening that the American government could no longer afford to divert its energies.

America Reacts to the First World War

The First World War broke out in August 1914, and with startling suddenness escalated into a worldwide conflict in which the combatants fought with unparalleled ferocity. Every weapon imaginable or technically possible at the time was put to use in this unbelievably desperate struggle. Why it broke out, no one seemed able to explain satisfactorily. But the fact was that the First World War became a total war in which millions of men rushed to arms and were flung at each other in such huge charging masses that in some battles more than a hundred thousand men died in a few hours. The planet had never before witnessed anything like it.

The Central Powers (Germany and Austria-Hungary, together with Bulgaria and the Ottoman Empire) faced the Allies (Great Britain, France, and Russia, together with Italy and some smaller states). The Germans swept into France through neutral Belgium on a broad front, being brought to a halt just short, so it seemed, of victory. Trenches hundreds of miles long, stretching from the English Channel to Switzerland, were quickly dug, and enormous armies disappeared into them for four terrible years of periodic charge and countercharge. The huge Russian front saw a confused and bloody grappling that in 1917 ended in the collapse of the czarist government and, after a brief interval, the emergence of the Soviet Socialist Republic under V. I. Lenin, who promptly made a separate peace with the Central

Powers. The United States entered the war in April 1917. The million men it placed in France within a year tipped the scale on the Allied side, and with their front collapsing the Germans asked for an armistice in November 1918.

The dead were uncountable. No one will ever know exactly how many died, but they numbered at least thirty million, including civilian deaths. All European civilization was bled white, for a large proportion of an entire generation had been swept away. No graver wound had ever been suffered by European culture save perhaps the Black Death of the Middle Ages. In 1914, it had seemed that democracy and a better life for all were on the march everywhere; at World War I's end, democracy seemed either destroyed or dying, millions were starving, and a new era of barbaric totalitarianism was emerging. The Austro-Hungarian Empire was destroyed, as were the empires of the Germans, the Ottomans, and the Russian czars—surely no great loss to humankind. But an entire way of life, encompassing tens of millions of people and stretching over vast reaches of the earth's surface, lay in ruins. In many ways the greatest tragedy of the twentieth century is the first World War, not only for what it destroyed directly, but for what it led to.

What did Americans think in 1914 when Europe suddenly fell into this savage war? They were utterly shocked. President Wilson tried from the outset to be neutral in thought and deed, and by and large the mass of the American people agreed. But at least a third of the population in 1914 was either foreign-born or the children of foreign-born, and so the war put cruel strains on everyone. Some 8 million Americans were of German or Austrian descent, about 4.5 million were of Irish heritage, and both groups were outspokenly hostile to Great Britain.

For millions more, however, Germany had long been a threatening menace on the horizon. There was the potent image of the German military caste, whose spike-helmeted visage now appearing in newspaper photographs seemed almost bestially warlike. More than this, the majority of the American people were of British lineage, and everything in the deepest chords of memory pulled them toward the British side. Democrats looked to Liberals with a sense of comradeship; Republicans looked to Conservatives in brotherly respect; and Socialists admired the Labor party.

Language, culture, religion, way of life, economic and social ties, a lively and continuous interchange of books and ideas across the Atlantic, the common heritage of representative government and personal rights—these all made it a foregone conclusion that from the outset American sympathies would be primarily with the British and the similarly democratic French.

Wilson Searches for Peace

Wilson did not ask the nation to go to war, however, until he had spent two and a half years in a futile search for some means of keeping the United States out of the combat. His first step was to strike a neutral course, since an overwhelming percentage of the American people had no desire to enter the frightful conflict. But how to be genuinely neutral? Without the huge production of American factories and American loans to the Allies so they could buy that output, it seems probable that the Central Powers would have won. This trade soon skyrocketed to massive proportions. American exports to the Allies before the war had been valued at about $800 million annually. By 1916, they had soared to $3.2 billion. By 1917, some $2.2 billion had been loaned to the Allies to support this trade (and only about $30 million to the Central Powers).

Clearly, an economic revolution of gigantic proportions was transforming the American economy. Not only did factories all over the land boom along day and night to fill the armament orders, they also turned busily to providing goods for the worldwide markets that the British and other European countries now had to abandon in their concentration on the war. The German government urged that the United States declare an embargo on the sale of munitions, for the British navy soon effectively ended any trade between the Central Powers and the United States by clearing the seas of enemy merchantmen. Such a move by the United States, however, would in fact have been unneutral, for command of the sea lanes was dictated by the facts of war, not by American actions. An embargo resulting from conscious American actions would have changed the outcome of the war, in all probability—and most Americans did not, in any event, wish for a Central Powers victory.

The Submarine Crisis

The submarine was a new invention, and like the atom bomb in a later war, it transformed the whole nature of the conflict. The Germans in 1915 felt driven to use submarines for several reasons: their land armies had not won; the war had settled down into a bloody stalemate; and the British blockade would eventually win the war if allowed to go on long enough. Moreover, Germany's admirals were excited over their new weapon—of which in 1915 they possessed only about twenty—and were absolutely confident that it could win the war if unleashed. (This was not the first time, nor was it to be the last, that military men, enamored of some new weapon, were to present this argument to a national government and thereby bring about unexpected results of vast importance.)

The submarine, however, had a grave tactical problem. A small and slow craft, its hull was necessarily thin since armor plating rendered it heavy and useless. When under the sea it was lethal and usually impregnable; when surfaced it was potentially at the mercy of the kind of small-caliber cannon that British merchantmen carried. (Actually, skillful tactics generally negated this threat, so that no German submarine was sunk by an armed merchantman before April 1917.) This made the following of "cruiser rules" risky. (Cruiser rules required vessels attacking merchantmen to give sufficient warning before sinking them to allow sailors to disembark and enter lifeboats.)

Therefore, the Germans announced that every enemy ship located in a huge area around Britain would be torpedoed by submarines without notice. Neutrals were warned that the mechanics of war made their vessels liable to unintended attacks. The German announcement was almost purely a bluff, for the tiny number of submarines they possessed could do little to check the streams of vessels carrying cargoes to Great Britain and France. However, few elsewhere in the world realized this. Especially in America, this unprecedented and apparently cowardly form of assault created a shock wave of revulsion and horror. Neutral nations were intensely concerned, for it seemed highly unlikely that a German officer peering through a periscope lens awash by sea and fog could accurately distinguish

← **U.S.A.** 1917

NORWAY

Oslo •

FINLAND
Indep. July, 1917

Lake Ladoga

• Helsinki

• Petrograd

SWEDEN

Stockholm •

ESTONIA
Indep.
Feb. 1918

RUSSIA
1914

NORTH SEA

Edinburgh •

LATVIA
Indep.
Nov, 1918

Riga •

Battle of Jutland
May-June, 1916

DENMARK

BALTIC SEA

Riga offensive
Sept, 1917

LITHUANIA
Indep. Feb. 1918

Memel •

Smolensk •

Copenhagen •

GREAT
BRITAIN
1914

Konigsberg •

• Vilna

Kiel •

Danzig •

Masurian Lakes
Sept, 1914

• Minsk

London •

Amsterdam •

• Hamburg

NETH.

Berlin •

GERMANY
1914

Tannenberg
Aug, 1914

POLAND
Indep. Nov, 1918

• Pinsk

Brussels •

BELG.
1914

Cologne •

Leipzig •

Warsaw •

• Brest-Litovsk

Kiev •

GERMAN INVASION
AUG-SEPT, 1914

• Dresden

• Lublin

Paris •

Mainz •

• Metz

Prague •

Cracow •

Lemberg •

GALICIA

Kerensky offensive
July, 1917

LUX.

• Strasbourg

Rhine R.

FRANCE
1914

BAVARIA
• Munich

Danube R.

Vienna •

Galicia offensives
Aug, 1914

Brusilov offensive
June, 1916

Berne •

SWITZ.

Vittorio-Veneto
Oct-Nov, 1918

Pressburg •

• Graz

UKRAINE

Milan •

Piave June, 1918

• Budapest

AUSTRIA-HUNGARY
1914

• Odessa

Genoa •

Venice •

• Trieste

Invasion of Serbia
1914

RUMANIA
1916

• Marseilles

BOSNIA

Belgrade •

Bucharest •

Danube R.

*BLACK
SEA*

SPAIN

ITALY
1915

Sarajevo •

Withdrew from
Triple Alliance 1914

CORSICA

MONTENEGRO
1915

SERBIA
1914

BULGARIA
1915

• Rome

• Sofia

Constantinople •

SARDINIA

ALBANIA

OTTOMAN EMPIRE
1914

• Naples

MEDITERRANEAN

← **PORTUGAL** 1916

Salonika •

Gallipoli

GREECE
1916

Dardanelles campaign
1915-1916

• Smyrna

SICILY

SEA

Athens •

CRETE

0   500

Miles

1916   Date of entry into the war

————   Maximum advance of the Central Powers

– – – –   Maximum Russian advance

••••••••   Line of the Brest-Litovsk Treaty Mar, 1918

————   Armistice lines, eastern front Dec., 1917

Central Powers   Allied Powers   Neutral Powers

between enemy and neutral vessels. Furthermore, neutrals (such as Americans) regularly traveled as passengers on British liners. Acutely concerned with protecting every detail of international law, Wilson warned constantly that neutral rights had to be protected or else the entire fabric of international law would crumble. In response to the German announcement of unrestricted submarine warfare, he stated that the United States would hold Germany "strictly accountable" if any American lives were lost or American ships sunk.

In late March 1915 the first American life was lost when a British liner was sunk. Then, in an event that shocked the world, the British liner *Lusitania* was sunk, carrying almost twelve hundred persons, including more than a hundred Americans, to their deaths. An earthquake of anger swept the American nation, and President Wilson demanded of Germany that its submarines henceforth refrain from attacking any unarmed passenger liner, whether enemy or neutral. When another such ship was sunk, he took the grave step of warning that diplomatic relations might be broken off, at which point the Germans relented and agreed to make no more such attacks.

The Preparedness Campaign

Now Wilson reluctantly began to equip the nation with military strength, for his negotiations with Germany had demonstrated how difficult it was to achieve anything from a position of weakness. But when he asked Congress for large increases in the navy and army, every antimilitarist group in the country broke into clamorous protest. Wilson now stumped the country appealing for support. Eventually the army was expanded moderately— to about 200,000 men—the state militia was renamed the National Guard and made subject to the president's call, and a formidable array of battleships and other powerful naval craft was authorized.

In the Democratic nominating convention of 1916, speakers found that the delegates went into frenzies of cheering at any mention of Wilson's success in keeping the nation out of the war. Thenceforth, this became the Democratic battle cry: Wilson was not only a full-fledged progressive, as the reforms described in the previous chapter indicated, he had also kept the nation at peace. Wilson chimed in by charging that the Republicans were the "war party." Winning a cliff-hanging victory on these issues, he then turned again to the sober business of fulfilling his pledge.

Wilson Seeks to Mediate

Wilson's hope was to serve as mediator between the warring parties, and he worked hard at this from the time the war began. He sent his confidential adviser, Colonel Edward M. House, on tours of the warring capitals to try to find some basis for negotiations, but to little avail. Wilson had made it clear that the kind of peace settlement to be worked out in such a conference would be one in which they had little interest—a peace of genuine reconciliation in which neither side gained or lost anything. Wilson was calling, in effect, for a new diplomacy to replace the old. Liberals in America and in the Allied countries had been arguing since the war began for a settlement that would establish a new world order in which the practice of secret negotiations would be ended, entangling alliances would be terminated, balance-of-power diplomacy would be replaced by an international parliament where all nations would be treated with equal consideration, and military strength would not be the dominant consideration. Massive disarmament should take place, for it was firmly believed that huge armies and navies were themselves the catalysts that brought on such horrifying conflicts. National groups ruled by alien governments (for example, the Czechs in the Austro-Hungarian Empire) should be given self-government. In the world at large, there should be freedom of the seas and an end to economic barriers between nations.

This was the kind of new diplomacy for which Wilson contended. He insisted on open negotiations, no indemnities (after the defeat of a nation in war, payments forced from it to compensate the victor for its losses), no punishments, no gobbling up of new territories. Making himself the leader of the new internationalism, he said repeatedly that the peace to be made should consider the people's wishes, not simply those of powerful government leaders. The British supported the notion of an international parliament, a league of nations, for the suggestion that such a body be created had in fact first come from them. But the rest of the new diplomacy was unacceptable to the Allies. A whole network of secret treaties had been worked out in which each nation was promised major territorial gains at the expense of the Central Powers. Furthermore, the Allied governments recognized that Wilson's real allies within the European nations were the labor unions and the reforming parties—the parties of movement—who wanted a "people's peace." They feared that surrendering diplomacy to the control of such parties would whet appetites for social revolutions, and this they abhorred.

As the war went on and became ever more bloody, discontent began welling up in the civilian populations of the Allied countries. They read the horrifying casualty lists; they saw whole generations of young men fall like wheat before a scythe; they learned of the mounds of dead that stretched for miles and miles after each "victory." There was a point during the conflict, Walter Lippmann once wrote, when the First World War became "hyperbolic." That is, its fantastic pressures simply burst the bounds of western Europe's institutional arrangements, and the people lost faith both in their leaders and in the systems under which they had been ruled. At this point, with mutiny threatening in the French army and the British digging deeper into the barrel of available manpower, the masses began looking to Woodrow Wilson as their new Messiah, their deliverer from carnage and death.

not possess enough submarines to justify the risk of war with the United States, and in early May 1916 it agreed that its navy would visit and search all vessels before attacking them—a sharp limitation on its whole undersea campaign. It was a spectacular diplomatic victory for the president, but the agreement was precarious. Who could tell when the Germans would change their policy? And when they did, what would Wilson be able to do? The only weapon he had left was war itself.

Wilson feared that the mounting desperation of the struggle in Europe, of which the submarine issue was only one outgrowth, might inevitably pull the United States into the war. In January 1917 in a speech before the Senate, he called for a "peace without victory." In such a peace, he said, there should be limitation of armaments, freedom of the seas, self-determination for all peoples, and security against aggression for every nation, small and large. Then a "league of peace" should be formed to enforce the peace settlement. The European masses reacted gratefully to this appeal, and even the British indicated that they were ready to attend such a conference. But the moment was too late. The Germans had decided to launch unrestricted submarine warfare: to sink without warning every vessel, neutral as well as Allied, liner as well as merchantman, that approached the British Isles or the French coast.

Europe Remains Belligerent

But in 1916 this point had not yet been reached. The publics of the warring nations were so embittered against their enemies that their governments could confidently reject Wilson's proposals for a peace of reconciliation. Everyone wanted to punish everyone else. The Central Powers had ambitious dreams of conquest (as the peace treaty they later extorted from Russia in 1918 proved), and their admirals and generals, like those on the Allied side, constantly predicted victory.

Meanwhile, the submarine problem grew more serious. In March 1916 a French vessel, the *Sussex*, was torpedoed in the English Channel with heavy loss of life. More such attacks soon occurred, and Wilson issued what amounted to a threat of war if the Germans did not cease all attacks made without warning on enemy or neutral merchantmen. The German government still did

And the War Came

Germany made this decision because it now possessed almost a hundred submarines and its admirals had persuaded the government that an unrestricted campaign would win the war. The Germans knew that it would bring the Americans into the war, but they were convinced that victory would come long before American armies could have any effect on the western front. Totally severing the lines of supply to the British Isles, they believed, would swiftly starve war-weakened England into submission. It was a bold and fateful move.

Still the president hesitated. He broke relations with Germany as a minimum gesture. Then he learned that the German government (in the British-discovered Zimmermann Telegram) was trying to get Mexico to attack the United States if America entered the war by promising to give

Mexico the American Southwest. This news inflamed American opinion to a fever pitch. Then ship after ship began to be sunk. Public opinion swung rapidly toward war. Prominent newspapers urged it as the only answer, and formerly impartial public figures such as the philosopher John Dewey said that war was the last response left. Then in Russia a revolution took place on March 15, 1917, in which a moderately socialistic regime (the "Mensheviks") overthrew the czarist government, thus eliminating the only autocracy on the Allied side. The Allied cause could now be confidently declared to be that of democracy and human rights. Thousands of Americans gathered in protests against the sinking of American ships. By mid March, Wilson's own cabinet was unanimously urging him to go to war.

By this time Wilson had come to a decision: no great power could submit to its merchant vessels being destroyed day after day without losing all influence it possessed in the world. The United States must fight back, and going to war was the only way effectively to do that. He had totally lost hope that he could deal in any way with the militarists in command of German policy. Most of all, he was convinced that American entry into the war was the best means to bring the war to an end as soon as possible and rebuild a civilized world.

On April 2, 1917, he asked Congress to declare war in a speech that gave the nation high ideals to fight for—not the balance of power, or national interest narrowly conceived, but the future of humankind. Wilson was sufficiently a realist to know that American security absolutely depended on the continued independence and freedom of Britain, with its huge navy and its commitment to democracy. Germany, he was convinced, was an unbearable menace to the safety of any freedom-loving world. In his own words, it "was a madman that needed restraining." The prospect of the world order that autocratic, militaristic Germany would create after a victory could not be tolerated.

By temperament, however, Wilson was a moralist, an idealist, a dreamer of great dreams. His mind, as always, could be seized most warmly by noble epics of human achievement. And so he spoke to the nation in his war message not of practical considerations or of limited objectives but of the need to eliminate autocracy, and, by eliminating the methods by which autocracies carried on their international relations, make the

Yanks parade through London on August 15, 1917, before being shipped to France. Huge American reinforcements soon helped check German offensives and turn the tide of the war.

United States Signal Corps, The National Archives

world a safe place for democracy. America was going to be fighting for the rights of neutrals, for peace and justice, and for the right of self-government by oppressed peoples. He called for a new world order, not for a restoration of the old.

In these words, Woodrow Wilson asked for a declaration of war against the imperial German government: "The present German submarine warfare against commerce is a warfare against mankind. It is a war against all nations. . . . Our motive [in responding] will not be revenge or the victorious assertion of the physical might of the nation, but only the vindication of right, of human right, of which we are only a single champion. . . . There is one choice we cannot make, we are incapable of making: we will not choose the path of submission and suffer the most sacred rights of our Nation and our people to be ignored or violated. . . .

"Our object now . . . is to vindicate the principles of peace and justice in the life of the world as against selfish and autocratic power and to set up amongst the really free and self-governed peoples of the world such a concert of purpose and of action as will henceforth insure the observance of those principles. Neutrality is no longer feasible or desirable where the peace of the world is involved and the freedom of its peoples, and the menace to that peace and freedom lies in the existence of autocratic governments backed by organized force which is controlled wholly by their will, not by the will of their people. . . . [We] know that in such a Government, following [its secret, autocratic] methods, we can never have a friend; and that in the presence of its organized power, always lying in wait to accomplish we know not what purpose, there can be no assured security for the democratic Governments of the world. . . . The world must be made safe for democracy. Its peace must be planted upon the tested foundations of political liberty. . . . We are but one of the champions of the rights of mankind. We shall be satisfied when those rights have been made as secure as the faith and the freedom of nations can make them."

In effect, Woodrow Wilson had made America's entrance into the First World War the climax of progressivism. The ideas, energies, and skills built up in the revitalization of democracy at home now turned under his leadership to the cause of world regeneration. The American people responded wholeheartedly to this grand vision. Unhappily, they were not prepared for the fact that in the peace conference that eventually took place Wilson faced men devoted to the old diplomacy. It was, therefore, impossible for him to secure many of the things for which he had so eloquently appealed. Wilson's brilliant war speech, one of the greatest utterances in American history, sowed the seeds of a massive disillusionment in the future.

America Mobilizes

The United States entered the war at a critical time, for, as Wilson soon learned, the British and French were at the point of total exhaustion and near defeat. Unhappily, however, the preparedness campaign Wilson had already launched was slow to pay any dividends. Conscription was enacted, but the first draftees did not begin training until the fall of 1917. Meanwhile, the nation was stumbling along trying to find some way of marshaling its economic and military energies. Early in 1918 the president, relying on legislation earlier passed by Congress, took near dictatorial powers to bring the economy under rigorously centralized direction—thus putting into practice the central concepts of nationalist progressivism. The War Industries Board took over the task of coordinat-

ing the manufacture of all war goods: raw materials were allocated efficiently; production was standardized; prices were fixed; and the purchases of American and Allied armed forces were coordinated. William McAdoo, secretary of the Treasury, took over direction of the railroads, which had fallen into total confusion. Similar steps were taken with regard to food production, under the direction of Herbert Hoover, an engineer who had gained worldwide fame as the man who kept food moving into Belgium during the German occupation. Since wheat prices were set at such a high level that farm production skyrocketed, marginal lands everywhere in the nation were pressed into service. In a year's time exports of food rose from about twelve to over eighteen million tons, and at the same time farm income rose perhaps 30 percent.

The war affected the economic situation of America's city dwellers in varying ways. Salaried workers found their incomes down 22 percent by war's end due to inflation, but on the other hand thousands of men became millionaires. Labor benefited greatly from the war, for Wilson gave strong support to their demands for collective-bargaining agreements with employers. Since some five million men were ultimately drawn into military service, working men had an unprecedented leverage in wage disputes. Wilson established the National War Labor Board, which negotiated settlements in hundreds of disagreements, usually on the side of the unions. From about 2 million members in 1916, the AFL grew to 3.26 million by 1920. Even the wages of unskilled workers rose, and perhaps half a million black Americans left the South to take up northern jobs.

Civil Liberties Crushed

Wilson's liberalism, however, failed miserably in one crucial test: he could not stand criticism. Entering the war was a frightful wrench for him, and he was forced to justify it to himself by seeing the war as one fought for the highest and most crucial interests of all mankind. He therefore saw any critic of the war as an enemy of human welfare. An Espionage Act was passed in 1917, and a Sedition Act in 1918, which revived the worst features of John Adams's Alien and Sedition Acts of 1798. Anyone aiding the enemy, obstructing recruiting, hampering the sale of war bonds, or even daring to "utter, print, write, or publish any disloyal, profane, scurrilous or abusive language" about the government, the Constitution, or the military was to be harshly punished—and many were.

Furthermore, a nationwide spy system was established to search out heretics. Union meetings, peace gatherings, and all such assemblages were honeycombed with informants. People guilty of no discernible crime were rushed off to jail, held without bail, and, reportedly, in extreme cases physically abused. A woman who received a Red Cross solicitor in a "hostile" manner, a socialist who wrote a letter to a newspaper charging wartime profiteering, a Californian who laughed at rookies drilling in San Francisco, a New Yorker who spat near some Italian officers—all were put in jail. *The Masses*, a socialist periodical, was shut down, for the American Socialist party had come out against participation in the war, which it condemned as nothing more than an argument between capitalists. Eugene V. Debs was given the barbarous sentence of ten years in jail for making an antiwar speech. Robert Goldstein made a movie, *The Spirit of '76*, which was hostile to British soldiers, and he too was sentenced to ten years in jail. When a woman wrote, "I am for the people, and the government is for the profiteers," the same punishment was meted to her. Worst of all, the Supreme Court upheld these actions in *Schenck* v. *United States* (1919), in a decision in which Justice Oliver Wendell Holmes, Jr., said that no one, in the name of free speech, had the right to shout "Fire!" in a crowded theater. By extension, this apparently justified the government in doing whatever it thought best during a time of war.

Progressives Respond

American progressivism had been largely indifferent to world affairs, but now the challenge of war forced a radical shift of attention. Many were devoted pacifists, such as William Jennings Bryan, or were doubtful about the rightfulness of the cause. Robert La Follette was one of the few in Congress who refused to rise and cheer when Wilson asked for war. But the president was successful in persuading progressives that the war was vitally related to a better future for humankind, and soon most of them swung enthusiastically behind American involvement. Now their task, as they saw it, was not only reforming America but reforming the world as well. In this spirit, Bryan and La Follette left their doubts behind and supported the cause.

Many progressives were also excited by the social possibilities that the war effort opened up within the nation itself. A sense of national unity emerged, and the progressive mind seemed always to respond eagerly to anything that induced collective action. Powerful governmental agencies in Washington, D.C., demonstrated as nothing ever had before what remarkable things could be done when the nation's energies were directed into socially useful directions—and the war was thought of as socially useful. A new sense of the possibilities inherent in cooperation between business and government emerged as business leaders came to Washington to direct the new agencies.

All sorts of reforms now seemed possible. The Department of Labor built thousands of homes for working families. Social workers labored in training camps, the Red Cross, and other agencies to aid, educate, and "uplift" thousands of poor people brought in from the hills, the farms, and the slums. The drive toward prohibition of alcohol reached victory in the Eighteenth Amendment (1919), and the vote for women was achieved in the Nineteenth Amendment (1920). Government operation of the railroads transformed them into a surprisingly efficient system. It seemed a time of true national collectivism, a time in which the regulatory state had finally emerged.

Even Wilson was inspired by the new possibilities. In 1919, while laboring in the peace conference at Versailles, he cabled a message to Congress calling for "a new organization of industry . . . [a] genuine democratization of industry . . . [a] cooperation and partnership based upon a real community of interest and participation in control." Progressives talked excitedly about the potentialities of national planning. McAdoo recommended that the railroads remain under government direction, and Josephus Daniels, secretary of the navy, recommended the same for the radio system. Progressive Republicans like William Allen White were enthusiastic about the possibility of national old-age pensions and public operation of the natural resources of oil, water, forests, and mines.

At war's end, such people in the United States and in Europe cherished a magnificent vision of the future. The fighting had created terrible disasters, but the experience of winning had revealed that each nation possessed the means of taking control of its resources and making human life rich and satisfying. When everyone was dedicated to an end greater than self-gain (save for those who became millionaires), there had been a vast release of energy. Molds had been broken, lives had been shunted into new channels, and new outlooks had emerged. The world seemed swept by winds of promising change, and for a time at least it was a young person's world full of hope in the midst of disaster.

The Fourteen Points

Wilson went to war in order to win a different kind of peace from the one he knew was on the minds of the Allied leaders. For this reason he referred to the United States as an "associated" rather than an "allied" power. The United States military operation was a separate affair, and Wilson consciously steered his diplomacy clear of any association with secret treaties of annexation or demands for vengeance. Once the United States had entered the war, he repeatedly called for a liberal peace. There were moderate elements in the German Reichstag (legislature), and he hoped that by his appeals he would inspire these antiwar groups to take control of German policy and make peace. He was, in fact, inclined to make separate peace negotiations if the Allies refused to respond to any overtures that might come from the Germans. He even hoped that the German army would not collapse entirely, for then the Allied governments would have the Germans wholly at their mercy.

Meanwhile, a huge American army and navy were being assembled to fight Germany. The German army mounted offensive after offensive. In July 1917 the first small American units came into the fighting line. In November the war was powerfully affected by events in Russia. There the Bolsheviks (Communists) under V. I. Lenin overthrew the moderate socialist government that had ruled since the czar's fall from power, and promptly asked for peace with Germany. They published the secret annexationist treaties that they found in the Russian archives, thus humiliat-

ing the Allied governments. Lenin, in a statement to the world, called the holocaust a squabble between capitalists who were using the common people as cannon fodder. He appealed to the masses of the world to rise in revolt against the capitalist system and open the way for worldwide equalitarian communism.

Now Woodrow Wilson came forward to give, in effect, the reply of the Western capitalist democracies to Lenin's appeals. He wished to prove to the suffering peoples of Europe that the West, too, could create a liberal and humane peace settlement. In January 1918 he issued his famous "Fourteen Points" address. It contained in eloquent language an appeal for a new world order. Wilson was also quite specific on the issue of self-determination in such territories as Alsace-Lorraine and the Balkans, and for the oppressed Czech and Polish peoples in the Austro-Hungarian Empire. Finally, the president took careful pains to assure the German people that the West intended no vengeance against them but only desired an end to the autocratic regime that had deluged Europe with blood and suffering.

The Fourteen Points were essentially a ringing international statement of the Liberal-Democratic world view. All trade barriers were to be removed—a principle of the purest Adam Smith lineage. Smithian economics conceived of the international community as most productive and peace-loving when all nations could freely produce what they were best suited to make, and without hindrance exchange their products for those of other nations. The ideal, in other words, was a world economy based upon an international division of labor. The seas should be open to all, even in time of war. Militarism, for generations the special object of Liberal-Democratic distrust, should be eliminated by general disarmament. The secretive diplomatic maneuvering of elitist, autocratic governments should be swept away; all international affairs should be placed before the public gaze, as is government within a democracy. And an international government, a league of nations, founded in parliamentary principles, with equal representation for all countries, should rule the world.

It is important to remember that the Liberals in Britain and the Democrats in the United States, who gave Wilson's liberal internationalism its most fervent support, were both political parties that in their own nations represented the outgroups: the Scots and Irish in Britain, and the non-WASP minorities in the United States. In other words, both parties had long sought equal status for minority groups (save, in America, for Afro-Americans). It is therefore hardly coincidental that the Liberal-Democratic internationalism to which Wilson now gave such eloquent expression argued for the equality of all nations, large and small; for a multilateral world democratic order to replace dominance by a few great powers; and for the right of each people, each ethnic community, to govern itself.

The immediate impact of the Fourteen Points, with their luminous image of a new world order, was enormous. The Allied governments, dominated by stern nationalists devoted to the old diplomacy of realism and balance-of-power tactics, in which the great powers ran the world, gave them no open endorsement. But the European peoples at large responded enthusiastically. Even the German people, long-suffering, patient, and trustful, began to grow restless. Then in March 1918 came a fateful event—the Treaty of Brest-Litovsk. By brutal uses of force, the Germans extorted an enormous region from Russia comprising almost 400,000 square miles and fifty million people. Now it was clear that Wilson's hopes for an overthrow of German militarism from within were groundless. In an angry outburst that amounted almost to a second declaration of war, he asserted that there was now only one answer: "Force, Force to the utmost, Force without stint or limit, the righteous and triumphant Force which shall make Right the law of the world, and cast every selfish dominion down in the dust." It was the world's tragic fate that the very use of this overwhelming force would make it impossible for Woodrow Wilson to achieve a "peace without victory." When the Allies won, the Germans were militarily crushed. They had to accept whatever the victorious powers handed down.

The Final Year of War

The war, however, was far from over. The collapse of Russia had freed the German army to shift forty tested divisions from the eastern to the western front, where they mounted a climactic offensive in 1918 designed to end the war. When the assaults began in the spring, there were still less than 30,000 Americans (about two divisions) in action. By July, however, their numbers had risen to 85,000, and the immense Allied counterattack that came in August 1918 included more than a quarter of a million Americans. The buildup continued with astonishing swiftness: soldiers were flooding into France on a veritable bridge of boats from the United States. In September 1918 there were enough Americans to form the First Army, which with half a million men assaulted and overwhelmed the German lines in the Verdun region. In a few weeks, more than 1.2 million American soldiers leaped out of the trenches in a combined assault with the British and French and fought their way grimly forward for more than a month through the wilderness of the Argonne forest.

Such assaults were incredibly costly. In the Argonne campaign the Americans suffered 120,000 casualties. But the German line was now collapsing massively, and the German high command urged the German government to make peace. Appealing to Wilson for a settlement on the basis of the Fourteen Points, to which the president had got the reluctant Allies to agree, the German government signed the armistice on November 11, 1918, and the war was over. It left behind 112,000 dead Americans (by comparison, seven years of war in Vietnam produced, by 1972, 56,000 dead), and millions of slain Russians, Germans, Italians, Rumanians, Austro-Hungarians, Serbians, Belgians, French, and British.

The Peace Conference

At war's end Wilson was seized with the zeal not only of a peacemaker but of a prophet as well. When he went to Europe and briefly toured the Allied capitals in 1919, millions of people cheered him with almost adoring frenzy. He must have felt that he had the cause of mankind in his hands. But there were grave barriers in the way. He had already made serious errors at home. In the congressional elections of 1918, he had appealed for a Democratic victory on the ground that if the Republicans won (as they did, gaining a majority in both houses, for reasons not particularly associated with the war), the world would interpret that victory as a rejection of his ideals. Although he would need the assent of the Senate to any

Infantrymen of the Second Division inch their way through thick smoke and fog in the Argonne Forest. These close-packed assaults into massed machine guns and artillery on the other side produced appalling slaughters.

United States Signal Corps, The National Archives

peace treaty he signed, he chose not one senator to accompany him to Versailles.

There, with both Germany and Russia excluded from the conference—the latter because of the separate peace already signed and its possession of a communist regime—he stood alone in advocating a liberal peace settlement. The wonder is that he won as much as he did of his Fourteen Points. France was adamant in its desire to gain permanent security against Germany, for on two occasions within living memory, in 1870 and 1914, German armies had poured across the French borders. Premier Georges Clemenceau would hear practically nothing of the Fourteen Points.

Britain and France demanded that Germany be forced to pay all the costs of the war. Endless disputes went on, Wilson insisting that Germany could never pay such a huge sum and remain economically alive. However, he finally had to accept British and French demands for reparations, which amounted eventually to the enormous sum of more than thirty billion dollars. This issue complicated all international relations for many years after the war, causing the most intricate and insoluble difficulties and helping to lead, in part, to the rise of Hitler and the outbreak of the Second World War.

What about self-determination? Wilson agreed that Germany's colonies should remain in the hands of the Allied powers that had occupied them, but he got those powers to accept the "mandate" principle, according to which their occupation of the colonies was to be under international supervision, the eventual goal being independence for each colony. The Austro-Hungarian Empire had already collapsed, and the people of Czechoslovakia had moved ahead on their own to establish self-rule. The Balkan areas of the empire were separated into an independent Yugoslavia, which included Serbia and Montenegro; Rumania was greatly expanded by the addition to it of large territories; and Poland, Lithuania, Latvia, Estonia, and Finland came into existence as new nations. Meanwhile, the Ottoman Empire was carved up into mandated territories by the French and British, a direct violation of self-determination.

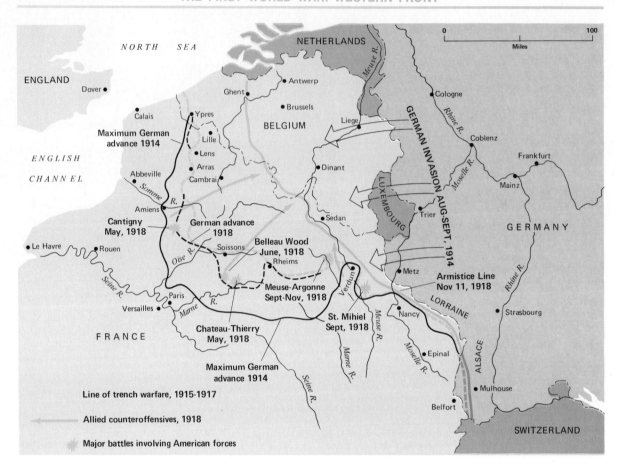

The problem of Russia was an enormously complicated one. A civil war was raging between anti-Soviet "whites" and the Soviet government, with its "Red Army." The French and British governments decided to intervene militarily in an attempt to crush the Soviet regime and help the White Russians return to power. While the war with Germany was still going on, they had even persuaded an exceedingly reluctant Woodrow Wilson to put a small force of American soldiers in the Russian port of Murmansk to prevent war supplies from being captured by the Germans and another in Siberia to assist a Czech army that wished to extricate itself from Russia and continue fighting on the western front. But in each of these cases Wilson scrupulously sought to take no role in internal Russian politics, and he insisted that the people of Russia be allowed to solve their own problems. All military interventions, he said at the peace conference, should be ended at once.

"Trying to stop a revolutionary movement by troops in the field," he said, "is like using a broom to hold back a great ocean."

In all this he kept his eye focused on his greatest objective—the establishment of a league of nations. In issue after issue at the Versailles Peace Conference he either failed or got only partial victories. The British would not agree to freedom of the seas; tariffs did not tumble; self-determination was often violated; key negotiations were usually secret, contrary to what he had called for. But in the end he got his league. As created in the Treaty of Versailles, the League of Nations was a two-house body, composed of an Assembly representing all member nations, and a Council of nine (five of its members to be the United States, Great Britain, France, Italy, and Japan). Joined to it was a Secretariat to provide administrative functions, a World Court, and an array of special commissions concerned with spe-

New independent nations

Allied occupation zone

Plebiscite area

cific problems. The Covenant, or constitution, of the league called for a number of admirable objectives—the reduction of arms, the arbitration of disputes, and the collective security of all members. This last was embodied in what Wilson called the heart of the Covenant, Article 10, in which each nation undertook "to respect and preserve as against external aggression the territorial integrity and existing political independence of all the members of the league." *Collective security* was to replace the *balance of power*.

The Fight Over Ratification

Wilson returned from Versailles to the United States in a defiant mood. He had had to make so *many* compromises. His lordly soul was deeply wounded, his disappointments keen and bitter. In the United States he knew opposition to the treaty was brewing, but he had passed beyond the point of compromise. Once again he was a stern Presbyterian, a confident president, who was absolutely positive that he was right. *"The Senate,"* he said to a reporter, *"is going to ratify the treaty."* He went to that body in person to present the treaty, and insisted that its key feature, the League of Nations, was the dream of all the world's masses. "Dare we reject it and break the heart of the world?" he asked. It was God Himself who had brought this great project into being.

But it was not going to be so simple. The lordly president might rumble and clench his teeth in the White House, but up on Capitol Hill a mile away, his treaty had to contend with powerful antagonistic forces. Woodrow Wilson, after all, was proposing a revolutionary change in America's relationship to the outside world. For more than a century the United States had pursued its own course in what it considered its own hemisphere, and the record of that policy seemed to many quite satisfactory. Now the president was demanding that the United States become a member of a wholly unprecedented new world government that few understood and the eventual effects and power of which no one could foretell. In the best of circumstances this would be a difficult thing to carry through. But Wilson was faced by a Senate in which the majority was Republican, and that party had always contained most of those who believed that the United States should go it alone in the world. The wonder is that he got so near to the two-thirds majority that he needed.

The crucial question concerned Article 10 of the League of Nations Covenant. Under its provisions, so it appeared, the league could summon out the armed forces of the United States, whether or not Congress approved. Wilson tried again and again to calm this fear, but it would not down. Irish-Americans thundered that American boys would be sent to Ireland to put down Irish revolutionaries. German-Americans scoffed that American armed forces would soon be putting down colonial troubles in the expanded French and British empires. No matter how long the issue was debated, observes the historian Ronald N. Stromberg, "Article 10 was the stumbling block. . . . The ensuing long and bitter debate over its meaning was often obscure, yet nonetheless real. Men *felt* that a vital issue was involved."

Progressives Turn Against Wilson

Progressives were touchy on issues of civil liberties, and Wilson's record there had deeply offended them. Furthermore, they were repelled by a treaty that seemed to embody so little of the liberal peace Wilson had said he would create. Once again, the men of power seemed to have had their way, producing a peace that combined selfish nationalism, fear, and repression. Thus, progressives regarded the treaty as a betrayal and condemned Wilson ferociously. To them, the notion that power could be built and used to good ends had turned out to be a mockery: strong government was a dangerous blunder; World War I and America's entrance into it, a terrible error.

The dreams of domestic reform that had so captivated the progressive world in early 1919 soon were dashed. Congress had no intention of going any further in the direction of collectivism. Disillusion was epidemic, and it centered on the Treaty of Versailles. Ray Stannard Baker, a veteran muckraker, gave the common opinion when he said, "It seemed to me a terrible document; a dispensation of retribution with scarcely a parallel in history."

Senator William E. Borah, a progressive Republican senator from Idaho, was a leading isolationist opponent of the League of Nations treaty. On the Senate floor in February 1919 he denounced its principles, first by quoting numerous statements of George Washington that called on America to stay free of Europe's troubles and entanglements, and then by asking: "Are there people in this day who believe that Europe now and in the future shall be free of selfishness, of rivalship, of humor, of ambition, of caprice? If not, are we not undertaking the task against which the Father of our Country warned. . . ? If a controversy ever arises in which there is a conflict between the European system and the American system, or if a conflict ever arises in which their interests, their humor, their caprice, and their selfishness shall attempt to dominate the situation, shall we not have indeed quit our own to stand upon foreign ground?

"Why should we interweave our destiny with the European destiny? Are we not interweaving our future and our destiny with European powers when we join the league of nations the constitution of which gives a majority vote, in every single instance in which the league can ever be called into action, to European powers? . . . The league nowhere distinguishes or discriminates between European and American affairs. It functions in one continent the same as another. It compounds all three continents into a single unit, so far as the operations of the league are concerned. . . . The very object and purpose of the league is to eliminate all differences between Europe and America and place all in a common liability to be governed and controlled by a common authority. [It will bind Americans to protect the British Empire, and give to that country, through its dominions, five votes to one for the United States.] Conceal it as you may, disguise it as some will attempt to do, this is the first step in internationalism and the first distinct effort to sterilize nationalism." Borah then quoted from the writings of the Russian Communist Leon Trotsky calling for an international world order, linking his words with the recent death of Theodore Roosevelt. "I sometimes wonder, Can it be true? Are we, indeed, yielding our Americanism before the onrushing tide of revolutionary internationalism? Did the death of this undaunted advocate of American nationalism mark an epoch in the fearful, damnable, downward trend?"

Wilson's bitterest personal and political enemy, Henry Cabot Lodge, was chairman of the Senate's Foreign Relations Committee. He had first persuaded enough Republican senators to sign a letter saying they would not approve the treaty in its existing form to ensure that it would be defeated. Then he used his position as chairman of his committee to delay things as long as possible. He read the entire treaty word for word, usually to an empty committee room. Then he called in every possible enemy, particularly the "hyphenates," as they were then called: Irish-Americans who hated Britain for not freeing Ireland; Italian-Americans who were bitter that their homeland had not benefited more in the peace settlement; and German-Americans who condemned the reparations and other aspects of the document.

In the face of repeated pleas that he accept reservations to the treaty, Wilson stood firm. Article 10, he said, could not be deleted without destroying the whole conception of the league. Many men, Republicans as well as Democrats, were ready to accept a treaty with a more modified approach to internationalism, but Wilson would have none of such halfway measures. When Lodge's hearings stretched on and on, Wilson decided to go to the people once more. He was a tired and sick man, he had labored almost beyond human endurance for many years, and his physician warned him against exertion. But the combative Scot and Presbyterian visionary, the messianic prophet, were too strong within him.

He was determined to have his way, and this appeared to be his only hope. He left Washington in September 1919 to travel in one month more than eight thousand miles and make almost forty addresses to cheering audiences. In Pueblo, Colorado, he collapsed from exhaustion. Sped back to Washington, he suffered a stroke that largely removed him from effective executive leadership. The treaty's chances were now gravely impaired, especially since Wilson was almost completely isolated from public contacts once he had recovered enough to make his wishes known.

By this time Lodge had reported the treaty to the Senate with a long string of reservations. The most crucial of them concerned Article 10; it stated that Congress would always retain final authority over the use of American armed forces. If Wilson had given the word, enough Democrats would have joined with enough Republicans to provide a two-thirds majority and ratification of the treaty. But once again he refused, instructing all Democrats to vote against the treaty containing reservations. In November 1919 the vote was taken and ratification was defeated. In response to an outcry of protest from across the nation, the treaty was brought up for a second vote; once more Wilson was unyielding; and once more it was defeated.

The Ethnics and the Election of 1920

Woodrow Wilson, now a fretful man who seemed almost to have begun to harbor delusions, looked forward to another battle. He believed that the presidential election of 1920 would become a great national referendum on the question of the League of Nations, and that behind that cause the Democrats would win. But the political ground had profoundly shifted from how it had lain in 1916. The First World War had been an enormously explosive political event, and all alignments had shifted. For German-Americans, the declaration of war upon their homeland began a cruel time of martyrdom. They had sturdily supported the cause of the Central Powers against the Allies, as had, indeed, the Scandinavians. Once America was in the war, to do that was to be a traitor. Stunned, their morale shattered, on every hand subjected to harsh and violent prejudice, the Germans greeted the Armistice of 1918 a

transformed people in America. Their newspapers were dying; their language was being rapidly shunned, even by their own people; and the shame that they felt replaced their old soaring pride as the only large ethnic group in the United States whose homeland culture could rival that of the British in sophistication, scholarly and scientific distinction, and world stature. Children turned against parents, rejecting the traditional Germanism for Americanism. Even the mother church of German Lutheranism in St. Louis, Missouri, resolved in 1918 to change its name to "Trinity Church" and to specify English as its official language.

The Germans hated Wilson's Treaty of Versailles, and were to vote massively against his party. The Italians were deeply offended that the treaty denied long-held Italian territorial ambitions around the Adriatic Sea, and attacked the League of Nations as a British plot. Thus the Democrats lost heavily in those urban regions in the northern states where they had been starting to gain a foothold, as well as in the heavily German and Scandinavian farming states of the upper Middle West.

Also, Wilson's administration was so heavily made up of Southerners and his policies during the war, especially in their favoring of cotton growers over wheat farmers, seemed so strongly colored by Southern ways of thinking that many in the northern and western states recoiled. Far western states, with their rabid anti-Japanese prejudices, were alarmed at the relatively strong push that the Treaty of Versailles gave to Japan's world status and its ambitions in China. Even the Irish turned against the treaty, attacking it for its failure to give freedom to Ireland and for the great power within the League of Nations that it gave to Great Britain.

In short, the coalition that Wilson had built in 1916 was shattered. The Democrats tried to compensate by turning, in their national convention of 1920, to the Middle West for their presidential nominee, James M. Cox, governor of Ohio. Franklin D. Roosevelt of New York, Wilson's engaging young assistant secretary of the navy, became the vice-presidential nominee. Against Warren G. Harding, also of Ohio, Cox waged a courageous campaign for internationalism and the League. But he was crushed in the balloting. The amiable Harding, who did little more than mouth platitudes about "normalcy" during his campaign, received more than sixteen million popular votes, to some nine million for Cox. At the same time, the Republicans gained huge majorities in both houses of Congress. The nation seemed clearly to have spoken. The president-elect, within two days of his victory, announced that the League was "now deceased."

President Wilson had yet another four months to live in the White House before Warren Harding's inauguration in March 1921. He spent that cruel time sunk in gloom. The Nobel Committee awarded him his peace prize, which was some consolation, but there seemed little left of his life work. He rode to the Capitol on inauguration day with the president-elect by his side, making no response to the cheering crowds, his face drawn and haggard, and listened somberly as the oath was administered to the new president. He lived quietly on for another three years in Washington, still turning over in his mind his disappointments and thinking of himself as the symbol

of international liberalism. Not long before his death, a crowd gathered before his home on Armistice Day 1923. He emerged, thanked them, and then suddenly spoke again with his old force:

Just one word more; I cannot refrain from saying it. I am not one of those who have the least anxiety about the triumph of the principles I have stood for. I have seen fools resist Providence before, and I have seen their destruction. . . . That we shall prevail is as sure as that God reigns. Thank you.

Bibliography

Books that were especially valuable to me in writing this chapter: On Wilson, see my references for chapter 27. I also drew much from Arno J. Mayer's *Wilson vs. Lenin: Political Origins of the New Diplomacy, 1917–1918* (1964), which shows Wilson in a struggle for world opinion. On the Gladstonian dimension in Wilson's foreign policy, see Robert Kelley, "Asquith at Paisley: The Content of British Liberalism at the End of Its Era," *The Journal of British Studies*, 4 (1964): 133–59. N. Gordon Levin, Jr.'s *Woodrow Wilson and World Politics: America's Response to War and Revolution* (1968) is fundamentally important, as is Laurence W. Martin, *Peace Without Victory: Woodrow Wilson and the British Liberals* (1958). I found Barbara Tuchman's *Guns of August** (1962) a superb evocation of the shattering first days of the First World War. Otis L. Graham, Jr.'s *The Great Campaigns: Reform and War in America, 1900–1928* (1971) contains perceptive analysis. R. E. Quirk's *An Affair of Honor: Woodrow Wilson and the Occupation of Veracruz** (1962) was valuable to me.

Concerning ethnic Americans and the First World War, I relied upon: Philip Gleason, *The Conservative Reformers: German-American Catholics and the Social Order* (1968); Frederick C. Luebke, *Bonds of Loyalty: German-Americans and World War I* (1974); David Burner, *The Politics of Provincialism: The Democratic Party in Transition, 1918–1923* (1968); Joseph P. O'Grady, ed., *The Immigrant's Influence on Wilson's Peace Policies* (1967); Louis L. Gerson, *The Hyphenate in Recent American Politics and Diplomacy* (1964); John M. Allswang, *A House for All Peoples: Ethnic Politics in Chicago 1890–1936* (1971); and Alan J. Ward, *Ireland and Anglo-American Relations, 1899–1921* (1969).

Woodrow Wilson in 1921, wan, aged, and defeated, seems to look back on the wreckage of his dreams of world order. To the end, however, he remained defiantly convinced that the future would prove him right.

The Granger Collection

How Have Historians Looked at the Topic?

The military transformation of the United States during the early twentieth century and Theodore Roosevelt's energetic role in the process is lucidly described in Howard K. Beale's vigorous and critical *Theodore Roosevelt and the Rise of America to World Power** (1956). Sidney Lens's recent *The Forging of the American Empire* (1971) contains a provocative and disturbing analysis. The virtues and defects of Taft's and his successor's policies are explored in Dana G. Munro's interpretative study *Intervention and Dollar Diplomacy for the Caribbean, 1900–1921* (1964). John M. Blum's *Woodrow Wilson and the Politics of Morality** (1956) contains an excellent short account of Wilson's interventionist policies in Mexico, and two admirable monographs help to round out the picture: R. E. Quirk, *An Affair of Honor: Woodrow Wilson and the Occupation of Veracruz** (1962), and C. C. Clendenen, *The United States and Pancho Villa* (1961).

Why did America go to war in 1917? In his war message, Woodrow Wilson eloquently proclaimed one rationale that future historians would echo. "The world must be made safe for democracy." Both Burton J. Hendrick's *The Life and Letters of Walter H. Page*, three vols. (1922–26) and Charles Seymour's *The Intimate Papers of Colonel House*, four vols. (1926–28) substantiated Wilson's idealistic purposes.

Sharply opposing views developed swiftly. C. Hartley Grattan in *Why We Fought* (1929) held that the desire for profits was the prime motivating factor behind the American entry into World War I. Walter Millis's biting indictment *Road to War, 1914–1917* (1935) accepted Grattan's emphasis on greed but added folly and sentimentalism as causal links. In perhaps the most skillfully argued revisionist study, *America Goes to War* (1938), Charles C. Tansill carefully concluded that the huge trade in munitions and the extension of private loans were determining factors behind American intervention.

In his war message Wilson emphasized the importance of submarine warfare—"a warfare against mankind"—in catapulting the United States to belligerent status with Germany. In two books that scrutinize Wilson's diplomacy in great detail, *American Diplomacy During the World War* (1934) and *American Neutrality, 1914–1917* (1935), Charles Seymour advanced the thesis that American intervention was the natural outcome of German submarine warfare.

World War II gave birth to a new school of historical interpretation centering on the question of America's national security. Writing during that conflict, Walter Lippmann postulated that Wilson and his advisers had chosen to intervene in World War I because they believed that American security would be endangered if Germany won. Lippmann's influential *United States Foreign Policy: Shield of the Republic* (1943) was seconded by Hans J. Morgenthau's *In Defense of the National Interest* (1951) and George F. Kennan's *American Diplomacy, 1900–1950** (1950). The position of the realists (as the advocates of the national-security thesis have been called) has been further fleshed out in Robert E. Osgood's *Ideals and Self-Interest in American Foreign Policy* (1953), which describes Wilson as essentially an idealist, and in Edward Beuhrig's *Woodrow Wilson and the Balance of Power* (1955).

The acknowledged authority on Woodrow Wilson, Arthur S. Link, has painstakingly probed Wilson's foreign policy in several excellent and invaluable volumes. Further historiographical insight can be gained from Warren I. Cohen's masterly study *The American Revisionists: The Lessons of Intervention in World War I** (1967). Russell F. Weigley, *The American Way of War: A History of United States Miltary Strategy and Policy** (1973) is essential on the fighting.

* Available in paperback.

29

TIME LINE

AMERICAN LIFE AND THOUGHT BETWEEN THE WARS

UPI

Tomorrow
I'll be at the table
When company comes.
Nobody'll dare
Say to me,
"Eat in the kitchen,"
Then.
Besides,
They'll see how beautiful I am
And be ashamed—

*I, too, am America.**

So wrote Langston Hughes, young poet, Missouri-born, Ohio-educated, who was just nineteen when he arrived in fascinating Harlem in 1921. Many black writers wanted to write "white" style, using "white" themes, but Hughes wrote of black life, black sorrows, black hopes, and he used black rhythms, black speech, much of it cast in the meter of "the blues," black America's musical gift, with jazz, to American culture. A flood of verse poured from him; soon it was being widely published, widely read, praised, condemned.

Polite black writers talked of doctors and dancers, Hughes wrote of prostitutes, laborers, and drunks, of "the people who have their nip of gin on Saturday nights and are not too important to themselves or the community. . . . Their joy runs bang! into ecstasy. Their religion soars to a shout. Work maybe a little . . . rest a little . . . Play awhile. Sing awhile. O, let's dance!" The crash of 1929 closed down the night lights of Harlem, where thousands of whites had roamed to find excitement, and the Harlem Renaissance faded, but Hughes continued to write: short stories, novels, plays, poetry. Hundreds of thousands in later decades read his words, newspapers printed his columns, and still it came—lyrics, history, librettos, adaptations, popular recordings of his work, together with world travel, awards, fame. Through it all he would return to his third-floor room, overlooking a Harlem backyard, and write. At his death in 1967 one of the great American writers, he had made it possible for Afro-Americans to speak in their own voice, of their own soul's ache and soul's hope, of their courage and their love.

* *Selected Poems of Langston Hughes* (New York: Knopf, 1959), p. 275.

Half a million black people congregated in Harlem in the 1920s, making it the national capital of Afro-American life. They came from California, Indiana, Utah, the Caribbean, the Southern states—from everywhere. And here black culture, like white literary and artistic culture in these years, exploded with unprecedented power and beauty. New ways, new thoughts: above all, a new pride in blackness, in black talents, black visions.

The America that entered the 1920s is, for the first time, recognizable to us now. Millions of automobiles occupy the streets in flowing streams; people are moving about in their daily lives like the Americans of half a century later. They flock to the movies, they listen to radios, and more than half of them live in cities, many of which are very large. The mass-consumption society toward which American industry had been heading for decades has fully arrived even in much of the countryside. The scattered, loosely organized, agricultural country of half a century before—a nation consisting largely of inward-turning island communities far distant in travel time and in ways of living from everywhere else in the country—has been replaced by a United States tightly interlinked by railroad and automobile, beginning to use the airplane, alive with a buzzing network of telephone lines, highly industrialized, and listening together to the president on the crystal set. American culture in the 1920s looks familiar, in its leisure habits (save for prohibition), its ideas about human nature and the natural universe, and especially in its sexual morals, its women, and its young people. The novels of these years are not, like those of the nineteenth century, about a culture so different that it seems almost foreign. Rather, they depict people and ways of living and thinking that seem in some ways odd, rather like the speeded-up movies of the period, but akin to ourselves.

To look at the two decades between the first and second world wars, however, is to see America in sharply contrasting moods. The prosperous 1920s were lively, confused, and individualistic, a time of rebellious youth and of vibrant romanticism in the arts. The 1930s concentrated on solving one great problem—the depression. This made that decade collectivistic and disciplined, for people had to pull together in the face of their common problems. In the arts, realism replaced romanticism as the dominant approach. The contrast between the decades reveals one of the tidal rhythms in American public life. During times of prosperity when no single crisis such as a depression or a war focuses the national mind, a period of "cultural" politics flourishes. The issues that erupt into public controversy involve such questions as the relations between ethnic groups, the life styles being adopted by young people, changes in sexual practices, "immoral" literature, and religious beliefs. Novelists turn inward, stressing personal questions and ignoring social problems. At the same time, optimism reigns in the business community, which thrives on the national well-being. Smug in its security, the middle class trumpets the values of Main Street from pulpits and service-club lecterns. In reaction to these values, alienated intellectuals cry out for self-expression at any cost, producing forms of dress, hair styles, and ways of living that antagonize everyone else.

Periods of cultural politics, in brief, are filled with contradictions, since the nation moves in many directions at once. Periods of "crisis" politics, however, see a move toward national unity and a serious frame of mind. In the economically depressed 1930s people concentrated on such practical issues as jobs, homes, poverty, bankruptcy, strikes, and "capitalist oppression." All eyes turned to Washington, D.C., for national leadership. The arts turned away from personal questions to examine major social issues, becoming polemical and ideological.

Cultural and crisis politics are not mutually exclusive. The key fact, however, is that when the country's situation changes, the national mind concentrates upon new things and lets old ones fade. This is why the generations shaped by one period find the next so incomprehensible; why the depression-reared veterans of World War II, trained to think in sober terms of cooperation, jobs, and national security, found the individualistic, rebellious children of affluence in the 1960s so hard to fathom.

The 1920s: Seedbed of Modern America

Pre-1914 America had been shaped by the life style of the small town and the countryside. Dominated by white Anglo-Saxon Protestantism, the "WASP" culture, it was genteel and moralistic. People characteristically thought and spoke in religious imagery. Cultural life was decentralized, as symbolized by the numberless traveling troupes of players who presented stock dramas in local "opera houses." There were a number of large cities, but they were tightly compacted and sharply marked off from the quiet America that surrounded them. In the countryside and the smaller town, where most everyone lived, nothing seemed as settled as a way of life made up of polite periodicals, Sundays in the local Protestant church, quilting bees, and people who looked, talked, and thought alike.

By the 1920s, the invention of the automobile and the development of mass production had provided almost everyone with a car. Hard-surfaced roads spread over the countryside with startling speed. City ways of life invaded the countryside, and farm folk found it easy to motor into town for shopping and entertainment. The radio, and most dramatically the movie, inaugurated a culture that bound the nation together as it never had been before. The new media were shaped by a few central institutions, located mainly in Hollywood and New York City. What people saw and heard in that darkened movie theater in River City, Iowa, was not genteel and moralistic but earthy, flippant, and sexually liberating.

The new mass culture, in short, was urban and cosmopolitan. It was dominated by men of the recently arrived urban ethnic groups—Italians, Greeks, and especially Jews—who had learned in the large cities how to cater to common tastes. This produced an unprecedented opportunity for such men to leap into a position of cultural leadership denied for generations to such older ethnic groups as the Irish and the Germans. Enterprising veterans of the world of New York

City mass recreation, the moviemakers migrated to southern California for the continual sunlight and varied scenery. Out of their studios came a flood of fascinating new manners and morals, new heroes and heroines.

The New Youth

In this rapidly modernizing society, there was a rebellion of youth against traditional morals and styles of life—at least among the WASP middle class of the cities. Indeed, the 1920s are the years in the twentieth century when "youth" first emerged as a large, self-conscious, much-discussed, and much-glorified element in American life. Grown-ups were obsessed with these young people, frightened of them in many cases, pleased with them in others. They were peculiarly the symbol of the changes rapidly sweeping American life in the 1920s; they were the "carrier movement" of the new values. Consumer markets were reshaped to meet the appetites of this new free-spending youth culture. College life suddenly glowed with romance and national attention, for here the golden youth found their most exciting fields of play, with their immense football stadiums (constructed in great numbers in these years), gin parties, and fast, loud automobiles. Newspapers and magazines discussed youth con-

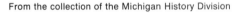

Along with prosperity came the inescapable traffic jam of riders rushing to work or escaping for weekend pleasure outings. Narrow highways also produced fatal head-on collisions.
From the collection of the Michigan History Division

stantly, books about them and scholarly studies proliferated. Over and over, one word to define their mood was used: *alienation*.

Traditionalists, who looked upon all of this in alarm, said it was the war that had created the "flaming youth" of the period, for war's appalling death and disillusionment had made them cynical, irreverent, rebellious, and disenchanted with the older generation as fools and false idealists. Thus the *Ladies Home Journal*, typical of many mass-circulation magazines, described youth as lost in alcoholic stupors, locked in erotic embraces in the back seats of automobiles, and given over entirely to pleasure seeking. They were seen as hard-boiled and smug, ravenous to experience life directly for themselves, and ready to reject older morals as hypocrisy. The rumored sexual license of youth was the ultimate symbol of disorder and rebellion, of the stark breakdown of American life. (It was now that "petting" became common; "going all the way" was still strongly rejected, morally, among the young.) The clothing worn by young women, brief and frankly revealing, was thought demoralizing. Cosmetics had traditionally been used by prostitutes; now young WASP ladies, copying the amorous screen actresses, seemed brazenly to flaunt immorality in their painted lips and rouged cheeks. Dancing, jazz music, slangy and often profane language, jokes about sex freely bandied between men and women: it was appalling. *The Ladies Home Journal* even launched a campaign to have jazz, exported to the rest of the country from New York City and especially from black America, outlawed.

It was perhaps the behavior of young women that caused the most intense concern. The new equality that they demanded was not the political rights or economic opportunities that the older generation of women reformers had labored for; it was equality with males in self-expression, self-determination, and personal satisfaction. The concept of virtuous womanhood, noble womanhood, seemed clearly to be in eclipse, while sexual promiscuity threatened to invade American life. The right to sexual satisfaction seemed to mount an irresistible assault on the sanctity of the marriage contract and above all on the home, the keystone of society.

Americans of a more liberal, modernizing bent did not condemn, but rather they praised, the new youth. Much about cultural progressivism before the First World War had aimed at lib-

eration of life styles and the challenging of Victorian morals, and cultural progressives now saw a more open and honest and individualistic American life being pioneered by young people. By this time (as we will see later in the chapter), the ideas of Sigmund Freud were widely known among progressive intellectuals, indeed were broadcast in popular magazines, and the morals of young people—much less flamboyant than painted by their critics—were thought to be moving in the right directions: away from harmful repressions and the neuroticisms they were said to foster.

The Changing American Family

Traditionalists had much to complain about in the American family as well. Popular magazines unmercifully attacked indulgent mothers, who, it was said, allowed their children to tyrannize the household. From the WASP middle-class urban household there seemed to come children who had been trained to be independent about their personal liberties and rights while ignoring self-control and responsibilities to society. The *Literary Digest* thundered in 1922 (after a survey) that the nation's pressing need was for parents to reassert their authority over children. Fundamental moral training was not being provided, critics maintained. At the same time, it was pointed out, American Protestant churches seemed to have lost all their prestige and standing among young people, so moral instruction would not come to them from that direction. "Liberal Protestantism," preached to the respectable, well-educated congregations of middle-class America, had by turning away from the old-time emphasis on the Bible lost its bite, its authority.

In truth, the American family, as we have seen, had been engaged in a modernizing transformation for a long time. The chief effect of this change was to put the *child* at its center, in middle-class WASP homes, even more than in the past. To find the roots to this change means looking at demographic facts. After 1850 the birth rate in the United States, already in decline, began dropping rapidly. This meant that the whole society was in fact growing older. In 1900, 35 percent of the society was under fifteen; by 1929, this figure had dropped almost a fifth, to 29 percent. In the same period, the median age of Americans rose from twenty-three years to twenty-seven. Thus, the "youth" segment of the population (fifteen to twenty-four) grew in comparison with small children (from being half as large in 1870 to two-thirds as large in 1930). Also, to supervise these children and young people there were proportionately more older people (for each person fifteen to twenty-four in 1870, there had been two older persons; in 1930, there were three). Put another way, mature adults had to care for a smaller number of young people, and there was more time to give them attention, more opportunity to provide elaborate care in their rearing. The trend toward raising "high-quality" children was intensifying. At the same time, child-labor laws and longer and longer schooling (extending into college) meant that young people had an ever lengthening period in which to prepare for being fully adult, or, conversely, in which to play at adult recreations while being free of adult responsibilities. With more older people around to do society's work, the labor of young people was not needed as pressingly. Coincidentally, an increasingly complicated economy demanded more skills and more education, and thus longer periods in the classroom.

This lengthening of schooling, in its turn, meant that families had a new external agency that worked in partnership with them in the rearing of children and young people to a far greater degree than ever before: the school and college. Being off at school gave American youth long periods of time in which their close associates were not parents or employers, but simply other young people of their age—their peer group. This was a profound change, for the peer group became a powerful new source from which to take instruction in how to live. Of course, the youth peer group was interested in perpetuating not the restrictive morals of the older people but instead the liberating morals that young people traditionally lean toward. Living with parents or employers meant unconsciously mimicking adult behavior; living with a peer group produced a strikingly different life style. To the consternation of adults, new values, fads, and styles circulated with great speed in this peer-group universe.

The Significance of Smaller Families

It is interesting to observe that families in *both* the working and middle classes were getting smaller, and that in both social spheres families were about the same size: close to five persons in 1900, down from six a generation earlier. However, from about 1900 onward, middle class families started getting smaller than the families of laborers. A crucial cultural event had happened. Whatever the reasons, middle-class (i.e. Protestant) American women had begun deciding that birth-control devices were not morally repugnant. Thus, by the 1920s middle-class families were down to one or two children. (Skilled workers were moving in the same direction, though not as fast. In the South and the Middle West, all of this lagged, families staying larger than those in the East but even so, becoming smaller than before).

Now husbands and wives could have sex regularly without having children. This was a milestone in family history. The companionate marriage was now fully possible. Married women were no longer just mothers; they could be wives. Husbands and wives established more democratic, sharing relations: they now planned together how many children they were going to have, planned together their increasingly costly education—now more possible, since there were fewer to educate—and together became more attuned to the family and its needs as a consciously managed concern. Women were much more in control of their lives and their families than in the past, and could claim more equality with husbands in family decision making. Especially as women became better educated, the numbers of children they bore became smaller and their role in the marriage veered strongly toward companionate arrangements.

It is not surprising that in this new setting— when marriages could serve the need of both partners for love and not simply such basic requirements as procreation for women and sexual release for men—the trend toward later marriages reversed. In 1920, proportionately more adult Americans were married than in 1890, and marriages occurred at earlier ages: from twenty-six for men and twenty-two for women in 1890 to below twenty-five for men and close to twenty-one for women in 1920. Thus, even though birth rates were low in the 1920s, the marriage rate among young people was high. (Remember that having regular sexual intercourse was still felt to require marriage.) Meanwhile, female sexuality, so long held down, could be released. There was a great lifting of the prevailing fear of childbirth, coincident with a fading of the convention strongly held to in "nice" circles that sexual activity was for women a duty and not potentially pleasurable. Of course, the complexities and powerful tensions of human sexual relations were by no means thus easily erased. Half a century after the 1920s they continue to display themselves, if probably in much less intense forms.

The New Marriage

People could now expect far more, in personal, emotional terms, of their marriages than their parents and grandparents could have: more loving intimacy, more physical expression, greater companionship, more freedom from the hierarchical duties that large families required. In the 1920s, there was much writing about a new ideal in family relations: family democracy. In the older family of the farm, with its large numbers of children and many shared daily tasks among the animals and in the fields, the pattern had to be one in which there was regimentation, hierarchy, careful disciplining, and the assignment of job responsibilities. Parents who had many children tended to be more distant with them, and to assign roles by age and sex.

In the smaller urban family, especially in those supported by the head of the household (that is, a family in which children did not go to work at an early age), the pressing economic functions of the family dissolved. At the same time, each child could be dealt with on his or her own terms, as an individual rather than as someone occupying a particular job-related slot in the family organization. And after 1920, infant mortality dropped significantly, so that babies could be freely loved without the need to hold back for fear of their death. This did not mean that large rural families were not quite capable of being households of love and affection, but that their latitude to be so was less, other things being equal. Democratic relationships were simply more possible in the new, smaller, more affluent city family—even if its members, not having actually experienced the life of the older family, may not have fully appreciated this fact.

In the 1920s marriage authorities were talking of the good marriage and the healthy family being characterized by compatibility between husband and wife in personal terms, and not simply a stoical bearing of whatever developed. Another characteristic was equality of privilege and responsibility between husband and wife, and this included the area of sexual pleasure. In other words, family life was now subject to this test: Was the family a happy one? Did it fulfill the needs of its members for love? Thus, what traditionalists saw as a revolt against marriage in the sexual permissiveness of young people was in actuality a revolt within, and certainly not against, marriage. In the countryside, as an early 1930s national White House survey demonstrated, the older hierarchical family still endured, rooted in discipline and authority and assigned roles. But in the cities, fundamental changes were clearly in motion.

One thing remained: the new ideal was shared by both young men and women in the middle classes, but its greatest impact was upon women. Marriage was to be an important part of a man's life, but it was still regarded as the primary and almost exclusive goal for even middle-class women. In general, men strongly disapproved of the idea of wives working, and women strongly agreed with them. There was of course a common expectation among young women that they would work for a while before marriage, or even in the early years after the wedding in order to help the new household get founded, but it was anticipated that soon thereafter children would begin to arrive and motherhood would end working. The doctrine of the two spheres held firm. At Vassar College, nine out of ten women said they preferred marriage over a career (in a 1923 study). Thus, although the ideal of equality within the marriage was firmly established in middle-class culture (how much it was actually practiced is not known), it applied only within the home, not outside of it.

The Children

Urban middle-class children showed distinctive characteristics. Studies revealed that they tended to confide more in their parents, and to be less hostile toward them, than rural children. They were punished less frequently, and more often received open and physical demonstrations of affection. Of course, they also had fewer chores, if any at all. Middle-class families did fewer things together, such as going to church or working at shared tasks, so that urban children were more on their own. Boys certainly lacked the opportunity to work with their fathers in their tasks. Likewise, with all their labor-saving aids mothers had far less need of their daughters' assistance.

One outgrowth of the new family was a concern that the "cult of the child" might be producing monsters. Even family sociologists, who generally praised the affectionate family, worried about its implications for the larger questions of discipline and responsibility in society at large. The more affluent the family, and the more child-centered, the more the children came to be self-conscious; to regard themselves as (obviously) very important personages; and to instinctively think that they were entitled to far more than either the children of earlier generations or those of contemporary less affluent and less indulgent families. The older home had at least been a clear and definite place, whose inner discipline helped create a sense of security and knowledge of one's identity. The newer home left much of this up in the air. Freedom always exacts its price, in any location, and the freer child with more opportunity to choose his or her life direction was therefore a more anxious, less stoical child.

Mothers confessed to being far more worried about child care than they believed their own parents and grandparents to have been. No longer was it possible, they said, for middle-class mothers simply to take children for granted, to raise them instinctively according to old patterns. (As we have observed, this anxiety was actually generations old.) Freudian psychology emphasized how crucially important were the child's early years, and this put heavy burdens upon mothers, who now had the children's unconscious to worry about, their repressions and stored-up anxieties —topics that would have been hooted at by earlier generations. Thus, of all the aspects of housework in the new family setting, mothers found child rearing to be their chief worry. "I try to do just what you say," a young mother is reported to have said to a family sociologist, "but I am just a nervous wreck trying to be calm."

Alarm at Rising Divorce Rate

Americans in the 1920s were seriously alarmed at the rising divorce rate. Indeed, for decades state legislatures had tried to stem the tide, putting up ever more stringent requirements before divorces could be secured; but to no avail, for they kept increasing. Between 1867 and 1929, the American population grew three times in numbers; marriages grew four times; but divorces grew twenty times. By 1930, every sixth marriage being made in a given year ended in a breakup. Some critics blamed the women's movement. According to them, women were becoming too independent-minded and breaking away from marriage. It was working outside the home, said others: women had too many opportunities to make money, leading them to forget their marital duties.

In fact, however, the marriage rate was rising too (from 8.8 per 1,000 eligible persons, per year, in 1870 to 12.0 in 1920—a 50 percent increase). If anything, Americans were more in love with love and marriage than ever before, more intent on creating homes for themselves and enjoying private life. When divorces occurred, remarriage soon followed. Women were indeed growing more independent-minded, and they worked more. However, the strongest force behind the divorce trend was not a rejection of marriage, but rising expectations as to what marriage should bring.

In the 1870s (when the divorce rate had been at 1.5 per thousand existing marriages, annually), expectations had been classically simple. "Husbands," writes Elaine Tyler May in *Great Expectations: Marriage and Divorce in Post-Victorian America* (1980), "were to provide the necessities of life, treat their wives with courtesy and protection, and exercise sexual restraint. . . . A wife's duty," May goes on, "was to maintain a comfortable home, take care of household chores, bear and tend to the children, and set the moral tone for domestic life. She was to remain chaste and modest in her behavior, frugal in matters of household expenses, and her conduct was never to reflect badly upon her home and her husband's good name."

In the 1920s, the old set of behaviors was still desired, but there was now a new expectation of "marital happiness"—as well as a divorce rate of 7.7 per thousand existing marriages, a five-fold increase from half a century before. For women marriage was still far more at the center of their daily lives than it was for men, who had their outside careers to absorb them. Thus, women were the partners most likely to seek divorce (though they were by no means alone in this). More eager for perfection in domestic life, women were the more easily disappointed. Perhaps they were

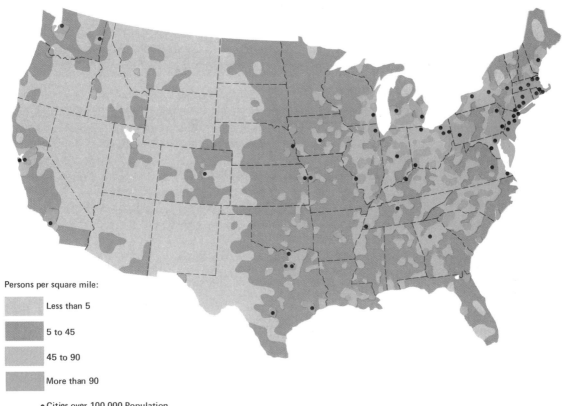

Persons per square mile:

Less than 5

5 to 45

45 to 90

More than 90

● Cities over 100,000 Population

more affected, too, by the Hollywood model for marriage which by the 1920s was pouring into the national consciousness from the new movie theaters. California had traditionally been more liberal, even in the 1870s, in its laws allowing for divorce (South Carolina, at the other extreme, actually banned divorce entirely in 1895). Thus, it was hardly coincidental that out of Los Angeles and its suburb Hollywood came the formula that youth and beauty and a more loving relationship made for the perfect marriage.

There should be excitement and strong mutual affection *and* domesticity in the home. "Given greater marital options," May observes, "hopeful brides began to desire more than merely the security of a roof over their heads . . . the men had to live up to extremely high expectations." Not that women en masse became giddy Hollywood starlets rejecting motherhood and the wife's traditional responsibilities. If anything, as earlier observed, childrearing absorbed ever more of women's attentions, more of their love and concern. Indeed, women worried and talked about the impact of the rising divorce rate upon

children, and they continued to be among the most forceful preachers of the ideal of motherhood. It was simply that, on the whole, the balance between the sacrifices expected in a marriage, and the satisfactions it was expected rightfully to provide, was shifting—and would continue to shift, as we shall observe in Chapter 38.

The Harlem Renaissance and the "New Negro"

The "New Negro" of the 1920s startled white America. The huge migration out of the South, the sense of pride black Americans drew from their role in the First World War, and the wartime emphasis upon democracy and human rights flowered in a cultural explosion in the 1920s. Centering in Harlem but eventually spreading around the country, a world of black novelists, dramatists, poets, scholars, and musicians made white America take black culture seriously for the first time. Jazz was enormously popular, moving swiftly from its New Orleans beginnings around 1900 into the national youth world, both white and black. Attacked by traditionalists as scandalously sensual, it contributed to the general breaking loose of American daily life from Victorian gentility.

Meanwhile, black writers defiantly, bitterly, and impatiently explored the hypocrisy of American affirmations of freedom and equality, and the reality of black life. Proclaiming that in the black soul there was a deeper humanity and a broader sensitivity to social truths than that displayed in white culture, black intellectuals experienced a soaring of the spirit, a bountiful pride and hope for black self-expression and self-realization. High culture in its traditional forms was passionately pursued as black men and women sought to demonstrate that they could excel at the most sophisticated levels of European and American literary and artistic performance. James Weldon Johnson in *The Book of American Negro Poetry* (1922) revealed the richness of contemporary black expression in this medium; Jean Toomer's *Cane* (1923) brilliantly illuminated black life. Langston Hughes, the Harlem Renaissance's leading spirit, poured out a rich miscellany of writings and gave wide inspiration to black intellectuals. Meanwhile, black writers were appearing in many periodicals, published by white and black editors, and white intellectuals watched in fascination this fresh outpouring of creative achievement. Black players began appearing on the stage in other than humorous roles: in Eugene O'Neill's *The Emperor Jones* (1920) and *All God's Chillun Got Wings* (1924), among other productions. Black musicals, black spirituals, black painting—all of these gave voice to a rising articulateness in the black community, a message to white America that the old days of silence and cultural timidity were gone.

Massive Immigration Transforms America

America has always been a land of immigrants, but never had so bewildering a diversity of peoples erupted in the United States as during the era of the great migration from 1880 to 1930, when there were twenty-seven million newcomers from abroad. During the nineteenth century the white American population had been descended almost entirely from the British Isles, Germany, and Scandinavia—that is, from northern Europe. Now, southern and eastern Europeans of many tongues and faiths and ethnic identities poured into the country. The peak of immigration from Germany had been in 1882. From Italy it was 1907, Russia 1913 (mainly Jews), and Czechoslovakia and Poland, 1921.

The numbers were huge. For example, from 1881 to 1910, more than three million Italians left their homeland for the United States. The next most numerous body of immigrants were Jews, who in the same years arrived as a host of two million people from all over eastern Europe. Then there were the various Slavic peoples, who constituted one out of four of the new arrivals: Russians, Ukrainians, Slovaks, Slovenes, Poles (the largest of the Slavic groups; one million came before 1914), Croatians, Serbs, and Bulgarians. There were more from eastern and southern Europe: a million Magyars from Hungary, 300,000 Greeks, almost 150,000 Portuguese, perhaps 80,000 Armenians, thousands of Syrians. From the Orient came 90,000 Japanese to settle in the West Coast states, which earlier had received perhaps 100,000 Chinese during the California gold rush and the building of the transcontinental railroads. (The Burlingame Treaty of 1882 with China had terminated Chinese immigration, and the "Gentleman's Agreement" with Japan in 1907 had largely closed down that source of migrants.) Many of the new immigrants would return home. Nine out of ten of those from the Balkans did so. In fact, between 1908 and 1914, for every three immigrants arriving one left the country. Since groups like the Greeks and Japanese came almost without women at all—most Italian immigrants were also men—the tendency to return home after making a stake in America was very strong.

The majority remained, however. Four out of five settled in the Middle West and Northeast. In fact, two out of three made homes either in New England or in the three Middle Atlantic states of Pennsylvania, New Jersey, and New York. Others headed westward to highly urbanized states such as Ohio and Illinois. Italians and Jews concentrated especially in New York City. Indeed, that city, Chicago, Detroit, Cleveland, and Boston were found, in the census of 1910, to have populations in which only one person out of four was not either an immigrant or the child of one. In San Francisco, only that proportion did not speak a foreign language.

The Reception of the Immigrant

The new immigration encountered massive distaste from the earlier arrivals. The Italians, so numerous in the new wave, received an especially outspoken barrage of insults. They were overwhelmingly from the poverty-stricken south of Italy and from Sicily, where illiteracy and an intense village-centered clannishness dominated life and a darker skin was common. The latter characteristic aroused color-conscious racism, and in the Southern states Italians were sometimes required to attend black schools. A people among whom ancient family and village feuds created the highest rate of homicide in Europe, in the United States Italians were singled out as peculiarly violent, given to crimes with knives. Sentor Henry Cabot Lodge referred to southern Italians as only "half-civilized," the "Chinese of Europe." A newspaper in the 1890s could hardly contain its disgust: "The sewer is unchoked. Europe is vomiting. She is pouring her scum on the American shore." California became a unique center for Italian settlement, an "Italy in America." In that state, so like Italy in climate and geography, Italians entered almost every segment of the economy: banking, wineries, farming, dairies, and fisheries. Since elsewhere in America Italians tended to congregate in industry, the construction trades, and small merchandising, the success of Italians in California farming and finance was particularly notable.

Jews had been coming to America from Germany since far back in the nineteenth century, though out of 15 million Americans in the 1830s, they numbered only 15,000. Anti-Semitism, an ancient attitude among peoples as diverse as Arabs, Russians, Germans, and Americans, surfaced in a major way in the 1870s in the United States, since by that time there were about 250,000 Jews in the country. They prospered extraordinarily. No other immigrants have ever risen so rapidly in wealth, and this produced a sour envy among older-stock Americans and other immigrant peoples. The ancient Shylock image attached to Jews began to be accompanied by a stereotype portraying them as loud and pushy, and in love with conspicious and vulgar display. Shortly, Jews were being excluded from hotels in the summering places of the northeastern states, and from private schools and social clubs.

Then came the immense influx of eastern European, highly orthodox Jews whose diet, dress, and styles of hair as well as speech were thought bizarre and unkempt not only by native Americans but also by the older German Jewish population. Now discrimination intensified. Newspapers took help-wanted ads specifying "Christian only." Universities established quotas. And dense inner-city neighborhoods became crowded Jewish ghettos, as in the old country. In these great communities, such as the one in New York City, highly religious Jewish peoples could find the rich cultural life they needed in order to maintain the viability of their synagogue worship and their language.

Nonetheless, Jews continued to demonstrate by their hard work and their passion for education that they were the most upwardly mobile of all American ethnic groups. Many, indeed, in striving to prove that they were as American as the WASPs themselves, sought, like many other immigrants, to discard their cultural identity and heritage, taking on WASP ways of dress, worship, and family life. Despite this willing acculturation, Jews in many parts of the United States in the 1920s were almost completely excluded from social contact with WASPs. In a cruel irony, Jews appeared to attract greater dislike as they became more economically successful. (With other ethnic minorities, such as the Germans and the Japanese, the opposite has been true.) The cultural historian John Higham suggests that this happened perhaps because people traditionally believed that Jews were more intelligent and more able than other peoples, and therefore felt more threatened by Jews.

Traditional America Revolts

This flood of new peoples was dramatically apparent in the 1920s. Large cities were now more than ever before the cultural centers of American life, and they were peculiarly the places where this babble of new tongues, styles of life, cultures, and religions congregated. The result was the last full-throated crusade of traditional WASP America to impose cultural homogeneity. The advent of prohibition in 1919 (by means of the Eighteenth Amendment)—adopted partly as a wartime measure to conserve grain and increase national efficiency by attacking drunkenness, partly in a surge of war-induced idealism, and especially as an anti-German and antiethnic crusade (the German beer industry was an object of particular hatred)—was the greatest triumph of traditional Yankee moral values. This confident WASP campaign to "purify" the country swept on into the postwar years.

The immediate threat to be battled was felt to be that alarming ideology: communism. Since the victory of the Soviets in Russia in 1917, it seemed to frightened Americans (and much of western Europe) to be sweeping titanically out of that country in a red tide fueled by hatred and waves of propaganda. After the First World War surges of disorder swept over Europe and the United States, and the turmoil was blamed upon the Communists. Strikes broke out everywhere in America as labor unions struggled to catch up with the skyrocketing cost of living. Every protest of workingmen was met with screaming headlines and an avalanche of abuse. Even steelworkers, who were simply trying to end their twenty-four-hour shifts and their seven-day week, were accused of marching to the orders of Moscow. At the same time, bombs began exploding while radical socialists went about the country crying for an end to capitalism.

In the fall of 1919 Attorney General A. Mitchell Palmer (whose home had been the target of one explosion) launched raids on many radical centers. Hundreds of members of the Union of Russian Workers were promptly deported to Russia. Then one night more than four thousand people were arrested as Palmer launched his most sweeping nationwide assault on the national conspiracy that he insisted was seeking to destroy the United States. Brushing aside civil rights, his agents invaded homes, union headquarters, and meeting halls to make their arrests. Many of those detained had no perceivable connection with any kind of radicalism. During the excitement, the legislature of New York expelled five legally elected legislators who were members of the Socialist party. J. Edgar Hoover, head of the Justice Department's alien-radical division, insisted that letting imprisoned men out to see their lawyers "defeats the ends of justice."

The Red Scare was soon over, for the raids turned up no evidence of a conspiracy and practically no arms at all. Even Warren Harding belittled the wild talk about Communists. But one thing continued to alarm the nation: aliens seemed at the center of every radical movement. As a consequence, nativism surged upward after many years of relative quiet. A sharp, brief recession hit the country in late 1920, just when immigration from Europe, quite low during the war, suddenly grew rapidly. How could the United States go on endlessly finding room for more people, it was asked, when it could not find work for those already here? Fanning the fires of nativism even more was the fact that many immigrants, culturally conditioned to be heavy consumers of alcohol, openly flouted prohibition. Indeed, many leading bootleggers were recent immigrants. Thus the nation came to identify aliens not only with the term *radical* but with the term *criminal* as well.

The Ku Klux Klan

The Ku Klux Klan emerged as the vehicle for the fears aroused by these new influences. Revived in Georgia in 1915, it expanded rapidly across the nation after 1920. Democratic in the South, it was strongly Republican elsewhere. The Klan not only harassed black Americans—especially the "New Negro" who returned from the fighting in France with a new sense of personal dignity—it also spread accusations that Catholics and Jews were behind the breakdown in traditional America's ways of life. Fundamentalist Protestantism had exploded in the South and the Middle West, and many Fundamentalist ministers, who preached a literal interpretation of the Bible and a vicious anti-Catholicism, gave the Ku Klux Klan their enthusiastic blessing. The Klan organized boycotts of Catholic businessmen, publicly condemned Catholic officeholders, and in some cases physically attacked Catholic churches and priests. It also developed an elaborate religious ritual featuring burning crosses, hymns sung to Klan verses, and kneeling prayers.

Perhaps five million Americans had enrolled in the Klan by the middle 1920s. The midwestern states experienced an enormous growth in the order, Indiana and Ohio becoming the leading states in the nation in membership. Even in Oregon the Klan was large enough to have a strong

The Ku Klux Klan parades down Pennsylvania Avenue in Washington, D.C., in 1926. Then an organization with millions of members, its open flaunting of bigotry has lost its respectability in the last half-century.

impact on the state's politics, and burning crosses flared on California hillsides as well. By this time, however, its leadership was following the pattern classic to such organizations: excess piled on excess, financial chicanery, and internal bickering. A growing national opposition to such vigilanteism checked the Klan's growth. Never strong in the big cities, which were its particular object of hatred, the Klan was vigorously condemned by ethnic legislators from large urban centers. Eventually it began a long decline and subsided into a fringe movement in the Southern states.

Hiram W. Evans, Imperial Wizard of the Ku Klux Klan in 1926, expressed the protest of his "Nordic American" organization against modern America: "The Klan . . . has now come to speak for the great mass of Americans of the old pioneer stock . . . as distinguished from the intellectually mongrelized 'Liberals.' . . . [These] Nordic Americans for the last generation have found themselves increasingly uncomfortable, and finally deeply distressed. There appeared first confusion in thought and opinion, a groping and hesitancy about national affairs and private life alike, in sharp contrast to the clear, straightforward purposes of our earlier years. There was futility in religion . . . strange ideas . . . moral breakdown . . . economic distress. . . . We found our great cities and the control of much of our industry and commerce taken over by strangers, who stacked the cards of success and prosperity against us. Shortly they came to dominate our government [with the result that] the native Americans were constantly discriminated against, in business, in legislation and in administrative government. So the Nordic American today is a stranger in large parts of the land his fathers gave him . . . one much spit upon, and one to whom even the right to have his own opinions and to work for his own interests is now denied with jeers and revilings. . . . Our falling birth rate, the result of all this, is proof of our distress."

The war revealed how many un-American, disloyal aliens were in the United States, and Nordic Americans "decided that . . . an alien usually remains an alien no matter what is done to him, what veneer of education he gets, what oaths he takes, nor what public attitudes he adopts. They decided that the melting pot was a ghastly failure, and remembered that the very name was coined by a member of one of the races—the Jews—which most determinedly refuses to melt. . . . They learned . . . that alien ideas are just as dangerous to us as the aliens themselves.

"We are a movement of the plain people, very weak in the matter of culture, intellectual support, and trained leadership. We are demanding . . . a return of power into the hands of the everyday, not highly cultured, not overly intellectualized, but entirely unspoiled and not de-Americanized, average citizen of the old stock." (*North American Review* [March 1926])

Nativism and Immigration Control

In the mid 1920s, antialien nativism reached its climax. In state after state, laws were passed forbidding the foreign-born from entering professions in medicine, pharmacy, architecture, and surveying, and even from driving buses or making wills. Nativists insisted that the nation could absorb no more immigrants. The "100-percent American" groups, such as the American Legion, also condemned immigration as the principal root of radicalism. The AFL demanded immigration restriction out of fear of job competition.

A new note, however, was now entering the controversy. No longer were people interested only in cutting down immigration: what they sought was to exclude certain kinds of immigrants while leaving the door partly open to immigrants from northern and western Europe. The writings of Madison Grant, who during the war had issued a gloomy book entitled *The Passing of the Great Race* (1916), became popular. An upper-class New Yorker of rarefied Anglo-Saxon stock, he had acquired something of a national reputation as a scientist. Disgusted by all the strange-looking immigrants from central and eastern Europe who had crowded into his city since 1890, he wrote that these people contained racial characteristics in their bloodstreams that were certain to debase the American stock. Others picked up the theme, warning that steps needed to be taken swiftly to preserve a "distinct American type" in the United States. Adherents of the theory seized eagerly on such official statements as one issued by a State Department office in 1920 that described the 120,000 Jews who had entered the nation that year as "twisted . . . unassimilable . . . filthy, un-American."

Immigration restriction had been talked about since the 1880s and had actually been instituted during the war, when a literacy test was established. But the upsurge of new arrivals after 1920 convinced nativists that much more needed to be done. In 1921 an immigration-restriction law was passed that established quotas by which each European nationality could send to this country only 3 percent of its numbers living in the United States in 1910. A temporary measure, it was supplanted in 1924 by permanent legislation that excluded Orientals entirely, allowed free immigration to continue from Canada and Latin America, and put the quota system for European immigration in its final form. Shifting the basis of computation at first to the census of 1890 (after 1929, the census of 1920 was to apply), at which time the immigration from eastern and southern Europe had only barely begun, the law limited the annual inflow of each nationality to a number equal to 2 percent of those in the country on that date. This meant that Britons, Germans, and Scandinavians would for a number of years have disproportionately large quotas while Italians, Poles, and the other eastern- and southern-European groups would have small entry quotas. Legislators from these urban ethnic groups complained bitterly against the measure, but when the crucial votes were taken in Congress a huge chorus of "ayes" from the small towns and the countryside turned the tide. "America must be kept American," said President Calvin Coolidge as he signed the legislation.

Thereafter, the total inflow of immigrants from Europe was to be limited to approximately 150,000 persons year. Thus was a new era in American history begun. The country's population slowly shifted from a condition in which the great cities were composed primarily of recently arrived European immigrants or their children to one in which the native-born overwhelmingly predominated. Each generation after 1924 saw a slow blurring of the differences among Americans of European origins in language, styles of dress, and customs.

Mexican-Americans Swell in Numbers

The Immigration Act of 1924 had an ironic effect, considering what its framers intended: by cutting off the supply of European labor that traditionally took up the lowest-paid and most undesirable jobs in the economy, and yet leaving the door open to unrestricted immigration from Western Hemisphere countries, it vastly increased the non-WASP Catholic population in the United States. The needs of agricultural business in the southwestern states and California for stoop labor from Mexico (to tend new crops in the fields had insured that the law would not exclude Mexicans, and now immigration from that country, already in its first large surge, shot upward steeply. (The statistics on legal immigrants show a sharp drop after 1925 to very low levels, but this is because the Mexican government, alarmed at the drain of labor to America, clamped down on legal migration, which simply diverted the flow into illegal channels.)

For forty years after the Mexican War of the 1840s the Spanish-speaking population in the Southwest and California had been small. In 1900, Texas, New Mexico, Arizona, California, and Colorado held only about 100,000 people of Mexican birth (of these, only 8,000 were in California). However, immigration across the border from Mexico had been on a slow rise since it began in the 1880s, because the states in this region were developing, and cheap labor was needed for railroad construction and maintenance, in mining, and in agriculture. Then in 1911 came an eruption of violent revolution in Mexico, and everything changed. Bloody warfare rocked Mexico until 1920, during which perhaps a million Mexicans lost their lives and possibly another million crossed the American border to settle in the United States. What for generations had been a small minority group in American life—those of Latin American descent—now began its immense twentieth-century growth into what is now the largest minority ethnic community in the United States after the Afro-American, drawing upon heavy influxes from Puerto Rico, Cuba, and Mexico. By 1930, in the five states earlier mentioned, the total of Mexican-descended residents reached more that 1,250,000 (in California, 368,000).

This immense Mexican immigration, which had risen to 90,000 legal arrivals a year by 1925, created large pools in America of unorganized, cheap labor and sizable *barrios* (Mexican-American residential areas) within southwestern cities. The immigrant workers built the irrigated farming industry of this region by providing an essential supply of laboring hands. In return they received bare subsistence wages, housing like that given slaves a hundred years before, no education, prejudicial treatment in social relations, and the status of America's most pitifully exploited workers —the migrant farm laborers. Mexicans also continued to labor in the railroads, mining, construction, and in various urban occupations. Indeed, many Mexican immigrants were middle-class people, especially those who were political refugees from their homeland.

Therefore, the Mexican *barrio* became much more than just a community of laborers. It became a fragment of Mexico itself, or perhaps more accurately, a kind of half-way house suspended between Mexican and American culture, with its own business and professional class. Here the Mexican immigrant could find an island of Mexican life, in which there was cultural persistence and cultural security. The barrio was not simply a place of residence for exploited workers, it was a haven in which Mexican immigrant culture could take root in America, flourish, and gradually evolve into that special phenomenon, Mexican-American culture.

Mexicans and Politics

Very few of the immigrant Mexicans became American citizens. Only 5.5 percent of the 320,000 Mexican-born living in the United States in 1930 who were over twenty-one years of age

had gone through naturalization. Perhaps this was because their homeland was next door, a fact that has made the Mexican-American minority group sharply different in its attitudes from most such groups in American history. Many harbored hopes of returning to Mexico; there was always much coming and going across the border. Since few were naturalized, few voted in American politics. Indeed, between 1900 and 1930, Mexicans in America participated primarily in *Mexican* politics. Many of the political refugees formed organizations which were active in support of various political factions in Mexico during the Revolution. As so often is the case among immigrants, politics meant for them the politics of their homeland. Where Mexican-American citizens did vote, as in New Mexico and in Texan border cities like El Paso, in San Antonio, and in South Texas, they usually voted solidly for local Democratic political machines. For this reason, and other factors of poverty and language and cultural differences, the Mexican-American group, for all its size, had little leverage in American politics. Therefore, their ability to improve their condition—especially since American labor unions usually refused to admit them—was practically nonexistent.

During World War I, Mexican-Americans began for the first time to appear in midwestern cities such as St. Louis, Chicago, and Detroit, where they labored in steel plants, automobile plants, and packing houses. (During and after the Second World War, this movement would grow tremendously.) Los Angeles, by 1925, was the second largest Mexican city, after Mexico City itself. Living in crowded ghetto conditions, urban Mexican-Americans entered at the bottom of the social scale under the Poles, Italians, and Slavs, who by this time were beginning to move upward —and to look down with dislike on the new arrivals. So significant was this movement into nonagricultural employment that in 1930 the census stated that while 180,000 Mexican-Americans worked on the farms, about 150,000 were common laborers on the railroads and in other industries.

The depression of the 1930s, however, brought an end to this first huge immigration of Mexicans into the United States. Jobs were no longer available; laws were passed prohibiting the employment of aliens on public works; contractors were discouraged from hiring noncitizens; migrant American farmers displaced from the dust bowl of Texas and Oklahoma moved heavily into the farm labor market; and probably a half-million Mexicans returned to their homeland. To keep them off welfare, whole trainloads were shipped southward; some 200,000 were moved out in the year 1932 alone. This was a grievous experience for thousands of people. It confirmed the view of most Mexican-Americans that Anglo-American society could not be trusted, and that the United States government was a power to be avoided. Welcomed when their presence produced profits for employers, Mexicans were abruptly expelled when things got difficult.

Millions of peoples entering America from many cultures had an often bewildering experience. America was so *different* from southern Italy, from the Orient, or from the ancient Mexican way of living that for many centuries had centered in and radiated outward from the high valleys of central Mexico. One of Mexico's great poets, Octavio Paz, has reflected upon his two years in America in the 1940s. In Los Angeles he observed his country's "Mexicanism—delight in decorations, carelessness and pomp, negligence, passion and reserve" —existing beside but never mixing with "the North American world based on precision and efficiency." The Mexican, he wrote, "succumbs very easily to sentimental effusions," and therefore adopts a stern reserve, shown in the "scowling expressions" of young Mexicans living in southern California. They hide, Paz suggests, a "sense of inferiority— real or imagined"—induced in part by the Mexican's "dazzled impression of [America's] grandeur . . . When I arrived in the United States I was surprised above all by the self-assurance and confidence of the [American] people, by their apparent happiness and apparent adjustment to the world around them. [They are critical of their society, but] . . . it is a criticism that respects the existing systems and never touches the roots. . . . [The] United States is a society that wants to realize its ideals, has no wish to exchange them for others, and is confident of surviving, no matter how dark the future may appear." By contrast, Paz goes on, in the Mexican's character, derived from Mexico's long history of bloody exploitation by dictators, is a "willingness to contemplate horror: he is even familiar and complacent in his dealings with it. The bloody Christs in our village churches, the macabre humor in some of our newspaper headlines, our wakes, the custom of eating skull-shaped cakes and candies on the Day of the Dead, are habits inherited from the Indians and the Spaniards and are now an inseparable part of our being. Our cult of death is also a cult of life, in the same way that love is a hunger for life and a longing for death. . . . The North Americans are credulous and we are believers; they love fairy tales and detective stories and

we love myths and legends. . . . They are optimists and we are nihilists. . . . We are suspicious and they are trusting. We are sorrowful and sarcastic and they are happy and full of jokes. North Americans want to understand and we want to contemplate. They are activists and we are quietists; we enjoy our wounds and they enjoy their inventions. They believe in hygiene, health, work and contentment, but perhaps they have never experienced true joy, which is an intoxication, a whirlwind. In the hubbub of a fiesta night our voices explode into brilliant lights, and life and death mingle together, while their vitality becomes a fixed smile that denies old age and death but that changes life to motionless stone. . . . North Americans consider the world to be something that can be perfected, and . . . we consider it to be something that can be redeemed. (*The Labyrinth of Solitude: Life and Thought in Mexico* [1961], pp.18–24)

And yet this picture, with its dramatic contrasts, was overdrawn. As we have seen, Mexicans in the United States had always been a heterogeneous group, both working and middle class, rural and urban, exhibiting diverse cultural characteristics. Many, by the 1940s, were already demanding and fighting for the same "American Dream" as other Americans—if often an American Dream in Mexican terms: that is, with an ultimate objective of returning to Mexico itself, in improved status and wealth.

Fundamentalism Fights Darwinism

The struggle waged in the 1920s by traditional WASP America to go back to older ways of life reached a dramatic climax in a spectacular trial in Dayton, Tennessee, in 1925. Early in the decade Fundamentalist Protestants had launched an attack on the teaching of Darwinian evolution in the public schools. The theory, they insisted, was a monstrous insult to God and a corrosive influence on morality. The true story of creation, they said, lay in the first two chapters of Genesis. How could young people believe in God's moral laws, laid down in the Bible, if science was allowed to challenge the Book's literal truth?

William Jennings Bryan led the campaign to outlaw Darwinism, a fact that immediately led the entire nation to watch the controversy closely. The anti-Darwinist campaign was especially successful in the South, where older forms of Protestantism held firm. Kentucky's legislature fell just one vote short of passing a law outlawing the teaching of evolution in 1922, and the governor of Texas, "Ma" Ferguson, simply erased Darwinism from the state's textbooks. "I am a Christian mother," she said, "and I am not going to let that kind of rot go into Texas textbooks." Then in Tennessee in 1925, a powerful lobbying effort led by Bryan secured passage of a law making it illegal to teach "any theory that denies the story of the divine creation of man as taught in the Bible. . . ."

The stage was set for tragicomedy. John T. Scopes, a biology teacher in Dayton, agreed to challenge the law with the support of the American Civil Liberties Union, an organization then rooted in big-city ethnic minorities. He lectured on Darwinism and was soon hailed into court. Clarence Darrow, a brilliant, cynical defense attorney and a religious skeptic, offered to defend Scopes. Bryan arrived to help lead the prosecution, conceiving the trial as a "duel to the death" between true Christian belief and atheistic science. There was no question that Scopes had violated the law, and he was convicted of that act and duly fined (a higher court set aside the penalty on a technicality). But in the process Darrow put Bryan on the stand and pilloried him mercilessly on religious issues. Jonah, testified Bryan, was in fact swallowed by a big fish; Joshua made the sun stand still; the languages of the world came from the tower of Babel; and Adam and Eve were the first human beings, Eve having been fashioned from Adam's rib. Much of the nation laughed derisively at Bryan, for his statements made him seem to many like an uneducated fool. Indeed, Bryan's reputation ever since has been buried under the ridicule he received in that steaming July. He left the trial confident that he was right, and ready for renewed struggles in his battle for the Lord, but within days, apparently because of the rigors of his ordeal, he died.

The New View of Humanity: Sigmund Freud

Traditional America could exclude aliens and pass antievolution statutes, but it could not keep away a flood of cosmopolitan modernism. The United States in the 1920s was eager to listen to modern science and to new ideas from Europe. None was more fundamentally important than a view of the nature of humanity that came from the Viennese physician Sigmund Freud. In the 1880s he had discovered that he could cure women of hysteria by getting them to talk freely about their most intimate experiences and fears. Soon he became convinced that sexual difficulties lay at the root of his patients' neuroses. For years, alone and despised, he tried to find out through his patients' revelations why his "talking cure" seemed to work.

He concluded that beneath the conscious mind lay another layer, the unconscious, into which people thrust unbearable thoughts and experiences. Such repression often left conflicts unresolved. Psychoanalysis would release these pressures through catharsis, thus allowing the patient to gain a rational understanding of the source of his or her problems. Freud was fascinated by the unconscious. Dreams, he concluded, opened a window into the region, though they clothed the repressed conflicts in symbols that had to be carefully examined to disclose their real content (for example, guns might represent male sexual organs). Freud came to believe that of all the forces that struggled in the unconscious, the most powerful originated in the body and its instinctual drives. For this reason, he described the irrational side of man as often more potent than the rational.

Freud said the human personality was composed of three elements. First there was the *id*, in which all the animal forces of passion, greed, and selfishness expressed themselves. Then there was the *superego*, or the moral teachings of parents and society, embodied in the conscience. And between these two powerful entities, seeking to bring their conflicting forces into harmony, there was the *ego*, or the conscious self. Here was an image of humanity in which madness and sanity seemed intermixed, in which primitivism (the id) struggled constantly with civilized intellect (the ego) for mastery. All people, no matter how proper and genteel, were capable of acting destructively toward themselves and toward others. What happened to the belief that our lives could be controlled by conscious, trained intelligence? Freud's depth psychology was like the discovery of perspective in painting. No longer could one take others simply as they seemed on the surface. Now there were hidden dimensions to be considered, powerful forces that rumbled far down in the interior.

Freud's way of looking at human nature was not new. The Greeks had known that people were moved by dark passions over which they seemed to have little control. The Bible is filled with similar observations. John Calvin and the Puritans had been keenly aware of the primitive flames in each person and of the precarious control that reason seems to hold over them. The romantics of the early nineteenth century believed the human personality to be primarily passionate. Friedrich Nietzsche, the German philosopher, had already written about the unconscious. But the predominate outlook in Western civilization after 1850 had been a confident faith that the human person is fundamentally a reasoning creature—had we not uncovered the secrets of the universe by science?—and a decent one as well. The long peace after the Napoleonic Wars gave strength to the notion that civilized humanity had outgrown primitivism. But Sigmund Freud was now saying again that we are forever engaged in a series of insistent inner conflicts that begin at birth and do not end until death. Human personality, he said, is best understood as a battlefield where civilized reason fights ceaselessly to control primitive passions, much as a rider (the ego) tries to master a wild and untamed horse (the id). Even children, he said, were moved by sexual urges.

America and Freud

In America more than anywhere else Freud's ideas were picked up rapidly, beginning about 1910, and spread widely through the country. Even before the First World War, intellectuals in New York City were discussing them excitedly. By the 1920s Freudianism seemed everywhere. Word-association parlor games spread like wildfire, their professed objective being to reveal the unconscious meanings people attach to things. Young intellectuals who called Freud a liberator used his ideas to scoff at religion and morals. Freud had never preached sexual license—indeed, he was rather puritanical in his views of sex—but in popular culture this was forgotten and creators of sensationalist movies and stories let the sex theme run riot. Even the Sears, Roebuck catalogue began listing books on sex, including *Ten Thousand Dreams Interpreted* and *Sex Prob-*

lems Solved. Writers of fiction such as Sherwood Anderson became obsessed with sexual symbolism. As to psychoanalysis, many seemed to take it up as a new fad.

Sigmund Freud's teachings were received in the United States more enthusiastically than in Europe for several reasons. For one thing, Freudian psychology was individualistic. Europeans tended to explain things about a person by pointing to his membership in a particular social class. But Americans liked to think that each person can be explained only in his or her own terms: look into one's unique childhood, Freud's theories suggested to them, and the answers will be found. Furthermore, American culture has been significantly more happiness-oriented than that in Europe. Humbled and disillusioned by centuries of suffering and wars, Europeans have tended to think that life in the best of circumstances is a difficult and unhappy business. But the innocent Americans, in their national experience given an apparently unbroken string of successes and inspired by the notion that they were showing the world how to find prosperity and contentment, believed that life should be a fundamentally enjoyable experience. Running through American history, even in times of doubt and dismay, has been a sturdy optimism. In Freud's teachings, so it seemed, a new way to happiness had been found.

The Optimism of the 1920s

Nothing seemed as deeply rooted in American life in the 1920s as this national optimism, which rose high over the dark prophecies of the Ku Klux Klan and the nervous fears of traditional America. The American population delighted in the "miracles" that new inventions had brought them—electric lights, airplanes, automobiles, radios. The list seemed endless, and progress in all directions appeared inevitable. These new devices brought greater power and ease to every individual, providing a leisure undreamed of by older generations. Automobiles and airplanes broke down space, giving ordinary people an exciting sense of mastery over distance. People watched Charles Lindbergh make the first solo nonstop airplane flight over the Atlantic in 1927 with a confident sense that it opened a new and fruitful era for mankind. The radio multiplied the power of the ear, the movie that of the eye. New amusements, comforts, and ways of life flooded in on every side.

For all of this, the business community felt a proud responsibility. Businessmen constantly proclaimed the arrival of what they called the New Era. Technology had opened many doors; opportunities seemed endless; and the mass market had grown so huge that it seemed no earlier age of industry could compare with the current one. Industrialists and financiers believed themselves to be not conservatives, as they were usually depicted, but daring innovators. They reached a level of national popularity perhaps never achieved before in American history, and certainly never again. Calvin Coolidge worshiped business as much as he detested government. "The man who builds a factory builds a temple," he said. "The man who works there worships there." The Republican administrations of the 1920s bent every possible effort toward cooperation with and assistance to the business community. The *Wall Street Journal* observed complacently that "never before, here or anywhere else, has a government been so completely fused with business." At the same time, a cult of success suffused popular literature. A steady stream of articles and books on how to get ahead and make a million was poured out. An almost lavish admiration of powerful industrialists and financiers emerged. Such great men as Henry Ford, it was often said, were the men to follow. If it were not for these leaders, said one business writer, "the multitude would eat their heads off, and, as history proves, would lapse into barbarism. . . . The masses are the beneficiaries, the few, the benefactors."

Optimism Among Intellectuals

This same optimism abounded among social scientists. Psychology came into enormous popular vogue. Books appeared that explained everything from the psychology of golf to that of selling life insurance. Psychologists confidently used intelligence tests and other clinical devices to predict personal success and to counsel businessmen. In 1925 the writings of John B. Watson on behaviorism suddenly caught the national fancy. He predicted that by proper conditioning anyone

could be transformed into anything he or she wished to be. The human, he said, was simply a machine who responded to stimuli. In brief, there were no limits to anyone's potentialities, given appropriately "scientific" training.

Sociologists were also emerging into national prominence on the basis of another "scientific" technique—the survey. By this means, quantitative studies of all aspects of social life were made. Sociologists were confident that a point would soon be reached when trained minds, ruminating over these growing mountains of accurate social information, would distill from them the social laws that govern human life. These, in turn, would allow sociologists to provide guidance to politicians, who would enact appropriate legislation. A similar confidence in their abilities was exhibited by economists, who were relying on scrupulously conducted studies of business affairs to keep the nation's economy booming toward prosperity.

Ranging through this academic confidence like a presiding spirit was the philosopher John Dewey. He was convinced that people could shape the future in any way they wished if they depended on the trained intelligence of experts and utilized central planning. At the core of everything, he believed, should be a new educational system that would train young people to test all assumptions by experience and scientific data. Ignorance and bad thinking, Dewey's teaching implied, were the only barriers to social progress. Everything restrictive in what was old and traditional he lumped under the term *cultural lag*, an irritating stumbling block to be swept away. In the end, Dewey suggested, reason would wipe away human and political tensions.

The same kind of utopianism dominated the world of liberal Protestantism. In the big-city churches and seminaries the social gospel was triumphant. It saw humanity not as irremediably twisted by its nature but as impaired only by ignorance of how to live a truly Christian life. The future could be made perfect. The ministers of God should work confidently in social reform to bring about "a growing perfection in the collective life of humanity, in our laws, in the customs of society, in the institutions of education, and for the administration of mercy."

Social gospelers believed that it *was* possible to follow the Ten Commandments: one need

Charles Lindbergh, being given a delirious ticker-tape parade in New York City after his solo flight in 1927 over the Atlantic. The "Lone Eagle" became the new symbol of a hopeful America.

United Press International Photo

only work at it hard enough. The Reverend Charles M. Sheldon's famous question "What would Jesus do?" should be the guide for everyone in daily life. It would guide businessmen in their business decisions; labor in its struggles; statesmen in the issues of peace and war; bankers in their uses of other people's money. Science, in this view, would be a helpmate in building the kingdom of God on this earth. Humanity was good; the leaven of Christianity would work within society; and the priniciple of love would eventually rise triumphant.

Economic Collapse

Then came the stock-market crash of 1929 and the massive depression that followed. At first Americans regarded these events as another ripple in the business cycle, similar to many in the past. But this depression was far graver than anything that had occurred before. The economy sagged lower and lower, year after year. The re-sult was a massive loss of confidence—in the system, in the nation's leaders, and in the American dream. The optimism of the 1920s disappeared under a tidal wave of pessimism. Searching for scapegoats, the public lashed out furiously at bankers, stockbrokers, and industrialists. The business community plummeted in public esteem. The confident idea of inevitable progress was deeply shaken. When Americans looked abroad, they saw another foreboding development—the collapse of democracies and the spread of dictatorships. The whole system of Western civilization seemed to be in rapid decay.

Ward James, an elderly teacher in the 1960s, reminisced on the emotional impact of the Great Depression: "There was a feeling that we were on the verge of a bloody revolution, up until the time of the New Deal. . . . I remember a very sinking feeling during the time of the Bank Holiday. . . . Everyone was emotionally affected. We developed a fear of the future which was very difficult to overcome. Even though I eventually went into some fairly good jobs, there was still this constant dread: everything would be cut out from under you and you wouldn't know what to do. It would be even harder, because you were older. . . .

"Before the Depression, one felt he could get a job even if something happened to this one. There were always jobs available. And, of course, there were always those [who said] even during the Depression: If you wanted to work, you could really get it. Nonsense.

"I suspect, even now, I'm a little bit nervous about every job I take and wonder how long it's going to last—and what I'm going to do to cause it to disappear.

"I feel anything can happen. There's a little fear in me that it might happen again. It does distort your outlook and your feeling. Lost time and lost faith. . . ." (quoted in Studs Terkel, *Hard Times* [1970])

Deep Roots to Pessimism

There was one group in American life, however, who looked on the depression almost with a sense of relief. America's writers had been saying for a long time that the system was corrupt, and now they appeared to have been proved correct. A remarkable literary flowering had taken place in the 1920s, the first genuinely brilliant outpouring of talent since, perhaps, the days of Emerson and the transcendentalists in the 1830s and 1840s. Ernest Hemingway, John Dos Passos, F. Scott Fitzgerald—these were but a few of the gifted writers of the era. They threw aside the central values of the progressive movement. The progressives had been confident, hopeful people. They had been strong on morals and filled with a faith that people can solve their problems if they apply reason and science. The confident social scientists of the 1920s were their true inheritors, and John Dewey the prophet of their philosophy.

As early as 1914, however, young intellectuals began rejecting this moralistic confidence. Listening to ideas coming from Europe, they insisted that irrationality, intuition, and passion were so strong that the dreams of the progressive would never come true. Cynical about the prospects of America's business civilization, young writers either went to live in Paris or fled to Greenwich Village. From these locations they wrote novels scorning the American way of life. Sinclair Lewis held up small-town life to international ridicule in *Babbitt* (1922). In 1930 he was given the Nobel Prize for Literature.

H. L. Mencken, editor of the *Mercury*, led the attack on American life in the 1920s. Democracy, he said, was a ludicrous farce enthroning the moralism and hypocrisy of the "booboisie" (businessmen) and the Bible Belt (areas inhabited by religious Fundamentalists). In such a world, Mencken scoffed, the real person of thought will always be crushed by the Rotarian and the peasant. Look at the United States, he asked, and observe its elements—prohibition, censorship of "dirty" books, and the Ku Klux Klan. He believed that the progressives' faith in the people was absurd. In reality, the people were nothing but a mob—spiritless, brutal, and ignorant. "Politics under democracy," he said, "consists almost wholly of the discovery, chase, and scotching of bugaboos." No gentleman could hold office in such a cheap charade, and as a consequence vermin made the laws of the United States.

Many besides the young writers were doubtful about the long-range healthfulness of modern life and skeptical of the faith in trained reason that had sprung from the Progressive Era. For them, the most shocking fact of all was the First World War. Throughout Western civilization, thoughtful persons had had their faith in the essential goodness of humankind deeply shaken by the horrors of fighting. In Europe, theologians like Karl Barth and Emil Brunner were so horrified that they rejected almost all they had been taught and began considering a "theology of crisis." The young Reinhold Niebuhr (whom we will consider later in this chapter) felt his social-gospel faith collapsing around him. For these and other such individuals, the war began a long search for a new way of thinking about humanity and its relationship to God.

The New View of the Universe: Relativity

Great changes were taking place in the natural sciences. For more than two hundred years, educated people had believed that the scientific method would ultimately unravel all the secrets of the physical universe. They found security in the view that the cosmos was a simple affair that could be understood by common sense. One could even make mechanical models of it. The universe consisted of physical bodies (mass) scattered through measurable space, and a force called energy. Space, scientists believed, was filled with an invisible gaseous element called ether, a sort of enormous ocean through which the physical bodies of the universe moved. These beliefs were based on the fundamental assumption that the universe we look out on is as it appears to us. Linked to this was another assumption: that if we discover physical matter to act in certain ways on earth, it would act in that way throughout the universe. The laws of earthly physics, in other words, were the laws of the cosmos.

In 1905 Albert Einstein, a young European theorist and mathematician, swept these assumptions away with his special theory of relativity (followed in 1916 by his general theory of relativity). An international sensation occurred among scientists that by the 1920s had spread to the general educated population, producing an outpouring of startled and fascinated editorials, popular articles, and scholarly books. Einstein began by making famous a theretofore little-noted experiment, conducted in Ohio in 1887 by Albert A. Michelson and Edward W. Morley, that proved that ether did not exist. Physicists were shocked, for they had built all their theories about light, energy, and other radiations on the assumption that they were transmitted through the universe by ether much as water transmits waves. Michelson and Morley proved something else as well: that the speed of light is a constant 186,000 miles per second whether the person measuring its speed is moving toward the light source or away from it. How could this be?

Einstein's solution was deceptively simple, yet astounding in its implications. When we speed up or slow down, all our measuring devices change proportionately. If the earth suddenly accelerated enormously in its movement through space, people's yardsticks would become shorter, their clocks would slow down, their hearts would beat more slowly, and radioactive atoms on earth would emit electrons at a reduced rate. Things would seem to be the same, but in relation to what they had been before, they would be different. A century of earthly time, as people presently measure it, could become an instant of time to someone whose speed through the universe had been increased. A man on a voyage through space at great speed would live by his own measurements perhaps a year or two during that voyage, but he would return to find that a couple of centuries had passed by earthly measurements.

All measurements, in other words, are relative to the location and movement of the observer. Time is not an independent thing that exists outside the system of reference within which it takes place. The same was true of space, for distance is a function of time. This meant that scientists could no longer believe that the universe was as they observed it. To an observer situated elsewhere, on some other planet moving at a different speed, the universe would appear quite differently. People could not rely on common sense. Humankind is surrounded, in short, by a mystery that could be described only in mathematical formulas dealing with relationships, not with things as they appear. Scientists were dismayed. What can I do, asked one famous physicist, if I cannot make a model of something and look at it?

Other Scientific Changes

There was more. The discovery of radium in the 1890s had demonstrated that atoms are not fixed and unchanging building blocks, but in certain conditions seem to decay by spraying energy outward. What was happening, explained Einstein, was the transformation of mass into energy. These were interchangeable physical phenomena, not separate things, as had always been assumed. In the most famous formula in this new kind of physics, Einstein described the relationship between energy and mass as $e = mc^2$: energy equals the mass times the speed of light squared. By this formula it could be proved that if matter traveled at the speed of light, it dissolved into radiation, or energy. If it congealed and became inert, it was mass. Once again, Einstein had taken a stable universe with fixed elements and replaced it with flux and flow.

What was the nature of radiation? In 1900 Max Planck theorized that it was emitted in little chunks called quanta. Others held to the older theory that radiation traveled through space in the form of waves. The problem was that both theories worked. Did this mean that we would never know the right answer? For generations people had believed that the scientific method would ultimately yield final answers to every scientific question. Now it appeared that a limit had been reached, that there was a point beyond which we could not go in our search for knowledge. In 1927 a German physicist, Werner Heisenberg, incorporated these thoughts into his "principle of uncertainty." It was pointless, he said, for a physicist to worry any longer about what a single electron was in actuality. For one thing, this was an attitude hanging over from the old physics that Einstein had destroyed—the search for the essence or substance of things. The new Einsteinian physics showed that all we could really find out was the relationship of things, not their ultimate reality, which is hidden from us. Besides, scientists dealt with electrons in streams or showers, each containing billions of electrons. To search out one and tie it down would be futile. Indeed, even if a person had a supermicroscope and could actually look at an electron, the force of the light directed on it would push it away. Thus it was absolutely and forever impossible to determine what an electron was. In short, we can never perceive ultimate reality by the use of our senses.

One thing was certain: if Einstein was right, locked within the atom were enormous stores of energy. By the 1930s scientists were talking excitedly about what might happen if an atom were split and its energy released. Atomic physicists at Berkeley, Cal Tech, and Columbia began building atom-smashing equipment, and their early experiments demonstrated that the physical elements of the universe, long assumed to be fixed and unchanging, could actually be changed from one form to another by knocking off electrons from them.

Popular Response to Scientific Changes

The popular mind was excited by these new developments. So far as Einstein could be understood, he was saying that it was no longer possible for ordinary people to comprehend the universe, and that what scientists actually did understand was strange and unsettling. Time, space, matter, energy—all these dissolved, shifted, and blurred. Everything depended on where the observer was located; relativity replaced fixity; ultimate things were hidden. At the same time, new scientific discoveries in other areas deepened the popular sense of unease. Big telescopes had been built around the turn of the century at Mt. Hamilton, California, and in Chicago that revealed strange new things. There were other universes: galaxies like our own buried deep in space, at unimaginable distances. Furthermore, everything in the

cosmos seemed to be part of some massive explosion, for all the galaxies were moving away from one another at increasing rates of speed. No longer could people believe that they lived in a tidy island universe sailing serenely and alone through space. Something far greater—and more humbling—was occurring in the cosmos.

Meanwhile, biologists were discovering that mutations within a cell nucleus could produce startling changes in plants and animals. The cells themselves, as one writer described them, were "subtle mechanisms of chemical balance, pulled now one way, now another, in endless trial and error relationships." The discovery of vitamins suggested that growth and change, even personality, could be affected by the presence or absence of certain chemicals in the body. By the 1930s Americans had learned that they could no longer be content with the simpleminded emphasis on sexual motivations that had earlier seemed to be the ultimate explanation of human personality. Sigmund Freud himself had long since moved on from his earlier emphasis on the unconscious and its physical passions to an exploration of the conscious self—the ego. This opened up many new views of the complicated relationships that sprang not merely from each person's childhood but from his or her current situations as well. Theory piled on theory, seemingly endless controversies developed over proper methods of treatment, and the public mind was further confused.

Meanwhile, social scientists were also losing the confidence of the 1920s public. Their studies of society came under the same criticism that Einstein had leveled at the old physics—that much of what sociologists believed to be true was true only from the standpoint of a particular observer. Relativity applied to knowledge about society as well as to knowledge about the universe. From country to country and from class to class, people's fundamental ideas, their world views, change, said the sociologist of knowledge Karl Mannheim. This is because they all have a particular location in society from which they see things, which necessarily allows them to be aware of some things and unaware of others. A laboring man has one perspective on the world, his employer another, and neither is necessarily wrong or right. Thus no one can ever know the final truth about government, society, or any large problem, for no one can ever see everything as a single fact. Such relativity in ideas was incompatible with the long-held belief that there were certain things that were true in all times and under all circumstances.

Equally well publicized was the new science of semantics. Scholars such as Stuart Chase, Thurman Arnold, and Kenneth Burke made the educated public newly aware that thought is expressed in particular words, and that the way people think is shaped by the words available to them in their culture. Certain Indian tribes speak languages in which the concept of time hardly appears; members of such tribes would probably have little difficulty in understanding Einstein's theories of relativity. But the ordinary American is obsessed with time and unconsciously thinks in terms of a collection of tenses that place events in rigid time relationships. There are aspects of reality in which our kind of language is a hindrance, yet we are unaware of this and persist in trying to put things in inappropriate terminology. Americans throw around words such as *democracy, capitalism,* and *free enterprise,* but what do they mean? Precision in language: this was what the semanticists called for. Life changes, but people's words do not, and this leads to their constant inability to think clearly about their problems. From this the educated person drew once more the lesson that things taken for granted before—the very words that people used—could no longer be relied on with the same surety.

The New View of Humanity and God: Reinhold Niebuhr

In the early 1930s a new religious voice burst on the American scene, that of Reinhold Niebuhr. Soon he became the most influential thinker in American Protestantism. Niebuhr had watched national and international developments from his pastorate in Detroit in a mood of growing disenchantment. The First World War had horrified him. Then the facts of industrial life in Detroit convinced him that it was fruitless to preach sermons about love and kindness, for the actual conditions of survival made it impossible for people to be always loving and kind. As early as 1927 he began criticizing the ministers of the social gospel for not realizing how evil people can be. Liberal Protestantism, it seemed to him, was fundamentally wrong in its hopefulness for humankind. Then came the depression, which conclusively destroyed the easy optimism of the 1920s and re-

vealed deep and apparently fatal flaws in capitalism. How could anyone believe any longer in the faith of John Dewey and the social scientists: that trained intelligence could solve all problems, that ignorance alone stood in the way of utopia?

In the 1930s Niebuhr moved to Union Theological Seminary, near Columbia University in New York City, where he continued to meditate on modern life, teach, and write his powerful books until his death in 1971. What he taught came to be called neoorthodoxy. That is, he revived what in former centuries had been the orthodox religious view of humankind—that people are inherently sinners and can never avoid the consequences of their sins. By the term *sins,* Niebuhr was concerned not with such actions as dancing and drinking, but with humanity's cruelty and selfishness.

The first thing to reject, Niebuhr maintained, was the liberal Protestant social-gospel belief that the kingdom of God and this world are somehow ultimately compatible and will eventually become one and the same. Niebuhr believed that they are permanently separate. Furthermore, they are in constant tension. People live in history, where power and practical considerations make it impossible to live the truly Christian life of self-sacrificial love. God and His teachings stand outside the world, providing it with the standards towards which people must always strive, but which they will never, by their very nature, be able to attain. God entered history as Christ to provide proof of His love and a standard by which life should be lived. But that standard remains what Niebuhr called an "impossible possibility," for human life is ultimately paradoxical: it is a blend of warring opposites. People love, yet out of fear are driven to aggression. They sacrifice themselves for others, and yet at that very moment they are the most subject to falling into sin through the lure of self-pride. It is the human condition for a person's every action to be potentially destructive as well as creative.

In his greatest work, *The Nature and Destiny of Man* (1940), Niebuhr consolidated his teachings into a powerful exploration of his belief that we are inherently sinners. He explained this by pointing to the central tension that lies at the core of life itself. Human beings possess a unique capacity: transcendence. That is, they can stand outside themselves and observe their situation, make themselves the object of their own thought.

They even possess a capacity to stand back and view the universe and thus to become aware of their own insignificance. Knowing that they will die, people struggle constantly to save themselves. This produces an inescapable selfishness in every human personality that can never be overridden. If people had enough faith in God, they would be able to find ease in His love and power to save them. But, being human, they never are able to muster enough faith to lose their fearful self-regard: they are inescapably selfish. This, according to Niebuhr, is humankind's original sin. All the other imperfections of humanity spring from that failing.

What, then, was the social message that Niebuhr derived from his neoorthodox theology? First, people must sweep away all false idealism and acquire a completely realistic view of themselves and humankind. This will prevent the disillusionment that so often leads to cynical withdrawal. Search for relative justice; for "proximate" solutions; for improvements that can be achieved within a person's limited capacities. Never be utopian, or believe that anything can be done innocently. Be sober about humankind's potentialities, but be hopeful. One of Niebuhr's favorite texts was from St. Paul, about being "perplexed, but not driven to despair. . . ." Commitment, struggle, a clear-eyed view of human nature, a readiness to plunge into the contaminating game of politics and power—these were the stern strictures issued to the nation's reformers by Protestant Christianity's most powerful voice.

The Arts in Depression America

Paradoxically, the nation's economic collapse brought its exiled writers flocking back from Paris's Left Bank. Art for art's sake went out the window; agonized searches for personal realization faded; and literary figures suddenly found in stricken America a new focus for their creative energies. Plays, novels, articles, and paintings that stressed Marxian analyses of social strife poured out on the national scene.

Whatever the inspiration, a social consciousness emerged among creative workers that eclipsed the personalist orientation of the 1920s. Together with this went a powerful awakening to a new concept, that of *community*. Books like

Ruth Benedict's anthropological study *Patterns of Culture* (1934) attained an enormous readership, for she sensitively described the innumerable ways in which all mental life is shaped by the encompassing cultures in which people live. Looking about them, writers rediscovered traditional America: its farms, villages, common folk, farm implements, square dances, harvest celebrations; its sweating laborers in the steel mills, in the mines, in the automobile factories. This vast continental community exerted an enormous appeal for writers such as John Steinbeck, whose *The Grapes of Wrath* (1939) was not only a powerful novel of social protest but a loving depiction of common folk in intimate relation to the land. From Archibald MacLeish and Robert Frost came a new kind of poetry, one that celebrated the folkish, rural beauty of America. Civilization (technology, efficiency, science) became the enemy, and culture (ways of life, symbols, speech, and values) became the new hope. An outpouring of writings, films, recordings, and paintings depicted every aspect of American life. The common people were treated with a warmth and sensitivity quite unlike the "booboisie" cynicism of the 1920s.

It was this new urge toward group consciousness and collective action that made the New Deal so exciting for most intellectuals. The Civilian Conservation Corps, which sent boys into the forests, the Tennessee Valley Authority, erecting vast dams throughout a wilderness to control floods and bring hope to impoverished farmers—these and many other programs seemed to revitalize the whole American community. There was despair in the depression, but there was excitement as well. To the most alienated, Marxism exerted an irresistible appeal. Few actually joined the Communist party, but a great many, in their search for social philosophies to explain the chaos, found Marxian socialism a congenial home. Until the disillusionment created by the purge trials that Joseph Stalin instituted in 1936, American intellectuals generally found Soviet Russia a fascinating and alluring example of what could be achieved by rigorous socialist experimentation.

The theater, likewise, swung toward social consciousness, in part through the extraordinary achievements of the Federal Theatre Project (FTP). Launched in 1935, it strove to place drama companies in cities all over the nation, and thus make use of local talent and traditions. The FTP blazed up meteorically, and productions appeared in every corner of the country. Its plays were often controversial social commentaries, especially the *Living Newspaper* series, which dramatized current political issues. Much condemned as socialist and anti-American, the FTP died in 1939 when Congress refused to support it any longer. Meanwhile, a left-wing theater movement following the slogan "Drama is a weapon" sprang up in New York City. In plays by dramatists such as Clifford Odets and William Saroyan, anticapitalism was the chief theme and collectivism the principal objective. The common man appeared as the hero in this kind of drama while moneyed interests were the villain. Labor unions, which seemed the epitome of group consciousness, figured prominently.

Painters and sculptors also turned away from the personalist experimentation of the 1920s to grope for a direct relation to social conditions. Turning realistic, they fell in love with the forms and shapes of the American scene. Painters' canvases were covered no longer with the abstract forms of modern art that ordinary Americans found incomprehensible, but with protests against capitalistic injustice. Their search was for an "art of the people." Landscapes, people at work, slum life, store windows, Coney Island bathers, farms, tractors, small towns—these were the topics of the day. Thomas Hart Benton of Missouri and Grant Wood of Iowa led an extraordinary upsurge of painting by midwesterners based on the scenes and people of their region. Benton's heroic mural of John Brown in the Kansas capitol and Wood's austere painting of a midwestern farm couple, *American Gothic*, were powerful symbols of the new realism of the decade. The Federal Arts Project hired hundreds of artists to paint similarly realistic murals in post offices and other public buildings throughout the nation.

By far the most powerful art form of the 1930s, however, was the "talkie" motion picture. Appearing first in 1927, the talkie struggled through a period in which technical and artistic problems produced static presentations, then flowered into an enormously flexible medium of tremendous cultural impact. Each week, eighty-five million Americans of all ages and income groups attended a movie. As studios competed to capture the largest audiences and revenues, they

The heroic power of John Stewart Curry's mural of John Brown, done for the Kansas capitol under the WPA art program, reveals the rediscovery of American themes and American folk drama by artists and writers in the depression years.

Courtesy of the Kansas Department of Economic Development, State Office Building, Topeka, Kansas

produced an enormous outpouring of Hollywood trash. Ernst Lubitsch, a German-born Hollywood director, commented, "The American public—the American public with the mind of a twelve-year-old child, you see—it must have life as it ain't." There were some significant movements toward social realism in the development of the documentary film, as in such powerful creations as Orson Welles's *Citizen Kane* and in the newsreel series *The March of Time*. But Hollywood producers generally shied away from controversial themes. They had had their struggles with would-be censors in Congress and in local communities, and they had no stomach for more such strife. The Motion Picture Producers and Distributors Association in 1934 fended off such efforts by establishing a production code that was particularly concerned with moral obligations. Sex was downgraded, violent FBI agents instead of violent criminals were glorified, and an endless stream of blameless movies about nice kids in nice neighborhoods—the Andy Hardy series, for example—poured out of Hollywood.

If not at the movies, the average family spent two to three hours a night listening to the radio. Primarily concerned with presenting humorous series—"The Jack Benny Show" and "Amos 'n' Andy," for example—the radio also began to introduce classical music into the home through broadcasts of symphony orchestras and the Metropolitan Opera. Radio theater had brilliant moments in such regular presentations as the "Mercury Theatre of the Air," created by Orson Welles, and CBS's "Columbia Workshop." Far more prominent were the soap operas that glutted the air and filled the housewife's working day. And, perhaps most important, radio news broadcasting emerged as a powerful nationalizing influence in the 1930s. From its thin beginnings in the 1920s, the newscasts took over at least a third of all air time, bringing the entire nation news not only of national events but of crises in Europe and the rest of the world as well. Americans could now listen to Hitler speaking, a fact that made the threat of fascism seem terrifyingly close.

In sum, the American people in the 1930s were assaulted from all directions by a cultural life that was nationalizing in tone and impact. The radio seemed to make the whole nation one meeting hall; everyone went to the same movies; literature and the arts concentrated on American themes as they had not done for many years. The

rediscovery of America that the writers and artists experienced was the cultural counterpart of the nationalism we shall be observing in the New Deal. A new awareness of society and its needs, a fresh interest in American traditions and values, and, paradoxically in a time of economic collapse, a surging confidence in what in the 1930s began to be referred to as the American way of life—these were the cultural hallmarks of a turbulent decade.

Bibliography

Books that were especially valuable to me in writing this chapter: William E. Leuchtenberg's *Perils of Prosperity, 1914–1932* (1958) remains fundamentally important in understanding the mood of the 1920s. Paula S. Fass gives us a fascinating account of youth, solidly based in demographic analyses, in her *The Damned and the Beautiful: American Youth in the 1920's* * (1977), and Carl Degler's *At Odds: Women and the Family in America from the Revolution to the Present* (1980) as well as Sheila M. Rothman, *Woman's Proper Place: A History of Changing Ideals and Practices, 1870 to the Present* (1978) are valuable. Elaine Tyler May's *Great Expectations: Marriage and Divorce in Post-Victorian America* (1980) aided me greatly.

Nathan Irvin Huggins's probing study is the essential work on the *Harlem Renaissance* * (1971). The vastly complex story of American immigrants is skillfully explored in many works, of which I learned much from: Philip Taylor, *The Distant Magnet: European Immigration to the U.S.A.* * (1971); Leonard Dinnerstein, Roger L. Nichols, and David M. Reimers, *Natives and Strangers: Ethnic Groups and the Building of America* * (1979); John Higham's magnificent sequel to *Strangers in the Land* * (1955), *Send These to Me: Jews and Other Immigrants in Urban America* * (1970), as well as his edited volume, *Ethnic Leadership in America* (1978); and Alexander DeConde, *Half Bitter, Half Sweet: An Excursion into Italian-American History* (1971).

Don S. Kirschner has given us a fascinating book in his *City and Country: Rural Responses to Urbanization in the 1920s* (1970). On the Ku Klux Klan, an excellent guide to and analysis of the newer historical literature is Carl N. Degler's "A Century of the Klans: A Review Article," *The Journal of Southern History*, 31 (1965), 435–43.

For a major insight into urban and ethnic culture and politics, see John M. Allswang, *A House for All Peoples: Ethnic Politics in Chicago 1890–1936*. Lawrence W. Levine, *Defender of the Faith: William Jennings Bryan, The Last Decade, 1915–1925* (1965) is an absorbing and revealing study.

I have followed closely, in tracing the experience of Mexican Americans, Matt S. Meier and Feliciano Rivera, *The Chicanos: A History of Mexican Americans** (1972). Abraham Hoffman, *Unwanted Mexican Americans in the Great Depression** (1974) discusses the deportations. Manual Gamio's pioneering work is essential: *Mexican Immigration to the United States** (1971) and *The Life Story of the Mexican Immigrant* (1971). A major new work is Mario García's close-grained study, *Desert Immigrants: The Mexicans of El Paso 1889–1920* (1981). The gifted poet Octavio Paz takes us far inside the Mexican mind and experience in his arresting book, *The Labyrinth of Solitude: Life and Thought in Mexico** (1961).

The literature on Sigmund Freud is large and rich. See Paul Roazen, *Freud and His Followers** (1974). In addition to Reinhold Niebuhr's *The Nature and Destiny of Man,** two vols. (1941, 1943), one of the most profound works of the twentieth century, see the valuable book edited by Charles W. Kegley and Robert W. Bretall, *Reinhold Niebuhr: His Religious, Social, and Political Thought** (1961), as well as Donald Meyer's brilliant book, *The Protestant Search for Political Realism* (1960). L. Pearce Williams, ed., *Relativity Theory: Its Origins and Impact on Modern Thought** (1968) was helpful to me; a recent work is Nigel Calder, *Einstein's Universe** (1979). Merle Curti's great work, *The Growth of American Thought* (3rd edition, 1964) was important to me for these decades, as in all periods of American thought to the 1960s. In particular, Charles C. Alexander's excellent *Nationalism in American Thought, 1930–1945** (1969) guided my understanding of New Deal era thought.

How Have Historians Looked at the Topic?

For years the decade of the 1920s was viewed as an abnormality, a period of disillusionment and frivolity squeezed between the holocaust of World War I and the terrors of the depression. This image was first presented in a lively book by Frederick Lewis Allen, *Only Yesterday: An Informal History of the 1920s** (1931), and it has been preserved practically intact in other histories until recently.

The scholarship of the 1960s has revealed aspects of the Roaring Twenties that question that decade's image of superficiality and cynicism. In *The Discontent of the Intellectuals: A Problem of the Twenties* (1963), Henry May asserted that the "lost generation" of writers and artists stood apart from the majority of Americans, who continued to endorse traditional American values. This judgment is supported by David A. Shannon in his penetrating volume *Between the Wars: America, 1919–1941* (1965). In a brilliant, probing book, *The Nervous Generation: American Thought, 1917–1930** (1970), Roderick Nash reveals a "thick layer of respect for time-honored American ways" beneath the eye-catching iconoclasm of Mencken and others. Lawrence Levine sees the same tensions from a different perspective in his fine article "Progress and Nostalgia: The Self-Image of the 1920s," in Malcolm Bradbury, ed., *The American Novel in the 1920s* (1971).

The trend in the new research is to mark the 1920s as a troubled decade in which fear of change lived side by side with the fact of change. The growing literature on women and youth reflects this paradox. Kenneth A. Yellis probes the condition of women following World War I in a provocative article, "Prosperity's Child: Some Thoughts on the Flapper," *American Quarterly,* 21 (Spring 1969). David Kennedy's biography of Margaret Sanger, *Birth Control in America* (1971), illustrates women's continuing struggle to assert themselves as well as the conservative uses to which birth control was put. The first part of June Sochen, ed., *The New Feminism in America** (1971), focuses on early-twentieth-century feminists' analyses. William H. Chafe carefully scans the broader scope of women's experiences in *The American Woman: Her Changing Social, Economic, and Political Roles, 1920–1970* (1972). Paul Carter offers a provocative assessment of the youth cult in *The Twenties in America** (1968).

Traditional America's postwar reaction to radicals is graphically depicted and astutely analyzed in Robert K. Murray's *The Red Scare: A Study in National Hysteria, 1919–1920** (1955).

Donald Johnson describes the origins of the American Civil Liberties Union in *The Challenge to American Freedoms* (1963).

The effects of the exclusionist immigration policy are studied in Robert Divine's *American Immigration Policy, 1924–1952* (1957). Roger Daniels offers an excellent account of the campaign against the Japanese in *The Politics of Prejudice: The Anti-Japanese Movement in California and the Struggle for Japanese Exclusion** (1970).

The persistence of the Ku Klux Klan is chronicled in a stimulating and thorough study by David Chalmers, *Hooded Americanism: The History of the KKK* (1965), and the strength of urban Ku Kluxism is explored in Kenneth Jackson's *The Ku Klux Klan in the City, 1915–1930** (1968).

The achievements of the business community during the 1920s are described in a perceptive and important study by Alfred Chandler, Jr., *Strategy and Structure: Chapters in the History of American Industrial Enterprise* (1962). Morrell Heald's *The Social Responsibilities of Business: Company and Community, 1900–1960* (1970) is a valuable overall view. Business attitudes and practices are succinctly treated in J. W. Prothro's *The Dollar Decade: Business Ideas in the 1920s* (1954). The modernizing impulses of the era are apparent in Otis Pease's *The Responsibility of American Advertising* (1958). Allan Nevins and F. E. Hill's *Ford: The Times, the Man, and the Company** (1954) and *Ford: Expansion and Challenge* (1957) are indispensable on the period's leading industrialist. Daniel Aaron's *Writers on the Left* (1969) analyzes the effects of the depression on literary intellectuals. The pessimism engendered by the deepening depression is portrayed through the words of those who experienced it in Studs Terkel's *Hard Times** (1970).

* Available in paperback.

30

THE NEW ERA: TRIUMPH AND DISASTER

New York Public Library

Al Smith of New York City had a nasal, grating voice, and as speaker of the state's assembly he had no dignity. He pounded his gavel with great swinging blows and bellowed out his parliamentary rulings. At times he even ate his lunch on the podium and talked through the food in his mouth. But Smith was a brilliant organizer, he knew the inner details of every bill before him, and under his leadership things got *done*. New York had never seen anything like it. In 1918 this man, who had only a grade-school education, became governor of New York, the first Irish Catholic ever to mount so high in American public life. WASP-dominated America was astonished. Elevated public office was everywhere presumed to be reserved for Anglo-Saxon Protestants.

As speaker and as governor he drove through bill after bill of social legislation: workmen's compensation, limits on hours of work for women and children, health centers for the poor, requirements for safe and healthful working conditions, maternity care and nursing services, minimum-wage laws, a day off in seven for laborers, and better housing. He gathered academic experts around him, brought into his team gifted social workers such as Frances Perkins, reorganized a chaotic state government, got home rule for the cities, created a network of state parks and beaches, and battled the electric-utility giants. Of course, as an Irish Catholic of traditional views he condemned prohibition and opposed the vote for women, but he also demanded justice for the helpless.

Why not the White House for this gifted man? The presidency was traditionally thought of as the next step for great governors of the nation's most populous state. Since New Yorkers reelected him repeatedly, Democrats nationally began turning to him. In 1924 Smith was almost nominated, and in 1928 he won that accolade. But a tornado of vicious anti-Catholicism rose up to overwhelm him in the voting booths. Cultural hatreds tore American life from top to bottom in the 1920s, and Smith was their lightning rod. Only in New York State could an Irish Catholic yet rise to a governorship. Besides, Smith was proudly New York City to his core: in his style and his lower East Side accent, which the invention of radio ("rad-dio" to him) broadcast to the nation; in his Tammany background and his city tough's brown derby; and in his links to alcohol and the saloon. Countryside and small-town America hated New York City as the symbol of everything corrupt and wicked. WASPs recoiled from the thought of an Irishman from its streets and slums, forever smoking his uptilted cigar and wearing his "snappy" clothes, at the head of the nation. The first great Irish Catholic in American public life, Al Smith watched in bewilderment as his candidacy was crushed—and four years later witnessed his aristocratic, Harvard-educated successor in the governor's chair, Franklin Roosevelt, enter the White House. It was a bitter blow, and one he never understood.

In 1920 Republicans once more took over the dominant position in Washington, D.C., which since the mid 1890s they had assumed was rightfully theirs. The basic outlines of the fourth, or Progressive Era, party system (1894–1930) reasserted themselves after the eight-year detour into Wilsonian governance. The South was back in its place as the solitary Democratic bastion, and the country once more was run by the Republican Northeast, Middle West, and Far West. The war had driven back into Republican voting ranks the ethnic minorities. From 1920 to 1932 the Republican party reached the very peak of its national preeminence, in what until 1929 the Republicans called the New Era, but then encountered disasters so stunning and fatal that they lost their traditionally dominant position.

We have learned by this time to see certain longstanding characteristics in the Republican party. From the time of Alexander Hamilton, a distinctive complex of peoples and ideas had gathered together behind the Federalist-Whig-Republican tradition. This tradition was the political expression of the nation's core ethnic community, the Yankees. From their heartland in New England, Yankee Americans and their culture had spread westward into the interior of New York and Pennsylvania, on into a broad band of territory extending through the central Middle West to Iowa, and across the continent to Oregon. Thinking of themselves as the "host" culture in American life, by the twentieth century they had been joined, especially in the small towns and farming countryside—the special center of traditional native-born America—by northern European peoples from Germany and Scandinavia. The result was a WASP monolith whose political expression was the Republican party.

Driven by a strong impulse to shape the cultural life of the entire nation, with its many peoples, in the WASP image—pious Protestant; thrifty; nondrinking, or at least temperate in the use of alcohol; Sabbatarian; puritanical in matters sexual and cultural—the Republican party was also the most outspokenly nationalist and "patriotic" in economics and foreign policy. From Henry Clay's time the Republican side of American politics had believed in building a self-contained American industrial system by excluding foreign products, if necessary, by means of high protective tariffs. Republicans had urged that the government be a partner, not a critic, of capitalist entrepreneurs by offering them all possible aid and encouraging a flourishing business climate. The businessman should be left largely in charge of the nation's economic life, and his profit-seeking impulses encouraged so that he could create wealth and jobs for all. Solutions to the nation's ills would rise naturally out of a healthy private-enterprise system, not through government intervention, save to assist that system. Toward the world, Republican nationalism had consistently inclined the party to prefer a "going-it-alone" attitude.

Critics said Republicans were interested only in the wealthy. But there was in Republican ideology an idealism that looked beyond the welfare simply of one class to that of the whole nation. Like their Federalist and Whig ancestors, Republicans simply believed that the nation would be strongest and most prosperous if it encouraged those who seemed by their success in life to be the most hard-working, self-disciplined, and imaginative. This translated in practice into a sincere elitism. The nation's great spirits, its men of power and vision, should be given the widest opportunities for enterprise and leadership. Young people should be constantly urged to take such leaders as their models and build similar lives of accomplishment. These were ancient Calvinist notions, and the Calvinist churches—the Congregationalists, the Presbyterians, and the Reformed congregations from Germany and Holland—had traditionally been Republican. Regions in America like western Michigan, where the cities of Holland and Zeeland proclaimed the generations-old solidly Dutch origins of the people, were Republican to the core. Austere, industrious, self-denying, and devout, their way of living was in miniature the vision for the nation at large that their party held to in good years and bad.

Such were, in fact, the larger outlines of the Republican era from 1920 to 1932. The administrations of Warren G. Harding (1921–23), Calvin Coolidge (1923–29), and Herbert Hoover (1929–33) bent every effort toward freeing businessmen from supervision, lowering their taxes, providing them protection through higher tariffs, and giving them open access to the nation's resources. Harding and Coolidge were passive presidents in the traditional Republican mold (the depression forced Hoover partially out of this pattern). During their years in office, the nation and the government looked in admiration to powerful industrialists and financiers for leadership and inspiration. Rooted in WASP America, the Republican party became the instrument of an aroused nativism that condemned eastern and southern Europeans as inferior beings and led to the passage of antialien legislation. In foreign affairs, there was a conscious and determined turning away from the internationalism of Woodrow Wilson. Important reform legislation continued to be enacted by a Congress in which progressives played a major role through the decade, but much of it was struck down by White House vetoes.

Meanwhile, the Democratic party in the 1920s was undergoing a crucial transition. On the one hand, the immigrant ethnic groups in the core of the nation's great cities began in the mid 1920s to return to the Democratic side. The millions of "new immigrants" from eastern and southern Europe who had been pouring into the country since 1890 had passed through their apprenticeship in democratic forms of government and were beginning to vote, following the lead of the firmly Democratic Irish Catholics. But the other great taproot of the Democratic party lay in the overwhelmingly rural and Protestant world of the Southern and border states. Here were the people most alarmed at the rise of the great cities and the urban way of life. Within the Democratic party in the 1920s, therefore, a hammering conflict took place between the older America—rural, moralistic, anti-Catholic, prohibitionist—and the newer America, to be found in the great metropolises. Multi-tongued, liberal, a compound of Jewish scholarship, Roman Catholicism, and the corner saloon, the Democrats of the growing urban centers were sure to win, but not until after bitter battles within the party. In the 1924 national convention it took the Democrats more than a hundred ballots to choose a presidential nominee—the colorless John W. Davis.

The Nation

In the twentieth century the American population's growth slowed. From 1900 to 1910 the rate of increase was 21 percent, but from 1910 to 1920 it dropped to 15 percent. In the latter year, when the nation held a population of 106 million people,

the birth rate stood at 27.7 per 1,000. By 1930 it had fallen to 21.3, and ten years later it had sagged to about 19 per 1,000, a replacement rate that would not be sufficient in the long run to maintain the population at a stable figure. Demographers forecast that sometime after 1960 the American population would peak and then decline.

The drop in the rate of growth was associated with the continuing massive movement from the countryside to the cities and with the fact that city families tend to be smaller than those in the countryside—though, as we have seen, the population decline was only slower in the countryside, since both rural and urban women had been for generations moving toward smaller families. During the period 1910–30 some 6.5 million people participated in this cityward movement, some 4.5 million of them going to the four great metropolitan centers of New York, Chicago, Detroit, and Los Angeles. This meant that in 1920, for the first time in American history a majority of Americans (51 percent) lived in communities of 2,500 people or more. At the same time, the number of workers engaged in some form of manufacturing outnumbered those in agriculture by about 5 to 4.

Immigration, which always brings in people primarily in the vigorous, reproductive years of life, came practically to a halt (from Europe) after the restrictive legislation of the early 1920s. Some 3 million people had flooded into the United States from 1911 to 1915, but only 68,000 arrived (legally) and stayed during the entire decade of the 1930s.

Some four out of ten Americans held membership in a Christian church in the 1920s. Of these, two thirds were Protestant, one third Catholic. The decrease in immigration brought about a reduction in the proportion of the foreign-born from 15 percent in 1910—where it had held relatively steady through many decades—to roughly 9 percent in 1940. A major change was also beginning to take place in the distribution of the nation's Afro-American population. In 1865 the proportion of blacks living in the Southern states was 92 percent. By 1920 this figure had dropped to 85 percent, for the First World War had seen the beginning of a heavy migration northward to industrial jobs. Thereafter, this movement accelerated, so that by 1940 nearly one fourth of all Afro-Americans lived outside the South.

The Presidency: Warren G. Harding

The election of 1920 brought to the White House a man ill suited to his task. Warren Gamaliel Harding had been an ordinary politician who looked wonderfully like a president but who lacked any real talents save a warm and gentle demeanor that made the country like and trust him. He had been editor of a newspaper in Marion, Ohio, served as a state legislator, gave William Howard Taft's nominating speech in 1912, and in 1914 was elected to the Senate. There he supported big business, advocated high tariffs, and opposed taxes on war profits. Following Henry Cabot Lodge's leadership, he firmly resisted American membership in the League of Nations as "a surrender of national sovereignty." As he said in his 1920 presidential campaign, "Stabilize America first, prosper America first, think of America first, exalt America first!"

Harding was a devoted public servant who worked slavishly at his task. He was much too weak a personality for the stern demands of the

Warren G. Harding, campaigning in Ohio. A warm-hearted and devoted public servant, he was much loved, won the presidency in a huge landslide, and was mourned at his death.

Wide World Photos

presidency and not very bright—Woodrow Wilson said he had a "bungalow mind"—but he wanted the "best minds" around him and made some strong appointments. He chose Charles Evans Hughes as secretary of state, Herbert Hoover to head the Commerce Department, and Andrew Mellon, one of the nation's richest industrial magnates, to be secretary of the treasury. The president turned most of the nation's affairs over to these men. This credulous, simpleminded man was widely popular. He seemed to express what the nation yearned for, what he himself had summoned up in a famous word he coined for posterity—*normalcy*.

Retreat in Foreign Affairs

The Harding administration pulled back immediately from Wilson's internationalism. Harding's guiding slogan was "America First." The president declared that the League of Nations idea was dead, and Secretary of State Hughes refused for some time even to answer mail from that body. It was manifestly impossible, however, for the United States to retreat completely to its pre-1914 isolation. Its whole position in the world had been transformed by the war. Western Europe owed huge sums to the United States, which caused Washington to be intimately involved in the complicated negotiations concerning intergovernmental debts and German reparations. American manufacturers had invaded markets all over the world, giving the United States heavy economic stakes in Latin America, China, and elsewhere, all of which required close attention. And the simple fact of America's having been massively involved in a great world war made it impossible to think any longer in isolationist terms. The world's affairs had burst irrevocably into the American consciousness.

The most pressing immediate problem at the outset of the 1920s lay in the western Pacific, where Japan, Great Britain, and the United States appeared headed for a showdown. All three nations had launched huge navy-building programs during the war that were only now coming to fruition. This meant that the Pacific would soon be bristling with heavily armed ships, and there would be rising tension. The war had left behind much mutual distrust and several points of grave conflict. Would Japanese forces remain in Russian Siberia, where it appeared they were preparing to tear off a huge chunk of territory? Would Japan leave China alone and evacuate the Shantung Peninsula? What was to happen to all the new island territories the Japanese had taken from the Germans during the war? In 1920 the progressive and isolationist senator from Idaho, William E. Borah, took the crucial step: he secured passage of a congressional resolution asking the president to call an international conference to ease the naval race.

The Washington Conference

The Washington Conference was the Harding administration's one major accomplishment. In November 1921 representatives of the nine nations involved in Far Eastern affairs gathered in Washington, D.C.: the United States, Great Britain, Japan, France, Italy, China, the Netherlands, Portugal, and Belgium. A tremendous fanfare attended the opening of the gathering, for the Republican administration hoped to make the conference their successful replacement of the much-maligned peace conference at Paris.

At the opening session of the conference, Secretary Hughes electrified the gathering by avoiding generalities and specifying an astonishingly long list of naval vessels that should be halted in construction or scrapped if already built. A total of 70 major ships would be eliminated: 15 American vessels plus 15 more under construction; 19 British battleships plus 4 under construction; and 10 Japanese ships plus 7 under construction. In addition, no more ships of the battleship class were to be built for the next ten years. The result of these changes, Secretary Hughes pointed out, would be to establish a 5:5:3 ratio in capital ships among Britain, the United States, and Japan; Italy and France would stand at the ratio of 1.75:1.75.

No one had even remotely expected so dramatic a proposal. Hughes was suggesting, one man said, to sink more British battleships "than all the admirals of the world had destroyed in a cycle of centuries." The American people were delighted, and similar responses came from all over the world. But long and difficult negotiations ensued. The Japanese insisted that they would accept their ratio only if everyone else agreed to build no more naval bases and fortifications in the Pacific area. In the Five-Power Pact this demand was met, and the proposed ratios were agreed to. A Four-Power Pact was also signed by the United States, Great Britain, Japan, and France, in which these nations guaranteed the security of one another's possessions in the Pacific islands.

The result of these agreements was to turn over military dominance of the Pacific to Japan. Recognizing that Japanese supremacy was being tacitly agreed to, Britain and the United States urged the Japanese to pledge that they would keep their hands off China. Under this pressure, the Japanese signed the Nine-Power Pact, which finally elevated America's Open Door policy to the status of international law. In this treaty, Japan and the other eight conference participants agreed to respect China's sovereignty, independence, and integrity; to maintain open commercial privileges for all nations in that country; and to avoid seeking any special rights that would impair those of other nations. Hughes also got Japan to agree to evacuate the Shantung Peninsula, give China control of the Shantung railway, and clear out its forces from Russian Siberia.

Hughes achieved in these pacts one of the great successes in international diplomacy. The United States gave up much, but what it relinquished was only a potential naval supremacy, and it was in any event doubtful that Congress would have been willing to provide the funds to complete the naval building program. The clear fact was that a frightening naval race was ended, and that peace in the Far East was secured in a way that held out strong hopes for the future. Unhappily, Congress's later stupidity in totally excluding the Japanese from the United States in the immigration legislation of 1924—not even allowing them the dignity of a tiny quota—was an insult which went far to destroy the good feelings that emerged from the Washington Conference.

Harding's Death

While his secretary of state was winning international laurels, the president was slowly becoming aware that his cronies were using their opportunities to line their pockets. "My Goddamn friends," he said to editor William Allen White, "they're the ones that keep me walking the floor nights!" The worst scandal involved the secretary of the interior, Albert B. Fall, who gave oil magnate Edward L. Doheny a lease on the naval oil reserves at Elk Hills, California, and received in return a satchel containing $100,000 in cash. Rumors of this deal were soon being passed about Washington, D.C. Then came an added shocker: another Harding appointee committed suicide rather than face an investigation.

In the summer of 1923, the worried president went on a trip to Alaska and the Pacific Northwest. Ill with the beginnings of heart failure and unable to sleep, he played bridge compulsively, day and night, trying to find peace of mind. But his worries and his physical weakness did not disappear, and by the time he had finished his Alaska visit he was drawn, exhausted, and at wit's end. Shortly the news went out to the nation that the president was gravely sick. On August 3, while attended by his wife, he suddenly shuddered and died, apparently from a heart attack. The public was shocked and grieved, for as yet it knew nothing of the scandals. Calvin Coolidge, as Harding's vice-president, now succeeded him, and the American people turned with confidence to their new leader, a classic puritan and an honest Yankee.

Calvin Coolidge: "Puritan in Babylon"

The new president was a simple, frugal, tightly controlled man from a small town in Vermont who lived in an ordinary rented duplex. He was scrupulously honest, and never spent his evenings drinking and playing cards. A thoroughgoing, tight-laced Yankee, he seemed to carry with him the tang of maple woods and sharp winter mornings. From the beginning of his political career he had admired and firmly supported large corporations. He advocated a protective tariff, conservative money policies, and freedom for the entrepreneur. "The chief business of the American people," he said in one of his more pithy utterances, "is business." Accordingly, Coolidge felt that the government should do nothing more than aid businessmen and withdraw from every other activity save foreign relations. Reducing governmental expenditures, he said, was "idealism in its most practical form." As president, he devoted himself to a masterly inactivity. When visitors came to see him, he followed a policy of being silent. "If you keep dead-still they will run down in

three or four minutes," Coolidge said to Herbert Hoover. "If you even cough or smile they will start up all over again."

He was a president, in brief, who believed the country's ills were to be solved by the silent operations of the business system. Beyond cleaning up corruption, he offered no constructive action to a country in need of leadership. Nevertheless, he was widely popular. The American people seemed most of all to want to turn away from their problems, and for such a time the new president was admirably suited.

The Farmer's Changed Situation

By the opening of the New Era, the American farmer had enjoyed more than twenty years of prosperity. America's growing cities provided essential markets; gold discoveries in South Africa, Alaska, and Colorado produced steady price inflation, which coincidentally raised farm prices; and the burning grievances that had exploded in the Populist crusade had died down. Ironically, this transformation in the farmer's situation took place at the same time that his numbers, in relation to city people, were shrinking. The fact was that the farmer had begun to learn how to organize himself in ways similar to those used by businessmen. He had also learned to apply technology to the farm far more sweepingly, in the long run, than has been true in any other part of the national economy. In the years before the First World War it became increasingly common for farmers to keep detailed financial accounts, learn scientific mixtures of feed for stock, concern themselves with soil chemistry, and turn to research laboratories for disease-resistant crops.

In the 1920s, however, American farmers were faced with a grave challenge. World War I had created an enormous worldwide demand for American foodstuffs that carried farmers to their highest peak of prosperity. But in 1920 an inevitable slump began. Millions of soldiers in Europe and elsewhere in the world returned to their farms, and soon world overproduction of farm crops sent prices rapidly downward. By 1921 the prices of wheat, corn, and hogs had fallen to below half their level in 1918. The result was that farm income dropped from ten billion dollars in 1919 to four billion dollars in 1921. There was some recovery afterward to about six or seven billion in the later 1920s, but even so a low farm income, in comparison with that of city residents, lasted until the middle 1930s. As a result, farmers' share of the national income dropped from 16 percent in 1919 to less than 9 percent in 1929.

Such a drop in income had serious effects on farmers' morale. Farm people had enthusiastically moved into the mainstream of American life in the preceding twenty years, the "golden age" of American agriculture. In doing so they had undertaken a much more costly standard of living. Rural roads, schools, and hospitals required heavy taxes. Electricity in the home, automobiles, trips to town, clothing and furniture like the city folk had—all represented real gains in life that farmers bitterly resisted giving up. All remembered the crude living conditions of their parents and had no intention, if they could help it, of returning to those conditions, especially while the cities were enjoying prosperity. Indeed, a million farmers moved to the cities in the 1920s, leaving about ten million behind.

Farm Radicalism

This discontent resulted in a reawakening of farm radicalism. The Grange and the Farmers' Union came alive once more, and a newly formed organization, the American Farm Bureau Federation, took up reform enthusiastically. Meanwhile, senators and congressmen from farm areas, responding rapidly to the new crisis, met in Washington in 1921 to form a nonpartisan organization called the Farm Bloc. Pulling together legislators from both northern and southern states, it wielded great power in Congress for many years.

The most dramatic expression of the new agrarian radicalism was an organized revival of the Progressive party. The first step was the convening of the Conference for Progressive Political Action in 1922, which so successfully ignited the old fires that the candidates it endorsed in the elections of that year were strikingly victorious. Soon Senator Robert M. La Follette of Wisconsin was at the head of the movement. As in 1912, its objective was to capture the Republican presidential nomination for La Follette. When that proved unattainable, the Progressive party was formally revived and La Follette chosen as its candidate. On a platform calling for public ownership of waterpower and the railroads and for at-

tacks on business monopoly, La Follette campaigned vigorously, drawing almost 5 million popular votes in the presidential election of 1924. (Coolidge, the Republican nominee, received almost 16 million popular votes and 382 electoral-college ballots; John W. Davis, the Democratic nominee, garnered 8.4 million popular votes and 136 electoral votes; La Follette carried only Wisconsin, receiving its 13 votes in the electoral college.)

Farmers Seek Aid

The chief scene of action, however, lay in Congress, where the Farm Bloc worked hard to secure legislation to aid the agrarian sector. In the Fordney-McCumber Tariff—enacted by the Republican Congress soon after Harding became president, it raised rates from the 26-percent average of the Underwood Tariff to 33 percent—they got some (ineffective) tariff protection against foreign meat and other commodities. Then for six years farmers mobilized a heavy campaign behind the McNary-Haugen plan, which would have had the government purchase the entire farm crop at a "parity price" (one that would make farmers as prosperous, relative to the rest of the population, as they had been in the years 1910–14) for sale domestically and abroad. Sternly vetoed by President Coolidge, who believed farmers should operate as individual businessmen and take their profits and losses as they came, McNary-Haugen eventually faded from sight. Farmers were learning that their fundamental problem was overproduction, and as the 1930s approached they were beginning to think of plans for cutting back their output to match the market at home, foreign markets having been cut off by new European tariff walls.

Andrew Mellon Aids the Rich

President Coolidge found his political inspiration in the writings and career of Alexander Hamilton. So did his secretary of the Treasury, Andrew W. Mellon, who was fond of posing before a portrait of the great Federalist. Mellon enthusiastically preached that the country's wealthy men should be freed from taxation so that they could develop the nation's resources and create jobs by invest-

Andrew Mellon, Treasury secretary in the Harding-Coolidge years, symbolized in his elegant, multimillionaire person the spirit that governed 1920s economic policies.
Culver Pictures, Inc.

sums of money that went into stock-market speculation and helped to build the boom culminating in the crash of 1929.

Republicans and the Regulatory Commissions

The progressives of the years 1900–1916 had concentrated on one key objective: establishing a group of independent agencies, staffed by experts, to oversee crucial sections of the economy. The reasoning behind their support for these commissions—the Federal Trade Commission, the Federal Reserve Board, a strengthened Interstate Commerce Commission, and other agencies —was that the public interest needed watchdogs in Washington to keep a close eye on the business community. The Republican administrations of the 1920s disagreed fundamentally with this outlook. Believing that the business community should be freed of irksome regulations, the Republican presidents filled the regulatory commissions with men friendly and cooperative to businessmen. The Tariff Commission was staffed with men who favored high tariffs. Indeed, some commissioners themselves were financially interested in the industries being protected.

Hoover and the New Era Philosophy

Herbert Hoover's Commerce Department, eagerly supporting the new philosophy of cooperating with businessmen, worked hard at building what Hoover called the "associative state." The department's catchwords were "efficiency" and "voluntaristic capitalism," its aims the elimination of industrial waste and duplication and the institution of scientific management, planning, and rationalization. Investigative commissions of experts were to study problems and propose answers: research and expertise would sweep away all difficulties. Meanwhile, Hoover urged on a vast expansion of the hundreds, and eventually thousands, of voluntary trade associations that existed in the business world. Their goal was to bring producers in a particular line of industry together, at which point they could cooperate in eliminating waste, standardizing specifications, and establishing common accounting and produc-

ment. He therefore appealed constantly to Congress to reduce taxation on higher incomes. At first he was unsuccessful, for the progressive-inspired tax policies of the war period, which involved heavy taxation of high incomes and corporations, were strongly supported by midwestern and southern progressives. Rebuffed by Congress, Mellon refunded huge sums to heavy taxpayers anyway, a total, the nation was startled to learn in 1928, of some $3.5 billion.

With Coolidge's victory in 1924, Mellon and the business classes vigorously renewed their campaign for tax reductions. By this time the country was so prosperous that Congress could no longer find much reason for insisting on high tax levels. The result was a victory for Mellon in 1926, for the Revenue Act of that year slashed corporation and high-income tax rates. The result, unknown at the time, was to release huge

tion techniques, safety procedures, market assessments, and voluntary limits on production to meet anticipated markets. It was industrial self-regulation, often skirting dangerously close to the antimonopoly provision of the antitrust laws, but officially sanctioned. A true nationalist progressive, Hoover believed that his networks of committees, planning staffs, and voluntary associations would create "regulated individualism," a middle way between the unrestrained laissez-faire of old and European-style socialism.

At the same time, a renewed movement toward business consolidation took place in the 1920s, with the result that by the end of the decade half of the total corporate wealth in the nation was controlled by a central core of about two hundred corporations. Monopoly, checked in the progressive years, was on the march again, and apparently with the federal government's blessing.

The Power Controversy

By the 1920s electrical power had become enormously important in the life of the United States. Some 6 million kilowatt hours were produced in 1902; by 1929 the number had risen to 117 million. Industry was being transformed, for the use of small electric motors allowed factories to disperse widely over the countryside; they no longer needed to rely on huge steam-power plants. At the same time, electrical power was revolutionizing the home, providing light, heat, and other conveniences that eased the urban housewife's drudgery. The result was a voracious demand that stimulated a scramble for power sites. In 1920 a supervisory agency, the Federal Power Commission (FPC), was created. Composed of the secretaries of war, the interior, and agriculture, it was given authority to issue fifty-year licenses for the private exploitation of federal hydroelectric sites, the government retaining the right to buy the whole operation at net cost when the lease expired. The FPC was also empowered to regulate rates, services, and financial operations if the states did not do so.

Under the Republican regimes, however, the FPC had little interest in standing as a watchdog over the private power industry. Instead, what it wanted was the rapid development of hydroelectric sites, and it relied on the businessmen concerned to use their leases in ways that were fair to the general public. The commission issued approximately 450 licenses between 1920 and 1930.

Because of the huge demand for power, great profits could be made from the building of utility networks. The result was a rush into utility investment and development reminiscent of the railroad boom of a half-century before. Entrepreneurs merged small companies with larger ones in order to rationalize the distribution of power. Then financiers created holding companies that combined the networks in order to profit from the issuance of stock. The holding companies themselves provided no major services, but were primarily devices for draining off the profits made by the producing companies they owned. Imaginative entrepreneurs such as Samuel Insull of Chicago piled holding company upon holding company, sometimes to the seventh level. Soon enormous burdens of debt were heaped on the producing companies, which in turn had to charge higher rates in order to meet the debt charges created by the holding companies' stocks and bonds.

When a public clamor arose against these practices, the utility companies, like the railroads long before them, boldly tried to dominate public opinion by influencing all sources of public information. They launched multimillion-dollar public-relations campaigns lauding private enterprise and condemning all proposals for regulation as socialism. They brought pressure to bear on newspapers, or bought them outright. The National Electric Light Association formed a textbook committee that coerced state agencies into giving up schoolbooks that criticized stockwatering and high utility rates or urged the need for public controls. A national program of public lectures was begun, and local politicians often found it financially advantageous to leave the utilities alone.

George Norris and Muscle Shoals

Many critics of the utilities began to advocate public production and distribution of electric power. It had become such a vital necessity of life, such individuals said, that no one should be allowed to profit from it. Electric power should be produced as cheaply as possible, distributed at the lowest possible price, and made available to Americans in all regions of the country, not only

THE NEW ERA: TRIUMPH AND DISASTER

in prosperous areas where profits could be made. Many municipalities, persuaded by such appeals, established their own power-production facilities that distributed electricity in the same way that municipal agencies distributed water.

The bulk of the electric power in the nation, however, was produced and distributed by private companies. Radicals proposed that the whole system be nationalized, but for most people this was too revolutionary an idea. One device, however, remained open: for the federal government to undertake the production and distribution of power in regions up to that time ignored by private industry as unprofitable. This would allow the creation of a yardstick by which private utility rates could be judged. At the same time, the availability of cheap power could revitalize vast areas where people now lived in poverty and despair.

One location immediately offered itself—the Tennessee Valley. Where the Tennessee River dips into Alabama, at Muscle Shoals, the government had started to build a large dam during the First World War in order to produce nitrates for ammunition. This required enormous supplies of electric power, to be produced by hydroelectric facilities at the dam. The facility was near completion when Harding took office, and the federal government immediately began looking for a private firm to lease the plant and sell power to private distribution companies.

But George W. Norris, progressive Republican senator from Nebraska, had already taken up his great cause: making electric power cheaply available to the masses by bringing it under public control. He had already conceived of a public corporation that would control the waters of the entire sprawling Tennessee watershed for the public welfare. It would not only build many dams to produce cheap power but would also control floods, revive navigation, fisheries, and recreation, and spread industry and jobs throughout an enormous region, then one of the most backward and poverty-stricken in the nation. As the nucleus for this system, he argued, the plant at Muscle Shoals should not be given to a private firm, but should be operated for the people of the Tennessee Valley. Republicans condemned his plan as bald socialism, but Norris was not to be turned aside. On two occasions in the 1920s he pushed a bill through Congress to build a federal Tennessee Valley project, but both Coolidge and Hoover

vetoed it. The Muscle Shoals dam was completed in 1925, and its power was sold to a local private company for distribution, but still Norris was not discouraged. He had saved Muscle Shoals from sale to a private corporation and in the 1930s, under the New Deal, his dream for the Tennessee Valley would become reality.

President Herbert Hoover's veto in 1931 of the Muscle Shoals proposal expressed the Republican response to all such projects: "I am firmly opposed to the Government entering into any business the major purpose of which is competition with our citizens. . . . This territory is now supplied with power and to obtain . . . an income it would be necessary to take the customers of the present power companies [by undercutting] the rates now made by them. . . . There are many localities where the Federal Government is justified in the construction of great dams and reservoirs, where navigation, flood control, reclamation or stream regulation are of dominant importance, and where they are beyond the capacity or purpose of private or local government capital to construct. In these cases power is often a by-product and should be disposed of by contract or lease. But for the Federal Government deliberately to go out to build up and expand such an occasion to the major purpose of a power and manufacturing business is to break down the initiative and enterprise of the American people; it is destruction of equality of opportunity amongst our people; it is the negation of the ideals upon which our civilization has been based.

"I hesitate to contemplate the future of our institutions, of our government, and of our country if the preoccupation of its officials is to be no longer the promotion of justice and equal opportunity but is to be devoted to barter in the markets. That is not liberalism, it is degeneration. . . .

"The establishment of a Federal-operated power business and fertilizer factory in the Tennessee Valley means Federal control from Washington. . . . The real development of . . . Muscle Shoals can only be administered by the people on the ground, responsible to their own communities, directing them solely for the benefit of their communities and not for the purpose of pursuit of social theories or national politics."

Strong Economic Growth

The persistent story of the 1920s in America, however, was solid, deep, extraordinary economic growth. Productivity per man-hour in industry soared at a rate never before achieved and workers' real income went on a similar steep rise. The average worker produced two thirds more in

1929 than in 1919, because of capitalists' heavy expenditures in new and more efficient machinery and a coincident rise in workers' education and skills. The nation as a whole spent twice as much at the end of the 1920s on education as it had at the beginning of the decade (from 1.17 percent of the gross national product to 2.22 percent). Consequently, almost 30 percent of the seventeen-year-olds in the country had graduated from high school in 1929, whereas a decade earlier the figure had been not quite 17 percent. At the same time, industrialists spent their funds not so much on expanding their plants, as they had done in the past, but, in a trend forecasting the modern industrial system that emerged after 1945, in research and development and in the application of scientific knowledge to technology. The use of low-cost electric power invaded industrial operations, creating greater efficiency and productivity, and the chemicals industry rapidly expanded.

In addition, the organizational revolution continued in business life. College-trained engineers, accountants, and business analysts brought in efficient budgeting, cost accounting, specialized divisions, and mass-assembly operations, as well as heavy expenditures in advertising and marketing to stimulate sales. The swiftly growing automobile industry, which turned out millions of vehicles in the 1920s, turned to the use of statistical procedures for forecasting and managing production. Regular changes in style were introduced—so that consumers would discard otherwise usable goods and purchase new ones—together with a great and powerful innovation: credit purchasing. In the midst of all of this swift change, workers' wage increases far outstripped increases in the prices of producers' goods, and because of farm overproduction food prices remained low. In the 1920s both national income and national product surged at a strong rate of almost 2 percent a year, so that real earnings were buoyant. Between 1900 and 1910 real workers' income (accounting for inflation) had risen about 20 percent; from 1910 to 1920, some 12 percent; but in the 1920s the rise was 23 percent. (At the same time, corporate profits rose 62 percent.) For production workers, hours at work were at the same time declining, approaching forty hours a week by 1929. The termination of massive in-migration aided this trend, because immigrants traditionally worked long hours willingly.

Mass consumption, though clearly not as great as it was to become after 1945, was another "modern" feature of the 1920s economy. In 1900 there had been only 8,000 registered automobiles in the country; by 1920 this figure had risen to almost 240,000; by 1932, it was reaching 25 million! Nothing as dramatically transformed ordinary people's way of life as the automobile, the hard-surfaced road, and the sudden ease of travel over wide distances. Life acquired a richness and a constant source of interest and novelty that it had never had before. The conquest of distance! Realizing this centuries-old dream was suddenly coming into the range of everyone's life. At the same time, during the 1920s the production of radios rose 25-fold; that of refrigerators increased 150-fold; and households within cities were rapidly electrified. People also bought more and better food, clothing, entertainment, and schooling—and probably bootleg liquor.

Even so, in 1929 a Brookings Institution study found 42 percent of American families still at or below a "subsistence-and-poverty" level. While there was a long-range trend toward a more even distribution of wealth in the population as a whole (the evidence is not very reliable; approximations are necessary), six out of ten still earned less than $2,000 annually (the poverty level was $1,500). The twelve-hour day was wide-spread in the economy; child labor still occupied a major role in production; and laboring people who tried to organize were harshly and often violently suppressed.

Republican "Involvement" in the World

The Republican attitude toward the outside world continued, through the 1920s, to be paradoxical. The Harding and Coolidge administrations were isolationist and nationalist at heart. The force of events, however, and the United States' unavoidably transformed status in the world, brought about an inevitable involvement in international politics, oftentimes in a major role. The League of Nations was shunned; membership in the World Court was seriously discussed, for a time pursued, and then rejected. The protective tariff was reestablished; the open door to immigrants was replaced with a filtering system designed primarily to admit northern and western Europeans;

and the policy of refusing to make binding political commitments that would require the use of force to maintain collective security against aggressors was continued. However, the Washington Conference and its agreements in 1921 was followed by participation throughout the decade in extended conferences in London and elsewhere that sought vainly to reduce naval armaments worldwide. Americans took major roles in complex negotiations connected with European war debts and reparations, and exhibited a reluctant but growing cooperation with the League of Nations in nonpolitical matters connected with the opium trade and the "Traffic in Women and Children" (kidnapping and sale, worldwide, for prostitution).

Most dramatic of all these involvements, if in the long run the effort to be most ridiculed, was the Kellogg-Briand Pact of August 1928. In this document fifteen nations, and eventually practically the whole world, agreed to renounce war "as an instrument of national policy." For years the idea that war could be ended simply by its being outlawed by the nations of the world had circulated within the American peace movement. Senator William E. Borah first suggested it in the Senate in 1923; a Columbia professor, James T. Shotwell, urged it upon Foreign Minister Aristide Briand of France in 1927; and suddenly it exploded into prominent international discussion. Charles Lindbergh's electrifying solo flight over the Atlantic to Paris in May 1927 created an exciting sense of revived links with America's Revolutionary-era ally. Briand proposed to the American secretary of state Frank B. Kellogg that their two countries create such a pact between themselves. To avoid the implication of a special relationship with France, which might be taken as a kind of alliance against Germany, Kellogg expanded the notion into a universal renunciation of war by all nations. Months of complicated diplomacy followed in which Kellogg fended off efforts to attach qualifications and exemptions, dreamed of a Nobel Peace Prize (it was awarded to him in 1929), and secured the convening in Paris of a grand meeting of the representatives of fifteen nations to sign the pact.

It was, however, purely a self-denying ordinance. No machinery whatever was established to implement it, and in time the pact became the classic symbol of the futility of interwar diplomacy. Grand-sounding words without commitments were useless in preventing warfare, indeed were effective only in creating cynicism and loss of mutual faith.

The Political Rise of Herbert Hoover

One American figure stood out with uncommon brightness at the end of the First World War— Herbert Hoover. His life had been purest Horatio Alger. A poor Quaker boy, he went to Stanford University as soon as it opened in the 1890s, became an engineer, and launched an international career that by 1914 had made him a rich man. Living in London when the First World War broke out, he was asked as a neutral to direct the relief operations that brought food to the people of war-ravaged Belgium. In this enormous effort Hoover's superb administrative skills soon made him internationally renowned. When he attended the peace conference at Paris, no one else seemed to represent quite so luminously the selfless concern for humanity that Woodrow Wilson was then vainly calling on the victorious powers to exhibit.

When Hoover returned to the United States, no one knew his partisan affiliation. He had had nothing to do with politics: he was an engineer, an expert, a twentieth-century man. For him the key concepts were efficiency, strong administration, and "scientific" solutions—classic notions from the heart of the Progressive Era. When he declared himself a Republican, that party was delighted. In fact, Quakers had always been overwhelmingly Republican, just as they had been Tory in Revolutionary times. A pious, hard-working, moralistic folk with deep English roots, they had been hostile to the Scotch-Irish and the Catholic Irish; fervently antislavery and anti-Southern; and devotedly in favor of temperance. No more Republican setting could be found than the small Iowa village of West Branch where Hoover was reared. Its Quaker memories rooted it within the Protestant, "respectable" tradition, as distinguished sharply from the moral corruptions and Catholicism of Chicago, that appalling city that so fascinated the rural Middle West and symbolized the Democratic party.

Harding made Hoover secretary of commerce, a post he held until he ran for the presidency in 1928. As earlier discussed, he made the office, formerly almost ignored, the most vital and exciting center of federal activity in Washington. Hoover was a missionary of capitalism who hated both socialism and unchecked individualism. A confirmed elitist, he had a horror of mob rule. As he wrote in his book *American Individualism* (1922), "the crowd only feels: it has no mind of its own which can plan. The crowd is credulous, it destroys, it consumes, it hates, and it dreams—but it never builds." Hoover believed that American individualism, founded on the twin principles of equality of opportunity and of service, would provide the hope of the future. Although he recognized poverty in the United States, Hoover insisted that the government should not do anything directly about it, for the operations of private enterprise were progressively eliminating the problem.

As the years passed, Herbert Hoover rose ever higher as the expressive symbol and philosopher of the American business system. There seemed no end to the expansion of the economy, and the glow of national prosperity lighted him for all the nation to see and admire. When Calvin Coolidge indicated that he "did not choose to run" for the presidency in 1928, the Republican party turned almost en masse to the brilliant engineer, organizer, and publicist Herbert Hoover.

Democrats in the 1920s: Frustration and Conflict

During the years of Republican triumph the Democrats lurched from disaster to disaster, wounded deeply by the cultural shifts of these years. Southern Democrats disliked everything that Democrats in the northern states represented: urbanism, "foreigners," Catholics and Jews, and drinking. The Ku Klux Klan, so popular in the South, was hated in the immigrant wards. Above all, Southern Democrats disliked the man who was emerging as the voice of northern Democrats, Alfred E. Smith, governor of New York. A Catholic who was reared in a tenement on New York City's East Side and in his speech and style a kind of American cockney, Smith had different memories from those held by the populistic Southern Democrats. They were aroused by the threat of monopolistic corporations and the protective tariff. Rooted in Smith's remembrances, on the other hand, were the stinking slums in which he

had lived, the degradation of endless labor in the foul air of crowded factories, the filth of public toilets, and the callous exploitation of child labor. He appealed for social reforms in the cities. Minimum-wage laws, eight-hour days, workmen's compensation, state provision of medical services, publicly provided cheap electrical power—these were his objectives. Furthermore, as a Catholic he was keenly interested in civil liberties, revolted by the Ku Klux Klan, and inspired by the idea of a pluralistic American society that would make an equitable place for all those who were not WASP.

In 1924, rural Southerners were not ready for the man with the East Side twang. He was "wet" on the liquor issue (he opposed prohibition), and they were "dry." He was a Catholic, they were Protestant. The Democratic convention of that year could not even unite in condemning the Ku Klux Klan. For more than a hundred weary ballots it wrangled between nominating Smith or William G. McAdoo, Woodrow Wilson's son-in-law, who had become the hero of the rural Democrats led by William Jennings Bryan. It was this deadlock that led to the choice of John W. Davis, a lackluster Wall Street attorney of no public standing, and to the smashing triumph of Calvin Coolidge.

Four years later, in 1928, there was no doubt that Governor Smith was the only Democratic candidate of sufficient stature to challenge Hoover for the presidency. Meanwhile, too, the Democratic party had swung over vigorously to the cause of rural radicals who demanded some kind of governmental aid to agriculture and other progressive-inspired reforms such as the public control of electric-power production and distribution. With Smith supporting these causes, a political basis existed for a union of Southern and northern Democrats. He was accordingly nominated by the Democratic party in 1928, while in New York State, the polio-crippled Franklin D. Roosevelt had been induced to come out of his semiretirement and campaign for the post of governor of that state, which he won.

Significance of the 1928 Presidential Vote

Smith lost by a wide margin to Hoover: the popular vote was fifteen million on his side and twenty-one million for the Republican nominee. However, Smith's showing was a critical portent of future politics. The dozen largest cities, which for years had voted Republican, swung over to the Democratic column. The new-stock immigrants of the northern cities, who had started to go Democratic before the First World War and had then fallen off because of their anger at Woodrow Wilson's war policies, were now swinging massively and finally into the Democratic column. Prohibitionism in the northern states was overwhelmingly a Republican policy, with its origins in small-town, WASP America, and the ethnic minorities bitterly hated it as an insulting slap at themselves. In truth, WASP America drank relatively little; it was Italian wine, German beer, Irish whiskey, and other ethnic beverages, and the saloon—overwhelmingly an ethnic institution—that prohibitionism attacked. Cities like Chicago, with their huge ethnic populations, ignored prohibition en masse. Anti-Catholicism was widespread in the northern states, as was nativism, the Ku Klux Klan, and the campaign for restricted immigration, and all of these were deeply identified with the Republican party. Rural America hated the city as an evil, corrupting place. Iowa farmers thought Chicago foreign, radical, dirty, repellent, in every way a force to be battled against by the Republican party. They felt their Protestant nation was in grave danger from the immigrant hordes who occupied its great urban centers. Jews, they were startled to find, had suddenly become the second largest religious group in Illinois, taking that honor from the Methodists!

Seeing the Republicans as their enemies—in their antilabor and probusiness views as well as in their hatred of immigrant culture—the Jews, Italians, Poles, and Yugoslavs poured in waves into the Democratic party. Most strikingly, so too did the Germans, who had got over their anger at the Democratic war against their homeland, and even the Scandinavians, a strongly ethnic group since far back in the nineteenth century (though they were to be relatively temporary Democrats).

From 1920 to 1928, seventeen million new voters passed the age of twenty-one, and the majority were from the new ethnic groups. Thus, although Herbert Hoover was able to win some 300 counties in the South, he did so on the basis of prohibition, which because of its impending repeal (in 1933), would be a dead issue by 1932. The Democratic party was now in the position where it would soon, with the help of the Great Depression, become the majority party.

Hoover: Triumphant President

Few presidents have taken office in such encouraging circumstances as Herbert Hoover. He was enormously popular. Everything about him symbolized and proclaimed the triumph of the New Era, which Republicans were fond of contrasting with Woodrow Wilson's New Freedom. As for the nation, it was as rich as all of Europe. Some 40 percent of the world's wealth was contained within its borders. The American business system seemed one of the wonders of the world, a compound of assembly-line production, time-and-motion efficiency studies, advertising, easy credit, low interest rates, and a continuing flood of new products. Its most dramatic sight was the automobile: Americans owned by 1929 an average of one per family. Henry Ford, a genuine folk hero, represented in industry the astonishing potentialities of mass production for a mass market.

Hoover convened Congress in a special session to do something to quiet the angry farmers and to revise the tariff. His party looked to him in admiration. But it was not long before the honey-

Al Smith (*left*), Democratic candidate for president in 1928. Brash, pro-drink, reared in New York City and an Irish Catholic, he represented everything that rural, WASP, and small-town America was against.
Wide World Photos

moon was over, for Hoover fundamentally disliked Congress and all politicians and wanted to have as little as possible to do with either. This distaste was impossible for him to hide, for he was a tactless man. Congressional leaders visiting Hoover at the White House would find him distrustful and pessimistic. Henry L. Stimson, his secretary of state, remarked that "it was like sitting in a bath of ink to sit in [the president's] room." Hoover, in fact, had utterly no social graces. Glum, reserved, terribly shy, at his nightly formal dinners with large groups of guests he commonly said no more than "hello" and "goodbye." Whatever happened in Congress, Hoover seemed always to interpret it as the product of some political grudge against himself.

Hoover clearly believed that nothing was fundamentally wrong with agriculture and that it needed only a dose of business methods. Rather than provide a price-support mechanism, he secured passage of a bill creating the Federal Farm Board, whose function would be to make farm marketing more efficient. The Farm Bloc succeeded in tacking onto the bill a $500-million appropriation that the board was to use in making direct purchases of crops in the market in order to stave off price declines. This step was pitifully inadequate to deal with so enormous a problem, but it represented a major breakthrough in the nation's agricultural policy.

For industry, Hoover had in mind a tariff revision that would allow him greater authority to raise or lower rates, following recommendations of the Tariff Commission. His central goal was to ensure greater efficiency by enabling the president to equalize the costs of production here and abroad. The result, after months of wrangling and back scratching, was the Hawley-Smoot Tariff, which increased rates on more than a thousand imports, but did not give Hoover the added flexibility he requested. The general tariff level was raised to 40 percent, which halted entirely the importing of a great number of foreign products. Hoover had been lauded as the expert economist who would take politics out of tariff making, and now the nation had a bill that was more blatantly protectionist and politically inspired than ever. A thousand economists appealed to the president to veto the bill, but he signed it. This had grave repercussions, for Britain and Germany soon retaliated by raising their tariffs against American goods, thus reducing international trade just when it needed to be increased.

The Great Crash

There were numerous economic danger signals in 1929 (though the government was ignorant of them since as yet it did not gather detailed economic statistics). In Wall Street, however, speculation went merrily onward. For a half-dozen years money had poured into the stock market from millions of investors in the United States and Europe. Profits seemed endless. The Federal Reserve Board, following Coolidge's urgings, made credit easily available. With no public supervision, the stock markets could make purchases ridiculously easy, asking investors to put down no more than 10 percent on a stock (a practice called margin purchasing), the stockbrokers themselves making up the balance by issuing loans. As the speculative craze mounted, stock was "split" (for example, for every two shares of its stock presently existing, a corporation might issue a third one), so that there would be more for investors to buy, and "blue-sky" corporations appeared that had practically no assets whatever save a stock-market listing. Buyers competed so eagerly for loans that interest rates soared from about 5 percent to 20 percent, with the result that money poured in from abroad in order to be lent out at high interest rates. Where normally the price of a stock might stand at eight or ten times its earnings, prices now soared to as much as twenty times earnings. The mania spread everywhere. Following the stock market and making speculative plunges became as common as following the baseball scores. Almost two million Americans by 1929 were investors in American securities.

The American stock market was like an enormous vacuum cleaner sucking in capital from all over the world and draining dry every other line of enterprise. Why put your money in conservative projects when fantastic profits could be made by buying and selling on Wall Street? European nations grew gravely worried, for the siphoning off of capital severely weakened their economies. Economists in England warned repeatedly that a crash was coming if something was not done. Finally, in September 1929 the Bank of England raised its rediscount rate to 6.5 percent, thus halting the flow of gold to America. This action seemed to trigger a cascade of events, beginning with the decision by many American and European investors to pull back, sell out, and safeguard themselves. The crucial element in the whole speculative spiral had been confidence.

Now it began to wane, and the result was inevitable. On Wednesday, October 23, 1929, a flood of "sell" orders deluged Wall Street, and since there were not as many buyers as before, stock prices began to tumble. From then on, the ghastly disaster grew more and more frightening. There were even brief periods in which nobody at all would agree to buy, no matter how low the prices. The visitors' gallery at the New York Stock Exchange was closed so that the panic on the floor would be less visible. The torrent of transactions put the stock ticker farther and farther behind, thus heightening the tension and increasing scare selling. The news spread hourly throughout the nation, and stock owners besieged their brokers' offices with appeals to sell and get out.

Bankers with enormous resources, such as those of the House of Morgan, stepped in at once to make huge purchases and thus stop the slide. Economists, the Treasury Department, even the White House issued reassuring statements. But the fear was too widespread. After a few days of quiet, on October 29 the uproar began again. Worried brokers, frantic to get their loans back, forced customers to sell. Another avalanche of sell orders descended on Wall Street, reaching an all-time high of sixteen million shares in one day. Within a month, the total value of stocks listed at the New York Exchange had dropped some twenty-six billion dollars, or 40 percent of their former level. The New Era had collapsed.

Why the Depression?

A recession had in fact already been under way, for businessmen in 1928 had greatly overestimated what the American public would buy, and had produced too many manufactured goods. Thus, factories had shut down operations and laid men off, waiting for merchants' swollen inventories to drop downward again—a normal and cyclical procedure. The stock-market crash suddenly wiped away enormous stores of capital, however, and in time the whole economy was made shakier, for it was now less able to be fed by a steady flow of investment. The crash also had a profound psychological impact: it pricked the bubble of belief in ever expanding prosperity, drained away confidence in the stockbrokers and bankers who had been leading the speculation, and led distrustful ordinary citizens to withdraw their money from investments and hold it as cash.

The confused, dazed crowd jamming Wall Street on the day of the 1929 stock-market crash expressed the mood that was soon to spread across the nation. Capitalism seemed to have collapsed.

Brown Brothers

The scene was not one of potential disaster, however, for the economy had weathered such fluctuations before. For many years scholars have explained that the great depression that actually developed was caused by *underconsumption*. That is, in the 1920s businessmen kept too much of their profits to themselves instead of paying them out in higher wages, so that ordinary Americans could not buy the huge output of the factories. Income, it has long been said, was so highly unbalanced—most of it being placed in the hands of the wealthy, who then squandered it in disastrous speculation—that fewer and fewer could buy what businessmen wished to sell. Farmers in particular were a depressed class, because farm prices had been slumping so long, and this made the economy even more likely to tumble into complete collapse when a triggering event like the stock-market crisis occurred.

Although these things had their influence, the facts are that national income was better distributed than at any earlier period; that potential demand was still high; and that it was quite possible for the federal government within its then existing resources to have pulled the nation out of the self-feeding downward spiral that slowly began to accelerate, plunging the nation deeper and deeper into what in time became a massive depression. What we now realize happened was a grave failure of policy within the Federal Reserve Board. Before the crash, the board had made speculation worse by responding sympathetically to the bankers' clamor for more and more funds, and by making credit easier to secure. Then after the crash, in 1931, the board grew worried that too much gold was leaving the country as Europeans, believing the American economy too weak, withdrew it. To prove conclusively that the American dollar was sound and valuable, the board made borrowing much more difficult by greatly raising the discount rate and thus sharply reduced the money supply. By 1933 the nation had a third less money with which to carry on its economic life. This was tantamount to shutting off the oxygen to a person who through overexertion was momentarily finding it hard to breathe. The result was catastrophic.

Thousands of banks closed; "runs" on their resources put the public in a panic. The economy now headed downward, with increasing speed. Investment in new factories and equipment practically ceased, falling from $10 billion in 1929 to $1 billion in 1932. Approximately 110,000 businesses closed their doors from 1929 to 1932, while the aggregate profit of all corporations declined from almost $8.5 billion to $3.4 billion. The railroads found themselves hauling only half their former volume of freight. In 1930 industrial production was about 25 percent below its peak in 1929; by 1932 it had sagged to 50 percent below that high point. Within six months of the crash, unemployment stood at three million; by 1933, it had reached twelve to fourteen million. Life in industrial cities was almost indescribable. While in the nation as a whole 25 percent of the working force was unemployed, in Ohio cities such as Cleveland half the workers were without jobs in 1933; in Toledo the figure was 80 percent! Huge urban areas lived in famine conditions like those of ancient times.

Hoover's Response

Knowing what the stock-market collapse foreshadowed, President Hoover quickly moved into action. His firm conviction was that the catastrophe was a great natural event about which the government could do little save to encourage people to be confident. The nation, he said, could no more "legislate [itself] out of a world-wide de-

pression [than] we can exorcise a Caribbean hurricane by statutory law." If businessmen would be unselfish, and if they would cooperate and keep faith in the system, recovery was certain. His own role, he felt, was to serve as "an influential advisor and well-placed cheerleader." He also briefly increased federal spending on public works. Fundamentally, however, he regarded the emergency as one that would soon be solved by cooperative, voluntary action by businessmen. He called business leaders to the White House and appealed to them not to lay off workers or lower wages. He emphasized, meanwhile, that he had no intention of interfering in any way with private enterprise.

Hoover made it clear from the beginning that he intended to handle the depression on his own, not by appealing to Congress for legislation. In response, for a considerable period both parties in Congress were content to leave the matter in his hands. By the end of 1930, however, evidence was accumulating that the depression was very severe, and some congressional critics of Hoover's passivity began calling for enormous increases in spending for public works. The president replied testily that "prosperity cannot be restored by raids upon the public treasury." Senator Robert Wagner of New York secured passage of the the Federal Employment Stabilization Act, which established a board to plan and carry through an accelerated program of public works, but Hoover made little use of it. Meanwhile, the nation sunk into apathy. Told constantly by politicians and experts alike that the economy would right itself automatically, the public settled into a fatalistic mood.

Action Begins

By the summer of 1931, however, it was no longer possible to continue in passivity. Herbert Hoover had by this time reluctantly given in, having found that voluntary action had grave weaknesses. Financiers everywhere were looking out for their own skins and shunning cooperation. In his state of the union address, Hoover called for the establishment of the Reconstruction Finance Corporation (RFC). To be modeled on the War Finance Corporation of 1917 and 1918, the RFC would save the collapsing banks, railroads, and insurance companies. Progressives in Congress criticized the proposed project for ignoring the sufferings of the unemployed. Fiorello La Guardia of New York called it a "millionaire's dole." A Republican congressman wailed that the RFC would be "the most decided step toward communism any civilized government has ever taken with the possible exception of Russia." Farm Bloc legislators angrily pointed out that it was only another aid to banks and railroads, long the special concern of a government indifferent to the farmers. But the emergency was clear; the bankers, impatient of political theory, were desperate for the RFC; and the measure creating it was enacted swiftly. Given $500 million in capital and the power to borrow additional huge sums, the RFC aided more than 5,000 companies in the year 1932 alone, practically all of which loans were paid back.

Democratic Progressives Revolt

The Democrats in Congress had thus far remained relatively inactive. Their leaders were largely Southern, and, lacking ideas of their own as to how to solve the depression, were content to leave decisions up to the president. The election of 1930 had delivered the House into Democratic hands, but Speaker John Nance Garner of Texas prided himself on cooperating with the president rather than carping at his policies. In 1932, however, all this fraternization blew apart.

A concerted drive began to force the president to agree to vastly expanded programs of relief for the unemployed, principally through federal public works. Hoover had doggedly insisted that relief was a private and local matter, that the nation's moral fiber and the vigor of its state governments would be destroyed if the federal government took up a direct role in relief. He particularly condemned all public works except those that would produce a self-liquidating revenue: toll bridges, power dams, and slum-clearance projects, for example. The president was determined to keep a balanced budget and to hold down spending. Every proposal for expanded public works came under withering Republican criticism as a "dole" (a simple handing-out of money to the suffering, a practice condemned as destroying initiative and self-pride.) But local governments and relief agencies had long since exhausted their funds, and they appealed for federal action. When Congress passed a bill calling for three billion dollars to be dispensed for public works, the president vetoed the measure. The man who had been the savior of Belgium and the worldwide symbol of compassion to the suffering had become "heartless Hoover." He seemed to care more for his principles of political theory than for the unemployed.

"I finished high school in 1930," mused Ed Paulsen, a United Nations official, in 1970, "and I walked out into [the depression]. . . . I'd get up at five in the morning [in San Francisco] and head for the waterfront. Outside the Spreckles Sugar Refinery, outside the gates there would be a thousand men. You know dang well there's only three or four jobs. The guy would come out with two little Pinkerton cops: 'I need two guys for the bull gang. Two guys to go into the hole.' A thousand men would fight like a pack of Alaskan dogs to get through there. . . .

"So you'd drift up to Skid Row. There'd be thousands of men there. Guys on baskets, making weird speeches, phony theories on economics. . . . They'd say: O.K., we're going to City Hall. . . . We'd shout around the steps. Finally, [the mayor'd] come out and tell us nothing. I remember the demands: We demand work, we demand shelter for our families, we demand groceries, this kind of thing. . . . I remember as a kid how courageous this seemed to me, the demands, because you knew that society wasn't going to give it to you. They'd demand that they open up unrented houses and give decent shelters for their families. . . . This parade would be four blocks long, curb to curb. Nobody had a dime. . . . The guys'd start to yell and there come some horses. They used to have cops on horseback in those days. Then there'd be some fighting. Finally it got to killing. . . .

"We were a gentle crowd. These were fathers, eighty percent of them. They had held jobs and didn't want to kick society to pieces. They just wanted to go to work and they just couldn't understand. . . . These fellas always had faith that the job was gonna mature, somehow. More and more men were after fewer and fewer jobs. So San Francisco just ground to a halt. Nothing was moving."
(Quoted in Studs Terkel, *Hard Times* [1970])

The Personal Catastrophe of Unemployment

It did not matter to the unemployed person that his condition was produced by nationwide conditions, that millions were unemployed throughout the industrialized nations of the world. The tragic impact of prolonged unemployment was eventually deep humiliation, loss of self-respect, and hopelessness. The first response upon losing a job was to wait confidently for some other job to turn up; then to start a feverish search; then to become discouraged and emotionally disorganized; and finally to sink into apathy.

This was a traditional human reaction. "Whenever I'm out of work," an English worker had said in the late nineteenth century, "I feel like a bloody dog." In the 1890s a young German commented on "the inexpressibly depressing effect of being obliged to trudge from factory to factory, from shop to shop, always offering one's abilities and capabilities, and always in vain." In the 1930s, this shattering experience became the fate of tens of millions in the world. "I'm beginning to wonder what's wrong with me," ran a typical observation from a man out of work for a month. He later said, "Even my family is beginning to think I'm not trying." If not resigned to their fate, the unemployed became bitter, gloomy, and inclined to drinking bouts and wild rage. They were expected to support their families: why were they failing at it? Few people could stand the strain of prolonged joblessness without paying a heavy psychological price in lethargy and despair. The unemployed, it was observed, usually "walk heavily and slowly." They drift away from their older associations, feel a sharp break with their past life. George Orwell, the English novelist, found a jobless family in a mining town "sprawling aimlessly about . . . one tall son sitting by the fireplace, too listless even to notice the entry of a stranger, and slowly peeling a sticky sock from a bare foot." The American historian Ray Allen Billington, a New Deal worker in the mid 1930s, remembered the jobless and "their bleak, downcast eyes, their broken spirit." Over and over the strange fact presented itself: "People seem to blame themselves." A widely read novel put this frame of mind succinctly: "It got you slowly, with the slippered stealth of an unsuspected, malignant disease. You fell into the habit of slouching, of putting your hands into your pockets and keeping them there; of glancing at people, furtively, ashamed of your secret, until you fancied that everybody eyed you with suspicion."

In a country like America, which had been built upon the idea that each person was responsible for his or her own success, and where there were almost no social systems for taking care of the jobless, the pain of unemployment was perhaps more piercing and inescapable than in any other society, though its tragedy was nonetheless felt everywhere. Indeed, the lack of political protest, the passivity that millions displayed, may have been created by the numbing effects of joblessness. The very fact that the depression was worldwide led many to believe that their own governments were not, in any event, to blame. There were mass meetings, marches of unemployed soldiers demanding war-related bonuses, and countless small outbreaks, but they were disorganized and spotty. Most of the jobless seemed, in fact, to reject radical politics. Communists orated powerfully, but few came to listen. Radicals made a great deal of noise in the 1930s, but relatively small numbers adhered to their causes. In late 1932, when there were perhaps 13 million unemployed in America, only 100,000 voted the Communist presidential ticket and no more than 882,000 cast Socialist ballots. Among 3 million unemployed in Britain, only 15,000 were members of the Communist party. What people expected was for the traditional political parties to respond, to create a credible reaction to the depression. They believed in the system, overwhelmingly. They had lost faith in themselves, but not in the regenerative power of the essentially free-enterprise economy that had until recently so buoyantly pushed on to ever greater heights. Americans still seemed to believe in the capacity of the American political system—the system of representative democracy. They expected to see arise, out of the inborn creativity and strengths of the American people themselves, a set of answers to this latest of the great challenges to face them.

The Election of 1932

Franklin D. Roosevelt, governor of New York, swept Herbert Hoover and the Republicans out of power in 1932 with a finality that left them shattered for the next twenty years. The nation had had enough of principles; now it wanted action, which Roosevelt seemed to promise. Not since before the Civil War had the Democrats won such a great majority in the Senate, nor since 1890 in the House. They gained in every part of the United States, winning a majority of the congressional race everywhere except in traditionally Republican New England. The Democratic victories on the Pacific Coast were the most astonishing, for there the Democrats increased their portion of the popular vote for congressmen from 20 percent in 1930 to 51 percent in 1932. Roosevelt received almost 23 million popular votes to Hoover's 15.8 million, while winning the electoral votes of all but five states: Pennsylvania, Connecticut, Vermont, New Hampshire, and Maine. When inaugurated in March 1933, the new president found a transformed Congress ready and eager to follow executive leadership. The New Era was gone; the New Deal now triumphantly seized the reins.

Bibliography

Books that were especially valuable to me in writing this chapter: John M. Allswang, *A House for All Peoples: Ethnic Politics in Chicago 1890– 1936* (1971) explores the voting trends and the conflicts over prohibition and other issues among ethnic groups; David Burner, *The Politics of Provincialism: The Democratic Party in Transition, 1918–1932* (1968) is valuable on the same score, focussing especially on North-South tensions. Robert K. Murray has given us a surprising picture of a much-maligned president in his *The Harding Era: Warren G. Harding and His Administration* (1969). Ellis W. Hawley's *The Great War and the Search for a Modern Order: A History of the American People and their Institutions, 1917– 1933** (1979) is a valuable recent history of these years from new perspectives, stressing the "organizational revolution." John Braeman, ed., *Change and Continuity in Twentieth-Century America: The 1920s* (1968) provides a number of essays by different scholars which illuminate varying aspects of the decade, and it has been joined by another fine selection of historians' articles, Joan Hoff Wilson, ed., *The Twenties: The Critical Issues** (1972). I have also found John D. Hicks's *Republican Ascendancy, 1921–1933** (1960), in The New American Nation Series, a solid and judicious history of the period.

L. Ethan Ellis has written a balanced account of *Republican Foreign Policy, 1921–1933* (1968) which makes it clear that isolationism was not the only quality inherent in it. Arthur Schlesinger, Jr.'s first volume in his monumental study of the era of Franklin Roosevelt, *The Crisis of the Old Order 1919–1933* (1957) presents a rich account crowded with details and color. Richard Hofstadter's discussions of American farm life in his *The Age of Reform** (1955) remain valuable. In all aspects of the economic history of the period, W. Elliot Brownlee's *Dynamics of Ascent: A History of the American Economy* (1978) has been an essential guide to me. A rush of new scholarship on Herbert Hoover has given us quite a new perspective on the Quaker president. Joan Hoff Wilson's *Herbert Hoover: Forgotten Progressive** (1975) is an outstanding example of the recent studies. Gabriel Kolko's *Main Currents in Modern American History** (1976) has keen insights on Hoover and Republican economic policies. Breaking new ground is John A. Garraty's almost unprecedented study of *Unemployment in History: Economic Thought and Public Policy** (1979), which allows us to understand the miseries of millions in this condition. The belated response of Congressional Democrats to the Depression appears in Jordan A. Schwarz, *Interregnum of Despair: Hoover's Congress and the Depression* (1970).

Other Works on the Period

Burl Noggle: *Teapot Dome: Oil and Politics in the 1920s* (1962); Donald R. McCoy, *Calvin Coolidge: The Silent President* (1967); Joan Hoff Wilson, *American Business and Foreign Policy, 1902– 1933* (1971); Thomas H. Buckley, *The United States and the Washington Conference, 1921– 1922* (1970); Robert Sobel, *The Great Bull Market: Wall Street in the 1920s* (1968); Lewis Galambos, *Competition and Cooperation: The Emergence of a National Trade Association* (1966); Irving Bernstein, *The Lean Years: A History of the American Worker, 1920–1933* (1960); Robert Zieger, *Republicans and Labor, 1919–1929* (1969); John D. Hicks and Theodore Saloutos, *Twentieth-Century Populism: Agricultural Discontent in the Middle West, 1900–1939* (1964); Gene Smith, *The Shattered Dream: Herbert Hoover and the Great Depression* (1970); Gary Dean Best, *The Politics of American Individualism: Herbert Hoover in Transition, 1918–1921* (1976); Clark Chambers, *Seedtime of Reform* (1963); William Preston, Jr., *Aliens and Dissenters: Federal Suppression of Radicals, 1903–1933* (1963); George E. Mowry, *The Urban Nation, 1920–1960** (1965).

* Available in paperback.

31

Court rules National Recovery Administration unconstitutional, subsequently invalidates other major parts of New Deal, such as Agricultural Adjustment Administration; Louis Brandeis and followers, hostile to centralized planning and distrustful of business, grow influential; Works Progress Administration; Federal Art Project; Federal Writers' Project; National Youth Administration; Rural Electrification Administration; Social Security Act; Utility Holding Companies Act; Federal Reserve System made much stronger; control over the money supply made a public responsibility; graduated income tax includes higher rates for wealthy; National Labor Relations Board; Congress of Industrial Organizations formed

1937 Supreme Court "packing" battle; Supreme Court begins approving New Deal legislation; economy slumps

1938 Huge spending program launched for recovery; antitrust campaign begun; Bituminous Coal Act; Farm Security Administration; United States Housing Authority; Agricultural Adjustment Administration reenacted in new form; Fair Labor Standards Act

FRANKLIN D. ROOSEVELT AND THE NEW DEAL

UPI

Louis D. Brandeis was the first Jew to enter the Supreme Court. When Woodrow Wilson nominated him in January 1916, the uproar was extraordinary. For years Brandeis had been "the people's lawyer," fighting organized capital to aid the poor, the helpless, and the community at large. Harvard-trained, brilliant, he had made a fortune in legal practice before beginning his crusades against railroads and trusts, and for conservation and labor. From 1912 on he was in Woodrow Wilson's camp, shaping the ideas and concrete reforms of the New Freedom. The money trust, he said, was the great danger to American life; it must be battled at every turn. Thus, his nomination to the Supreme Court stunned financiers. The *New York Sun* called him "utterly and even ridiculously unfit." *Life* magazine pointed to a public concern about "the Jewish mind." Though

he was Kentucky-born, people said Brandeis was not really American.

As Mr. Justice Brandeis, he was for many years a famous dissenter in a conservative court. Legislatures and Congress, he believed, had wide powers under the Constitution to regulate economic and social affairs, but the Court's majority disagreed, striking down measure after measure aimed in this direction. The New Deal pleased him, if not most of his colleagues. Always distrustful of "bigness" in private business—it was inherently inefficient and exploitive, he said—he knew that only a strong national government could provide the necessary counterforce. On the other hand, he also distrusted too much "bigness" in government too, and he enthusiastically approved of the Court's decision in 1935 to strike down the New Deal's most centralizing agencies. Regulation and trust busting: fine. But not an all-powerful government directing everything in detail.

Hundreds of closely reasoned, fact-crammed opinions were handed down by Brandeis in his years on the Court, and slowly he won the majority of the justices to his views, both on social reform and on protection of civil rights and freedom of speech. In his mid seventies in the New Deal years, Brandeis was a towering figure. He had a strong and beautiful face, and the brooding strength of an Old Testament prophet. Writers, economists, reformers, congressmen: they all visited his weekly teas, each waiting for their chance to chat with the great justice. Human intelligence, he insisted, cannot run huge things well: rely upon smallness and localism. Go back to Texas or Oregon to do your work, he would urge young activists. America would be regenerated, Brandeis would say, not in Washington but in its cities and states. In the economy, always keep competition alive. Free enterprise, not monopoly, would release the human spirit and human productivity.

In his eighty-third year he retired; two years later, in 1941, he died without much discomfort, of heart failure. Four years earlier, in 1937, the Court had finally stepped back and begun allowing the government to guard and protect the social welfare. Brandeis the dissenter had prevailed.

Overview

"I pledge you," Franklin D. Roosevelt had said during the 1932 election campaign, "I pledge myself, to a new deal for the American people." On inauguration day in March 1933, the tall man with the large shoulders moved slowly on his crutches and crippled legs to the high white rostrum in front of the Capitol. With every fourth workingman out of a job, urban-welfare systems out of funds, the banking system shut down, and panic spreading through an immobilized nation, his task was to jolt the United States out of despair. "First of all," he cried out in his high ringing voice, "let me assert my firm belief that the only thing we have to fear is fear itself—nameless, unreasoning, unjustified terror that paralyzes needed efforts to convert retreat into advance." The nation, he said, was in a kind of war, and now the challenge was for the president to give vigorous leadership. "This nation asks for action, and action now."

This was indeed what he provided. With his inauguration it was as if a cornet trio playing thinly in the nation's capital was suddenly replaced by huge brass bands marching in from all directions, every instrument blaring at top volume. The national government exploded into furious activity and grew rapidly in size. Tiny budgets became huge ones; Congress worked day and night, month after month; message after message arrived at the Capitol from the president, calling urgently for more and more legislation; and a cornucopia of new federal agencies opened up, cascading offices and bureaus all over Washington, each of them bringing in experts from universities, banks, labor unions, farms, and corporations to supervise some crucial sector of the national economy.

Roosevelt's New Deal passed through two phases. From 1933 to 1935, the First New Deal operated on the assumption that overproduction was the fundamental problem, and it tried to solve this by instituting massive programs of centralized planning designed to reduce output and therefore raise prices. This would help the producers of goods. After partial success, the First New Deal collapsed in a welter of confusion and impasse. The Second New Deal, which began in a rush of legislation in 1935 and lasted into 1938, acted on the idea that underconsumption was the main problem and that helping the consumer was the most important goal—a classic Democratic

pattern. Aid to the unemployed was vastly expanded so that their purchasing power would increase; labor was aided in its organizing drives; and other programs helped farmers, the old, the blind, and the helpless. Full public control over the currency was established by a major strengthening of the Federal Reserve System; gigantic utility holding companies were broken up; and income taxes were aimed at high incomes.

Franklin D. Roosevelt: Progressive Democrat

The president was a kindly man who had known personal suffering—an encounter at age thirty-nine with infantile paralysis that left him permanently crippled—but never poverty. Reared as a much-loved only child in a gentle Episcopalian household, Roosevelt spent his early life on his father's Hudson Valley estate at Hyde Park, New York. Then came Groton, Harvard during the era of William James, Columbia Law School, and the beginnings of a Wall Street attorney's career. In 1910 Roosevelt entered politics as a state senator from his home district, Hyde Park. His father had been a Cleveland Democrat, and at Harvard Roosevelt worked hard for antiimperialist causes at the time of the Spanish-American War. In the New York legislature he was a progressive Democrat who chiefly battled against "bossism" and Tammany Hall.

Roosevelt admired Woodrow Wilson and pushed vigorously for his election. Wilson summoned young Roosevelt to Washington and appointed him assistant secretary of the navy. Dynamic, quick to learn, Roosevelt was an eager and effective administrator. When Wilson's League of Nations dream was killed, Roosevelt took up the cause as the Democratic party's vice-presidential nominee in 1920. In 1921, paralysis struck him down. Refusing to give in, he plunged into a years-long program of physical therapy. His courageous struggle against illness won him a national sympathy he could never have received as the handsome Hyde Park aristocrat.

Soon he was back on the political scene, nominating Al Smith at both the 1924 and 1928 national Democratic conventions and catching warm attention with his gallantry and eloquence. While Al Smith was going down to smashing defeat in 1928, Roosevelt was being elected governor of the state of New York. In this post he worked hard to make certain that the immense hydroelectric potential of the St. Lawrence River would be saved for public control, not handed over to private enterprise. When the depression struck he established the first state relief agency in the United States, tried to help workers and farmers, and provided jobs for the unemployed in state conservation projects. Soon a corps of academic experts, headed by Columbia University's Raymond Moley, gathered around Roosevelt to feed him ideas in preparation for the bid for the White House in 1932 that everyone expected. Confident, aggressive, with more than twenty years of experience in public life behind him, Franklin Roosevelt was ready for action when he finally assumed the presidential power he had long dreamed of.

What outlook would he bring to the presidency? No one really knew. Many thought him just a pleasant and smiling man, little equipped for the rigorous demands of the White House. In truth, his campaign speeches consisted mainly of bland generalities. He was certainly no radical. He had a strong sense of community, distrusted unchecked individualism, and warmly sympathized with suffering people. But he nourished no brooding ill will against the American system. He was a progressive Democrat, not a Marxian socialist. He wanted to save capitalism, not supplant it. His principal characteristic was a readiness to experiment. The theme that ran through Roosevelt's devotions was the belief that God wished men to be happy on earth, an outlook that made the goals of social reform more important to him than dogmas about laissez-faire and limited government. A product of the Progressive Era, he was a humanitarian pragmatist more interested in action than in orthodox principles. He became a president more excited by the prospect of ending child labor than worried about whether doing so violated hallowed maxims of government.

The Banking Crisis

Roosevelt's first challenge as president was to reopen the banks. This was a vital matter. The awesome spectacle of closed bank doors in every city in the land made people feel that in some catastrophic sense the American economy had come full stop. The president moved boldly. Assuming the mantle of commander in chief in time of war, he made use of First World War statutes, still on

The jaunty F.D.R., here photographed in a typical pose, lifted the nation's morale just by his manner and his high-spirited optimism. Brilliant as a crisis manager, always ready to experiment, he was both loved and hated by multitudes.

Wide World Photos

the books, to declare a bank holiday and halt all trading in gold so as to end its panic-induced flight from the country. Within a few days the president had bills before Congress empowering him to investigate the banks, allow sound ones to reopen, give loans from the Reconstruction Finance Corporation to those in need of help, and liquidate any that were hopelessly bankrupt. Note the essential conservatism of his actions: he did not urge nationalization of the banks (making them publicly owned). Rather, the weak ones were to be weeded out, the sound ones helped, and the system allowed to proceed as before. This was not socialism, but revived free-enterprise capitalism.

Congress quickly passed the legislation, Roosevelt made his first radio "fireside chat" to explain what was being done, and on Monday, March 13, banks reopened in the twelve Federal Reserve bank cities. Confidence rebounded. Deposits poured back into the banks, people talked excitedly of the decisiveness of their new national leader, and business immediately picked up. In the following two years, Treasury investigators weeded out thousands of unsound banks and thoroughly rehabilitated the national financial system.

The Hundred Days

Roosevelt now pushed forward on a broad front during the famous Hundred Days, a three-month period in the spring of 1933 when Congress enacted the most sweeping program of reform legislation in American history. Fifteen major laws went on the books; they dealt with banking, the gold standard, relief, mortgages, hydroelectric power and regional planning, the stock market, and national planning in industry and agriculture. A wartime outlook, inherited from the experiences of the First World War, linked these separate programs together. In the years 1917 and 1918, laissez-faire had been cast aside and the federal government had taken over direct supervision of the national economy. The result had been an amazing outburst of planned productivity that fascinated business leaders, public administrators, and intellectuals. From then on, the dream of national planning never left the American consciousness. Academics like John Dewey looked eagerly to the building of a centralized state that would utilize planning to achieve both prosperity and social justice.

Wartime psychology creates a national pulling together. People tend to look on the country as a great team under centralized direction in which each member cooperates with every other for the good of the whole. So, now, the leaders of the First New Deal regarded national planning and social cooperation as their guiding ideals. Capital and labor should cease their strife and work together; businessmen should set aside competition and cooperate; government and business should form a mutually helpful partnership. The national economy had reached its full growth, so it was believed—was not overproduction and surplus the chief problem?—and therefore the task now was to manage a completed national estate. Ways must be found to fit production to the limited market. Everyone should be accorded his fair share of the profits available, which meant letting businessmen agree among themselves on what prices they would charge and how much each would produce.

Roots in the New Era's Associative Capitalism

There was little that was new here. Essentially, what big business was urging upon Washington in the early decision-making weeks and months of the New Deal was that Herbert Hoover's trade associations be given legal powers. In 1931 Gerard Swope, president of General Electric, had issued a widely praised proposal to make the trade associations immune from antitrust laws and give them the authority to jointly establish prices for goods, how much each firm would produce, and common investment policies. Called "the most gigantic proposal of monopoly ever made in history," among FDR's advisers it had great appeal. Everyone save radicals wanted to preserve capitalism; people also liked the idea of social engineering, planning, centralized controls; and about the entire notion hung the aura of Theodore Roosevelt's New Nationalism, which FDR had always rather admired. For three years corporations had been losing money while competing desperately for markets and underpricing each other. Perhaps restoring confidence and rationality by this means would turn things around. The model of the 1917–18 War Industries Board fascinated almost everyone; it had, indeed, left an indelible imprint upon many minds as to how productivity could be efficiently directed from the center. Between 1930 and 1932, in fact, half a dozen major proposals had surfaced in Congress calling for the creation of some sort of central planning body, and they had come from people as widely separated as corporation heads and labor-union leaders.

In addition, Franklin Roosevelt leaned in this direction. The "shared common life" of the country was a theme he continually returned to. Planning, he had written, is "the way of the future." Planning for what, and by what means, was not yet very clear to anyone, but the idea seemed open to all sorts of definitions. For Roosevelt, the words "collectivism" and "planning" went together as antidotes to the ruinous individualism that the Republican years appeared to have demonstrated. The historian of the planning idea, Otis L. Graham, Jr., concluded in his *Toward A Planned Society: From Roosevelt to Nixon* [1976]), that FDR was, in fact, "an instinctive collectivist." By 1932 the conservationist outlook that had always been one of his major items of faith had matured, in the presence of a great economic disaster and the urgent counsel of many people, including his group of Columbia University professors—his "brains trust"—into "an organic view of society which assumed the need for continuous public intervention to compensate for imbalances that were not inherently self-correcting." An economy left entirely to private enterprise produced great imbalances toward one side or the other, which led to social injustice, a confused and irrational economic system, and damage to the environment. Thus, government must intervene as a manager: it must regulate, compensate, and control, and all with the aim of protecting the public interest and insuring stability together with progress.

Planning in Business

Out of this atmosphere emerged the chief creation of the Hundred Days—the National Recovery Administration (NRA). Businessmen were allowed jointly to make fair-trade codes concerning prices and production, and such agreements were to have the force of law and be exempt from the antitrust statutes. In return, employers (under Section 7A of the NRA Act) were to permit their laborers to organize unions and bargain collectively concerning wages and hours. For unorganized workers, employers had to agree to pay minimum wages and stay within a ceiling of maximum working hours per week. Linked to the NRA was a $3.3 billion public-works spending program to stimulate the economy, to be administered by a Public Works Administration.

Under the leadership of a flamboyant administrator, General Hugh Johnson, the NRA plunged into furious activity. Within weeks some 2.5 million employers had signed a standard code governing labor relations, so that 16 million workers came under the program's protection. By shortening hours and spreading the work, the NRA produced jobs for about 2 million additional workers. Some 700 detailed codes relating to particular industries were then devised, primarily by the businessmen involved. Enthusiasm soared, a "boomlet" spurted up in the economy, and the words "competition" and "individualism" were much condemned.

Very shortly, however, the NRA was in trouble. Progressives in Congress complained bitterly about the lifting of the antitrust laws, for they feared the emergence of massive government-sponsored monopolies. Since Johnson believed that businessmen should govern themselves, what came about was not central planning but a jumble of codes, each of which governed only one industry without regard to the entire economy. Since it was big businessmen who primarily influenced the writing of the codes, small businessmen felt they were being squeezed out. They insisted that they could not pay the wages or charge the prices that big business had inserted in the codes. And what about enforcement? The belligerent Johnson bristled when asked this question and barked that violators would "get a sock right on the nose." But in fact they were not prosecuted. Johnson relied only on social compulsion to force businessmen to comply with the codes, and this proved grievously insufficient. Soon the offices of the NRA in Washington were in bedlam, and protest was swelling across the country. Faced with severe problems, businessmen by the thousands simply ignored the codes.

The NRA, however, did achieve important things in its brief, meteoric rise. The idea of legally specified maximum hours and minimum wages was established on a national basis, so that later, in the Fair Labor Standards Act, it became firm policy. The problem of child labor was practically eliminated, especially in the textile industries, where children had been used more than in any other industry. Section 7A of the NRA law made it illegal for employers to hinder the formation of labor unions, and legalized collective bargaining. This had a tremendous influence on the labor movement. Furthermore, for all its failings the NRA broke the mood of economic fatalism. It accustomed people to think in terms of vigorous federal regulation and stimulation of the economy.

Planning in Agriculture

As the NRA was being launched, the government also moved for the first time into agricultural planning—another program that planned only one segment of the economy. (The development of an overall integrated plan linking all social and economic elements into one broad national set of objectives was never attempted during the New Deal after the collapse of the NRA, and before then only sloppily and partially.) The root problem on the farms was enormous overproduction, which was causing a disastrous agricultural depression. Farm income stood at one-third what it had been in 1929; farm prices had dropped in that period more than 50 percent; and the ratio of prices received by farmers to the prices they paid

FRANKLIN D. ROOSEVELT AND THE NEW DEAL

for manufactured goods (the parity ratio) had sunk from 89 in 1929 to 55 in 1932 (on a scale using the parity ratio of 1910–14 as base 100). Mobs of farmers halted foreclosures, sometimes physically abusing judges who issued foreclosure orders.

Shortly after his inauguration, Roosevelt sent to Congress a proposal calling for strong federal control of agriculture. The producers of seven basic commodities (wheat, cotton, corn, hogs, rice, tobacco, milk and dairy products) would receive federal payments if they cut their acreage or reduced production. Congressman Joseph Martin, a New England Republican, cried out "We are on our way to Moscow," but the bill boomed through Congress. The task of the Agricultural Adjustment Administration, so created, was to raise farm income to 100 percent of parity by restricting production. At the same time, the law provided a means of ending the farm-mortgage crisis: the refinancing of mortgages through federal land banks. In 1935 a program of compulsory crop controls, voted on in each instance by the farmers concerned, was established. The result was that during Roosevelt's first term, gross farm income rose by 50 percent.

Unhappily, the benefits of this program did not extend to the poorest of all in the countryside —the millions of sharecroppers and tenants. Landowners often expelled their sharecroppers, especially in the South, upon reducing their acreage to qualify for the federal payments. The Farm Bureau, voice of the larger landholders, grew in power while sharecroppers, "tractored off" the land, joined the exodus of farm unemployed that swelled further the population of the hard-hit cities.

Regional Planning

Another great project of the Hundred Days was to take up the longstanding issue of public power. Senator Norris and President Roosevelt toured the Tennessee Valley, paying close attention to the Muscle Shoals facility. However, Roosevelt had far more in mind than the public production and distribution of electric power. A devoted conservationist, he wanted to use the immense physical powers of the Tennessee River to revitalize the whole 40,000 square miles of impoverished countryside that drained into that stream. In the Tennessee Valley the nation could be shown how

regional planning and expert conservation could create a new design for living. The American people, Roosevelt believed, lived too much in congested cities. The countryside must be made attractive again, so that young men would stay and till the soil rather than leave for factory jobs.

Within a month of his inauguration, Roosevelt asked Congress to establish the Tennessee Valley Authority (TVA), "a corporation clothed with the power of government but possessed of the flexibility and initiative of a private enterprise." It was charged to provide a yardstick by which to judge private-power rates elsewhere. In addition, it was to halt floods, provide river navigation, produce fertilizers, revive fisheries, provide recreational resources, reforest denuded watersheds, and lead in bringing about regional planning. In the next nine years the TVA laid the basis for a wholesale revitalization of the entire Tennessee Valley watershed by the building of twenty dams and the improvement of five already in existence. By 1960, its total investment in this and other diverse physical facilities had reached two billion dollars—and the Tennessee Valley had become a model that drew public leaders from all over the world to see how the harnessing of a basic resource could yield such dramatically fruitful results.

Relief Programs

On taking office Roosevelt moved swiftly to help the fifteen million people who were out of work. His first effort was combined with his favorite cause—conservation of national resources. Huge numbers of young men were wandering aimlessly in city streets: why not put them to healthful and socially productive labors in the forests? Within days of the inauguration, Congress responded to Roosevelt's request by establishing the Civilian Conservation Corps (CCC). By June 1933 more than 300,000 young men were at work in more than a thousand forest camps. In the ensuing years a total of 2.5 million CCC men planted trees, built reservoirs, erected flood-control works, constructed bridges and fire towers, cleared out plant diseases, scoured beaches, and rebuilt campgrounds. Continuing until well into the 1940s, the CCC was easily the most popular of the New Deal agencies.

Roosevelt also got Congress to establish a Federal Emergency Relief Administration

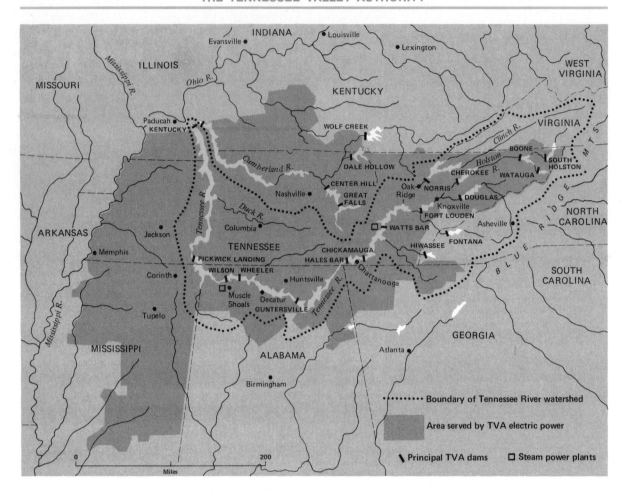

(FERA), which would grant some $500 million to the states for relief programs. "It is socialism," cried Robert Luce of Massachusetts, but the problem was too urgent for such philosophizing, and the bill was rushed through. With Harry L. Hopkins as its chief—he had run Roosevelt's relief program in New York State—the FERA urged that work relief, instead of the dole, be utilized by the states. "I have seen thousands of these defeated, discouraged, hopeless men and women," said Hopkins, "cringing and fawning as they come to ask for public aid. It is a spectacle of national degeneration." When many states lagged in their relief efforts, however, Roosevelt approved the establishment of a Civil Works Administration (CWA), also under Harry Hopkins, by means of which work relief would be provided directly by the federal government. By the end of 1933, so vigorously did Hopkins move, four million men were employed by the CWA. (Ten mil-

lion more remained out of work. Federal work-relief programs were designed to take up only part of the burden; private enterprise, it was hoped, would do the rest.) Hundreds of thousands of projects were launched: building or improving country roads, employing teachers in impoverished schools, erecting schoolhouses, developing playgrounds, and constructing hundreds of airports, parks, waterways, and swimming pools.

Financial and Monetary Reforms

The Banking Act of 1933 completely separated commercial from investment banking, thus making it impossible for unscrupulous bankers any longer to use the funds entrusted to their care by depositors for speculation in the stock market. Furthermore, the Federal Deposit Insurance Cor-

Men working on a Civil Works Administration project in Central Park Zoo, New York City. This kind of program, vastly expanded later in the Works Progress Administration, put millions of men to work in socially valuable projects.

Photoworld FPG

poration (FDIC), another new agency, insured bank deposits up to $5,000. In order to aid the millions of home owners who faced imminent loss of their dwellings, Congress established a Home Owners Loan Corporation that eventually refinanced 20 percent of all the mortgaged homes in the United States. On the day it began operation, distraught home owners formed lines many blocks long while waiting for its doors to open. Meanwhile, a Truth-in-Securities Act (followed by the Securities Exchange Act of 1934) put the stock exchanges under federal supervision for the first time. A Securities and Exchange Commission was created to ensure that investors were given truthful information concerning stocks and bonds and that fraudulent activities would be checked.

Roosevelt was under enormous congressional pressure from rural Democrats of Populist leanings to inflate the currency. This, they insisted, would raise the price level, aid farmers, and stimulate business activity. Responding positively, Roosevelt secured legislation taking the nation off the gold standard (so that it could directly control the volume of its own currency, rather than being subject to international influences in this regard); removed all gold from pub-

lic commerce (save that used for industrial, medical, and jewelry purposes); and put it in Fort Knox to serve as a national trust for backing the currency. Then he set the price at which the American government would buy gold at a level higher than its price on the world market (eventually, thirty-five dollars an ounce), so that gold began flooding into the country. By 1940, Fort Knox held more than three times as much gold as it had in early 1934, and the nation's money supply had soared dramatically. It was this monetary expansion, observes W. Elliot Brownlee, "that seems to have been the fundamental factor in the nation's economic recovery."

Roosevelt was not by philosophy a deficit-spending president, but this expansion in the money supply gave him what he needed: the funds to begin a wide array of social-welfare programs adopted for their intrinsic importance, and not because they poured federal money into the economy and aided recovery, though that was their effect. The president talked continually of keeping the budget balanced, and he meant what he said, raising taxes and cutting back on spending whenever he thought he could, but the total effect of the social-welfare programs was to create deficit spending.

A Booming Recovery

The startling thing now to realize, as revealed by research in economic history, is that the American economy did in fact rebound dramatically from the 1933 depths of the depression. At that point, national production and income were down a third from 1929, and unemployment had reached 25 percent. Then things turned sharply upward: from 1933 to the first peak, in 1937, national productivity soared at an astounding 12 percent a year. America has not to the present time had another four-year period with such a rapid growth of real product and income, and never before had a peacetime expansion surged over so long a period (fifty months) unbrokenly.

In short, the American economy, contrary to the usual historical stereotypes, did not lie prostrate and shattered throughout the 1930s while the New Deal labored frantically to bring it alive. In 1937 real income was marginally higher (3 percent) than it had been in 1929; per-capita income reached the 1929 level in 1939. Recovery was far from complete, for 14 percent of the labor force was still unemployed in 1937 (about seven million people), but that was a distant cry from the 25 percent of a few years earlier. Put in the simplest equation, half of those without jobs in 1933 were at work in 1937. A recession ensued in 1937–38 that broke the momentum of this upward surge, but the recovery resumed thereafter. It did not require the mobilization of World War II to end the depression.

Roosevelt in Power

By late 1934 the foundations of the First New Deal had already been shifting. The spirit of wartime unity evaporated rapidly. National income spurted by more than 20 percent in 1934, and people once again indulged in the luxury of carping and criticizing. The president himself dominated the scene. He had been in the White House almost two years, and the country had grown used to the spectacle of an endlessly busy president who was not only charming and courageous, but also tough, crafty, forceful, and dominant. Hampered by his paralyzed legs, he spent most of his working days in the Oval Room of the White House's west wing, where twice a week he welcomed crowds of reporters for press conferences (337 of them in his first term; 374 in the second;

279 in the third). In the 1920s, Washington, D.C., had not generated much news, the press corps in the town was small, and its standing in the news industry was not high. Now, however, news was pouring out of the national capital, and the president himself was the reporters' best source, their most cooperative and eager supplier. "God, did he make news!" writes David Halberstam in his extraordinary book on the rise of the media, *The Powers That Be* (1979). "Every day there were two or three stories coming out of the White House. [FDR] . . . intended to make the whole federal government his, make it respond to his whim and vision, he did so, and in that struggle he became this century's prime manipulator of the new and increasingly powerful modern media."

Roosevelt was hated by most of the big newspaper publishers, who were conservative Republicans, but he dominated their front pages. And while Hoover had ignored the swiftly-growing new media giant, radio, Franklin Roosevelt was skilled at its use even before he became president. His warm voice and his perfectly crafted speeches poured into the nation's living rooms from millions of radio sets, making the President of the United States for the first time a living presence to the American people. Then he would turn to the movie cameras for the weekly movie theatre newsreels and do it all over again. FDR, in short, was the nation's first *media* president; in fact, it was he who in effect created the modern news media industry. The men who had covered the Washington beat before his time had simply been regional reporters looking for news which related to their part of the country. By the time the era of Roosevelt was completed, the national capital overflowed with reporters, now nationally respected and on the verge of being media personalities themselves, who were skilled in national and international affairs and wrote their stories for the entire country.

The American people at large (or at least most of them) formed a deep affection for and trust in the president. He clearly cared about suffering people, and he provided brave, zestful, imaginative leadership. FDR was a laughing and optimistic man in a country that desperately needed that kind of reassurance, and in his unaffected way he was also a genuinely religious man who turned easily to the Bible and to his God for encouragement, as did most ordinary Americans. He knew dark moods. A Washington correspondent once observed him in an unguarded moment in a holiday retreat with "a kind of drawn grimace of his mouth and over his forehead like a man trying to see something in his mind and suffering." Then all at once, when he saw the reporter, "the smile came back over the look in his eyes and he called out: 'Hello there, Billy. Picking flowers?'" As the correspondent and his companion turned and left, they could "hear his big laugh back of them in the spruce." He was genial, warm, a fun-loving father who annually presided over monster egg-rolling contests involving thousands of children on the hallowed grounds of the White House lawn on Easter mornings.

It was inevitable that such an overpowering personality, who freely used the potentially vast constitutional powers of the presidency, would create both an adoring following of people who loved him and an unalterable opposition of those who hated him. Was he a destroyer of capitalism, as many trumpeted? an advance agent of Moscow, a Jewish communist—as whispering campaigns depicted him to be? The business community has never liked Democratic presidents. The bankers were the first to recoil from the administration, for not only did congressional committees subject them to withering public exposure as they investigated the nation's sick financial system, but Roosevelt in his speeches seemed to give such antagonism his blessing. The president, said one wealthy man, "is a communist of the worst degree. . . . Who but a communist would dare persecute Mr. Morgan and Mr. Mellon?" Then, as the shock waves of the NRA's encouragement of labor and its policies on higher wages and shorter hours began to be felt, the dismay spread wider. Medium-sized and small businesses were directly hit by these measures in ways the big corporations never were: they were squeezed hard to pay higher wages, as well as personally outraged by suddenly defiant workmen. Soon all their frustrations and anger crystallized in hatred of Roosevelt.

The New Deal's Style

Much of the hostility toward the New Deal was revulsion at the whole style of Roosevelt's administration. Just as conservatives had recoiled against the libertarian dress and intellectualism of Thomas Jefferson, so they now took offense at Franklin Roosevelt's Washington. Everywhere there were college professors in shirt sleeves,

cocktails and parties, and brash young men of power. To a significant extent, every great period of reform in American history has been produced by a fresh generation in positions of leadership. So it was with the New Deal. To established political leaders, the spectacle was appalling. Equally upsetting was the rather playful way in which the New Dealers tossed about ideas and refused to be humbled by traditional concepts. Frank Kent, a conservative political analyst, called the New Deal nothing but "third rate college professors and unsuccessful welfare workers." How in the world did such men ever come into such power?

In 1937 the sociologists Robert S. Lynd and Helen Lynd found the business leaders of Muncie, Indiana, convinced that "there has been 'an insane man in the White House,' with 'our best mindless thinkers advising him.' . . . 'We businessmen here aren't just a bunch of Tories,' commented a local banker heatedly, 'but we're scared to death that a lot of reckless political wild men will take everything away from us. We believe in change and know it's going on. We believe in looking ahead, but we don't believe in trying to do it all at once. It'll take two or three hundred years to get the perfect state. Change is slow and big changes won't come in our lifetime, so meanwhile we intend to go ahead and not worry too much about what these changes will be or ought to be. . . .

We've no faith in Roosevelt—his angel wings and smiling words cover up a worse political machine than Hoover ever had. He isn't honest—he talks one way and acts another. He has no courage—or rather courage at the wrong time. He isn't fit to be President and can't hold a candle to Hoover. . . . Sure we need planning. But these bright boys that jam Washington don't know their stuff. Who's a big enough man to plan? We businessmen are afraid of bureaucrats and planners. I've walked through Washington offices, and I never saw so much loafing in a business office. . . . [The] common stockholders [of a business] control [their managers] and if they don't make money, they're turned out. But government employees don't have to make money. . . . By what God-given right do these fellows in Washington think they can do a job so big? It's the very immensity of national planning that makes it impossible. . . . You can't make the world all planned and soft. The strongest and best survive—that's the law of nature after all—always has been and always will be." (*Middletown in Transition* [1937])

Across the country, however, the president was "all but crowned by the people," observed the veteran editor William Allen White after the midterm election of 1934. "There has been no such popular endorsement since the days of

Thomas Jefferson and Andrew Jackson." In that balloting, historic precedent was shattered. The administration's party almost always loses seats in such elections, but instead a flood of voters pushed the massive Democratic majorities even higher. The House witnessed the election of 322 Democrats and only 103 Republicans.

Eleanor Roosevelt: The Nation's First Activist "First Lady"

Much of the White House's extraordinary quality of unprecedented vitality came from Franklin Roosevelt's remarkable wife, Eleanor, the first First Lady to be an active public figure. Before even arriving in Washington she had for ten years been a teacher, a publicist, and a business executive. While FDR had been governor of New York she had had a commercially sponsored radio contract, her newspaper column, "My Day," appeared regularly in national newspapers, and she even edited a nationally-circulated magazine, *Babies—Just Babies*. On controversial topics, she had always been good copy for reporters, for she was a strong Democrat and she cared about the issues. FDR, stuck in his wheelchair, asked her to be his eyes and ears while president, and she traveled endlessly throughout America, visiting and talking and inspecting, and returning home to inform the president what she had seen, and to play a major role in his "kitchen cabinet" —his informal circle of advisers. The first press conferences ever given by a First Lady were held by Eleanor Roosevelt. She insisted on speaking only to women reporters, who were barred by the men reporters from their meetings with the president.

Though Eleanor Roosevelt banned specifically political topics in such press conferences, she was a compassionate woman and she condemned labor sweatshops, counselled women to buy only from merchants who gave their employees decent working conditions, urged the ending of child labor, and pleaded for an outgoing, internationalist foreign policy to help a gravely afflicted world. She was direct, she had no airs— Eleanor Roosevelt thought herself a plain and unattractive woman—and there was a warm graciousness in the tall First Lady's manner which captivated the public (though many women as well as men ridiculed this activist president's wife, saying she neglected her husband and her family, and condemned her reformism as un-American.)

She spoke endlessly to women, urging them to take a reforming role in the nation to help it rise out of the depression. *It's Up to the Women*—a 40,000-word book comprised of her articles and speeches which quickly appeared after she entered the White House—not only contained chatty advice on menus and household budgets, but also appealed to women to lead the campaign for social justice, support and even become members of labor unions, create consumers' groups to monitor prices, and get into politics. The "understanding heart of women," and their special vitality, she said, must shape the new order of things. Women should lead the movement to end war; help youth; work to abolish poverty, and to enhance the rights of minorities (black Americans quickly recognized in Eleanor Roosevelt one of their most determined advocates in the New Deal leadership). Selfishness, greed, an unmastered hunger for profit: these, she said, had brought the United States to its present disaster. Now Americans must learn the lesson of "interdependence," of community, of working collectively to solve their national crisis. In fact, Eleanor Roosevelt was much more radical in her reform ideas than her husband.

Almost daily she had conferences with Harry Hopkins, the relief administrator, on work projects for unemployed people, especially for women and the young. She prodded and pushed FDR leftward, and she got him to appoint many women to important positions in the New Deal administration—a largely unprecedented phenomenon in the national government. Eleanor Roosevelt was not long in the White House before women had a far larger role in the national organization of the Democratic party. In 1934 her regular radio talks began again (with commercial sponsorship), so that by this medium and her newspaper column, she could resume her favorite role: teacher, only this time to the nation. Appeals for progressive education; campaigns against illiteracy; speeches at women's prisons; lecture tours around the country: wherever she went her cultivated diction and singular clarity of speech, her high-pitched voice, and her unaffected dignity of bearing captured attention and affection. Eleanor Roosevelt, in her remarkable determination to serve the nation, greatly broadened and elevated the ideal of the woman in public office.

The Fifth Party System Takes Form

From about 1894 the nation's politics had been operating within the larger outlines of the fourth, or Progressive Era, party system. Built essentially on the shrinking of the Democratic party into a Southern and partially a western party inspired by William Jennings Bryan and his rural radicalism, the fourth party system had seen the ethnic minorities of the northern cities swing Republican in the depression of the 1890s. The fourth party system, therefore, had been characterized most of the time (the Wilson years were the exception) by a solidly Democratic South and a solidly Republican North, Middle West, and Far West. WASP America had been in the ascendant, politically, economically, and culturally.

The great depression that began in late 1929 shattered that system. The WASP coalition broke apart as almost every voting group in the United States turned Democratic. Even Scandinavians, legendary for their traditional Republicanism, joined Catholics and Jews in voting for FDR in cities such as Chicago. In 1932, Franklin Roosevelt received almost as large a vote in the WASP countryside and smaller towns as in the metropolitan areas. The elections of 1934 confirmed the new pattern. By 1936 Roosevelt's voting base was so enormous that only Maine and Vermont were left in the Republican column. The fifth, or New Deal, party system, which endured until the turning point elections in the years 1968–80 (to be discussed later), had arrived. Its powerful Democratic base in the cities, where the ethnic majorities had returned en masse to their ancient Democratic home, was revealed in the fact that between 1932 and 1936 the Democratic plurality in the nation's twelve largest cities leaped 80 percent, an unprecedented occurrence. And the countryside, North and South, was Democratic. The Republicans had ignored for too long the economic distress of the farmers, traditionally (in the North and West) one of their great sources of strength. A new collectivism, the inexorable product of overproduction, had taken over the rural mind. The Roosevelt revolution was transforming the political landscape.

The Democrats, in short, were becoming once more the nation's majority party. Black America swung almost in a body away from the Republicans and moved to the Democrats. As tens of thousands of Afro-Americans moved out of the South (where they were effectively denied the vote), they joined the northern city masses and voted loyally for Roosevelt. Not only did he provide jobs for the city unemployed, but his administration—notably through the voices of Eleanor Roosevelt, Interior Secretary Harold Ickes, and relief administrator Harry Hopkins—also spread the notion that its sympathies were warmly problack. How substantial were the benefits that black America received from the New Deal is a matter in question, but the overwhelming majority of black voters clearly felt that the president was doing everything he could for them in a difficult situation.

Ideas Begin Shifting

Despite his popularity, Roosevelt knew at the beginning of 1935 that things were not as well the nation seemed to think. The surge of the Hundred Days was over, and the economy was settling on a new plateau. Panic had disappeared, the downward spiral was halted, but there were still ten million people unemployed, and the number seemed fixed. No one was more baffled than the president himself. He kept a steady stream of businessmen, academics, and government leaders coming to the White House to talk about the state of the nation and to search for new ideas.

As the government drifted along, radical prophets spoke up. Governor Floyd Olson, Farmer-Labor governor of Minnesota, said he hoped "the present system of government goes right down to hell." He went on to demand that the "key industries of the United States [be] taken over by the government." The Reverend Charles E. Coughlin of Detroit built a huge radio audience with attacks against capitalism and the "timid" New Deal. Bankers, he said, were the origin of the world's sufferings. "Modern capitalism," Coughlin insisted, "is not worth saving." He recommended that the government nationalize the banking system and take over the production of power, light, oil, and natural gas.

Most spectacular of all the new radicals was Huey Long, a senator from Louisiana. As governor of that state, he had inaugurated sweeping reforms while erecting an unchallenged dictatorship unparalleled in American history. Soon he launched a "Share-Our-Wealth" program, which called for government confiscation of all incomes above a certain level and their redistribution to less affluent people. Thousands of local clubs were founded so that his message could be spread, and millions received his mailed literature. Huge crowds fought to see him when he spoke in northern cities.

It was clear that the First New Deal could never survive this bubbling radicalism. Everywhere one listened, whether it was to Long's Share-Our-Wealth campaign or to the Marxian revolutionary talk that filled Greenwich Village cocktail parties and burst into a wide array of cultural outlets sponsored by the Communist party, anticapitalist oratory abounded. With one fifth of the work force still unemployed, it was no longer enough to preach wartime unity and centralized planning.

The Brandeisians and the Spenders

In the Supreme Court building Justice Louis D. Brandeis, now an intense old man with flaring white hair, nodded his head vigorously when such things were said to him. From the beginning of the New Deal, a key group of Roosevelt's lieutenants had gathered about this fascinating old battler from the days of Wilsonian liberalism. He roundly criticized the First New Deal because it accepted and warmly cooperated with the largest business corporations. It was foolish, he believed, to say that the answer to the nation's problems was the building of a large federal government, for this went beyond human capacities. The real solution, Brandeis said, lay in whittling everything down to human size, in returning control to local regions rather than lodging it in a Washington bureau. Only then could democracy and individualism revive.

Brandeis's chief disciple was Felix Frankfurter, a professor at Harvard Law School, who, as a close confidant of Roosevelt, had placed bright young men in major posts throughout the Roosevelt administration. As a group they had been uneasy under the First New Deal, condemning its fostering of monopoly and its friendliness to businessmen. Now, led by Frankfurter, they urged Roosevelt to recognize that business-government cooperation had failed, that centralized planning was a snare and a delusion, and that the real need was to take up once more the traditional Democratic assault on corporations and banks.

Frankfurter, however, believed that it was not sufficient just to renew the assault on wealth and power; that, by itself, would not bring prosperity. In search of ideas, he went to Britain in 1934, where he spent a year in close conversation with intellectuals and government leaders. He returned with word of a solution proposed by the English economist John Maynard Keynes—huge government spending. The essential idea was to place purchasing power directly in the hands of the consumers so that they could begin buying once more. This would require heavy spending through unemployment relief, public-works construction, agricultural subsidies, and other such programs. It would also require bringing the banking system under full public control in order to make effective regulation of money policy possible.

Roosevelt distrusted the idea, for he was conservative in his fiscal beliefs and talked always of the need for a balanced budget, as did most world leaders at this time. But the spending proposal dinned constantly in his ears, coming from American sources as well as from Britain. A group of American economists—chief among them Paul Douglas of Chicago—had been saying for some time that governmental spending would create lasting recovery, and the idea was spreading to such leaders of the banking community as Marriner S. Eccles of Salt Lake City, who urged it on congressional committees. Always the pragmatist in search of solutions, Roosevelt finally agreed, and in January 1935 he startled Congress with a request for the largest single appropriation of funds in American history to that time—five billion dollars for a program of work relief. What happened, in fact, was that America, preeminently the world's free-enterprise country, turned toward government spending to counteract depression far more dramatically than any other of the industrialized nations, save Germany and Sweden.

The Works Progress Administration

Thus was born the Works Progress Administration (WPA), whose goal was the employment of 3.5 million workers. The "social conscience of the New Deal," it signified once and for all that the federal government cared for the suffering millions as well as for the organized interests. Through 1941 it spent more than eleven billion dollars on some 250,000 small-scale construction projects, building or improving more than 2,500 hospitals, 5,900 school buildings, 1,000 airfields, and nearly 13,000 playgrounds. At the same time, the WPA employed actors, writers, and artists. Its Federal Theatre Project supported drama companies throughout the nation. The Federal Writers' Project created about 1,000 publications and sponsored innumerable local historical-research projects. Artists were employed by the Federal Art Project to launch teaching programs in painting and crafts and to decorate the interiors of hundreds of public buildings with murals and other artworks, "some of it good," observed Roosevelt, "some of it not so good, but all of it native, human, eager, and alive. . . . " Young people were aided by the National Youth Administration, which gave part-time jobs to 600,000 students in college and 1.5 million in high school.

Of enormous cultural impact in the nation—perhaps more sweeping in its effects than any other piece of New Deal legislation—was the creation of the Rural Electrification Administration (REA). Designed to spread electrical lines into the countryside, it transformed country life. "Every city 'white way,'" wrote one observer, "ends abruptly at the city limits. Beyond lies darkness." Nine out of ten farms had no electricity. Farm wives labored in almost medieval conditions while their city counterparts enjoyed illumination and electric appliances such as refrigerators, washing machines, and vacuum cleaners. The REA enabled farmers' cooperatives to borrow millions of dollars from the government to dispel the darkness. Four out of ten American farms had acquired electricity by 1941, and by 1950 nine out of ten.

The Supreme Court Takes a Hand

Meanwhile, the basic laws of the First New Deal had been making their way upward through the courts, undergoing challenges as to their constitutionality. Everyone knew that the legislation was threatened by the makeup of the Supreme Court, which contained four justices who were hard-core conservatives unbendingly opposed to a vigorous federal government. In 1935, the New Dealers' fears were borne out. In a unanimous decision warmly concurred in by Justice Brandeis, the Court threw out the NRA as unconstitutional in the case of *Schechter Poultry Company* v. *United States*, on the ground that Congress had wrongfully delegated its lawmaking powers to an executive commission. In addition, the justices ruled that the Schechter Poultry Company was engaged wholly in local trade, whereas the federal government's authority extended only to the control of interstate trade. The fulcrum of the First New Deal was broken.

In subsequent cases the Court laid waste to much of the rest of the First New Deal. It threw out the AAA on the ground that agriculture was a local activity and not interstate commerce, and it nullified the Coal Conservation Act, which had established federal regulation of coal production, on the same ground. In sum, the Court (usually by majorities of five to four) effectively denied Congress any powers over farming, mining, manufacturing, and labor relations. Then, in *Morehead* v. *New York* (1936), it even held that states could not regulate hours, wages, and labor conditions on the principle that the Fourteenth Amendment guaranteed freedom of contract.

The Second Hundred Days

In June 1935 President Roosevelt responded by sending an avalanche of major new bills to Congress, thus launching the Second Hundred Days and what is usually termed the Second New Deal. Five pieces of legislation, he insisted, had to be passed before the legislators could leave the Capitol for their summer vacations: a social-security bill, legislation directed toward putting the money supply under public control, a law to aid labor unions, a public-utility holding-company measure, and a soak-the-rich income-tax law. In the succeeding months Congress bent wearily to its work and hammered through every one of Roosevelt's proposals, which in sum constituted perhaps the most far-reaching reform program it had ever enacted.

Frances Perkins, the first woman to hold a cabinet post, had as secretary of labor been urging that the New Deal make a much broader attack upon the problem of personal insecurity, especially among the helpless and in the family: the old, the physically handicapped, the mothers of children with no father to provide support. Perkins was the symbolic figure of the social-worker revolution that for forty years had been remaking the whole nature of city government in the United States. For twenty years in New York State she had been an effective social reformer, and out of this long experience with suffering people she came to her high office in Washington convinced that something needed to be done for them on a *national* level. The needy in every state had to be helped, not simply those in the wealthier and more enlightened states. Perkins could not count on the aid of organized labor: it distrusted anything done by the government. But she could count on such urban liberal reformers as Senator Robert Wagner of New York.

For many years, among American reformers there had been a great interest in the programs of unemployment and old-age insurance that had long been in existence in Great Britain and Germany. The United States, it was clear, was far behind in these public manifestations of social humanitarianism. And in FDR there was finally a president who cared about such things. "I see no reason why every child," he said to Perkins, "from the day he is born, shouldn't be a member of the social security system . . . cradle to the grave. . . . " It should be an insurance system, solidly based in regular contributions by both employees and employers, so that no future politician could take the program's funds away for some other purpose. Thus, it was to be self-supporting, by means of its own special taxes.

Proposed in January 1935, the social-security bill produced an uproar from conservatives. From Alfred Sloan of General Motors: "It will destroy initiative, thrift, and individual responsibility"; James Donnelly of the Illinois Manufacturers Association: it would "sooner or later bring about the inevitable abandonment of private capitalism"; Charles Denby of the American Bar Association: "the downfall of Rome began with [such measures]"; George Chandler of the Ohio Chamber of Commerce: no one will work, no one will save to provide for old age or widowhood, there will be moral decay, financial bankruptcy, and the collapse of the United States government. John Tabor, a New York congressman, was equally alarmed: "Never in the history of the world has any measure been brought in here so insidiously designed as to prevent business recovery, to enslave workers, and to prevent any possibility of the employers providing jobs for the American people." Every Republican in the House of Representatives save one voted against the bill.

When Roosevelt swung behind the bill,

however, it rolled to passage by large majorities in both houses. In its final form the bill solved one of the great arguments that had raged over social security: it assigned to the states the responsibility of implementing the system. Washington would only collect and redistribute the money to the states, on a matching basis. This approach had great drawbacks, however. In fact, one of the problems left behind by the New Deal was its heavy reliance throughout on the state governments, long one of the weakest links in the federal system, to carry out the social reforms enacted by Congress. It was county-level officials who established the welfare departments, staffed them, supervised them, and paid their employees. The result was a crazy-quilt unemployment-compensation and welfare system with widely varying benefits, often warped in strange ways by segregation and other forms of racism. However, by this means state and county governments were brought directly in touch with millions of Americans in an unprecedented way—a helping, supportive way—and this initiated a long learning process that has had an immense impact on American life. The old, the jobless, the sick, the needy, the blind, the mothers who had children to care for and no husbands, the children themselves: all were now aided by the Social Security Board, through local agencies. A historic break had been made with all past American social policy. Many people were left out at the beginning (domestic and farm workers, among others), but as the years went by, successive administrations enlarged the outreach of the system, until in the 1960s it even began to provide for medical care. A wide door had been opened to the kind of social-welfare state that urban liberalism had been heading toward for many years.

New Economic Legislation

The strictly economic legislation of the Second New Deal was founded not—as in the First New Deal—on telling businessmen what to do, but on telling them what not to do. This essentially Brandeisian idea was embodied best in the bill concerning gigantic utility holding companies. Long condemned by the public, utility holding companies—sometimes piled on top of one another to the seventh level—had seemed the expression *par excellence* of inefficient, exploitive "bigness."

The goal of the bill was to restore a kind of economic democracy to the utility industry by breaking it up into much smaller and more realistic units. The electric-power companies seemed like great octopuses that exploited vast regions for the sole purpose of paying stock dividends on functionless holding companies. They had corrupted state legislatures in order to escape meaningful regulation, and now they poured millions of dollars into a frantic effort to stave off federal action. But Congress was aroused, and the bill went through, empowering the Securities and Exchange Commission to break up any holding company, beyond the first level, that was not in the public interest. Within three years, practically all the great utility empires were dissolved.

The banking legislation of the Second Hundred Days completed the process begun under Woodrow Wilson. His Federal Reserve System had given public authorities only limited influence over the actual supply of money that bankers issued, leaving the day-to-day operations of the Federal Reserve System in the hands of private bankers. It was time, critics said, to end this arrangement. The national government must finally assume as its sovereign responsibility the crucial power to regulate the size of the money supply. Then, and only then, would it be able to manage the nation's economy and prevent the onset of depressions. If Roosevelt was radical at all, it was in his inherited Democratic distrust of bankers, and he warmly supported a bill drawn up by Marriner Eccles that would transfer control over the money market from the bankers in Wall Street to the federal government in Washington, D.C. This led to a loud and turbulent struggle, for bankers had long regarded control of the money market as theirs practically by divine right. Ogden Mills cried out that the bill would "throw us back five hundred years." But Franklin Roosevelt was not to be denied. The bill as passed created a new Federal Reserve Board in Washington that had all necessary powers to put the money supply under public control. To ensure his victory, Roosevelt appointed Eccles the first chairman of the board.

The delighted Roosevelt, excited and confident now that his new program was rolling so well, then began pushing for a soak-the-rich tax bill. The Democrats gave the bill a standing ovation in the House when they heard it read, but an outcry of rage welled up from the rich and from the business community (Roosevelt had also proposed heavy taxes on corporation income). William Randolph Hearst called the proposal "essentially Communism." The struggle over the bill went on all summer, with the result that the final measure was fairly mild. Corporations were taxed very little; inheritances were left alone; but rates on high incomes were raised. Ironically, however, the "wealth-tax" bill did little to redistribute wealth. By the end of the 1930s upper-income groups were still commanding the same share of the national income they had received before the depression.

Organized Labor in the Economy

Perhaps the most transforming of all the laws enacted during the Second New Deal was the one that created the National Labor Relations Board. Thereafter, the relationship between capital and labor, at all times one of the most fundamental in any society, was drastically changed.

It is important to understand some basic realities concerning labor and labor unions. The economy is complex. Therefore, the history of each union, indeed of each worker, varies widely in each part of it. When particular industries are in a precarious condition—when competition is harsh and constant, markets fluctuate, and not only is the cost of doing business high but such cost cannot easily be passed on to the consumer—employers tend to be resistant to unionization to begin with, or to any wage demands made by unions that may raise the cost of operations (or to changes in working conditions that will do the same). They fight back angrily, even violently, to resist workers' requests. In such circumstances strikes and industrial warfare are frequent (as in the case of the large steel and automobile industries before unionization, or agriculture even now). Where these conditions do not exist, industrial relations are relatively peaceful, since employers have assured profits and can raise their prices to make up for added costs. Union organizers learned early on that it was usually easier to work with large, quasi-monopolistic firms than with smaller, struggling operations.

Also, there has not historically been a close relationship between unionization and the general level of worker income. It is true that in depression years unionized workers are better able to prevent wage declines. However, the great surge in average income in the 1920s, when the material conditions of life and national productivity improved proportionately more than in any other decade, did not occur in highly unionized industries. The total demand for labor in a particular part of the economy appears to have been far more powerful than collective bargaining in raising wage rates. Unions, in fact, have commonly recognized this. When a particular industry has been in difficult straits, they have tended not to push for exceptional wage gains. "If the company doesn't have it," one union leader observed, "we can't get it."

Workers' wages, furthermore, tend to rise more easily in those industries where employers have been able to invest more and more money in machines to do a lot of the work (making their operations, as economists say, capital-intensive). Employers in such circumstances are more ready to raise wages because the proportion of labor cost in the final product is less and less. In the textile, furniture, food and beverage, and printing and publishing industries, where the proportion of labor cost ran as high as 50 percent in the 1920s (as against 35 percent in the economy nationally in 1929), workers tended to be the most poverty-stricken, and labor-management conflict the harshest and most consistent. When in the coal mines in the 1940s and on the docks at a later period labor unions allowed major shifts to the use of machines, the number of jobs declined sharply, but wages were higher. All of this is not to say that unionization has had no effect whatever on wages. From the 1960s on, for example, unionized workers have received wages at levels up to 15 percent higher than the nonunionized (though sometimes there is no differential at all), a fact having a major impact upon the standard of living.

The urge to unionize has not historically relied simply upon the demand for higher wages and better working conditions and hours, though these have been pressing considerations, especially during the depression. It has arisen also from the hunger of workingmen to get some control over their lives, some limitations upon the autocratic bossism that they hated. The labor historian Herbert Gutman has shown how powerful an emotion this was in stimulating the emerging labor-union movement of the late nineteenth century, and given the small proportion of working people who were successfully unionized in the

1920s (perhaps 10 percent), this anger at "proletarianization" persisted. Furthermore, workers in steel production, among other industries, still worked extremely long hours in the 1920s and 1930s, wage rates were often extremely low, and the conditions of work dangerous and demeaning.

Organized Labor Struggles to Rise

Employers in the 1920s launched a powerful nationwide antiunion crusade, calling for what was termed the American Plan: nonunion "open shops." Workers were required to sign "yellow-dog" contracts agreeing never to join a union. Big steel producers refused to sell steel to firms that hired union labor, and the National Open Shop Association paid spies to infiltrate the ranks of workers and find out which of them were secretly members of unions. Some twenty-two state manufacturers' associations agreed never to negotiate with a union—that is, never to accept the principle of collective bargaining. The United States attorney general vowed that the government's power would always be used to maintain the open shop. Courts issued hundreds of injunctions ordering unions to cease strikes and return to work. On occasion, unions were forbidden even to carry on discussions among themselves, write, telephone, or in any other way communicate about a strike. The National Guard, called out time and again, aided employers. Thus, of 36 million available workers in 1932, only 1 in 10 belonged to a union. Of the 50,000 workers in the steel industry, only 8,600 of them were organized; of 8 million retail clerks and salesmen, only 7,200 of them belonged to a union.

Under President Hoover, labor had won a major victory in the passage of the Norris–La Guardia Act in 1930. After forty years of struggle, labor finally received recognition of its right to organized existence: court injunctions could at least no longer be used to prevent the formation of a union. Then under Roosevelt came Section 7A of the NRA law, which required that employers allow their workers to organize. The result was a massive awakening of long-dormant unions. Organizers rushed about proclaiming the news. John L. Lewis of the United Mine Workers told miners that the president wanted them to organize. From 60,000 members in 1932, the United Mine Workers soared to 300,000 in 1933 and 1934. While

FRANKLIN D. ROOSEVELT AND THE NEW DEAL

other older unions grew in similarly explosive fashion, the mass-production industries were invaded by unions practically for the first time.

Employers fought back, however, by refusing outright in some cases to admit the principle of unionization into their NRA codes, and by forming hundreds of company unions (dominated by the employer) to keep out the AFL and other independent unions. NRA officials stood back, often allowing an employer to bargain with a small union and ignore another that represented the majority of his workers. Labor, therefore, soon began striking to get what it was entitled to. In fact, for five years, from the middle of 1933 to early 1938, America witnessed a full-scale outbreak of class warfare such as had not been seen for generations. It was appalling, frightening, a daily sensation in the newspapers, a transfixing spectacle for middle-class America that went on month after month, year after year. Anarchy, revolution, the tearing down of law and order, the rising of tens of thousands of formerly powerless ethnic workers to seize control of the national economy: these, to many Americans, seemed to be the alarming issues being fought out.

The result was a massive outpouring of support and sympathy to any effort aimed at putting down the apparent insurrection. Troops were again mobilized by local authorities to break up picket lines and allow strikebreakers through. In 1933, 15 strikers were murdered on picket lines; the next year, 40 more; in 1935 and 1936, 48 died. When in Rhode Island strikers and troops clashed in the streets, an employers' journal declared that "a few hundred funerals will have a quieting influence." Some 18,000 strikers were arrested from 1934 through 1936, and it is impossible to know how many were simply beaten or wounded. In January 1936, workers unveiled a dramatic new tactic. At the Firestone plant in Akron, Ohio, workers simply sat down at their places, refusing either to work or to leave, and production halted. This tactic, the sit-down strike, spread like wildfire across the country, producing an electric sensation. Workers were *taking over* the employers' property!

The bloodiest encounter was the Memorial Day Massacre in South Chicago in 1937. A column of several thousand strikers marching toward a steel mill, singing songs and chanting slogans, was halted by a force of police who suddenly opened point-blank fire. Five died instantly; five died later; almost sixty were wounded, either by bullets or by savagely swung billy clubs that crushed ribs, arms, eyes, and skulls. Chicago newspapers praised the massacre of the "murderous mob"; it had helped halt the "revolutionary tide."

In 1937, Chicago police massacre strikers, revealing the attitude of local governments around the nation to the growing union movement. Years of such near warfare rocked the nation well into the 1950s.

Chicago Historical Society

The National Labor Relations Board Created

Until the violent outbreaks of the mid 1930s, the federal government had simply held back from labor-management relations. Franklin Roosevelt had never been more than mildly friendly to organized labor. Indeed, middle-class liberals like Frances Perkins had long ago given up on the labor unions, believing they had no new ideas for social reform, and had turned their attentions to improving the conditions of workers' lives by direct legislation. Section 7A of the NRA Act had only *allowed* organization; it had not actually forced employers to accept the unions.

For a long time, however, Senator Robert Wagner of New York, ever labor's devoted friend, had been urging the national government to move in strongly to redress the unequal balance between employers and employees and thereby make a powerful impact upon national recovery and social justice. Only if this were done, he said, would stability and peace reemerge on the country's labor-management front. Furthermore, only if this were done would labor be able to get a large enough share of profits, in the form of higher wages, to be able to consume more, have a higher standard of living, and therefore contribute to the revival of the economy.

But his bill languished in Congress, deprived of the president's support. Then in 1935, when Roosevelt switched directions and launched the Second New Deal, everything changed. The creation of the National Labor Relations Board (NLRB), through enactment of the Wagner bill, inaugurated a historic change in the relation between Washington and the labor movement. The government now moved vigorously to ensure not only the right of organization but also the right to bargain collectively in fair and equitable conditions. The NLRB was given power to order employers to bargain with the unions that represented the majority of their workers, after elections that it supervised. It could also prevent employers from utilizing "unfair" practices designed to force employees away from the union. No similar prohibition of unfair practices was established against the unions.

In its first five years of life, the NLRB handled nearly 30,000 cases, two out of three of them dealing with unfair employer practices. It settled over 2,000 strikes, and held almost 3,500 elec-

tions in which workers were free to decide whether or not to have a bargaining agent—that is, a particular union to speak for them collectively to the employer. By 1945, the NLRB had presided over 36,000 cases involving unfair labor practices and 38,000 cases involving employee representation. Some six million workers had cast ballots in NLRB-supervised elections—24,000 of them.

Labor-management relations were simply revolutionized. Employers could no longer interfere with the rights of workers to organize and to strike. Indeed, to enforce this point, the NLRB required employers to give some 300,000 employees almost $9 million in back wages. Labor spies were prohibited; antiunion propaganda was prohibited; the yellow-dog contract was outlawed; and blacklists, as well as any other employer device for discriminating against workers on the ground of their union activities, were outlawed. It was now lawful to picket peacefully, and to establish a "closed shop" (in which only members of the union could be hired). Company unionism (unions created by employers) was practically destroyed. A social revolution a century in the making had been brought to its effective conclusion, as far as public policy and strong administration could achieve its goals.

Labor Divides

Labor was now free to push ahead on all fronts. But it had deeply divisive problems within its own ranks. Perhaps the most dramatic involved the traditional loyalty of the AFL to organizing workmen only by their skills and crafts, not by industry. This produced weakness and disarray in the face of powerful employers. In 1933 two young men in Akron, Ohio, organized 4,500 formerly unorganized rubber workers in the tire factories into a single union. When it applied for affiliation with the AFL, however, officials from that body arrived at the plants and divided the workers into nineteen craft unions: box makers, blacksmiths, masons, carpenters, pipe fitters, printers, sheet-metal workers, and so on. To get such a heterogeneous group of small organizations to agree on a common policy against the employer would be practically impossible. Furthermore, the newly unionized workers tended to be much angrier at capital, to which they had been subservient for so long, and far more ready than older AFL members to strike over many different issues. The auto unionists went out on a total of 100 strikes in 1933, and the same occurred in the aluminum and cement industries, among many others. In each case, workers demanded the right to have one union industry-wide. When faced with this challenge in the steel industry, the AFL expelled three fourths of the members of a new union because they insisted upon such tactics.

Around John L. Lewis, the powerful and flamboyant head of the United Mine Workers, an opposition to William Green and the other established leaders of the AFL developed. In late 1935, Lewis and other disaffected AFL union heads split the AFL wide apart by forming the Congress of Industrial Organizations (CIO). Its goal was to build industrial unions in mass-production factories, where the craft-oriented AFL had as yet made little impression. Early in 1937 Lewis won a stunning victory in the steel industry when United States Steel recognized the CIO union as the employees' bargaining agent. Like other large employers, "Big Steel" was ready to accept the new labor-management relationship that the Wagner Act called for. The auto industries resisted, which led to massive labor outbreaks in 1936 and 1937, but in time labor won. By 1938, the CIO contained 3.7 million members. Meanwhile the AFL, amazed at the CIO's successes, was stung to new activity. It too began organizing unskilled workers in large numbers, so that by 1938 it had 3.4 million members.

John L. Lewis, head of the United Mine Workers and president of the CIO, put labor's case in September 1937: "Five of the corporations in the steel industry elected to resist collective bargaining and undertook to destroy the steel-workers' union. These companies filled their plants with industrial spies, assembled depots of guns and gas bombs, established barricades, controlled their communities with armed thugs, leased the police power of cities, and mobilized the military power of a state to guard them against the intrusion of collective bargaining within their plants.

"During this strike eighteen steel workers were either shot to death or had their brains clubbed out by police, or armed thugs in the pay of the steel companies. . . . The murder of these unarmed men has never been publicly rebuked by any authoritative officer of the State or Federal government. . . .

"Labor does not seek industrial strife. It wants peace, but a peace with justice. . . . The United States Chamber of Commerce, the National Association of Manufacturers, and similar groups . . . are encouraging a systematic organization of vigilante groups to fight unionization under the sham pretext of local interests. They equip these vigilantes with tin hats, wooden clubs, gas masks, and lethal weapons and train them in the arts of brutality and oppression . . . financed under the shabby pretext that the C.I.O. movement is communistic. . . . Do those who have hatched this foolish cry of communism in the C.I.O. fear the increased influence of labor in our democracy? Do they fear its influence will be cast on the side of shorter hours, a better system of distributed employment, better homes for the underprivileged, social security for the aged, a fairer distribution of the national income? . . . Labor has suffered just as our farm population has suffered from a viciously unequal distribution of the national income. In the exploitation of both classes of workers has been the source of panic and depression. . . ." (John L. Lewis, *Vital Speeches* [1937])

Black Americans and Organized Labor

These events produced epochal changes for blacks in the organized-labor movement. In general, most AFL unions had excluded black Americans for decades, the United Mine Workers and the Longshoremen being major exceptions. These were essentially industrial unions, though affiliated with the AFL, and this type of union has always tended to be more egalitarian and racially tolerant, since it enrolls all workers in a given industry rather than just a select skilled group. In 1917–19 white workers, who hated blacks not only on racial grounds but as competitors for unskilled jobs and as strikebreakers, had set off huge race riots in Chicago and other midwestern cities. The great migration of blacks out of the South to work in the North during the First World War had doubled the black population in Chicago, from 50,000 to over 100,000. In 1910, blacks made up only 6 percent of the work force in that city; in 1920, 32 percent. They often regarded the white employers as their natural allies, not the racist unions.

An extraordinary black leader, A. Philip Randolph, brought the first all-black union with a national base into existence in 1925: the Brotherhood of Sleeping Car Porters. By "all the gods of sanity and sense," he said, "Brotherhood men are a crucial challenge to the nordic creed of the white race's superiority. For only white men are supposed to organize for power, for justice and freedom." Against enormous odds, both within and outside of the black community, he built his union into a powerful and nationally recognized body by the late 1930s.

Then came John L. Lewis's Congress of Industrial Organizations, which was of great aid to the cause of black laboring men. It was not completely successful in suppressing racial segregation and discrimination within its ranks, especially in the South, but it nonetheless made an incalculable contribution to opening the ranks of organized labor to black men and women. Militantly progressive on the whole range of social issues, the CIO espoused racial justice as one of its central concerns. CIO affiliates capitalized on the acute labor shortages of World War II to gain major concessions for black workers from employers. In 1939 the median income among nonwhite workers was 41 percent that of whites; by 1950 it was 60 percent, wages for black persons during this period having risen much faster than those for whites. Indeed, the years 1942–45 witnesses the most important income changes for black Americans since the Civil War.

The Election of 1936

When Roosevelt began touring the country for his 1936 presidential campaign, enormous crowds turned out to cheer him. He had, in truth, impressive accomplishments to report to the nation. Six million jobs had been created since his inauguration, and national income was 50 percent higher in 1936 than it had been in 1933. The output of factories had almost doubled. Corporations had lost two billion dollars in 1933, but in 1936 they made a profit of five billion dollars. During the same period the net income of farm operators grew almost four times. There were still eight million people unemployed, but prosperity seemed clearly on the way. Gone were the long soup lines, the apple sellers, the pathetic "Hoovervilles" (shantytowns) outside every city.

The result was one of the most sweeping victories in American history. Only Maine and Vermont cast their electoral votes for Alfred M. Landon, the Republican nominee. Republicans in Congress were reduced to practically a corporal's guard. Landon received 16.7 million popular votes, but an avalanche of 27.7 million votes went

to Franklin Roosevelt. Without question, the American people wished to see the Second New Deal continued.

Second-Term Disasters

Roosevelt opened his second term with a speech clearly signifying that he intended to push ahead on the social-welfare front. "I see one-third of a nation ill-housed, ill-clad, ill-nourished," he said. But what he actually began with was a proposal that the Supreme Court be reorganized. The nation was stunned. Nothing had been said of this in the previous campaign; no congressional leaders had been warned; and Roosevelt's argument for his proposal was obviously a deception. The federal court system was clogged with work, he said, because the judges were too old to cope with the work load. His only desire, he told Congress, was to make the system more efficient. He asked for power to appoint up to six more Supreme Court justices (and forty-five justices in lower federal courts) to supplement the work of those judges who refused to retire at age seventy. Everyone knew this was not his real motive. The fact was that the Supreme Court was dominated by a conservative majority, and Roosevelt wished to give it a New Deal coloration. Even liberal Democrats in Congress rose up in rebellion, and public opinion swung strongly in their support. Perhaps no leading American politician had made so disastrous a miscalculation since 1854, when Stephen A. Douglas wrote the Kansas-Nebraska Act. FDR was openly challenging one of American republicanism's oldest and most honored principles: separation of powers. The instant nationwide response revealed how alive and powerful in the American mind the venerable national ideology still was.

Roosevelt clung doggedly to his request, frittering away months of Congress's time and further alienating the public. Meanwhile, Justice Owen Roberts swung over to the liberal side and began providing a majority vote in favor of New Deal laws. When the National Labor Relations Act was ruled constitutional, it was clear that Roosevelt would have no further resistance from the Court. In effect, that body had made a historic decision: finally agreeing with Louis Brandeis, it was going to give up its decades-long struggle to impose its own economic beliefs on Congress and the president. Thereafter, until it took up the issue of civil rights in the mid 1950s, the Supreme Court consciously turned away from the activist philosophy that had motivated it from the days of Grover Cleveland.

The Second New Deal Revives

In April 1938, after a severe economic slump in 1937 caused by a drastic cutback in federal spending, Roosevelt began moving decisively again. He returned to the spending philosophy, securing from Congress close to four billion dollars for public works and huge increases for the WPA. At the same time, he gave warm support to an antitrust campaign begun by Thurman Arnold in the attorney general's office. Whereas Theodore Roosevelt had employed 5 attorneys in his antitrust campaign, Arnold had almost 200 searching out business wrongdoing. The chief objective was to break the "managed-price" stranglehold that great corporations seemed to exert on the economy; that is, instead of lowering prices when demand dropped off, they kept prices high and simply reduced production. This, it was said, was a fundamental reason why the national economy could not recover from the depression. If big corporations were broken up, as the Brandeisians urged, then they could no longer ignore the market, but in response to competition would be forced to lower prices and keep production high, thereby creating jobs.

Meanwhile, Congress enacted the last major reforms of the New Deal. It had refused to allow Roosevelt to "pack" the Supreme Court, but it approved a number of procedural changes that greatly hastened the Court's work. The Bituminous Coal Act revived the centralized-planning arrangements that the industry had had under the NRA, making it in effect a public utility. The Farm Security Administration was established to help migratory farm workers secure better housing and assist tenant farmers in buying their land. By 1946 it had helped 870,000 farm families rehabilitate their properties and had lent funds to 41,000 farmers for the purchase of their land. The United States Housing Authority began the task —which is still a long way from being completed —of cleaning up the slums. By making loans to public-housing agencies, it brought more than 160,000 new housing units for low-income families into existence by 1941.

The AAA Returns

The New Deal's farm program was revived in February 1938 by the passage of a new AAA statute. Based on the principle of soil conservation, it authorized the secretary of agriculture to decide how much acreage should be planted each year in the staple crops so as to meet the nation's needs. At the same time, it provided compulsory quotas that stringently limited production (after approval in each case by a vote of two thirds of the farmers producing the crop). The principle of parity-price supports thus became established as national policy. Production, however, continued to rise mountainously despite acreage limitations. To ease the problem, Congress empowered the Agriculture Department to purchase and store surpluses, which were to be distributed to the needy, sold abroad, or released in time of shortage. The huge supplies of food thus stored were of inestimable value during the Second World War.

In May 1938 Roosevelt secured his last major reform from Congress, the Fair Labor Standards Act. Designed to aid those who did not have the protection of a union, it sought to make permanent the wages and hours standards that had been established in the now-defunct NRA codes. Southerners vigorously opposed the measure, for it would establish a nationwide floor under wages, and Southern leaders insisted their only hope was to maintain a wage differential by which labor would be cheaper in their region than in other parts of the country. The law, as passed, established a forty-cents-per-hour minimum wage (no Southern textile worker had reached that level yet) and a forty-hour maximum work week (time and a half to be paid for overtime). It also made illegal the use of child labor in any industry that shipped across state lines, a provision that finally won the long fight for this cause. Some thirteen million workers were protected by the law, and many of them received immediate pay raises. At first many exemptions weakened the program, but in succeeding years these were eliminated.

The New Deal in Retrospect

What balance sheet may be struck concerning the New Deal? It did not solve unemployment completely. Primarily because Roosevelt could never bring himself to spend enough, there were still six million people out of work in 1941. Only the Second World War swept away this deep scar, though it now appears that recovery was building enough momentum to have eventually achieved this goal without the war. Was it a revolution, as conservatives then and later alleged? Liberal historians such as Arthur Schlesinger, Jr., have been saying so for decades, though calling it a desirable revolution that moved America toward social justice. In recent years dissent has risen. Columbia historian William E. Leuchtenburg, after an extensive examination of the New Deal's limitations as well as its accomplishments, carefully concluded that it was only a "halfway revolution." Its accomplishments never matched its rhetoric. Massive aid went to business in the form of loans, to organized labor in the form of an active NLRB, and to millions of commercial farmers in the form of price supports. But the assistance given to the really helpless was tentative and incomplete. Tenant farmers and sharecroppers lost heavily under the AAA program and belatedly received only the limited assistance of the Farm Security Administration, which aided but a small proportion of those in need. Millions of farm and domestic workers were excluded from the social-security program, and the WPA employed only a minority of the jobless. Much of the New Deal depended on the state governments, which were notoriously lackadaisical. The noble ideals of the federal laws relied on the readiness of county supervisors and welfare departments to implement them, and too often their hostility negated the legislation. "Unemployables"—the sick, crippled, old, and helpless—were specifically left for state governments to aid, and in many regions this meant no aid at all.

Other historians, such as Barton Bernstein and Howard Zinn, have maintained that the failure of the New Deal went deeper than Leuchtenburg indicated. They believe that it sprang from a fundamental ideological conservatism. Roosevelt could have created, they insist, a truly humanitarian socialist system that could have equalized incomes and eliminated economic exploitation. But being a liberal and not a radical, he was subservient to capital. Instead of nationalizing the banking system, he refurbished it and handed it back to private bankers. Instead of really taxing wealth, Roosevelt talked loudly and then allowed Congress to leave the rich alone. Though he could have nationalized the great steel and automobile industries, he simply gave them enormous loans from the RFC. Wherever one looked, say these

historians, the New Deal was interested solely in the middle class and its economic security, not in the poor and helpless. Even in its loud antitrust campaign, little was accomplished. To those who had much—the skilled laborers, wealthy farmers, powerful bankers, industrialists—much was given; to those who had little—tenant farmers, blacks, unorganized workers, slum dwellers, the poor, the unemployable—very little was given. At the end of the New Deal decade, the rich had just as much money as before, and "the one-third ill-fed and ill-housed, and the two-thirds alienated and desperate," writes Paul Conkin, "still existed." If anything, the business classes were more secure than ever—more free of the threat of socialization, more confident that when in trouble the government would help them out.

Difficulties and Achievements

The historian Otis L. Graham, Jr., has judiciously remarked that these criticisms ignore too much. They give the New Deal too little credit for the enormous changes it wrought and the opponents of the New Deal too little credit for the powerful weapons that they could and did use against change of any kind. Consider the barriers to major reforms: the Supreme Court; the Southern oligarchy that dominated congressional committees; the great difficulty in getting major legislation through Congress, with its antiquated and obstructive rules, even in the best of times; the fundamental conservatism of the American population; the massive anti-Roosevelt campaigns carried on constantly by most of the newspapers; the fact that almost no one knew enough to be more than confused about most of the great problems of the day, which led to constant differences of opinion, bickering, and disarray within the ranks; the deep-rooted individualism of the whole society; the fact that the poor were then, and almost always have been, so weak, so uneducated, so unskilled in the ways of politics as to be politically apathetic. "The full context," Graham writes, "has not been supplied." Considered against the full range of ideas and possibilities current in America in the 1930s, "the New Dealers appear well toward the innovative and daring end of the spectrum, with stronger democratic instincts and a stronger commitment to racial justice and a more steady humanitarianism than all but a scant minority of their contemporaries." Considering

FRANKLIN D. ROOSEVELT AND THE NEW DEAL

the obstacles against which the New Dealers worked, the remarkable fact lies not in their failures but in their achievements.

So warned and chastened, contemporary historians now draw up the balance sheet of the New Deal with less unquestioning enthusiasm than in the past, but at the same time with an awareness that it constitutes a crucially important transformation in American history. The federal government experienced a vast expansion in its authority over the nation's economy, and since then it has used that authority vigorously. The list is almost endless: farm prices supported and farm plantings centrally planned; the money supply made a federal responsibility; stock exchanges regulated; bank deposits insured and banking practices supervised; the relations between employers and employees made a matter of public concern, and closely controlled; whole regions provided electric power by government facilities; utility systems given public direction; and economic recessions subject to ever vigilant federal attention, with increased public spending lying in wait to prevent the onset of another depression. For the mass of the population, New Deal legislation established a minimum standard of living: minimum wages and maximum-hours; old-age and disability pensions; unemployment insurance; monthly payments to mothers living alone with dependent children; direct assistance to the blind and crippled; insured bank deposits; higher wages through organized unions; and the sense of security that comes with the knowledge that in times of disaster the federal government will step in to provide essential aid.

The New Deal and the Democratic Party Tradition

Franklin Roosevelt's Democratic coalition closely resembled the earliest such coalition of them all: that put together by Thomas Jefferson. When the ethnic minorities of the Middle Atlantic and Middle Western states flooded back into the Democratic party under FDR, that same powerful combination that Jefferson had built reappeared, and once more took command of the nation's government: a linking of the white South to the ethnic minorities of the North. A predominantly WASP national government now became, under the Democrats, multiethnic and pluralistic. Catholics began to be appointed to judicial posts and to major administrative offices in great numbers, and so were Jews. Black Americans had little specifically aimed at helping them during the New Deal, but clearly they believed that the Roosevelt administration was doing as much for them as it could in a difficult situation, given white supremacy in the South and the dominance of white Southerners in congressional committees. They swung massively into the Democratic column in the North and West, where—as contrasted to the South—they were allowed to vote and therefore were politically important. Roosevelt also made Italians, Poles, and other ethnic groups feel that he cared. Mostly important, FDR, with his Jeffersonian love of the soil and of farming, converted traditional Republican-leaning WASP farming regions into Democratic country with his unprecedented programs of agricultural assistance.

The Strong Presidency

Roosevelt reintroduced into the national government a predominantly Democratic institution: the strong presidency. Jefferson had been a strong president, in contrast with those immediately before and after him, for he worked closely and successfully to lead Congress in directions he had chosen. Andrew Jackson was a "tribune of the people" in this mold (that is, a leader who sought consciously to lead the people and protect their rights), and his protégé James Polk was a surprisingly modern president in his skillful and hard-driving direction of Congress in reorganizing the economic system.

The strong-presidency concept, in which the chief executive conceives of himself as the spokesman of the people at large, rather than simply as a chairman of the board, and therefore as the nation's leader in shaping major new policy initiatives, reappeared in Grover Cleveland and Woodrow Wilson. Abraham Lincoln, though he vigorously used the existing executive powers of the presidency to prosecute the Civil War and free the slaves (as commander-in-chief), never sought leadership of Congress in the Democratic style. Indeed, as a former Whig, he did not believe in it. The same attitude toward the presidency was displayed by his many Republican successors, save Theodore Roosevelt, who to a great extent felt impelled to leave the Republican party in 1912 on this ground. Herbert Hoover detested working with Congress, totally lacked the arts of popularity, and pushed major legislation only when forced to by the depression.

With Franklin Roosevelt, however, the Jeffersonian tradition of the strong presidency was fully revived. Power again gravitated from Capitol Hill down to the White House, sitting a mile away on Pennsylvania Avenue. Henry Clay used to complain at the top of his voice about the "autocracy" of Andrew Jackson, and Republican senators almost hourly did the same in FDR's time. Here was no "government by boards of trustees" which Woodrow Wilson had so acidly condemned, no group of oligarchs in which the chief executive was little more than a presiding figurehead. Herbert Hoover's mail could be handled by one man; it took fifty to handle Franklin Roosevelt's. By the latter years of his administration, he had gotten Congress to create a large Executive Office of the President with a growing staff to give him the assistance he needed to run the expanded federal government and try to persuade it to follow one line of policy (perennially almost impossible). In later years this "imperial presidency" that FDR brought into being would be much expanded and used by other men in ways that would have appalled Roosevelt. In his time, however, the Democratic party exulted in his revival and expansion of the "tribune of the people" presidency as a bold and necessary weapon in the battle for social justice.

Democratic Libertarianism and Egalitarianism

We have seen that Democratic ideology traditionally was libertarian and egalitarian, and under Franklin Roosevelt these emphases continued. The New Deal was, in cultural terms, openly libertarian. Moralistic Republicanism had tried to preach to the ethnic minorities, seeking to remake them in the WASP image by changing their life style and ways of enjoying themselves. But Roosevelt's New Dealers took them on their own terms. The Roosevelt administration sang no hymns and chased no "wicked" influences; it was culturally tolerant and pluralistic. Indeed, the New Deal era began with the ending of the great prohibition experiment (the Twenty-first Amendment was declared ratified in December 1933) and the century-old WASP crusade on its behalf.

Furthermore, the New Deal openly and fervently preached egalitarianism (though gingerly, with regard to black Americans), for the Democratic party continued to be the party of the minority groups. Over and over, New Deal figures insisted upon the equality of all faiths and the need for positive toleration. Hitler's murderous assault upon the Jews in Germany taught Americans how potentially destructive were all forms of bigotry—the long-range influence of this realization upon black-white relations would be delayed, but of great significance. Liberal Democrats as well as many Republicans denounced ethnocentrism and racial stereotyping with mounting horror.

By the New Deal's latter years, the whole relationship of Catholic and Jewish America to American life in general was markedly different. Intellectuals rejected "scientific" racism, and the "100% American," in the usage of that term which had involved rabid anti-ethnic, pro-WASP prejudice, was much condemned nationally and shrunken in influence. The cultural historian John Higham writes in *Send These To Me: Jews and Other Immigrants in Urban America* (1975) that the late 1930s witnessed "the rise of the broadest, most powerful movement for ethnic democracy in American history." It was aided by the rise of the new unionism, which embraced whole industries and therefore included all minorities working in them (the older craft unionism had been ethnically exclusive). This culturally tolerant mood would reverse itself during the Second World War, as the internment of Japanese-Americans demonstrated, but under President Harry Truman, in the postwar years, the crusade against racial and religious prejudice would revive and push forward again with wide support.

The Historic Shift Toward Government Intervention in the Economy

What changed with arresting historical impact was the final scuttling of that ancient Democratic concept: economic laissez-faire. Democrats traditionally had taught that the economy should be left strictly alone, for every time the government intervened supposedly to enhance prosperity and national strength, it wound up (they believed) helping the already wealthy and powerful and intensifying the exploitation of the poor (as in the erection of protective tariffs). However, beginning with William Jennings Bryan, and with Woodrow Wilson eventually coming on board, the idea of *positive* liberty began to take hold. Urban minorities in industrial states discovered from 1910 onward that a Democratically-controlled government could free working people and the socially helpless from the grossest forms of exploitation in industry, and in housing and other areas of social need. With Franklin Roosevelt, who drew upon Bryanite populism as well as upon urban liberalism, these ideas rose up to and took over the national government.

Republicans recoiled from their old principle, now taken over by the Democrats: that the nation is one great community which should use its common government to create a prosperous and socially-just economy. In the realm of the economy itself, Republicans remained committed to powerful nationalizing institutions, as in the great banks, investment houses, and industrial and transportation corporations. Concerning government, however, they took up the now-discarded Democratic principles of laissez-faire and localism, mourned the passing of economic libertarianism, and became the voice of economic as well as of cultural (WASP) tradition.

Now it was the Republicans, traditionally the future-oriented party of modernization, who looked backward in yearning and mourned the loss of an (allegedly) simple republic in which people had been on their own, with no government stepping in to aid the lowly and therefore—in Republican belief—take away their initiative and self-respect. It was one thing for a relatively small government to aid businessmen by protective tariffs, the granting of rights to hydroelectric sites, and other traditional friendly assistance; it was another for a vastly swollen government, collecting huge sums in taxation, to help the unfortunate and closely regulate the successful. The government had for so long been the businessman's partner; now it had suddenly become his critic and his disapproving supervisor. To people used to being on top, the reversal in roles was appalling. It was only human, therefore, for Republicans to look back nostalgically to what they remembered as the golden years, in which WASP America had been preeminent in all aspects of national life; to the years of McKinley and Taft, of Harding and Coolidge. And it was no less human for the Democrats to become the exultantly future-oriented party under Franklin Roosevelt. Now it was they who preached the old Yankee concept of *community;* of everyone hanging together, like a great family, and working collectively toward common goals. FDR's New Deal seemed to them the very wave of the future.

Traditional Hostilities Retained

The New Deal was classically Democratic in that it was consumer-oriented (save in agricultural policy). Thus, FDR's Democrats condemned traditional enemies: bankers, businessmen, industrialists, the entrepreneur, and monopolists. During the Second New Deal they even turned again to the ideas of Adam Smith and called for a revival of competition as the essential disciplining mechanism in the economy. Internationalist in its economics (as we shall see in the next chapter), the New Deal steadily lowered the tariff through reciprocal trade agreements with other nations.

Because New Deal Democrats sometimes looked abroad to social welfare regimes in Europe to find ideas, they faced the charge that they were un-American, disloyal, the lackeys of a subversive alien power centered in Moscow. Since the time of the Alien and Sedition Acts in Thomas Jefferson's years, the Democratic side of American politics had been often attacked as un-American. Federalists had insisted that Jefferson's close ties with and advocacy of French republicanism made him, and his party, a subversive threat to the American nation. Grover Cleveland had been attacked as an agent of a foreign, anti-American power (Great Britain) when he called for reductions in the protective tariff—which would open American markets much more widely to British goods. As the party of Roman Catholics, of Jews, and of other non-WASP minorities, as well as of the white South, for generations the Democrats had been accused of being allied to disloyalty. How could such people be loyal to a Northern-dominated, WASP America? So the heated Republican allegations of alien influence and of un-Americanism that the New Deal absorbed continued a long tradition in American politics. Republicans, consistently more nationalistic and more outspokenly patriotic, have been the party most attractive to those inclined to believe that Democrats harbor conspiracies against national security and true Americanism.

It is not limited only to Republicans to nourish paranoid convictions about the other side. Since their founding as a party generations ago, Democrats have traditionally attracted to their ranks those Americans who instinctively distrust wealth and power, and who believe that behind Republican corporation and banking doors, economic conspiracies against the community at large are constantly being hatched. The classic picture has been that of greedy, callous, and exploitive industrialists scheming to dig unjustified profits out of the public at large, and spreading instructions by means of their network of country clubs and luxurious cocktail parties. Roosevelt himself believed that the slump of 1938 was caused by an organized strike of capital against the New Deal. The prospect of powerful monopolies getting hold of the economy and squeezing out competition has been a traditional Democratic fear, and in 1938 it was wholly in his party tradition for Franklin Roosevelt to set up an antitrust operation that dwarfed anything undertaken under Theodore Roosevelt and William Howard Taft.

A Later Generation Has Doubts

Subsequent generations of reformers, rising to prominence in the 1960s, have wondered whether the New Dealers' faith was properly placed. Massive bureaucracies seem to get out of control and exert their authority inflexibly. In time, strong government agencies appear to be easily taken over by the very interests they were designed to control. Huge corporations continue to flourish, receiving bountiful government aid, while the poor still live in stinking slums and have to go to court to force bureaucracies to provide legally ordained assistance. Most of all, the Vietnam War and the Watergate crisis have led to grave and searching doubts about the wisdom of creating a strong presidency and a large government. How could this have occurred? it is asked. Were the New Dealers genuinely concerned with aiding the poor, or were they really concerned with helping the already wealthy and powerful? Were they willfully blind to the dangerous potentialities of a strong presidency?

The ambiguity is irresolvable, for all large political ideas contain contradictory tendencies. A strong president could well become a tribune of the people, protecting them from the powerful, but he could also become a danger to democratic government. Strong bureaucracies can sternly restrain profit-hungry corporations, and they can become their allies. Social philosophers have long observed it to be the human condition that what is apparently good has within it the seeds of its own corruption, that each principle, as each person, possesses in the same instant both destructive and creative potentialities that are often at work simultaneously. There is no reason to doubt the sincerity of the Franklin Roosevelts and the Frances Perkinses, nor is there any reason, conversely, why their ideas should have been uniquely free from human paradox. As we saw in our examination of the accomplishments of the Jacksonian era, each reformist ideology, when it becomes an established and traditional pattern, presents features that later reformers find repellent. If the laissez-faire dreams of the Jacksonians eventually turned sour, creating not only economic freedom for the enterprising but also, in time, gigantic corporations that gravely worried following generations, it is hardly surprising that in our own years the strong-government mystique of the New Dealers stimulates searching doubts.

Bibliography

Books that were especially valuable to me in writing this chapter: Franklin Roosevelt's complex character is best discovered in Frank Freidel's multivolume biography, *Franklin D. Roosevelt* (1952–73), which is as yet uncompleted. *Roosevelt: The Lion and the Fox* (1956) by James MacGregor Burns remains a valuable one-volume life. The nature of the New Deal is judiciously assessed in William E. Leuchtenburg's *Franklin D. Roosevelt and the New Deal, 1932–1940** (1963), a book I've drawn much from. Otis L. Graham, Jr.'s brilliant *Toward A Planned Society: From Roosevelt to Nixon** (1976) is essential on the role of planning; and on labor and other aspects, I've been aided by Gabriel Kolko's *Main Currents in Modern American History** (1976). Arthur M. Schlesinger, Jr.'s *The Age of Roosevelt,** three vols. (1957–60) is history in the grand, abundant tradition, and important reading on a host of aspects. As an overall evaluation, Otis L. Graham, Jr.'s acute essay, "New Deal Historiography: Retrospect and Prospect," in his edited volume,

FRANKLIN D. ROOSEVELT AND THE NEW DEAL

*The New Deal: The Critical Issues** (1971) provided me valuable insights. Richard Hofstadter's analysis of the New Deal in *The Age of Reform** (1955) remains valuable reading, as is his sketch of FDR in *The American Political Tradition** (1948).

On the crucial question of whether the New Deal achieved significant economic recovery, and was on its way before the impact of the Second World War, I have been guided by W. Elliot Brownlee's *Dynamics of Ascent: A History of the American Economy* (1978). Irving Bernstein's masterful study, *The Turbulent Years: A History of the American Worker, 1933–1941* (1970) was essential on this central theme. An important new overall study is Gerald D. Nash, *The Great Depression and World War II: Organizing America** (1979). The crucial role of FDR and the media is skillfully explored in David Halberstam's *The Powers That Be** (1979). The remarkable First Lady is sensitively presented in Joseph P. Lash, *Eleanor and Franklin: The Story of Their Relationship Based on Eleanor Roosevelt's Private Papers* (1971). Raymond Wolters, *Negroes and the Great Depression: The Problem of Economic Recovery* (1970) opens up a crucial issue, and so does Monroe Lee Billington, *The Political South in the Twentieth Century* (1975). Christopher G. Wye's article, "The New Deal and the Negro Community: Toward a Broader Conceptualization," in *The Journal of American History*, 59 (1972), 621–39 is another important assessment. On voting patterns, see John M. Allswang, *A House for All Peoples: Ethnic Politics in Chicago 1890–1936* (1971); V. O. Key, Jr., *The Responsible Electorate: Rationality in Presidential Voting, 1936–1960* (1966); John L. Shover, "The Emergence of a Two-Party System in Republican Philadelphia, 1924–1936," *The Journal of American History*, 60 (1974), 985–1002; and Allan J. Lichtman, "Critical Election Theory and the Reality of American Presidential Politics, 1916–40," *The American Historical Review*, 81 (1976), 317–51. See also Robert Kelley, "Ideology and Political Culture from Jefferson to Nixon," *The American Historical Review*, 82 (June 1977), 531–62, for my own evaluation in a broader perspective.

Other Works on the Period

E. E. Robinson, *The Roosevelt Leadership* (1955); Milton Friedman, *Capitalism and Freedom* (1962); Barton Bernstein, ed., *Towards a New Past** (1968); Paul Conkin, *The New Deal** (1967), and *Tomorrow a New World* (1958); Sidney Fine, *The Automobile Under the Blue Eagle* (1963), and *Sit-Down: The General Motors Strike of 1936–1937* (1969); Ellis Hawley, *The New Deal and the Problem of Monopoly* (1966); Harmon Zeigler, *The Politics of Small Business* (1961); Grant McConnell, *The Decline of Agrarian Democracy** (1969); David E. Conrad, *The Forgotten Farmers* (1966); Thomas K. McGraw, *TVA and the Power Fight, 1933–1939* (1972); Michael Parrish, *Securities Regulation and the New Deal* (1970); Milton Friedman and Anna Schwartz, *A Monetary History of the United States, 1867–1960* (1963); Robert LeKachman, *The Age of Keynes** (1966); Joseph A. Pechman et al, *Social Security: Perspectives for Reform* (1968); Charles McKinley and Robert W. Frase, *Launching Social Security: A Capture-and-Record Account, 1935–1937* (1970); William F. McDonald, *Federal Relief Administration and the Arts* (1969); Otis L. Graham, Jr., *Encore for Reform** (1967), an intriguing analysis of how the progressives of Theodore Roosevelt's day reacted to FDR's New Deal; and Everett Carl Ladd, Jr., with Charles D. Hadley, *Transformations of the American Party System; Political Coalitions from the New Deal to the 1970s,** (1978).

* Available in paperback.

32

TIME LINE

slavia, North Africa, and Russia; Roosevelt freezes Japanese funds in America when Japan takes over southern Indochina; Roosevelt and Winston Churchill meet off Newfoundland, issue "Atlantic Charter"; attack on Pearl Harbor; America enters Second World War

1942 Year of disaster for Allies; American government removes Japanese-Americans and Japanese nationals from West Coast to internment camps; Arcadia Conference forms United Nations against Axis powers; Coral Sea and Midway Island naval victories halt Japanese advance; American forces invade North Africa

1943 Tide turns against Axis; Russian victory at Stalingrad begins German retreat; Roosevelt and Churchill meet at Casablanca, announce unconditional surrender to be demanded of Hitler at war's end; Allied forces invade Sicily and Italy; island-hopping campaigns in Pacific

1944 Bombing of Japan begins; Allies invade France; Russians sweep westward into central Europe; Battle of the Bulge; Philippines retaken

1945 Yalta Conference; Harry S. Truman becomes thirty-third president of the United States upon death of Roosevelt; Potsdam Conference; atom bombs dropped on Japan; end of Second World War

AMERICA AND THE SECOND WORLD WAR

UPI

Born to a wealthy New York City German-Jewish family in 1904, Robert Oppenheimer was a fascinating man. Incontestably a genius, by the 1930s he had become a gifted scientist who also wrote poetry, read Dostoevsky, commanded many languages (he read Plato in the original Greek and the Hindu *Bhagavad-Gita* in Sanskrit), and had created America's first great center of theoretical physics, at the University of California, Berkeley. Thin, frail, but almost superhumanly energetic, his flow of thought and words awed colleagues, as his complex character mystified them. Oppenheimer loved to roam the high mountains and mesas of New Mexico on horseback, and during the Second World War, in 1942, he brought physicists from all over the nation to a remote mesa northwest of Santa Fe—

Los Alamos. Here, within a guarded fence, he created a self-contained community of scientists and engineers whose task was to puzzle out how to make and build atomic bombs from fissionable uranium. Soon there were thousands at work on the mesa. "Oppie" was the spirited skipper, and morale was high.

Then in July 1945 he stood transfixed before the enormous fireball of the test firing in the New Mexico desert, appalled at its power. The ethical question of being a munitions maker had always worried him, though the thought that America had to have the bomb before Hitler got it eased his conscience. Now he was torn by doubts. Within weeks Hiroshima and Nagasaki were vaporized, and Robert Oppenheimer, his face and name splashed in the national press, had become the charismatic new hero of the new age of science. To his death he would never again find freedom from the glare of publicity.

At Los Alamos in 1945, guilt at the thought of the thousands of dead soon flooded in to replace the former excitement of success. Now the scientists talked of nothing but how to stop the atomic race, how to keep the world from incinerating itself, how to put the sinister genie back in the bottle. "Mr. President," Oppenheimer said to Harry Truman, "I feel I have blood on my hands." He began working tirelessly in a failing campaign to get atomic energy denationalized and placed under international control, and to prevent the making of the even greater horror, the hydrogen bomb.

However, Oppenheimer's wife and close relatives had been communist activists, the physicist himself had worked intermittently before the war in left-wing causes in Berkeley, and he had long been under suspicion. From his Los Alamos laboratory, it was learned, Soviet spy-scientists had sent crucial atomic information to the Russians. Oppenheimer was alleged to be opposing the hydrogen bomb on orders from Moscow, and in 1954 he was decreed a "security risk" by the Eisenhower administration and severed from all connections with the atomic program. The atomic age, tragic for the world, had brought tragedy as well to the personal life of J. Robert Oppenheimer. In the 1960s belated honors came—the Atomic Energy Commission awarded him the Enrico Fermi Award with its $50,000 prize in 1963—but little of life was left to him. In 1967 he was gone.

The Great Depression ended the precarious peace of the 1920s. When the world economy collapsed, spreading misery and dismay among millions, explosive forces were set off that eventually erupted in the Second World War. The Western democracies responded to the sufferings of the depression by setting up programs for internal reform; but Germany, Italy, and Japan reacted by launching campaigns of external aggression. The American people wanted to be free of foreign wars, and Congress passed a series of neutrality acts to ensure noninvolvement. The horrors perpetrated by Adolf Hitler, however, steadily eroded isolationism. Both President Roosevelt and the American people finally concluded that they could not survive as a nation if Hitler gained dominance over Europe. Desperate to ward off this prospect by preventing Great Britain's defeat, Roosevelt led the nation away from neutrality to armed belligerency in order to give Britain every aid short of war. At the same time, on the other side of the world he sought by strong nonmilitary actions to halt Japan's aggression. On December 7, 1941, Japan responded by attacking the American fleet at Pearl Harbor; Germany and Italy honored their treaty commitments to Japan by declaring war on the United States; and America was catapulted into the Second World War.

The Isolationist Temper

The isolationism that dominated United States foreign policy in the 1920s and 1930s was a traditional state of mind to Americans. The First World War deepened the separatist outlook. There was a giant recoil from intervention after the Versailles Peace Conference, when Americans became disillusioned. For a brief time the country had followed the soaring dream of Wilsonian idealism, but soon it all seemed a bloody and foolish mistake. In the 1930s scholars examining the origins of the First World War alleged that the nation had been dragged into the conflict by munitions makers and British propaganda.

Furthermore, war had lost its glamor. The boyish enthusiasm with which men joined the colors in 1917 had been followed by the shock of trench warfare, machine guns, enormous artillery barrages, and poison gas. Gallant cavalry charges had disappeared; brutish clanking tanks took their place. War became another name for mass butchery. The invention of the movie camera brought home to millions of Americans, sitting appalled in darkened theaters in the 1930s, the horror of warfare.

For generations a peace movement had existed in the United States. It had always been relatively ineffectual, but now it grew to heights of unexampled influence. One wing argued strongly for the United States to prevent war by acting on the principle of collective security; that is, by banding together with other nations to present a common front to aggressors. Other groups, more radical—such as the War Resisters' League—preached isolationism. The League of Nations, they said, was weak, which proved collective security delusory; militarism was taking over everywhere; and the only answer was to refuse to build armaments and follow totally noninterventionist policies.

Americans were puzzled and angry that European nations resisted paying off the loans they had secured from them during the First World War. (The debts totaled some ten billion dollars, which with interest over a projected repayment period of more than sixty years came to twenty-two billion dollars.) Calvin Coolidge put the matter simply: "They hired the money, didn't they?" Europeans pointed to their own millions of dead and countered that America should write off the money owed as its contribution to the common cause. Besides, there was little possibility that the European countries could pay the debts off anyway, since their economies had been shattered by the war. The question embittered all transatlantic relations and contributed much strength to the isolationist movement. President Hoover proposed a year-long moratorium on war-debt payments in 1931 in an attempt to ease the international financial crisis, and from then on the European nations stopped repayment.

Withdrawal from Latin America

In the 1920s it was clear that the United States no longer had to fear European aggression in Latin America. In consequence, new policies began to be instituted. Secretary of State Charles Evans Hughes withdrew American troops from the Dominican Republic in 1924. In 1928 the newly elected president, Herbert Hoover, made a tour of Latin America before his inauguration to spread the idea that America intended to be a "good neighbor." In 1930 the Clark Memorandum, named for a State Department official, terminated the Roosevelt Corollary to the Monroe Doctrine, in which Theodore Roosevelt had declared it America's right to ensure that Western Hemisphere nations paid their debts. The marines were withdrawn from Haiti in 1932, and from Nicaragua in 1933.

Franklin Roosevelt carried on and strengthened the Good Neighbor policy. In late 1933 he sent Cordell Hull to the Pan-American Conference in Montevideo, Uruguay to support the declaration that no nation had the right to intervene in the affairs of any other. In May 1934 he signed a new treaty with Cuba that finally ended the island's protectorate status, maintained since the Spanish-American War. In 1936 the American government formally gave up its legal right to intervene in Panamanian affairs, and the president traveled to the Inter-American Conference in Buenos Aires to declare to a cheering assemblage that the United States had given up entirely the principle of military intervention in Latin America. Henceforth the American government was committed to the principle that any differences between Western Hemisphere nations were to be settled by joint consultation, not by an overbearing Colossus of the North alone.

The Far East in Crisis

When the depression hit Japan, sending the export of raw silk from Japan tumbling by half and putting millions out of work, military expansionists began pointing to Manchuria. They urged that Manchuria become a settling place for surplus Japanese, as well as a vital economic underpinning for Japan's sagging commerce. In late 1931 Japanese army officers in Manchuria took the matter in their own hands. Declaring that their soldiers had been attacked by the Chinese, they launched a campaign to take all of Manchuria by force.

The officers' action openly violated the Open Door policy and the Nine-Power Pact. European nations held back while the United States urged action. In January 1932 the United States declared that it would not recognize any Japanese action that impaired "the sovereignty, the independence, or the territorial and administrative integrity of the Republic of China or . . . the open door policy." This refusal of recognition was designed to bring pressure on the Japanese by making American financiers reluctant to invest in affairs regarded as illegal by American authorities, but all it did was stir up Japanese anger. United States' nonrecognition also excited national and international derision, for the American government clearly had no intention of backing up its policy with force. Unchecked thereafter by any power, the Japanese were free to do as they wished in China.

Lowering Tariffs

With the Democrats back in power, a concerted drive to lower the tariff was soon begun. This was a particularly urgent need because the high rates of the Hawley-Smoot Tariff, created under Hoover, had set off a chain reaction of international reprisals. Indeed, a rage of economic nationalism was sweeping the world. Each country was seeking to keep out all foreign competition, erecting walled-off trade areas within their boundaries open only to their own producers. Democrats preached the message of low tariffs and open international trade. This approach, they insisted, would help bring the world out of its economic slump, for it would open up markets and lower prices for consumers. Roosevelt's secretary of state, the venerable Tennesseean Cordell Hull, had come to believe during Woodrow Wilson's administration that lowering tariffs would not only spread prosperity but would also help buttress world peace by reducing economic rivalries.

In June 1934, at Hull's urging, Roosevelt secured passage of the Trade Agreements Act, a law of historic importance. Reformers had insisted for decades that true tariff reform could never be achieved if tariff legislation was always subject to the back scratching and bargaining of congressional sessions. Only if the president—presumably an impartial judge—was given authority to raise or lower tariffs as appeared most helpful to the whole nation would an intelligent trade policy finally be established. The president was now empowered to negotiate bilateral agreements with other nations (agreements between the United States and one other country) by which he could raise or lower the tariff up to 50 percent if he could get similar adjustments in foreign tariffs. Once made, reductions would be applied to everyone under the most-favored-nation principle (all nations in regular treaty relations with the United States were guaranteed the trading rights given to "the most favored nation" by the American government) and in this way major tariff changes would be achieved across the board. This new presidential negotiating power produced agreements with twenty-one nations by 1940, affecting two thirds of all American foreign commerce.

Fascism Versus Communism

Five weeks before Franklin Roosevelt became president, Adolf Hitler was installed as chancellor of Germany. Nothing like Hitler had appeared on the stage of Western civilization for centuries. Benito Mussolini had become dictator of Italy in 1926 behind the banner of his *Partito Nazionale Fascista*, thus showing the way for the later rise to dictatorial power of the Germany leader. (The term *fascist* has been generally used to denote both Italian fascism and German Nazism, the latter being the abbreviation used for Hitler's movement, the *Nationalsozialistische Deutsche Arbeiterpartei*.) But Mussolini's political murders and foreign aggressions fade in comparison with the monstrous genocides practiced by Adolf Hitler. His pathological drives—an earlier age would have called them demonic—plunged the world into a succession of horrors so overwhelming that a war of global dimensions was inevitable.

Fascism was in the 1930s often described as the philosophy created by driving the beliefs of the political right wing to their extreme. Similarly, communism—from this point of view—was produced if the beliefs of the left were pushed to their extreme. An alternative theory was that fascism and communism, both being founded on authoritarian methods, were two sides of the same coin. Certainly it is true that in the same years that Hitler was killing millions of Jews, Joseph Stalin was killing millions of Russian peasants who resisted his agricultural collectivization. The butcheries associated with both the communist and the fascist movements give each an appalling historical burden to bear.

There were, however, fundamental differences between fascism and communism. Fascism, especially as expressed in Hitler's Nazi party, glorified the "race" of a given nation, preaching its superiority to other peoples. Communism glorified a particular class—the proletariat—around the world, asserting that the middle and upper classes were the enemy of the proletariat (the workers and farmers) and must be eliminated. There was a tribalism about fascism that drew its strength from deep, instinctual emotions, primarily those of fear and hatred of other peoples. It was not, therefore, an exportable political philosophy. How could non-Germans accept Hitler's principle that the German people were superior to all others? Communism, by contrast, proclaimed the universal equality of a particular stratum of all peoples, and could therefore flow across national boundaries and evolve into a movement in practically every country. Where fascism described humankind as a pyramid the apex of which was the superior race, communism described humanity as a horizontal entity in which everyone was to be equal to everyone else. Whereas fascism enjoyed flamboyant uniforms and badges of rank that clearly demarcated superiors from inferiors, communism adopted plain dress and styled everyone "comrade." Hitler screamed to his huge, cheering audiences that the essential reality of the German race lay not only in its blood but also in its spirit. The communists taught that material forces, not spiritual ones, were history's driving influences. Anticapitalistic, they insisted that all productive property must be owned by the state and that no person should be directly employed by any other person. Fascism, on the other hand, emphasized the rights and prerogatives of private property as long as all power resided ultimately in the state. It was often called a dictatorship of the upper class, whereas communism was described as a dictatorship of the lower class.

Fascism Glorifies Irrationalism

There was a brutal kind of tribal masculinity about fascism. Mussolini enjoyed being photographed either bare-chested or stomping around in a huge, beetling steel helmet. Hitler adored the spectacle of marching masses of jack-booted troops. Physical strength was idolized, and every problem was to be solved by the mailed fist. Polit-

Adolf Hitler and top Nazi officials attend a 1934 party rally. Ahead of him were brutal aggressions against many nations, millions of deaths, and world catastrophe.

Wide World Photos

ical enemies were simply killed. Any talk about mental difficulties was squelched, for it hinted at weakness. Sigmund Freud was hounded out of Vienna, and psychiatrists fled by the thousands. Indeed, it was distinctly unsafe to be an intellectual of any sort in a fascist country, for dissent and thoughtful reflection were not allowed. Fascism lauded instinct and distrusted rational intelligence. Absolutely crucial was obedience. Hitler would rise to towering rages at any suspicion of resistance. Throughout his life he had a pathological aversion to anyone telling him what to do. He was the *Führer* (leader), who had always to be complete master of every situation and circumstance. Whatever he said was, by definition, absolutely correct.

Hitler had many hatreds. He hated political democracy, for it guaranteed argument and criticism, making dictatorship impossible. Marxian communism was another enemy; of all political philosophies it seemed to him the most dangerous. But most of all he hated the Jews. "Wherever I went," he wrote of his early life, "I began to see Jews, and the more I saw, the more sharply they became distinguished in my eyes from the rest of humanity. . . . Later I often grew sick to the stomach from the smell of these [people]." They seemed foul and corrupt to him. He had wild sexual fantasies about Jews, writing of the "nightmare vision of the seduction of hundreds of

thousands of girls by repulsive, crooked-legged Jew bastards." It was a hatred that he fed on to the moment of his death. His last testament, written in 1945 just before he reportedly commited suicide, contained a final accusation that the Jews had caused the Second World War and were destroying Germany.

Hitler's regime tried from its beginning literally to eliminate the Jewish people of Europe. As soon as he became chancellor, Hitler dismissed all Jews from government service, the universities, and the professions. Two years later, all marriages between Jews and people of "German blood" were prohibited, and all civil rights were taken away from the Jewish population. In the fall of 1938 there was an indiscriminate killing of Jews, during which SS (Schutzstaffel) troops, Hitler's secret police, confiscated most Jewish property. Survivors were thrust into ghettos. When World War II began, they were systematically murdered, usually in huge death camps. In the part of Europe occupied by the German army, six million out of a total prewar population of 8.3 million Jews were put to death or died from starvation and disease. The genocide was so barbaric that, like the size of the universe or the dimensions of an atom, it cannot be comprehended by the mind. This barbaric crime against humanity was joined by the obliteration of millions of the peoples of the USSR during the Second World

War. Even in a century as filled with horrors as our own, these monstrous crimes take on a special frightfulness.

Hitler's Aggressions Begin

Hitler announced in 1935 that henceforth he intended to ignore the restrictions of the Treaty of Versailles. He began building up a military system and in 1936 moved boldly to remilitarize the Rhineland—the district between the Rhine River and France—despite the warnings of his general staff that if the other powers resisted his action, Germany was unprepared to respond successfully. The French, however, limited themselves to written protests, and the British government, which had long considered the Versailles treaty unfair to Germany, did not resist.

Convinced that Britain and France would never oppose him, the German dictator began looking toward his ultimate objective—the conquest of eastern Europe and the Soviet Union. As he declared in his last political statement, the conquest of the U.S.S.R. was "the be-all and end-all of nazism." His secret plan was to destroy the Soviet government, kill off or enslave half the inhabitants of the country, confiscate their land, and make the fruitful Ukrainian region a vast territory of German settlement. First he had to acquire Austria, then Czechoslovakia, and finally Poland. In March 1938 his troops took over Austria, which he incorporated into the German nation. Six months later at Munich he got the British and French to agree that the Sudetenland, the large section of western Czechoslovakia containing German-speaking peoples, should be granted to Germany. After another six months passed, he occupied the rest of Czechoslovakia.

Now Hitler worked diligently to neutralize the Soviets before moving into Poland. In secret talks he agreed to divide Poland with the U.S.S.R. and to let them take over the Baltic nations of Estonia, Latvia, and Lithuania. The world was therefore astonished to learn in August 1939 that the former enemies had signed a nonaggression pact. This event destroyed any hopes for continued growth that might have been entertained by Communist parties in the Western democracies, for all radicals save the inner core of dedicated Communist-party members were revolted by the pact with Hitler. Within days,

Hitler's armies were flooding across Poland's borders and the desperate British and French had declared war, having given up the belief that the German leader could be contained by something other than force. The Second World War had begun.

The Neutrality Acts

In the mid 1930s the American Congress reacted to the rising international storm by determinedly turning inward. The disenchantment over the First World War had struck so deep that people could no longer believe that anything but further harm would come to the nation by trying to solve international crises. The very notion of collective security was rejected. On top of such an attitude, furthermore, was the towering congressional anger against the European "chiselers" who would not pay their war debts—ironically, the very nations threatened by Hitler's Germany—Britain and France.

The Senate created a committee under progressive Gerald P. Nye of North Dakota to explore the reasons why the United States had become involved in the First World War. A sensational show featuring accusations against war industries was put on. Stretching over two years, it never actually proved anything, but nevertheless left firmly implanted in the public mind the belief that bankers and arms manufacturers had dragged the country into war. This led to the First Neutrality Act, passed in August 1935, which charged the president to impose an arms embargo on all belligerents during a time of international war, thus making it impossible for him to discriminate between aggressors and victims. In 1936, the Second Neutrality Act prohibited the making of any loans to a country involved in a war. In the Third Neutrality Act, passed in 1937, Americans were forbidden in time of war to travel on ships owned by belligerents, and no American merchant vessel was to be armed. In 1939, after war began in Europe, the sale of arms was put strictly on a "cash-and-carry" basis. In sum, Congress legislated out of existence all of the factors that, it was believed, had dragged the United States into the First World War. The result was to immobilize the American government in a time of grave world crisis.

America Retreats from the Far East

When Franklin D. Roosevelt came to the White House, he held back from further action on the Far Eastern crisis. Meanwhile, the government proceeded to make another kind of withdrawal from the Far East—giving independence to the Philippines. Antiimperialists had called for this step for many years, and Filipino nationalists had agitated for the same objective ever since the First World War, when Woodrow Wilson's appointee as governor general, Francis B. Harrison, had encouraged feelings of self-sufficiency by granting considerable power to the Philippine legislature. By the 1920s, American producers of sugar, tobacco, and other products also grown in the Philippines were beginning to support the independence idea, for they wanted to exclude the growing volume of imports from the Philippine Islands, which enjoyed a guarantee of complete free trade established in the Underwood Tariff of 1913. The Republican presidents of the 1920s, however, firmly opposed independence. Under Franklin Roosevelt, the Tydings-McDuffie Act was passed in March 1934. Tariffs were to be

raised only gradually against Philippine goods, and full independence was to be granted in 1946.

In China there was a brief calm following Japan's conquest of Manchuria. But then in July 1937, a newly militant Japanese government began the Second Sino-Japanese War, the objective this time being the conquest of all of China. Roosevelt refused to invoke the First Neutrality Act, thus allowing arms to reach the Chinese, though the lines of communication had to wind through India and Burma.

Roosevelt Turns Outward

By his second term, Roosevelt could no longer remain passive in his foreign policy. The "community of the damned"—Japan, Germany, and Italy—was forming. The deepest values of Western civilization were clearly at stake. The kind of world that Hitler was plunging toward would be a world based on nothing but jungle law. Increasingly, the president was convinced that the United States had to play a major role in the world to defend basic human values. This meant, to begin with, initiating rearmament, and in early 1938 he obtained funds from Congress to build the navy up to a strength allowing it to defend both ocean frontiers. Later in the year, Hitler's pogrom against German Jews horrified the American public. When Hitler sent his troops into Austria, forcibly joining that country to the Third Reich, a turning point was passed. From then on, isolationism was on the defensive, for the German dictator's actions made that philosophy increasingly absurd. After Poland was struck from east and west by German and Russian armed forces in September 1939, Roosevelt was able to secure a repeal of the arms-embargo feature of the First Neutrality Act. This freed the American government to begin selling goods on a cash-and-carry basis to its friends while denying them to Germany, since that nation would find it difficult to get to American ports through the British fleet. (Loans, however, were still prohibited, as was travel by Americans in the war zones.)

Several months of quiet followed the conquest of Poland. Americans breathed easier, for they were confident that the British and French would eventually defeat Hitler, thus making it unnecessary for the United States to do more than sell arms to the western Allies. Then in several

THE SECOND WORLD WAR: ALLIANCES

Allied nations

Axis nations

Neutral nations

JAPAN
→

lightning campaigns begun in April 1940, Hitler conquered Denmark, Norway, Luxembourg, Holland, and Belgium. Hardly pausing to catch their breath, his armed forces then poured into France, administering a swift defeat. On June 22, 1940, the *Führer* secured a total French capitulation.

America Becomes an Armed Belligerent

The fall of France set off a wave of panic in the United States. Mayor Fiorello La Guardia of New York cried out that the American government could not even defend Coney Island. Roosevelt had already gone before Congress, in May, to give a sensational speech that described how bombers could fly from West Africa to Omaha, and asked funds—speedily granted—for the building of 50,000 war planes. Only Britain now stood between America and Hitler's total victory in western Europe, and the American government immediately came to one fundamental decision: the British must be saved at all costs. By various means, using go-between private companies (because explicit government aid would have brought the U.S. into the war and the country was not ready for this yet), Roosevelt rushed thousands of aircraft and guns to Britain to replace the equipment their armies had had to leave behind as they fled France. A Gallup poll revealed that 70 percent of the American people now believed that a German victory would directly imperil the nation. With this tidal wave of opinion behind him, Roosevelt persuaded Congress to establish in September 1940 the first peacetime draft in American history. Meanwhile, everyone watched in horror as Hitler launched a bombing campaign against Britain's cities in preparation for an expected invasion.

The supply lines crossing the Atlantic between North America and British ports were under unremitting attack from German submarines. Therefore, the American government gave the British fifty destroyers of World War I vintage, in return for ninety-nine-year rent-free leases of sites for naval bases on eight British possessions in the Western Hemisphere, running from Newfoundland through the Caribbean islands to British Guiana. By this time, it was apparent that the cash-and-carry law was not aiding the British, since they had begun to run out of money and did not have the ships to carry to their islands all the war matériel they needed. In January 1941 Roosevelt asked Congress for authority to lend or lease war goods to the British, thus taking the dollar sign, as he put it, out of the transaction. This would effectively prevent any recurrence of the festering war-debt problem that had poisoned the interwar decades. Speaking to the press, he made use of a brilliantly chosen parable. Neighbors are always happy, he said, to lend their hoses to a man whose adjoining house is on fire, for it will reduce the danger to their own dwellings. All they ask is that he return the hose when the emergency is over, if it is still usable. "We cannot and we will not tell [Great Britain and her Allies]," he said, "that they must surrender, merely because of present inability to pay for the weapons which we know they must have."

Every anti-British, isolationist, or antiwar group split the air with protests. All recognized that the lend-lease proposal would be a crucial turning point, making the United States in effect a nonfighting partner in Britain's struggle against Hitler. Republican Senator Robert A. Taft of Ohio snorted, "Lending war equipment is a good deal like lending chewing gum. You don't want it back." Burton K. Wheeler of Montana made the most violent attack: lend-lease, he said, was the "New Deal's 'triple A' foreign policy—to plow under every fourth American boy." Debate raged throughout the land, in every grocery store and stock-market board room. Lend-lease was not an administrative decree; it was a course of action reached after the fullest possible nationwide discussion among the people. The national decision was clear: even at the risk of war, Britain must be saved. With letters expressing this viewpoint deluging them, congressmen came to their final vote after weeks of debate in mid March 1941. They passed the Lend-Lease Act by heavy majorities in the two houses. Roosevelt immediately secured an appropriation of more than seven billion dollars and began making the United States into what he called the "arsenal of democracy."

The Battle of Britain

During the following months the pressure mounted higher and higher. Great plumes of smoke rose over the British Isles as clouds of German bombers rained explosives on the civilians

AMERICA AND THE SECOND WORLD WAR

below. In the Battle of Britain, British fighter planes mounted a heroic and eventually successful struggle against the bomber attacks. Meanwhile, German submarines sunk scores of merchant vessels, and Roosevelt set up naval convoys that sought to protect munitions-carrying vessels as far eastward as Iceland, where the local authorities granted rights for an American military occupation. American destroyers and aircraft ranged over the North Atlantic searching out German submarines and radioing their location to British naval forces. When the destroyer *Greer* engaged in a shooting encounter with a German submarine (which the *Greer* had actually instigated), Roosevelt ordered the navy thereafter to "shoot on sight [these] rattlesnakes of the Atlantic." He secured congressional authority to arm American merchant ships and to allow them to enter war zones, a boon to the hard-pressed British.

Meanwhile, Hitler sent German armies racing into Greece and Yugoslavia. Then his *Afrika Korps* thrust swiftly to the Egyptian frontier, threatening to drive the British out entirely and seize the Suez Canal, which would have snapped crucial supply lines. On June 22, 1941, Hitler stunned the world by suddenly sending an armed force of hundreds of divisions into the Soviet Union. Dizzied by his swift successes, he did not prepare his troops for winter campaigning, since

THE SECOND WORLD WAR: EUROPEAN THEATER, 1939–1942

he expected to defeat the U.S.S.R. before cold weather set in. Hitler's armies plunged rapidly into the depths of the Soviet Union, and the Nazi occupation officials who followed began systematically killing off tens of thousands of village officials. Hundreds of thousands of Soviet troops were captured and sent to prison camps, where they were allowed to starve to death. European Russia was to be cleared out for German settlers.

This astounding event transformed American opinion toward the U.S.S.R. From being hated as Hitler's accomplice in aggression, the Soviet Union overnight became a much valued and much praised ally. Americans watched the progress of Hitler's armies in alarm, for clearly a Hitler victorious over the limitless resources of the Soviet Union would be practically unstoppable in his career of world conquest. Roosevelt soon promised aid to Joseph Stalin, the Soviet dictator, and in November 1941 allocated one billion dollars in lend-lease aid, which was followed by many billions more.

The Atlantic Meeting

In early August 1941, Roosevelt and Churchill met off the Newfoundland coast in a gathering of British and American naval vessels. Churchill had come to plead for greatly increased aid. Roosevelt, on his side, was determined to win some agreements that looked toward the kind of world that would be constructed after the war. In all important details, it would be the Liberal-Democratic world order that Woodrow Wilson had vainly sought to create. From FDR's days as a Harvard student, he had been a determined anti-colonialist. He wanted to do everything possible to get the British (and the French, for that matter) to free their colonies. "I can't believe," he said to Churchill, "that we can fight a war against fascist slavery, and at the same time not work to free people all over the world from a backward colonial policy. . . ." Later on he brought pressure to bear on the French, trying to prevent their return as colonial masters to the countries of Indochina—Vietnam, Laos, and Cambodia. He also hoped to see protective tariffs lowered worldwide, thus inaugurating the world of open trading that, like Wilson before him, he had long envisioned and worked for. Of highest importance, to cap off this structure and maintain peace, would be the

construction of a new international body to replace the League of Nations. In its final version, the president and the prime minister's joint statement, the so-called Atlantic Charter, was a cautiously worded hope expressed to the world that upon the defeat of the aggressors, trade barriers would be lowered, no nation would make territorial acquisitions, the peoples of the world would be allowed to govern themselves, and a "permanent system of general security" would be established. The two leaders also called for a world blessed by freedom from want and fear.

Japan Moves Southward

In September 1940 Japan, Germany, and Italy signed the Tripartite Pact, which pledged them to aid one another in case of attack by the United States. This faced President Roosevelt with the sobering fact that war with any one member of the Rome-Berlin-Tokyo Axis would lead to war with all. And yet any thrust southward that Japan made to capture French, British, and Dutch colonies—and sources of raw materials—would weaken the Allies in their struggle against Hitler. When France fell, thus opening its colony of Indochina to Japanese incursions, the last and most fateful chapter in Japan's movement toward war with the United States began. When it became apparent that Tokyo was planning to move into Indochina, preparatory to moving on the resource-rich Dutch East Indies, Roosevelt took steps to warn off the Japanese. He put the export of oil and scrap metal to Japan under a licensing procedure, which allowed him to choke off supplies should he decide to, and ordered that aviation fuel be sold only in the Western Hemisphere. This was a great shock to the Japanese, for about 80 percent of the scrap iron, steel products, and oil needed for their armies and navies came from America.

Militant expansionists in Japan now moved to take over greater power in the Japanese government. The new foreign minister, Yosuke Matsuoka, said that Japan was going to go "hell bent for the Axis and for the New Order in Asia." In September the French government agreed to let the Japanese move into northern Indochina, where they controlled seaports, built air bases, and ran the railroads. The Japanese government then began a long series of negotiations with the

The U.S.S. *West Virginia* and the U.S.S. *Tennessee,* both battleships, lie burning on Pearl Harbor's floor after the surprise Japanese attack of December 7, 1941. These pictures were long kept from the nation.

80-G-32414 in the National Archives, Navy Department

United States to secure American acceptance of the "New Order." Briefly, the American government was to cease giving any support to Chiang Kai-shek, the Chinese Nationalist leader, accept Japan's dominance over China and the Far East generally, and drop its embargo against the sale of strategic goods to Japan.

Roosevelt's Response

President Roosevelt refused to accept these demands. This was a crucial point. The United States could have had peace if it had agreed to give up its decades-old policy of trying to keep China an independent nation open to the trade of the world. But Roosevelt firmly believed that he could make the Japanese halt their aggressions by keeping the pressure on. He therefore told the Japanese that the only acceptable settlement would be for Japan to get out of China, respect the Open Door once more, and give up its military expansionism. Given the state of Japanese opinion, this demand was impossible for the Japanese to meet. Many in the Tokyo government believed that Japan would lose if it went to war with the United States (a view held by the Japanese emperor Hirohito himself). But they could not bring themselves to accept so total a national humiliation. Hoping that the United States would give in, the Japanese continued negotiations until the very end. Meanwhile, on July 2, 1941, a momen-

tous conference of all Japan's leaders, with the emperor in the chair, considered the whole matter afresh and resolved to continue to push southward. Shortly afterward, Japanese troops occupied southern Indochina, in preparation for an attack on Malaya and the Dutch East Indies.

Roosevelt responded by freezing all Japanese funds in the United States and halting the shipment of oil and war supplies to Japan. Now the Japanese war minister, Hideki Tojo, soon to be prime minister, warned that war was the only answer. It was essential, he said, to "break through the military and economic barrier" that the United States had erected. Beginning in September 1941, the high command held war games preparing for an attack on America's fleet at Pearl Harbor. This, it was believed, would give Japan sufficient temporary military superiority to take a vast ring of islands in the western Pacific Ocean, from which it would thereafter maintain an impregnable defense of the "Greater East Asia Sphere of Co-Prosperity." When it became clear that the United States would not retreat from its policies, a great fleet set out from the northern Japanese islands. Soon it reached the vicinity of the Hawaiian Islands, and on December 7, 1941, it executed a massively successful bombing and torpedo attack on the American fleet at Pearl Harbor. When the planes ceased their wheeling and diving on the stricken vessels below and disappeared from view, heading back to their untouched aircraft carriers, they left behind five battleships sunk of the eight then at Pearl, fourteen more ships sunk or disabled, and almost 2,400 dead soldiers and sailors. Amazement and anger struck the United States. On the following day Congress declared war on Japan; three days after that, Germany and Italy honored their treaty pledges by declaring war on America. Thus was the United States finally catapulted into World War II.

The Effects of Pearl Harbor

While the attack was certainly a tactical victory for the Japanese (though the crucial American aircraft carriers, then at sea, were spared destruction), in a larger sense it was perhaps their gravest strategic defeat. The bombing absolutely destroyed isolationism and unified the American people as they had never been in any of their pre-

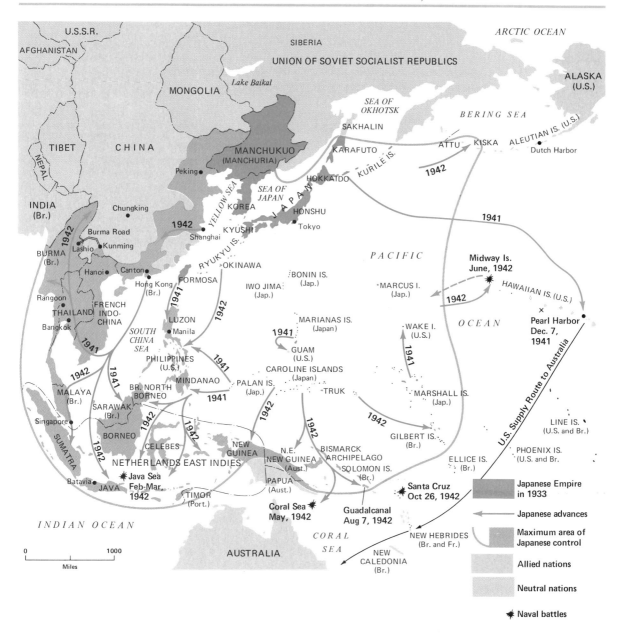

vious wars. Massive unanimity welded the nation into a fighting force of unparalleled power. "My convictions regarding international cooperation and collective security for peace," said one Republican isolationist senator, Arthur H. Vandenberg of Michigan, "took firm hold on the afternoon of the Pearl Harbor attack."

From a more distant viewpoint, it can be said that Pearl Harbor shaped all of America's responses to foreign-policy crises in the next quarter of a century. A generation of American leaders went into the Second World War convinced that in the future the only way to secure world peace would be to maintain armed vigilance and a readiness to strike at aggression in its earliest stages. Furthermore, Hitler's barbarities and Japan's ruthless attacks on China and finally on America's own young men hammered deeper into the national consciousness an unquestioned belief long held by Americans that their country represented, then and afterward, the forces of good; that its use of the mailed fist, in whatever circumstance, was morally right. America's national ideology, its faith in itself as the world's leading exemplar and spokesman of *democracy* (which now summed up for Americans what the word *republicanism* had meant to them in the 1800s), was vastly revived by this desperate struggle against Hitler and the Japanese. The Second World War was a great theater in which America's role (as Americans conceived of it) was to lead the fight for human freedom.

Indeed, to the American people the Second World War became in a certain sense "America's war." Never very knowledgeable about the rest of the world anyway, Americans quickly inflated their country's role in this immense conflict to one of absolute preeminence. The newspapers, the radio, and the newsreels concentrated on American troops, armies, fleets, air forces; on Americans struggling back from early defeats to glorious victories; on American troops, with the British, invading the European continent through France and eventually battering down Hitler's forces. What was rarely understood, then or later, was the almost inconceivably enormous fighting that went on inside the Soviet Union. At any one time over 200 of Hitler's army divisions were deep in that country, locked in a hideously bloody battle with a Soviet army of at least equal size. (In the entire war, the United States mobilized only about 90 divisions of combat troops.) People died by the tens of millions in what the U.S.S.R. today calls The Great Patriotic War against the fascists. Millions died among Hitler's armed forces, and 20 million more among the Soviet troops and citizenry. For every American who died in the Second World War (about 300,000), 50 Soviet citizens perished—a fact never forgotten in the Soviet Union, which by its own understanding is the country that defeated Hitler while the Anglo-American allies mounted small sideshows in the west.

Seized by a totally different conviction— that the United States had saved the world from tyranny—Americans would end the Second World War in a peculiarly exalted mood. Never before had they done anything as a people, certainly nothing so immense, in which they had been so uniformly in agreement that they were doing the right thing. That sense of national unity and national pride, and that conviction that they were freedom's saviors, would profoundly affect all of America's foreign and domestic policy for many years after 1945. Until the disaster of the Vietnam War, Americans unquestioningly conceived of their nation as not only the world's leading democracy, but as the country almost divinely chosen (for many, the United States *was* divinely chosen) to lead the "Free World," as they put it, against the forces of autocracy.

One outgrowth of the Japanese attack was the forced removal of 70,000 Japanese-Americans and 42,000 Japanese-born (by law denied citizenship) from their West Coast homes to bleak concentration camps in the interior. Lieutenant General John L. DeWitt offered this justification: "The area lying to the west of the Cascade and Sierra Nevada Mountains in Washington, Oregon and California, is highly critical not only because the lines of communication and supply to the Pacific theater pass through it, but also because of the vital industrial production therein, particularly aircraft. In the war in which we are now engaged racial affinities are not severed by migration. The Japanese race is an enemy race and while many second and third generation Japanese born on United States soil, possessed of United States citizenship, have become 'Americanized,' the racial strains are undiluted. To conclude otherwise is to expect that children born of white parents on Japanese soil sever all racial affinity and become loyal Japanese subjects, ready to fight and, if necessary, to die for Japan in a war against the nation of their parents. That Japan is allied with Germany and Italy in this struggle is no ground for assumption that any Japanese, barred from assimilation by convention as he is, though born and raised in the United States, will not turn against this nation when the final test of loyalty comes. It, therefore, follows that along the vital Pacific Coast over 112,000 potential enemies, of Japanese extraction, are at large today. There are indications that these are organized and ready for concerted action at a favorable opportunity. *The very fact that no sabotage has taken place to date is a disturbing and confirming indication that such action will be taken.*" (United States Army, *Final Report: Japanese Evacuation from the West Coast, 1942* [1943]) [Italics added.]

Overall Strategy

The first military decision made at the war's outset was to concentrate on defeating Hitler while fighting a holding action in the Pacific. The next was to form an alliance with Britain so close that even military commands were jointly staffed. It is doubtful that any two nations have ever created so intimate a partnership in time of war. No such intimacy could be achieved with the U.S.S.R., however. Its distrust of the western Allies was too deep. Joseph Stalin could well remember when British and French forces had tried to bring down the Soviet government by direct intervention following the First World War. He had witnessed Britain and France seemingly engaged in pushing Hitler eastward, and cheering on his anticommunist activities. More important, however, were the suspicions all communist regimes have entertained toward any capitalist government, and the deep-rooted feeling of Russians for many generations that they were surrounded by hostile forces. Although Roosevelt and Churchill tried again and again to break through Stalin's massive distrust, they rarely succeeded.

The very closeness of the Anglo-American relationship heightened that distrust. The fact, too, that the western Allies were too weak until 1944 to mount an invasion of Hitler's Europe—especially the British, who were also obsessed with getting control of the Mediterranean, and feared renewing the immense and bloody land battles on the Continent that they had suffered through during the First World War—delayed the opening of the Second Front for which Stalin clamored, and this made him even more disbelieving. Of course, the Soviet dictator was hardly a man of normal sensibilities. As later disclosures made horrifyingly clear, he had built a regime that had murdered millions of Soviet citizens in order to clear away all obstacles to his will. The whole Soviet government, however, joined him in his inability to believe in the West's good intentions. Although billions of dollars of American war matériel were rushed to the Soviet front (without it, it is doubtful that the U.S.S.R. could have remained in the war), an American observer in Moscow commented that the Russians "cannot understand giving without taking, and as a result even our giving is viewed with suspicion." Roosevelt worried constantly over this situation. He was convinced that a peaceful postwar world would be impossible unless the Russians were somehow led to adopt new attitudes of trust and cooperation. This point of view lay at the roots of his wartime diplomacy.

Meanwhile, he led in the creation of a "Grand Alliance." At the Arcadia Conference, convened in Washington at the outbreak of the war, the "Declaration by the United Nations" was issued to the world. Signed by twenty-six nations —twenty more signed before the war's end—it pledged acceptance of the Atlantic Charter's principles and bound the signatories not to enter into any separate armistices or peace treaties with the common enemy. In the same month, January 1942, a meeting of the foreign ministers of the American republics was held at Rio de Janeiro. Out of this meeting came the declaration that an attack against one nation in the Western Hemisphere was an attack against all. Following this unprecedented act—a fruit of Roosevelt's long-standing efforts to win Latin American friendship—all Latin American countries broke relations with the Axis (Chile not until 1943, and Argentina in 1945). Brazil even dispatched a combat division to the fighting in Italy when the Allied campaign against Hitler reached that point.

Year of Disaster: 1942

In 1942, however, the war went from disaster to disaster. The United States was unprepared for an all-out conflict. German submarines sunk vessels by the hundreds, at a pace far greater than they could be replaced. German armies fought to the outer defenses of Alexandria, Egypt. The Japanese took Singapore and sunk practically all the British fleet in the Pacific. Guam and Wake Island were swiftly overrun, and after a long struggle on the Bataan Peninsula, American forces in the Philippines were defeated. The American commander, General Douglas MacArthur, fled to Australia. Before long Japanese forces had taken the Dutch East Indies, with their immense resources of petroleum and other raw materials, and were mounting threats to India (through Burma) and Australia (through New Guinea). In May and June of 1942 the American navy suddenly halted this seemingly unstoppable advance by winning naval victories in the Coral Sea and near Midway Island with the aircraft carriers luckily spared the disaster at Pearl Harbor. In the summer of 1942 American troops began the slow, winding process of rolling back Japanese power by landing on Guadalcanal, which they wrested from the Japanese army after a difficult campaign. Thereafter the American campaign in the Pacific consisted of a series of stepping-stone operations in which the enemy was dug out of island after island. Shaking with malarial fever, sapped by dysentery, plucking off leeches, fighting often hand to hand in jungle slime or over sharp coral, thousands of Americans fought a kind of war of which few in the United States had ever dreamed.

Meanwhile the Soviet front was on the verge of total collapse. In 1942 the huge German army renewed its offensive and struck deeper into the U.S.S.R.'s vitals, reaching perilously close to sweeping up all of the nation's industrial and petroleum resources. In response, American military planners worked desperately to open a second front in Europe sometime during that year. But it was impossible: the British were not strong enough and the United States was far from ready. However, an attack had to be made somewhere: Roosevelt had pledged to Stalin to open a second front. Therefore, in early November 1942 a large, primarily American Allied force arrived off the northwestern coast of Africa and launched an invasion to the east. Their objective was to catch the German forces, then concentrated mainly between Tunisia and Egypt, from the rear. (The Soviets scoffed then, and still maintain, that this entire effort was a meaningless, diversionary, minor campaign that bothered Hitler very little, and left the Soviets still fighting the main war against the Germans.)

Dwight D. Eisenhower

This campaign brought swiftly to international notice an American general of rare qualities, Dwight D. Eisenhower. Commander of the North Africa invasion, he had been plucked out of relative obscurity early in the war by America's chief of staff, General George C. Marshall. A career officer who had served since the First World War (in which he supervised noncombat units), Eisenhower displayed a remarkable capacity for leading large organizations and inspiring trust in his subordinates. Warm, open, unpretentious, he was a peaceful man who seemed to look on warfare not as a glorious opportunity for renown but as a painful necessity pursued only to protect innocent people against aggressors. In this new kind of warfare, in which gigantic armies of millions of men needed to be gathered together and skillfully coordinated, he was a genius at planning and administration.

Although Eisenhower's North African invasion went well at first, his troops were painfully inexperienced. The Germans knew this. In a bold counterattack they administered a severe defeat to the eastward-rushing American forces at Kasserine Pass. This had the effect of forcing a much more cautious pattern of advance on the Allied armies. Not until months had passed were the Americans and British able to converge on the German armies, basket them in Tunisia, and, in May of 1943, totally defeat them.

At Home: The New America

Unlike millions abroad, Americans were not bombed, strafed, or invaded during the Second World War, nor did they experience mass devastation of cities and farmlands. Spared these sufferings, they in fact enjoyed a dramatic soaring of their standard of living. The last scars of the depression were wiped away by massive government spending (which taught unforgettable lessons to postwar planners; the idea of compensatory government spending to prevent depressions was now firmly fixed in the national mind). Farm income rocketed to unprecedented heights, agricultural debt was practically wiped away, and at the same time millions from the farms moved permanently to the cities to benefit from high pay in war industries. Agricultural productivity rose 25 percent while the farm population was dropping almost 20 percent.

People began moving about the country at a rate never before witnessed, producing a great mixing of ethnic groups, religions, and political loyalties. War industries pulled them not only into large cities, but into many Southern and Western regions where aircraft plants and shipyards demanded workers. Over a million people flooded into California, initiating the tidal wave that would make that state in time the nation's most populous. At the same time, so many women were brought into industry that the work force by war's end was almost one-third female. Labor unions, in a situation where men were in short supply, grew markedly in strength. Meanwhile, the government halted all antitrust activities, large corporations began merger movements to become even larger and more powerful, and businessmen went in droves to Washington to take up dollar-a-year jobs (they were still on salary with their original firms) to administer war production. By 1945, the nation's business community had recovered its prestige and was playing a major role once again in the federal and state governments.

AMERICA AND THE SECOND WORLD WAR

Income taxes were heavy, especially on higher incomes, as a means of raising money for fighting the war, and there was actually a significant narrowing of the income gap as ordinary people made high wages and rose in standing. In 1939 the wealthiest 5 percent of the American people had received almost 24 percent of the nation's income, but by 1944 this figure had dropped to slightly under 17 percent. Poverty, so widely visible during the depression, seemed to vanish. In another major departure from all past national policy, the government began for the first time calling upon the universities to conduct research and development projects, which in these wartime years were almost wholly weapons-connected. In 1945 the Massachusetts Institute of Technology had more than $100 million in contracts. This relationship, now firmly established, would expand in the postwar years into a major element in higher education, the economy, the sciences, and the search for knowledge.

The federal government itself was transformed, never to go back to its former condition. In 1940 there were a million federal civilian employees; in 1945 there were 3.8 million. A government that in the former year spent $9 billion spent just under $100 billion in the latter. When peace resumed, nondefense spending did not return to the $7.2 billion of 1940; indeed, in 1947 it would reach $25 billion. If people had learned to begin looking to Washington in the depression years, during the war that city became, and would remain, the overwhelmingly dominant center of national life. Its relationship to industry would never again be the same. A government that at the wartime peak was spending $250 million *each day* for war goods was creating a network of links to corporations all over the nation that would in later peacetime years evolve into the military-industrial complex. Entire industries were created to feed wartime needs, such as that for synthetics, and immense bomber plants were constructed.

Unlike the situation in the First World War, there was no national crusade to search out and imprison "subversives" for every critical statement about the war and its conduct, in part because the war effort received such massive national support. Though Germany was the national enemy, German-Americans no longer received the hatred they had absorbed in the earlier conflict. In fact, to a remarkable degree, the war in Europe was defined as a war against Hitler and his regime and philosophy, not against a people. The same was not at all true concerning the Japanese, who in California and the West had been generally subject to harsh prejudice before Pearl Harbor, and were interned during the war. Propaganda against the Japanese was candidly, insistently racial in tone.

The War's Tide Turns: 1943

By 1943, the Soviet Union had been able to mount huge counterattacks against the Germans. In January of that year, in a bloody struggle to capture Stalingrad, Hitler had pushed his forces into such an extreme position that the Red Army was able to encircle and capture over 200,000 German troops. At this moment, Roosevelt and Churchill were meeting in Morocco at Casablanca to coordinate their war plans. They resolved to pour every possible resource into winning the crucial battle of the North Atlantic, for unless the flow of ships and supplies to Britain grew easier, no invasion of continental Europe was possible. Similarly, they decided on a day-and-night bombing campaign against Germany. The barbarities wreaked on Britain by Germany—and on other European countries—in the bombing of civilians were now to be the fate of Hitler's Reich. (American bombers specifically sought to bomb only military and industrial targets, in daylight; the British Royal Air Force aimed instead at mass terror bombing of cities at night. By war's end, 305,000 Germans would die from aerial bombing and close to 800,000 would suffer injuries.) Then, to expand the victory in North Africa and open the Mediterranean Sea completely, Roosevelt and Churchill agreed on an invasion of Sicily, to be followed by an invasion of mainland Italy.

At the conference's end, President Roosevelt announced to newsmen that the conferees had agreed that the war with Hitler was to be fought until "unconditional surrender" was won from the dictator. This set off a long-lasting controversy. Senator Burton K. Wheeler called the policy "brutal" and "asinine." Many agreed with him then and afterward that the plan would make the war longer and bloodier, for the Axis governments would fight to the end if the only terms were to be complete and hopeless surrender. Furthermore, if the German government were to be completely wiped out, a power vacuum would be created in the center of Europe into which Soviet power would flow. In truth, however, this was the only policy on which both the western Allies and the U.S.S.R. could reach agreement. Anything less than that would lead to endless haggling over terms and intensified mutual distrust. Furthermore, the president was deeply impressed by Hitler's continual insistence that the First World War had never really been lost, that traitors high in the German government had agreed to an unnecessary armistice. Roosevelt was determined that the powerful German people be confronted with final and unarguable defeat, that no voice could ever again say that in another aggressive war a German victory might be grasped.

In July 1943 the Allies invaded Sicily. Soon afterward the Italian people threw off their dictator, Mussolini, and signed an armistice with the Allies. German armies now flooded the Italian peninsula to take up the fight against Allied troops. A long and terribly wasting campaign had to be fought, Allied lines inching slowly northward after landing near Naples in September. One result, however, was to draw off large bodies of German troops from the Soviet front, which helped the Red Army initiate a sweep westward that began rolling the German armies back toward their homeland.

The Pacific Campaign Thrusts Westward

Though apparently denied highest priority by the Germany-first decision made at the war's outset, the American forces in the Pacific found means by skillful campaigning to thrust westward into the island ring Japan had conquered. In fact, so successful and crucial was the effort against Japan that the Pacific war effectively gained equality with the war against Germany. In late 1943, when 1.8 million Americans were deployed in the fight against Hitler, 1.9 million were campaigning against the Japanese. The "Europe-first" priority was never fully realized.

Operating out of Australia, General Douglas MacArthur aimed at the Philippine Islands. His soldiers leapfrogged through the Bismarck islands, utilizing the northern coast of New Guinea and the islands of the Solomons. At the same time, far to the north, a combined naval and land force under Admiral Chester W. Nimitz

fought through the islands of Micronesia in the Central Pacific, on to the Marianas, and then northwestward toward Japan itself. MacArthur's attacks, being confined to the heavily forested regions of the southern jungles, were slow and foot-slogging. Nimitz's force, by contrast, struggled through brief and bloody battles on the beaches of heavily defended small islands. Hundreds of aircraft pounded the islands in preparation for invasions, and powerful flotillas of battleships followed up with storms of bombardment. Even so, the Japanese were strongly entrenched, and they fought almost literally to the last man. When the marines waded onto Tarawa's coral beaches in November 1943, they went through a roaring four-day hell in which 1,000 Americans were killed and 2,300 wounded. In February 1944 Kwajalein was stormed, then Eniwetok, followed in June 1944 by the conquest of Guam, Saipan, and Tinian. The Japanese fleet struck back, but in the battle of the Philippine Sea (June 1944) was disastrously defeated, losing practically the last of its aircraft carriers.

The impact of these cumulative Japanese defeats wrought chaos in Tokyo. General Tojo and his cabinet were dismissed, and the government began preparations for a last-ditch stand. The Americans were now inside the inner defenses of the Japanese Empire, and they seemed irresistible. Late in 1944 the first B-29 Superfortresses flew off the newly captured airfields of the Marianas—on Guam, Saipan, and Tinian—to begin the bombing raids that eventually reduced the great cities of Japan to rubble.

The Invasion of Europe

Millions of men, thousands of aircraft, and tens of thousands of tanks, half-tracks, and artillery had been gathered in Britain by June 1944. This huge army, as Eisenhower later wrote, was like "a great human spring, coiled for the moment when its energy should be released and it would vault the English Channel in the greatest amphibious assault ever attempted." The main landing was to be made on the coast of Normandy, and another force was to enter the south of France from the Mediterranean somewhat later. On the evening of June 5, hundreds of vessels left a series of ports on the English south coast and headed for France, carrying an assault force of 150,000 Americans,

American B-17 "Flying Fortresses" of the Eighth Air Force drop bombs on Europe. With the relatively accurate bombsights, they tried in daylight to hit military targets, as against the nighttime area bombing of the British Royal Air Force.

United Press International

Britons, Canadians, and Free French. Thousands of fighter planes and bombers raced in over the French coast to strafe and bomb all approaches leading to the invasion beaches, while an armada of ships stood offshore and lobbed heavy shells into fortifications. The terrible fighting of D-Day, June 6, ended with the Allied troops securely lodged in their beachhead. A hectic month of buildup followed during which thousands of troops and tanks were poured into the Normandy beaches preparatory to sweeping across France. ("The . . . landings and . . . successful buildup on the beachheads would almost certainly have been impossible," writes the military historian Russell Weigley, "if the bulk of the German army had not been committed in Russia.") In July the German ring around the beaches was broken. General George Patton took command of the Third Army then racing through the holes torn in the German lines, and led a lightning advance that soon spread chaos within the enemy forces. Having suffered its worst defeat since Stalingrad, the German army began reeling back, and the liberation of France was under way. In August 1944 the German command holding Paris surrendered, and General Charles de Gaulle walked down the

Champs Elysées in triumph, having led the Free French forces through every kind of travail to this soaring hour.

Counterattack

It was now the autumn of 1944, and Hitler's empire was crumbling. The Soviet armies were moving rapidly westward: they were deep within Poland, had taken Rumania and Bulgaria, and were approaching Hungary. The Italian compaign was in its last stage. During three months of disastrous fighting, Hitler had lost over a million men, mainly captured. Clouds of bombers rained destruction on German cities. At this moment Hitler decided on one last, bold counterattack. Choosing the forested Ardennes region in France, he planned to pull together his last reserves, break through the Allied lines (which were lightly defended at this point), race to the English Channel, and win an armistice with the western Allies. Then he could turn to deal with the hated Russians. It was a plan born of madness. The terrible bombing of Berlin had left Hitler with trembling hands, partial paralysis of one leg, and a hysterical manner of thought and speech. He gathered three full armies and thousands of planes and tanks for the great thrust. Then in the bitter snows of December 1944, when the Allied armies had settled down for a brief respite, he launched his attack.

The Battle of the Bulge in the Ardennes Forest frightened the Western world. Everyone had thought Hitler beaten; now his armies suddenly came tearing out of the dark forests sending a torrent of tanks and heavily armed men westward. A hole forty-five miles wide was torn in the Allied lines. However, a crucial crossroads town, Bastogne, was held by an airborne division; the Allied forces north and south of the gap wheeled to crush off the attack; thousands of aircraft struck the German supply lines; and by early January the thrust was blunted and beginning to be turned back. Within a month the Bulge was straightened out, and Eisenhower was free to take up his advance once more.

However, the war's end had been profoundly changed by the Battle of the Bulge. Just as the struggle was being won, Roosevelt, Churchill, and Stalin were meeting in Yalta. Their decisions at that crucial gathering (to be

AMERICA AND THE SECOND WORLD WAR

discussed in the next chapter) were vitally affected by the fact that the western armies had just suffered a stinging rebuff and were still 400 miles from Berlin, while the Soviet forces were sweeping commandingly westward and were only 30 miles eastward from that city. Hitler's preparations of the Ardennes offensive had led to this situation, for he had drawn away large forces from the eastern front. Punching through Hitler's thin lines, the Soviet armies had been able to quickly take the rest of Poland and to race on into Germany. At this point, when future zones of occupation were being agreed on at the Yalta Conference, it was impossible for the western Allies to insist that Berlin belonged to them.

In February 1945 Eisenhower's armies hammered through the Siegfried Line, Germany's concrete fortifications just within its borders, and crossed the Rhine. By April his troops were at the Elbe River, a hundred miles westward from Berlin. There they halted, awaiting the arrival of the Soviet armies, for the Elbe was the agreed-on dividing line for occupation by the two armies. The war in Europe effectively came to an end on April 29, 1945, when Hitler, surrounded in his Berlin bunker by the holocaust of the Russian attack, is reported to have raised a pistol to his mouth and shot himself. On May 7, a German delegation led by Field Marshal Alfred Jodl, chief of the German general staff, surrendered unconditionally to the Allies in a brief ceremony held in a schoolhouse in Rheims, France. In a suburb of Berlin, representatives of the German high command surrendered to the Soviet forces on the following day, May 8.

THE SECOND WORLD WAR: EUROPEAN THEATER, 1942–1945

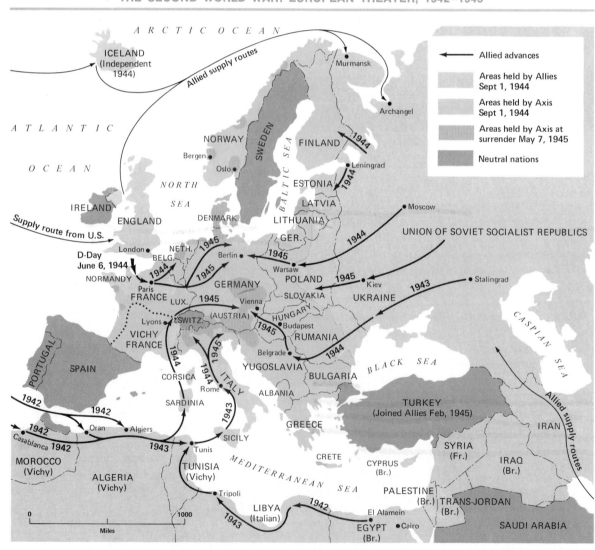

Victory in the Pacific

Meanwhile, the Japanese were being hammered inward in the western Pacific. A joint British-American campaign began driving them out of Burma in early 1944, thus opening up transportation routes to China so that Chiang Kai-shek's armies could be resupplied for assaults against the Japanese forces. General MacArthur's troops continued making long jumps of about 200 miles each through the southwestern islands to the Philippines. In October 1944 he invaded those is-lands, wading ashore on the beaches of Leyte to issue a dramatic broadcast to the Philippine people: "I have returned! Rally to me!" Then the battle of Leyte Gulf, the largest naval battle in the history of warfare, led to the almost total destruc-tion of the rest of the Japanese fleet. In January 1945 the American army invaded Luzon, the prin-cipal island of the Philippines, and drove the Jap-anese out of Manila. By July of that year, the Phil-ippine Islands had been completely reconquered.

Northward, Admiral Nimitz's forces fought a bloody battle to take Iwo Jima in February 1945

THE SECOND WORLD WAR: PACIFIC THEATER, 1942–1945

in order to provide a closer air base for the bombing of Japan. (In the war against Japan the American air forces freely adopted terror bombing of Japanese cities, inflicting enormous casualties upon civilians, a military policy they had held back from in Germany.) In the following month Tokyo was fire-bombed in the most horrible air raid of the Second World War: more than 80,000 people were killed and a million more rendered homeless. Then came the biggest land battle of the Pacific war, the invasion of Okinawa. A force of 100,000 Japanese waited when, on April 1, 1945, American troops landed to begin their assault. Hundreds of suicide pilots, called *kamikaze*, dived in massed attacks on the American naval forces, subjecting them to a searing ordeal rarely experienced by any battle fleet in history. More than thirty ships were sunk, and hundreds were damaged. In the process, however, the Japanese air force was largely eliminated.

A New President: Harry S. Truman

Eleven days after the invasion of Okinawa began, Franklin Roosevelt was seated in a little house at Warm Springs, Georgia. For many months he had been in poor health, worn down by the burdens of war. In 1944 he had accepted his party's nomination for a fourth term and had defeated Thomas E. Dewey of New York, as in 1940 he had defeated Wendell Willkie. He had met twice with the Russians in the previous year and a half, at Teheran in December 1943 and at Yalta in February 1945. The photographs of him at Yalta were a shock to the public, for the gay, smiling president of former years had been replaced by a shrunken, weary, haggard man who stared somberly at the camera. His visit to Warm Springs was made in search of renewed vitality. But now, suddenly, as an artist sketched his portrait, he grasped his head and said, "I have a terrible headache." He lost consciousness and two hours later died of a massive cerebral hemorrhage. The nation and the world were stunned. To the end of their lives, millions remembered the exact moment when they learned that Franklin Roosevelt had died, for the news seemed to shake the firmament of their accustomed world.

Equally shocked was the vice-president, Harry S. Truman, for a great weight now fell on his shoulders. A peppery, scrupulously honest man who had served as senator from Missouri, he brought little but courage and common sense to the White House, for he knew almost nothing of what had been going on in the executive branch. The world was still in flames, Hitler's Reich was collapsing in its last volcanic agonies, and the Soviet armies were streaming westward. Complex negotiations awaited him in San Francisco, where in less than two weeks fifty nations would gather to form the United Nations. After that would come a crucially important conference with Joseph Stalin and the British in Potsdam, just outside of Berlin, where fundamental decisions about the postwar world would be made. Equally grave was the news brought to the president within days of his entering the White House that for years the United States had been developing an atomic bomb and that it might need to be used to achieve the final conquest of Japan.

Japan Surrenders

By July 1945 the Japanese home islands were practically defenseless. The imperial battle fleet was gone, and submarines had sunk most of Japan's merchant vessels. Cut off from food supplies, the Japanese people were nearly starving. American bombers ranged over the cities, burning out vast urban areas. An American naval force cruised up and down the Japanese coast untouched, bombarding at will. Okinawa had fallen in June; nothing was left to provide an outer defense. The military leaders, however, were filled with a fanatic zeal to fight until the end, and they had never been under the jurisdiction of the civilian government. The generals kept talking of one last battle in the homeland, where by the superior spirit and sacrificial courage of their own soldiers, the Japanese people would defeat the Americans. The loss of life on both sides would be astronomical, but Japan and its honor would be saved.

From the Potsdam Conference, the western Allies and China announced on July 26 that unconditional surrender would be demanded only of the Japanese armed forces. No mention was made of the fate of Emperor Hirohito, which led high Japanese officials to fear that he would be tried as a war criminal. This strengthened the military's determination to fight on. Now, however, there was a powerful new factor in the equa-

AMERICA AND THE SECOND WORLD WAR

tion. Early in the morning of July 12, 1945, a group of scientists and technicians had stood transfixed in the New Mexico desert watching a dazzling ball of flame, erupted by the world's first nuclear explosion, rising and swelling steadily larger. They had not anticipated an explosion so vast and terrifying. The fear flashed through them that it would not stop growing until it had swallowed up the earth and the heavens above. As he watched, the scientist Robert Oppenheimer suddenly found these words from the Hindu holy book, the *Bhagavad-Gita*, racing through his mind:

> If the radiance of a thousand suns
> were to burst into the sky
> that would be like
> the splendor of the Mighty One—
> I am become Death, the shatterer of worlds.

General Leslie R. Groves, director of the atomic-bomb project, had an utterly different kind of response. Turning to a military colleague, he exulted, "The war's over. One or two of those things, and Japan will be finished."

By August, a B-29 was on Tinian Island ready to carry an atomic bomb to drop on Japan. President Truman was warned that unless some great demonstration of America's overwhelming power was made, the war could be ended only by an invasion that would cause the deaths of untold thousands. We now know that this may not have been true. Emperor Hirohito had already decided that the war had to be ended somehow. The Japanese government had sent out peace feelers, and intense discussions were taking place within the highest imperial circles on how best to respond to the Potsdam declaration. "Had the Allies given the Prince [Konoye] a week of grace in which to obtain his Government's support for acceptance of the proposals," the historian Robert J. C. Butow has written after a close examination of Japanese archives, "the war might have ended—without the atomic bomb and without Soviet participation in the conflict."

Truman's Decision

To the new American president, halfway around the world, there seemed no alternative. Over and over again the Japanese had shown that they pre-

ferred death to surrender. Even their women and children had run off the cliffs of Saipan to die on the rocks below, choosing to join their slain husbands and fathers rather than suffer the shame of capture by the Americans. Accepting the view that dropping the bomb would actually save lives by making an invasion unnecessary, President Truman authorized an attack on Hiroshima. On August 6 the entire city, with its 80,000 people, was destroyed. Two days later, the Russians declared war against Japan, eager to join in the booty before it was too late. When no surrender came from the Japanese, a second bomb was dropped on Nagasaki on August 9.

Soon after the Hiroshima bombing, President Truman issued a statement: "Sixteen hours ago an American airplane dropped one bomb on Hiroshima, an important Japanese Army base. . . . It is an atomic bomb. It is a harnessing of the basic power of the universe. The force from which the sun draws its power has been loosed against those who brought war to the Far East." It was developed, he said, in a race against the Germans involving over a hundred thousand workers, scientists, and engineers. "What has been done is the greatest achievement of organized science in history. . . .

"We are now prepared to obliterate more rapidly and completely every productive enterprise the Japanese have above ground in any city. . . . If they do not now accept our terms they may expect a rain of ruin from the air, the like of which has never been seen on this earth. Behind this air attack will follow sea and land forces in such numbers and power as they have not yet seen and with the fighting skill of which they are already well aware.

"The fact that we can release atomic energy ushers in a new era in man's understanding of nature's forces. Atomic energy may in the future supplement the power that now comes from coal, oil, and falling water. . . . I shall recommend that the Congress of the United States consider promptly the establishment of an appropriate commission to control the production and use of atomic power within the United States. I shall give further consideration and make further recommendations to the Congress as to how atomic power can become a powerful and forceful influence towards the maintenance of world peace."

During these frightful days, the Japanese government was stunned into a series of nonstop crisis discussions. The militarists still vowed a fight to the death, but when the news finally reached Tokyo of what had happened to the two bombed cities (the violence of the blasts had destroyed communication lines), Emperor Hirohito convened the Supreme War Council to debate anew the fate of Japan. From this gathering a message went to the United States saying that if the emperor were left at the head of his people and not tried as a war criminal, Japan was ready to accept unconditional surrender. When told that the emperor would be subject to the orders of General MacArthur as supreme commander, the Japanese again began arguing among themselves. At this moment the emperor rose before his council and for the first time intervened directly. "We demand that you will agree to it," he said. "We see only one way left for Japan to save herself. That is the reason we have made this determination to endure the unendurable and suffer the insufferable."

Peace was made. On August 15, American forces ceased fire, and on September 2, 1945, surrender documents were signed on the deck of the battleship *Missouri*, swinging at anchor in Tokyo Bay. The greatest war in history was ended. In the major fighting countries some seventy million men had been mobilized (not counting the U.S.S.R. where the figures are unavailable). Counting civilian casualties, perhaps fifty million people had died. Germany and Japan lay in smoking ruins. The same was true of large areas in the Soviet Union, and throughout Europe and Asia. The task ahead was less exciting and perhaps more difficult than fighting the war, though happily it would be pursued largely in peace: building a new world order on the ash heap of the old.

Bibliography

Books especially valuable to me in writing this chapter: The important thing to grasp about American foreign policy thinking in the prewar and wartime years is the powerful hold of Wilsonian internationalism, especially his concept of collective security, upon Franklin Roosevelt and others like him of his generation. Here, Jean-Baptiste Duroselle's *From Wilson to Roosevelt** (1963) is valuable, and especially Roland N. Stromberg's *Collective Security and American Foreign Policy From the League of Nations to NATO* (1963). So, too, the isolationist mentality must be grasped, and I found Selig Adler's *The Isolationist Impulse: Its Twentieth Century Reaction** (1957) essential. As a general guide, a small volume by John E. Wiltz, *From Isolation to War, 1931– 1941** (1968) has keen insights, and the opening chapters in James MacGregor Burns's *Roosevelt: The Soldier of Freedom* (1970) are important. Alan Bullock's *Hitler: A Study in Tyranny** (1953) remains a fundamentally valuable analysis. A. Russell Buchanan's *The United States and World War II*,* two vols. (1964) is thorough and judicious. Books on the Second World War itself are legion. I benefited from reading the memoirs of various generals, notably those of Dwight Eisenhower and Omar Bradley. *The Age of Global Power: The United States Since 1939** (1979), by Norman A. Graebner, is the work of a distinguished diplomatic historian, and valuable reading. Gerald D. Nash's *The Great Depression and World War II: Organizing America** (1979) provides an excellent picture of the domestic scene, as does also Richard Polenberg's *War and Society: The United States, 1941–1945* (1972). I relied upon Russell F. Weigley's *The American Way of War: A History of United States Military Strategy and Policy** (1973) for an informed look at broad decisions and strategy, especially the balance between the Eu-

Thousands of feet high, a cloud of smoke mushrooms over the vaporized Japanese city of Nagasaki after American airmen dropped the second atom bomb, August 9, 1945. This specter has hung over the world ever since.

Wide World Photos

ropean and Pacific theaters. Robert Leckie's *The Wars of America,** 2 vols. (1968) is fascinating. For the Soviet side of things, and their interpretation of the war, I turned to Nikolai V. Sivachev and Nikolai N. Yakovlev's recently published volume, *Russia and the United States: U.S.-Soviet relations from the Soviet point of view* (1979) (published in The University of Chicago Press's series, The United States in the World: Foreign Perspectives, Akira Iriye, ed.) and to N. Sivachev and E. Yazkov, *History of the USA since World War I* (1976). On the crucial question of the dropping of the atom bombs and their effects on Japan's war plans, I drew upon Robert J. C. Butow's brilliant *Japan's Decision to Surrender* (1954 and 1967).

Other Works on the Period

Herbert Feis, *The Road to Pearl Harbor** (1950) and *Churchill, Roosevelt, Stalin* (1957); Paul W. Schroeder, *The Axis Alliance and Japanese-American Relations, 1941* (1958); Roberta Wohlstetter, *Pearl Harbor: Warning and Decision** (1962); William Langer and Everett Gleason, *The Challenge to Isolation, 1937–1940** (1952), and *The Undeclared War, 1940–41* (1953); Bruce M. Russett, *No Clear and Present Danger: A Skeptical View of United States Entry Into World War II* (1972); Gabriel Kolko, *The Politics of War: The World and United States Foreign Policy, 1943–1945* (1968); Gar Alperovitz, *Atomic Diplomacy: Hiroshima and Potsdam** (1965); Robert A. Divine, *Roosevelt and World War II* (1969); Dorothy Borg, *The United States and the Far Eastern Crisis, 1933–1938* (1964); Barbara Tuchman, *Stilwell and the American Experience in China* (1970); Audrie Girdner and Anne Loftis, *The Great Betrayal* (1969) and Roger Daniels, *Concentration Camps USA: Japanese Americans and World War II* (1971) [the Japanese detention camp story]; Alton Frye, *Nazi Germany and the American Hemisphere: 1933–1941* (1967); James V. Compton, *The Swastika and the Eagle: Hitler, the United States, and the Origins of World War II* (1967); Warren F. Kimball, *The Most Unsordid Act: Lend-Lease, 1939–1941* (1969).

* Available in paperback.

33

TIME LINE

1946 Stalin declares need for buildup of strength against capitalist world; Churchill gives "iron-curtain" speech; Truman stiffens policies toward Russia

1947 Cold War begins; Truman Doctrine; European economy in crisis; Marshall Plan announced; George Kennan describes containment policy against Russia

1948 Organization of American States created; Congress approves Marshall Plan

1948–49 Berlin Airlift

1949 North Atlantic Treaty Organization created; Russia explodes atom bomb; Chinese Communists gain control of mainland China

1950–53 Korean War

1950 China enters war as United Nations force approaches Chinese border

1952	Dwight D. Eisenhower elected thirty-fourth president of the United States
1954	Southeast Asia Treaty Organization established as bulwark against Communist advance; United States forms alliance with Nationalist Chinese government
1957	Eisenhower Doctrine announced; Russians launch *Sputnik 1*; Khrushchev trumpets superiority of Russian technology
1958	United States occupies Lebanon under Eisenhower Doctrine; United States puts small satellite in orbit, fires first intercontinental ballistic missile; Russia joins America in halting atomic tests in atmosphere
1959	Khrushchev meets with Eisenhower in America
1960	American U-2 airplane shot down over Russia; Communist China breaks with Russia; John F. Kennedy elected thirty-fifth president

THE COLD WAR

UPI

His greatest impact upon the world, however, came in five peacetime years, from 1945 to 1950, when as Supreme Commander for the Allied Powers he sweepingly reorganized Japanese life. For decades Asia had been his obsession; he knew Nipponese folklore, politics, and economy as did few Westerners. And after the massive air raids and the atomic bombs, the Japanese were a crushed, dazed people. Soon his courtliness and compassion to the defeated made him a national hero, one almost idolized by the Japanese.

MacArthur, the autocratic general, believed his great task was to introduce *demokrashi* to Japan. All his precepts seemed drawn from William Jennings Bryan. He broke up the *zaibatsu,* the feudal oligarchy that had owned and ruled the country, and denied it any role in public life; sternly ended Shinto and emperor worship and made them no longer the state religion; freed labor, urging it to unionize; and dissolved both the former industrial monopolies and the great landholdings, widely distributing land to those who tilled it. As soon as Japanese troops were demobilized, he ended all former Japanese restrictions on political, civil, and religious freedom. Political prisoners were released, and newspapers were told they could publish anything they liked, for the Supreme Commander wanted an informed electorate. American republicanism in an almost undiluted form, as MacArthur had learned it in the years of Grover Cleveland and William McKinley, had come to Japan.

There came with it a new philosophy to be taught in the public schools: that government is the servant, not the master, of the people. MacArthur wrote a democratic constitution that renounced war forever "as a sovereign right." Indeed, he regarded the new constitution, which is still in force, as "the single most important accomplishment of the occupation," though others would point to his land reforms as well. When fourteen million Japanese women joined Japanese men in going to the polls in April 1946, a profoundly new life for Dai Nippon had begun. Indeed, MacArthur's concern to liberate women was genuine. After giving them the vote, he opened both high schools and universities to them and eliminated contract marriage and concubinage. Hundreds of women were elected to public office; soon they were in the cabinet.

Many Asians now regard Japan as so Westernized as no longer to be Asian. To the extent that this is true—traditional Japanese values still make that country sharply different from anything in the West—to the autocratic general from America goes a large share of the responsibility. Few men in history have left so large and enduring a legacy.

Even his wife called him "General." Douglas MacArthur was vain beyond belief, domineering, publicity-hungry, a man thirsting for adulation. He was also one of the great generals of history, a brilliant commander who won sweeping, daring victories in the Pacific so skillfully that the casualties among his troops were remarkably low. Born in 1880, in America's twentieth-century wars Douglas MacArthur became a towering figure. Winston Churchill called him "the glorious commander." His peacock ways were everywhere ridiculed, but, like Ulysses Grant, he fought and he won—which to MacArthur seemed only right, for in his own eyes he was a man of destiny.

The American people greeted the end of the Second World War with a carnival outburst of joy and release. Crowds poured through city streets laughing and singing; men in uniform danced wildly with women from the munitions factories; and a discordant symphony of happy sounds—car horns, train whistles, trumpets, and brass bands—greeted the hopeful new world of peace. Within a year, however, a chill was falling, for the suspicion was spreading that a new world conflict was coming, one as ominous as that which had just ended. A year after that, and the Cold War between the Soviet Union and America had been launched. Stocky Winston Churchill, bulldog-faced and scowling, told a college audience in Fulton, Missouri, that "from Stettin in the Baltic to Trieste in the Adriatic, an iron curtain has descended across the Continent." From Joseph Stalin, Russia's prime minister, came the foreboding announcement that communism and capitalism were inevitably fated to clash. On March 12, 1947, Harry Truman faced the assembled houses of Congress and grimly announced what is known as the Truman Doctrine: the United States would support free countries in resisting Communist takeover. The immediate challenge, he said, was to protect Greece and Turkey from imminent collapse by pouring millions of dollars into their economies and armed forces. Congress quickly approved. The Cold War, gestating for almost two years, was now in the open.

It came as a stunning shock to the American people. As soon as the Second World War had ended, under pressure from the American people the nation's huge military system had been demobilized in a tearing rush: millions of young Americans were brought home and released to civilian life; ships were mothballed; tanks were dumped into the sea; cannon were spiked; and aircraft by the thousands were put out to rust in western deserts. In a brief time the world's most powerful nation, confident that its wartime allies were friendly and that the United Nations would ensure a peaceful future, put away its arms and turned in on itself. Now, unexplainably, came a new threat and the beginnings of a long and frustrating confrontation with a seemingly brilliant adversary who appeared to skillfully exploit every world problem to America's disadvantage. Americans were startled to learn that millions of people regarded them not as kindly liberators but as capitalistic exploiters. "Yankee Go Home" was scrawled on the walls of buildings around the globe.

The psychological effects of this plunge from a peak of exultation to the depths of anxiety were profound. Americans were convinced that they were a good and moral people. Was their country not the great democracy to which all the world's peoples (Americans believed) looked in admiration? Had they not defeated the bloody fascists and brought liberty to the world? they asked themselves. Had they not spread their treasure freely to their friends and asked nothing in return? They were massively bitter, therefore, toward the Soviets and their international coworkers. Americans took up the Cold War with a grim obsessiveness and self-righteousness that produced a near wartime national atmosphere. Used to thinking of great crusades, they hated this new enemy and thirsted for its complete destruction as they had that of Mussolini and Hitler.

At the same time, they were afraid. The map seemed to show the red of communism spreading over ever larger regions of the world: into eastern Europe, erupting in violent upheavals in western Europe, flowing over China, and bursting across the borders of South Korea in a flood of Soviet-made tanks. Given the American tendency to think of the world in simplistic terms, they came to believe that every controversy abroad was another outcropping of the Cold War. Wherever they looked, the hand of the wily Soviet seemed to be manipulating the strings that made the puppets dance. A paranoid fear so gripped the minds of many Americans that they believed communism had secretly taken over the schools, colleges, and churches. Most frightful of all to such people was the thought that Communists had seized control of the State Department and perhaps even the army. For years, because of such anxieties, the nation was rocked by a national witch hunt that put the Red Scare of the 1920s to shame. What else could one expect of a people unversed in the complexities of world politics? The total victory Americans had been led to expect in all their former controversies seemed mystifyingly to elude them. Someone, it was believed, must be selling the nation out.

Crisis followed crisis, and billions of dollars poured out of the Treasury to rebuild the military system, as well as the economies and armies of scores of the "free-world" allies. From the Marshall Plan, the Communist takeover of Czechoslovakia, and the Berlin blockade in the Cold War's early years (1947–49), through the Korean War in the 1950s, to the orbiting of *Sputnik 1* (1957), the building of the Berlin Wall (1961), and the Cuban missile crisis (1962), the Russian-American global confrontation kept the world in an uproar. Not until almost fifteen years of this continuous friction and intermittent warfare had passed were the American people, seasoned and disillusioned, ready to put aside their anger and accept the idea of peaceful coexistence with Soviet Russia, which on its side had also decided to deescalate the terror. Largely ignored in the general relief was a bubbling crisis in remote Indochina, where before long a new and, for the United States and Vietnam, far graver conflict would soon begin.

The Yalta Conference

This complicated chain of events had its beginnings shortly before the end of the Second World War. In February 1945 Roosevelt, Joseph Stalin, and Winston Churchill gathered in the Black Sea resort of Yalta on the Russian Crimean peninsula to plan out the postwar world. It could not have been a more dramatic or fateful confrontation.

The three men and their large groups of advisers came to the meeting with sharply divergent objectives, and at a time of sweeping Soviet victories. While the participants carried on their negotiations, the Red Army was already in occupation of Rumania, Bulgaria, Hungary, Poland, and other vast reaches of eastern and central Europe. Winston Churchill had watched the westward flooding Soviet armies in horror. "Good God," he exclaimed to an associate in late 1944, "can't you see that the Russians are spreading across Europe like a tide?" Franklin Roosevelt had also observed the same phenomenon, which forecast complete Soviet domination over these countries, but he was an optimistic man and he came to Yalta in hope. He was convinced that through gestures of friendship he could persuade the Russians that they need not fear any future Western aggressions against themselves, and that they could relax their grip on the small nations their armies then occupied, letting them govern themselves as they wished. Like Woodrow Wilson before him, FDR was determined that the principle of self-determination should govern the world, allowing all peoples the freedom to choose their own governments. He had convinced Churchill to agree to this principle in the Atlantic Charter, had secured agreement to that charter by almost fifty nations, and expected to be able to persuade Stalin to accept the concept.

He found Stalin unyielding, however, when the most important eastern European country, Poland, was discussed. Stalin's armies occupied it, a Moscow-trained communist government had been put in control, and the Soviet premier had no intention of seeing it put in jeopardy. All Roosevelt and Churchill could get Stalin to do was to approve a Declaration on Liberated Europe which pledged democratic governments for the nations freed from Hitler. As it eventually worked out, Stalin refused even to allow Western observers to be present at the free elections he had promised in Poland—and then they were never held.

Differences in Experiences and Ideas

Why were the Soviets so adamant? Since the Kremlin operates in secret and its files are not open, it is impossible to know with certainty, but this first stand-off between the U.S.S.R. and the West can be made more understandable by considering the background. Russia and America were profoundly different from each other in their national experiences, and in their basic values and ideas. Out of these differences sprang inevitable disagreement.

By 1945, the American people had had many generations of internal stability (only one four-year civil war in 170 years). Theirs was a successful country, affluent, and relatively untouched by the Second World War, in which American losses were lighter than they had been almost a century before in the Civil War. Secure, rarely if ever genuinely threatened in their rich and isolated continent, the American people had felt free to be individualistic, independent-minded, and prickly of their liberties. As the first democratic nation, the United States of America was inspired by a dream of carrying its national ideology, democracy, to the world at large. Its citizens assumed that the wave of the future was

THE COLD WAR

with them and with their way of living. Indeed, Americans assumed that their values and ways of living were the ones most instinctive and basic to human existence, as people generally do in all cultures of the world. What could be more natural, Americans felt, than that all peoples should be allowed the right democratically to choose and run their own governments, with guarantees (as in the United States) of basic human rights? What could be more willful, unnatural, and obstructive than to oppose this principle? What, furthermore, could be more expected than that the peoples of the world would trust Americans, the lovers of freedom and liberty?

Russia is an ancient country with no protective geographic boundaries. It has been invaded again and again in its long history. This centuries-old experience has burned itself into the Russian mind. Even today, the outsider living in Russia finds its people remembering and referring to the "Tatar Yoke": the 150 years in the 13th and 14th centuries when Russia was under the rule of invading Mongol tribes. In the modern centuries, warfare has continued regularly to ravage the Russian people, and for many years before the Second World War there was almost constant turmoil inside the country and great loss of life. From 1914 to 1945 the Russian people suffered through the First World War, an ensuing civil war between the communists and their enemies (the "Reds" v. the "Whites"), a great famine in the 1920s, and under the dictator Joseph Stalin in the 1930s, forced farm collectivization and savage purges within the government and party—followed by another great world war. The death toll in these long bloody years is estimated by demographers to have reached 65 million, of which at least 20 million occurred during the Second World War.

Consequently, the Russians were not in 1945 (nor are they yet) a trusting people. Foreigners have been regarded warily by the Russian people for centuries. There is a national paranoia over "spies" from the outside. Anyone wandering about with a camera in Moscow, unless near the tourist sights around the Kremlin, is regarded distrustfully by ordinary Muscovites, not simply by the police. The Russians have felt surrounded by enemies since long before the communist revolution took place under V. I. Lenin in 1917, and after that event occurred, this attitude

grew stronger. In 1945, much of the U.S.S.R. lay in shattered, smoking ruins, and the Soviets were determined to guarantee their future military security by their own efforts, not by trusting others.

It would be inconceivable, in their minds, to stand back in the countries their armies now occupied in eastern and central Europe and allow Western-style democratic regimes—capitalist, and middle-and upper-class dominated—to take over. The memory of two massive German invasions since 1914 also made the Kremlin believe that Germany must be crushed, and that the countries in Slavic Europe through which the German armies had come (Poland, Czechoslovakia, Hungary, Rumania, and the Balkans) must be directly under their control so that such invasions could never occur again. They knew, and later candidly admitted to protesting American diplomats, that free elections in the countries of eastern Europe, whose peoples for centuries had hated the Russians—had indeed looked down upon the Russians in contempt as (in their belief) a boorish, uncivilized people—would simply mean the creation of anti-Russian, and therefore anti-Soviet, governments there.

The Issue of Self-Determination

The Russians had never accepted the principle of self-determination. They had not even accepted it within the U.S.S.R., a fact which requires some explanation. Americans usually do not realize that "Russia" and "the Soviet Union" are not the same thing. The Soviet Union is composed of 15 republics, of which far and away the largest is Russia itself. In 1970 there were 241 million people in the Soviet Union, made up of more than 90 ethnic groups: Georgians, Estonians, Moldavians, Uzbeks, Azerbaijanis, and many others. The largest of them, the Russians, numbered 128 million, or slightly more than half the Soviet population. Moscow is their ancient capital, sited in the heartland of the Russian republic. It was Russian armies marching out from this heartland that over the centuries conquered the smaller nationalities (ethnic groups) and formed the Russian Empire under the czars. Thus, in contrast with the United States, where ethnic groups live mixed in with one another in the various states, in the Soviet Union (lineal descendant of the Russian

Empire), each nationality has lived for centuries in a particular region. In other words, the ethnic groups live separately from each other, with little intermixture of settlement—save for the Russians, who have migrated out into the non-Russian republics in large numbers.

After the communist revolution of 1917, V. I. Lenin informed the national minorities that they could henceforth be independent, if they wished to, but when a number of them promptly took advantage of this offer, Moscow sent the Red Army to force them back inside the old imperial boundaries, which became the boundaries of the Union of Soviet Socialist Republics. As a federated nation, the U.S.S.R. is dominated, politically and governmentally, by the Russian republic. Russians make up most of the legal government and the leadership of the Communist Party of the U.S.S.R. There are close to a hundred different languages spoken by the Soviet Union's scores of ethnic groups in their own regions, but all are required to learn the Russian language, the Russians themselves being officially termed the "elder brothers" in the U.S.S.R. Under the dictator Joseph Stalin (himself a Georgian, who greatly admired Russians), there was savage repression of ethnic loyalties in the non-Russian republics.

As to democracy itself, Lenin had simply followed the centuries-old Russian tradition in government when after the 1917 communist revolution he had insisted that to establish justice and protect the new Soviet nation from its enemies, all power must be centralized, as it had been under the czars. All political parties, save for the Communist Party of the U.S.S.R., were soon suppressed, for unanimity was felt to be essential. In the Russian village, from which most Russians have only recently come (or where they still live), from time immemorial all decisions of the village *mir*, the council of village elders, had to be unanimous. We have observed the same habit in colonial New England villages, where being of one mind and one voice was also assumed to be the only possible way.

In their long history the Russians have never had any experience whatever with democracy, and they distrust it. The turmoil and confusion and periodic invasions they have lived through lead them to prefer order, team spirit, hanging together in the face of common enemies,

and stability. Freedom of speech and press means to them morally unrestrained license to say and do abusive, destructive, harmful things. Someone should be in charge, supervising what is said and printed. Democracy looks too individualistic and chaotic—and, Marx and Lenin said, too subject to being skillfully dominated by the wealthy and powerful. Where Americans fear tyranny most of all, and have carefully divided up authority into many different and competing bodies, national and local, Russians fear anarchy: lawlessness, or political disorder due to the absence of strong authority. Firm leaders are admired; many continue to revere the memory of the dictator Stalin, for all his crimes. Dissidents, critics of the regime and the system, receive savage public condemnation. The principle of centralized authority is supreme. In the Soviet Union, literally *everything* is centralized in Moscow. The 15 republics do not even have the power to raise taxes. Every factory, no matter how small or remote, produces only what it is told by Moscow to produce.

Therefore, when Franklin Roosevelt came to Yalta talking of democracy and human rights and self-government, he got nowhere with Joseph Stalin and his associates. They had no interest in FDR's dream of a liberal-democratic world order, modeled on the American and British democracies, in which every nation, no matter how small, would be independent and self-governing, and an overarching United Nations would insure the universal rule of (Western-style) law. Stalin and Lenin before him had only contempt for democratic parliamentary government, and the rights of small nations were in the eyes of Soviet leaders to be brushed aside in the interests of a larger, communist-style—and Russian-dominated—unity.

The Mission of Russia

Thus, while the Americans at Yalta dreamed of a new world order, so, too, did the Russians. They had a powerful faith of their own, Soviet communism, and an understandable determination to carry it to all the world. This impulse is not something new. For many generations the Russian people have believed that Russia has a great mission in the world, just as the Americans have believed this of their own country since their Revolution. Russia with its empire, czarist and Soviet, is and has been a very large country, more than twice as large as the United States. With this large size has gone an instinctive belief that, somehow, Russia has a destiny to guide the world. Under the czars, the dream was that Holy Russia would inspire the world by a truly Christian and spiritual civilization. It was this conviction which helped to inspire Russian armies as they defeated the ruling Mongol tribes, and then as they continued their outward surge from the Moscow region to conquer, step by step, the vast multi-ethnic region which became the Russian Empire. The dream of a great Russian mission to lead the world in true and better paths changed in form and substance as a result of the communist revolution of 1917, but it remained nonetheless a compelling national inspiration. The Russian people are passionately patriotic, and in 1945, after having at enormous cost thrown back the greatest invading host in their history, and having finally conquered vast reaches of that part of Europe from which the invading armies had come, they were filled with pride in themselves and determined to see their influence and power expand.

Balance of Power Diplomacy

The Soviet determination to insure the safety of the U.S.S.R. led to a sharply different foreign policy philosophy than FDR's: great-power "spheres of influence" or "balance-of-power" diplomacy. In this system, the great powers come to agreements on the regions of the world they will individually dominate, and by their own strength they impose order and peace in the regions each power controls. Peace in the world at large, in this system, is kept by periodic negotiations between the great powers.

Franklin Roosevelt, and his long-time secretary of state, Cordell Hull, disagreed with this philosophy. They believed it had caused the two world wars. Throughout the Second World War they had persistently rejected the idea of basing agreements on the coming postwar world in the ancient doctrine of spheres of influence. Rather, they insisted upon the one-world, multilateral concept in which all nations are thought to be equal, no nation is dominated by any other, and an international body, the United Nations, keeps order. FDR believed, as Woodrow Wilson had believed before him, that only such a world order could insure world peace. At Yalta, however, the fundamental fact was that Stalin and the Soviets intended to proceed on the basis of a balance-of-power principle. The choice before Roosevelt and Churchill was either to recognize openly that fact and allow the Soviets their sphere of influence in eastern Europe, or to continue the war and drive the Soviet armies back within their own borders. The latter was impossible. The former, given the fervent convictions of the American people, was also impossible. Thus, the United States would continue after 1945 to insist that the Soviets behave according to the principles of self-determination and the equality of all nations, and work in willing good faith within the structures of international organizations. On their side the Soviets proceeded to ignore these demands, indeed to find them infuriating, and to hold on to the regions under their control by force of arms. In fact, Stalin had taken Estonia, Latvia, and Lithuania in 1940, joining these small Baltic countries to the Soviet Union against their will, and after the Second World War he incorporated more huge regions into the U.S.S.R. itself: large portions of Norway and Finland, of prewar Poland, of eastern Czechoslovakia, and of Rumania. The Red Army-occupied nations in eastern and central Europe would not become legally part of the U.S.S.R., but would nonetheless remain under strict Soviet control.

Agreements Made at Yalta

These were the realities of Soviet intentions at Yalta. Nevertheless, FDR hoped more than anything else that he could persuade the Soviets to come to the projected San Francisco conference at which the United Nations was to be formed, and become a part of that body. It would provide, FDR believed, the ultimate protection for small nations by ensuring world peace, and thereby easing the fears that made great powers aggressive. Thus, Roosevelt worked hard at Yalta to establish a good relationship with the Soviet leaders by yielding gracefully to their demands where he had essentially no choice, and in this way hopefully laying the basis for a postwar world in which all nations would work together on a basis of mutual trust. A harsh treatment of the U.S.S.R. at Yalta would have destroyed at the outset any hopes for achieving such a goal. Later, when things did not work out as he had hoped, he would be subjected to much posthumous condemnation, but he was playing for big stakes and the long haul.

The Russians were frightened that Germany might once again launch a new invasion, and they got the western Allies to agree, in principle, that that country would be dismembered. They also asked for reparations. Roosevelt seemed as anxious as the U.S.S.R. to punish Germany by dismemberment and the extraction of reparations, but the British retained vivid memories of the postwar period after 1919, when an economically sick Germany, borne down by reparations demands, dragged all of Europe into depression. The only final agreement concerning Germany made at Yalta was to settle on zones of occupation by the various armies.

America's military leaders had warned Roosevelt that Soviet help would be desperately needed in the final campaigns against Japan. At Yalta, Stalin volunteered his desire to enter that war as soon as possible after Germany was defeated. In return, Roosevelt agreed that Russia should be allowed to take back what that nation had lost to Japan in the Russo-Japanese War of 1904 and 1905: the Kurile Islands and southern Sakhalin, together with control over Manchuria's railways and its ports of Darien and Port Arthur. All of this Roosevelt made conditional on the approval of Chiang Kai-shek's government. (When the Chinese discovered that the Russians in the Yalta agreement were ready to recognize China's complete sovereignty over Manchuria, they hastened to approve enthusiastically.)

Last, the Americans won approval for the project they considered most crucial—formation of the United Nations. At first the Russians argued closely on the matter of voting: they were openly scornful of small nations and recoiled from the prospect of being outvoted by them. When they learned that the great powers—to include France, China, the U.S.S.R., Britain, and the United States—would have the right of veto over any actions by the United Nations Security Council, they dropped their objections. Stalin regarded the General Assembly with amused indifference, for even though every nation in that body was accorded equal voting power, the assembly would have no power to do anything other than talk and pass resolutions.

Good Relations Break Down

The Americans left Yalta pleased with the results of their work. But within two months Franklin Roosevelt was writing Stalin of his "astonishment," "anxiety" and "bitter resentment" that the Russians were refusing to install a democratically based government in Poland. In a few days he was dead, and the new president, Harry Truman, was listening to W. Averell Harriman, American ambassador to Moscow, say that the United States was faced with a new "barbarian invasion of Europe." Truman bluntly demanded of Stalin that the Polish government be reorganized, but Stalin flatly refused. Poland, he said, was vital to Soviet security. "The Soviet Union," he went on, "has a right to make efforts that there should exist in Poland a government friendly toward the Soviet Union." The Soviets would never understand that an America with millions of Polish and Catholic citizens would retain a close interest in the fate of that country, nor would they realize how crucial was the principle of self-determination to the American people. They could only conclude that every American complaint aimed simply at harming Soviet interests, and in fact masked an attempt at aggression and at meddling within spheres vital to them. Why could America, they asked, rule Japan unilaterally and the U.S.S.R. be denied this right in Poland?

The breach widened steadily. Charge and countercharge went back and forth, the U.S.S.R. and America interpreting each other's actions in the worst possible light. In July 1945 Truman, Stalin, and the new British premier, Clement Attlee, gathered in Potsdam, a suburb of Berlin, to discuss their differences. They were able to agree on little. The new Soviet threat made American planners decide that Germany should be unified, rebuilt in democratic form, and given a healthy economy so it could serve as a bulwark against Soviet expansion. On this issue there was no possibility of compromise with the Soviets. Their fears of Germany and hopes for the spread of communism made them hold fast thereafter to their zone in Germany and turn it into a Communist state. They wiped out the Prussian landlord

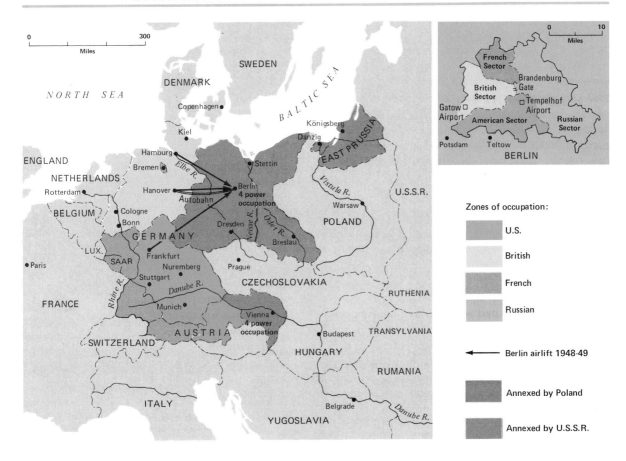

Zones of occupation:

U.S.

British

French

Russian

Berlin airlift 1948-49

Annexed by Poland

Annexed by U.S.S.R.

class, nationalized east Germany's industries, and forced all parties to accept Communist control. At the same time, they would agree to no arrangements that would merge their eastern zone either economically or politically with the western zone. The division of Germany was complete. By force of arms, certainly not by the choice of the people of east Germany, communism had leaped far westward from the Soviet Union to implant itself deeply in the heart of Europe.

The Atom Bomb and Russian-American Relations

When the atom bombs were dropped on Japan in August 1945, the whole balance of international power suddenly shifted, and a psychological earthquake occurred in the Soviet Union. If the Soviets' tendency was to distrust the capitalist West in the best of circumstances, now their fears escalated sharply. In Washington, con-

versely, the bomb seemed to give men a sense of power advantage. Truman remarked to Henry Stimson, who had been secretary of war under Roosevelt, that it "gave him an entirely new feeling of confidence." However, when Secretary of State James Byrnes went to a meeting with the U.S.S.R.'s foreign minister, Molotov, in September 1945, delighted with "the presence of the bomb in his pocket, so to speak, as a great weapon to get through the thing," he found the Soviets more hostile and unyielding than ever.

The American government went almost immediately to the United Nations (in October 1945) with a warning that some international means of control over atomic energy had to be worked out. In March 1946 it proposed that all atomic production be placed under an international agency; that international inspectors be given free access to every country to ensure against violations; and that the big-power veto in the Security Council be abolished in all matters pertaining to violation of atomic agreements. The Soviets had never trusted the United Nations, for in all of its deliberations they were clearly in a minority. They totally rejected the American plan. Instead, they wanted the United States to destroy its stockpile of weapons and halt all nuclear production, after which a program of international control would be established. In response Truman observed, "We should not under any circumstances throw away our gun until we are sure the rest of the world can't arm against us. If we accepted the Russian position, we would be deprived of everything except their promise to agree to controls." The impasse was total; another deadlock had occurred.

President Truman found the world scene in January 1946 deeply alarming. The Soviets were mounting intense pressure against Turkey to give them control over the Dardanelles; their armed forces were still in northern Iran, where they seemed busy establishing another puppet regime; and after a brief period in the fall of 1945 when they had relaxed their grip in eastern Europe (they had allowed elections in Hungary, which went smashingly against them), they had clamped down hard. Millions of refugees fled to western Europe to get away from the Russians. Truman now told Byrnes to drop conciliatory gestures. "Unless Russia is faced with an iron fist and strong language," he wrote Byrnes, "another war is in the making. I'm tired of babying the Soviets."

In February 1946 Stalin made a speech in Moscow that chilled the non-Communist world. There could never be any lasting peace with capitalism, he insisted. The Soviet Union must prepare itself for many years of austerity while it built the necessary industrial strength to meet the capitalist challenge. Justice William Douglas echoed the feelings of many when he said this speech was "the declaration of World War III." Shortly afterward, when Winston Churchill made his "iron-curtain" address in Fulton, Missouri, he pleaded with Americans to use their possession of atomic strength to create "a unity in Europe from which no nation should be permanently outcast." Stalin trumpeted that Churchill's words were "a call to war with the Soviet Union," and scoffed that it was "the law of historical development" for all Europe to become Communist. Soon an intense ideological campaign was begun within Russia to drive out Western influences, make Stalin into a kind of god, and instill the purest Stalinist dogma. The Cold War was in full cry.

The Crisis of 1947

By 1947 the United States stood face to face with a harsh reality: Europe was in a state of collapse. Its railroads, factories, electrical systems, banking houses, supplies of capital, farms, markets—all had been utterly devastated by the Second World War. The governments of each European

Hamburg, Germany, lies devastated after wartime bombing. In such conditions lay the economic and social plight of much of stricken postwar Europe. Quonset huts provided temporary housing.

Wide World Photos

THE COLD WAR

country staggered from crisis to crisis, overwhelmed by millions of refugees, desperately trying to feed starving populations and unable to find capital anywhere. American production and prosperity soared as European countries clamored for our goods—they could produce very little themselves—but soon they began running out of dollars. They tried borrowing, but were unable to make payments. Famine, unemployment, and black despair spread everywhere. Communist parties flourished in France and Italy, asserting that the only solution was to jettison capitalism entirely and turn to the Soviet system.

Great Britain teetered on the edge of total economic disaster. Its empire lay in ruins, its trade had disappeared, its currency reserves were depleted, and its factories were both overworked and obsolete. Its millions of city dwellers, who made up most of its population, were desperately in need of food and raw materials from abroad, but they could not produce enough to pay for them. For two years Britain's armies had occupied Greece, helping its government fight off a Communist-inspired rebellion. In February 1947, however, London's ambassador officially informed the American government that the British could no longer carry this burden. Unless the United States took their place, Greece would have to be abandoned.

Here was the turning point. Was the United States going to cast off its traditional policy of peacetime isolation and move massively into Europe with direct aid to its faltering governments, or was it going to hold back and—as it was almost universally believed—watch communism take over? The loss of Greece to the Communists would be bad enough, but the psychological impact of this event on the staggering nations of western Europe would be enormous. Washington buzzed with meetings. Emergency gatherings were held in the State Department and the Pentagon, and a steady stream of advisers came and went from the White House, where President Truman discussed the crisis with his new secretary of state, General George C. Marshall. To the president, the question was fundamentally a simple one: the United States had fought to crush totalitarianism; the new Soviet menace "facing us seemed every bit as grave as Nazi Germany and her allies had been"; and the time had come "to align the United States of America clearly on the side, and the head, of the free world."

The president therefore went before Congress on March 12, 1947, and not only asked for $400 million in economic and military aid to Greece and Turkey but also announced the Truman Doctrine: "I believe that it must be the policy of the United States to support free peoples who are resisting attempted subjugation by armed minorities or by outside pressures." Thus, before a cheering Congress, the American president called not simply for action in a limited sphere but for a policy of global scope as well: that Americans assist "free peoples" anywhere who were in danger of overthrow by the Communists.

The Marshall Plan

Secretary of State George Marshall was an austere and forbidding man whose magisterial leadership of the American armed forces during the Second World War as chief of staff had made him one of the giants of the age. Revered in Washington and throughout the country, he had the kind of moral authority that enables men to lead nations into historic actions. He knew that aid to Greece and Turkey was not enough, that all of Europe was desperately sick. He therefore summoned George F. Kennan, the State Department's brilliant and experienced expert on the Soviet Union, and instructed him to prepare a comprehensive plan for meeting the Soviet challenge and saving Europe. "He then added characteristically," Kennan later wrote, "that he had only one bit of advice for me: 'Avoid trivia.'"

The proposal that Kennan and his planning staff drew up became the bold and imaginative program known as the Marshall Plan. Promising immense gifts of money to rebuild the European economy, it caused excitement in the European governments. The plan was based on three premises. First, it was offered to everyone in Europe, Communist and non-Communist alike. George Kennan put the reason for this succinctly: "We would not ourselves draw a line of division through Europe." Second, it assumed that communism's basic appeal was economic, that a healthy Europe, able to offer jobs and hope to everyone, would not voluntarily choose the Communist system. As the secretary of state said when he announced the proposal in a speech at Harvard in June, the plan would fight "hunger, poverty, desperation, and chaos."

Third, it was hoped through this means to push Europe away from nationalism and toward internationalism. At least since the days of Woodrow Wilson, and especially under Democratic presidents, foreign-policy planners in America had believed that the long-range solution to the world's problems lay in building an international structure of institutions that would allow nations to make their plans and decisions jointly. A multilateral world should replace one in which nations acted unilaterally (entirely on their own). Franklin Roosevelt had placed enormous faith in the United Nations. Under Truman this same internationalist tendency persisted. Washington poured huge sums into the United Nations and vigorously supported its specialized agencies: the Economic and Social Council, the World Court, the International Labor Organization, the Food and Agriculture Organization, the International Monetary Fund, the World Health Organization, and the Educational, Scientific, and Cultural Organization. During the Second World War the United States had required all recipients of lend-lease to commit themselves to the principle of lower tariffs, and in 1947 the government led in the creation of the General Agreement on Tariffs and Trade. This agency worked worldwide to effect bilateral negotiations that progressively reduced tariff barriers. Thousands of commodities were affected by these agreements, in which more than sixty countries, accounting for four fifths of the world's trade, participated. Similarly, in Latin America the Truman administration worked steadily toward the formation of a hemisphere-wide international body, the Organization of American States, which finally appeared in March 1948.

In this spirit, the Marshall Plan assumed that nothing would work in Europe that rested simply on a series of uncoordinated economic programs developed within each nation. Therefore, Secretary Marshall told the Europeans that the United States would help them only if they jointly decided what their needs were and how they could be solved. "By insisting on a joint approach," Kennan wrote, "we hoped to force the Europeans to begin to think like Europeans, and not like nationalists." Responding enthusiastically, delegates from sixteen European nations gathered quickly in Paris, formed the Committee of European Economic Cooperation—the beginning, people said hopefully, of European federation—and plunged into intensive studies of their economic requirements. By September, a two-volume report had been sent to Washington, D.C., and Congress began deliberations on this historic change in America's foreign policies.

America Grapples with Dilemma

Republicans controlled Congress—having won it for the first time since 1930 in the 1946 off-year elections—and they reacted warily to the proposal. They were even more firmly hostile to the Soviets than Truman, and continually urged ever harsher policies. Before long they began attacking Truman as "soft on communism." Moreover, they had little patience with economic aid as a proper response to the Communist challenge. They tended to favor military strength and constantly hammered for a bigger army, navy, and air force and a foreign-aid program that would concentrate on building up the armed strength of the non-Communist governments. Senator Robert Taft of Ohio, Republican leader in Congress, scoffed at the Marshall Plan as a kind of "European TVA," which for an economic conservative of his rigorous views was the ultimate curse. Furthermore, conservative Republicans have traditionally leaned toward nationalist, unilateral approaches to world affairs—in the tradition of Alexander Hamilton and Theodore Roosevelt—and the prevailing internationalism of Truman's administration made them angry. Had they not condemned America's entry into the League of Nations and scoffed at the World Court in the interwar years? Now that they were finally in control of Congress again, they had a chance to make their views influential once more.

This presented, indeed, a grave dilemma for the American people. Was the Soviet threat mainly a military one, or did it feed primarily on misery and privation? On this assessment rested crucial differences in policy. Throughout the Cold War and after, the American government wavered on the issue. The argument went on endlessly in Washington and in the press, sincere people on both sides calling their opponents fools, militarists, or even traitors. In good part the issue was partisan. Republicans—particularly the hard-lining anti-Communists on the right wing—looked at the Communist insurrection in Greece and said: put it down by swift military force. But the Democrats had a more complicated response. Southern Democrats, with the strong martial culture of their region behind them, often agreed with the Republicans. But liberal Democrats thought in terms of social reform—in addition to which, they traditionally distrusted the military, a distrust the military heartily returned. Their answer to a Communist movement was: take away its appeal by economic aid and social reform; foster land reform, build schools, and give hope and opportunity to the common people so that they will lose interest in communism.

The Policy of Containment

The Second World War, however, had hardened many of the liberal Democrats. It was no longer possible, they believed, to get along in the world solely by peaceful methods. Reinhold Niebuhr, now at the peak of his influence among liberal Democrats—George Kennan called him "the father of us all"—criticized the optimism that led liberals to reject armaments and rely simply on international organizations to maintain peace. Liberals, he said, had foolishly ignored the side of human nature that is selfish, distrustful, and aggressive. There is deep-seated will-to-power created by fear that makes international tensions inevitable. In such a world, Niebuhr maintained, every nation must be tough-minded and meet threats by counter-strength.

In this spirit George Kennan published in *Foreign Affairs*—under the pseudonym "X"—the philosophy of "containment," which became the basis of American policy toward Russia. The Communists, he said, would unendingly press outward, taking advantage of every weak spot in the non-Communist world. Moscow did this both because it believed the world should be Communist (its version of "missionary diplomacy") and because repeated invasions of Russian territory over the centuries had made Russians fearful and insecure. Negotiation would gain very little. America should instead build "situations of strength" around the vast Russian perimeter so that the Soviets' outward thrusts would be met by effective resistance. Since the Communists believed that the capitalist system was in any event doomed to collapse, they would draw back from actually going to war. If the United States was strong, vigilant, and patient, this "duel of infinite duration" would eventually end in a peaceful stalemate.

Kennan explained his containment policy in these words: "The first of [Moscow's beliefs] is that of the innate antagonism between capitalism and Socialism. . . . It means that there can never be on Moscow's side any sincere assumption of a community of aims between the Soviet Union and powers which are regarded as capitalist. . . . If the Soviet Government occasionally sets its signature to documents which would indicate the contrary, this is to be regarded as a tactical maneuver. . . . [Thus] the phenomena which we find disturbing in the Kremlin's conduct of foreign policy: the secretiveness, the lack of frankness, the duplicity, the war suspiciousness, and the basic unfriendliness of purpose. . . .

"But we have seen that the Kremlin is under no ideological compulsion to accomplish its purposes in a hurry. Like the Church, it is dealing in ideological concepts which are of long-term validity, and it can afford to be patient. . . . Thus the Kremlin has no compunction about retreating in the face of superior force. And being under the compulsion of no timetable, it does not get panicky under the necessity for such retreat. Its political action is a fluid stream which moves constantly, wherever it is permitted to move, toward a given goal. Its main concern is to make sure that it has filled every nook and cranny available to it in the basin of world power. . . .

"In these circumstances it is clear that the main element of any United States policy toward the Soviet Union must be that of a long-term, patient but firm and vigilant containment of Russian expansive tendencies. [But we must] remain at all times cool and collected and . . . demands on Russian policy should be put forward in such a manner as to leave the way open for a compliance not too detrimental to Russian prestige. [Containment will be achieved] by the adroit and vigilant application of counterforce at a series of constantly shifting geographical and political points. . . ." ("The Sources of Soviet Conduct," *Foreign Affairs*, 25 [July 1947])

Success in Europe

The Soviets condemned the Marshall Plan as a capitalist plot to create war, refused to permit iron-curtain nations to participate, and established the Cominform (Communist Information Bureau) to instigate revolutions. France and Italy were brought to the brink of civil war by violent, Communist-led strikes and sabotage. In February 1948 Moscow obliterated the non-Communist parties in Czechoslovakia—the last iron-curtain country with a vestige of democracy—and installed full Communist control. In April 1948 Congress finally approved the Marshall Plan and provided the first six billion dollars to get it rolling. (In all, twelve billion dollars was eventually spent in carrying it out.) In response, the Soviets closed off surface access to Berlin. President Truman's reply was the Berlin Airlift, which for almost a year (June 1948 to May 1949) flew mountainous supplies of food and other necessities to West Berlin. Truman thus demonstrated conclusively to western Europe that it could count on the United States in a crisis. Meanwhile, he ran for reelection in 1948 against Governor Thomas E. Dewey of New York and won a stunning upset victory.

The Truman administration now moved ahead to build a system of collective military security that would make Europeans confident that they could rebuild their economies without fear of a Soviet attack. In April 1949 the North Atlantic Treaty, leading to the creation of the North Atlantic Treaty Organization (NATO), was signed. It aimed not only at linking the United States militarily to western Europe (eventually including Greece and Turkey) but also at providing a matrix out of which, many hoped, some larger transatlantic federation might emerge. In the NATO treaty a council was provided for, as well as an agreement that "an armed attack against one or more of [the members] in Europe or North America shall be considered an attack against them all." An elaborate military system was built up, deployed throughout Europe, and set in readiness for any eventuality.

The Marshall Plan and NATO were remarkably successful policies. This was so for several reasons: they were in pursuit of objectives clearly vital to American interests; the goals and methods adopted were within America's means to achieve; and what Americans did had the support of those they were trying to protect. With infusions of American capital and the adoption of cooperative methods, the European economy began booming. A basis was established for a stalemate that eventually allowed East and West to live together. In 1949 the Soviets exploded their own atomic bomb, thus moderating their fears of American atomic weaponry and creating a "balance of terror." Having found through their joint efforts in the Marshall Plan how successful cooperation could be, the western European nations during the 1950s launched a series of multinational agencies that pointed toward a federated Europe: the Common Market, the European Coal and Steel Community, and the European Payments Union.

The Soviet Viewpoint on the Second World War

Within the U.S.S.R., these events are described quite differently. Soviet historians explain the Cold War to Soviet students, in fact, by closely interlinking it with their understanding of the Second World War. It will be important for a moment, therefore, to look backward upon that event as they see it.

Before 1939, Soviet historians write, the West was trying hard to settle its difficulties with Hitler and release him to sweep eastward through Poland to conquer the Soviet Union. When the U.S.S.R. made its much-condemned Nonagression Pact with Hitler in 1939, this was only to give the Soviets time to prepare for the attack they knew was coming (Western historians describe Stalin as, by contrast, totally surprised by Hitler's assault). To create a deep buffer against the coming invasion, in 1940 the U.S.S.R. took over eastern Poland and reunited (as Soviet historians put it) the small countries of Estonia, Latvia, and Lithuania with itself. (These countries had successfully separated from the Russian Empire of the czars upon its collapse in 1917.) Had such steps not been taken, Soviet historians insist, the U.S.S.R. would not have been able to resist the Germans as stoutly as it did. This, in turn, would have released Hitler's armies to invade and conquer Great Britain.

Once the Second World War expanded in 1941 to include America, Soviet students are told, the United States held back "to delay direct participation in combat operations as long as possible," as the historian Nikolai N. Yakovlev writes in an English-language history of Soviet-American relations that he coauthored with Nikolai V. Sivachev (*Russia and the United States: U.S.-Soviet relations from the Soviet point of view* [1979]). Why? In order "to be the last in line among the great powers to enter the war." This tactic, it is explained, was aimed at allowing America to enter the postwar world relatively undamaged, but massively armed and ready to dominate the

THE COLD WAR

world. For example, the United States was able to quickly produce huge supplies of arms, and it could have invaded western Europe in 1942 instead of 1944 (the Soviets assert) and thereby taken pressure off the Soviet Union. However, the American strategy was to appear on the scene only after others had weakened the Germans first. As to Japan, the United States first tried to get it to attack the U.S.S.R., and then, after Pearl Harbor, kept its battle with that country at a strictly limited level, a modest holding campaign. The United States intended for the Soviets themselves to ultimately take on the major role of defeating Japan, after destroying Hitler. American diplomacy from 1941 on pushed Moscow to get involved in the Pacific conflict.

Who defeated Germany? Without question, Soviet historians write, the victory against Germany had its beginnings in the Soviet Union. It was there that the fascists were massacred and first made to turn back. (We have seen that there is no disputing this point.) "Everything else in the final analysis," Yakovlev observes, "was derived from conditions on [the Soviet] front": Hitler's inability, through lack of sufficient strength, to punch on through to the Near East at the Suez Canal, to prevent the Western invasion of France, or to defeat that invading force. As to the American and British campaign in North Africa, in Soviet eyes it was not only insignificant, it was a violation of the earlier pledge made (they insist) by FDR to invade the European continent in 1942. While 258 divisions of fascist troops, by Soviet estimate, totaling over six million men, were deep inside the Soviet Union and being fought off, the British and Americans could manage only slow victories over 20 or so divisions. Three fourths of Hitler's forces were in fact on the Soviet front, they write. Even after the invasion of the Continent by the Western armies in 1944, only a third of Germany's strength opposed the British and Americans. In the Battle of the Bulge, it was the Soviets who halted Hitler's westward thrust against the Americans and the British by intensifying their attacks on the eastern front—on his rear, so to speak—and forcing him to withdraw many divisions to hold the Russians off. Thereafter, the Western armies fought against only token German forces, whereas a massive defensive effort was made by the Germans to delay the westward-sweeping Soviet army. The Soviet forces, meanwhile, were "bringing liberation to the peoples of Europe [so that] the peoples of Eastern and Southeastern Europe [could] set out on the road to building a new life. . . . The peoples of these countries were repudiating regimes that the United States and Britain, under the banner of 'democracy,' were attempting to restore there once more, while the USSR had sufficient opportunity to guarantee that the violent enemies of socialism would not rage on its borders once again. It was here that the essence lay of the discord that clouded Soviet-American relations as early as the end of the war in Europe. . . . Those in the United States who had gotten into the deplorable habit of reasoning in terms of 'the American century,' did not want to resign themselves to this."

The Soviet View of the Cold War

The Soviets depict the Cold War as an American-led effort to overturn the U.S.S.R.'s massive successes in the Second World War. It was this motive, they write, that led to the atomic bomb being dropped on Japan. The Soviet attacks upon the Japanese armies in Manchuria were already sealing the fate of Japan (they maintain) and there was no need for the atomic blasts, but America wanted to intimidate the Soviets. In reality—the Soviet version runs—the Soviets had no aggressive intentions after the war. Indeed, "talk of the 'aggressiveness' of the USSR" was known by many in the Truman administration to be untrue. But a perverted "totalitarian model" of socialism in the U.S.S.R. was cleverly developed in America, and this led to equally perverted notions as to future Soviet policy. Paranoid fears of the Soviets even swept the world of American scholarship. Also, Dean Acheson, Truman's secretary of state, believed firmly that "the Kremlin [gives] top priority to world domination," as he recorded in his memoirs. This unthinking prejudice against the U.S.S.R. led many bigoted Americans to drive sensible people out of the American government. Thereafter in Washington, "the belief had spread that the United States could pursue any course it wished in foreign policy, since they had the atomic bomb on their disposal."

Meanwhile, the Soviet government, Soviet historians write, was trying to normalize all relations with the West, in accord with the historic principle of peaceful coexistence announced long ago by Lenin, and in line with the U.S.S.R.'s acute need to restore its war-torn economy. Military forces in the Soviet Union were greatly reduced—to about 2.8 million men under arms. And while America "clung tenaciously to its bases in many countries, and under conditions of peace endeavored to secure additional ones," Soviet troops were withdrawn from many countries they had liberated. At the United Nations, in the meantime, "with the utmost patience, literally as one would do with children or with hysterical unbelievers," Soviet diplomatic representatives carefully explained that their country believed in peaceful coexistence and wanted a cooperative world.

The U.S.S.R. urged repeatedly that all troops be withdrawn from countries other than those of the occupying power, it urged arms reduction, and it called for "a ban on atomic weapons." But it was hopeless, Soviet students are told: Washington was bent on a mindless course of militant anticommunism. It devised a theory of "containment" aimed at bringing such pressure to bear upon the U.S.S.R., through an inevitable arms race, that in ten to fifteen years it would collapse. "In essence," Yakovlev concludes, "the entire postwar period was permeated by the persistent striving of the United States to alter the balance of power in the world to its own advantage." Or, as Nikolai Sivachev and Eugene Yazkov write in a work based on their lecture course in American history at Moscow University, *History of the USA since World War I* (1976), in American policymaking, "by the end of the war almost everything [was cast] . . . in an imperialist, hegemonic [i.e., dominance-seeking], and expansionist color scheme." Indeed, the very policy of restoring the economic unity and health of Germany, adopted under President Truman, was formed not out of a sense of justice to the German people, but in order to preserve "the military and industrial might of fascist Germany in the future struggle against the USSR and the democratic forces of Europe." Furthermore, the "ruling circles" in America were not happy at the end of the war in Europe, for as they looked ahead they "were clearly troubled by the future which promised an upsurge in the forces of peace, democracy and socialism as its main feature." With this in mind, they worked hard to undermine the United Nations by establishing NATO and other regional alliances, for what had seized American leaders was not the ideal of advancing democracy, but "the advancing notions of American imperialist dominance."

(Despite these strongly stated views, the Soviet historian Nikolai Sivachev and his colleagues have since 1974 annually invited an American historian to lecture to their students at Moscow University, under no restrictions, even though the Americans' viewpoints on history diverge widely from their own. Indeed, the lecture course given by the American professor is required of all students majoring in American history [who are fluent in English], including weekly small-group discussions of the latest historical scholarship in the United States, and a final examination is given by the American at the end of the term. When in 1979 it was my responsibility to present these lectures, at their request the then-current edition of this textbook served as the students' basic reading, despite the fact that its cultural interpretation of politics runs counter to the historical materialism of Marxism-Leninism. Thus the students, in order to pass the final examination, had to master interpretations new to them in American history which were ideologically unorthodox. As yet, American professors have not been invited to lecture on the post-1941 years, though it should be said that American scholarship on this period is available to the students.)

Debates Among Historians of the United States

For many years, American historians presented a totally opposite view to that of Soviet historians: that the Cold War, without question, was begun and kept in motion by the Soviet Union. There seemed little reason to doubt the purity of American motives. The United States had long since acquired the fixed notion that it was the warrior for freedom in the world. At least since the bloody Stalin purge trials beginning in 1935, most Western intellectuals had turned against the U.S.S.R. as a dangerous, inhuman dictatorship. Although these feelings had been muted during the common fight against Hitler, they erupted with great force again at the onset of the Cold War. There was a firm belief that America was in fact aiming only at building a world of liberty and justice, whereas the Soviets were at war against those human values wherever they could get the opportunity. The United States had fought bitterly to defeat a German dictatorship that had gobbled up small countries, and now the U.S.S.R. seemed to be doing just what Hitler had done. That President Truman and his associates were sturdily and courageously holding back an arrogant and brutal tidal wave of Soviet force appeared beyond question.

The Vietnam War has severely shaken this confidence. In that conflict American motives were (eventually) harshly condemned by millions of Americans, including most scholars. A group of "revisionist" historians—William Appleman Williams, Walter LaFeber, and Gabriel Kolko chief among them—maintain that the Cold War was produced by a global American drive for power and markets. They stress that the Soviets were only trying to protect their own security by building a ring of friendly buffer states between themselves and the Germans. The United States, meanwhile, was the aggressive power: it wantonly tore apart a possibly peaceful world because capitalism is inherently aggressive. The historian Gar Alperovitz, in his controversial book *Atomic Diplomacy: Hiroshima and Potsdam* (1965), asserted that President Truman dropped the atom bomb on Japan in order to frighten the Russians and cause them to retreat from eastern Europe.

In a more recent study (*Main Currents in Modern American History* [1976]), Gabriel Kolko presents an analysis of the Cold War in which the Soviet Union almost disappears from the stage. He focuses instead upon what he sees as "Washington's desire once and for all to create an integrated, cooperative world capitalism . . . under United States leadership." Such a world order was sought as a solution to America's own economic needs. It was soon learned, Kolko writes, that joining this effort to a spurious (i.e., deceitful and illegitimate) anti-Communist crusade throughout the world would get Congress to authorize the loans, credits, and grants (as in the Marshall Plan) that would tie non-Communist nations to the American economy. Thus, the Cold War was born. Kolko explains the angry attacks that Americans unleashed against the Soviets as springing from their arrogant belief that America was the world's master, and their fury at what seemed to be the U.S.S.R.'s presumptuous attempts to frustrate its capitalist plans. In truth, America's trumpeted faith in "internationalism" and free trade was only propaganda designed to cover up its real goal: to prevent other nations

from building up competitive economies, behind protective tariffs of their own, that would challenge American economic supremacy.

As we observed at the beginning of this book in "The Historian's Task," a scholar's underlying view of life shapes his or her interpretations. Since Western scholars have had no access to Soviet records, Stalin's motives may only be guessed. On the other hand, no systematic evidence of a capitalist conspiracy—and certainly none suggesting a plot so skillfully designed and led—may be found in American records, though there is certainly ample evidence to indicate that the United States wanted markets abroad and desired a world open to American investment. When Henry R. Luce, editor and publisher of *Time* and *Life* magazines, as early as 1941 trumpeted a call that the "American Century" was opening, he gave voice to dreams of American predominance and world leadership that would be hungered for by many in the years to come. But the revisionist historical argument is based in preexisting assumptions about human motives, capitalism, and American society which imply more than this. It assumes that people's real motives lie solely in economics, whatever may be the grand ideals in which they clothe their actions. The fear of a spreading wave of tyranny, and the hopes repeatedly expressed in Washington that a world of self-governing and cooperative nations might be built, cannot be regarded as revealing America's real goals. As to capitalism, it is so inherently corrupting that the leaders of capitalist nations are captured by Wall Street. They mouth clichés about democracy while serving wealthy masters. America, in short, is monolithic, directed essentially from its centers of capitalist power, rather than being the pluralistic, complex, many-voiced society that most observers see.

The revisionist outlook, it will be clear by this point, is not shared in this book, though in earlier pages Russian fears over their own security from attack and their distrust of democracy and capitalism have been made clear. Indeed, the revisionist perspective is not shared by most American historians, which by itself does not necessarily mean that the revisionists are wrong. The general attitude now is to be more skeptical of American policy than formerly, while assuming that power struggles between great and powerful nations devoted to competing ideologies are practically inescapable; that is, it does not require a conspiracy to create them. In this sense, there is felt to have been a certain inevitability about the Cold War. Once mutual distrust and loudly voiced hostility was unleashed, fears on both sides intensified unrealistically, leading each country to overreact. Certainly the American government and the American people whipped up their anxieties and emotions to the verge of hysteria, and in that mood they did appalling things. Certainly, too, there was much to fear in the Soviets' outward thrust. That both governments masked their plans in secrecy and employed all the apparatus of covert intelligence intensified fears on both sides. But where revisionist historians see a monolithic America, and a conscious conspiracy within it to create an unreal anti-Communist mood, most historians see a pluralism of motives, an immensely complicated and many-centered American society which does not march to one drummer, and blunders made by leaders well and sincerely motivated who had real dangers to face and a precious heritage to defend.

As the primary objective of American leadership, the dream of building a democratic world order was often gravely flawed in practice, but historians generally accept it as in broad terms a true statement of American purposes—and one not to be trivialized. American idealism has deep roots; so, too, have America's concern for its own self-interest and its desire for power and predominance. These impulses exist separately and yet are intertwined in nations as they are in individual human beings, who are also pulled in contradictory directions by motives of benevolence and selfishness.

In the last analysis, it is hard to regard Stalin and the Soviets as tolerantly as revisionist historians have sometimes appeared to do; to make them into such relatively innocent bystanders. As the Soviets themselves revealed in 1956 after Stalin's death in a spectacular and world-shaking outburst of self-criticism, under the dictator atrocities on a Hitlerian scale were committed both inside and outside the U.S.S.R. Millions died in the mass purges of Stalin's secret police and in the forced collectivization of Soviet agriculture. That the Stalin regime was capable of destructive designs on world peace and the security of other nations seems the normal accompaniment of such madness. Communist ideology is in fact hostile to crucial human values which are widely held in the West; the Soviets were at least

as eager to induce the outward spread of their ideas as the United States and its democratic allies were to see their principles eventually triumph in the world. It is difficult to accept the view that Moscow's sphere of control expanded after World War II only because it felt threatened by American actions. Tremendous pressures toward outward expansion existed within the U.S.S.R.

The Far East Transformed

After 1945 Asia was transformed. The huge British, French, and Dutch empires crumbled away, allowing such countries as India and Indonesia to become independent nations. America consolidated its power in the Pacific by taking over as United Nations trusteeships the former Japanese-mandated islands swept over by United States armies, and it also occupied Okinawa. Having conquered Japan practically unaided, Washington made certain that it ruled that country without interference. General Douglas MacArthur became supreme commander over the occupation of Japan and thus over its way of life. A sweeping social revolution was ordered as the Americans sought to remake Japan in the United States image.

The total result? Difficult to assess, most experts agree. Japan has an ancient and powerfully rooted culture, and clearly it could not be totally remade during a brief occupation by foreigners. Americans were naive to think they could transform Japan into a Far Eastern United States. The Japanese took what they wanted and rejected the rest. At the least, however, American reforms instigated an opening up of Japanese life that released floods of social change within the family, the factory, and the nation. Japan remained an elitist nation bound together in habits of deference toward those above, but one profoundly shaken by the new values of individual freedom and self-expression.

In China, Chiang Kia-shek lost little time after 1945 in beginning an all-out attack against the Communists. But his regime was riddled by corruption, indifferent to the rural masses, worn down by long years of war, and unable to inspire the Chinese people. The American government sought vainly in 1947 to bring peace between the

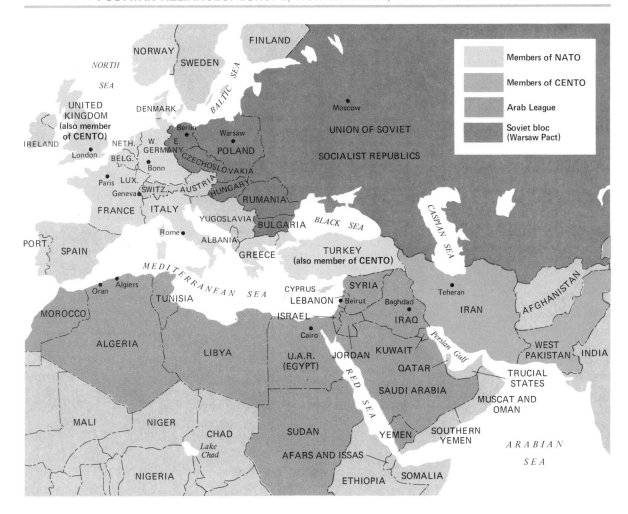

two factions, but in a civil war compromise is impossible—as the war in Vietnam was later to demonstrate and as earlier civil wars in the United States, France, England, Greece, and elsewhere had abundantly shown. Soon the Communists were surging out of their base of power in Manchuria into North China. The Nationalist army rapidly collapsed. Many of Chiang's generals changed sides, taking their American equipped armies with them. Following a desperate retreat, the Nationalist government fled to the island of Formosa (now Taiwan). In October 1949, the People's Republic of China was proclaimed over the Chinese mainland, its capital at Peijing.

The American people were shocked. Almost immediately a storm of protest blew up, concentrating on one endlessly reiterated theme: the Truman administration, influenced by traitorous influences, had "lost China." Such critics brushed aside the counterargument that 800 million Chinese were beyond the control of any American policy, right or wrong. Great numbers of Americans believed that there was no limit to the power of the United States to work its will in the world. This notion, built into the American mind through generations of domestic success and by victories in two huge world wars, was called "the illusion of American omnipotence" by Denis Brogan, a perceptive British observer. Illusion or not, it was to be a major force behind United States foreign policy at least until the late 1960s, when years of failure in Vietnam began to teach the American people a new lesson about the limits of power.

Members of SEATO

Nations having bilateral treaties with the U.S.

Communist bloc

The Korean War

On June 24, 1950, the Soviet-equipped army of North Korea flooded over the border into South Korea, using hundreds of tanks sent by Russia within the previous two months. Word was flashed to President Truman while he was visiting his home in Missouri. It was his habit to think historically, and now he looked at the Korean invasion not by itself, but in a historical continuum beginning in the 1930s. Then, the Western democracies had held back and allowed Manchuria, Ethiopia, and Austria to be taken, only to find that the appetite of aggressors was increased rather than diminished by such victories. Now, he believed, the time had come to demonstrate that collective security could in fact work.

President Truman believed in the United Nations and in multilateralism, and he immediately appealed to the United Nations Security Council for joint action. Since the Russians were then boycotting its proceedings, the Council was able to quickly pass a resolution condemning North Korea and calling on that nation to withdraw. When that failed, the United Nations asked its members to "furnish such assistance to the Republic of Korea as may be necessary to repel the armed attack and to restore international peace and security in the area." Following this step, which no world organization had ever taken before, a United Nations Command was created, and the United States was asked to appoint its commander.

Within a short time American forces were battling in South Korea, to be joined later by thousands of troops from Britain, Turkey, Australia, France, and the Philippines. (Eleven more nations helped out in lesser ways.) Under the leadership of General Douglas MacArthur the United Nations force held onto Pusan, in the southeast corner of South Korea. With typical boldness, MacArthur then decided on an amphibious invasion far up the peninsula behind North Korean lines at Inchon, the harbor for Seoul, South Korea's capital. In September, almost three months after the war had begun, he sent tens of thousands of marines and army soldiers splashing ashore. By intense fighting they quickly thrust their way to Seoul. Meanwhile the United Nations forces had burst out of their Pusan perimeter, and in a brief time more than a hundred thousand prisoners were taken, the shattered North Korean army fleeing northward back across its borders.

General MacArthur now appealed to the United Nations for authority to cross the thirty-eighth parallel and drive the Communists out of the entire Korean peninsula. After a highly charged debate, the General Assembly called on him to do so, despite warnings from Communist China. As the U.N. force approached the Chinese border it was suddenly assaulted by hordes of Chinese soldiers who caught MacArthur's troops awkwardly spread-eagled across the peninsula. In the disaster that followed, the United Nations army suffered shocking casualties. Large units had to fight their way back into South Korea to get behind lines hastily thrown up far south of Seoul, which had once again fallen to the Communists. The Korean War, on the verge of being so brilliantly won, was now doomed to grind on for three more years.

The "Great Debate"

During the bloody seesaw warfare that ensued, Republican leaders like House Minority Leader Joseph Martin demanded an expansion of the war: the bombing of China, the blockading of its coast, and the "unleashing" of Chiang Kai-shek to begin an invasion of China from Formosa. (President Truman had put the Seventh Fleet between Formosa and the mainland to prevent either side from invading the other.) But Truman was determined to keep the conflict a limited war for limited objectives. At all costs he wanted to prevent its escalation into World War III. General MacArthur chafed bitterly under this restriction, insisting that there was no substitute for total victory. In April 1951, when he publicly lined up with the Republicans by allowing Congressman Martin to read in the House an appeal by the general for total victory over the Chinese, Truman dismissed him for insubordination.

This set off a tremendous national furor, for the general was admired and adored by hundreds of thousands. Congress immediately began a "Great Debate" over the issue of the war's strategy. The debate raged nationally through every medium, eventually producing a consensus: that the military must not be allowed to challenge civilian authority, and that a major land war in Asia

Soldier of an American army unit advances under fire from Communist forces during the Korean War. Many months of trench warfare across the middle of the peninsula eventually ended in a cease-fire in 1953.
U.S. Army photograph

would be, as General Omar Bradley put it, "the wrong war, at the wrong place, at the wrong time, and with the wrong enemy."

In Korea, the United Nations Army, now under the command of General Matthew Ridgway, massacred whole armies of Chinese with its superior firepower (China lost well over a million men in Korea) and pushed back northward. By the time Ridgway had established a line across the peninsula in the general vicinity of the thirty-eighth parallel, the weary Chinese were proposing an armistice. Negotiations over its terms dragged on for two years, beginning in July 1951, while the deeply entrenched armies continued their bloody raids and counter-raids.

The Election of Dwight Eisenhower

The Truman administration was destroyed by the Korean War. The endless, inconclusive fighting; the "limited-war" concept, which grated against

the nerves of a nation long habituated to total victory; the very existence of the Chinese Communist regime, for which Truman was blamed—these controversies created a massive loss of confidence in the government. The Republicans chose the luminous war hero, Dwight D. Eisenhower, as their presidential nominee in 1952. Against the Democratic nominee, Adlai E. Stevenson, witty and cerebral governor of Illinois, Eisenhower swept to a landslide victory. (He massively defeated Stevenson again in the election of 1956.)

Eisenhower entered office having pledged to end the war in Korea. Fortunately for him and for the world, Joseph Stalin soon died, and in the ensuing "thaw" in the Cold War the Chinese proved cooperative about armistice terms. In July 1953 an armistice was signed setting the truce line along the existing line of entrenchments. (A formal peace treaty has never been settled on, and the northern border of South Korea is still heavily fortified against a renewal of hostilities.) After more than two million casualties on both sides

686

(including more than a million South Koreans, 142,000 Americans [33,000 dead], and 17,000 in British, Australian, New Zealand, French, Belgian, Dutch, Greek, Turkish, Colombian, Ethiopian, and Siamese units), the Korean War was over.

The New Foreign Policy

Under Eisenhower and his secretary of state, John Foster Dulles, the Republicans reintroduced into the conduct of America's foreign policy some attitudes long traditional on their side of American politics. There was no return to "Fortress America" isolationism, as might have happened had an old-line Republican like Robert Taft gained the presidency, but there was, nevertheless, a shift toward a unilateral, nationalistic foreign policy. President Eisenhower admired wealthy industrialists and financiers, and he appointed a cabinet of millionaires. Consequently, there was no move to lower tariffs. Aid that would strengthen the industrial systems of foreign nations was largely shelved, and a much stronger emphasis was placed on purely military assistance. In the underdeveloped countries, the administration relied on the influence of American business and showed little patience with proposals that the United States foster social reform. Republicans had always believed that the best results for everyone, rich and poor alike, flowed from opening up resources and opportunities to modern business and thereby creating jobs and a rising standard of living.

The Truman administration had worked endlessly to maintain close relations with its allies, making sure that great decisions were arrived at after multilateral discussions, but John Foster Dulles had little patience with this difficult, time-consuming process. He tended to announce United States foreign policy from Washington, expecting the nation's allies to defer to his leadership. European governments were offended. The result was a steady deterioration of the NATO alliance as the foundation of American foreign policy.

Dulles was a devout Presbyterian, a Wall Street lawyer for more than forty years, and a moralist who saw the world as a battleground between good and evil. The American system of free capitalism was, to him, practically divine in ori-

gin, and communism was pure evil. As he said in 1953, the Soviet system "believes human beings are nothing more than somewhat superior animals . . . and that the best kind of a world is that world which is organized as a well-managed farm. I do not see how, as long as Soviet Communism holds those views . . . there can be any permanent reconciliation. This is an irreconcilable conflict." In this view Truman's containment policy, which aimed merely at holding the line, was fundamentally immoral. The eastern European countries must be liberated, and the Soviet system itself destroyed. How did he propose to do this? By a constant drum fire of moral outrage bringing such unrelenting pressure on the Soviet Union that—he believed—it would crumble from within.

Meanwhile, he believed that all nations must choose sides between good and evil. To be neutral, in Dulles's opinion, was to be on the Soviet side. India chose a neutral course; therefore the American government regarded the Indians as enemies and formed a lasting alliance with Pakistan instead. Heavy shipments of military equipment were sent to governments that declared themselves anti-Communist, even if, as critics asserted, their policies within their own countries were reactionary and oppressive. Time and again this form of anticommunism lined up the American government behind regimes that were undemocratic, as in Spain, Pakistan, and Brazil. Horrified at the Communist victory over the French in North Vietnam in 1954, Dulles insisted adamantly that the patched-together government of South Vietnam be maintained in power, even though repeated Central Intelligence Agency analyses warned that it was corrupt, unpopular, prolandlord, and oppressive. The Seventh Fleet, which Truman had placed between Formosa and China, was ostentatiously removed so that Chiang Kia-shek's army would be "unleashed" for an invasion (which it was never strong enough to mount). An intense propaganda campaign was beamed toward the iron-curtain countries that all but promised them direct aid if they rose in rebellion against Russia.

The New Defense Posture

At the same time, the Eisenhower administration stated that never again would the United States get involved in a conventional, Korean-type war against Communist aggression. The Kremlin was warned of "massive retaliation"; that is, if another such invasion began, the American government would attack Russia itself with nuclear weapons. The army, the tactical air force, and other such conventional military systems were allowed to dwindle to almost token levels, while the jet bombers of the air force were relied on as the striking force. Great emphasis was placed on creation of a full range of nuclear weapons. Secretary Dulles described the American strategy in the Cold War with Russia as "brinkmanship"—going to the brink of war to force compliance, without actually tumbling over the edge. The world was horrified at this tactic. It provided another reason for western European disenchantment with American leadership and for the success of those who urged Europe to take its own independent course in the world.

The Dulles Alliances

Secretary Dulles decided to complete a ring of American-dominated military alliances around the Soviet Union and China. In September 1954, following the defeat of the French in North Vietnam, he had "shored up" Southeast Asia by creating the Southeast Asia Treaty Organization. It included Britain, France, Australia, New Zealand, the Philippines, Pakistan, Thailand, and the United States. Three months later he completed a defensive treaty with the Nationalist Chinese government and pledged America to defend Formosa and the Pescadores (a group of small islands between Formosa and mainland China). Following that, Congress passed a resolution authorizing the president to fight if need be to protect Formosa.

In February 1955 Dulles succeeded in forming the core of another hoped-for regional-defense arrangement when he got Turkey and Iraq to sign a defense alliance called the Baghdad Pact. Soon Britain, Pakistan, and Iran joined in. Gamal Abdel Nasser, Egypt's ruler, quickly took advantage of the resentment this pact created in Russia by making a huge arms agreement with Moscow in September 1955. From this point on, a special relationship burgeoned between Egypt and Russia, one that greatly strengthened the military power of the Arabs. Nasser nationalized the British-owned Suez Canal in order to get its revenues, thus taking a potential stranglehold over essential supplies of oil to Europe. When Israel suddenly invaded Egypt in October 1956, the British and French joined in, seeking to regain the canal. (At almost the same time, the Russians were putting down the 1956 Hungarian rebellion, largely shielded from world attention by the attack on Egypt.)

The Atlantic alliance was practically destroyed by the Suez incident. Britain and France had gone ahead without consultation with Washington, and Eisenhower immediately drew back from their undertaking, calling on the United Nations to halt the fighting and establish a peacekeeping force in the area. The British and French were totally humiliated—and angered at the United States. Trying to salvage some order out of chaos and to fend off the Communists, in March 1957 Dulles secured congressional approval of a new policy, known as the Eisenhower Doctrine. It proclaimed that the American government would use its armed forces against any Communist or Communist-dominated aggressor in the Middle East if the attacked country sought American help. In mid July 1958 Lebanon appealed for assistance under this doctrine, alleging Syrian-supported Communist insurrection, and American troops landed to prevent the collapse of the government. (They were withdrawn in late 1958.) In the midst of this crisis Secretary Dulles virtually pledged American membership in the Baghdad Pact, later renamed the Central Treaty Organization (CENTO) when Iraq withdrew.

The Sputnik Crisis

In October 1957 the world was electrified by a spectacular event: Russia launched *Sputnik 1,* the first globe-circling satellite. Hundreds of millions of people around the earth stood next to their dwellings and watched in fascination as the tiny, gleaming satellite appeared over the horizon and then pursued its serene, relentless path across the heavens, carrying with it the triumphant message of Russian technological brilliance. Khrushchev boasted delightedly that this dramatic event demonstrated the superiority of the Communist system, and he launched an in-

THE COLD WAR

tensive propaganda campaign designed to persuade wavering neutralist nations to join the Soviet side.

The Soviet Union's dramatic achievement began a year of national crisis in the United States. Eisenhower urged an increase in defense spending, especially for missiles—formerly given little attention—and nuclear submarines. He vigorously pushed through a centralization of the Defense Department, giving the secretary of defense vast new powers to unify the efforts of the military services and control the joint chiefs of staff. In January 1958 the tension was eased when the army successfully placed a small satellite in orbit, using a World War II–type rocket. The culmination of this phase—getting missile development in full motion—was the successful firing of the first Atlas intercontinental ballistic missile in November 1958.

Renewed Tensions in Europe

The most persistent problem in Europe during Eisenhower's years in office was the status of Germany. Largely through Dulles's insistence, the German Federal Republic (West Germany) was accorded independence in May 1955, given the right to rearm, and brought into NATO. The spectacle of a rearmed Germany outraged the other European nations, especially France. In late 1958 the Soviet Union suddenly reopened the long-inactive question of West Berlin. Khrushchev called for declaring it a "free city," expelling Western occupation forces, and placing its contacts with the West wholly under the control of the East German government.

Eisenhower, now bereft of Secretary Dulles, who died of cancer in early 1959, responded boldly. Seized with the conviction that he could bring the world back to peaceful conditions by direct acts of personal diplomacy, he invited Premier Khrushchev to the United States for a visit and face-to-face talks. When this went well, the president embarked in December 1959 on a spectacular tour of eleven nations, from France to India, where he spoke to immense, enthusiastic crowds about the American ideals of peace and friendship in freedom. Then, in February and March 1960, he journeyed through Latin America, where once more tumultuous crowds cheered him. There he proclaimed a "Hemi-

President Dwight Eisenhower, in search of eased relations with Russia and a damping of the Cold War, welcomes Soviet premier Nikita Krushchev to the United States in 1959.
Bob Henriques, Magnum Photos

sphere Crusade" for economic development and reaffirmed American aims of political and economic stability in the Western Hemisphere. Hopes rose throughout the world that this extraordinary man might be able to reach a lasting friendly relationship with the Soviet Union and end the Cold War.

In May 1960 the president left for Paris, where he met with the British, the French, and Khrushchev. At this moment occurred one of those events, relatively minor in themselves, that deflect world history. An American U-2 reconnaissance plane, flying high over Russian territory and deep within its borders, was shot down. Eisenhower refused to take refuge in the customary denial of responsibility. The Soviet premier exploded, gave a frightening tirade, broke up the conference, and returned to Moscow, where he soon revived the Cold War by threatening talk and gestures. Much of the free world blamed Eisenhower for the timing of the flight. During the rest of Eisenhower's administration, the bitterly disappointed president stayed home in the White House, watching a political storm build up in which his conduct of the presidency came under unending attack.

Bibliography

Books that were especially valuable to me in writing this chapter: Diane Shaver Clemens's *Yalta* (1970) is a trenchant analysis; Richard F. Fenno, Jr. provides a useful compilation of historians' interpretations in *The Yalta Conference* (1972). My analysis of the background in Russia's experience and ideas, and of Soviet attitudes toward the Second World War and the Cold War, draws upon what I learned during study of these matters while serving as a Fulbright/Hays professor of American history at Moscow University in the winter and spring of 1979. The following books were useful to me in exploring these issues: the dissident Soviet historian Roy A. Medvedev's brilliant study, *On Socialist Democracy* (1975); Ronald Hingley, *The Russian Mind* (1977); Nicholas V. Riasanovsky, *A History of Russia* (1977); Hélène Carrère d'Encausse, *Decline of an Empire: The Soviet Socialist Republics in Revolt* (1979); Hedrick Smith, *The Russians* (1976);

Robert G. Kaiser, *Russia: The People and the Power* (1976); James H. Billington, *The Icon and the Axe: An Interpretive History of Russian Culture* (1970); Nikolai V. Sivachev and Nikolai N. Yakovlev, *Russia and the United States: U.S.-Soviet relations from the Soviet point of view* (1979); N. Sivachev and E. Yazkov, *History of the USA since World War I* (1976); Erich Goldhagen, ed., *Ethnic Minorities in the Soviet Union* (1968); Peter Vanneman, *The Supreme Soviet: Politics and the Legislative Process in the Soviet Political System* (1977). Norman A Graebner's *The Age of Global Power: The United States Since 1939* (1979) gave me the insights of a distinguished diplomatic historian. Of course, one reads Gar Alperovitz's *Atomic Diplomacy: Hiroshima and Potsdam* (1965) and Walter LaFeber's *America, Russia, and the Cold War, 1945–1966* (1968). I drew upon Gabriel Kolko's views as they are presented in his recently published *Main Currents in Modern American History* (1976).

George Kennan's *Memoirs, 1925–1950* (1967) give us a most remarkable book to which I kept returning, and of the flood of Kennedy books, Theodore C. Sorensen's *Kennedy* (1965) and Arthur M. Schlesinger, Jr.'s *A Thousand Days: John F. Kennedy in the White House* (1965) provide large stores of factual information not available elsewhere. David Halberstam's *The Best and the Brightest* (1972) was important to me. I was teaching American history in the Cold War years and I drew upon periodical contemporary literature to help form my opinions as to the politics of the Cold War period. Thomas G. Paterson, ed., *Containment and the Cold War: American Foreign Policy since 1945* (1973) provides an excellent compendium of documents and historical interpretations, and the following were also useful: Paul Y. Hammond, *The Cold War Years: American Foreign Policy Since 1945* (1969); David Rees, *The Age of Containment: The Cold War* (1968); Glenn D. Paige, *The Korean Decision: June 24–30, 1950* (1968); Robert Leckie, *The Wars of America,* 2 vols. (1968); Dwight D. Eisenhower, *The White House Years: Mandate for Change, 1953–56* (1963) and *Waging Peace, 1956–1961* (1965); Alonzo L. Hamby, *Beyond the New Deal: Harry S. Truman and American Liberalism* (1973); Charles C. Alexander, *Holding the Line: The Eisenhower Era, 1952–1961* (1975).

Other Works on the Period

Seyom Brown, *The Faces of Power: Constancy and Change in United States Foreign Policy from Truman to Johnson* (1968); Paul Y. Hammond, *Organizing for Defense: The American Military Establishment in the Twentieth Century* (1961); Dean Acheson, *Present at the Creation: My Years in the State Department** (1969); Michael A. Ghin, *John Foster Dulles: A Statesman and His Times* (1972); Denna F. Fleming, *The Cold War and Its Origins*, 2 vols. (1961); William A. Williams, *The Tragedy of American Diplomacy** (1959); Harry S. Truman, *Memoirs*, 2 vols. (1955–1956); Herbert Feis, *From Trust to Terror: The Onset of the Cold War, 1945–1950** (1971); David Rees, *Korea: The Limited War* (1964); Roger Hilsman, *To Move a Nation: The Politics of Foreign Policy in the Administration of John F. Kennedy** (1967); Robert W. Tucker, *The Radical Left and American Foreign Policy* (1971); Robert James Maddox, *The New Left and the Origins of the Cold War* (1973); Adam Ulam, *Containment and Co-Existence* (1967).

* Available in paperback.

34

TIME LINE

1952	Dwight D. Eisenhower elected thirty-fourth president of the United States
1953	Major industries agree on guaranteed annual wage; Earl Warren appointed chief justice of the United States; House Concurrent Resolution 108 terminates federal services to Indians and places tribes under state supervision
1954	In *Brown* v. *Board of Education of Topeka* Supreme Court strikes down the separate-but-equal doctrine in public schools and facilities
1955	Merger of AFL and CIO
1957	Violence mounts against blacks in South; First Civil Rights Act; Little Rock crisis; *Sputnik 1* launched by Russians
1958	National Aeronautics and Space Administration created; first intercontinental ballistic missile launched; National Defense Education Act gives federal aid to education
1959	Landrum-Griffin Act regulates internal governance of labor unions; Alaska and Hawaii admitted to the Union
1960	John F. Kennedy elected thirty-fifth president of the United States

COMPLACENT YEARS: TRUMAN AND EISENHOWER

UPI

It was a German workingman's family in a factory town in West Virginia in the 1920s, and it was Sunday. After church and the noon meal were over, Valentine Reuther, an immigrant socialist and a labor-union leader, would gather his three teen-aged boys to debate their prepared topics: child labor, women's suffrage, prohibition, the draft, labor's rights. Life was a serious business, millions were exploited, and social compassion was the only answer.

Son Walter, at age nineteen in 1927, left for Detroit to be a tool and die maker in the auto industry. He was bookish, a trade union radical who went to college in his off-hours, organized a Social Problems Club, and labored for socialism. In 1933 the Ford Motor Company fired him, and he worked his way around the world, for some months laboring in a Soviet automobile plant near Moscow. Then it was back to Detroit to lead successful sit-down strikes, absorb beatings by Ford-hired thugs, and become a national figure. By the early 1940s Walter Reuther was winning many millions in additional wages for Ford workers, time and a half for overtime, seniority rights that protected workers from arbitrary discharge, and grievance procedures. In 1946, though not yet forty, the spectacular Reuther became president of the United Automobile Workers. Imaginative, energetic, widely suspected for his youthful radicalism, he was a celebrity, admired by his followers and hated by conservatives.

In 1945 he demanded a 30-percent increase in wages with no increase in prices. Force the auto makers to open their books, he cried; they can afford it! Strike after strike followed, long, wearing, and bitter. The employers' books remained closed, but the higher wages came. Reuther then led a campaign to drive Communists out of the labor movement, first out of the UAW, then out of the parent CIO itself. In April 1948 a shotgun blast through his kitchen window almost killed him, but he recovered to become labor's most far-sighted postwar leader. First came the "escalator clause," which brought relative quiet to industry by automatically raising wages with rises in productivity and in the cost of living. Then followed long struggles to win pensions, the guaranteed annual wage (insuring laid-off auto workers, during periodic shutdowns, most of their regular wage for a year), and multi-year contracts and thereby establish stability in wages and working conditions. In 1952 Reuther became president of the CIO, then helped form in 1955 the great labor merger, the AFL–CIO.

Year after year, Reuther labored for national social reforms that extended far beyond the bounds of trade unionism. He marched in the civil-rights cause, having fought racism since the 1920s, and used his high position in the Democratic party to work for public housing, urban renewal, and full employment. Indeed, he was the only major AFL–CIO leader to encourage César Chavez and militant farm workers' unions. When Richard Nixon sent American troops into Cambodia, Reuther's was one of the most prominent of the national voices that rose in protest. But on May 9, 1970, a small jet aircraft plowed into the ground during a storm in northern Michigan, and Walter Reuther was dead. "The world," said United Nations Secretary-General U Thant during the international mourning, "has lost a wise, courageous, and statesmanlike humanitarian. . . ."

Overview

The Japanese had hardly surrendered when President Harry Truman called on Congress to fire up the banked coals of the New Deal and enact a long series of major domestic reforms. But Congress was not interested. Three years later, after he had won a stunning reelection victory in 1948, Truman tried once more, but again with no success. From 1945 through the latter 1950s, the nation worried about the Russians and about Communists at home, but it was fundamentally complacent about the nature of its own society. Problems rumbled under the surface—urban decay, festering race relations, tragically costly health crises among the poor—but they were largely ignored.

After all, most Americans were riding a crest of affluence such as they had hardly dreamed of during the 1930s. Tens of millions of people found themselves moving upward into a middle-class way of life that included golf, split-level homes, luxurious automobiles, trailers, boats, land and gardens, recreational weekends, and costly hobbies. The war had poured wealth into countless homes, and now people wanted to spend and enjoy. Millions of soldiers came home with attitudes that accented this national mood. In jungles and remote deserts, in farthest Asia and in sandy army barracks on the Texas plains, men and women had whiled away months of tedium and moments of frightening combat by daydreaming of the good life to come. They were not critical of America; they wanted to share in it. Their dream was to put together what most of them had never had before—a secure life in comfortable circumstances.

The United States yearned for quiet, not for radicalism. Protest met with massive disapproval. The old political cries for socialism, communism, or liberal reformism had lost their appeal. The predominant mood was disenchantment with ideologies of any kind. The status quo: this was what people idealized, called "Americanism," and elevated to the status of a folk religion. The fears aroused by the Cold War heightened this conservatism. Anyone politically left of center risked being stigmatized as a Communist. The national mood of suspicion laid the basis for the Second Red Scare, which began in 1950 when Senator Joseph McCarthy walked the land like a new Caesar.

The Truman-Eisenhower era was fundamentally complacent, but it was a turbulent time in many respects. From the nationwide eruption of labor agitation in the late 1940s, through the Red Scare of the early 1950s, to the burgeoning outbreak of race hostility thereafter, problem after problem thrust forward. A tide of reformism grew, held back by the determined resistance of the Eisenhower administration until it erupted in a tumbling flood of social change in the kaleidoscopic 1960s. And underneath the complacency was a deep anxiety, produced by the frightful blood bath of the Second World War and the existence of the atomic bomb.

Harry S. Truman: Jacksonian Democrat

From 1945 through 1952 Harry S. Truman presided over this inward-turning nation, seeking vainly to spur it to renewed domestic reform. A peppery, combative, courageous man, Truman brought Jacksonian qualities to the White House. He was unpolished, small-town in background—Independence, Missouri, was his home—largely self-educated, and proudly a "man of the people." Certainly his personal style had overtones of the truculent prickliness of the general from Tennessee, and, like Jackson, he distrusted powerful corporations and worried about the common man. Furthermore, he quickly became an active chief executive in the Democratic tradition. Not for him were the long, droning, nap-filled afternoons of Calvin Coolidge. In domestic affairs he worked hard to push Congress toward social reforms, and in foreign relations he led the nation out of its traditional isolationism into the role of world leadership it has tried to carry on ever since.

In domestic matters Truman fell far short of his goals. He was faced with an informal coalition of Southern Democrats and northern Republicans who halted practically all his efforts at social and economic reform. Southern whites wanted no part of his efforts to aid black people, and conservatives in the North opposed his attempts to revive the New Deal. Truman's personal qualities also gravely hampered him. Although courageous, he somehow never attained the kind of moral leadership that presidents need to bring the country along with them. A nation accustomed to the majesty of a Franklin Roosevelt could not take seriously a president who surrounded himself with small-time political cronies, burst out peevishly at opponents, and once scribbled off an angry letter to a music critic who had slighted his daughter's singing voice.

But Harry Truman saw where the nation's ills lay, and long before the national mind was prepared to do something about them he was raising warning flags and calling for action. In his first major message to Congress, in September 1945, he urged in his "Fair Deal" program not only the expansion of social security and an increase in the minimum wage, but such far-sighted measures as national health insurance, a major assault on slum housing, federal aid to education, guarantees of equal access to jobs for Afro-Americans, support of scientific research, and vigorous new conservation programs that would spread TVA-like regional systems across the United States.

Major Achievements

Truman got little of these reforms, but he did get major pieces of legislation passed. One was the Full Employment Law of 1946, which permanently committed the national government to intervene continuously in the economy to ensure that a depression would never occur again. To implement the law, a three-man Council of Economic Advisers was established to provide the president with professional expert knowledge. A second act concerned atomic energy. There was no question that this powerful new force could not be turned over to private enterprise; it was too important for that. But should it be controlled by the military, as it was during the war, or placed under civilian direction? President Truman was unshakably convinced that civilians should be in charge, and against strong Republican opposition—but with the country behind him—he won his battle. The Atomic Energy Act of August 1946 created a five-member Atomic Energy Commission, which had exclusive control over research and production. At the same time, the law made certain that the president possessed the sole power of ordering the use of atomic bombs in combat.

On his reelection in 1948, Truman tried once again to launch his Fair Deal, this time with a bit more success. The National Housing Act au-thorized the building of over 800,000 public-housing units for poor families, as well as the provision of subsidies to renters, slum clearance, and rural housing. More money went into the building of power facilities in the West, for reclamation, and for aid to tenant farmers who wanted to buy their land. The minimum wage was raised from forty cents to seventy-five cents an hour, and the Social Security System was vastly expanded, ten million more people coming under its protection. Truman also finally got Congress to allow 400,000 Europeans, displaced by the war, to immigrate to the United States. But this was the sum of it. The major events of the Truman administration lay not in legislative victories but in crises in the nation and the world.

The War's Effect on the National Economy

While Asia and Europe lay in ruins, the Second World War transformed the United States into a boomingly prosperous nation. Out of a population of 135 million, about 300,000 soldiers died in the war, compared with over half a million in the British Commonwealth, almost 3 million in Germany, and 10 million in Russia (in addition to 10 million civilian deaths). Put another way, America lost 1 in 450 of its population, Britain 1 in 150, Germany 1 in 25, and Russia 1 in 10. Even in the Civil War the United States had suffered far more heavily: there had been 600,000 deaths out of a population of 30 million. When civilian casualties, which ran to the many millions, are added to the losses of the other nations in the Second World War, America's remarkable good fortune stands out even more.

The national economy grew explosively. The United States produced $91 billion worth of goods in 1939; by 1945 the total had soared to $167 billion. Per-capita disposable income (stated in the value of 1960 dollars) grew a third, reaching $1,669 for each man, woman, and child in 1945. Together, individuals and corporations had saved more than $48 billion; state and local governments, $10 billion more. The result was a boom that began as soon as the war ended, instead of the depression widely feared. The gross national product continued skyrocketing, rising beyond the $300-billion level in 1950 and the $400-billion level in 1955 and exceeding $500 billion in 1960. By that time per-capita income had climbed to $1,969, an increase of two thirds in twenty years.

Never before had the ordinary American been so affluent. Population rose about 28 percent from 1945 to 1960, reaching 180 million, but since the gross national product had leaped 56 percent during the same period, individual incomes could soar. While all this took place the number of working people grew enormously, from 55 million in 1945 to almost 67 million in 1960. The income of workers in nonagricultural occupations rose steadily. In the late 1950s, however, an old problem—unemployment—returned and persisted as recession after recession frustrated economic planners in the Eisenhower administration.

Women, the Family, and the Population Boom

Fueling the upward rise of the economy was a dramatic reversal in population growth after 1940. For many years the birth rate had declined, sharply, but the war changed all this. The abundance of jobs and high pay sent marriage rates soaring, and many servicemen were eager to marry before leaving home or going overseas. A powerful impulse to form families and have children, as an individual assertion of the life force in the face of millions dying, and indeed in the face of one's own possible death, moved many young people. Then in the postwar years the dream of building a large, healthy family seized millions, for it seemed the most creative and life-affirming thing two people could do in order to restore a world of peace and fruitful order. The world had been torn apart, by depression and international war. Now, in forming families and creating once more a tangible and stable future, people were rebuilding that world where it meant the most to them: in their own individual lives.

The model for women of being wife-companion to their husband and of investing their life and spirit in their children, which had reached full development in the 1920s, surged again during the postwar years. During the depression there had been little opportunity in such stringent times for much investment in comfortable and attractive homes, or in children. During the Second

World War huge numbers of women entered the labor force, doing every conceivable kind of work, but practically everyone regarded this as an interlude. Almost universally, women said they wanted to return to homemaking at war's end.

And so they did in a rush, from 1945, and in circumstances of widely shared affluence. (Actually, 31 percent of all women were working in 1950, as against 27 percent in 1940, but they worked in prewar-type jobs: in office work rather than in manufacturing or in the professions, which were largely closed to women. Much of the work, also, was part-time: it provided supplementary rather than necessary income.) With strong encouragement from Washington, which offered practically 100-percent low-interest loans and built great nets of highways to ease transport, white working and middle-class Americans moved in a massive tide to the suburbs. They were realizing an ancient dream. For years ordi-

The explosion of new families with many children in the postwar years, affluence, low-interest government housing loans, and freeway building sent housing tracts marching over fields and hillsides, as here in Los Angeles in 1953.

J. R. Eyerman, Life Magazine, © Time Inc.

nary people had hoped to own a home in the countryside, with its green yards and quiet streets, away from the crowded, noisy, violent city. Between 1950 and 1960 two thirds of America's rise in population occurred in the suburbs; the major cities rose slightly under 9 percent, and the suburbs by half.

The comfortable, roomy, secluded suburban home was the theater ideal for women's long developing role as wife-companion and loving mother. A family life of great privacy could be constructed. And everything in American life encouraged the firm belief that women could make their highest contribution to a healthy, flourishing national life by rearing large families of happy, emotionally sound, loved, and carefully trained children and by making an intriguing home life for themselves and their husbands. The kitchen was to be a scene of high culinary skills—with affluence and an abundance of foods, the American meal took on a richness and variety never before experienced—and the bedroom was the center of the marriage. Dr. Benjamin Spock, in his *Baby and Child Care* (1946), which sold in the millions, urged mothers to construct an atmosphere of warmth, intimacy, and trust between themselves and their children. Breast feeding came back into fashion, and especially designed slings allowed babies to be carried for hours by mothers to enhance contact. YMCAs and other public and recreational gymnastic facilities popped up by the thousands to provide vigorous athletics for children and family.

Surely no generation of women was more centered in their children, or more conscious of their psychological development. Sigmund Freud's disciples had long made it an accepted truth that what happened to children in their first few years would shape the rest of their lives. Homemaking and motherhood, therefore, came under higher and higher demands. As to women themselves, Helene Deutsch, in her massive work *The Psychology of Women* (1945), which was widely accepted as the authority on the subject, wrote that only in motherhood, in relations (fairly passive) with men, in a person-absorbed tenderness, and in a readiness to suffer for others would women find emotional health and personal happiness. The pain of childbirth itself, Deutsch held, was essential to women. In mass American life, this emphasis upon female sexuality was trivialized by commercial advertising, which could appeal to the newly affluent American woman to realize herself by consuming a wide variety of beauty aids. Being virginal at marriage identified the ideal young American woman; being fruitful thereafter, and raising three to four children, if not more, was the ideal of the young American matron.

Privacy: each child had his or her own room; the service rooms, such as the kitchen, pointed to the street; and the living room looked to the interior garden. Husbands and wives connected suburban living with spending evenings alone together, not with family or friends. The other side of this soon emerged, for some women: loneliness and a sense of isolation. Whereas for their neighbors the busy life of full-time suburban motherhood might be rewarding, if tiring, for such women it was almost beyond endurance. Suicides among women mounted, the use of tranquilizers skyrocketed, and psychological counselors found their offices busy. Large families could mean almost unending activity: tending to laundry, music lessons and swimming lessons, the garden, the dishes, guided play, and chauffering the children. Finding herself through her children was not every woman's particular joy, as by the 1960s some would begin to say.

The Boom in Household Formation

Meanwhile, millions of young couples had their big families and felt that although it was not an easy life, it was in fact the good life. Not since the Progressive Era had American families had so many children. From 19.4 births per 1,000 in 1940, the rate had leaped to 25.8 by 1947, where, with minor reductions, it remained throughout the 1950s. The result was that between 1940 and 1950 the American population grew more rapidly than in any prior decade in the nation's history (by 14.5 percent). In the 1950s even this surge was surpassed, as the total population reached almost 180 million, or some 18.5 percent over its mark in 1950.

More marriages and children meant an insatiable demand for washers, dryers, furniture, clothes, automobiles, homes, roads, schools, firehouses, new residential areas, lawn sprinklers, radios, televisions, rugs—the list of the many needs of these new households is endless. This,

COMPLACENT YEARS: TRUMAN AND EISENHOWER

in turn, brought a swift expansion in the industries producing these products. There was also a tremendous mobility in the growing population. People migrated to the places where jobs were most plentiful or to the "sun states" of Florida, Arizona, and California, where a new way of life could be taken on. The movement from country to city continued: the nation's farming population of thirty million in 1940 had become less than twenty-one million by 1960. In the former year 56 percent of Americans had lived in cities; in the latter, 75 percent. The "white flight" from the city core left behind growing slum regions with rapidly increasing minority-group populations whose reduced incomes could not provide the necessary taxes for schools and other services. The largest American cities actually declined in population as the suburban communities spread over the surrounding countryside.

Black America continued to flee from the South. In 1940 three million Afro-Americans lived in non-Southern states; by 1960 the number had grown to seven million. At the same time, only 7 percent of Americans were foreign-born in 1950, and by 1960 the figure had dropped to 5 percent. In urban areas across the country whole ways of life disappeared as third-generation ethnics, now thoroughly removed from the ways of the old country, adopted styles of living closely resembling those of their Anglo-Saxon neighbors.

Since immigration from Western Hemisphere nations was unrestricted, the hundreds of thousands of Mexican-born who after 1910 had begun moving into Texas, Arizona, and California to work as agricultural laborers had expanded to a total of 2.5 million Mexican-Americans living in the United States by 1945. Furthermore, the opportunities of wartime employment brought a flood of Puerto Ricans to the northeastern states (especially to New York City), where approximately 750,000 lived at war's end.

The New Farm Crisis

While the income of urban people rose, that of farmers fell alarmingly in the Truman-Eisenhower years. Between 1952 and 1960, farm income dropped 23 percent. For this reason farm families continued their flight to cities: in 1956 alone, one eleventh of the farm population left the land. The basic cause was overproduction, which

in turn was created by soaring mechanization and greater efficiency. In 1949 the Agriculture Act of that year had set parity-price supports at the 90-percent level. The result was government purchasing of billions of dollars worth of crops, skyrocketing production, and bulging federal warehouses.

Ezra Taft Benson, Eisenhower's conservative secretary of agriculture, shifted the government away from rigid to flexible price supports, believing that lower subsidies would cut production and force farmers to become more businesslike, efficient, and self-reliant. The Agriculture Act of 1958 reduced price supports to a general level of 65 percent of parity. At the same time, a program was adopted in 1956 whereby farmers would be paid for taking land out of production and putting it into a "soil bank" from which the nation could draw in future emergencies. Millions of acres were thus withdrawn, especially by "agribusinessmen" who owned large holdings.

Explosive Labor

The war had hardly ended when organized labor erupted in its last major outburst in American history. The war had brought millions more workers into nonagricultural jobs, the total number of workers rising from 27 to 38 million, and the increasing efficiency of the machinery they used made each worker increasingly productive. By 1945 the nation's factories were producing 100 percent more than they had in 1939, but mandays of labor had increased by only half. At war's end there were 6.8 million workers in the AFL, 6 million in the CIO, and over a million in other unions.

Everyone was worried, however, that the nation was going to collapse into another depression. Union leaders looked at the 12 million men and women in the services who would soon be flooding the labor force in search of jobs, and they feared disaster. When Washington's labor statisticians reported that unemployment was rising, labor's fears seemed confirmed. Union leaders decided that the best way to ward off a depression was to keep wage rates at a high level, so that there would be plenty of purchasing power in the general population. Pointing to capital's huge wartime profits and to increased productivity per worker, labor leaders such as the United Automobile Workers' Walter Reuther insisted that employers could raise wages without raising prices.

Then a different kind of demand came from John L. Lewis, head of the United Mine Workers. He called not only for higher wages but also for employers to finance "fringe benefits," consisting of health and welfare services. This led to a coal strike that soon created heating and industrial crises through a shortage of coal. In May 1946 the railroad workers began a strike that threatened to paralyze transportation. Then, in the spring of 1946, wartime price-control legislation was allowed to lapse, and the cost of food and other necessities rose with breathtaking suddenness. All the raises that labor had won were canceled out in a brief few weeks, while corporate profits boomed upward to their highest point in history—and more strikes began.

The public, however, was angry at the unions. The national economy staggered along from day to day through a seemingly endless series of crises: strike votes; bold pronouncements by union leaders; decisions to withhold essential services; and apparently dictatorial demands. Furthermore, this controversy tapped once more that deep-running force in American life: the habit of using and respecting authority. Protests by those below often produce enormous anger in those above. We have seen this anger stirred up in the British mind by the protests of American colonials, in Southern whites by the protests of Southern blacks, in Anglo-Saxon Protestants by the protests of Irish Catholics. Employers were massively offended by the demands of labor that they open their books, pay higher wages without raising prices, and "submit" to the union. Millions of unorganized Americans, running their small shops or living on restricted incomes, identified with the employers and shared their outlook. Where do the "damned unions" get off trying to tell their employers how to run their businesses? So ran the argument, as a nation still devoted to individualism, and sentimentally in tune with established authority, condemned organized labor.

The Taft-Hartley Act

In November 1946 the Republicans won a sweeping victory in Congress, taking control of both houses for the first time since 1928. Now they had

their chance to turn the tables on labor. The Wagner Act of New Deal days, they said, had made the unions far too strong. They could halt production by jurisdictional strikes (where two competing unions struggled for membership), secondary boycotts (refusal by other unions to handle the goods of a factory or business under strike), violation of contracts, refusal to bargain, and open coercion of employees to join a union.

The resulting Taft-Hartley Act, which expressed primarily the ideas of the National Association of Manufacturers, listed for the first time a group of "unfair" labor practices of which the unions were guilty, and henceforth declared them illegal: the closed shop (the requirement that a worker had to be a union member before he or she could get a job); coercion of nonunion workers; secondary boycotts and jurisdictional strikes; demanding pay for work not performed; and refusal to bargain in good faith. Employers could now sue for breach of contract. And where a strike threatened the national health or safety, the president could secure court injunctions that would provide eighty-day "cooling-off" periods before the strike could begin. To reduce possibilities for union graft, all unions were required to register with the secretary of labor and provide regular financial reports.

Labor fought back hard against the Taft-Hartley Act (which Truman vetoed, only to be overridden). But Southern Democrats were as unalterably opposed to the unions as were northern Republicans. They adamantly protested any force that might raise wage rates in the factories that had been moving to the South because labor costs were cheaper. Furthermore, no part of American society was more devoted to the habit of authority than the South. Factory owners were respected and admired in the South as captains and generals had been in the Civil War. Union "dictation" was not to be abided. The Taft-Hartley Act, therefore, withstood all assaults.

The Annual-Wage and Cost-of-Living Principles

As inflation continued pushing prices higher, labor fought round after round of wage-increase battles with employers, one hardly ending before the next one began. Then in 1948 Walter Reuther got General Motors to agree to automatic "cost-of-living" pay raises, which would be granted in accordance with rises in the consumer price index as measured by the federal government's Bureau of Labor Statistics. This principle spread rapidly through the economy, affecting even government workers.

In 1953 the United Automobile Workers began another campaign with crucial implications: a demand for a guaranteed annual wage. The first national response was the traditional one: the notion was rejected as absurd. For many months the issue was debated intensively. Finally, Ford agreed to such a contract, which quickly became standard in similar industries. It provided that when qualified workers were unemployed, the company would pay them about two thirds of their normal earnings for a period of six months, to be received on top of any government unemployment benefits. (By 1967, this had been expanded to 95-percent pay for a year.) These measures eased the buildup of annual pressures within the economy for wage increases, so that the vast turbulence of the late 1940s, when millions of workers struck for long periods, died away.

Except in the South. Here lay the core of antiunion sentiment, for the South was the last unorganized region in the United States. In the early 1950s, when labor pushed unionization throughout the South, local officials and self-appointed labor haters openly took the side of employers and used violence against the organizers. Scenes occurred that were reminiscent of those in Detroit during the depression. The difference, however, was that the unions were now powerful national organizations with vast resources at their command. They persisted in their drive: in 1951 alone some 1.5 million new members, mainly in the South, joined the unions. (Despite these efforts, the South remains the least unionized section in the United States.) By the mid 1950s union membership had reached some 16 million nationally (8 million in the AFL, 7 in the CIO), or about one third of all workers in nonfarm industries.

Labor Merger: Formation of the AFL–CIO

The time was now ripe for the AFL and the CIO to join forces. The lines that formerly divided them had blurred, for the AFL had already

In a climactic moment ending twenty years of feuding within organized American labor, George Meany and Walter Reuther celebrate the merger of the AFL and the CIO in 1955. The labor-management scene henceforth became much more stable.

Wide World Photos

swung far over in the direction of industrial unionism. In 1955 long negotiations ended in the creation of the AFL–CIO, which brought more than 85 percent of all union members under one administrative roof. George Meany became president, and Walter Reuther vice-president.

The last major piece of legislation concerning organized labor was the Landrum-Griffin Act, passed in 1959. This law reflected the federal government's recognition that unions had arrived as permanent elements in the national economy, and that—like railroads, banks, and other public-utility-like institutions—their internal organization needed careful public supervision. The law governed the way in which unions conducted their elections, held strike votes, and administered their funds, which by this time had grown enormous through pension and welfare receipts.

The Threat of Automation

The gravest problem remaining to labor was automation. The gross national product, it was pointed out, had grown 40 percent from 1954 to 1964, but employment had risen only 12 percent. The United Automobile Workers once numbered 1.5 million workers; by the mid 1960s this work

701

force had dwindled by a half-million. In 1947 it took 1,300 man-hours of labor to produce 1,000 tons of coal; in 1962 the figure had dropped to 500. During that time employment in the coal mines declined from 400,000 to 123,000. Because of these influences, the organized-labor movement reached its peak in 1956 and began declining in numbers thereafter.

The significance of automation, however, has yet to be proved. It was increasingly difficult for unskilled workers to find jobs, and more of them became permanently unemployed. Out of this trend has come, in good part, the persistent problem of poverty in the midst of affluence. However, automation has had another major effect: it has created hundreds of thousands of jobs in wholly new industries, such as computers and electronics. Furthermore, the national economy has been moving steadily in a new direction where the largest proportion of its workers are engaged not in the production of goods but in the provision of services: soft water, clean diapers, health, education, landscaping, interior decoration, accounting, government, and countless other occupations. This has made old-time swings in the business cycle less likely to occur, for the market for services is not subject to abrupt changes.

The Democrats and Disloyalty

Since Thomas Jefferson's day a conviction that the Democrats are disloyal to the American way of life has circulated among important sections of the American population. Democratic foreign policy has traditionally been internationalist in tone and methods, and "100-percent Americans" of strongly nationalistic views have bitterly distrusted the Democrats on this ground. Add to this a tendency on the Democratic side to distrust the military and to rely on "soft" methods of economic aid and painstaking multilateral diplomacy, and the resulting combination infuriated many people. Often such critics were curiously unconcerned with combating communism abroad: what they feared day and night was communism at home. They were ready to explain the nation's ills by saying that subversive "pinko" radical intellectuals from Harvard had taken over Washington, D.C.

In ordinary times these kinds of people have had little leverage on the American public. Like those on the far-left wing of American politics who constantly trace every national problem to alleged conspiracies among the wealthy corporations, right wingers who constantly preach the message of disloyalty are usually given small attention. But when the nation is struck by great fears, much of the public is swayed by these attitudes.

The world, after all, was a terribly disordered place in Truman's years. It rang with the chilling threat of atomic war, of huge armies still marching, and of young Americans still dying. No one could relax for years on end. For this reason the Second Red Scare, unlike its predecessor from 1919 to 1920, went on and on. It spread throughout the country, affecting Seattle and Birmingham, Boston and Los Angeles. Librarians were harassed by book burners, teachers were hounded by reactionaries who condemned any mention of Russia or the New Deal, and liberal ministers were driven from their pulpits. The national mood made these goings-on seem legitimate; the violent haters were relatively free to give vent to their wild theories of subversion and treachery. Right-wing vigilantes in local communities were exhilarated to find themselves regarded as front-rank soldiers who could do no wrong in their "battle for America."

Impact of the Second Red Scare Upon the Republican Party

In the anti-Communist crusade that overran American life for many years after 1945 the Republican party found powerful new sources of strength and vitality. When in the 1930s FDR and the Democrats had seized the strong-government ideology that for so long had been Republican property, the Republicans' leverage on the national mind had been greatly reduced. Now, however, in the process of linking the Democrats to a hated foreign power and ideology—Soviet Russia and communism—the Republican party coincidentally escaped the fate of their ancient forebears the Federalists, who had simply faded away when in Thomas Jefferson's time their political opponents had stolen their ideological thunder.

The postwar anti-Communist crusade actually began during the prewar New Deal years, when aroused Republicans, genuinely alarmed that America was losing its free-enterprise system, and that foreign ideas of collectivism and a social welfare state were taking over, attacked FDR bitterly for taking the nation on the road to Moscow. Indeed, many Democrats, especially in the South, agreed. Government had intruded into ordinary life in massive fashion. Businessmen found their liberties infringed upon in what seemed countless infuriating ways. And with the rise of labor, apparent child of the New Deal, proud and lordly men found themselves in the galling position of having to take "dictation" from people they had long thought of as beneath them. Power relationships in American society had been profoundly changed, a fact that built a proportionate rage in those whose position had been diminished.

Roosevelt's wartime internationalism, his drive for lower tariffs, and his apparent assent at Yalta to a vast expansion of Soviet power into eastern and central Europe fueled the attack. Harry Truman's reelection in 1948 was the crowning indignity. Now the Republicans, still confident that they were the voice of the "real" America, would be excluded from the presidency for yet another four years, making twenty in all! The cry that Democrats were disloyal to America now mounted ever higher in intensity, and it went on year after year. In the process the anti-Communist, anti-Democrat crusade vastly revived the Republican party, for millions of Americans throughout the country agreed with that party's anti-communism and its fears for America. Behind their war hero Dwight Eisenhower, the Republicans' Andrew Jackson, in 1952 the Republicans would take control of both the White House and Congress for the first time since 1932. A functioning national two-party system would apparently return to full operation.

It must be understood that the anti-Communist crusade was a *cultural* crusade. The questions were not simply those of foreign policy and national security, but revolved around a central query: what was happening to the national way of life? Was the American nation being destroyed from within by communism? FDR's collectivism, the United Nations ideal, and all the new concepts which had entered into the American mind with the New Deal—strong government caring for the poor, strong labor unions, strict regulations upon free enterprise: these liberal and reformist dreams seemed to have flowed into school textbooks, into church teachings, and into race relations. To the older, WASP America, the New Deal had been a wrenching experience. FDR had indeed changed the nation in dramatic ways, and now the backlash grew louder and more bitter in tone. By linking the anti-New Deal attack to the Soviet Union abroad, which seemed to be taking over the world, it picked up strength in ever wider elements in American life.

When cultural fears predominate in the country, as was increasingly the case in the Cold War years, Republicans have traditionally benefited. As the party of the WASP host culture, they seem to be, in their own minds and even in those of other people, the unique possessors of all that is genuinely American. Furthermore, in the anti-Communist crusade, in which the enemy was collectivism at home and the Soviet Union abroad, there were no white minorities to be offended by this anti-Democrat assault, as there had been in the earlier Republican crusades against drink and the parochial schools. Russia and godless communism were the enemy on ethnic as well as on religious grounds of Poles, Germans, Hungarians, Czechs, Slovaks, and all Catholics. Thus many Democrats from northern ethnic precincts joined the anti-Communist crusade of the Republicans, together with many Southern whites, who had been alarmed at pro-black policies emanating from the Democratic-controlled White Houses.

The First Phase: 1938–1950

As long ago as 1938 the House had established the Un-American Activities Committee, which shortly was sending out to the populace the grave news that the Boy Scouts were Communist-infiltrated. In 1940 Congress passed the Smith Act, which made it a crime for any person in the United States to urge the violent overthrow of any government, or to organize or become a member of any group that taught such goals. Designed primarily to combat fascism, soon after the Cold War began it was revived for use against suspected Communists. In 1946 Americans were startled to learn of a Soviet espionage ring in Canada. Demands were soon made that the federal government flush out any employee whose general attitudes and affiliations made it reasonable to suspect that he or she might be a security risk. The Republican-controlled Congress prepared to enact necessary legislation, and President Truman sought to defuse the issue by establishing a rigorous loyalty program by direct executive order.

Begun in 1947, Truman's program subjected every government employee to a searching review. The procedures paid little attention to civil rights. On the bare ground that no one had a right to be a government employee, the loyalty-review boards made a travesty of courtroom procedures, even though dismissal as a security risk would blot a person's entire career. They entertained any and all accusations, accepted Federal Bureau of Investigation reports as beyond question, refused to let the accused confront their accusers or even know their identity, freely condemned people on the basis of associations with other people often unknown to the accused—and spread dismay, alarm, and timidity throughout the government service. This program went on from 1947 to 1951 and resulted in the discharge (not for actions, but for supposed tendencies) of 212 employees out of about 2.5 million.

Long lists of supposedly disloyal organizations were published by the United States attorney general in 1947, without prior hearings or even an explanation of why each organization was so named. In 1948 the government charged eleven leaders of the American Communist party under the Smith Act. All were eventually found guilty, fined heavily, and put in jail for terms of three to five years.

The Hiss Case

In August 1948 a former State Department official, an Ivy League graduate named Alger Hiss, was accused before the House Un-American Activities Committee of having been a Soviet spy. Congressman Richard M. Nixon, a member of the committee, would not let the case die. A sensational trial of Hiss in 1949 for perjury ended in a hung jury, but an equally dramatic one in 1950 resulted in his conviction. The jury decided that he had actually been part of a spy network within the government in the 1930s, and right-wingers pointed with alarm to the fact that he had been on Franklin Roosevelt's staff at Yalta. The stunned country was now willing to listen to charges that the Democrats were soft on communism.

Earlier had come a series of shocking events, piled closely on one another, that seemed to confirm the nation's hysteria. A young woman in government service, Judith Coplon, was charged with giving the Soviets crucial information on how the Federal Bureau of Investigation organized its counterespionage system. Then the Russians exploded their first atomic bomb in September 1949. How could they have so rapidly achieved the nuclear expertise to have done this? Spies in the government, said the Truman haters —and sure enough, in February 1950 a Soviet spy ring was uncovered in the Los Alamos atomic installation, which led to the execution of Julius and Ethel Rosenberg in July 1953. Hard on the heels of Russia's atomic-bomb exploit came the collapse of the Nationalist government in China, widely explained as the result of the Truman administration's alleged lack of concern about Communists.

Joseph McCarthy Transfixes the Country

In February 1950 an obscure young Republican senator from Wisconsin, Joseph R. McCarthy, said in a public address in Wheeling, West Virginia, that the Department of State was crammed with Communists; that he and the secretary of state knew their names; that he had, in fact, a list of them in his possession (which he never produced). These Communists were "still working and making policy," he said, and the government refused to get rid of them. For almost four years after this speech, the United States grappled with one internal problem almost to the exclusion of everything else: was Senator Joseph McCarthy telling the truth? Committee after committee of the United States Senate examined this question and reported that he was not, but huge audiences continued to shout and cheer when McCarthy spoke. He received vast sums of money from right-wingers, for in their eyes he was the new savior.

The Catholic Church in Europe was locked in an unrelenting struggle to maintain its freedom from Communist control in countries such as Poland and Hungary, where the Russians had taken over, and millions of Catholics in America were passionately hostile to "godless communism."

They were joined in this by fundamentalist Protestants—especially in small-town, rural, "Bible Belt" regions—who had long equated radicalism with the devil. Furthermore, Irish Catholic Joe McCarthy, in his attacks on the eastern, Ivy-League-trained, intellectual elite that for decades had run the nation's foreign policy, was assaulting the very fortress of the Anglo-Saxon Protestants, whose status had long been resented by the outgroups. For people who nourished old hatreds and an ancient sense of being excluded, the McCarthy campaign was a way of declaring that they, not the Anglo-Saxon elite, were the true patriots.

McCarthy brought the Truman administration practically to a halt by massively eroding its credibility. He destroyed the careers of State Department officials with unproved charges and smeared the reputations of both Dean Acheson and George Marshall, the secretaries of state who had shaped Truman's Cold War policies. "The Democratic label," he said, "is now the property of men and women who have . . . bent to the whispered pleas from the lips of traitors . . . men and women who wear the political label stitched with the idiocy of a Truman, rotted by the deceit of an Acheson. . . . "

The McCarran Act

Out of this atmosphere came the McCarran Internal Security Act, passed over Truman's veto, which required Communist and "Communist-front" organizations to register with the federal government (so they could be prosecuted, apparently) and authorized the government in times of national emergency to gather up and imprison suspected subversives. As soon as the Eisenhower administration was installed in January 1953 it got busy rescreening all government employees under the loyalty program. A year later it proudly stated that 2,200 workers had been fired—though not one of them was a proven Communist.

But for McCarthy this was not enough. After a brief silence following Eisenhower's inauguration, he was soon at his crusade again. Though few of those whom he attacked could admit that he was anything but a totally unprincipled dema-

gogue, recent research seems to indicate that for all his crudities, McCarthy genuinely believed in his anti-Communist campaign. Many far-right-wingers would in subsequent years say Eisenhower was a dupe of the Communists, and now McCarthy began saying, in effect, just that. He accused the new president of running a "weak, immoral, and cowardly" foreign policy composed of "appeasement, retreat, and surrender." The president was furious, but he refused to demean himself by openly contesting the senator. People of great standing and authority were horrified by McCarthy's sensational career and enormous sway over the public. "When I think of McCarthy," said President Eisenhower's banker brother, Arthur, "I automatically think of Hitler." He was, indeed, an unlovely sight. He liked to be thought of as a tough guy, cultivated a reputation as a heavy drinker (which he was) and a terror with women, and swaggered forth in a heavy-shouldered way with a sullen look on his face. "McCarthy," wrote an unadmiring veteran Washington reporter, Richard Rovere, "was surely the champion liar. He lied with wild abandon; he lied without evident fear; he lied in his teeth and in the teeth of the truth; he lied vividly and with a bold imagination; he lied, often, with very little pretense to be telling the truth."

But McCarthy died, politically and literally, by his own excesses. In the fall of 1954 his wild charges that the army was harboring Communists were subjected to a long series of committee hearings that fascinated the nation, for they were the first such dramatic occasions ever to appear on national television. Millions of viewers found to their disdain that the senator was a rather repellent figure, a bully who twisted facts, bulldozed his way rather than let others speak, tried to slur an innocent young lawyer simply to get at the other side, and made himself ludicrous by his heavy-jowled, endlessly reiterated bellow, "Point of Order! Point of Order!" Soon the television comics were making fun of him, and, almost as swiftly as it had risen, his national reputation collapsed. The Senate censured him, relieved now that the frightening ogre had been made into a petty politician. He spent his last days hurrying through the Senate's corridors, trying to get reporters to listen to some new "sensation." In May 1957 he died of cirrhosis of the liver. Although fallen in the general public's eyes, he was mourned by many. He remains a martyred hero to thousands.

Dwight Eisenhower and Republicanism

Dwight Eisenhower had been swept into the White House over Adlai Stevenson in 1952, for the nation was sick of the Korean War, thoroughly tired of the Democrats, and eager for a president it could trust and admire. This good-hearted man, whose warmth and dignity attracted grateful support from millions of Democrats as well as Republicans, could give the country what it needed: calm and unity in place of the McCarthy hysteria. Indeed, Dwight Eisenhower was to be a president who soared high above his party in the people's estimation, for only in 1952 were the Republicans able to gain a majority in Congress behind him. For six of his eight years in office, the nation persistently put Democrats in control of that body.

He was a Republican, however, and it is important to understand what this meant. In both foreign and domestic affairs he fell toward the liberal side of his party, but he was still incontestably a man of the right wing in national politics. He remained firmly committed to the global-leadership role that Truman had built for America— thus rejecting isolationism, which many in his party espoused—but within that role he and John Foster Dulles were more unilateral and nationalist in their mode of operation than Truman and far less concerned with sponsoring social reform abroad. Within the nation he made one historically important liberal contribution: he would have nothing to do with any campaign to repeal the New Deal, thus permanently fixing its reforms in the American system. Indeed, he even broadened the coverage of social security, supported federal aid to the schools, and approved the creation of the Department of Health, Education, and Welfare.

Nonetheless, he built a thoroughly Republican administration. The Democrats had traditionally stressed ideas in their administrations, which tended to be rather confusingly organized. The Republicans, on the other hand, stressed neat and businesslike methods while paying much less attention to intellectuals and reform proposals. The new president installed a symmetrically organized staff system in the White House, like that of a military organization, in which discussions and decisions flowed upward to him through an ascending pyramid of officials who refined the issues so that he, as president, had mainly to say only yes or no. As a commander, he had scrupulously delegated responsibilities to subordinates, and now he did the same, largely turning over the direction of the great departments in the government to his cabinet members.

Differences in Governing Style

This was what presidents on the right wing of national politics had been doing since the days of the Whigs and the Federalists. Republican administrations, unlike Democratic ones, traditionally rejected the idea of the strong executive who runs the government with a firm hand, keeps close tabs on departmental affairs, and provides active leadership to Congress and the people. Republican administrations, too, place considerable emphasis on decorum, modes of dress, and stately procedures. Not for them the shirt sleeves of the Democrats, the party atmosphere, informality, and general raffishness of the New Deal. Homburgs were carefully chosen for the new president's inauguration, and the style of entertainment in Washington, always shaped or the model displayed at 1600 Pennsylvania Avenue, became well mannered and subdued.

Dwight Eisenhower had a strong admiration for the great men of the business and financial world, and he formed his cabinet principally of millionaires. Wherever he could as president, he turned things over to private enterprise: government-built rubber plants; hydroelectric sites; and control of natural resources. He spoke of the Tennessee Valley Authority as "creeping socialism," and in the Dixon-Yates controversy of 1954 tried to arrange for the Atomic Energy Commission to buy electric power from a private plant rather than from TVA sources. To the federal government's independent regulatory commissions— such as the Federal Communications Commission (radio and television), the Federal Trade Commission (advertising and marketing), and the Securities and Exchange Commission (stock markets)—he appointed new members who were friendly to the businesses they were supposed to regulate, rather than critical of them. Hostile toward government spending, he spent his eight years slashing budgets and battling inflation.

He believed deeply in the separation of powers and abruptly terminated the practice of trying to shepherd laws through Congress by the daily and painstaking influence that his Democratic predecessors had sought to apply. He felt that his duty as president was to present his proposals as logically and persuasively as possible and leave their disposal to the wisdom of Congress. He did not use the White House as a "bully pulpit," as Theodore Roosevelt had called it, nor did he give any presidential leadership to the Republican party, for which many of its members harshly criticized him. A quiet term in office, a time of healing, moderation, and settling down: this was his intention, and so, in large part, did his tenure as president turn out. Convinced that the business community was the proper source for national leadership, that most people would do best to solve their problems without government help, and that the country was fundamentally healthy and needed only good administration, Dwight Eisenhower rarely, if ever, tried to lead the country in new directions.

The End of Ideology

In truth, the Truman-Eisenhower years were not from any standpoint an encouraging time for reformers. The country was not in a mood for great changes in its national life. Radicalism was dead. To be an intellectual, a questioner and a critic, was unpopular. The United States of America was regarded by the dominant white Anglo-Saxon Protestant culture as a good and shining example to the world. This mood sprang naturally from the team-spirit feelings induced by the tensions of the Cold War and by the anxieties about the future of humankind that lay in the back of people's minds as they thought of that awesome mushroom cloud which had risen over Hiroshima.

Far from turning in new intellectual directions, in the mid 1950s Americans flocked to the churches. Their membership rose twice as fast as the general population, and new church buildings were built by the thousands in the growing suburbs. A hundred million Americans turned to God as they searched for meaning in life in the most traditional of all sources. A profound revival in theology took place. Protestant, Catholic, and

Jewish seminaries were crowded with young clerics who searched ancient and modern sacred writings with an intensity unknown since before Charles Darwin's theory of evolution had cast doubt on the Bible. Reinhold Niebuhr, who had for years been insisting that humanity is irretrievably selfish and sinful, became a kind of national sage and prophet in the post-1945 years.

Existentialism and Disillusionment

Existentialism in theology and philosophy attained enormous vogue among intellectuals. Rooted in the writings of the nineteenth-century Danish theologian Sören Kierkegaard, and in the books of two Frenchmen—Jean-Paul Sartre and Albert Camus—that, written in the 1940s, were widely read in America, existentialism was a bleak, cheerless outlook for humanity. Life, existentialists said, is a terrible riddle in which we cannot find meaning, no matter how hard we try. The conditions of existence are such that fear and anxiety are built into us. Thus, all persons are entirely on their own: they must live simply for themselves, in a meaningless universe. Existentialists like Sartre lost faith in the idea of God, and became atheists. Others followed Kierkegaard's leap of faith to a belief in Christ as humanity's only salvation from itself; that is, they became, like Reinhold Niebuhr, Christian existentialists. As such, they taught that humanity cannot achieve sweeping changes in its condition, but only "proximate" improvements; that original sin keeps us forever limited in our compassion for others.

The mood among pre-1960 intellectuals who were concerned with politics and public affairs was reflective, disenchanted, and disengaged. They had lost the reformist optimism of the 1930s, which had fueled the New Deal. Instead, they now viewed life as complicated, ironic, and paradoxical. Reform movements of any kind, for all their noisy laborings, seemed to such scholars to produce but small results. In a book widely read in college and university classrooms, *The Age of Reform* (1955), the Columbia historian Richard Hofstadter depicted a politics in the United States that, on balance, seemed to consist largely of the discharging of feelings rather than of realistic attempts to deal concretely with social problems. Public life appeared primarily as a great socio-drama in which the masses expressed their fears and anxieties and were satisfied with symbolic victories—gestures and words—over their enemies. To Hofstadter the American people explained their problems not by realistic analysis, but by relying on the simpleminded belief that conspiracies lurked behind the scenes, either in the financial world or in the government. Soon scholars were finding what Hofstadter called "the paranoid style" behind every ideological movement from the Jacksonian Bank War to the free-silver movement.

Much of this attitude was shaped by the appalling spectacle of McCarthyism, which taught the intellectuals of the 1950s new lessons about the mass of the people. It seemed that nothing was as powerful among Americans as a mindless hunger for simple solutions. The Progressive Era's faith in the intelligence and goodness of the common people, which these scholars had inherited, died away. For the first time in many years there was much talk about the wisdom contained in conservatism. There was a revived interest in the ideas of John Adams and Edmund Burke, great conservative thinkers of the 1790s (the first, America's president; the second, an eminent British parliamentarian). The true conservative, it was said, knew that people reason badly, are swept by passions, greedily look after their own interests, and need to have their energies tempered by living within strong institutions of law and order.

Thus, a strain of elitism ran through the thought of the 1950s. So, too, a kind of weary and sophisticated disenchantment colored what older scholars told younger ones. Political and social wisdom, they said, lay in recognizing that evil cannot be wiped away; that people cannot escape tragedy and despair. Tension and uncertainty, together with shrunken hopes, are irremovable parts of life. "In the Western world," wrote Daniel Bell in *The End of Ideology* (1960), " . . . the ideological age has ended."

The Revolutionary Warren Court

While the presidency, the Congress, and the nation's intellectuals were immobilized in deadlock, conservatism, and disillusionment, the Supreme Court of the United States suddenly thrust itself forward, uncharacteristically, to become a great spearhead of reform. Eisenhower's most important single appointment was that of Earl Warren, governor of California, as Chief Justice of the United States in 1953. Ironically, in this action the president devoted to inactivity helped to create one of the most amazing phenomena in American life: a Supreme Court that suddenly seized so bold and active a role that it was widely called revolutionary. The president is rumored to have called Warren's appointment the "biggest damfool mistake I ever made." Thousands of Americans who emblazoned "Impeach Earl Warren!" signs about the country agreed. No Supreme Court since John Marshall's, 150 years before, matched the Warren Court in the breadth and sweeping importance of its decisions. Even the Marshall Court pales by comparison, for its decisions related just to the powers of the federal government, whereas the Warren Court plunged deep into social and political life.

Earl Warren, like Eisenhower, was a generous, simple, and courageous man whose mind worked with fundamental considerations of decency and fair play, rather than with the fine intellectuality of the law. But unlike Eisenhower, he had been a political leader of a large and populous state and had acquired an appetite for grappling with large problems. He had begun in California politics as a regular Republican who attacked "communistic radicals," wanted to force school children to salute the flag even when conscience forbade them, and in wartime led the clamor to uproot all persons of Japanese ancestry and send them to concentration camps. Perhaps this last experience shook him, for ever after he showed an acute sensitivity for the rights of individuals. Three times governor, he astonished his conservative supporters after 1945 by proposing major social reforms, including prepaid medical insurance.

The Supreme Court in American Life

The Supreme Court has often been at the center of great political storms, because in the American system it has the power of ruling whether a law conforms to the national constitution. Many of the cases and issues it considers would never come before the judiciary in other countries. In other words, the Court is a great agency of public policy.

COMPLACENT YEARS: TRUMAN AND EISENHOWER

Should it be active and forward-thrusting in this role, or as passive as possible, leaving the making of policy primarily to the popularly elected branches: Congress and the president? This question has perennially been debated. Under Chief Justice John Marshall in the nation's early years, the Court actively pushed forward not only to establish its own power and its authority over the issue of constitutionality, but to define the relative powers of states and the federal government (it leaned strongly toward the latter). In the late nineteenth and early twentieth centuries, the Court strongly enforced its concept of what was sound economic policy for the nation (laissez-faire), invalidating law after law that would now be thought of as within the ordinary operations of government. During the New Deal the controversy peaked: the Court at first tried to throw out much of what FDR was accomplishing, and then adopted the principle of "judicial restraint."

According to this principle, the Court should avoid constitutional issues whenever possible, making decisions in this area only when it can be shown conclusively that constitutional rights are being violated that can be protected *only* by the Court's intervention. In other words, the country should ordinarily work out its arguments in the legislature, among the people's elected representatives. Also, the Court should invalidate a law only if on its face, and inescapably, it violates a specific constitutional prohibition, such as that against infringements upon freedom of speech. Essentially a principle associated with Democrat-appointed justices (such as Louis Brandeis and Felix Frankfurter), judicial restraint was supreme by the mid 1940s.

Within a decade, however, it was fast falling out of fashion. The demand for racial justice had simply become too strong and, in constitutional terms, persuasive in the country. Moreover, the courts have traditionally been more responsive to questions of *discrimination* than either the executive or the legislative branch. Also, the notion had become powerful in the country that freedom and liberty were no longer provided simply by the government standing back and doing nothing; rather, the state should take positive steps to insure a just society. Joined to these concepts was an increasing sensitivity, after the experience with Hitler and the continued observation of Stalin's communist dictatorship, to questions of personal liberty and privacy. People should be allowed to say things and print things even if others regard them as obscene; the government should not be allowed to intrude into private lives. A new sense of individuality, in short, was abroad in American life.

Racial Segregation

The great issue before the Court when Earl Warren became chief justice was that of racial segregation in the public schools. It was embodied in the case of *Brown* v. *Board of Education of Topeka*. In 1952 a group of cases concerning school segregation came to the Supreme Court. Of these, the one begun by Oliver Brown of Topeka, Kansas, and supported by the National Association for the Advancement of Colored People, was first in order. Brown's eight-year-old daughter, because she was black, was kept from a school just five blocks from her home and forced to travel two miles to a black institution.

Clearly, a decision based on this case would be of national importance. Initial arguments were heard in late 1952, and were renewed in the fall of 1953 after Warren became chief justice. The ruling principle was clear. In 1896 the Supreme Court had ruled in *Plessy* v. *Ferguson* that compulsory segregation on railway trains did not violate the "equal protection of the laws" clause of the Fourteenth Amendment, provided that the separate facilities furnished to each race were actually equal. This principle, which had already been applied throughout the South, had since become operative to a certain extent all over the nation in many things besides railroading. In 1953 it was still the law of the land. The Court under Earl Warren could have followed this precedent again, in the ancient and necessary practice of courts. Following precedent establishes stability: it insures that societies do not go forward in great lurches, but step by step. Following precedent can protect freedom. It also helps give the law great moral force, for society in general will accept what the law says as "right" and obey it willingly, without the constant oversight of the police, if that law is not simply the personal notion of a judge and therefore frequently changeable, but is instead something stable, time-tested, and enduring. What would the Court do in light of these weighty considerations?

On May 17, 1954, Warren read his decision, in which the Court agreed unanimously (a fact that gave the decision far more authority than it would otherwise have possessed). Even though all physical facilities and other tangible elements may be equal between two schools, one for white children and the other for black, this practice, Warren said, "generates in black children a feeling of inferiority as to their status in the community that may affect their hearts and minds in a way unlikely ever to be undone." Modern scholarship amply demonstrates this, the chief justice observed, regardless of what people knew about psychology in the 1890s. "We conclude," he said, "that in the field of public education the doctrine of 'separate but equal' has no place. Separate educational facilities are inherently unequal." Segregation, in short, was against the law.

This was an event of the most profound importance. Suddenly, as if in a great inrush of fresh air, the national atmosphere began to change. And it did so in ways which revived (against strong resistance and condemnation) one of the most ancient of all impulses in American life, the impulse toward *equality*. The powerful egalitarian potential of the Constitution, that eternally republican document, was once more released in national life when the crucial words in the 14th Amendment guaranteeing to all Americans the "equal protection of the laws" were put to use to uplift black Americans. For generations the party of the minority groups, the Democrats, had as we have seen emphasized egalitarianism in the interests of the white minorities, and it perhaps makes historical sense that the Supreme Court which finally began applying that venerable principle in American republicanism to black America consisted entirely of appointees by Democratic presidents, save for the new Chief Justice, a liberal Republican from California.

How strange the scene was, in a certain sense. The powerfully liberalizing (and, to those higher in the social hierarchy, alarming) concept of egalitarianism, a force of genuinely revolutionary social potential when set free and put in motion, erupted from the courts, thought traditionally to be conservative and hostile to change. It burst upon American life in a decade, the 1950s, when every other influence, whether from the presidency, the Congress, the Cold War, or the cultrual mood abroad in the country, was anti-reform and opposed to liberalism. And the crusade, as we shall see, now strengthened and broadened into a wide campaign for equal treatment in many crucial aspects of American life, from voting and access to public facilities to higher education and employment. The years from 1954 to about 1966 became in a real sense a great era of egalitarianism in American life, one of the few such surges in this direction in American history.

This sweeping transformation did not begin easily, however. From the standpoint of effective government in the United States, the Supreme Court's bold 1954 breaking away from clear precedent (the former "separate but equal" principle) produced a great practical problem: such a violation of precedent is hard to enforce. Until the moment that the new principle is enunciated, millions of people have accepted the other arrangement as good, proper, and established, as hallowed by time. The new ruling does not have that aura; it does not yet carry the quality of being "the law." People have a tendency, therefore, to dismiss the decision as just the opinion of a small group of men that time may change with changes in membership. It is for this reason that law made by legislatures usually carries more moral authority than a precedent-shattering decision by a court. The process by which law is made by the legislative branch is usually long, much argued publicly, and the product of compromise and many votes. White Southerners naturally, therefore, took the *Brown* decision to be an irregularity. Voluntary compliance was almost nonexistent, for people doubted that the law was in fact "the law." *Brown* v. *Board of Education*, however, was one of the milestone statements of human rights in America, a statement heard around the world. At a time when the other branches of government were completely passive on the subject of equality and were likely to remain so, the Supreme Court of the United States had stepped forward to fill the breach. America's moral beliefs, taken in their highest expressions, and the country's actual practices, had gotten far out of alignment, and this step was needed to begin the process of bringing them into harmony again.

The Constitutional Revolution Broadens

The Warren Court had an impact upon much else in American life. It not only swept away the legal basis for discrimination, it wiped out "rotten boroughs" in the states by ruling that everyone must be represented equally in state legislatures and in the federal House of Representatives; rewrote practically all procedures in criminal justice by ensuring crucial rights to the accused; broadened the artist's right to publish works shocking to public taste; and in major ways made it more difficult for the government to penalize individuals for their beliefs or associations. All of these decisions were denounced by critics as destroying the nation. But long before his term as chief justice ended, Earl Warren had become a world-honored figure symbolizing the humanitarian values that, many still hoped, lay at the core of the American system.

Astonishing to many was that in the matter of racial relations the Warren Court went far beyond the principles laid down in *Brown* v. *Board of Education*. That case had struck down a conscious and specific action by a state to establish segregation. But how about the many thousands of daily situations in which government did not appear to be involved? Individual citizens who owned hotels or restaurants had for generations put up signs saying Whites Only or Blacks Only. Black people were denied equal access to jobs simply by ordinary citizens' refusal to hire them, even if otherwise qualified, and by similarly informal means they were denied access to housing. No law specifically backed up these arrangements, and to white people in general, they were perfectly proper things to do. People were at liberty, it was almost universally said, to do what they wished with their own property. If nonwhites protested and tried to get service at a lunch counter reserved for whites, they were guilty of trespass and could be prosecuted. School systems could be, and were, segregated not by law (de jure segregation) but by simple decisions as to where attendance lines were drawn (de facto segregation).

To address this kind of segregation and its imposition of inferiority upon millions of Americans, the Court again broke dramatically with precedent. Nothing had been more established than the notion that the Fourteenth Amendment, which mandated equal protection of the laws, applied only to actions by government, not to what people did as private citizens. Furthermore, it was established constitutional doctrine that states and the federal government were by the Four-

teenth Amendment refrained only from *imposing* segregation. It was not their responsibility to take positive steps to eliminate racial injustice. Both of these longstanding principles were set aside. The Supreme Court ruled that the courts could properly direct citizens not to discriminate in their private actions (whatever might be their private thoughts). Thus, the Fourteenth Amendment could be used directly to prohibit private racial discrimination—it became, in effect, practically like a statute law—if "to some significant extent," the Court stated, "the State in any of its manifestations has been found to have become involved in it." Property owners could no longer demand police action to prevent trespass if a young black person sat at a lunch counter reserved to whites and demanded service.

The Court went further: it held that the governments of the United States are obligated under the Fourteenth Amendment to take *affirmative* steps to insure that no discrimination occurs in places of public accommodation established under public law. They must, for example, insure that private clubs organized under the laws do not discriminate; corporations may not do so either. By not doing anything, the Court stated, government "has not only made itself a party to the refusal of service, but has elected to place its power, property and prestige behind the admitted discrimination."

A great and historically important constitutional change had come to the governing system of the United States of America in these decisions of the Warren Court. Government at all levels was henceforth to move affirmatively to insure the realization of human rights. Just as it had taken positive steps to insure a prosperous economy, education, medical care, and pensions, it must insure equal access and equal treatment to all American people.

The Black Revolution Gains Momentum

On all sides segregation was struck down: in public parks, buses, trains, and airplanes, at public golf courses and other recreational facilities, in libraries and other public buildings, in elections and marriage laws. And on all sides the implications of the Warren Court's rulings, though they may have created difficulties in enforcement, vastly stimulated the still relatively quiet black revolution.

Prior to the *Brown* case, black Americans could appeal only to moral considerations and the consciences of white people—notoriously weak reeds. Henceforth, however, black Americans could point out that the statutory discriminations that tied them down and kept them in a secondary caste were *illegal*, and so were most of the discriminatory actions of individuals. The Supreme Court had time and again in past generations hammered at the principle that a constitutional right, such as free speech or religion, is something that is "personal and present"; that is, it resides in the individual person. It is a permanent possession that is not created or affected by laws passed in some city council or state legislature. Now the "Second Reconstruction," the sweeping change in the position and role of black Americans in national life that took place in the 1950s and 1960s, could begin.

Roots of the Second Reconstruction

The Second Reconstruction had actually been in preparation for many years. The steady migration of Afro-Americans out of the South had brought them much closer to the power centers in national life, which are located in the northern cities. In 1910, about 90 percent of black Americans lived in the Southern states; in 1920, 80 percent did; and by 1960, the figure had declined to 60 percent. From 1940 to 1960, almost 3 million blacks left the South: some 600,000 of them went to California, 500,000 to New York, 370,000 to Illinois, and nearly 190,000 to Michigan. Even in the South blacks had shifted from rural areas, where they were isolated and powerless, to the cities (a third lived in cities in 1940; more than half did in 1960). By the time John Kennedy was elected in 1960, 73 percent of black Americans lived in cities, a slightly higher proportion than that among whites. For many blacks the change meant moving from rural misery to urban misery. But it also meant that they had gathered in compact masses and thus had acquired much more potential leverage on public policy than they ever had living in isolated rural areas.

The Second Reconstruction sprang in part from the long-range impact of the system of segregation. On the basis of segregation, Afro-Americans were finally given a large system of schools —if limited in educational scope. On this basis, too, separate black communities emerged within major cities: for example, the Beale Street area in Memphis, the Auburn Avenue area in Atlanta, and of course Harlem. Such communities had their own black doctors, lawyers, bankers, businessmen, and ministers. This meant that the segregated schooling system could greatly expand what in fact it had never lost—instruction in the liberal arts and sciences. The basis of every black child's education had been training in literature, geography, the sciences, and history. Even in the rural schools the traditional curriculum survived, vocational arts never being given more than secondary emphasis. Segregated colleges grew in number, reaching more than a hundred by the 1930s. They met the daily needs of the black community by offering courses in business, economics, journalism, medicine, teacher training, and theology. Indeed, black education was similar in substance—though certainly without anything like similar resources and public funds— to the kind of education given white youngsters. By Franklin Roosevelt's presidency, therefore, a new middle class was emerging among Afro-Americans that was preparing itself for leadership. We have seen that a "new middle class" trained by the universities of the late nineteenth century produced the Progressive movement among white Americans in the years after 1900; the creation of a similar group among black Americans had the same effect in the mid twentieth century.

Impact of War and Depression

The two world wars and the Great Depression provided quickening stimuli. The First World War brought huge numbers of blacks out of the South and excited them with the dreams of democracy and equality that Woodrow Wilson spread to the world. Soon they found that this was a white man's dream in which they were not to share, for the image of a new democratic order was destroyed by race riots, lynchings, and continued discrimination.

During the 1920s black America turned in on itself, producing the remarkable flowering of the Harlem Renaissance. The depression of the

1930s, however, broke open the mold again. When black voters flooded into Democratic ranks, they acquired a political power they had not had before. Since the New Deal programs were dominated by segregationist whites at the local level, blacks never shared equally in benefits, but even so the change in their situation was remarkable. At least they knew that the government meant for them to share equally. There were great disappointments for blacks in the depression decade, but their hopes had been stimulated.

Then came the Second World War. Afro-Americans entered it without the illusions they had held in 1917. Many openly called it a white man's war, and a few even supported the Japanese cause. The way blacks were treated during the conflict confirmed their cynicism. War industries gave them only menial jobs, rigid segregation existed in the services (the marines excluded blacks entirely), and even the Red Cross blood program refused to mix blood from whites and blacks. Once more, however, this was a war fought for widely trumpeted humanitarian values of equality and decency, and this intensified the Afro-American's conviction that his place in American life should be upgraded. Many agreed with the black columnist George Schuyler's remark, "Our war is not against Hitler in Europe, but against the Hitlers in America."

Rising Militancy

White Americans reacted in anger. Black newspapers were barred from military camps, and Franklin Roosevelt was even asked to approve the prosecution of some black editors for sedition and harming the war effort (he refused). Racial tensions escalated, and riots broke out in 1943. But black militancy continued to rise. Hope and cynicism existed side by side. "What an opportunity the crisis has been . . . for one to persuade, embarrass, compel and shame our government and nation . . . into a more enlightened attitude toward a tenth of its people!" said the Pittsburgh *Courier*. Protest against discrimination mounted.

In 1945 Walter White, the executive secretary of the NAACP, wrote that "World War II has given to the Negro a sense of kinship with other colored—and also oppressed—peoples of the world. . . . [He] senses that the struggle of the Negro in the United States is part and parcel of the struggle against imperialism and exploitation in India, China, Burma, Africa, the Philippines, Malaya, the West Indies, and South America. . . . [There will be] world-wide racial conflict unless the white nations of the earth do an about-face on the issue of race. . . .

"Will the United States after the war perpetuate its racial-discrimination policies and beliefs at home and abroad as it did during the war? . . . Will decent and intelligent America continue to permit itself to be led by the nose by demagogues and professional race-hate mongers—to have its thinking and action determined on this global and explosive issue by the lowest common denominator of public opinion? . . . The United States, Great Britain, France, and other allied nations must choose without delay one of two courses—to revolutionize their racial concepts and practices, to abolish imperialism and grant full equality to all of its people, or else prepare for World War III. . . . A wind is rising —a wind of determination by the have-nots of the world to share the benefits of freedom and prosperity which the haves of the earth have tried to keep exclusively for themselves. That wind blows all over the world. Whether that wind develops into a hurricane is a decision which we must make now and in the days when we form the peace." (*The Rising Wind* [1945])

A. Philip Randolph pointed out in January 1941 that all the efforts by committees and isolated black leaders sponsored by the NAACP and other black organizations had failed to change governmental policies. Mass action was needed. Out of this recommendation quickly came a plan for an all-black march of 50,000 people on Washington to force action by the president and Congress. Alarmed, Franklin Roosevelt agreed to establish the Fair Employment Practices Committee, the first national agency to explore discrimination in jobs and work for equal employment. This concession halted planning for the march, for it was regarded as a great victory—though it fell far short of the March on Washington Movement's stated goals, which called for massive direct action to throw open jobs to blacks and end discrimination against them in unions, government employment, and the military services. By war's end, however, discrimination in war industries and in unions connected with them had greatly declined. Whereas in 1940 every third black worker was on a farm, by 1947 the situation had changed so drastically that the figure had dropped to one in six.

Postwar Race Relations

After the war, several disturbing trends became apparent: when factories slowed down during recessions, blacks were the first to be fired; blacks were rigorously excluded from management positions and sales jobs; they were given limited opportunity in the professions and were treated only a little better in skilled and clerical positions. These conditions, together with continued legal discrimination in public facilities in the South and adjoining states and the increasing congestion and dreariness of slum life, kept black militance from waning.

At war's end the battleground was initially the struggle to keep the Fair Employment Practices Committee alive, despite unending attacks against it by Southern congressmen. President Truman took actions that were unusually helpful to the black cause. He eliminated discrimination in the armed services by executive order in 1948, working a revolution that many said would bring chaos but was accepted with surprising—and significant—compliance. From then on, the military services became an often chosen means for young black Americans to break out of poverty (though their chances of becoming officers were low in the

army, lower yet in the air force, and practically nonexistent in the navy).

In 1948 Truman also established a program to eliminate discrimination in the federal civil service and in factories and businesses supplying the government. What the program did, of course, was to push discrimination into the realm of extralegal, informal measures, but some important gains were made, especially in government employment. At the same time, President Truman urged a program on Congress that called for laws against lynching, protection of voting rights (long denied to blacks in the South), and continuing efforts against discrimination in employment. He got none of this legislation. In the presidential election of 1948 Strom Thurmond led a bolt of Southern Democrats from the party, running for the presidency as the States' Rights candidate and winning four Southern states in an attempt to prevent Truman's reelection.

The Drive for Equal Education

Black America, however, put its greatest hopes in education, as, indeed, all Americans had done since Andrew Jackson's era. The first campaign led by the NAACP after 1945 was to break open segregated higher education. In 1948 Oklahoma was forced to admit a black student to its university by court order. Similar edicts were then issued elsewhere in the South and the Border States: Kentucky in 1949; Louisiana, Missouri, Texas, and Virginia in 1950; North Carolina in 1951; and Tennessee in 1952.

Conditions were now ripe for the emergence of a determined and persistent mass movement. Hundreds of thousands of blacks belonged to the NAACP, and it had funds to pour into the necessary legal battles. Furthermore, the rise of new independent nations in Africa and the Middle and Far East quickened the whole community of black America. Why, it was asked, should blacks continue as a secondary caste when everywhere black and brown men were throwing off white rule and proudly governing themselves? The "revolution of rising expectations" that was sweeping oppressed peoples around the world from China to French Canada, Brazil, and Ghana had seized the Afro-American mind as well. Also, the fact that the United States trumpeted itself as the protector of freedom in the Cold War intensi-

In an eloquent tableau, three men seated in a public location in a Southern town in the 1950s symbolize the state of race relations.

Henri Cartier-Bresson

714

fied the aspirations of black Americans for an equitable share in that freedom.

White Resistance

The classic *Brown* decision in 1954 by the Warren Court, outlawing legally-ordained segregation in the public schools, was followed by endless frustration for blacks. A year later, when the Court ordered school districts to proceed with all "deliberate speed" to implement this principle, the South stubbornly resisted—and northern school districts did so only slightly less rigidly. Segregation in law was now illegal, but segregation in practice continued. As late as 1965 black children in the South had been admitted to white schools in less than 25 percent of the school districts. Indeed, in actual numbers only a little more than 6 percent of the black students in the old Confederacy were attending schools with white students.

In 1956 Southern senators and congressmen issued a "Southern manifesto" prepared by Senator Richard B. Russell of Georgia: "The unwarranted decision of the Supreme Court in the public school cases is now bearing the fruit always produced when men substitute naked power for established law. . . . We regard the decision . . . as a clear abuse of judicial power [in that the separate-but-equal principle,] restated time and again, became a part of the life of the people of many of the States and confirmed their habits, customs, traditions, and way of life. It is founded on elemental humanity and commonsense, for parents should not be deprived by Government of the right to direct the lives and education of their own children. . . .

"This unwarranted exercise of power by the Court, contrary to the Constitution, is creating chaos and confusion in the States principally affected. It is destroying the amicable relations between the white and Negro races that have been created through 90 years of patient effort by the good people of both races. It has planted hatred and suspicion where there has been heretofore friendship and understanding.

"Without regard to the consent of the governed, outside agitators are threatening immediate and revolutionary changes in our public-school systems. If done, this is certain to destroy the system of public education in some of the States. . . .

"We commend the motives of those States which have declared the intention to resist forced integration by any lawful means. . . . We decry the Supreme Court's encroachments on rights reserved to the States and to the people, contrary to established law, and to the Constitution.

Eisenhower and the Black Revolution

President Eisenhower was favorably disposed to the Afro-American cause and appointed the first black cabinet-level official, J. Ernest Wilkins, assistant secretary of labor. He even brought a loyal black Republican, E. Frederick Morrow, into the White House as the first presidential assistant of that race. But Morrow was constantly frustrated in his efforts to get the White House to take a leadership role. Eisenhower and his advisers believed that blacks were pushing too hard. Furthermore, they were extremely worried about offending white Southerners, and they believed government action could not seriously affect race relations.

By early 1957 black homes and churches in the South were being bombed by whites determined to frighten off blacks in their attempts to make the Supreme Court decision an actuality. Meanwhile, the Eisenhower administration was filling international channels of communication with protests against the way the Soviets were treating the Hungarians, and was welcoming Hungarian refugees to America. Why, asked black newspapers and leaders across the country, did Eisenhower not give the same concern to his own black fellow Americans?

In August 1957 the first civil-rights law since 1875 was passed by the Democratic Congress. It created the Commission on Civil Rights to study and report on the equal protection of the laws, prohibited interference with the right to vote (including primary elections), and provided new procedures for securing federal protection of this right. The last two provisions were based on the fundamental belief that if blacks in the South could secure the vote, all their other problems would eventually be solved. Shortly afterward, however, Governor Orval Faubus of Arkansas sharply escalated the crisis by using the state's National Guard to prevent the enrollment of blacks in a white high school in Little Rock, Arkansas. The president was now forced to respond, for Faubus's action directly violated a court order. In a profoundly important step, he took control of the National Guard away from the governor, utilizing legislation passed decades before (ironically, with Southern support) to strengthen the Guard by linking it to the federal government. Then he used troops to ensure that black students could peacefully enroll in the white high school. Thus, at the hands of a reluctant president the federal government took direct action for the first time in almost a hundred years to aid black Americans in the South.

Eisenhower remained deeply convinced, however, that state and local authorities should handle the race problem. He took no steps beyond ensuring compliance with specific court orders and stating publicly in the strongest terms, as he did on September 26, 1958, that racial segregation was contrary to American ideals of equality. His assistant, Fred Morrow, could only report sadly, after all his efforts to swing blacks behind the Republican banner, that "the Republican leadership [around the country] was aloof, still looked upon Negroes as a lower class, and talked down to them rather than giving them any chance of equality." At the same time, northern Democrats were "making it possible for Negroes to share in party councils and [were] appointing them to jobs of influence and prestige in northern states and cities." At the end of the Eisenhower years, the black vote was still solidly in the Democratic camp, despite the presence also within that party of the white Solid South.

The Forgotten Minority: American Indians

The last time the American Indian was discussed in these pages was in relation to the Dawes Act of 1887. White Americans then believed that they had solved the Indian problem. Indeed, for half a century the Dawes Act remained basic national policy. American Indians, on their 241 federal Indian reservations, faded from national consciousness, becoming a forgotten minority. In fact, however, much was going on, even if obscured from view.

In 1889 the Indian tribes possessed 104 million acres of land, an expanse of territory equivalent to the state of California. But the principle of the Dawes Act of 1887 had been to divide this immense holding into allotments and require each Indian family to live on a small homestead, usually 160 acres. On homesteads, it was believed, Indians would learn the habits of the white majority—pride in individual property ownership, labor by the clock and calendar, and the production of articles for commerce. After allot-

ment, "surplus" tribal lands would be sold. Off-reservation boarding schools were built for young Indians so as to complete the process of destroying Indian culture. Traditional Indian religious practices were suppressed.

In a decades-long tragedy, Indians had their land taken from them in return for pieces of paper that most did not understand. Many, indeed, retreated to remote woods, refusing to sign anything at all, even when this meant a total loss of all property, for the whole process was detestable to them. In some places—notably Oklahoma, where the immensely valuable oil lands of the Five Civilized Tribes were located—county courts arbitrarily declared adult Indian men and women in need of guardianship and assigned control of their lands to whites. Despite all Indian protests, huge areas were opened to white settlement, save in such inhospitable land as that of the Navaho and Hopi of the southwestern states. The Five Civilized Tribes of Oklahoma had owned almost 20 million acres in 1898; by the 1930s their land had dwindled to about 1.5 million acres. Overall, America's Indians possessed only some 47 million acres in 1934, most of which consisted of empty desert land. As the Indian Task Force of the Hoover Commission was to say in 1948, "The practice of allotting land and issuing fee patents obviously did not make Indians 'competent.' It proved to be chiefly a way of getting Indian land into non-Indian ownership." Most Indians faced a wretched future. They were illiterate, lived in shacks and hovels, suffered from malnutrition, and gave way to complete hopelessness.

A New Spirit Toward Indians

By the 1920s the white generation that had most exploited the Indians had passed on. The wars of the plains were over; most of the good Indian land was gone anyway; and a new spirit began to take the place of the old vindictiveness and contempt. The unbridled abuses began to be noticed. What earlier administrations had proudly reported as "progress"—the rising proportion of allotted land —was now seen to be instead a story of poverty and suffering. The Hoover administration began to spend funds for agricultural assistance, better schools located near the tribal settlements, and a more professional Indian service.

In the 1930s Indians were further benefited

when Franklin Roosevelt appointed John Collier commissioner of Indian affairs. A gifted man wholly devoted to the idea that Indian culture and ways of life were unique and valuable, to be preserved and strengthened, Collier was the moving spirit behind the passage of the Indian Reorganization Act of 1934. A landmark in Indian history, the act scuttled all past policy and for the first time since 1887 recognized the existence of the tribal system and empowered the tribes to govern themselves. Allotment of land was halted, and funds were appropriated to help the tribes buy back land they had lost. (The funds actually spent were limited but crucially helpful, especially in the form of revolving loans, where the money repaid would then be loaned out again.) Meanwhile, Collier fostered pride in what he called "Indianhood" by encouraging ethnologists and historians to write books about the Indian past and culture. Indian religious practices, condemned as superstition by Christian missionaries, were allowed to flourish again.

Some ninety-five tribes drew up constitutions, and most formed corporations for conducting their business affairs in common. Incredible though many found it, the spirit of tribal membership and the culture that had given it life and reality for centuries still lived. Indeed, from various sources tribal lands actually grew by some four million acres in the next twenty years. Unfortunately, the problem of increasingly complex fragmentation of ownership, as successive heirs of allotted land received ever smaller fragments of property, could never be solved. In general, such land was leased by white farmers and cattlemen for nominal sums. For thousands of Indians, therefore, even the new regime meant little. They continued to live in poverty on their reservations, or they drifted to cities to work as unskilled laborers.

The Post-1945 "Termination Policy"

After 1945 the humanitarian spirit waned. Farmers, lumbermen, and stock grazers, whose operations had been greatly expanded by the Second World War, looked covetously at the Indians' remaining land. Congressmen agitated for a repeal of Collier's Reorganization Act and the breaking up of tribal governments. In 1950 the man who

had been in charge of Japanese internment camps during the war, Dillon S. Myer, became Indian commissioner. He immediately began a policy of terminating all federal services to selected tribes and placing them under state supervision. His work was formally approved in 1953, when the Congress passed House Concurrent Resolution 108, which stated national policy to be "to make the Indian . . . subject to the same laws and entitled to the same privileges and responsibilities as . . . other citizens . . . and to end their status as wards of the United States, and to grant them all of the rights and privileges pertaining to American citizenship." Indian Bureau administrators dating from the days of John Collier resigned or were fired. The keynote, once again, was "development" of Indian lands under the guise of "freeing the Indians."

These new policies sent a wave of anxiety through the Indian world. Every year the National Congress of American Indians and most intertribal councils petitioned Congress for an end to the policy, but with little success. In the years from 1952 to 1956, the government "freed" 1.6 million acres of land for sale to whites; the revolving-loan fund established in New Deal days to allow expansion of Indian lands was frozen; and members of the bureau talked of migration to the cities as the final solution to the Indian problem. Thousands of Indians were recruited by the bureau for city jobs, given moving costs, and aided in finding housing. Relocation centers were established in major cities such as Chicago, Denver, and Los Angeles. The overwhelming majority of these Indians left their tribal locations because their land was being pulled out from under them. The busiest office in the Indian Bureau was the "Realty" branch, which labored steadily at working out terminations and putting Indian land up for sale. By the 1960s, about 40 percent of America's Indian people had become city dwellers, leaving 370,000 behind on the reservations.

Federal Aid to Education Begins

In 1957 the Russians launched their first orbiting satellite, *Sputnik 1*, an event that created a storm of controversy in the United States. Everywhere there were meetings, talks, discussions, and proposals on what should be done to make up for the apparent failure of the nation's educational system in the areas of science and technology. Public educational institutions throughout the country began radically changing curricula, particularly in the direction of providing enriched programs for "gifted" students. Suddenly there was a new emphasis on high performance. High-school and college students found themselves in a much more intensive academic environment, and a new seriousness—some called it overemphasis—concerning grades emerged.

In August 1958 Congress enacted the first general education law since the Morrill Act of 1862. Entitled the National Defense Education Act, it authorized more than one billion dollars over the ensuing four years in federal aid to education at every level, from elementary school through graduate training. The act also established funds for loans and fellowships to college students; for the strengthening of science, mathematics, and language teaching; for testing and counseling programs; and for the dissemination of scientific information. Thus began a massive federal program that has continued ever since.

The "New" Eisenhower

By the beginning of 1959 a "new" Eisenhower had appeared, convinced at long last that his passive conception of the presidency had been wrong. Now he began using the vast powers of his office vigorously. He spoke regretfully of the proposals he had let die in Congress in previous years through a distaste for politics, and began cajoling and threatening congressmen in order to secure favorable votes. Out of this attitude came his bold new approach to foreign relations, including personal tours around the world and face-to-face talks with Nikita Khrushchev. He was able to preside over two historic events in 1959 that changed the shape of America: the opening of the St. Lawrence Seaway, which made the whole Great Lakes waterfront an extension of the seacoast, and the admission of Alaska and Hawaii as the forty-ninth and fiftieth states in the Union.

Despite the president's new dynamism, however, Republican chances in the upcoming presidential election of 1960 looked dim. Eisenhower was still loved and could perhaps have been reelected despite his age—a possibility ruled out by the Twenty-second Amendment, passed in 1951, which limited a president to two

terms—but that popularity had never rubbed off on his party. Besides, his long years of calculated inactivity while in office had driven deeply into the American mind a feeling that the nation's growing problems were coming to a crisis while the Republicans did nothing. Recession after recession hobbled the economy, probably induced by the administration's tight-money policies; in 1960 yet another one began. Although the American economy's growth rate had never risen above 3 percent a year in the Eisenhower era, the economies of the Soviet Union, China, Germany, and Japan were bounding upward. Race relations were growing worse; Eisenhower's diplomatic campaign had collapsed in confusion and embarrassment when the Soviets shot down the American U-2 reconnaissance plane over their territory in May 1960; and John Kennedy was arousing widespread excitement with his promise that he would "get the country moving again." In November this arresting young man, the first Catholic ever to enter the presidency, won a dramatic victory over Richard M. Nixon—though by a narrow popular-vote margin.

So it was that in January 1961 Dwight Eisenhower sat on the white inaugural platform in front of the Capitol, the oldest president in the nation's history, and listened while John F. Kennedy, the youngest man to be elected president, gave his inaugural address. An older order passed off the stage with Dwight Eisenhower when he left Washington for his Gettysburg farm. The turbulent 1960s had begun.

Bibliography

Books that were especially valuable to me in writing this chapter: Harry Truman's own memoirs provide a fascinating glimpse into his character: *Memoirs by Harry S. Truman*, two vols. (1958), and Alonzo L. Hamby, *Beyond the New Deal: Harry S. Truman and American Liberalism** (1973) is broad, solid, and essential. Earl Latham's *The Communist Controversy in Washington: From the New Deal to McCarthy** (1966), together with Richard H. Rovere's compelling and pungent account of *Senator Joe McCarthy** (1960) give together a balanced view of this lurid era. David M. Oshinsky, *Senator Joseph McCarthy and the American Labor Movement* (1975) and Michael P. Rogin, *The Intellectuals* and McCarthy: The Radical Specter (1967) flesh out the picture. For a case study of a particular group under fire, read Thomas C. Reeves' excellent Freedom and the Foundation: The Fund for the Republic in the Era of McCarthyism (1969). Two milestone works by John Kenneth Galbraith are essential: The Affluent Society* (1958) and The New Industrial State* (1971).

On women and the family, I continued to be guided by Sheila M. Rothman, Woman's Proper Place: A History of Changing Ideals and Practices, 1870 to the Present (1978); Carl N. Degler, At Odds: Women and the Family in America from the Revolution to the Present (1980). William H. Chafe, The American Woman: Her Changing Social, Economic, and Political Role, 1920–1970* (1972), and Michael Gordon, ed., The American Family in Social-Historical Perspective* (1978) are also valuable. W. Elliot Brownlee's Dynamics of Ascent: A History of the American Economy (1978) remains an important source on this and all other aspects of economic development.

The labor history of this period is explored in a number of works, including Henry Pelling's American Labor* (1960); Thomas R. Brooks, Toil and Trouble: A History of American Labor* (1964); and Philip Taft, Organized Labor in American History (1964). The Eisenhower administration is judiciously narrated in Charles C. Alexander, Holding the Line: The Eisenhower Era, 1952–1961* (1975). I was also guided by a thorough study by James L. Sundquist, Politics and Policy: The Eisenhower, Kennedy, and Johnson Years (1968). James T. Patterson has written a superb biography in his Mr. Republican: A Biography of Robert A. Taft (1975). Gary W. Reichard, The Reaffirmation of Republicanism: Eisenhower and the Eighty-Third Congress (1975) gives us a closeup look in a crucial time period. An acute study by a member of Eisenhower's White House staff, Emmet John Hughes, The Ordeal of Power* (1963), and Dwight D. Eisenhower's own memoir, Mandate for Change 1953–1956* (1963) provide an intriguing focus upon the president himself. Daniel Bell's The End of Ideology (1960) provides a keen insight into the mind of the era, as does George B. Nash's The Conservative Intellectual Movement in America: Since 1945* (1976). Richard Hofstadter's The Age of Reform* (1955) and his The Paranoid Style in American Politics* (1965) reveal tellingly the outlook of one of the nation's leading intellectuals, and the literature on Reinhold Niebuhr and existentialism is extensive.

Archibald Cox's learned book, The Warren Court: Constitutional Decision as an Instrument of Reform (1968), written from the standpoint of one of the nation's leading legal scholars and public figures, aided me greatly. So too did The Warren Court: A Critical Analysis (1969) edited by Richard H. Sayler, Barry B. Boyer, and Robert E. Gooding, Jr.; The Supreme Court from Taft to Warren* (1958), by Alpheus Thomas Mason, and Politics, the Constitution, and the Warren Court* (1970), by Philip B. Kurland. The black revolution following World War II has stimulated an outpouring of books, of which I found the following valuable: John Hope Franklin, From Slavery to Freedom* (1967); Anthony Lewis, Portrait of a Decade* (1964); Benjamin Muse, Ten Years of Prelude: The Story of Integration Since the Supreme Court 1954 Decision (1964); Louis E. Lomax, The Negro Revolt* (1962); The Autobiography of Malcolm X (1965); Allan Weinstein and Frank Otto Gatell, The Segregation Era 1863–1954: A Modern Reader* (1970); E. Frederic Morrow, Black Man in the White House* (1963). Concerning Indian America, Wilcomb E. Washburn, The Indian in America* (1975), in the New American Nation Series, was a fundamental reliance for me, and I drew also from: Vince Deloria, Jr., Custer Died For Your Sins: An Indian Manifesto* (1969), and Alvin M. Josephy, Jr., The Indian Heritage of America* (1968).

* Available in paperback.

35

TIME LINE

1945–60	Huge migration of Southern black Americans to North
1948–53	Birth rate increases 50 percent
1955	Bus boycott in Montgomery, Alabama; emergence of Martin Luther King as black leader
1959	Fidel Castro establishes anti-American Communist regime in Cuba
1960	John F. Kennedy elected thirty-fifth president of the United States; Students for a Democratic Society formed; Second Civil Rights Act; lunch-counter sit-in in Greensboro, North Carolina; Student Nonviolent Coordinating Committee formed; black nonviolent protests against segregation spread widely in South
1961–63	Congressional opponents block most of Kennedy's reform proposals
1961	Student Nonviolent Coordinating Committee and Congress of Racial Equality lead freedom rides in an attempt to desegregate interstate transportation; Twenty-third Amendment gives the District of Columbia the right to vote in presidential elections; Peace Corps

established; Alliance for Progress; Bay of Pigs disaster; Kennedy announces goal of placing a man on the moon; Berlin crisis intensifies, leads to partial United States mobilization and increased spending for conventional arms; Russia resumes testing of atomic bombs in atmosphere; Housing Act; Area Redevelopment Act

1962 University of Mississippi forced to admit James Meredith; Kennedy orders end to racial and religious discrimination in federally financed housing; Trade Expansion Act; Cuban missile crisis results in de-escalation of Cold War; Medicare defeated; in *Baker* v. *Carr* Supreme Court establishes one-man-one-vote principle in apportionment of legislative bodies

1963 Birmingham police crush black nonviolent protestors; Kennedy makes national appeal for first-class citizenship for black Americans; March on Washington; President Kennedy assassinated; Test Ban Treaty agreed on; Lyndon Baines Johnson becomes thirty-sixth president of the United States; Higher Education Act and other enactments funnel funds to colleges and schools; Accelerated Public Works program; Kennedy proposes tax cut to stimulate economy

THE TURBULENT 1960S: THE EGALITARIAN SURGE BUILDS MOMENTUM

HISTORY IN AN INDIVIDUAL LIFE

With stunning force the bomb exploded against the front wall of the house. Then the phone rang: "Yes, I did it," a woman's voice said. "And I'm just sorry I didn't kill all you bastards." A crowd of angry black people quickly gathered at the house, ready to strike out in retaliation at the trigger-happy white policemen who also surrounded the property. Immediately a deep, controlled voice came from the porch, where Dr. Martin Luther King, Jr., had emerged from his shattered dwelling to stand: "We believe in law and order. Don't get panicky. Don't do anything at all. Don't get your weapons. He who lives by the sword will perish by the sword. Remember, that is what God said. We are not advocating violence. We want to love our enemies. We must love our white brothers no matter what they do to us."

It was late January 1955. The Montgomery, Alabama, bus boycott that the Reverend Dr. King had been leading was a year old, and the black revolution was just beginning, led by the tactics he preached. A deeply philosophic and learned man, King's doctorate from a New England university capped years of close study of Socrates, Plato, Kant, Hegel, Marx, Henry David Thoreau, Reinhold Niebuhr, the Social Gospel leader Walter Rauschenbusch, and the existentialists Sören Kierkegaard and Albert Camus. King had worked his way systematically to an acceptance of Rauschenbusch's belief in a loving and improving humanity; Niebuhr's warning that we must be content with piecemeal advance, given our inescapable selfishness as human beings; and above all Mahatma Gandhi's message that to win freedom from a powerful superior people, oppressed people must nonviolently absorb all punishment, return it with love, and awaken the conscience of the oppressors.

Mass indoctrination in nonviolence now began; black Southerners were taught what it meant and how to use it. Almost nightly in the black churches, which were the heart of black culture, there were lectures and films on techniques and tactics; skits on accepting appalling white abuse; instructions on sitting in, holding one's place, marching, and demonstrating, all without undignified shouting back at white taunts, without physical response. "If cursed, do not curse back. If struck, do not strike back, but evidence love and goodwill at all times. If another person is being molested, do not arise to go to his defense, but pray for the oppressor."

King meant it. Indeed, it was this awesome integrity, as well as his fluent rolling phrases and his charisma, the aura of being touched by destiny, that allowed him for a decade to hold millions of black people to this incredible course of self-denial, faith, and love. Its power was enormous, as became clear in time. The great dignity of black Southern America, marching unbendingly into the fire hoses and singing "We Shall Overcome" within the mass jails, reached into Congress and drew out the powerful civil-rights laws of the Second Reconstruction, despite massed white resistance. "Our ultimate end," King would say, "must be the creation of the beloved community." An America built upon love between the races? It was his dream—in Reinhold Niebuhr's terms, his "impossible possibility" toward which we must work constantly. His personal reward, however, was martyrdom: in Memphis, Tennessee, on April 4, 1968, an assassin's bullet ended the life of Martin Luther King, Jr. But not his inspiration, his achievement, or his enduring message.

We have seen that American public life swings back and forth between periods of crisis politics and periods of cultural politics. The thirty crisis years encompassed by the Great Depression, World War II, and the Cold War gave the people of the United States a team-spirit psychology. The nation had a common objective—the need to restore the economy, or to fend off a foreign enemy—and for most people it was natural to pull together. There was a strong tendency to follow the president loyally. In the depression years, people worked together in Roosevelt's New Deal programs. During the Second World War, millions of Americans joined ranks and obeyed marching orders. In the Cold War, another time of threat, the common task was, as Americans saw it, the salvation of the world from tyranny.

From their experiences in these years, the people of the United States derived a strong sense of community, of national belonging and purpose. Furthermore the postwar presidents—Truman, Eisenhower, Kennedy, Johnson, and Nixon— were all shaped by this long era of crisis. They unconsciously learned to think of their country in the imagery of the football team, the army platoon, and the naval vessel. Joint effort against a common enemy, orderliness and sobriety, self-sacrifice and the supremacy of group goals— such were the elements of their generation's life style.

But after 1960, when prosperity and relative security returned, a period of cultural politics, like that of the buoyant 1920s, began. The rise of black America explosively transformed national life. A new ethnic consciousness demanded pluralism and social equality, in place of WASP dominance. People broke away from established patterns and began doing their own thing, and the surge toward egalitarianism in many aspects of American life grew in strength and boldness. The media, as forty years before, were filled with excited arguments over such cultural issues as the way young people dress, behave, and relate to older people, the role of women, the status and temper of minority groups, changes in sexual practices and attitudes, and new styles of living. The sense of community faded. Romanticism shaped the new mood, which emphasized instinct and impulse rather than reason, joyous release rather than restraint, individualism and self-grati-

fication rather than group discipline. And in the 1960s there were millions of college students, instead of only thousands, as in the 1920s, so that when the revolt of college youth came it rocked the entire nation. At their outset, however, the 1960s offered a scene of national hope and renewed purpose, engendered by a remarkable young president who for almost three years riveted the country's attentions on the White House, on the reforms he proposed, and on his bold foreign policy.

John F. Kennedy Takes the White House

For more than a hundred years it had been an axiom in American politics that a Roman Catholic could not be president. Al Smith's smashing defeat in 1928 seemed the ultimate confirmation of this rule. The ancient distrust of Catholics by Protestants was too strong to overcome. In 1960, however, America was ready to close this chapter in its history, for the national mind was ready for this step. Protestant-Catholic hostilities were simply not the virulent force that for so long they had been. Though fundamentalist Protestants, especially in the South, still could cry out that the Pope was trying to subvert America and that a Catholic president would take his orders on all issues from Rome, this view was losing its believability. Christianity itself was fading in its hold on the national mind, at least in Protestant America. The great surge of religious interest in the 1950s had focused not so much on the figure of Christ as on the image of God the Father. Church leaders and religious thinkers in all faiths had stressed *ecumenicalism*—the unity of all faiths, their essential agreement on fundamentals, and their equality before God. After all, it was international communism that provided the enemy in the 1950s, not the Vatican and the Pope, and all could unite in their rejection of atheism. Furthermore, the rising emphasis upon equality made anti-Catholicism suspect.

The country was ready, therefore, to respond with interest and growing approval to a new figure rising rapidly in American politics in the latter 1950s: the young Irish Catholic Democratic senator from Massachusetts, John Fitzgerald Kennedy, whose millionaire father, Joseph, had been a prominent member of FDR's New Deal ad-

John F. Kennedy excited millions of Americans, especially young people, with a new sense of national vigor and purpose, poured dozens of major proposals into the Congressional hopper, but before much of his promise could be realized he was tragically assassinated in November, 1963.

United Press International

Kennedy seemed to express, in short, the hopes of millions in a world led by old men for a fresh leadership of youthful force and optimism. He was not sure in which direction he wanted the country to go, for Kennedy was not an ideological but rather a pragmatic man, but movement and decisiveness and courage were his guiding values.

Like Theodore Roosevelt, whom JFK resembled in many of his personal characteristics, Kennedy was the most spectacular national figure in a new generation of young people who were pushing ahead to win authority in every area of public life. This new generation, in drama, literature, scholarship, politics, and the leadership of minority groups, filled the national stage with urgency and new dreams. Eisenhower's vice-president, Richard M. Nixon, against whom Kennedy ran for the presidency in 1960, was of Kennedy's generation. Both had been young officers in the Second World War, and had entered the House of Representatives in 1946. But Nixon seemed in contrast to represent an older generation, cautious and still obsessed with older issues. The Democratic party traditionally identified itself with youthfulness and change, the Republicans with order and rule by older people, and these distinctions in style, mood, and pattern of living were sharply evident in the campaign. The Kennedys could be thought of as part of the jet set. The Nixons were restrained, small-town in origins and values, and sensitive about maintaining personal morals and lives of solid virtue. Kennedy, nonetheless, almost lost. The Protestant readiness to accept a Catholic president was still not wholehearted (Kennedy received only a 38-percent Protestant vote, instead of the almost 50 percent that usually went to Democrats). But an exceptionally high pro-Democrat Catholic and Jewish vote (80 percent, instead of around 65 percent), including an enthusiastic outpouring of blacks and of the normally low-voting Mexican-Americans, gave Kennedy a razor-thin margin of 118,000 votes out of 68.3 million cast.

The Kennedy Presidency

In his inaugural address Kennedy cried out that Americans must take up a long, self-sacrificial struggle to revive the nation's power, its spirit, and its economy after the repeated recessions of

ministrative team. Harvard-trained, a historian, crisp, intelligent, and both wealthy and sophisticated, Kennedy, with his striking good looks and his exceptionally beautiful wife, Jacqueline, had star quality. Soon there gathered around the two of them the adulation that a Hollywood-trained America, now increasingly obsessed with television, could give to such figures. And in truth, John Kennedy was an exciting, charismatic personage. Few young people, certainly, who heard or saw him could forget his driving voice, the stabbing finger accenting taut, cutting phrases. He was the cool hero—brave in wartime combat, witty, cerebral—and yet he seemed to *care*. Kennedy was impatient with a country that under Eisenhower had seemed to grow sluggish and bewildered. As he went back and forth across the country he condemned immobility and slackness, cried out for renewed national "vigah!"—his Boston accent charmed millions—and insisted that he could "get the country moving again!"

the Eisenhower years and the sense of national drift that had settled in. "Ask not what your country can do for you," he said; "ask what you can do for your country." The new president quickly built a traditionally Democratic administration. The oval office once more became the turbulent hub of everyone's attention, and a stream of messages calling for urgent national reforms, for the opening of what Kennedy called a "New Frontier" in American life, came forth from it. Kennedy was a master of television, and he held frequent press conferences that millions watched. Catholics, Jews, intellectuals, veterans of urban politics, liberal internationalists, Southerners, and blacks—these were the kinds of people brought to Washington to staff the new administration. Businessmen across the country drew back in alarm, and the Business Advisory Council, made up of wealthy bankers and industrialists, broke off its longstanding ties with the Department of Commerce. The familiar Democratic political style—irreverent, self-consciously brainy, and confident—pervaded Washington social life. An influx of young people to the capital stirred the public's hopes that the country's vital energies would be released and bold adventures launched.

Kennedy, however, faced serious obstacles. His very youth meant that congressional leaders, mainly older men deeply rooted in positions of power, felt he could be ignored. Preeminently men of small-town and rural America, they lacked his concern with the problems of big cities and of the young. Kennedy, after all, had won only a thin victory over Nixon, and the same coalition of Southern white Democrats and northern Republicans that had hamstrung Harry Truman's reform proposals was still functioning. Kennedy had to search for a broad middle ground where he could find general support, and so the policies of his administration were relatively moderate.

The basic strategy he adopted was to *educate* the country during his first term, to persuade Americans to accept a broad list of national reforms, and then to get them enacted after his anticipated reelection in 1964, an event that he talked about again and again. This meant sending to Congress a long series of proposals—whether or not that body, still dominated by elderly conservatives, could immediately be brought to pass them—so as to lay out before Americans their agenda for the future, as Kennedy was fond of

saying. Although an assassin had other plans for Kennedy, his program in effect followed this course.

Kennedy's Domestic Reforms

In his first three months in office, Kennedy sent thirty-nine messages and letters to Congress asking for legislation. Some of them had to do with reviving the economy, but most were concerned with changing the quality of life in a wondrously abundant, but seriously ill, society. There were messages on health and hospital care, education, natural resources, highways, housing and community development, farm needs, the reforming of independent commissions such as the ICC, civil rights, transportation, consumer protection, and aid for the mentally ill, the poor, and the elderly.

Kennedy followed the advice of his trusted secretary of agriculture, Orville Freeman, and supported basic new legislation for farmers. The problems were severe: mountainous overproduction due to skyrocketing mechanization; bulging government warehouses; low farm income (in the 1960s only one farmer in nine earned as much in a year as a skilled worker in the cities); and yet millions of starving poor here and abroad. Characteristically turning to scholarly experts in the field —the Eisenhower administration had preferred to listen to agricultural businessmen—Freeman put together a new national framework for farming. The Food for Peace program sent surpluses abroad, while an imaginative new concept with immense impact over the succeeding years, the Food Stamp plan, enabled the poverty-stricken to join in the benefits of high food production, while at the same time aiding farmers. Essentially, the government purchased excess farm products and distributed them to those whose income could be proven as being below the government's formally-established poverty income level. Recipients bought the stamps, paying $46 for $100 worth (which could be exchanged for that much food).

To farmers who would keep strict controls on production, holding it down to what the nation needed, the government made direct payments to replace their foregone profits. Land not used was to be kept in a national soil bank, as in the Eisenhower years. In other words, farm subsidies no longer took the form of keeping prices high by various government measures, but were effected by simple checks in the mail. Meanwhile, consumers could benefit from the fact that food prices were kept relatively low. Each year, farm income rose a billion dollars while surpluses were pared down to what constituted a reasonable national storage.

Kennedy and Education

The issue that Kennedy cared about most of all was education. He would often reel off disheartening statistics about the young: only six children of every ten in the fifth grade would finish high school; only nine of every sixteen high-school graduates would go on to college; a million young people were out of school *and* out of work; and school dropouts were a constant drain on public resources. In 1963, Kennedy obtained passage of the Higher Education Act, which produced more aid for colleges in five years than they had received in a century, since the Morrill Act of 1862. Hundreds of classrooms, community colleges, graduate centers, technical institutes, and college libraries were constructed under the act.

Kennedy then pursued the theme of "specialized" aid to the elementary and secondary schools, getting grants for vocational education, providing literacy training to the unemployed, launching efforts to halt the dropout and delinquency problems, and building libraries. Educational television also received important assistance. In total, a third of Kennedy's proposals to Congress on major issues had to do with education. The Office of Education, surveying the record, described the Kennedy years as the most significant for education in its hundred-year history.

The Medicare Proposal

In 1945 Harry Truman had asked Congress to establish publicly supported medical insurance for all Americans. Members of the American Medical Association rose up in massive wrath, condemning his plan as "socialized medicine," and Truman was turned down. However, rising medical costs and the low incomes of the elderly (who were growing every year more numerous) created unavoidable social distress. The tragedy was that the old could usually not get, or even retain, medical insurance at the time of their life when they needed medical care most of all. The savings of an entire lifetime could be wiped away by one illness, after which self-respecting men and women who had taken pride in being independent all their lives would have to accept the shame of being charity patients.

Within the offices of the Federal Security Agency, where it was well known that the aged were in a cruel situation, studies on the problem proceeded. One of the results of this research, a bill that would give some aid to the elderly, was proposed in Congress but for years was little noted. In 1957, however, the classic process by which America makes major reforms finally got under way: a systematic building of national opinion and support, a "constituency," for the idea. The AFL–CIO, its vice-president Walter Reuther pushing hard for social-justice reforms, got behind the measure. It then swiftly rose to become a great national issue, figuring prominently in the presidential campaign of 1960.

President Kennedy, however, lost one of his crucial battles in Congress when he tried to get a Medicare bill through that body that would have provided coverage to those over sixty-five, through the mechanism and funding process of the Social Security System. The American Medical Association once more condemned the idea, and its opponents were able to keep the bill locked up in the House Committee on Ways and Means year after year; it was never allowed to come up for a vote on the House floor.

Aid for the Cities

The president was deeply aware of urban ills. His administration sought to help cities by aiding the long court fight to redistrict state legislatures so that rural areas would have their influence decreased and cities would be able to claim their proper share of legislative power. Under the existing system, overrepresentation for rural areas was extreme. In California, a county with 15,000 people had the same representation as another with 6 million people. Attorney General Robert Kennedy helped bring the crucial cases—*Baker* v. *Carr* (1962) and *Reynold* v. *Sims* (1964)—before the Supreme Court. The Court ruled that the national House of Representatives and all state and local legislative bodies had to be apportioned on a one-man-one-vote principle, a revolutionary decision in American government. Once again, the egalitarian potential of the 14th Amendment's provision for the "equal protection of the laws" was dramatically released and put to work to transform a major element in American law and government.

Congress enacted a $6.1-billion Housing Act in 1961, which was of great potential value to urban families—a large proportion of them black—at low- and middle-income levels. The president failed to get approval of a job corps that would train unemployed young men and women, who were then just roaming the streets. Consequently, he established vocational schools and launched the Area Redevelopment Act of 1961. Concentrating on the most depressed communities, the act's objectives were to provide job retraining and stimulate the building of new industry. In the fall of 1963, Kennedy read Michael Harrington's brilliant book *The Other America*, was shocked to learn from it about the suffering of millions of forgotten, poverty-stricken citizens, and ordered that plans be prepared for a "war on poverty." He had already secured passage of an Accelerated Public Works program to employ the jobless, the first such enactment since the New Deal.

In 1962 President Kennedy, struggling hard to turn an unfriendly Congress into a cooperative one, went to St. Paul, Minnesota (as he did to other cities), to speak for the election of Democratic congressmen: "One of the favorite bromides in the world," he said, "is that there is no difference between our two political parties. I'm going to show you what the difference is this year. Last year we had a bill to increase the minimum wage for workers . . . to $50 a week, $1.25 an hour. Do you know that on this not very drastic piece of legislation 100 percent of the Republican Congressmen from Minnesota voted against it? Do you know on a bill a month ago that was killed, to provide assistance for higher education, by 1970 twice as many boys and girls are going to be applying for admission to our colleges as in 1960—they are our most valuable resource—on a bill to assist higher education in this country, 67 percent of the Republican delegation from the State of Minnesota voted 'no.' On a bill to provide for assistance to depressed areas, those with long-term, chronic unemployment . . . 81 percent of the Republican Congressmen in the House of Representatives voted 'no.'

"That's the issue in this campaign. On a bill to provide medical care for our older citizens . . . seven-eighths of the Republican members of the Senate voted 'no,' just as their fathers before them had voted 90 percent against the social security in the 1930s. . . . We have won and lost vote after vote by 1 or 2 or 3 votes in the Senate, and 3, 4, or 5 votes in the House of Representatives, and I don't think we can find jobs for our people, I don't think we can educate our younger people, I don't think we can provide security for our older citizens, when we have a party which votes 'no.'" (*Public Papers of the Presidents of the United States: John F. Kennedy, 1962*)

Stimulating the Economy

Rising over all other immediate domestic considerations, in Kennedy's mind, was the economy's lagging rate of growth. Many national problems would disappear, he believed, in a booming economy. Black people, city people, farmers, the unemployed, those too poor to move elsewhere to find jobs, those badly housed, poorly schooled, and ineffectively policed—all would benefit by renewed prosperity.

Equally important in Kennedy's view was the international rivalry with Russia, which could not be won, he believed, if the Russians had a flourishing economy and the American system fell farther and farther behind in its growth rate. Furthermore, the United States could not maintain its position in world trade if stagnation at home meant a reduced ability to compete abroad. With Britain, France, West Germany, Italy, and especially Japan more productive than ever before, the American dollar had lost its old-time power.

Kennedy came to office with traditional ideas about economic policy, most of which revolved around the belief that the national government should at all times work for a balanced budget. Within two years though, he had dug deeply into modern economic theory by quizzing economists across the country as to how he could boost the economy from its 2-percent annual rate of growth to at least 5 percent a year. He emerged from this experience the nation's first Keynesian president: that is, he adopted the basic economic theory of the Englishman John Maynard Keynes, who a generation before had written that the way a government revives a national economy is to spend more than it receives in taxes (deficit spending). Franklin Roosevelt had toyed gingerly with the idea, but Kennedy was the first to adopt it as policy and, in a time of relative prosperity, propose a sweeping reduction in taxes. He proposed a national budget that would *purposely* wind up twelve billion dollars out of balance in 1964.

Since at the time this idea was heresy in the eyes of congressmen and the general public, the president had to painstakingly persuade people of its value. Removing taxes, he said, would unleash the economy. As it boomed upward, it would eventually produce *more* revenue than before, even at the lower tax rates. (Inflation, which tends to be accentuated by deficit spending, and by cutting taxes and allowing people to spend more, was not yet a major problem in these years.) He sent his cabinet members and advisers around the country to lecture to public groups and business gatherings, and released a stream of news stories from the White House dealing with the new economic plan. Then in 1963 he announced his program for a planned national deficit, which began a long series of congressional hearings and national debate that ended—after his death—in the tax reduction he had called for. Thereafter, the national economy took off on the longest uninterrupted boom in the history of the United States—which, ironically, eventually produced a nation so affluent that by the end of the 1960s it was choking on its wealth, gobbling up natural resources at a frightening rate, and lurching into inflation.

Kennedy and the World at Large

Like most presidents, Kennedy came to the White House fascinated by foreign affairs, since in that great realm the president of the United States can move with a freedom of action far greater than that afforded him in domestic policy making. In truth, by 1960 the world was a far different place than it had been in 1945, the existing Cold War policies seemed in need of drastic revision, and new directions in foreign policy were called for. The British, French, and Dutch empires had disappeared, and this opened up an extraordinarily fluid situation in Asia, the Near East, and Africa. China made its momentous break with the Soviet Union in April 1960, striking out on its own independent path of—for many years—rigid and puritanical communism. Meanwhile, western Europe, which during the Eisenhower years had been offended by America's tendency to ignore its wishes and at the same time

had been emboldened by the booming success of its Common Market, took an increasingly separate line as well. France's president, Charles de Gaulle, urged that Europe become an independent force in the world, turning away from American leadership and downgrading NATO. Indeed, the French were soon to pull their military forces out of the NATO system.

To John Kennedy, the world was not the place envisioned by Cold War enthusiasts: he did not believe the West to be all good, nor the East all evil. Rather, he thought of the world as inevitably a chancy and untidy place in which it was important for the United States to operate from a position of strength, but in which it was possible and desirable to live in peace and mutual cooperation with the Soviet Union.

Nonetheless, everywhere in 1960 was heard the drumbeat of fear that perhaps Nikita Khrushchev was right when he insisted triumphantly that communism was the wave of the future. In the month of Kennedy's inauguration an exultant, belligerent Khrushchev gave a major address in Moscow in which he boasted of Russia's industrial growth, missile exploits, immense hydrogen bombs, and growing success in underdeveloped countries from Vietnam to Cuba. History and communism, he said, were partners; "there is no longer any force in the world capable of barring the road to socialism." World wars were to be condemned, the Soviet premier maintained, but "wars of liberation or popular uprisings" were to be fostered "wholeheartedly and without reservation." In this context, peaceful coexistence meant "a form of intense economic, political and ideological struggle between the proletariat and the aggressive forces of imperialism in the world arena."

These words cast a chill over Washington. Reading them, the new president observed that "we must never be lulled into believing that either [Russia or China] has yielded its ambitions for world domination. . . ." Kennedy became fascinated by the new military doctrine of counterinsurgency. "We must be ready now," he said, "to deal with any size of force, including small externally supported bands of men; and we must help train local forces to be equally effective. . . ." He began poring through books written by the leading world spokesmen for guerrilla warfare— Che Guevara and Mao Tse-tung. The army developed new concepts, equipment, and training to produce military units such as the Green Berets. With Dean Rusk as secretary of state, Robert McNamara running the Defense Department, the president's brother Robert as attorney general, and McGeorge Bundy and Walter W. Rostow as White House advisers on foreign affairs, the Kennedy team began to respond vigorously to Khrushchev's threats.

The Best and the Brightest

It is important to understand the spirit of the Kennedy administration. They were proud men who were confident that whatever the challenge, they could solve it. "A remarkable hubris [i.e., overweening pride of self-confidence] permeated this entire time," David Halberstam has written in his brilliant study of the Kennedy and Johnson administrations, *The Best and the Brightest* (1972). "Nine years earlier Denis Brogan had written: 'Probably the only people who have the historical sense of inevitable victory are the Americans.' Never had that statement seemed more true; the Kennedy group regarded the Eisenhower people as having shrunk from the challenge set before them." The revolutionary upheavals sweeping through such countries as Vietnam and Cuba were seen merely as the newest editions of a series of "problems" that Americans had been successfully solving generation after generation.

Insurgency was thought of as something that could be fended off with organization and technology. The men of the Kennedy administration liked to think of themselves as tough-minded; they wore the popular nickname of "the Irish Mafia" with some pride. The president himself was fascinated by power in whatever form, and he liked using it. Combating the new challenge of guerrilla rebellions in Vietnam and elsewhere seemed an exciting kind of military chess in which dash, intelligence, and professional skill would be rewarded with inevitable victory. This is where the Green Berets—the United States Army Special Forces—would play their special role.

At the same time, however, John Kennedy was a liberal Democrat, heir to the tradition of Adlai Stevenson, and he carried with his fascination for power a lively belief that the United States could win no victories unless it also worked for social reform abroad. He knew that the root cause of world turbulence lay in what Stevenson had called the "revolution of rising expectations," the realization by millions in the non-Western world that a better life was possible and their growing readiness to throw off what they had for a way of life more like that of the wealthy countries. Therefore, from the beginning he revived the social idealism expressed in the Marshall Plan and the concept of economic aid. Throughout Kennedy's administration ran this central conflict between a tough-minded, prideful military response that could lead the nation (and did) into overseas adventures of great potential danger, and a sensitive concern for human suffering that understood social turbulence as an outcry that would not stop until the revolution was completed.

Kennedy and the Third World

Some forty countries holding nearly a billion people had achieved independence since 1945 in Latin America, Asia, and Africa—the Third World. The United States had had a strange relationship to this process. On the one hand, the American government was traditionally anticolonialist and cheered it on; on the other, its NATO ties with imperial powers (France, Britain, Holland, Portugal) made it worry about doing anything that would unduly offend them. During the Eisenhower years, moreover, the Cold War psychology demanded that the new nations choose up sides, and condemned those that were neutralist—the great majority. Added to this was the predominantly business-oriented foreign policy of the Republican regime, which in each new country linked America with those of wealth and power against upwelling socialist movements.

President Kennedy was determined to transform this relationship. For some years before his election he had spoken publicly against colonial rule. In his campaign he had often referred to the Third World in terms of sympathy and understanding for the awakened hopes of millions of Africans, Asians, and Latin Americans for a better life. His election as president was cheered enthusiastically in these countries. To the White House came a steady stream of Third World leaders who were enchanted by the new president's knowledge of their problems and his genuine concern to offer American aid.

The most dramatic expression of Kennedy's

outlook toward the new countries was his creation of the Peace Corps. A descendant of Franklin Roosevelt's Civilian Conservation Corps, which also aimed at putting young people to work in ways that served the country, it was condemned by Eisenhower as a "juvenile experiment." The response of young people throughout the United States was so enthusiastic, however, that the program soon became one of the shining lights of the new administration. By 1964 some 10,000 young Americans were at work in forty-six countries, laboring to bring such self-denying assistance as they could to the impoverished of the world.

Latin America

The new president was especially interested in Latin America. With 200 million people, half of them illiterate, multiplying faster than any other peoples in the world and living in the grossest extremes of poverty and wealth, it was a vast region at once exciting and appalling. In 1959 Fidel Castro set up a violently anti-American Communist government in Cuba, and American attentions were suddenly forced southward. Cuba's quickly burgeoning ties with the Soviet Union transferred the Cold War to this hemisphere. "Operation Pan America," which was designed to raise income levels, stimulate land reform, and pull the Latin American countries together, had already been approved at a hemispheric conference in Washington in 1958. In 1960, Eisenhower pledged $500 million to underwrite development programs.

Kennedy swiftly seized these initiatives and broadened them into a bold appeal for an "Alliance for Progress." Modeled directly on the Marshall Plan, the Alliance for Progress included the demand that Latin American countries work out their plans together before the United States would provide the necessary capital. The United States pledged at least twenty billion dollars in aid over the next ten years in private and government funds, provided the Latin American countries made fundamental social reforms. Launched with soaring fanfare, the Alliance for Progress disappointed Kennedy. Entrenched privileged groups in Latin America, divisions among reformers, hostility from many Latin American countries, the almost constant eruption of military coups—these combined to hamstring the program, which limped along until, by the mid 1960s, it was heard of but rarely.

Even so, the Alliance was a catalyst for long-range change: governments began working out development plans; cooperative efforts developed into free-trade regional agreements; land reform pushed ahead; schools were built and teachers trained; water supplies were purified; roads opened up remote regions; and hopes were stimulated. Food production was at least keeping up with the explosive population growth, and for the first time wealthy Latin Americans began investing in their own economies instead of sending their money to Swiss banks. By 1966 investment had soared to a level ten times the amount of financial aid coming in from abroad. Although the countries were terribly hampered by galloping inflation, economic growth rates, especially in the countries along the Andes, were astonishingly high.

The Bay of Pigs Disaster

One of President Eisenhower's last actions had been to break diplomatic relations with Fidel Castro's Cuba because appropriate compensation for nationalized American sugar-producing facilities had been denied. Then, as Kennedy learned to his surprise on taking office, the Eisenhower administration had begun to train an invasion force composed of 1,200 Cuban exiles. The American government assumed that Castro, a Communist, was unpopular among his people and would be overthrown in a national uprising if outside assistance was provided. This presented President Kennedy with a crucial decision: Should he remain true to his liberal Democratic heritage and keep faith with Franklin Roosevelt's policy of strict nonintervention? Or would he be "tough-minded" and support an undertaking in line with his oratory about the need for a vigorous response to the Communist challenge? He chose a middle ground: he ruled out any involvement of Americans in the invasion itself. The 1,200 Cubans then training in the Guatemalan jungles would have to fight without the aid of the United States navy or air force. Kennedy's military advisers assured him categorically that this would work.

But it failed utterly. The invasion force was quickly smashed when it struggled onto the beaches of the Bay of Pigs in April 1961. The people of Cuba did not rally to its support. A massive miscalculation had been made that disgraced the Kennedy administration within three months

THE TURBULENT 1960s: THE EGALITARIAN SURGE BUILDS MOMENTUM

of the inauguration. Military derring-do, CIA-trained guerrillas: it had all proved a miserable mistake. It was a profound shock. The president, said one of his aides, "showed his fatigue for the first time. He looked sad. The exhilaration of the job was gone. He was no longer the young conquering hero, the first 43-year-old president . . . the young man smoking his cigar with his friends and telling them how much fun it was. All that was gone. Suddenly it became one hell of a job."

The Space Race

While the Kennedy administration was struggling to rise from this disaster, it was making a full investigation of the nation's space programs. The president had concluded that it was absolutely essential for the United States to gain supremacy in space technology, both for its immediate effects on national security and for its immense psycho-logical importance in rebuilding American confidence. Finding the space effort understaffed, underfunded, and uncoordinated, he decided to choose one great objective that would inspire the whole nation and allow everyone, scientist and technologist alike, to pull together. The objective? Placing a man on the moon. In the year 1961 this seemed an impossibly visionary conception, but the very grandness of it caught his imagination.

In June 1961, therefore, he called the Congress into joint session and, in a personal address, appealed for immense funds to be devoted to the project. "Now it is time to take longer strides," he said, "time for a great new American enterprise—time for this nation to take a clearly leading role in space achievement, which in many ways may hold the key to our future on earth." Responding enthusiastically, Congress began pouring out billions of dollars to finance an enormous exploit in space technology and space science that has extended into the 1980s.

On May 25, 1961, President Kennedy went before Congress to call for a landing of man on the moon before 1970. Astronauts John Glenn, Gus Grissom, and Alan Shepard are shown during their training for the first manned space flight.

NASA

Kennedy and Khrushchev

The president's main concern in foreign policy was to break the rigid Cold War and ease relations with the Soviet Union. To his dismay, he found Khrushchev unyielding. He would come to no agreements concerning Indochina or Berlin or any other world hot spot. Following American initiative, the Soviets had halted the testing of nuclear bombs in the atmosphere in 1958, and Kennedy pushed insistently for a test-ban treaty to make this arrangement permanent. However, Khrushchev would not listen to Kennedy's appeals. Instead, he made more threatening speeches, boasted of his missiles and bombs, and ordered a 30-percent increase in military spending. He was unbending as to the status of Berlin: control over access to West Berlin was to be given by Russia to the East German government. He bluntly warned Kennedy that he was prepared to go to war to end the existing situation. West Berlin was to become a "free city," and Western forces would be allowed to remain there only if East Germany agreed.

To Kennedy, the Berlin challenge amounted to a crucial test of the American will. In response, therefore, he took a fateful step: on national television in July 1961 he called for a partial mobilization of the armed forces and a major increase of more than three billion dollars in military spending. The time had come, he said, for the United States to regain flexibility by rebuilding its conventional forces: ground armies, air transport, air tactical units, support naval craft. Eisenhower's military posture of "massive retaliation," which relied largely on delivering bombs on Moscow, had made the country unable to respond to lower-level challenges. Most of his buildup, therefore, went to the long-starved army: an addition of some 875,000 men. Meanwhile, draft calls were greatly increased, reserve units were called up from civilian life, ships and planes were reactivated, and a tremendous sum was spent on non-nuclear weapons.

Khrushchev's response was to send another huge missile around the earth and to talk about a Soviet nuclear bomb equivalent to 100 million tons of TNT. In August the Soviets built a wall across Berlin to halt the flood of refugees that for many months had poured into West Berlin. They also resumed exploding atom bombs in the atmosphere, an action that the United States eventually copied. The world was once more faced with the horror of radioactive fallout saturating the atmosphere and causing unimaginable damage to human beings below.

The "Grand Design"

President Kennedy watched the growing strength of the European Common Market and concluded that the time had come to build a revived and strengthened Atlantic community. If this was not done, the tariff walls around the Common Market would rise ever higher, trade between North America and Europe would languish, and the world would fall back into the old divisive international trade wars. The answer lay deeply rooted in Kennedy's Democratic tradition: slash tariffs all round so as to ensure a steadily growing world of multilateral trade in which the resources and skills of the world would be openly shared to everyone's benefit. In early 1962 he asked Congress for revolutionary authority to greatly reduce American tariffs across the board—by as much as 50 percent in whole categories of commodities and manufactured goods—in some cases to abolish them entirely, provided similar concessions could be gained from Europe.

President Kennedy was a practical-minded man who did not like dealing in ideologies and soaring dreams, but this was a cause he pursued with evangelical zeal. Throughout 1962 he spent endless hours mobilizing a nationwide educational campaign designed to persuade Americans that in his "Grand Design" there was a real hope for a better world. "The two great Atlantic markets," he said, "will either grow together or they will grow apart." In farm regions, among businessmen, in labor unions—anywhere he could reach listeners, the president preached his message. The result was the passage in September 1962 of the boldest trade legislation in American history—a bill that alone, in more peaceful eras, would have marked the Eighty-seventh Congress for an important niche in history. "The age of self-sufficient nationalism is over," the victorious president exulted. "The age of interdependence is here. The Atlantic partnership is a growing reality."

Ahead, however, lay years of careful, hard-driving negotiations. The "Kennedy round" of tariff-reduction talks, convened under the authority of the General Agreement on Trade and Tariffs, did not begin until after the president's death. Negotiations among fifty-three nations from around the world (outside the Sino-Soviet bloc) began in Geneva in 1964 and ground on for three years, ending in May 1967 with the largest and widest tariff cuts in modern history. Thereafter, tariff barriers posed only a minor obstacle to world trade (though other administrative hurdles, such as import quotas, remained to be dealt with).

The Cuban Missile Crisis

The Cold War reached its frightening climax in October 1962. American reconnaissance planes flying over Cuba discovered a startling fact: the Soviets were placing intercontinental missiles on the island. The president was startled and shocked. With Soviet missiles sited within ninety miles of the southern American coast, the elaborate network of radar warning systems and military bases that the United States had built abroad would be short-circuited. It would be impossible for the United States ever to intercept a missile rising from Cuba since the warning time would be too short. In such an intensively charged international atmosphere as then existed, Kennedy felt that the implications of this move were enormous.

President Kennedy and Secretary of Defense Robert S. McNamara in a tense executive committee meeting during the Cuban missile crisis of 1962. Its resolution seemed finally to end the threat of world atomic war, at least as an immediate possibility, and the Cold War.

John F. Kennedy Library

The balance of power would shift massively to the Soviet side.

President Kennedy regarded this as the ultimate test of his administration. For two years he and his advisers had been learning how to manage crisis. They had bungled badly in the Bay of Pigs disaster. Would they do better this time? For ten days the White House bustled with secret meetings round the clock as every possible response was proposed, discussed, argued over, and balanced against alternatives. The most important condition Kennedy imposed on the debate was that Khrushchev was never to be backed into a corner. Options were always to be left open that would allow him to escape total humiliation. Meanwhile, aerial photos continued to pour in so that the conferees could watch almost hour by hour as the missile sites were rushed toward completion. At the same time, it was learned that more than a dozen Soviet vessels were on their way to Cuba, some of them with suspiciously shaped on-deck cargo boxes that could contain missiles.

On October 22, 1962, the president went on national television to inform the nation of these developments and announce his decision. This "sudden, clandestine decision to station strategic weapons for the first time outside of Soviet soil," he said, "is a deliberately provocative and unjustified change in the status quo which cannot be accepted by this country, if our courage and our commitments are ever to be trusted again by either friend or foe." He declared a blockade around Cuba that would allow everything but missile-bearing vessels through. At the same time, he ordered that a small army of more than sixty thousand men be rushed to Florida, thus making use for the first time of the new military flexibility that he had called for during the 1961 Berlin crisis.

Khrushchev's Response

The world was electrified with fear. What would be Khrushchev's response? Would the war that all had dreaded finally break out between the Soviet Union and the United States? To demonstrate solid hemispheric support of Kennedy's actions, the Organization of American States met and voted 19 to 0 (even Kennedy was surprised at this unanimous action) to authorize the use of force to maintain the blockade. After an agonizing wait, the Soviet ships began, one by one, to swing in wide arcs and head back to their ports. Soon a secret correspondence, initiated by Khrushchev, sprang up between the Soviet premier and the American president. It was a frank interchange in which the Americans were relieved to see Khrushchev finally expressing horror at the prospect of nuclear war. The crisis was over: the Soviets withdrew their missiles, and the world began to breathe again.

Kennedy's actions in the missile crisis have been harshly criticized by those who believe that the president was wholly unjustified in taking the world to the brink of nucelar war. At the time, Adlai Stevenson and the distinguished newspaper columnist Walter Lippmann had urged a different course: that the United States offer to remove America's long-established missile sites in Turkey in exchange for the elimination of Soviet sites in Cuba. American possession of intercontinental ballistic missiles had by this time rendered such overseas launch sites as those in Turkey of minor importance. In truth, there was a hollow ring to American protests about Soviet missiles within ninety miles of Florida when Turkey was even closer to Soviet soil, sharing a common border.

The End of the Cold War

In retrospect, however, Lippmann, who had been analyzing world events since the days of Woodrow Wilson, called this crisis the turning point of the Cold War. The world had been living in continuous fear of an atomic holocaust. Now it knew that when the two superpowers faced each other in a naked showdown, they would pull back from the brink. The atomic bomb was defused. All world history has been different since the missile crisis of October 1962.

The Soviet Union and the United States moved steadily into a new and relaxed relationship in which each accepted the stalemate. Talk of the Berlin crisis vanished, and in early January 1963 Khrushchev wrote a letter to Kennedy saying that "the time has come now to put an end once and for all to nuclear tests. We are ready to meet you halfway."

The Long-Range Impact of the Cuban Missile Crisis

What in fact happened, however, was a fundamental shift in Soviet policy. The Kremlin decided that the lesson of the crisis was not that they should stop regarding the Americans as weak and irresolute (Kennedy felt that this was the lesson he was teaching the Soviets). Rather, the lesson was that the Soviets should never again allow themselves to be so humiliated before the world. In order to prevent this possibility, they began a massive, long-range buildup of army, naval, air force, and missile strength, looking toward the day when America would not, by means of great superiority in these fields, be able to force the Kremlin ever again to back down.

This immense buildup of Soviet armed strength would take many years. There did not exist within the relatively underdeveloped Soviet economy the great industrial-military base that was necessary to acquire the vast strength in naval power, missiles, conventional armies, and air forces that was envisioned. There would also need to be a sweeping reorganization within the Soviet hierarchy and governing system as well. Khrushchev had brought disgrace upon the U.S.S.R.; his impulsive one-man rule within the Soviet Union had produced wild lurches and inef-

ficiencies in the nation's economy; and in 1964 he would be toppled from power by a group led by Leonid Brezhnev. By the late 1970s, it was dawning upon the West that a Soviet Union incredibly more powerful, militarily, than the country Khrushchev had led in 1962 had come into existence. In the intervening years, however, the conditions were ripe for a relationship of détente (cooperation and the relaxation of tensions) to slowly take form between the U.S.S.R. and the United States.

In June 1963 President Kennedy strongly signaled to an approving world his readiness to work toward détente. In a speech at American University in Washington, D.C., he urged Americans to drop their fears of a conspiratorial Russia, just as the Russians should stop believing terrible things of the United States. There must be "increased understanding between the Soviets and ourselves . . . increased contact and communication." Responding to the spirit of these remarks, Khrushchev made it possible for the Test Ban Treaty to be concluded. In October 1963 the treaty was initialed in Moscow. The president was jubilant. This, he felt, was his most important gift to the world, his greatest achievement. For years, he said, the world had struggled "to escape from the darkening prospects of mass destruction." Now, he went on, "a shaft of light cut into the darkness."

At American University Kennedy appealed to Americans to rethink their attitudes toward Russia: "It is discouraging to think that their leaders may actually believe what their propagandists write. . . . But it is also a warning—a warning to the American people not to fall into the same trap as the Soviets, not to see only a distorted and desperate view of the other side, not to see conflict as inevitable, accommodation as impossible, and communication as nothing more than an exchange of threats.

"No government or social system is so evil that its people must be considered as lacking in virtue. As Americans, we find communism profoundly repugnant as a negation of personal freedom and dignity. But we can still hail the Russian people for their many achievements—in science and space, in economic and industrial growth, in culture and in acts of courage. . . . Let us reexamine our attitude toward the cold war, remembering that we are not engaged in a debate, seeking to pile up debating points. We are not here distributing blame or pointing the finger of judgment. We must deal with the world as it is, and not as it might have been had the

THE TURBULENT 1960s: THE EGALITARIAN SURGE BUILDS MOMENTUM

history of the last 18 years been different. . . . Above all, while defending our own vital interests, nuclear powers must avert those confrontations which bring an adversary to a choice of either a humiliating retreat or a nuclear war. To adopt that kind of course in the nuclear age would be evidence only of the bankruptcy of our policy—or of a collective deathwish for the world. . . . We are unwilling to impose our system on any unwilling people—but we are willing and able to engage in peaceful competition with any people on earth. . . ." (*Public Papers of the Presidents of the United States: John F. Kennedy* [1964])

The Black Revolution

The Kennedy years will be remembered as the time when the Second Reconstruction burst into full momentum. Almost a hundred years had passed since the First Reconstruction, during which bold efforts were made to bring black America to civil and political equality with white America. Now those efforts, which had largely failed, were revived on a nationwide scale in the executive and legislative branches of the federal government, not simply in the courts, eventually culminating in sweeping reforms in national life far beyond those conceived of by the Radical Republicans of the First Reconstruction.

The event that catalyzed the black movement occurred late on a December day in 1955, when Rosa Parks boarded a bus in Montgomery, Alabama. She was a black, middle-aged seamstress, and she was tired. Without much thought she sank down on a seat in the front part of the bus traditionally reserved for whites. Normally, when asked by the bus driver to move to the rear she would have assented. But this day she could not bring herself to obey. Thus, Rosa Parks inspired a revolution which demanded that the "equal protection of the laws" be made a broad reality in American life.

A year-long boycott of the bus system in Montgomery, led by the young black minister Martin Luther King, Jr., ended in victory in November 1956, when the Supreme Court ruled that segregation on buses was unconstitutional. King then founded the Southern Christian Leadership Conference and crisscrossed the South preaching Mahatma Gandhi's philosophy of nonviolence. Oppressed peoples, King said, achieve their goals most successfully by appealing to the conscience

of their oppressors. He looked toward an integrated, interracial America, toward that "beloved community" in which blacks and whites would recognize their common bonds of humanity.

In 1960 a civil-rights act was passed that allowed the appointment of federal referees who were to aid blacks in registering for and voting in federal elections. Previously, only 28 percent of voting-age blacks had been registered in the South, compared with 70 percent in the North (roughly the proportion among the white population). In the states of the Deep South, the percentage of registered blacks was the lowest in the nation. In Mississippi, for example, the figure was 4 percent.

The Sit-Ins

In 1960 a group of young black college students in Greensboro, North Carolina, refused to leave their seats when denied service at "white" lunch counters. Sitting doggedly in their places, serenely facing verbal and physical abuse, they provided an inspiring example for a nonviolent army of thousands of Southern blacks. With the backing of the Supreme Court, thousands of demonstrators marched in Southern cities, demanding and usually winning open access to movie theaters, restaurants, hotels, and bowling alleys and enduring tear gas, fire hoses, and mass arrests.

In the midst of rising turbulence, Martin Luther King in late 1959 renewed his call for nonviolent tactics: "Token integration is the developing pattern. . . . There is reason to believe that the Negro of 1959 will not accept supinely any such compromises. . . . It is axiomatic in social life that the imposition of frustration leads to two kinds of reactions. One is the development of a wholesome social organization to resist with effective, firm measures any efforts to impede progress. The other is a confused, anger-motivated drive to strike back violently to inflict damage. Primarily, it seeks to cause injury to retaliate for wrongful suffering. Secondarily, it seeks real progress. It is punitive—not radical or constructive. . . .

"There are incalculable perils in this approach. . . . The greatest danger is that it will fail to attract Negroes to a real collective struggle, and will confuse the large uncommitted middle group, which as yet has not supported either side. Further, it will mislead Negroes into the belief that this is the only path and place them as a minority in a position where they confront a far larger adversary than it is possible to defeat in this form of combat. . . . It is unfortunately true that however the Negro acts, his struggle will not be free of violence initiated by his enemies, and he will need ample courage and willingness to sacrifice to defeat this manifestation of violence. But if he seeks it and organizes it, he cannot win. . . .

"In the history of the movement for racial advancement, many creative forms have been developed—the mass boycott, sit-down protests and strikes, sit-ins—refusal to pay fines and bail for unjust arrests —mass marches—mass meetings—prayer pilgrimages, etc. . . . There is more power in socially organized masses on the march than there is in guns in the hands of a few desperate men." (*Liberation* [October 1959])

The Churches and the Black Movement

America's churches, led by the National Council of Churches, poured passionate, often self-sacrificing energies into the cause of black rights. The NCC urged each church "to confess her sin of omission and delay, and to move forward to witness to her essential belief that every child of God is a brother to every other." Prominent in every civil-rights march, North and South, were priests, nuns, Protestant ministers, and rabbis, many of them present in the hope that their being in the ranks would ward off violence. In Washington, interfaith coalitions of religious leaders actively labored with Congress to push civil-rights legislation through reluctant committees and to win passing votes. "For the first time in American history," observed a commentator in *Religious Education*, "the United States Congress was presented with a united testimony by Catholics, Protestants, and Jews. . . ." At the same time, nine out of ten Supreme Court cases in which Southern police and courts had jailed civil-rights demonstrators, on charges of trespass and disorderly conduct, ended in the Court rejecting such convictions as unconstitutional. Television, now the medium through which most Americans got their late-breaking news, seized upon the civil-rights movement, filling American homes with a steady flow of graphic images and information. In a typical gesture, a major network beamed a three-hour documentary on the civil-rights movement, *American Revolution, 1963*, to the American public.

John Kennedy and the Second Reconstruction

President Kennedy was an Irish Catholic. Blacks and Irish Catholics had generations of hostile relations behind them. Since both were the urban poor of the North, they often competed for the same low-paying jobs. The Catholic Church's nineteenth-century opposition to liberalism had been another source of bad feeling. And then there was the simple matter of racism in congested inner cities. Northern whites in general were antiblack; Irish Catholics had no monopoly on such feelings. However, since Franklin Roosevelt's time blacks and Irish Catholics were at least in the same political party; Rome's hostility to liberalism had long since moderated; and a wealthy young Irish Catholic who attended Harvard and whose father was a major figure in the New Deal administration would tend to lean toward social justice. Even so, John Kennedy was no tearing reformer. As a congressman and senator, he introduced almost no such legislation, and for a time he even approved tentatively of Senator McCarthy's anti-Communist crusade. Then in 1960, as he responded to his emerging national constituency, JFK made it clear that he would be considerably more vigorous than Dwight Eisenhower in using the powers of the presidency to enforce the rulings of the Supreme Court on racial issues. Even so, his moderation on the topic kept the white South firmly in his camp during the election of that year. He certainly had no sweeping civil-rights legislation to propose to Congress when he assumed the presidency. That, he believed, would simply enflame the elderly and racially inflexible white Southerners who dominated Congress's committees. If that happened, then he would be unable to obtain any legislation to help the poor—including blacks—secure better housing, better schools, and better employment opportunities.

Kennedy's great innovation as president was to swing the moral and legal weight of the presidency strongly behind the idea of equal treatment for black people. Also, by putting his brother Robert in the post of attorney general, he tried to insure that the existing legal protections of black people against violence and against discrimination in education and other fields would be vigorously enforced. Thus, as JFK said, two branches of the federal government, rather than simply the court system, were now behind the black cause. "The Executive Branch," he said to a reporter, "is beginning to turn. This is a tremendous new source of power. Have you really focused on the possibilities?"

Executive Action

President Kennedy initiated extensive surveys of black employment in the federal government, found a miserable record (save in menial occupations), and began pushing hard to force the hiring of black professionals. He made a surprisingly large number of appointments of blacks to high-ranking positions involving policy making. Among the most notable appointees was Robert Weaver, former mayor of Cleveland, who was named head of what would become in the near future the Department of Housing and Urban Development. The journalists' news pool at the White House was desegregated, to the lasting gratitude of the nation's many black newspapers and magazines. A distinguished black attorney, Thurgood Marshall, was elevated to the Second Circuit Court of Appeals in New York (Lyndon Johnson would make him the first black American to serve as a justice of the United States Supreme Court). Kennedy worked hard (but unsuccessfully) to achieve home rule for the predominantly black District of Columbia, which was ruled autocratically by a Southern white–dominated congressional committee.

Within Washington itself, the Kennedys condemned racial bias in private clubs, and withdrew from the famous Cosmos Club because of its policy of segregation. In an unprecedented move, American black leaders were invited to social gatherings both at the White House and in Robert Kennedy's home in Virginia. A high-ranking inter-cabinet body was formed to negotiate with major corporations who sold goods to the federal government to get them to begin hiring blacks on a more equal basis. And far more than in the past, the White House was accessible to civil-rights leaders. Not only was the president's ear open to them, he met a large delegation from the National Association for the Advancement of Colored People (NAACP) in July 1961 to give formal moral endorsement to their work. Schools striving for racial desegregation were singled out for presidential praise, and ceremonies were held at the White House to celebrate the signing of corporate pledges to end job discrimination.

It was in enforcing civil rights in the South that the most dramatic steps toward racial equality were taken by the Kennedy administration. Robert Kennedy played an ever more assertive role in forcing Southern state governments to protect the legal rights of their black as well as their white citizens. In April 1960 the Student Nonviolent Coordinating Committee (SNCC) had been formed. In 1961 SNCC joined with the Congress of Racial Equality (CORE) to mount "freedom rides" into the South on interstate buses in order to implement a Supreme Court decision that outlawed segregation in bus, train, and air travel. Mobs assaulted the freedom riders, sheriffs arrested them, and their buses were set aflame. When blacks entered white waiting rooms, white youths threw coffee cups at them, chased them outside, and unmercifully beat and kicked them. The Kennedy administration rushed in federal marshals to keep order and got rulings from the Interstate Commerce Commission directing the removal of White Only signs. In 1962 President Kennedy dispatched troops to Mississippi to force the state university to admit James Meredith, a black student. At the same time, he issued an executive order forbidding racial or religious discrimination in federally financed housing.

Now SNCC workers, with the aid of white students from the North, funds from northern white foundations, and the encouragement of the Justice Department, moved into Mississippi in force. Their demand was for equal political rights for the masses, and their chief tactic was voter-registration drives. Voting registrars used every kind of device to prevent black registration, making the procedures so complicated that often only one voter could be registered per hour. Long lines of blacks stood outside voter-registration offices in the burning sun, hooted at and abused by roaming bands of whites. Meanwhile, SNCC workers endured a ghastly succession of physical assaults and illegal jailings while laboring toward their goals.

Birmingham: The Civil-Rights Movement Peaks Out

In the spring of 1963 the nation was presented with the shocking spectacle on television of Police Chief Eugene "Bull" Connor and his men assaulting thousands of nonviolent black men, women, and children in Birmingham, Alabama. Before the advent of television, white Americans outside the South had had little direct knowledge of how blacks were abused in that region. Now they could *see* what was happening—the police dogs, the brutality—and they were horrified. (The powerful impact of television in allowing Americans directly to observe events, and thereby in stimulating them to action, was a crucial element in these years of dramatic reform.)

Some 150,000 black citizens had marched on the Birmingham city hall protesting segregation in public facilities and in job hiring. When police arrested them they fell to their knees and prayed. Powerful streams of water from fire hoses sent them sprawling; bricks and bottles were thrown from onlooking crowds. But day after day the protest marches mounted. Thousands of young and old black people were soon in custody, chanting "Freedom! Freedom! Freedom!" Everywhere the question was raised, How could Southern blacks continue to follow Martin Luther King's nonviolent approach? In the face of "Bull" Connor's attacks, would they not themselves turn violent? Malcolm X, a leader of the Black Muslims, a black-nationalist movement, denounced King, telling a black audience, "You need somebody who is going to fight. You don't need any kneeling in or crawling in."

The President Appeals for Legislation

By mid June 1963 it was clear to President Kennedy that simple executive action was not enough to insure equal civil rights. Despite the hostility of Southern committee chairmen in Congress, he finally had to reach out to the third branch of the federal government and appeal for the enactment of fundamental new civil-rights legislation. Governor George Wallace of Alabama had just brought another spectacular confrontation to its climax by standing at the door of the University of Alabama's campus at Tuscaloosa on June 11 to denounce a court order requiring the registration of black students. By the physical interposition of his body he sought to express the formal opposition of the State of Alabama. Wallace ultimately stepped aside, when asked to do so by the commanding general of the Alabama-Mississippi National Guard (which the president had federalized that day in order to remove it from local control), but his defiant gesture threatened to stimulate more illegal violence against blacks and civil-rights workers.

In the White House Kennedy, like the rest of the country, watched these events on television. Late in the day he decided to ask the networks for time to address the nation. His advisers did not even have time to complete writing the speech he planned to give; part of it would be presented extemporaneously. Then, as historian Carl Brauer describes the event, the president delivered "one of the most eloquent, moving and important addresses of his Presidency. It marked the beginning of what can truly be called the Second Reconstruction, a coherent effort by all three branches of the government to secure blacks their full rights." Speaking with great intensity, the president asserted, "The heart of the question is whether all Americans are to be afforded equal rights and equal opportunities, whether we are going to treat our fellow Americans as we want to be treated. If an American, because his skin is dark, cannot eat lunch in a restaurant open to the public, if he cannot send his children to the best public school available, if he cannot vote for the public officials who represent him, if, in short, he cannot enjoy the full and free life which all of us want, then who among us would be content to have the color of his skin changed and stand in his place? Who among us would then be content with the counsels of patience and delay?"

Kennedy went on to explain in graphic terms how white Americans were far ahead of black Americans in such crucial matters as jobs and income. He attacked segregation and the denial of the right to vote. Then he asked, "Are we to say to the world . . . that this is the land of the free, except for the Negroes; that we have no second-class citizens, except Negroes; that we have no class or caste system, no ghettos, no master race, except with respect to Negroes? Now the time has come for this nation to fulfill its promise." He then asked Congress to enact a law that would guarantee equal access to all public accommodations; empower the attorney general to sue for enforcement of the Fourteenth and Fifteenth Amendments; and forbid discrimination in any state program—such as schools, welfare, and highway construction—receiving federal aid. In particular, he asked Congress to outlaw discrimination in employment and voting.

In August 1963 Martin Luther King led 250,000 protestors in an enormous March on Washington, which ended at the Lincoln Memorial. There he electrified his audience with a speech in which he cried out again and again, "I have a dream!"—of a new America in which there would be freedom and equality for all, in which black and white would be reconciled. Southern congressmen blocked Kennedy's civil-rights bill, however, until after his assassination in November. The new president, Lyndon Johnson, was able to drive it through in July 1964. In March 1965 Johnson called Congress into special session to ask for a voting-rights bill. As enacted the following August, it eliminated all qualifying tests for registration that had as their objective limiting the right to vote to whites. Thereafter, the proportion of registered blacks in the South spurted rapidly upward, reaching 53 percent in 1966 (33 percent in Mississippi). In the elections of 1968, over three million black Americans were registered to vote in the Southern states. The civil-rights phase of the black revolution had reached its legislative and judicial summit.

A New Day for the Indians

The vast awakening that swept black America in the 1960s did not stop there. It set off a surge of ethnic consciousness throughout the American population and a new mood in favor of equal treatment for minority peoples, which in combination made this decade a time of fundamental change among many of the "outsiders." Both Richard Nixon and John Kennedy proclaimed in their 1960 presidential contest, for example, that there would be an end to the campaign to break down Indian culture and "Americanize" the Indians, as embodied in the termination policies of the Eisenhower years. Congress freed loan funds; the Federal Housing Authority began actively helping Indians build their own homes; and so successfully were businessmen urged to build plants on Indian lands and thus establish employment opportunities that in 1968 alone their total investment on tribal lands was almost $100 million.

In 1968 Lyndon Johnson became the first American president to send Congress a special message asking aid for the Indians: "an opportunity to remain in their homeland, if they choose, without surrendering their dignity; an opportunity to move to the towns and cities of America, if they choose, equipped with the skills to live in equality and dignity." The National Council on Indian Opportunity, created by Johnson and headed by Vice-President Hubert Humphrey, channeled large funds into community improvement, the training of workers, youth activities, and health services.

Richard Nixon continued these progressive policies. The Bureau of Indian Affairs began to shift its emphasis to the issuing of grants to the tribes for the economic development of their resources. In 1969, however, the shape of the future was startlingly revealed when a group of Indians took over Alcatraz Island in San Francisco Bay (no longer in use as a prison facility) and demanded it be returned to them in compensation for the countless treaty violations and land steals that stretched back through American history. Subsequently, young Indian militants in almost every major American city began seizing federal property, demonstrating that the future location of the "Indian problem" was to be in the cities, no longer in the trackless immensities of the western states. Vine Deloria, Jr., author of the best-selling *Custer Died for Your Sins: An Indian Manifesto* (1969), estimated that three fourths of the Indian population had become both eastern and urban.

A revived concern with tribalism swept the Indian peoples, paradoxically opening a new chain of problems. Through steady population growth, tribes with only a few hundred members living on the reservation often had thousands listed on their tribal rolls, most of them scattered in distant cities. With their increasingly complex and mobile inner social structure, such groups could experience bewildering shifts and changes in internal policy if first one and then another group won brief voting triumphs in tribal elections. Thousands of young Indians entered the nation's colleges as the new ethnic consciousness swept the academic world. But where programs of Indian studies were launched, a question immediately arose: What is the Indian identity? Traditional or modern? Reservation-based or urban? Could tribal culture, for centuries taught only by the elders on tribal lands, become an academic discipline without losing its validity?

Education, material advancement, and

urban living seemed inevitably to destroy the Indians' ancient culture, or at least gravely endanger it. But clearly the new urbanized Indian youth still nourished the ancient grievances. In late 1972 hundreds of them, members of the American Indian Movement, took over the Bureau of Indian Affairs building in Washington, fortifying themselves within it for almost a week and rifling—indeed carting off—its files. In 1973 a long and wearing occupation of Wounded Knee in South Dakota by Indian activists almost led to a shootout with federal forces reminiscent of the nineteenth century. When it was over the question remained, What was the real shape of the Indian future? As urban Indians all over the nation continued seeking one another out and forming city organizations, it was ever more clear that whatever its form the Indian future lay in the metropolis. A tremendous awakening was under way among native Americans that was quite unlike anything in their past.

Kennedy and the Immigration Revolution

The revolution surging for the "outsiders" in American life moved on to utterly transform the nation's forty-year-old immigration-restriction policy, and thereby to shift markedly the ethnic balance in the American population. John Kennedy, the first representative in the White House of one of the immigrant groups traditionally most scorned in American history, led the drive to throw out the policy of sharply restricting immigration to northern European countries, as embodied in the immigration law of 1924, and to treat all nationalities equally. Shortly after the Second World War he had sponsored legislation to admit thousands of people displaced from their homes by the conflict, and in 1957 he had led to passage in the Senate another such law aimed at allowing the reuniting of families. As president he proposed in July 1963 that the entire system of restricting immigration to northern Europeans be scuttled. As he wrote in his last published book, *A Nation of Immigrants* (it appeared posthumously, in 1964), the existing principle contained "strong overtones of an indefensible racial preference." America should admit immigrants not on this basis, but simply on the ground that as individuals they possessed skills "our country needs and on the humanitarian ground of reuniting fami-

lies." The special discrimination against people in the Asia-Pacific region, who were limited to 100 immigrants a year per nation, should be ended as well, he insisted. "With such a policy," Kennedy asserted, "we can turn to the world, and to our own past, with clean hands and a clear conscience."

Americans were at long last ready for these steps, for a basic element in their picture of themselves as a nation was fading. Traditionally, the ruling myth was that the United States was a melting pot. Immigrants, it was said, were steadily absorbed into the dominant "American" (read WASP) population, and took on its ways of living. The long years of war and threats of war since the 1930s had intensified this image. Ethnic minorities did not assert their separate identities, for the national self-conception of one American people hanging together against great and powerful enemies in the world was dominant. The ending of the Cold War, however, and especially the volcanic rising of black America, suddenly made it acceptable for many different kinds of Americans to say that the United States was not, in fact, a melting pot. There was, of course, a broadly shared culture in American life: the stress upon individualism, for example, and on such values as getting ahead, efficiency, hard work, orderliness, and material improvement. But mixed in with this shared culture was a pluralism of subcultures, of different ways of living, believing, and speaking. Now it was insisted that diverging from the WASP core community and its ways was not a bad thing, not a mark of inferiority. Rather, it was an admirable assertion of cultural identities that had fully as much claim to equal respect and esteem as that of whites of northern European ancestry.

In the 1960s, therefore, the longstanding principle that immigration should give overwhelming preference to northern Europeans was set aside. It was not easy. The Immigration Reform Act was carried through under President Johnson in 1965 against stubborn resistance in Congress. As enacted, it provided simply that 170,000 immigrants, taken in the order of their applications, could annually enter the nation from Europe, Asia, and Africa, with no more than 20,000 to arrive annually from any one country; thus the system of different quotas for different nations was eliminated. Preference, for the first time, would go to people with valuable skills—to professionals, scientists, engineers, and other highly educated persons. In addition to these 170,000, up to 100,000 relatives of American citizens could enter the country in each year.

Opponents of liberalized immigration won at least one significant victory, however. Under the former system there had been no quota limits upon immigrants from Western Hemisphere countries. However, these individuals still had to go through the procedures of the Immigration and Naturalization Service, which must issue a visa (a stamped approval on one's passport) for each entering person, usually a time-consuming and—for poor people—expensive process. In issuing visas, the INS applied literacy, health, employability, and other tests, which together formed another set of barriers that many could not pass. Therefore, as we shall see, many thousands from Mexico entered the United States illegally from the 1920s onward. In the 1965 law this situation, which has grown into one of the knottiest controversies in American life, was complicated further by the establishment for the first time of a quota limit upon legal immigration from Western Hemisphere nations. No more than 120,000 annually were to be allowed into the country from this source (no upper limit per nation was applied, in contrast to immigration from Europe, Africa, and Asia).

This principle was agreed to, finally, by advocates of liberalized immigration because the figure of 120,000 was roughly equivalent to those already legally entering the United States from the rest of the Western Hemisphere in the early 1960s. Indeed, the Johnson administration argued for passage of the immigration-reform bill in good part on the ground that the new policy toward Latin America would have little real effect in any event. From Latin America, as a leading official said, "there is not much pressure to come to the United States."

Dramatic Effects of the New Immigration Law

Few forecasts have been so inaccurate. Immigrants poured into the United States after 1965, especially from Latin America but also from many other countries in the world. From 1965 to 1975, almost 400,000 legal entrants came each year. Amounting to a tiny fraction of the total American population of about 218 million in the 1960s, by 1976 this influx nonetheless accounted for nearly one fourth of America's total annual population *growth*. The inflow from Europe dropped steadily, so that in the mid 1970s more than half of all immigrants arrived from seven countries in Asia and Latin America: Taiwan, the Philippines, Korea, India, Cuba, Mexico, and the Dominican Republic. The striking reversal this involved is seen in the fact that while in 1969 three immigrants came from Europe for every two from Asia, in 1976 three came from Europe for every six from Asia. India alone sent more emigrants to the United States than Italy and Greece together; Thailand sent more than Germany; Egypt more than Ireland.

The new immigrants were sharply different from the old in that many of them were so professionally or technically skilled that they moved right into the ranks of middle-class America, or even higher. In the 1930s, by contrast, only one out of every five immigrants had held even a white-collar position in their home countries. Therefore, in the 1970s the countries losing these well-trained people complained bitterly of a "brain drain" to America.

Nationally, the center of ethnic balance shifted. In the pre-1960 United States it was the older cities of the northern and eastern states that had been heavily immigrant and ethnic, and this ethnicity was strongly Catholic and Jewish—certainly European in origin. But now the large immigrant communities were more likely to be found in California, Texas, and Florida. San Francisco's Chinatown, earlier thought to be dying, was dramatically rejuvenated.

In the 1970s, while the use of foreign languages in general was declining (the Census Bureau reported in 1975 that only one of ten Americans possessed a second language), those normally speaking Spanish in their daily life exceeded those speaking all other non-English languages combined. And with Oriental immigration surging for the first time in generations, in 1975 the number of homes using Chinese, Japanese, Korean, or Filipino as their daily language exceeded the number of homes using Italian, and almost equaled the numbers of households speaking French, German, and Greek. Asian and Middle Eastern religions—Buddhism, Hinduism, and Islam became significant elements in the religious life of America.

Given the skills of these new immigrants, especially those from the Orient, they did not congregate in such ghettos as Chinatown as exclusively as previous immigrants. For example, the Chinese immigrants, who came in many thousands from the nations of Asia, were largely professional, scientific, or technically skilled people who tended to spread out into middle-class living areas and to work in universities, laboratories, hospitals, architectural offices, or engineering firms. The family income of Chinese-Americans, indeed, was higher than the national average, as was their level of education. The vicious stereotypes that used to be applied freely to the Chinese were replaced by a new image of a highly educated, hard-working, and affluent people.

Few Japanese emigrated to America under the new law, for in their rapidly developing and highly sophisticated country there were plenty of opportunities for advancement. Japanese-Americans, for their part, acquired a new status and much respect. Between Japan and America a special relationship had sprung up after 1945. An inpouring of technologically sophisticated manufactures from Japan, and that country's booming postwar prosperity, gave Americans a fresh basis for admiration of that extraordinary people. Moreover, Japanese-Americans had made almost no postwar outcry against their wartime placement in concentration camps, but with their passion for hard work and education had devoted themselves to getting ahead. By the 1970s they too were above the national average in income and schooling. A study revealed that "high status Japanese Americans tend to live in mostly Caucasian neighborhoods, tend not to belong to Japanese American organizations, are less likely to be Buddhists, and are less likely to speak Japanese as well. They have been mobile not only *up* in the status hierarchy but also *out* of the ethnic community." Before the Second World War an overwhelmingly agricultural people living by themselves, by the 1960s the Japanese-Americans were spreading rapidly into the broad reaches of American life. From the state of Hawaii, largely Japanese in ethnic background, came the first from that people to sit in the United States Senate: Daniel Inouye. From California came the second: Samuel Hayakawa. Research in California revealed that intermarriage of Japanese and Caucasians was common in the 1960s. In the two cities of San Francisco and Fresno, half of the Japanese getting married in the 1970s chose Caucasian partners—a classic sign that social boundaries between peoples were disappearing.

So huge was the inrush of Latin Americans from the 1960s on that by 1979, according to the Census Bureau, more than 12 million people of Hispanic descent were living in the United States: 7.2 million from Mexico; 1.8 million from Puerto Rico; 700,000 from Cuba; 900,000 from Central and South America; and 1.4 million from other regions of the world. Like the Japanese-Americans, they were a people who before 1945 had been identified primarily with farming. But in the 1970s, three of six Hispanic Americans lived in the inner city and two in the suburbs.

Unlike the Orientals, however, the Hispanic Americans were not (on the average) high in education, skills, income, or social status. Most were farm or blue-collar workers; every fourth Spanish-speaking family was below the poverty line. And the phenomenon of the "undocumented alien," who could not prove legal residence in the United States, had by the 1970s grown to mountainous proportions. Since the Hispanic population in America is destined to continue growing rapidly, a closer look at its recent history, especially that of the Mexican-Americans, is in order.

Mexican-Americans in the Second World War Years

During the depression-ridden 1930s, when, as we have seen, perhaps 500,000 Mexicans held to be illegally in the United States were deported, great changes began to come to the life of Mexican-Americans. Farm workers began for the first time to fight back against their degraded living and working conditions by organizing unions and strikes—most of which failed to improve their situation. Then, during the Second World War, Mexican-Americans went into the fighting forces with the identical hope that had inspired black Americans to participate in the Civil War: to demonstrate their manhood and their rightful claim to equal status in American life. (The same motive also impelled thousands of young Japanese-Americans to fight in special American army units in the European theater, among them Daniel Inouye, who lost an arm in combat.) More than 300,000 Mexican-Americans served, primarily in the army. Indeed, the proportion of Mexican-Americans belonging to army combat divisions was higher than that of any other ethnic group save, perhaps, the Japanese. An especially high proportion volunteered for hazardous duty in the paratroops and the marines. Of fourteen Texans who won the medal of Honor, five were Mexican-Americans.

The wartime experience—both military service and participation in the war industries—energized the Mexican-American community. For the first time, great numbers of them worked directly with Anglo-Americans and earned high salaries. Then *la raza* veterans (*la raza* refers to the entire community of the Spanish-speaking) were helped in going to college and starting businesses by the G.I. Bill, which provided extensive aid to all veterans. But despite their achievements, *la raza* found that the Anglo-Americans still treated them in the old, prejudicial way.

Braceros and Wetbacks

During the Second World War a great need for farm labor in the southwestern states led to the *bracero* program. The governments of Mexico and the United States supervised the recruitment of Mexican nationals, who were brought across the border to labor for a year in the fields and then returned to their homeland. About 250,000 *braceros* were recruited from 1942 to 1947. Allowed briefly to lapse, the program was revived in 1948, and during the next sixteen years 4,500,000 Mexican nationals participated in temporary periods of agricultural employment on American farms. (Because race prejudice was traditionally more prominent in Texas, where from the beginning Mexicans were linked with blacks in Anglo-American eyes, the Mexican government did not allow *braceros* to be sent to that state.)

The program had sharply contrasting results. The average Mexican who participated did so eagerly, since he could earn far more in the United States than at home. But job conditions were often demeaning, and American laborers claimed, usually with good reason, that employers used *braceros* primarily to keep wage rates down. Far worse, however, was the status of the *mojados*, or "wetbacks," so called because thousands of these illegal entrants swam the Rio Grande to get to the United States. Totally unable to appeal to the authorities for aid against their

employers, they were paid the lowest wages of any manual laborers, lived in the worst housing, and were preyed on by everyone. They made an enormous contribution to the immense expansion of southwestern agriculture during and after World War II, but received little in return. Wetbacks, indeed, may well have been the principal source of cheap farm labor in the decade beginning in 1945. In 1954 the Immigration Bureau began a large campaign of deportation, rounding up wetbacks—many of them only alleged to be wetbacks—and hurrying them out of the country with little regard for due process. In 1953 some 875,000 allegedly illegal entrants had been arrested and returned to Mexico; in 1954 this figure swelled to more than a million. Altogether, from 1950 to 1955, 3,700,000 people alleged to be wetbacks were deported, only some 60,000 by means of formal proceedings; the rest left "voluntarily." Families were disrupted; even individuals who had been living in America for longer than ten years were suddenly expelled. This experience left the same lastingly bitter feelings that had resulted from the similar expulsion in the 1930s. In this case, however, those remaining behind noticed how wage rates jumped upward by as much as a third.

Mexican-Americans in Politics

Traditionally, Mexican-Americans participated relatively little in politics. This was so partly because (as earlier observed) relatively few were citizens. Also, they were poor. Political apathy among the poverty-stricken is a common feature of politics: poor people see little in their past experience that suggests that suddenly becoming politically active will change their situation. In the case of Mexican-Americans, government had never helped them; the world of politics was far away, it was usually hostile, and besides, it was Anglo. Because of a continual heavy influx of immigrants from the mother country, it was generally the case after 1945 that only a quarter of the Mexican-American population regarded English as their first language. This meant that the most powerful cultural distinction between a minority people and the majority—that of language, which carries with it a separate way of thinking—intensified the isolation of Mexican-Americans, certainly from American-style politics. Also, Mexican-Americans traditionally worked in the countryside, far away from county registration offices and balloting booths. In any event, the thousands of them who were migrant laborers could not establish residency in any one place long enough to vote, even had voting seemed a useful thing to do. American politics depends heavily upon an educated citizenry, and the dropout rate from high school of Mexican-American youths was very high, running at a steady 75 percent through the 1950s. A separate language can make Americanized schooling a fatally discouraging experience.

After 1945 Mexican-American veterans formed a number of organizations, notably the G.I. Forum, which was strongly political in its tactics, and also the Mexican American Political Association (MAPA). More and more Mexican-Americans were moving into cities; significant numbers were rising to middle-class status in income and occupation; and in general they were increasingly unwilling to accept the inferior roles they had long played in American society.

Upon this scene came John Kennedy. Wherever he went in the southwestern states and California during the presidential campaign of 1960, he was greeted by wildly cheering Mexican-American crowds (usually organized by MAPA). The "Viva Kennedy" organizations urged traditionally nonpolitical Mexican-Americans to the polls, with the result that they voted in record numbers. Some 85 percent of the Spanish-speaking vote went to Kennedy, providing the crucial margin in Texas and New Mexico, and probably even in Illinois. The 91-percent majority he gained among the thousands of Spanish-speaking voters in the Chicago area helped put him barely in the victor's camp in that state—and therefore in the White House. One of the nation's largest ethnic groups, the (then) nine million Americans of Spanish surname, seemed finally to have become politically active in American politics.

1960s Militancy

It was now that the term *Chicano*—a shortened form of *Mexicano* generally taken up by younger, more ethnically conscious Americans of Mexican origin—appeared as a new ethnic identification. They condemned what the historian Mario García terms "the Mexican American generation" of the

1940s and 1950s as passive and acquiescent, but in reality, as García observes, the Mexican-American generation had been no less active politically. In the years 1940–1960 they had agitated for civil rights for Mexicans, for desegregated schools (many from Texas to California were set aside only for Mexican-Americans), for better jobs and political representation. It was simply that the style and objective of the older generation had been different. It had believed in integration into the larger American culture, and in the validity of the American system. Chicanos tended to reject cultural integration, proudly asserting the equal validity of their ethnic identity, and they questioned the legitimacy of American values.

They were stimulated to this position in good part by the tremendous success of the black civil-rights movement, and the egalitarian ideology of Kennedy's New Frontier, Johnson's Great Society, and the foreign-policy rhetoric of America's fight for "democracy." Indeed, events outside America had a profound influence upon Chicano consciousness. For the young people of the movement, the dramatic new prominence in the world at large of leaders and movements drawn from the Hispanic cultural tradition inspired a sense of prideful emulation. Fidel Castro and Ernesto "Che" Guevara in Cuba seemed eloquently to demonstrate that the Spanish-speaking may be assertive toward Anglo-America. A true political militancy, therefore, arose for the first time among Mexican-Americans during the 1960s.

There was much of which to complain, from the standpoint of Mexican-America. Economically, Hispanics were far behind Anglo-Americans. As late as 1970 the income of the average Puerto Rican family, for example, was 40 percent below the national average, or about $6,000 a year. Mexican-American families were not much better off, averaging about $7,000 a year. Latin Catholics worked in the lowest-paid jobs, either in the fields as stoop labor or in blue-collar employment. Their jobless rate was high, and managerial positions, save in their own businesses, were generally closed to them.

Deeper than these influences, however, are the cultural values of Chicanos, which keep vitally alive feelings of ethnic distinction and anger at discrimination. Almost unique to them is the fact that their home country is next door (the same is true for Canadian-Americans, but on the whole they merge effortlessly into the American population). This closeness keeps Chicano cultural life regularly refreshened. Family ties are immediate and direct, and there is much coming and going. The massive number of fresh arrivals from Mexico, stimulated by grinding economic distress and uneven modernization in the home country, pours a steady stream of Mexican identity into the United States. Studies of undocumented Mexican aliens in California reveal that many of these immigrants are drawn from the most enterprising and courageous peoples in their homeland; that they believe in "the American dream" perhaps more fervently than native-born Americans themselves; and that they display what are usually described as classic American characteristics of hard work and getting ahead, even at great risk to themselves. Nonetheless, their illegal status and their need for protection from the authorities tend to intensify their pattern of communal separateness. Furthermore, Hispanic culture contains an intense masculine pride. With high unemployment among young males leading to a demeaning sense of dependency, a proud anger and a turbulence just under the surface go naturally together.

An added factor in the recent surge of Chicano activism is another cultural fact of pro-

One of the great political changes of the 1960s was the emergence of the Mexican-American peoples of California, the Southwest, and many American cities. César Chavez here leads a farmworkers march urging boycott of grapes. The term *Chicano* was widely adopted by the more militant among them.

Wide World Photos

found importance: for Mexican-Americans, North America has been their home for thousands of years. Like the American Indians, they are native to the continent. The immense region of the southwestern states and California carries an Hispanic overlay in its place names. The Spanish-speaking have lived in New Mexico's upper Rio Grande valley for centuries. Their ancient farmlands, laid out in long strips in European style, contrast sharply with the millions of square miles of Jeffersonian rectangular surveys the traveler observes in the land below while flying west from the Appalachians. In southern California, the tradition of a "Spanish" past expresses itself in architecture and in annual festivals. Catholic mission churches are scattered widely, their walls having been erected in the eighteenth century under the Spanish crown. Los Angeles and Santa Barbara, two centuries old as communities in the early 1980s, claim that distinction by reaching back to their founding in Hispanic times.

Since historic tradition in Mexico holds that the ancient peoples who settled the Valley of Mexico and created the extensive precolonial empire of the Aztecs came from somewhere in the far north, it is possible for intense Chicanos to speak of an *Aztlan*, a legendary homeland running from southern Mexico to the American high plains. Bitter to many, therefore, is the knowlege that in this huge area Mexican-Americans have been consigned to second-class status in the ghetto-like residential sections called *barrios*, where housing has been deficient, jobs ill paid, and public services often inadequate at best. In the 1960s Chicano cultural identity and cultural pride, especially among students, led to demands that prejudiced teachers and administrators be discharged and course offerings be changed to emphasize the Chicano past, present, and future. The Brown Berets were organized in that decade, consisting primarily of Chicanos of high school and college age in the southwestern states. Their goal was to unite the Chicano community by their own example of brotherhood and self-sacrificial discipline. Whereas for black Americans the adversary within their own community had been the "Uncle Toms" who would acquiesce in second-class status, for activist Chicanos the adversary was the *tio taco*—the Mexican-American who clung to the old stereotypes and role.

The most active Chicanos came from rural areas, where living conditions were the most pitiable. One Chicano leader, Reis Lòpez Tijerina, led a demand for the reversion of millions of acres of southwestern land to direct heirs of those who, under the Treaty of Guadalupe Hidalgo (1848), had had their land rights guaranteed but subsequently taken away by American courts. A true visionary (and a convert to evangelical Protestantism), Tijerina formed in 1963 the Alianza Federal de Mercedes (Federal Alliance of Land Grants), which envisioned the recapturing of immense lost territories for Chicanos and the building of a confederation of free city-states based on utopian principles. In 1967 he led an occupation of a courthouse in the New Mexican town of Tierra Amarilla. Men were wounded during the ensuing brief warfare with local authorities, and a massive manhunt with tanks and helicopters finally captured the fleeing Tijerina. Jailed in 1969, Tijerina served two years and emerged to find his movement fading.

César Chavez

Far more lastingly effective was the campaign launched by César Chavez for the organization of farm workers. The first Chicano to achieve a truly national standing and to become a unifying symbol for Mexican-Americans in the manner of Martin Luther King for black America, Chavez was, like King, an apostle of Gandhi's nonviolence policy. Deeply spiritual in his motivations, a gentle and thoughtful man, since 1962 he had been working in Delano, California, to form a union among grape workers. Director of the AFL–CIO United Farm Workers Organizing Committee, he had himself emerged from the extreme poverty of a family caught in the migrant farm workers' cycle of constant movement, illiteracy, and low wages. Keenly aware of the need to mobilize national opinion in support of his objections, he attracted students, ministers, and civil-rights workers to Delano, and by 1968, during which year Robert Kennedy gave his cause prominent support, he had successfuly organized a nationwide boycott of table grapes. In 1970 his long struggle came to an apparent end when the grape growers signed a three-year contract with his union. Later on, however, the growers began signing contracts instead with the Teamsters Union, apparently an organization whose objectives were more palatable. This led in 1973 to a new eruption of turmoil

and protest. In 1977 a landmark agreement was finally struck between Chavez and the Teamsters. The former henceforth would organize field workers, the latter those in packing houses. However, in the background for Chavez was the sobering fact that the increasing cost of farm laborers was stimulating landowners to turn to machines for the cultivation and picking of row crops. In the 1960s, migrant farm workers in the United States dropped in numbers from 400,000 to 250,000. Whatever the outcome, the figure of César Chavez provided lasting inspiration to the Chicano community.

Urban Chicanos

Meanwhile, urban Chicanos were joining in the mass uprisings of the late 1960s, notably through the efforts of the Brown Berets. After Chicanos were jailed in Los Angeles in 1968 for staging a demonstration, Joanne Gonzales proclaimed in La Raza Yearbook that their cause was to seek "Chicano Power for our people so that we can have control over our environment; control over our schools so that our children can receive a better education; control over the agencies which are supposed to be administering to the needs of our people; control over the police whose salaries we pay but who continually brutalize our people." Mexican-American leaders demanded an educational process that was both bilingual and bicultural, and that would thereby revive the equality of treatment guaranteed in the Treaty of Guadalupe Hidalgo. Teachers of Mexican ancestry were urged to retain and emphasize with pride their "Mexicanism," and authentic Mexican arts experienced widely enhanced prominence. The image of the Mexican-American in Anglo-American eyes, long summed up in the figure of a sleepy peasant under a large sombrero, was beginning to be replaced with the fresh understanding that Latin civilization was urban as well as rural, progressive as well as traditional, sophisticated as well as uncomplicated. By 1972, younger Chicanos were even seeking to found a new national political party: La Raza Unida. Chicanos were also heavily involved in the antiwar movement of the 1970s.

Nevertheless, Mexican-Americans found it hard to achieve unity. Their very identity was difficult to crystallize. "To start a long discussion among Los Angelenos of Spanish-Mexican descent," observed Paul M. Sheldon in *La Raza: Forgotten Americans* (1966), "simply introduce the . . . question, 'Who are we?'" Spanish, Mexican, or completely Americanized? Chicano culture, he wrote, contains an individualism that discourages unity; a family consciousness that places the focus of concern elsewhere than in politics; and traditional values often opposed to the hard-driving success ethic of the American urban world. Other influences hampering Chicano ability to organize were: the small Mexican-American middle class; the migrant character of so much of Mexican-American employment, both rural and urban; poverty; and the cultural instability created by the constant arrival of immigrants fresh from Mexico.

However, more and more Chicanos were entering into the mainstream of America life, and this made it increasingly difficult for them—as for the American Indians, who had also become increasingly urban—to retain a hold on ways of life that for many had become remote. Eighty percent of the Mexican-American people lived in cities in the 1960s, and therefore in what had become the heartland of American culture. Los Angeles held a million people having a Spanish surname. Puerto Ricans in the United States had always been an urban people: they numbered at least a million in New York City. Together, these two Latin Catholic groups comprised more than 400,000 people in the Chicago area. Total isolation in the rural countryside, perhaps in sight of the traditional architecture of a local Catholic church, was no longer possible.

Meanwhile, the political clout of this immense ethnic community remained sharply limited, for Latin Catholics continued to turn out in low proportions for balloting. The 1960 voter support for John Kennedy was a high point. After that, the Hispanic vote steadily eroded. Puerto Ricans in New York City cast less than half the number of votes in 1968 that they had cast in 1960. Only 6 out of the more than 500 members of Congress were Spanish-speaking by descent. Where labor unions were growing, as among the Spanish-speaking of Texas, the voting trend was upward, but in general the Hispanic Americans were still not as politically important as their numbers warranted.

The future, however, was another question. Ultimately, the voice of Hispanic Americans in national politics would have to grow. If by the end of the 1970s the Census Bureau could estimate that in twenty years the Hispanic population had grown by 33 percent—from nine to twelve million—there would soon be a time when those of Spanish surname would be the largest minority in the American population, surpassing black Americans. The phenomenon of the undocumented alien was startling. The Immigration and Naturalization Service had estimated in 1965 that there were about 110,000 illegal aliens in the country. In that year, however, the Immigration Reform Act had established for the first time an upper limit on legal Western Hemisphere immigration. By 1977 the INS was estimating that at least a million people were illegally in the United States; others in official positions estimated from four to seven million. By the end of the 1970s it was generally agreed that a million people were illegally entering the country each year. Without dispute, even the simplest projections of past population trends into the future meant that in succeeding years the United States would be a considerably different place from what it had been before the 1960s.

The New Industrial State

Deep-running changes were taking place also in the nature of the American economy. Though as we will be seeing in Chapter 39, the business world contains hundreds of thousands of small or medium-sized firms, an ever smaller group of great corporations has been taking an ever larger role in the national economy. In the 1960s the 500 largest corporations provided half the goods and services that the nation used. In 1962 some 12 percent of all manufacturing resources was owned by five large corporations; the 50 largest held over one-third. There were approximately 2,000 firms in the country with assets of over ten million dollars each, and they controlled eighty percent of all manufacturing. Three corporations—General Motors, Standard Oil of New Jersey, and Ford—together took in more dollars than all the farms in the country combined. Each of these companies had higher gross revenues than any single state in the Union; General Motors alone took in eight times as much money as the state of New York, and a fifth as much as the federal government. The corporate form of business had swollen so gigantically that in communications, electric power, a large part of transportation, most of manufacturing and mining, even in much of entertainment and merchandising, the corporation had become dominant.

And it was quite a different kind of organization than in Theodore Roosevelt's time. To make a Model T had been a simple business of ordering some steel from a local warehouse, and hiring a group of men to put together simple parts. Thus one man at the head of the business could run the show. But automobiles are now fantastically complicated; their designs must be worked out by teams of highly skilled specialists; and corporation presidents cannot possibly understand these intricacies, nor can their boards of directors or stockholders. Thus the "brains" of these immense firms are no longer in the head of a Henry Ford. They have instead descended deep into the organization, where the engineers, technologists, cost analysts, and marketing specialists are located. Only these men can know enough to make the crucial decisions—and then only when working together in groups. In *The New Industrial State* (1967), the economist John Kenneth Galbraith has called these staffs of specialists, who do all the planning and designing for the great corporations, the *"technostructure."*

Consumers ask for higher and better performance from every one of their products—surgical tools, television sets, water softeners, light bulbs, clothes washers, and scores of other manufactured things. To make these more precise and complicated articles, however, takes years longer than in the past. The auto manufacturer cannot simply go to a local steel warehouse and buy whatever happens to be in stock; he must search the world for special metals—molybdenum, titanium, aluminum—and prepare them in special ways. Contracts with thousands of suppliers must be negotiated, and the inflow of parts and materials closely coordinated.

The need for close coordination of the manufacture of complex products means that a long "lead time" is now built into the industrial process. Years can pass from the time a given product is conceived of until it rolls out on the assembly line. An immense investment in expensive equipment is required, as are large planning staffs, to ensure that the thousands of separate procedures and items all get thought out and brought together. Only very large corporations have the necessary funds and technostructure to plan and carry through such costly and long-range operations. But even they cannot afford to make a mistake, as the major auto manufacturers were discovering in the late 1970s, when small imported cars suddenly began driving them to bankruptcy because they had not anticipated this trend. The result is that these gargantuan firms do everything they can to gain control of all the factors that might influence their chances for success.

Major Corporations Try to Control All Factors

Modern corporations have tried to eliminate the influence of bankers by making certain that corporation profits are high enough to generate their own investment capital—surely one of the most epochal changes in the history of capitalism. By becoming huge, and therefore one of the few buyers for particular kinds of supplies, corporations like General Motors seek to be certain that their suppliers, eager for their trade, charge stable and acceptable prices (though in the inflationary spiral that struck in the 1970s this would prove to be impossible). Then, by being one of the few producers, giant corporations have great influence on prices, since their competitors are not likely to engage in much price-slashing, for they also desire a stable pricing structure on which they can base their planning. The consumer, for his part, can make little complaint, for he has not the foggiest idea of what it actually costs to manufacture, say, a bun-warmer. Then, to ensure that the products will actually be bought at the prices they set, the large corporations maintain large research, advertising, and sales organizations to stimulate the market. The corporations of the new industrial state are in fact far more bureaucratic, centralized, and remote from outside control than they had ever been in the past.

The sum result of these developments is that the classic picture of American capitalism as being controlled and disciplined by competition, in the free and uncontrolled marketplace, is less true than it used to be of the big corporations. Wherever the product is most complicated, and therefore the technology is most advanced and the investment of capital the heaviest, there the marketplace as a factor in the corporation's success is the most vigorously manipulated, though by no means always with success. How to reestablish full competition and thus lower prices? No longer can the ancient antitrust laws be applied to break up the huge corporations if the same kinds of products are still to be manufactured. Smaller corporations cannot produce them since they are too costly, in the need for lead time and a large planning staff, to carry out design and coordination. To end bigness, it would be necessary to do away with the kind of sophisticated products that the public now consumes and wishes to go on consuming.

The Technostructure

We have now, then, a new phenomenon in American life—the technostructure. It is important to ask, what are the motives of this new class of people who together plan and direct the operations of the great corporations? Unlike a blue-collar worker who puts together the products someone else designs, and belongs to an externally based union, the white-collar worker tends to regard the corporation much as a football player does his team: its success, since he is part of its "brain," is his to bask in. The white-collar workers of the technostructure, therefore, necessarily put highest value on high productivity and booming sales, as signs of success.

The technostructure also seeks to reduce the number of manual workers, for their wages, being largely controlled by unions, constitute another uncontrolled element in the total picture. (White-collar workers tend to remain unorganized.) Seeking certainty, the technostructure designs and buys machines to replace manual laborers. For this reason, blue-collar employment (craftsmen, operatives, laborers, aside from farmers and miners) decreased by 4 million jobs from 1951 to 1964, while total employment grew by about 10 million. White-collar employment (professional, technical, managerial, office, and sales workers) reached 45 million by the mid 1960s, but blue-collar employment dropped to 37 million. This was why the labor union movement peaked in the 1950s and then began dropping from 16.6 million members in 1956 to 14.9 million in 1962 (or

about 27 percent of the labor force, a proportion that has remained stable since the early 1960s).

The Corporations and the Government

One extraordinary result of these complex changes is to render obsolete a great deal of traditional political ideology. Decades of reformers answered the crisis of industrialism with one simple answer: let the government take over, either by regulation or by outright ownership. Modern technology, which requires highly skilled planners, makes this impossible. The British Labour party nationalized major industries after 1945, but it discovered that this approach did not produce what was anticipated. Great industries cannot be run by politicians, even civil servants; they are too complicated. Only the technostructure can control them and make them work; they must have autonomy from public control. And instituting civil service rules eliminates flexibility, i.e., the easy constitution and reconstitution of groups.

For groups now have the power that individuals used to have. The remarkable progress that has been achieved in science, scholarship, and industry has resulted from the process of taking ordinary men, training them very intensively in limited bodies of knowledge, and then putting them to work together. Large areas of the national economy are still being run by individual entrepreneurs or small groups of them, such as in farming, small mines, the world of the arts and professions, small merchandising firms, and most personal services. Even in manufacturing there are many thousands of smaller firms. But by far the greatest economic power lies in the great corporations, located at the heart of the economy where huge supplies of capital, expensive machines, immense work forces, extensive marketing and advertising establishments, and—most of all—heavily staffed research and development operations, are required.

Business-Government Links

However, it cannot be said that the corporations are entirely independent of the state. In extremely high-cost industries like aerospace, it needs the government to carry on, or finance, the necessary research and development. The sixty billion dollars that the Defense Department was spending annually in the 1960s supported an astonishingly large portion of the industrial system. Literally thousands of large and small firms depended on a large annual defense outlay—and still do. Furthermore, such outlays are usually on a "cost-plus" basis, ensuring profits. While the corporations depend on government support, the government, of course, depends on the corporations to supply it with its necessary goods. Firms like Boeing Aircraft, General Dynamics, Raytheon, Lockheed, and Republic Aircraft, which in the 1960s sold anywhere from two thirds to all of their output to the government, were actually seminationalized industries. It is important to point out that, once again, the technical issues are far too complex for Congress, the government's "board of directors," to understand, and it therefore cannot exert much control over weapons procurement.

If even the government cannot effectively control the corporations, what answer can be given to protests that they have become too remote from the public's needs; that they have, in fact, created terrible problems for modern society such as pollution and overconsumption of limited natural resources? We are only beginning to grope toward the answers. Galbraith has suggested that the very educational system that was built to help meet the needs of industry may in the long run provide solutions, for only in higher education is there a potential for working out new ideas that will create social innovation. The corporations look only to their own needs, and in the 1960s they were wonderfully successful in meeting them. This would change markedly in the economic crisis that would strike the nation from 1974 onward (to be discussed in Chapter 38).

Bibliography

As in all the post-World War II chapters in this book, it is difficult to pick out the books which have been most useful to me, since I lived through these years, followed public affairs closely, and formed my understandings from many sources. As a general overview of the 1960s, William O'Neill's candid and irreverent *Coming Apart: An Informal History of America in the 1960s** (1971) remains valuable; the passion John F. Kennedy evoked and the political network he built are described brilliantly in Theodore H. White's classic *The Making of the President, 1960** (1961). James L. Sundquist's scholarly *Politics and Policy: The Eisenhower, Kennedy, and Johnson Years* (1968) was valuable to me, as were three fundamental works: James M. Burns, *John F. Kennedy: A Political Profile* (1959); Theodore C. Sorensen, *Kennedy* (1965); and Arthur M. Schlesinger's *A Thousand Days: John F. Kennedy in the White House** (1965). Lawrence H. Fuchs, *John F. Kennedy and American Catholicism* (1967) explores a vitally important dimension.

President Kennedy's troubled response to Michael Harrington's *The Other America** (1962) set the War on Poverty in motion. On the president's economics, see Edward S. Flash, Jr., *Economic Advice and Presidential Leadership: The Council of Economic Advisers* (1965), Robert Lekachman, *The Age of Keynes** (1966), and Herbert Stein, *The Fiscal Revolution in America* (1969). John Kenneth Galbraith, *The New Industrial State** (1972) is essential on the great corporations. Norman A. Graebner's *The Age of Global Power: The United States Since 1939** (1979) provided an excellent guide to overall foreign policies, while Roger Hilsman's brilliant and absorbing *To Move A Nation: The Politics of Foreign Policy in the Administration of John F. Kennedy** (1967) gives a fascinating inside view by an important Kennedy administration official. David Halberstam's *The Best and the Brightest** (1972) is absolutely essential reading to catch the mood of the Kennedy team.

John Kennedy and black America is a major issue illuminated skillfully for me by Carl M. Brauer's *John F. Kennedy and the Second Reconstruction** (1977). Many other books were helpful in this complex story: Benjamin Muse, *The American Negro Revolution: From Nonviolence to Black Power** (1970); *The Mind and Mood of Black America: Twentieth Century Thought* (1960), by S. P. Fullinwinder; Charles Silberman's probing analysis of racism, *Crisis in Black and White** (1964); Howard Zinn, *SNCC: The New Abolitionists** (1964); Lerone Bennett, Jr., *What Manner of Man: A Memorial Biography of Martin Luther King, Jr.* (1968), as well as King's many writings; Hugh Davis Graham and Ted Robert

Gurr, *Violence in America: Historical and Comparative Perspectives** (1969); James Baldwin, *The Fire Next Time** (1963); Claude Brown, *Manchild in the Promised Land** (1965); Eldridge Cleaver, *Soul on Ice** (1968). On American churches and civil rights, I consulted Martin E. Marty, *The Righteous Empire: The Protestant Experience in America** (1970); Cushing Strout, *The New Heavens and New Earth; Political Religion in America** (1974); and Sydney E. Ahlstrom, *A Religious History of the American People* (1973). Concerning Indian America, see the bibliography for the preceding chapter.

The immigration revolution, as well as much else in post-war social history, is superbly explored in Richard Polenberg's *One Nation Divisible: Class, Race, and Ethnicity in the United States Since 1938* (1980), a book I learned from extensively. Valuable too was John F. Kennedy's valuable (and posthumously published) book, *A Nation of Immigrants* (1964). On the broad themes of immigration and ethnicity, I drew upon: Philip Taylor, *The Distant Magnet: European Immigration to the U.S.A.** (1971); Mark R. Levy and Michael S. Kramer's detailed study, *The Ethnic Factor: How America's Minorities Decide Elections** (1973); Lawrence H. Fuchs, ed., *American Ethnic Politics** (1968); Edgar Litt, *Beyond Pluralism: Ethnic Politics in America* (1970); Peter Schrag, *The Decline of the WASP* (1971); Matt S. Meier and Feliciano Rivera, *The Chicanos: A History of Mexican-Americans** (1972); Armando B. Rendon, *Chicano Manifesto** (1971); Leonard Dinnerstein, Roger L. Nichols, David M. Reimers, *Natives and Strangers: Ethnic Groups and the Building of America** (1979); John Higham, *Send These to Me: Jews and Other Immigrants in Urban America** (1970), as well as John Higham, ed., *Ethnic Leadership in America* (1978); Peter Matthiessen, *Sal Si Puedes: César Chavez and the New American Revolution** (1970); Manuel P. Servin, *The Mexican American: An Awakening Minority** (1970); Patricia B. Blawis, *Tijerina and Land Grants: Mexican-Americans in Struggle for Their Heritage** (1971).

Several recent books of importance have appeared on Chicano history: Mario T. García, *Desert Immigrants: The Mexicans of El Paso, 1880–1920* (1981); Albert Camarillo, *Chicanos in Changing Society: From Mexican Pueblos to American Barrios, Santa Barbara and Southern California, 1848–1930* (1979); Richard Griswold del Castillo, *The Los Angeles Barrio, 1850–1890* (1979).

* Available in paperback.

36

TIME LINE

1963 President Kennedy assassinated; Lyndon Baines Johnson becomes thirty-sixth president of the United States

1964–69 Period of massive turmoil in black ghettos in northern and western cities and on hundreds of university and college campuses

1964 Free-speech student protest at University of California at Berkeley; Twenty-fourth Amendment outlaws poll tax; Third Civil Rights Act; War on Poverty program launched with passage of the Economic Opportunity Act; creation of Office of Economic Opportunity; tax cut passed; Wilderness Act

1965 Johnson announces Great Society program; federal aid to education greatly broadened; Medicare enacted; Fourth Civil Rights Act; Water Quality Act; Appalachian program of redevelopment; Economic Development Administration established; Department of Housing and Urban Development created; Johnson escalates Vietnam involvement; Malcolm X assassinated; Watts riot; Fourth Civil Rights Act

1966 Republicans make strong gains in congressional elections; Stokely Carmichael creates Black Power slogan

1967 Detroit riot; National Conference on Black Power

1968 Democratic National Convention scene of massive police attacks against antiwar protestors; Martin Luther King assassinated; Black Panthers organize; women's-liberation movement becomes prominent; Poor People's Campaign; Fifth Civil Rights Act; Robert F.

Kennedy assassinated; Senator Eugene McCarthy almost defeats Johnson in New Hampshire presidential primary; Johnson withdraws from presidential race; police and antiwar protestors clash at Democratic National Convention; Richard M. Nixon elected thirty-seventh president of the United States

1969 Nixon adopts conservative economic and social policies and a pro-white "Southern strategy"; antiballistic missile authorized; Vietnamization announced; Neil Armstrong lands on moon; Warren E. Burger appointed Chief Justice of the United States; Nixon proposes family-assistance payments to replace welfare system; Nixon proposes New Federalism

1970 Kent State University massacre of student protestors; nation becomes widely concerned over pollution crisis; Nixon establishes Environmental Protection Agency, Council on Environmental Quality, and National Oceanic and Atmospheric Agency; Cambodian invasion leads to renewed turbulence on campuses; Democrats make good showing in congressional elections

1971 Nixon calls for "New American Revolution" in domestic policy, proposes family-assistance payments and revenue sharing; Laos invasion fails; My Lai massacre revealed; Nixon opens talks with China in historic reversal of policy; Nixon devalues dollar, raises barriers to imports, removes gold as basis for dollar in international trade, and establishes wage-price controls to battle inflation

1972 Intensive bombing of North Vietnam

THE TURBULENT 1960S: THE FLOOD TIDE OF REFORM PEAKS AND FALLS BACK

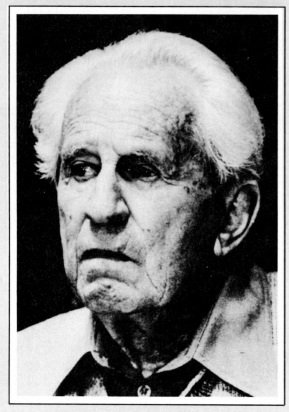

UPI

In Paris and Rome in 1968, thousands of radical students chanted the sainted names: "Marx—Marcuse—Mao!" Who was this strange third person, Americans asked, this Herbert Marcuse (mar-kóo-za)? He was an elderly German philosopher at the University of California, San Diego, who more than half a century before had fled Hitler's Europe to become an American. His densely written and closely reasoned books had been paid little attention until the students had seized upon them. Now he was hated by conservatives, and idolized by anticapitalist and anti-American radicals.

America, he said, had become the model for the world, and it was corrupt. Technological capitalism had here become so efficient, so alluring in the material things it poured out for the common people, that it was both repressing and draining away all revolutionary impulses. There must be a "Great Refusal" to go along with it. The power of *negative* thinking was needed. Humanity could be truly happy, Marcuse wrote (drawing upon his reading of Sigmund Freud), only when its sexual impulses, its desires for self-indulgent joy, were allowed to flow over and beyond all human relations, eroticizing the entire culture. But to get us to work hard and produce, capitalism repressed the instinct for play, instead making us organized, institutionalized, disciplined. The patriarchal family reinforced capitalism's wishes; it must be ended.

Society's discontents, in short, were psychological, and they were created by economic exploitation. In actuality, Marcuse insisted, we do not need all this disciplined work any longer: the economy is so productive that we can slow down and let technology support us. It is in fact the enormous psychological stresses that capitalism produces, its emphasis upon a constrained life style, that produces world wars, concentration camps, and atom bombs. Thus, society is destroying itself. Few were left, Marcuse believed, save for radical students, who were able any longer to see all of this. Certainly the workers in America, let alone the middle class, had no revolutionary impulses. They willingly participated in capitalism. Thus, in this overdeveloped, overrepressive society (as Marcuse saw it) in which all are enslaved who are part of the system, student radicals, as yet uncommitted to the aims of the economy, have an obligation to the people to take power and bring on the revolution that the people do not realize they need. Lenin had preached the revolutionary role of the intellectual elite, and Marcuse—a latter-day Marxist— echoed him. Freedoms of speech and the press must not be allowed to the revolution's enemies, for in their hands they destroyed the true interests of the people.

By these means, Marcuse insisted, a new consciousness could be released, one filled with beauty, luxury, calm, sensuousness, and gratification. Humanity would be transformed; liberation would create the good society.

Overview

On the twenty-second of November, 1963, a crisp and sunny day in Dallas, Texas, John Kennedy was riding in an open car, waving to the crowds lining the streets, when rifle fire rang out and he fell, dying, into Jacqueline Kennedy's arms. America and the world were stunned, horrified. Days of national mourning ensued, focusing on a stately funeral observance in Washington, D.C., attended by hundreds of thousands of Americans, by a great gathering of the world's leaders who solemnly paced down Pennsylvania Avenue, following Kennedy's casket, and by the watching lenses of the world's television cameras. It was a wrenching, tearing experience for a nation that had briefly enjoyed the sense that America was once more a country guided by exciting young leadership, as in the days of its beginnings, and directed by ideas that had caught the world's attention.

In former vice-president Lyndon B. Johnson of Texas, Kennedy was succeeded by a master of congressional relations. Joining his political skills to the momentum that had been built by his predecessor, and buoyed by an enormous vote of confidence in the presidential election of 1964, Johnson was able to push through all the legislation that Kennedy had asked for, and more. In 1964 and 1965 Johnson displayed presidential leadership as masterful as that of Woodrow Wilson or Franklin Roosevelt at their best. Indeed, he needed to be skillful, for the rising of black America swept into the northern and western states from 1964 onward, setting off nation-rocking explosions of racial violence. One after another the great reforms marched through Congress: the civil-rights laws; the inauguration of massive federal aid for public schools, housing, urban redevelopment, the War on Poverty, mass transit, and the arts and humanities; medical care for the elderly and the indigent; the revision of the immigration laws; a concerted drive to solve the problems of Appalachia; and the first steps toward controlling pollution.

Few presidents have stood at such a peak of national acclaim as did Lyndon Johnson in 1965; few have fallen so far, so swiftly, as did Johnson thereafter. In that year he escalated the Vietnam conflict into a full-throated war that destroyed much of that Asian country and took thousands upon thousands of Vietnamese and American lives. Soon the war issue tore the nation apart and ended Johnson's popularity. America's youth launched the first full-scale revolt of young against old in American history. The extraordinary Lyndon Johnson, who had been so powerful, was reduced to announcing—to a relieved nation—that he would not run for reelection in 1968.

With the advent of Richard Nixon, the turmoil slowly subsided. American troops were withdrawn, bit by bit, from Vietnam, and peace was at length achieved. The flow of reform proposals from the White House dwindled, and the emphasis moved to reduced government spending, federal passivity on race relations, and escalated attacks on suspected criminals and radical agitators. The president effectively ended the "Supreme Court revolution" by appointing four conservatives to the bench. He built an administration notable for its sober tone and its concern with efficient management and national planning. The leadership of this conservative president produced major changes in America's ways of governing itself, through the "New Federalism," and in national policies toward the environment.

The campuses and cities quieted while Nixon devoted himself to the sphere that most fascinated and absorbed him: foreign affairs. A measure of orderliness returned to national life after the whirlwinds of the late 1960s—until the scandal of Watergate broke in 1973. In 1974 Richard Nixon became the first president to face impeachment for having committed a felony while in office, and the first to resign that great office.

Lyndon Johnson: The President of National Unity

Johnson assumed the presidency in almost ideal circumstances for a new man in the job. Dwight Eisenhower and John Kennedy had built a large reservoir of trust in the White House among Americans at large. Both were extraordinary men who had been respected and admired by millions. Kennedy in particular had transformed the spirit of the country, though his legislative achievements had been few. The mission of America seemed brought to life again. A sense of movement and challenge, of being once more the focus of the world's admiration, briefly reunified the country. After the dark years of confusion and

McCarthyism that had so disturbed the national mood in the 1950s, JFK had helped rebuild a feeling of national purpose and pride. The aching void that millions felt after his death was grief not only for the loss of their leader, whom they had loved and admired, but for the feared loss of this new spirit.

As soon as Lyndon Johnson arrived in Washington from the terrible event in Dallas, he began swiftly pulling the country together. He was a man superbly equipped for the task: strong, confident, a veteran of almost thirty years in Washington, and for much of that time close to presidents. The momentum of Kennedy's drive to move America toward egalitarianism was not allowed to die—especially in the crucial area of civil rights, where, since Johnson was a Southerner, the nation had understandable doubts. One of the peak moments in the history of the United States occurred when in July 1964 the Third Civil Rights Act became law. Under its provisions, lawsuits begun by the attorney general over voting rights were expedited; all discrimination in public accommodations—hotels, restaurants, theaters, drinking fountains, swimming pools, parks—was declared illegal; the attorney general was authorized to bring suits to desegregate schools; the Equal Employment Opportunity Commission was created; and discrimination was barred in any state or local program that was supported by federal funds (public works, schools, agricultural research, hospitals, welfare programs, and the like).

At the same time, Johnson got Congress to enact the tax-cut bill that Kennedy had proposed; secured a renewal of the National Defense Education Act, under which a billion dollars was sent to the colleges for construction and scholarships; and proclaimed in January 1964 the War on Poverty, which he sought to make uniquely his own program. When the Republicans made the error of nominating Senator Barry Goldwater, a dedicated right-wing conservative, for the presidential election in 1964, Johnson overwhelmed him. The president won the largest vote of any candidate in United States history (61.1 percent; the former record was Franklin Roosevelt's 60.7 percent in 1936). Some forty-three million people voted for Lyndon Johnson, and twenty-seven million for Goldwater, who took the electoral votes only of Arizona, his home state, and a few states in the Deep South. Behind Johnson the Democrats won huge, lopsided majorities in both houses of Congress. The stage was set for one of those rare periods in American history when the traditional deadlock in the national government was broken and a host of reform proposals that for years had been battering fruitlessly against the legislative barrier could suddenly find the necessary majorities and become law.

The Johnson Presidency

Lyndon Johnson had great virtues as a president: he was exceptionally intelligent, energetic almost beyond belief, and eager to be another Franklin Roosevelt. Reared in near poverty in the west-Texas countryside, he was sympathetic to suffering people and wanted to help them. The first president to come from that huge and venerable denomination the Disciples of Christ (known also as the Christian Church), founded in Thomas Jefferson's day as an offshoot of the Presbyterian faith, he was always stressing, like his church, the essential unity of all peoples. It was his greatest virtue that although reared a Southerner, he was able to take a national outlook on the race question. Over and over his eloquent words calling for equal rights—uttered, on crucial occasions, before Southern white audiences—helped to move the nation far toward racial justice. From the beginning Johnson wanted to give something to everyone, and thus to have liberals, middle-of-the-roaders, and conservatives all believe that he was on their side. For three years the word *consensus* was his key term, and during much of that period the consensus strategy worked.

Most of all, however, he was a social reformer. He never forgot the Great Depression, during which he served as a young New Deal administrator, congressman, and protégé of Franklin Roosevelt. Government, to Lyndon Johnson, meant building dams and spreading irrigation waters to make the countryside green and flourishing; finding jobs for the unemployed; building schools and hospitals; helping the aged; healing the sick; and uplifting the downtrodden. When he talked about compassionate government (while proposing the War on Poverty) and decent government (while signing civil-rights laws), he meant what he said. Johnson wanted to be the guardian of his people, striding over the land like a kindly colossus and building what he called the Great Society.

The War on Poverty

He had long since launched his War on Poverty, announced with great fanfare in January 1964, less than two months after John Kennedy's death. Learning of the plans that were already under way among the White House staff, he remarked, "That's my kind of program. . . . Move full speed ahead."

The fundamental problem, only recently discovered, was that there existed a hard core of millions of poverty-stricken people, perhaps a fifth of all American families, who were being left behind as everyone else soared upward in income. The economy was becoming increasingly sophisticated and mechanized, and these people were without skills. Indeed, most of them were functionally illiterate and could not be retrained. The manpower-retraining programs that Kennedy's New Frontier had already begun had run head-on into this situation. Being poor, for these people, meant staying poor. It meant being weakened by illness most of the time because medical care was too expensive; being too poor to move around to find jobs; being so uneducated as to be unaware of basic information concerning the availability of jobs. The children of such families grew up in stunted surroundings, becoming themselves chronically sick and uneducated, entering the same cycle of low motivation, hopelessness, and lack of incentive that their parents were trapped in. The result was a culture of poverty that existed in the rural South and in city slums. The result, too, was a steady rise in crime rates, for the hard-core unemployed were prominent lawbreakers because of their frustration at having to live empty, boring lives in the midst of a bustling, prosperous America.

The War on Poverty, embodied in the landmark Economic Opportunity Act of August, 1964, was to serve as the economic counterpart to the great civil rights acts of the Kennedy-Johnson years. It concentrated on children and on youth. Aid was given to the older poor, but salvaging the young, the hope of the future, by improving their health, schooling, training, and general welfare

was the greatest concern. Head Start programs were established to give preschool children literacy training; the Job Corps was created to provide training and remedial education to city youth, both in slum-located centers and in forest camps where conservation was the objective. The Neighborhood Youth Corps provided experience for young people in serving those around them, and another program helped college students earn income. Funds were given to support work programs under the direction of local welfare departments, by which unemployed adults were given a chance to earn money. Loans were made available to small farmers, and to people who wanted to start small businesses in the cities. A domestic peace corps, the Volunteers in Service to America (VISTA), was created so that middle-class young people from all over the United States could use the skills they had learned in their homes and schools to aid the poor. Controversial federal grants were given to hundreds of public and private local community-action organizations whose concern was in some way to uplift the poor. These community-action programs were to be run in good part by the poor themselves. This led to endless controversies in thousands of communities, for the poor lacked managerial experience and handled funds in ways that angered the middle class, bringing charges of corruption and social radicalism.

Critics Attack the War on Poverty

The critics of the War on Poverty were legion. Sargent Shriver, who as head of the Office of Economic Opportunity was in overall direction of these many separate programs, had to struggle constantly with middle-class distrust of the undertaking. State and city governments disliked the community-action groups, which were not under their control. Republicans were staunchly opposed to them as a waste of public money. Barry Goldwater put the Republican view most simply by saying that there will always be poor people in American society and that their only problem is that they are too lazy to work. Southern Democrats were often hostile, since the Office of Economic Opportunity was deeply involved in helping black people, who were then rioting. Given organizations of their own, the poor were often militant and very loud-voiced—and Congress was enraged.

Funds, therefore, were always hard to extract from Congress. The first appropriation was only one billion dollars, hardly enough for a full-scale "war." When the swing of the political pendulum in later elections put more conservatives back in office, the War on Poverty was one of the first programs to suffer cutbacks. Unlike such great reforms as the Social Security System, it had no solidly based and well-organized public support behind it. Furthermore, poverty was terribly difficult to root out. Huge sums were spent without any dramatic effect. Head Start did not seem to fulfill its hopes, largely because the schools that children went into after Head Start were not equipped to keep them moving along at an enriched level. (Research published in 1980 would eventually reveal that Head Start children showed, by their teenaged years, significantly stronger records of academic success and constructive social performance than those without such early training.) Organizations of the poor rose and faded, leaving hardly a trace. Besides, the booming economy enabled masses of people to move above the poverty line: almost six million from 1964 to 1968. In time, President Johnson made little mention of the War on Poverty, and the many separate programs run by the Office of Economic Opportunity settled down into an almost random collection of routine operations rather than a committed national effort to eradicate poverty. Nevertheless, the total expenditures of the federal government in all programs to aid the poor, including such operations as social security, rose from about ten billion dollars in 1960 to thirty billion dollars in 1968.

Aid for the Schools

After his massive victory over Goldwater swept huge Democratic majorities into Congress, President Johnson was able fully to inaugurate his Great Society program. (At the same time, he moved fatefully to escalate American involvement in Vietnam, taking the nation to war—as will be discussed in the following chapter.) The first measures he proposed concerned medical aid and educational assistance, both of which had

tremendous stores of accumulated national support behind them.

What he now proposed was to concentrate on grants designed to aid disadvantaged children, whether in public or private schools. Large sums were given to the states in proportion to the number of children in families with annual incomes under $2,000. Government-purchased materials used in private schools would be considered on loan. General expenses, however, such as those for faculty and buildings, were not to be provided. Rather, the money went for libraries, special training programs for teachers, laboratory facilities, learning aids, and other special services. At the same time, Johnson pushed through another higher-education bill that provided billions of dollars to colleges and universities for scholarships, loans, buildings, libraries, dormitories, and other facilities. By the time Lyndon Johnson left office, 1.5 million students were in college who, without federal help, could not otherwise have afforded such schooling.

By 1968, Johnson had carried twenty-four major pieces of legislation through Congress that dealt with education, and federal expenditures in that area had risen from $375 million (in 1958) to $4.2 billion. The most important area of government action formerly controlled by state and local governments was henceforth to be shared with Washington, now the source of 10 percent of all national expenditures on education.

The Enactment of Medicare

The Johnson landslide of 1964 poured scores of congressmen into Washington who favored Medicare, and the president made it one of his top-priority items. The American Medical Association continued to fight desperately, but even the Republicans were giving in. In July 1965 the Medicare bill went through, providing millions of Americans over the age of sixty-five with a kind of security they had never known before. Under the Social Security System, funds were set aside to provide payment of doctor and hospital bills, nursing-home fees, and the cost of necessary drugs. A "revolution" had finally been concluded—one that, in the long run, the medical profession found to be extremely profitable for its members. Medicare, so violently condemned, soon became one of the pillars of American society that no one, any longer, would propose taking away.

The Great Society Rolls On

In March 1965 national television displayed before the horrified nation the state troopers of Alabama bombarding hundreds of praying blacks near Selma with tear gas and then beating them with clubs, whips, and ropes. The eruption of national outrage sent President Johnson before Congress to ask for passage of a fourth civil-rights act, which gave the federal government the power to send officials into the South to register black voters. Black registration in the states affected by the law swiftly rose from 30 to 46 percent of those eligible.

In his Great Society speeches Johnson had made the environment a principal concern. John Kennedy had presided over passage of the Clean Air Act of 1963, which enabled the federal government to begin exploring the problem of air pollution. Johnson now launched a series of White House conferences on pollution, out of which came the Water Quality Act of 1965. It gave the federal government powers bitterly resisted by industries for years: to establish standards as to the purity of the nation's rivers (if the states did not do so, or if their standards were judged inadequate), and to levy penalties for pollution. Then a $3.5-billion program was established whereby the federal government assisted hundreds of communities in the building of improved sewage facilities. Following this, the clean-air program was greatly broadened to empower the federal government to set standards for the exhaust emissions of automobiles and to accelerate necessary research.

Changing the Quality of Life

Johnson continued to pursue the main objective of his Great Society program: changing the *quality* of American life, now that affluence had demonstrated that for most Americans the question of *quantity* had been solved. At his urging, nine new national parks and recreation areas were established (making a total of fifteen since 1961), the first major addition to the nation's park system since the days of Franklin Roosevelt. The Wilderness Act, which the Sierra Club and other environmentalist organizations had been pushing for years, had moved forward with President Kennedy's support and was passed under President Johnson in September 1964. By its provisions, some nine million acres of wilderness were to be kept in that condition and another fifty million acres examined for inclusion in the system.

Meanwhile, an ambitious program for the revitalization of the depressed and despoiled Appalachian region swept through Congress in March 1965 with a $1.1-billion authorization. Since the area-redevelopment program of the Kennedy administration had come to a halt because its efforts were too thinly spread, in August 1965 the Johnson administration secured creation of the Economic Development Administration. Its task was to locate those centers of economic activity that, if given a boost upward, could reawaken the business life of entire regions. Having at its disposal some $500 million authorized for the building of crucial public works that would stimulate economic growth, it became the new national agency for regional development.

For the big cities, with their masses of ill-housed and restive poor—and their frightening riots—Johnson secured establishment of the Department of Housing and Urban Development.

The need for a national antipollution effort displays itself in 1966 in a panorama of polluted air hanging heavily over New York City. Such palls led to sharply increased rates of death resulting from respiratory failure.

Neal Boenzi/NYT Pictures

THE TURBULENT 1960s: THE FLOOD TIDE OF REFORM PEAKS AND FALLS BACK

Robert C. Weaver became its first secretary and the first black American to serve in the cabinet. Some $7.8 billion was provided for urban redevelopment and public housing, and in 1966 another enactment provided rent supplements to poor families so they could live in better quarters.

Did It All Help?

In the late 1960s and into the 1970s it became politically fashionable to say that the many reforms of the Kennedy-Johnson years "threw money at problems" but did not solve them. Welfare was a mess, critics said; retraining did not retrain; medicare became just a corrupt rip-off. By 1976, however, the dust was settling, and scholarly studies revealed these views to be incorrect. The system of programs that had evolved was admittedly complex, but then the problem of caring for the unfortunate was complex. Improved Social Security System aid, covering practically all workers, with benefits linked to the cost of living; unemployment compensation; public assistance to the aged, blind, and disabled; and Aid to Families with Dependent Children (fatherless families), the most controversial—in combination these programs functioned reasonably well, raising practically all citizens at least to the poverty threshold.

The food stamp program, inaugurated in 1961 by the Kennedy administration, was a revealing example of an admittedly expensive undertaking which nonetheless performed so well in aiding the poor while at the same time aiding others indirectly—in this case, the farmers—that despite the partisan attacks on the War on Poverty, even Republican administrations in later years broadened and strengthened it. Carefully modified to exclude all but the genuinely needy (those whose annual income could be proved to be below the federally-established poverty level), by the end of the 1970s it would be aiding 22 million people, or every tenth American, at a cost of $10.5 billion. In 1975 the Nixon administration even made the program mandatory in every county in the United States, and the need to actually purchase the stamps ($46 for $100 worth) would be dropped in 1979. In that year, a family of four that had only $400 a month in net income (after deductions for rent, transportation, and other necessary expenses) qualified for a direct grant of $113 in food stamps per month, which could be exchanged for that much food. By this program, hunger and malnutrition were dramatically reduced in America among the very poor. Three out of four of those receiving food stamps were children, elderly people, or single parents (primarily women) who were the heads of their households.

The Medicare and Medicaid programs of the Great Society went far toward ending the main worry of the aged and one of the great problems of the poor. (Medicaid is federally-subsidized state-level medical care for the poor: i.e., those who receive welfare support of varying kinds.) More medical care was in fact provided, and it was reallocated so that it reached people formerly ignored. The housing programs, both by direct construction and rent subsidies, helped bring low-income minority families out of ghettos and into better residential areas. Retrained persons actually improved their wages and began to acquire a much higher level of job stability. The higher earnings they received far exceeded the average cost of the programs, profiting both individuals and the whole society. Civil-rights laws vastly improved the political and social situation of minorities. Federal aid for higher education greatly expanded the availability of college and university facilities, and made it possible for tens of thousands with low incomes, especially among minorities, to secure the benefits of college study, another large step in the cumulative surge toward egalitarianism.

In short, while the Great Society did not end racial inequality, eliminate poverty, equalize income, or establish full employment—achievements beyond the reach of any human government in any reasonable time span—it did bring about very substantial improvements in the national standard of living by lifting the poor to a minimum standard of living and by opening new doors to a better life for many formerly ignored.

The Black Revolt Moves Northward

President Johnson was not fated, however, simply to enjoy a great administration of reform in the grand New Deal tradition. A complex man himself, he was to preside over complex and shuddering upheavals in national life that by the end of his administration would leave the country desperate for a return to order and stability and swinging strongly rightward in its politics. First, the black revolution broke sharply away from nonviolence. At almost the same time, America's youth began its own massive protest against the older culture and the Establishment. Finally, Johnson's tragic war in Vietnam, always in the daily news, escalated to appalling proportions. It produced angry protest by tens of thousands and brought the national government practically to a halt.

Martin Luther King, Jr.'s crusade had concentrated upon the South. In 1963, however, the revolt of black America spread to northern and western cities. At its peak, from 1964 to 1968, more than a hundred American cities were swept by riots, dynamitings, guerrilla warfare, and huge fires, which created scenes resembling the bombed-out cities of Europe after World War II.

What had brought on this upheaval? Was it because the status of black Americans was growing steadily worse? By all the major indexes, this was not true. Black Americans had been on a steady rise since the Second World War. Hundreds of thousands had left the red-dirt farms of the South for northern and western cities. By 1970 almost 11 million (47 percent) lived outside the South. Because they had better access to medical facilities, their death rate dropped rapidly (as much from 1950 to 1960 as in the previous fifty years). In 1940 the median education of blacks in the 25–29 age bracket was seven years; by 1959 it was eleven years, the same as that of the general American population. College attendance by Afro-Americans doubled from 1940 to 1960, then spurted rapidly: from 234,000 in 1964 (51 percent in predominantly black schools) to almost 400,000 in 1971 (a third in black institutions), or more than the total of young people attending college in Great Britain.

In 1960 some 16 percent of working blacks held white-collar jobs; by 1970 the percentage had risen to 28. Those in service occupations (cleaning and domestic work primarily) dropped from 32 to 26 percent; conversely, employment as craftsmen, foremen, and operatives rose from 26 to 32 percent. In 1950 the annual median income among black families was approximately $2,500; it rose 73 percent in the next ten years, reaching slightly more than $4,000 in 1960; and, after a further increase of more than 50 percent, it had reached $6,191 by 1970. Indeed, among young married couples at the end of the 1960s there was little difference in income between blacks and whites. Showing the growth of a sizable black middle class was the fact that every fourth black family earned more than $10,000 a year in 1970.

The Revolution of Rising Expectations

Ironically, however, when the mold is broken and standards of living begin moving upward, hopes rise even more rapidly. Revolutions do not occur among the totally oppressed, but among those whose status is improving and who are thereby emboldened to dream great dreams. Wartime studies demonstrate that morale is much better in organizations where promotions are slow than in those where they come rapidly. Black Americans lived in a country that professed high ideals of democracy and equality. For generations most of them had quietly accepted the fact that they were not to share in these ideals, but the hopes now being created resulted in a swiftly rising impatience with the status quo.

Conservatives in former times had insisted that education would make the poor discontented, and they were right. Education *is* subversive: it teaches people to be discontented if only a small and unequal portion of life's opportunities is offered to them. With more schooling, Afro-Americans were learning far more about the possibilities of life and acquiring skills they naturally wished to use. When great numbers of educated blacks found that many jobs and professions were still closed to them, their alienation was intensified. Then there was the impact of the mass-communications system: every day black Americans learned through television that whites had fine houses and many comforts while they did not.

Most significant, however, was the inescapable fact that whatever their advances, black people were being left behind by the whites. The yearly median income of white families was over $10,000 in 1970, making for a larger dollar gap between white and black families than had existed ten years before. Whites were moving more rapidly above the poverty line than blacks: every third black lived below that line, but only every tenth white. Afro-Americans held but a tiny fraction of managerial and professional positions, and their rate of movement into them was at a crawl.

In 1970, white unemployment averaged about 6 percent nationally and black unemployment about 9 percent, but within the slums it was frequently true that 25 to 50 percent of the employable black males lacked jobs. Housing conditions were incomparably better for whites. While the slums were being flooded by blacks, white Americans made a mass exodus to the suburbs, where abundant federal loans allowed them to buy new homes. In 1970 only 15 percent of black Americans lived in the suburbs, which were 95-percent white.

The City Changes Black Attitudes

Urban life had profound effects on Afro-American attitudes. Just making the move from an isolated farmhouse in Georgia to the teeming streets of Harlem was a profound psychological shock, similar to that experienced by millions of European peasants when they emigrated to America. Everything was changed. Most important, the ingrained pattern of submission to and dependence on whites, inherited from slavery and perpetuated on white-dominated Southern farms, gave way. Young blacks could cheer a galaxy of heroes, from Willie Mays and Jim Brown in sports to Sidney Poitier and Aretha Franklin in entertainment. Increasingly they realized that they were not inferior in talent, but only in opportunity. The leaders of the black rebellion showed how to leave behind Amos 'n Andy and become Martin Luther King or Stokely Carmichael. The ghetto itself made blacks a community in a way they never were when they were scattered over the Southern countryside.

The huge new black communities in the North had the potential of becoming a fresh and vital civilization. First, however, blacks saw that the inner-city regions in which they lived were too often foul, decaying slums. The plumbing did not work, and rats ran in the walls. Because the tax base was dwindling, schools were bad and garbage collection spotty. Stairwells, vacant lots, and side streets were choked with refuse. On the average, rents were as high as in white residential areas; in many cases they were higher. Bored, unemployed, and embittered residents frequently made a shambles of their living areas and preyed on one another by burglary, robbery, or drug ped-

dling. For the last hundred years, crime and violence had been steadily dropping in American cities; despite common myths, they were much safer and more peaceful places to live in than ever before. But in the 1960s this trend reversed itself, and blacks were everywhere blamed.

Since there was little money in the ghetto, there were few jobs. Factories were far away; employment was generally out in "white country." This required long rides on deteriorating, costly bus lines, if they even existed. Since it was often impossible for black men to find jobs and support their families, many became drifters, with disastrous effects on family life. In the New York area alone, in 1960 one fourth of the black families were headed by women, as against one in ten white families. The harried mothers were miles from potential jobs, frequently had little education, and lived in hand-to-mouth dependence on welfare.

When Martin Luther King began to lead the black revolution in the South, the tinder was dry in northern cities. Faced with degrading lives, young black men were desperate for a means of realizing their manhood. Fascinated by the rise of new black nations overseas and shamed by the knowledge that their Southern brethren, whom they had long looked down on as crude country cousins saying "yas suh" to the white boss, were standing up with massive courage against white attacks, they sought to join in. Pulled by their own version of the revolution of rising expectations, northern and western blacks were ready to set off the greatest social explosion in American life since the Civil War.

The Flaming Cities

The beginning rumbles occurred in 1963, when 200,000 persons marched in Detroit to protest discrimination, 3,000 students boycotted Boston public schools to protest segregation, and half the black children in Chicago—more than 200,000—did the same. Then, in the summer of 1964, came the first huge riots in northern cities. For hours on end roaring multitudes smashed through the center of Harlem, shattering windows, frightening policemen, and looting stores—attacking the symbols of white domination within the ghetto. Riots subsequently erupted in Brooklyn, Jersey

The massive Detroit riot of 1967, like those earlier in Watts, and other cities, left large areas of the central city area looking like bombed-out Europe after the Second World War.

Detroit Free Press from Black Star

City, and Paterson, then in Philadelphia and out west in Chicago. Everywhere the same deep feelings were displayed: despair, alienation, fierce anger—and, paradoxically, hopes for a better future. But these outbreaks were not religious in tone. Martin Luther King could lead a nonviolent crusade in the South, inspired by hymns and the Christian message of love; but northern cities held far fewer "believing" blacks. Particularly among the young—and later studies found young male blacks, usually school dropouts and unemployed, the leaders in the riots—there was little memory of what had been left behind in the South; they were conscious only of present unemployment and despair.

In the summer of 1965 the flames mounted higher. In August an enormous riot raged for five days in Watts, a suburb of Los Angeles. Thirty-five people were killed, 600 buildings were looted and burned, and thousands were arrested. Next came three days of violence in Chicago's West Side and another riot in North Philadelphia. In the summer of 1966 riots flared up again: in Atlanta, Chicago, Waukegan in Illinois, Lansing in Michigan, Omaha, Cleveland, New York City, and Dayton, Ohio. Then in Detroit, in July 1967, came one of the most massive of all the riots. It lasted for weeks, and more than forty persons died. (As in all the riots, the dead were mainly black Americans, shot down by police or National Guardsmen.) More uprisings followed in Michigan, Indiana, Illinois, Wisconsin, and Connecticut.

A Change of Mood

White Americans outside the South swiftly changed their outlook when the riots began. Sympathetic to blacks while the disorders were confined to the South, they now began to pull back. Terrified by the vast insurrections, they were much less inclined to support egalitarian legislation. Coincidentally, in the summer of 1966 a crucial shift in opinion surfaced among young black reformers. Young SNCC workers turned away in anger from the American political system, and from the whole notion of integration, liberal values, and nonviolence. Inspired by the writings of Malcolm X, who had been murdered by hostile Black Muslims in February 1965, some preached black nationalism: complete withdrawal from whites and the establishment of a separate black nation within the United States. In the summer of 1966, while on a march of protest into Mississippi, Stokely Carmichael, leader of SNCC, suddenly began a chant that swept the nation: "Black Power! Black Power!" Thousands of blacks chanted it in city after city while white America recoiled in fear. No one knew precisely what it

763

meant; Carmichael was never able to explain it; and moderate black leaders condemned the slogan.

Together with Black Power came the slogan Black is Beautiful. Indeed, much of the black movement now devoted itself to a nationwide campaign to change the self-image of blacks by introducing new themes in the arts, especially in the theater, literature, and television. Black men and women began appearing prominently in movies and television programs, not as the old, stupid stereotypes immortalized in the 1930s, but as real individuals. Fiction and nonfiction by black authors flooded bookstands and magazine pages. Universities established programs of black studies and searched nationwide for black professors. The stigma of black cosmetics (hair straighteners and lighteners) disappeared, and natural, "Afro" hair styles swiftly became popular.

White America, however, was frightened by the extremist rhetoric used by black militants. Just as the words used by northern abolitionists in the 1850s had frightened Southerners into extreme actions; just as Chicago anarchists had convinced Americans in the 1880s that revolution was imminent, thereby incurring nationwide jailings and scare legislation—so did Black Power advocates stir up an avalanche of white overreaction with their use of such volatile slogans as "Burn, Baby, Burn." "It's time we stand up and take over," said Stokely Carmichael. "Move on over, or we'll move on over you." In the National Conference on Black Power in Newark in July 1967, H. Rap Brown, Carmichael's successor as head of SNCC, said, "Go and get your guns, then lead the march." In 1968 the Black Panthers organized. They made a great show of being heavily armed and ready to battle the police in order, as they described it, to protect black communities from police lawlessness.

The Assassination of Martin Luther King, Jr.

Terrible events rocked the nation in 1968. By this time Martin Luther King, Jr., winner of the Nobel Peace Prize in 1964, had carried his campaign to the northern states, where he no longer worked only for equal civil rights, but for better housing, schools, and jobs as well. Preparing plans for an-

other march on Washington (of poor black and white people), he went to Memphis, Tennessee, in April to support a strike of city garbage collectors. A riot broke out, more than a hundred buildings were burned, and thousands of National Guardsmen were called in. Then, shockingly, King himself was assassinated as he stood on a motel balcony. This senseless act angered all black America. Riots erupted in more than a hundred American cities; some fifty persons died (forty-five of them blacks); fire and looting destroyed tens of millions of dollars in property; and more than 20,000 arrests were made.

In May 1968 the Reverend Ralph Abernathy, King's successor as head of the SCLC, led the Poor People's Campaign to Washington, where for a few months protestors camped at "Resurrection City" near the Lincoln Memorial. Congress responded by passing the 1968 Civil Rights Act, which rendered illegal any discrimination on racial grounds in the sale or rental of 80 percent of the nation's private housing, or some thirty-five million units.

Rebellion Among American Youth

The black rebellion, especially in its post-1963 phase of violent protest, got its driving power from a new generation of young black activists. Coincidentally, an earthquake upheaval against the older generation and its culture took place among white young people. They had grown increasingly disenchanted with the disillusioned conservatism of the preceding generation of intellectuals, who in the Truman-Eisenhower years had lost faith in reform and ideology. The younger generation had not personally known the Great Depression or the Second World War; they were not by their own experience trained to regard human life as something that, realistically considered (as the older intellectuals would say), could be changed only in limited ways. Indeed, they felt cheated of the brave adventures of the New Deal years that their grizzled and sardonic mentors described to them in university lecture halls. They knew that the world was filled with unsolved problems, and they were filled with the impatient confidence of youth.

Hungering for a cause to believe in, the new generation seemed to find it for a time in John

THE TURBULENT 1960s: THE FLOOD TIDE OF REFORM PEAKS AND FALLS BACK

Kennedy. During his thousand days in the White House, a rush of hope had inspired young people to think that a new America was being born. However, Kennedy was himself a product of the earlier years, he too was a disciple of Reinhold Niebuhr and shunned ideology, and even before his death many young radicals were turning away from him, saying that little was being achieved. After his death, such psychological moorings as young whites and blacks had in the Establishment were cut. The "quiet generation" of college students characteristic of the 1950s became the "wild generation" of student radicals and "hippies" who in the mid 1960s rebelled against the political and cultural authority of the older generation.

What had happened was not simply the death of John Kennedy but the ending of the Cold War. The great anxieties that had driven Americans together and had made them shun innovation and new ideas evaporated after the Cuban missile crisis of 1962 and the beginning of Soviet-American détente. After more than thirty years of national crisis, which had begun in the stock-market crash of 1929, Americans were finally free to begin "doing their own thing," as the language of the 1960s described it. The caution and careful realism that had restrained most people gave way to a great national explosion of romanticism. Soaring utopian dreams of human liberation from old constraints, of a "new consciousness," seemed to seize the younger generation, and many among the older generations as well. Perhaps not since Ralph Waldo Emerson and the communal transcendental utopians of the Andrew Jackson years, long before the Civil War, had America seen such an outpouring of romanticism.

Styles of life began changing swiftly. The "pill," "nudie flicks," *Playboy* magazine, and crucial Supreme Court decisions made the United States, long one of the world's most puritanical nations in sexual matters, one of its most liberated. The drug culture vastly expanded. Communes of "dropouts" who rejected mass culture and offended their neighborhoods became prominent. Older folk were shocked to see beards suddenly sprouting on millions of youthful faces, young men growing their hair long, and young women wearing men's clothing. People over age thirty reacted angrily to the flamboyant youth (always a small minority of the youth population,

in truth) who flouted traditional standards, glorified self-indulgence, and scorned discipline.

The revolutionaries of the 1960s were passionately convinced that humanity possesses enormous emotional and spiritual powers that lie untapped. Release them, they believed, and a new consciousness would emerge that would make all things possible. Revolutionary ideologies, the cry of "liberation," the use of drugs, and (later in the 1960s) the pursuit of Hindu mysticism in order to explore inner worlds—these became the characteristics of the "counter-culture." The new romantics rejected the religious revival of the 1950s. Norman Brown's *Life Against Death* (1959) and Herbert Marcuse's *Eros and Civilization* (1962) were the new inspirations for the culturally alienated. These works attacked industrialism as repressive, explained humanity's predicament in sexual and psychoanalytical terms, and preached liberation from all socially imposed restraints.

The Decade of Youth

The United States became in the 1960s a country practically obsessed with its young people. Everywhere one looked, or so it seemed, there were "flower children" begging in the streets, mobs of young activists storming through university campuses, drug enthusiasts, antiwar demonstrators, beads, long hair, bare feet, and communes. This was not, of course a wholly unprecedented phenomenon. But the scale of the turmoil in the 1960s—the "decade of youth"—sets it apart as a phenomenon the like of which we may rarely see again.

Census figures tell the tale. Between 1948 and 1953 the annual baby crop increased 50 percent, the biggest short-range increase in births ever recorded in this or any other country. In 1957 the birth rate started a decline that has continued into the 1970s, but the die was cast. In 1959 about twenty million Americans were children under the age of five; about eleven million were between fourteen and seventeen; but thirty-two million were aged five to thirteen. In that year the center of the nation's population gravity was still in the thirty-five-to-forty age group, but within four years it plummeted to the late teens. In 1964, seventeen-year-olds were the largest single age group in the country. Over the next seven years the number of seventeen-year-olds was each year greater than the previous year, and the same pattern was reflected among those aged eighteen to twenty-two, the classic college years.

No time of life involves greater changes than the period between seventeen and twenty-two, unless it be the time around retirement (for working men and women) or the period when the children leave home (for housewives). This is the time when youngsters traditionally move out from under the wings of their families, try out new cultural styles, rebel against authority, and begin building their own identities. Special conditions in mid-twentieth-century America intensified this process for the nation's young. Many no longer went right to work after high-school graduation at age seventeen, as in the past. Now at least half went on to college, thus stretching out their period of adolescence—their time of freedom from family and job responsibilities. Because of the large increase in graduate training, created by the growing complexity of the economy and its need for higher skills, this period of preadult life was extended even further for many young people, reaching into the late twenties.

Read everywhere in the 1950s and 1960s by those interested in understanding young people were the writings of Erik Erikson, such as *Childhood and Society* (1950) and *Young Man Luther* (1958). "I have called the major crisis of adolescence the *identity crisis;* it occurs in that period of the life cycle when each youth must forge for himself some central perspective and direction, some working unity, out of the effective remnants of his childhood and the hopes of his anticipated adulthood; he must detect some meaningful resemblance between what he has come to see in himself and what his sharpened awareness tells him others judge and expect him to be. . . . In some young people, in some classes, at some periods in history, this crisis will be minimal; in other people, classes, and periods, the crisis will be clearly marked off as a critical period, a kind of 'second birth,' apt to be aggravated either by widespread neuroticisms or by pervasive ideological unrest. . . .

"The need for devotion . . . is one aspect of the identity crisis. . . . The need for repudiation is another . . . a sharp and intolerant readiness to discard and disavow people (including, at times, themselves). This repudiation is often snobbish, fitful, perverted, or simply thoughtless. . . . The outstanding quality of these [young people] is *totalism,* a to be or not to be which makes every matter of differences a matter of mutually exclusive essences; every question mark a matter of forfeited existence; every error or oversight, eternal treason. . . . I have

called this the 'rock-bottom' attitude, and explained it as . . . an attempt to find that immutable bedrock on which the struggle for a new existence can safely begin and be assured of a future." (*Young Man Luther*)

The term *identity crisis* was picked up and applied in countless contexts in the 1960s, becoming one of the key concepts of the era. Like Freud's and Darwin's ideas, which were adopted and used indiscriminately, Erikson's were expanded to encompass the "identity crisis of Europe," or that (allegedly) of the aerospace industry, of President Johnson, and of the Black Panthers. More important, Erikson provided his age with a means for understanding the vast upheaval of young people in the mid 1960s.

Inevitably, this tidal wave in the population moved on, in the early 1970s entering the twenty-to-thirty age group. If young adults were involved in public affairs—as many, inspired by the turbulent 1960s, continued to be in the 1970s—it was usually not as rebels but as participants in "the system." This meant that in the 1970s party politics at the local level across the country would receive an inundation of youth, as in fact happened. Perhaps the most dramatic expression of this trend was the unprecedentedly swift passage in 1971 of the Twenty-sixth Amendment (less than three months from congressional enactment to ratification by the states), which gave the vote to all between the ages of eighteen and twenty-one.

Life Styles Among College Students

It is misleading to fashion a picture of young people in the 1960s exclusively around the college-based activist. The majority of young people go to work more or less directly from high school, and are often culturally and politically conservative. The proportion going to college, however, has grown greatly: in 1946 about 25 percent of the young people went to college; by 1970 it was about 45 percent. Research by social psychologists indicates that there is a wide range of cultural styles among those in college. For vocationally oriented students with a specific occupation in mind, college is a place of practical training. "Professionalists" head toward law, medicine, and executive positions in business and government. The "collegiate" student is the classic Joe College, who regards studies as a necessary but boring evil, plays the social game of sex, drinking, and drugs, and pursues long, fun-filled weekends. Then there are the "ritualists," who go to college simply because it is the "thing to do"; they do not know what else to do with themselves.

The "academics" are students seriously committed to scholarly achievement, usually in the sciences. The "intellectuals" are similar, but their interests—in the 1960s, usually ranging into the humanities and social sciences—are wider than those of the academics. They are headed toward some form of public service, but as generalists their objectives are not specific.

"Leftists" and "Hippies"

Then there was a small minority of students, the "leftists" and "hippies," that alarmed the public far out of proportion to its size. Constituting in the 1960s probably no more than 2 percent of the college population, activists and hippies populated the fevered imaginations of millions of older Americans. These two types of students differed sharply. Leftist activists believed that the system could be saved, and that personal involvement was the highest goal of life. For the most part highly intelligent, often concentrated in prestige schools that demand high grades for entrance, and springing from affluent, well-educated families, they called themselves the New Left. They were young people outraged at what they regarded as hypocrisy, mistreatment of others, and public evil. They operated from the fundamental conviction that American society is corrupt—certainly the oldest motivation among reformers in the modern centuries. In a sense they were reincarnations of the seventeenth-century Puritans, who were also outraged at corruption and consumed by an ambition to cleanse the (English) nation by radical measures.

The hippie, on the other hand, was so culturally alienated from American life that he withdrew from it. Almost always white, hippies were also from affluent families and felt little need to succeed at anything at all. As far back as the Adamites in the second century, there have periodically surfaced highly self-conscious groups of people who feel they have found the road to innocent, pure lives: withdrawal from society and a total rejection of its ways. Hippies, like their predecessors, denied reason and exalted feeling;

detested restraints; searched in Oriental mysticism for a means of transcendence, or in drugs of various kinds; and dispensed with the ideas of work, production, and achievement. The senses were to be freely deluged with "experiences," either ecstatic or manic; everything was to be "naturally" done; and laws and principles were to be discarded. Like the communitarian experimenters in the Age of Jackson, they established what they believed would be innocent communes of mutual love and sexual freedom.

In San Francisco, where the hippie movement began, they took up residence in the Haight-Ashbury district in 1967. They soon found that their life style too easily degenerated into a world of drugs, liver diseases (from infected hypodermic needles), filth, malnutrition, and crime. Widely hailed as prophets of the future, the flower-children movement faded rapidly, leaving behind, like the Shakers of old, quiet little pockets of gentle individuals who turned away from publicity and sought to live simple, noncompetitive lives.

The Movement and the Universities

In the 1960s young college radicals launched a campaign to transform America, calling it the Movement. The roots of this crusade lay in the late 1950s, when white students joined Martin Luther King, Jr., in his nonviolent programs for black equality. In 1960, the Students for a Democratic Society (SDS) was formed; soon its initials haunted ordinary Americans. Its "Port Huron Statement," which seems relatively mild in hindsight, appeared then as a veritable communist manifesto. It called for black dignity and equality; condemned wars and "anticommunism"; attacked as dehumanizing and irresponsible the power of bureaucracies in government, corporations, universities, and labor unions; and, in the part of the statement that set off the most turmoil, demanded that universities be used as bases for political assaults on "the system."

The tactic of nonviolence, as practiced by King and his followers, demanded enormous patience. It soon became intensely frustrating to white student activists who went to the South and were beaten, burned, shot, jailed, and murdered for their pains. In 1964 Mario Savio, a veteran of such efforts in Mississippi, turned his anger on higher education and led a free-speech uprising at the University of California at Berkeley. Set off by the university's attempt to deny the distribution on campus of political leaflets, it erupted into a tumultuous confrontation between students and institutional authorities that went on for months.

This pattern was repeated in varying degrees across the country. University administrations and faculty were subjected to abuse from the public, which was outraged that young people should be "dictating" to anyone, anywhere. Ordinary Americans still thought of colleges as playing a parental role—a role that had generally disappeared in the 1950s. Students, on their side, found the colleges easy marks for disruption, for the academic world was liberally oriented and reluctant to be punitive, and at the same time physically weak and practically indefensible. It was a grave business for students to risk their lives in the South or in direct assaults on military bases (where, presumably, the conduct of the war in Vietnam could be most directly affected); it was much easier to smash college windows and disrupt classes, using the excuse that as part of the Establishment the schools were implicated in the repression of blacks and in the Vietnam War.

The universities enacted many reforms in order to make their curricula more relevant to student interests and the nation's affairs, but they refused either to hand themselves over to student control or to let themselves be converted into bases for political action. President Johnson's escalation of the war in Vietnam in 1965, however, (to be described in the next chapter), made students far more angry with their society than before, and universities continued to bear the brunt of their assaults. As that war raged ever more violently after 1965, the youth rebellion grew into a nationwide upheaval. The slogan they had shouted in 1964 was Power Now! In 1968 it was Revolution Now!

The Movement and Revolution

By 1968 people were seriously discussing whether or not a revolution was possible or desirable. The Movement preached it with evangelical fervor; scholars such as sociologist Peter Berger were moved to write whole books to establish the opposite point of view: *"Revolution is not a viable op-*

tion in America, either practically or morally" (*Movement and Revolution* [1969]). Tactics now verged on terrorism, for "The Weathermen" and other extremist factions shouted over and over the message "Tear It Down." At San Francisco State College, Columbia, Harvard, Berkeley, Wisconsin, and scores of other institutions, a steady stream of arson, hit-and-run bombing, and other incidents often brought education practically to a halt from 1968 to 1970. Around the world the turmoil spread, from universities in Germany and France to those in Japan. It reached a climax on May 4, 1970, at Kent State University in Ohio. Students demonstrating against Nixon's invasion of Cambodia were fired on by National Guardsmen, and four fell dead. At this point almost 500 colleges and universities were on strike or closed down, and even Secretary of the Interior Walter J. Hickel was telling President Nixon that "youth in its protest must be heard."

The Movement, however, was more than a campaign to reform universities and end the war in Vietnam: it was a search by thousands of young Americans for a community to which they could feel a sense of belonging. They dreamed of an America based on love and openness, not on the technological, "rationalized," bureaucratic, centrally controlled, and militarized style of life that they were convinced dominated their country. The conduct of war was drifting to genocide; nature and the environment were being mindlessly polluted; and corporations were controlling everything. These young people were revolting against a society that they saw as overdeveloped, oversized, strangling in the coils of its immense power structures. Everything seemed to be moving toward depersonalization: automation and cybernation, computers and numbers, ascending pyramids of authority that insulated the decision makers from the people, and a rise in affluence that so deadened the ordinary people's sensibilities that they were willing to put up with being made small cogs in a huge machine.

Frustration Mounts

These ills, however, were much too pervasive for a student movement to affect. As their frustration mounted, activists retreated into a special world where they could convince themselves that the tactics of shock alone could somehow bring about the revolution they desired. By assaulting the sensibilities of the middle class, they hoped to overcome it; thus the ritualistic use of obscenities, the indulgence in violence, the preachings that the nation was on the verge of some unimaginable calamity. The reigning belief among activists was that absolute personal integrity—"authenticity" —had to be maintained at all costs, making compromise impossible, indeed degrading.

By late 1970 this irrational destructiveness was repelling the general student body. After years of massive protests on hundreds of campuses, involving countless "trashings" (window breaking and other forms of destruction), police-student conflicts, mass arrests, and the burning of buildings, the turmoil suddenly subsided. Almost as if by common decision, college students ceased turning out when the activists called for them to do so. The Vietnam War was being deescalated; the draft was ending; students were weary with immense disorders that produced little change; and, most important, the black revolution was dying down. As student activism had been born in that movement, so, perhaps, it subsided because for a time black America had ceased its protest.

The Tragedy of Lyndon Johnson

President Johnson was a great reforming president, one of the most ambitious and successful in American history. Yet in our own time his memory carries the heavy burden—for many people, the damning burden—of his having taken the United States into an overseas war that in time many Americans came to consider criminal. It is likely that this image of Johnson will dim, in later generations. Ultimately, the people in any country are most interested in the story of what happens at home; how their own society has evolved through time. Foreign relations have far less emotional power and interest. Johnson will come to be remembered primarily for his dramatic record in pushing the great surge of egalitarian reform to its peak. The human tendency to forget unpleasant things about oneself operates just as influentially in the memories of nations. About unpopular wars such as that in Vietnam little is actively remembered. In the cruel and bloody conflict Americans call the Philippine Insurrection (1899–1902), some 70,000 American troops suppressed the Fili-

pino desire for self-rule and independence after the Spanish-American War, leading to at least 20,000 Filipino deaths and horrifying tales of torture by American troops, wholesale destruction of property, and lawless executions of captured Filipinos. For a time American life was filled with outrage and controversy over the conflict, but it has since almost disappeared from American history. In the same fashion, perhaps Johnson's war will fade.

In the year 1968, however, Lyndon Johnson, practically under siege in the White House because of antiwar protest, had to concede publicly that his popularity was so low that he could not run for reelection. There was more to this development than simply blaming him for a much-condemned and failing war. Everyone has personal faults that become suddenly prominent when things are going badly. Johnson's shortcomings included an almost pathological passion for secrecy. He frequently made statements to reporters that they knew were not true, covered his tracks with small lies, and denied taking steps that were publicly known. He would state categorically that no one wrote speeches for him, though everyone knew who his speechwriters were. He had more than a hundred scholars studying national problems for him and making recommendations, but he never publicly admitted this, revealed their names, or released their reports. He wanted people to think that everything came from *him*. Distrust of what he said spread among reporters in his first two years in office, and then out to the larger public, until it stained everything he undertook. The war in Vietnam became one massive deception. Even when he announced that he could not run again for the presidency, many did not believe him.

Unfortunately, the president never understood the public's distrust. He regarded it as the creation of a conspiracy of eastern intellectuals and newspaper reporters. Johnson was always prickly about being a Texan and a graduate of San Marcos State Teachers College. If he were only a Harvard man, he would acidly say, they would all treat him well. As a self-professed "country boy," he recoiled from the big cities and the suburbs: their way of life he neither liked nor understood. Northeasterners in general seemed to him arrogant and conceited. These, of course, have been the classic feelings of outsiders, whether Scots rankling at the snobbery of the English, Boston

Irish resenting the condescension of old-line Yankees, or Mexican-Americans in California angry at being talked down to by Anglo-Saxon schoolteachers. And in truth, cultivated Londoners never laughed more readily at the clotted accent of a Glasgow Scot than New Yorkers at the broad west Texas drawl of Lyndon Johnson. Their attitude hurt the president deeply. "Want to know what's wrong with Lyndon?" asked John Connally, the president's shrewd and intimate friend. "He's ashamed of being a Texan." This made Johnson an obstinate braggart, a big man who felt compelled to put up a small man's boastful front.

The Johnson Ego

Urban Americans had liked John Kennedy's lightness, his wry taste for understatement and for not always taking himself seriously. But there was little wit about Johnson: his manner was heavy and pontifical, his humor coarse and earthy. Many Americans were offended by his immense ego, which had him spreading the initials *LBJ* on everything—from his shirts and his ranch to his wife and daughters. Always absorbed in himself, after he had undergone an abdominal operation the president thought that certainly the nation would be eager to see his scar, but when he yanked up his shirt to display it to photographers the public shivered in distaste. Then came the horror of Vietnam.

"Johnson's almost desperate need for loyalty was the other half of the coin of insecurity of this great towering figure [who] in so many important sections of [Washington] felt himself an alien, the Texas ruffian among the perfumed darlings of the East. It was a profound part of him; his sense of being alien, of the prejudice against him, was never assuaged. In October, 1964, when George Ball handed in his first memo against the [Vietnam] war, Johnson turned to an aide and said, 'You've got to be careful of these Eastern lawyers. If you're not careful they'll take you and turn you inside out.' He was haunted by regional prejudice. . . . Later, after he left office, he became convinced that it was his Southern origins, not the war, which had driven him out, that they had lain in wait for an issue, any issue, and had used the war, which was their war in the first place, to drive him from office. . . . He had triumphed over one area of Washington, the doers, the movers, men of the South and West, shrewd insiders, but he had always failed in another area, the tastemakers, so much more Eastern, more effete, judging him on qualities to which he could never aspire. . . ." (David Halberstam, "Lyndon," *Esquire* [August 1972])

The tragedy of Lyndon Johnson was very real. He loved America, and he hungered for its people to love him. But beginning in 1966 the bottom fell out; in fact there was no bottom there. The congressional elections of that year were a disaster for the Democrats. In time the president took to confining himself in the White House, peering distrustfully at the sightseers gathered at the fence and muttering that he could count on no one. Always resentful of criticism, he consulted with a smaller and smaller group of people within the administration. Johnson, in truth, was that man of whom Hamlet spoke:

So, oft it chances in particular men
That for some vicious mole of nature in them
. . . Carrying, I say, the stamp of one defect
. . . His virtues else—be they as pure as grace
. . . Shall in the general censure take corruption
From that particular fault.

This enormously egocentric man, caught in the pitiless eye of modern television and in the total exposure of modern communications, could build no reservoir of affection and trust in mid-twentieth-century America, the country he wanted so much to serve and to lead.

The Nation Swings to the Right

In 1968 the United States was swinging rapidly to the right. The surge of egalitarian reform, one of the most powerful in the nation's history, was over. This could be easily explained as a reaction against a bitterly unpopular war and as a characteristic and traditional turn toward conservatism after the great outburst of reform in Johnson's first two years.

Deeper and more fundamental, however, was a crucial shift that had taken place in American politics. The massive aid given to black equality in the 1960s, the first such boost in a century, had come from the Democrats. This meant that that party had become identified with black America in the same way that in the nineteenth century it had been identified with Irish America. The "Irishness" that had radiated from the Democrats in that time had offended Anglo-Saxon

Protestant Americans. Now the "blackness" that seemed equally to characterize the Democrats caused white America—or substantial portions of it—to recoil. The burning cities of 1968 led many whites to believe that blacks were an ungrateful, inherently violent, and "uppity" people whose rise to power would gravely threaten the nation. The United States as a whole, in other words, was becoming in a certain sense "Southernized." As never before, politics in the northern and western states began to throb to the same white-supremacy beat that for generations had provided the fundamental rhythm in Southern public life. Rocked by massive disorders and frightened at the swiftly rising crime rate—for which black America was everywhere blamed—the white majority turned toward the law-and-order appeals of the Republicans. The fifth, or New Deal, party system was starting to come to an end, though this would not be clear until the 1980s. The Republican party was beginning, finally, to revive.

An additional reason for the country's rightward shift was that the cultural issues that have traditionally aided the Republicans, in the reaction they produce, were dinning into everyone's ears: rebellious youth, women's liberation (to be discussed in Chapter 38), the drug scene, and new styles of life. Many Americans were uneasy about the upsurge of minority, ethnic America, which meant that the whole nature of national culture had turned in non-WASP directions. For generations Anglo-Saxon Protestants had run the nation's cultural life. We have seen how in the 1920s the new movie industry introduced a strong Jewish, Italian, and Greek influence into cultural life, but even then the movie moguls and the stars they hired Anglicized their names and built their plots around predominantly small-town, WASP themes. The novelists, historians, lawyers, and social scientists whom the historian Henry Steele Commager discussed in his widely read book *The American Mind* (1951) were practically all WASP: F. Scott Fitzgerald, Ernest Hemingway, Carl Sandburg, Sinclair Lewis, John Dewey, William James, Henry James, Charles Beard, Edmund Wilson, Oliver Wendell Holmes, and Lester Frank Ward. Intellectual life was expressed in *The Atlantic Monthly* (edited by Edward Weeks) and *Harper's* (edited by Frederick Lewis Allen). *The Saturday Evening Post, Collier's, The Country Gentlemen, The American Magazine*—these were the popular magazines, filled with stories

and articles redolent of WASP interests and values, that sold in the millions of copies in the 1930s and 1940s. If someone was a black, a Mexican-American, a Jew, an Italian, a Pole, a Greek, or a Russian, and wanted to make it in American cultural life, he or she had to learn the style, the accent, and the value system of the dominant culture. Whatever was "American" was WASP.

Decline of the WASP

But by the late 1960s, even though WASP America still ran the Establishment—corporations, country clubs, foundations, universities, the military, and the government—in cultural life a transformation had taken place. The names themselves tell the story: novelists Philip Roth, Bernard Malamud, Saul Bellow, James Baldwin; the scientists Robert Oppenheimer and Edward Teller; reformers Ralph Nader, César Chavez, and Saul Alinsky; the sociologists David Riesman and Lewis Feuer; social philosophers Paul Goodman and Herbert Marcuse; the psychologist of youth, Erik Erikson; the historian Richard Hofstadter. Scott Momaday, an American Indian, won the Pulitzer Prize for fiction in 1969, and the prize for nonfiction was split between Norman Mailer, a Jew from Brooklyn, and René Dubos, an immigrant from France. Aided by the flood of immigrant intellectuals who had fled Hitler's Europe in the 1930s, American cultural life had become pluralistic, ethnic, black, and anti-WASP. *The Saturday Evening Post* was dead (later it would be partially revived), and the black ghetto, rock music, Hindu gurus, Zen philosophy, Jewish anarchists, even Chairman Mao Tse-tung, were the new lodestones. Obscene words long excluded from ordinary conversation became commonplace utterances. The old mainstream of culture had lost its magnetic attraction; there were now many strands, accents, hair styles, and audiences.

The fact that many whose parents had come to America in the great migration from 1890 to 1920—Italians, Greeks, Jews—were prospering by the 1960s introduced a new complication. They and the older outsiders, such as the Irish Catholics, had become country-club members, owners of suburban homes, and college graduates. For them there was no revolt from WASP-dom, but acceptance into it. Identifying with the values and life style of traditional America, they too recoiled from the new cultural confusion. Many of the most militant spokesmen for WASP values in recent years have been these new recruits to that world, for whom Vice-President Spiro Agnew became a chief advocate and the symbol of the shift rightward.

The Ethnic Vote

Even so, it remained true in the 1960s, as from the beginning of American history, that the bulk of the ethnic outgroups continued to vote Democratic, though the pattern varied significantly. During the reign of the popular Dwight Eisenhower the Republicans had made heavy inroads (at least in balloting for the president) into the immense European Catholic bloc—the Irish, Italian, and Slavic (Polish, Czech, Russian, and Hungarian) voters—which had for so long voted as high as four-to-one for Democrats. John Kennedy pulled most of them back in 1960—especially the Slavic voters, consistently the most liberal and pro-Democratic among the European Catholics—but, at that, his majorities among the Irish and Italians were not top-heavy, nor were they substantial among the Jews and the black Americans. Only the Latin Catholics, particularly the Mexican-Americans, turned out in unprecedentedly high numbers for him, but their support was enough to produce the classic four-to-one vote that Democrats had always relied on among the ethnic outgroups to overbalance the huge WASP support Republicans could anticipate.

But by 1964 the tide was running strongly in traditional directions again. Kennedy's presidency, Lyndon Johnson's reforms on behalf of all groups, and the caustic right-wing conservatism of the Republican candidate in 1964, Barry Goldwater, unified the ethnic groups behind the Democratic banner. Blacks, European and Latin Catholics, and Jews trooped en masse behind Johnson. The massiveness of the black vote, both North and South, set the stage for the continuation of major reforms for blacks in Johnson's second administration. It also began a quiet revolution in the Southern states, where the emergence of a large black voting bloc put Afro-Americans in a crucial balance-of-power position. From this point on, as later events made clear, the support of black voters for a white candidate in local

Southern politics would practically assure his election.

The Accession of Richard M. Nixon

When Johnson announced that he would not run for reelection, a hectic Democratic race began. Soon Senator Robert Kennedy of New York, the martyred president's brother, was in the lead for the nomination, but his shocking assassination in June sent the contest into confusion again. Vice-President Hubert Humphrey was able to win the nomination, but through the summer and early fall his campaign could only limp along through a nightmare of obstructions mounted by howling young war critics who lumped Humphrey with the Johnson policy on Vietnam.

Meanwhile, the Republicans had turned to "Mr. Republican," Richard M. Nixon. Although he had not won an elective office on his own since 1950 (when he was elected a senator from California) and had lost narrowly against John Kennedy in 1960 and disgracefully against Pat Brown when he ran for governor of California in 1962, Nixon was still an amazingly potent and lively public figure. For more than twenty years he had been at the peak of national political life; only Johnson could match him in his long experience of closeness to power. Freshman congressman in 1946 (with John Kennedy), a household name since the days of Alger Hiss, always controversial, intensely disliked and rarely loved, he was the kind of career politician who had no roots anywhere but in public life.

The Election of 1968

Keying his presidential campaign to the law-and-order theme and giving the impression that he intended to get the nation out of Vietnam, Nixon went about the country speaking of the "crime crisis" and of the need for a reestablishment of authority in American life over young people and the turbulent cities. Spiro Agnew, the Republican vice-presidential nominee, called Humphrey "squishy soft" on communism. In the balloting George Wallace, former governor of Alabama and the presidential nominee of the American Independent party, sliced away a huge volume of

THE TURBULENT 1960s: THE FLOOD TIDE OF REFORM PEAKS AND FALLS BACK

votes on the right wing, since he was recognized as an openly antiblack candidate who advocated a hard line in Vietnam. Nixon won only a small popular-vote plurality—500,000 votes in a total of 74 million cast. With 43.4 percent to Humphrey's 42.7 percent and Wallace's 13.5 percent, Nixon had the smallest victory margin since Woodrow Wilson's in 1912. Indeed, for the first time since Zachary Taylor's election in 1848 a newly elected president assumed office with both houses of Congress in the hands of the other party, for the Democrats retained control in the Capitol.

There was a shaking, however, in the traditionally Democratic European Catholic voting bloc. Although blacks, Latin Catholics, and Jews turned out almost unanimously for the Democratic candidate, as they had in 1964, Nixon and Wallace together achieved a significant invasion of the European Catholic group. (Also, it should be pointed out, the numbers of Latin Catholics and northern blacks who actually went to the polls and voted continued a slide begun in 1964.) The Irish and the Slavic voters remained firm, casting about two thirds of their votes for Humphrey, but among the Italians he was able to garner only a bit more than half the ballots. Perhaps it was among this ethnic group, still heavily rooted in the inner cities, that the backlash against black rioting was strongest. For that matter, there have always been enclaves—such as New Haven, Connecticut—where Italians, much less devoutly Catholic than the Irish, have voted strongly Republican. Indeed, Nixon actually won a majority of the Italian vote in New York in 1968, the *first* time any Republican presidential candidate had ever carried any of the six major ethnic groups in any state. In state politics, Republican candidates found themselves pulling ever larger groups of Italians away from the Democrats— though only if they were liberal, not conservative, Republicans.

Nixon as Republican

President Nixon sprang from a classically Republican background and exhibited classically Republican outlooks. He believed America to be a good land where a life of comfort and self-respect was available to all who would work for it. Reliance on government for aid would be unmanly. The nation's leadership should come from its

business community; the "enemy" consisted of agitators and lawbreakers. The American system, if allowed to operate freely—that is, without the intrusion of government—would solve the country's social ills. Richard Nixon was the first chief executive to come from California. His identity, however, was not sectional but social and cultural: he sprang from the mainstream of WASP America. Small-town and lower-middle-class in his origins, he was reared in a world of sober coats and ties and consciously well bred manners. In his world, bold expansiveness, sophistication, and worldliness in personal style were frowned on. Neat and close-cropped hair, efficiency and order, closely buttoned vests—these were the hallmarks of Nixon's milieu.

The Nixons, like so many Republican families before them in American history, were zealously religious and moralistic. They were part of that classically Republican faith, Quakerism. English in ethnic origin, Tory in the Revolution, and Whig in Jackson's time, Quakers helped found the Republican party and traditionally disliked Democrats as drinkers, racists, and non-WASP Catholics. The Nixons were a family of true believers: in religion and politics they knew exactly who they were and where they stood. Skepticism had little standing. Nixon's father was a hot-tempered and argumentative man who laid down strict rules in his household and reached quickly for the strap to enforce them. The Nixon family was one in which team spirit and the importance of following orders were primary values.

Nixon's Enemy Fixation

It is not surprising, therefore, that the president who came from this setting was a self-righteous man given to preaching moralistic sermons to the nation. He was also an intensely combative and partisan man who for years carried the reputation of resorting to low blows in attacking his political opponents. What he enjoyed most of all in politics, he once observed, was the "battle itself." Richard Nixon knew who the enemy was, had absolute confidence in his own views, and had long suspected (and said) that the other side must somehow be disloyal to America. No belief, indeed, is more traditionally Republican. From the days of the Federalists to those of the mid twentieth century, "subversive" and "un-American" have been the most instinctive cries of the party's far right wing when attacking Democrats. The WASP party has traditionally felt itself to be uniquely American, the minority outgroups behind the Democrats to be ineradicably "foreign," and the Democratic party itself given to un-American ideas.

Team-spirit Americanism was strong in Richard Nixon. He wanted to see the United States "number one" in the world—in everything. He was fascinated by football, a notably military-style sport, and gave the generals and admirals far more prestige and influence in his administration than they had enjoyed under the Democrats. Veterans' organizations uniformly applauded the president, as they had former Republican chief executives, for they considered him a kindred spirit in his intense patriotism, dislike of liberals, and preference for men in uniform. Police forces, fire departments, and National Guard units looked on him as their natural leader, for he preached law and order, was unsympathetic to blacks and rioting youth, and believed that authority and a strong hand, rather than social reforms, were what was needed to bring peace to the country.

The Nixon Presidency

The Nixon presidential style, too, was in the traditional Republican mold. Here was a chief executive who would go months on end without a press conference, who secluded himself in a small office for many hours a day while he ruminated his policies. The active president, working diligently with Congress, educating and inspiring the nation with frequent addresses,—this model disappeared, to be replaced by the remote and silent Nixon, regarded as hermitlike even by his staff. Shy and retiring anyway, he was a terribly private man. As one who believed America to be fundamentally sound, he once observed, "I've always thought this country could run itself domestically, without a President. All you need is a competent Cabinet to run the country. . . . You need a President for foreign policy." Within the White House great stress was placed on orderliness and efficiency.

Congress receded, as is usually the case in Republican administrations, for the president made little use of it. There was an almost calcu-

Lyndon Johnson and his successor, Richard M. Nixon, on inauguration day 1969. Veteran Washington figures, they carried the "imperial presidency" to new and appalling heights, the one in a tragic foreign war, the other in both that war and the Watergate conspiracy.

Elliott Erwitt, Magnum Photos, Inc.

lated ignoring of the congressional barons, who fumed that they could not get through to the president: his huge staff of assistants (larger than that of any former chief executive) refused to let them have access. Nixon put much emphasis on the dignity of the presidency and toyed for a while with the idea of florid, European-style uniforms for the White House guard—until dissuaded by public ridicule. He was deeply impressed by France's Charles de Gaulle, the majestic president of the French Republic, who insisted that a national leader must maintain distance, aloofness, and mystery in order to establish effective rule. All this was to have serious repercussions, for the Watergate scandal that erupted at the outset of his second term—an event unprecedented in the history of the presidency for its extensiveness and grave moral implications—was widely attributed to the secretive, conspiratorial air that such presidential isolation produced.

Nixon's Administration

The president and America's intellectuals regarded each other with mutual distaste. Only a few were on his staff—notably Daniel Moynihan, for two years (1969–70) his adviser on urban affairs, and Dr. Henry Kissinger, his adviser on foreign relations and from 1973 his secretary of state. Nixon's was a strangely unusual Republican administration in that it had few ties even with corporate America, though the president certainly followed policies aiding big business. The veteran reporter Stewart Alsop, reflecting on the tone of this administration, wrote that the president "is not just square—he is *totally* square. His political strategy is based on the assumption that a majority of the American electorate consists of people like himself—middle-class squares." There was no humor, no jauntiness; there were no Jews (save Kissinger), blacks, or big-city ethnics. It was the evangelist Billy Graham who had the president's ear, not some liberal intellectual. The White House was light-years removed from the booming earthiness of Lyndon Johnson or the folksy Jacksonianism of Harry Truman.

In domestic affairs, Nixon entered office without any great goals in mind save to fight crime and disorder, to pull the white South into his party by sharply slowing desegregation, and to throttle back on social reform. The cities, low-income housing, the War on Poverty, welfare programs—these would be given less and less money, and then, in the president's second administration, would be drastically cut back. Richard Nixon did not seem, however, to have what could be termed an ideology. Staff members close to him later concluded that there did not seem to be an "inner" Nixon. "I don't know what the president believes in," observed cabinet member George Romney. "Maybe he doesn't believe in anything." A senior aide remarked, "If Nixon has an over-all policy, I wasn't able to find it when I was working over there." John Ehrlichman, counselor and then principal domestic advisor to the president (subsequently imprisoned for his role in the Watergate affair), admitted that his chief possessed no philosophy, but chose his steps on practical grounds, adopting shrewd tactics in whatever immediate situation he found himself. "Flexibility," Nixon once stated, "is the first principle of politics."

A Strong Swing Toward Planning

This guideline made the president extraordinarily ready, therefore, to take bold new steps in unexpected directions. The Nixon presidency certainly contained more surprises than most of its predecessors. Though the president was clearly understood to be a conservative Republican, at the urging of Daniel Moynihan he pushed forward an almost bewildering array of proposals, and reorganizations of the federal government, which looked toward *national planning*. That concept, so condemned by conservatives for decades as being too much like socialism and communism, had essentially been buried after efforts at national planning during the New Deal failed.

By the 1960s, however, America had vastly changed. In corporations, universities, and local governments; in such federal agencies as the forest service; in local zoning commissions; in the nation's business schools and among its business elite—everywhere were heard such terms as *systems analysis*, *cost-benefit studies*, and *projections*. All of this was linked to the explosive spread of computers in business and government. Robert McNamara had brought to the Kennedy-Johnson Defense Department a sophisticated, corporation-tested system of analysis and a flood of similar experts had come with him into the national government. "The modern executive, the lawyers and economists and statisticians and engineers who served with them," writes historian Otis L. Graham, Jr., in *Toward a Planned Society* (1976), "had by the late 1960s thoroughly absorbed the planning ethos." From all around him, and from men he admired, Richard Nixon heard advice to make the federal government an activist agency that, through planning, would take effective control of the national economy and direct it toward consciously chosen, rationally conceived, national objectives. He wanted, anyway, to do something bold, like John Kennedy, whose example strongly influenced him (Moynihan was his capture from the world of the Kennedys), and this new thrust appealed to him.

Centralized planning of the national economy was not, in reality, a concept wholly foreign to the traditions of Nixon's party. Before the New Deal of the 1930s had revolutionized American political ideology, and before the Democrats had taken over the idea of governmental activism (which for generations had been the property of Republicans), men like Theodore Roosevelt and Herbert Hoover—and before them Henry Clay and Alexander Hamilton—had insisted that the national government move vigorously to guide the economy so as to create prosperity and national strength. The ideal of strong administration, so central to the progressivism of Republicans like Gifford Pinchot (Theodore Roosevelt's planning- and central-management-oriented head of the Forest Service), appealed strongly to Republicans concerned with efficiency. Herbert Hoover has recently been termed by a leading historian, Joan Hoff Wilson, the "last of the Progressives" for his lengthy campaign during the 1920s to join busi- ness and government in a partnership working toward rationalized, standardized, and central- ized management of the economy. It is not sur- prising, therefore, that the second Republican president to sit in the Oval Office after Herbert Hoover's departure from it in 1933 should seize upon the planning ideal.

Steps in this direction had been taken by Kennedy and Johnson. They quickly learned, as all presidents do, that the "permanent govern- ment"—the vast federal bureaucracy and its irre- movable civil service—is almost impossible to move in new directions, whatever they are. Ken- nedy and Johnson wanted to launch great re- forms, but the bureaucracy was often indifferent. Kennedy's answer was to steadily enlarge the White House staff, and therefore his ability to monitor and urge to duty the many scattered fed- eral agencies in Washington. Meanwhile, studies of urban growth, rural decline, population trends, and other elements of national growth began to be made. In 1968, both national party platforms called for the evolution of informed, coherent pol- icies of national growth, and the National Gover- nor's Conference supported the idea.

Behind all of this was a nationwide upsurge in city planning, which was repeatedly urged on local governments by Congress in its housing, transportation, and urban-development grants. No national agency, however, pulled all this dis- organized planning activity together. Certainly the White House was not able to do it. Even to make the federal government itself choose spe- cific objectives and then guide its budgeting and activities in those directions seemed impossible. Lyndon Johnson was greatly impressed by Robert McNamara's planning system in the Defense De- partment—it was called the Planning-Program- ming-Budgeting System (PPBS)—and in 1965 he ordered the entire federal government to put the elaborate PPBS procedures to work. But people were untrained in its requirements, necessary planning data were not available, many forms had to be used to coordinate thinking, and "systems

analysis" was a concept foreign to most civil ser- vants. The effort faded after Johnson left the presidency and McNamara went to the World Bank.

Nixon's Planning Efforts

Spurred by Moynihan, in 1969 Nixon issued the first presidential message ever presented on *pop- ulation*. He called on Congress to create (which it did) a commission that would study how fast the American population was growing, what prob- lems this created, and what should be done about it. He actually called for research in birth-control methods (the words had never been used by a president in public before), and expanded family- planning activities. The president also estab- lished an Urban Affairs Council under Moynihan and directed it to "devise a national urban policy" in which the more than 400 separate federal pro- grams affecting metropolitan areas, and the real problems of the cities, would be harmonized. Per- haps Americans should be induced by federal ac- tion to live in different spatial arrangements; per- haps some areas should be targeted for rapid development, and others held back.

By the 1970s an exultant Moynihan was writing, "We are moving from program to policy- oriented government. . . . the idea of policy arises from the recognition that the social system is just that, a system. . . . In a system, every- thing relates to everything. If one part is changed, all other parts are affected. It thus becomes nec- essary to think of the total effect [of highway projects, housing projects, the issuing of defense contracts, the putting up of import quotas on par- ticular crops], not just the partial one." Shortly he got Nixon to agree to establish a National Goals Research Staff that would gather social data, ana- lyze them, select policy choices, and measure progress toward goals. Installed in the White House basement in summer 1969, it got hard at work, though uncertain exactly what it was to do, or how.

At the same time, the president doubled the size of the White House staff (to over 500 mem- bers) in order to gain closer control of the "perma- nent government" in Washington. The Bureau of the Budget, for many years the president's only direct means (and not a very effective one) of con- trolling what federal departments did, was expanded and named the Office of Management and Budget. It was charged with evaluating the performance of all federal agencies, gathering information, and training civil servants in improved managerial techniques. The elaborate PPBS installed under Johnson became a simpler Management by Objectives (MBO) system, in which federal agencies yearly described their objectives and the president decided which of them to give top priority in budgeting. In March 1970 a Domestic Council, modeled on the longstanding example of the National Security Council (which oversaw foreign relations and defense), was created with the authority to coordinate the work of all departments concerned with the nation's internal affairs. Having its own staff (like the NSC), it was to use task forces of analysts to study such issues as busing, the environment, health, crime, energy, and welfare.

The "New Federalism"

No single action in Richard Nixon's initial year in the White House more dramatically expressed the objectives Republicans believed he would work toward as president than his message to Congress calling for a "New Federalism." Nationwide, leading Republicans defined Nixon's mission in simple terms: to make the national government smaller; to stop it from meddling in social reform; to liberate capitalism from the constraints inherited from the Democratic administrations; and to return power to local regions. "The New Deal is dead," said a close Nixon associate. The president insisted that the time had come to reverse the flow of power so that it moved not upward from the states and localities to Washington, but back downward. The device: revenue sharing. That is, the immense flow of funds that came to the national government because for more than half a century it had largely monopolized the income tax—the most productive single source of revenue—should be redirected. The money *came* from the local communities, said Nixon; now Washington should send it back and, with few strings attached, let them spend it on objectives they chose.

This ran squarely against the idea of national planning directed from Washington. Clearly, every national administration gets launched in paradoxical directions. But revenue

sharing was one goal upon which Republicans had agreed since the days of the New Deal. State and local governments would be immensely revitalized by this historic turn in direction. As a result of revenue-sharing funds, county- and state-government staffs and their activities grew enormously. Earlier they had been buried in endless fiscal crises because their traditional sources of revenue (property and sales taxes) were limited and regressive (they bore heaviest on those with the lower ability to pay). Revenue sharing, finally enacted by Congress in 1972 in the form of a $30.2-billion grant to the states to be spent over a five-year period, would in the following years work a near revolution in American local government.

Pollution Control and Environmental Protection

One crucial realm in American national life, the quality of the natural environment—air, water, and land—lacked any supervision whatever. Surely nothing could call more insistently for attention in a setting in which national planning and the intelligent, rational use of resources was being demanded. In 1969 a great oil spill from a drilling operation in one of the nation's most beautiful natural environments, the Santa Barbara Channel off the coast of California, brought to climax the upwelling of concern about protection of the environment that had become one of the great cultural phenomena of the 1960s.

Richard Nixon had already established a cabinet-level body, the Environmental Quality Council, in May 1969. Now Congressional Democrats, led by senators Edmund Muskie of Maine and Henry Jackson of Washington, pushed through the National Environmental Policy Act of 1969. This historic law declared it to be national policy that the environment must be protected and restored. It established an independent agency, the Council on Environmental Quality, that was to provide research and guidance. Every federal agency was now required to think carefully before it did anything, by way of construction projects, to the environment. Furthermore, environmental-impact studies had to be conducted in advance: all possible adverse impacts were to be examined and reported, and proposed reasonable alternatives to be considered. Shortly

THE TURBULENT 1960s: THE FLOOD TIDE OF REFORM PEAKS AND FALLS BACK

Nixon secured establishment of an Environmental Protection Agency, which was to consolidate all antipollution programs, and called for action in regard to drinking-water standards, mass transit, land-use policies, the siting of federal power plants, the protection of coastal wetlands, and the preservation of endangered species.

Another new body, the National Oceanic and Atmospheric Agency, was to pull together all government research agencies in these two areas and concentrate scientific efforts to combat pollution. Meanwhile Congress, heeding environmentalists' arguments concerning massive air pollution (and economists' arguments concerning profitability), cut off all funds for the development of a supersonic transport plane, thus ending the project.

A major advance came in the passage of the Clean Air Act of 1970, which required the establishment of national emission standards for all "significant new pollution sources," including the automobile. In June 1971 the Environmental Protection Agency ordered stringent standards for the emission of hydrocarbons, carbon monoxide, and nitrogen oxides. If they had been fully implemented, they would have cut automobile pollutants by 90 percent by 1976. In response to the EPA's actions, the huge research programs that automobile manufacturers had already begun into types of engines that would reduce pollutants were accelerated.

At the same time, the EPA seized on a long ignored statute, the Refuse Act of 1899, that gave the federal government power to control all discharge of polluting substances into the nation's navigable watercourses. Scores of criminal actions were begun against polluters of navigable waterways in 1971, and injunctions were secured that halted discharges. Thus heartened, the state governments moved ahead on their own. California had long led the nation in its extensive program of research and public controls on air pollution. Now, in 1971, the state of Delaware enacted a law banning heavy industry along its entire coastline and severely controlled tanker-loading operations. In Maine an environmental commission began reviewing all developments involving twenty acres or more, and other states adopted strong regulations on pesticides, notably DDT. The phosphate content of detergents came under close public attention, for this material, washed into rivers and lakes, killed fish and plant life. New Jersey ordered that sewage sludge and industrial wastes not be discharged within 100 miles of its coastline, and other states moved to control the discharge of solid wastes. Everywhere environmentalists were able to take advantage of the provision in the National Environment Policy Act that required environmental-impact studies to be made before any federally funded project could be begun. States in which environmental concern was especially strong, such as California, enacted counterpart legislation to the National Environmental Policy Act (in California's case, the California Environmental Quality Act) so that henceforth environmental-impact studies of practically every proposed construction project—federal, state, or private—would have to be made.

In 1972 Congress enacted a massive program to clean up the nation's polluted waterways

The federal government in 1971 began reasserting its power to prevent pollution of waterways, typified here by the emptying of waste products from huge industrial processes into the Monongahela River, in West Virginia.
Bruce Davidson, © 1969 Magnum Photos

by 1985. President Nixon vetoed the bill on the ground of cost, but Congress overrode his veto (and Nixon immediately impounded the funds). Controls were also established over pesticides, and antinoise legislation aimed at all noise producers, especially airports, was enacted.

The Moon Landing

In July 1969 the twenty-four-billion-dollar space program achieved its most breathtaking success when astronaut Neil Armstrong descended to the moon from his *Apollo 11* spacecraft, saying "That's one small step for a man, one giant leap for mankind." The world was astonished by this incredible event (which, in later missions, quickly came to seem commonplace), and a jubilant President Nixon called Armstrong on the moon by telephone to communicate his congratulations. But this was a rare unifying event for Americans in this troubled year. There had already been a long, stinging fight in Congress over whether to continue spending on the antiballistic-missile system. The president had won a limited victory in March 1969, but there was a rising tendency to condemn a scale of national priorities that poured billions into fantastic weapons and a fruitless war while ignoring the country's domestic ills.

A More Conservative Supreme Court

The president had come to office a stern critic of the way in which the Supreme Court, under Earl Warren, had steadily broadened the rights of accused criminals. In May 1969 Warren retired, and the president promptly nominated Warren E. Burger, a law-and-order advocate, to replace him as chief justice. Burger received Senate confirmation the following month. Nixon was determined to place conservatives on the bench, and in May 1970 Harry A. Blackmun, a relatively conservative and thoroughly competent jurist from Minnesota, was approved as his next appointment. He quickly joined Chief Justice Burger in a decision limiting freedom of the press in obscenity matters. In 1971 the president was given the remarkable opportunity to change the whole character of the Court's outlook within one presidential term when John Marshall Harlan and Hugo

Black retired. Choosing Lewis Franklin Powell, Jr., a respected Virginia lawyer, and William H. Rehnquist, a young (forty-seven) and talented assistant United States attorney general, the president completed a group of four conservatives on the bench who would profoundly affect later decisions. The predictably liberal justices remaining in the Court were William J. Brennan, Jr., William O. Douglas (who resigned in 1975, to be replaced by John Paul Stevens of Chicago, a centrist), and Thurgood Marshall. Potter Stewart and Byron White were regarded as "swing men."

Nixon Turns Away from Environmentalism

From 1968 to 1971 the Nixon administration had taken the lead in reforming the country's governing system so that it would give public authority at all levels the power and the means to get control of the nation's economy and its social problems. The result of this effort to protect the environment, minister to distressed cities, manage growth, and address a population-growth phenomenon that seemed to spawn endless problems, however, was an instinctive distrust on the part of investors, developers, and entrepreneurs. They hated controls over what they were doing; they distrusted public inspection; they opposed limits on the freedom of individuals to develop their property as they saw fit; and they were irked by costly delays and modifications.

Nixon's veto of the 1972 water-pollution bill showed that he too was tiring of all this disturbing reformism. The activist surge of his early presidency was evaporating. The national-planning initiatives he had launched, the sweeping studies of American life that were being made, and the pollution-control mechanisms that had been established, all were producing results that traditional Republicans found highly bothersome. Therefore, after Daniel Moynihan left for a teaching post at Harvard University in 1970, controls upon growth were given little further publicity by the Nixon administration. The idea of trying to influence where people lived, or how many children they had, was increasingly out of favor. Liberal Democrats in Congress enacted the Coastal Zone Management Act in 1972, which empowered the states to protect such regions by close supervision over development, but Nixon allocated no funds in his 1974 budget for implementing the law. In 1972, as it watched Nixon's retreat from environmentalism, Congress created its own internal agency, the Office of Technology Assessment, and authorized it to monitor new developments in industry that were potentially dangerous to the environment.

The Nixon administration was concentrating now upon quite different matters: the re-election of the president in 1972, Nixon's forthcoming visits to China and the Soviet Union and the seemingly endless war in Vietnam. Indeed, the nation was haunted by that war, and by the national turmoil it induced. We shall now, therefore, turn our attention to the great issue that destroyed the Johnson presidency and wholly absorbed national attentions during the first Nixon term: the war in Vietnam.

Bibliography

Books which were especially valuable to me in writing this chapter: As before, James L. Sundquist's admirable early study, *Politics and Policy: The Eisenhower, Kennedy, and Johnson Years* (1968) was helpful, as was Hugh Sidey's *A Very Personal Presidency* (1968), and Eric Goldman's *The Tragedy of Lyndon Johnson** (1969). Theodore White continued his studies of the presidential elections in *The Making of the President, 1964** (1965) and *The Making of the President, 1972* (1972). Tom Wicker's *JFK and LBJ: The Influence of Personality Upon Politics** (1968) is a perceptive analysis by a leading Washington correspondent. The president's own views as given in his *The Vantage Point: Perspectives of the Presidency 1963–1969** (1971) is useful. A revealingly intimate portrait is in Doris Kearns's *Lyndon Johnson and the American Dream** (1976). A massive study by a leading member of the Kennedy and Johnson administrations is W. W. Rostow's *The Diffusion of Power 1957–1972* (1972).

The best analysis of Johnson's poverty program is contained in John C. Donovan's *The Politics of Poverty** (1967), an excellent book that explains why exposés of poverty continue to be written—for example, Robert Coles's *Still Hungry in America* (1969) and Kenneth Davis's *The Paradox of Poverty in America* (1969). Sar Levitan and Robert Taggart in *The Promise of Greatness* (1976) give us a retrospective look at the Great Society reforms which reveals their enduring accomplishments. Valuable also is James L. Sundquist, ed., *On Fighting Poverty: Perspectives from Experience* (1969). A harsh treatment of community action programs lies in Daniel P. Moynihan's *Maximum Feasible Misunderstanding: Community Action in the War on Poverty** (1970).

Concerning the black rebellion of the Johnson years, see books cited for the previous chapter. For a broad perspective upon youth uprisings, I benefited considerably from Lewis S. Feuer's *The Conflict of the Generations: The Character and Significance of Students Movements* (1969). Peter L. Berger and Richard John Neuhaus's *Movement and Revolution** (1970) was an eloquent statement from a sociologist and an activist Lutheran minister inside the movement. William L. O'Neill's *Coming Apart: An Informal History of America in the 1960s* (1971) skillfully evokes the mood; Hal Draper's *Berkeley: The New Student Revolt* (1965) probes the deeper meanings of the free-speech movement; and Robert Kahn's *The Battle of Morningside Heights* (1970) focuses on the Columbia University disruption. Essential to understanding the phenomena of the counterculture are: Kenneth Keniston's *The Uncommitted* (1965), which focuses on the bankruptcy of technological values; Theodore Roszak's *The Making of a Counter Culture** (1969), practically a classic of the movement; William Braden's *The Age of Aquarius* (1970); and another much-read work, Paul Goodman's *Growing Up Absurd: Problems of Youth in the Organized Society** (1960). Edgar Z. Friedenberg, a valuable observer of youth in these years, may be read in *Coming of Age in America: Growth and Acquiescence** (1967). Lewis Yablonsky is important on *The Hippie Trip** (1973), as is Irwin Unger in *A History of the New Left* (1974).

I found Peter Schrag's *The Decline of the WASP* (1971) and Michael Novak's *The Rise of the Unmeltable Ethnics: Politics and Culture in the Seventies* (1972) valuable in catching these shifts beginning in the 1960s. For other books on ethnicity in politics, see the books cited for the previous chapter, as well as Perry L. Weed, *The White Ethnic Movement and Ethnic Politics* (1973), and Stephen D. Isaacs, *Jews and American Politics* (1974). John H. Kessel, *The Goldwater Coalition: Republican Strategies in '64* (1968) is revealing on this score, as is Kirkpatrick Sale, *Power Shift:*

THE TURBULENT 1960s: THE FLOOD TIDE OF REFORM PEAKS AND FALLS BACK

The Rise of the Southern Rim and Its Challenge to the Eastern Establishment (1975), as well as a major work, Numan V. Bartley and Hugh D. Graham, *Southern Politics and the Second Reconstruction* (1975).

The fascinating Richard Nixon may be explored, first, in his *The Memoirs of Richard Nixon* (1978); in a forthcoming biography by Fawn Brodie; and in: Edwin P. Hoyt, *The Nixons: An American Family* (1972); Joe McGinnis, *The Selling of the President, 1968** (1969); Lewis Chester, Godfrey Hodgson, and Bruce Page, *An American Melodrama: The Presidential Campaign of 1968* (1969); Paul Hoffman, *The New Nixon* (1970);

Garry Wills, *Nixon Agonistes: The Crisis of the Self-Made Man* (1970). Daniel Moynihan has written a number of books springing from his experiences in the Nixon administration which provide inside views, as for example: *The Politics of a Guaranteed Income: The Nixon Administration and the Family Assistance Plan** (1973). Nixon's experiment with national planning, and his role in environmental protection, is closely examined in Otis L. Graham, Jr.'s brilliant book, *Toward a Planned Society: From Roosevelt to Nixon** (1976).

* Available in paperback.

37

TIME LINE

1954 France defeated at Dien Bien Phu; Geneva Conference divides Vietnam

1957 Rebellion under way in South Vietnam against Diem; Vietcong rise

1961 President Kennedy expands commitment to South Vietnam, sends in 16,000 advisers, and calls on Diem to democratize his regime

1963 Buddhists in South Vietnam rebel against Diem; Diem assassinated

1964 United States begins covert military operations against North Vietnam
Gulf of Tonkin incident

1965 President Johnson begins Operation Rolling Thunder, enormously escalates war, sends in ground troops; Johnson sends troops to Dominican Republic to quell revolt

1966 France withdraws from NATO; Johnson liberalizes travel rules and trade with U.S.S.R.; treaty with U.S.S.R. bans placing nuclear weapons in orbit; Johnson goes to Manila to help launch massive program of economic development in Southeast Asia; Senate ''doves'' criticize war; Nguyen Van Thieu elected president of South Vietnam

1967 American policy in South Vietnam condemned around world; Secretary of Defense Robert McNamara states bombing is useless; immense peace demonstrations in the United States

1968   Vietcong Tet offensive devastates South Vietnam, reflects failure of Johnson's policies; Johnson suffers national loss of faith in his leadership, forced to announce halt to escalation and bombing, withdraws from presidential race; negotiations for peace in Vietnam begin in Paris

1969   President Nixon adopts de-escalation and Vietnamization policies; Nixon and Henry Kissinger formulate balance-of-power foreign policy; Guam Doctrine announced

1970   Strategic Arms Limitation Talks with U.S.S.R. begin; Cambodian invasion

1972   North Vietnam makes massive conventional invasion of South Vietnam; United States revives aerial bombing; Thieu establishes dictatorship in South Vietnam; Nixon wins massive election victory over Democratic candidate, George McGovern; bombing attack on North Vietnam follows breakdown in negotiations; Nixon visits China and Russia

1973   Cease-fire in Vietnam; American forces withdraw; exchange of prisoners of war

THE END OF AMERICAN INNOCENCE: THE VIETNAM WAR

UPI

He became the star and strong man of the Kennedy administration: Robert Strange McNamara, Secretary of Defense. California-born and -reared, a graduate of the University of California, Berkeley, and Harvard, McNamara was a classic hard-working, austere, logical, bookish Presbyterian. He had been a brilliant management analyst and statistician in Air Force headquarters during the Second World War, and after many high-level years in the Ford Motor Company he had become its president. Now he was in the Pentagon again, not as a young lieutenant colonel but as top man.

McNamara and Kennedy were both convinced Cold Warriors. The Communist menace from Moscow must be held back at every point, they believed, or the world would go under. But the response must be flexible, imaginative, built around specially trained counterinsurgency forces who would foil the "wars of liberation" that Khrushchev called for from the Kremlin, while transforming threatened pro-West countries into societies built upon democracy and social justice. The war in Vietnam was soon called "McNamara's War," for the secretary believed firmly in its rightness and its absolute necessity. Being objective and unemotional; sticking to facts that can be measured, quantified, and analyzed statistically: this had made McNamara a legend at Ford, and he applied the same principles in his direction of the war. "Every quantitative measurement we have," he remarked confidently in early 1962, "shows we are winning this war." He would say, "If we can learn to *analyze* this thing, we'll solve it." Ultimately, McNamara seemed to be asserting, life is shaped by cool analytical minds that set emotion aside.

Optimism; determination; toughness; clear reason: these would do the trick. Sooner or later the North Vietnamese would realize that the United States of America meant business, they would look at their terrible losses, and—logically—they would make peace. Make the *cost* heavy enough, the trained economist and Harvard Business School graduate in him believed, and they would give in. But war, especially civil war, is not a logical affair. By focusing on the quantifiable, McNamara missed those very forces that matter the most in wartime: despair and lack of motivation on one side, and confidence and a passion to win, at *whatever* cost, on the other.

After 1965 McNamara grew inwardly edgy, worried, and doubtful, though outwardly ice-blooded. Close friends such as Robert Kennedy began condemning the war; thousands were in the streets, protesting. North Vietnam, he came to realize, would endlessly absorb bombing without being deflected from its cause. It was an impossible situation. Americans, he felt, should have got out in 1965, instead of escalating their military involvement. Disillusioned, a growing irritant to President Johnson, in late 1967 he was finally edged out of his post and given the presidency of the World Bank. Here he would labor until his retirement in 1980, pouring development funds into poor, backward nations and hoping by this means to give relief to the Third World, where formerly he had sent bombs, soldiers, and death.

Overview

The day before his inauguration in 1961, John Kennedy sat in the White House listening to Dwight Eisenhower talk worriedly about the Indochina situation. South Vietnam was on the verge of being overrun by a Communist-dominated insurgency, and in remote Laos the rightist government and left-wing forces were at war. In the conflict between communism and democracy Laos, Eisenhower said, was the key to all of Southeast Asia: if it went to the Communists, the other countries of that vast region would fall one by one like a string of dominoes. The United States, he remarked, might have to fight. From 1946 to 1954, America had poured billions of dollars into a French effort to put down Ho Chi Minh's Communist regime in North Vietnam. In 1954, the Geneva Convention had given the northern half of the Vietnam to the Communists. The United States, regarding this settlement as a disaster, pushed the French aside in South Vietnam and took over, buttressing its non-Communist government. Now that government was collapsing.

After his inauguration, President Kennedy secured the neutralization of Laos but felt impelled to pour major resources into South Vietnam in order to stave off a Communist takeover. In 1965, when a Communist victory was again very near, Lyndon Johnson decided to take America to war. He sent into South Vietnam what became a force of more than 500,000 American troops and began a bombing campaign against North Vietnam. In 1968, after three years of growing protest in the United States and the failure of his military tactics, Johnson was forced to recognize the limits of American military power and cease escalating the war.

In 1969, Richard Nixon became president of an American nation that was humbled at discovering that, like the ancient nations of Europe, it could be guilty of wrongfully using power. Nixon now changed the whole direction of American foreign policy. The new trend was toward withdrawal and a "low profile." While slowly pulling American combat troops out of Vietnam, Nixon drew back also from old commitments elsewhere. Then he startled the world by opening a Peking-Washington dialogue in 1971. In effect, the world order that had lasted since 1945 came to an end, and a new one was born. American military operations in Vietnam ceased in 1973.

Once ended, a war fades quickly from the national mind, unless it was fought within the country's own territory. While the fighting goes on the nation is wholly caught up in it, appalled and yet fascinated by the terrible events and persistently anxious about their outcome. When it is over, fascination is replaced by disinterest, especially if the conflict took place abroad. The American dead are remembered primarily by their family members; the foreign dead, and the devastation left in their countries, are hardly thought of at all.

Thus, the United States' war in Vietnam, though the longest conflict in American history, lasting from 1965 to 1973, left the American mind with almost startling swiftness once it was over. Perhaps it was speeded to this oblivion by the realization that it was in every way so doubtful an enterprise and in many ways so shameful in its execution. All that remained was a shuddering conviction that it had been a great mistake, not ever to be repeated. It was a war, however, that, perhaps above all others in the American past, should not be allowed to be so conveniently set aside and forgotten. It was a searing learning experience of the profoundest importance, paid for by the lives of many thousands of young Americans and many more thousands of Vietnamese. It is necessary to consider what happened, and to reflect upon it.

The Vietnamese Background

Vietnam is a country 1,200 miles long. Placed on the American West Coast, it would stretch from Los Angeles to Seattle; on the East Coast, from Boston to Florida. Curiously enough, Americans tended to think of Vietnam as a "small" country, to be easily blanketed by American military power. The Vietnamese population totaled some 38 million in 1970, divided almost equally between North and South.

Europeans first arrived in Vietnam in 1615, when a French Catholic mission made its appearance. The Catholic fathers had a profound cultural influence on the country, installing Catholicism as a flourishing religion (though Buddhism and other Asian religions outnumbered it), and putting the Vietnamese language into a Western-style alphabet. In 1885, Vietnam formally accepted French protectorate status. The Japanese occupied Vietnam during World War II, though allowing the French (now defeated by Hitler) to continue governing the country and maintain military forces there. In 1945 the Japanese informed Emperor Bao Dai, who had been the constitutional figurehead, that his country was independent. The emperor thereupon repudiated the old protectorate treaty of 1885, and French rule was legally ended. In August 1945 Ho Chi Minh, who for thirty years had worked to make his country independent, established a Communist-dominated government in Hanoi, the major city in the north, received the official imperial seal from Bao Dai, and established the Provisional Government of the Democratic Republic of Vietnam.

But the French were determined to recapture their former colony. Soon they helped non-Communist Vietnamese nationalists establish a separate government in the south, based in Saigon. Now the French and the North Vietnamese government both made a grave miscalculation: each side believed it was strong enough to defeat the other in a short war. But the fighting that broke out between them in late 1946 did not end for eight years. By this time the Cold War between the United States and the U.S.S.R. had begun, and the United States started giving its support to the French. Americans saw the conflict in Vietnam as a Communist–Free World struggle.

The French were doomed to failure. Indeed, Communist General Vo Nguyen Giap had already explained what would happen. No democratic society such as France or the United States, he insisted, could ever fight endlessly an indefinite, inconclusive war unless its own survival was at stake. In time, public opinion in the democracy would demand an end to the "useless bloodshed"; the legislative body would demand explanations for the astronomical expenditures; and the democracy's military leaders would desperately promise a quick end to the conflict. This would prove impossible, their credibility would be ruined, and eventually the political leaders would accept any kind of settlement in order to end an otherwise ceaseless guerrilla war. In May 1954 Ho Chi Minh's armies inflicted a catastrophic defeat on the French at Dien Bien Phu, and the war was over, for Giap was right: the people of France would no longer support a fruitless war. In the Geneva negotiations of July 1954, Vietnam was divided at the seventeenth parallel; the French

withdrew from Indochina, having suffered 172,000 needless casualties; and the American period of dominance in the South began.

The American Background

The American government took over as South Vietnam's protector in 1954 with little premonition of the tragedy that would follow. In fact, few people in the United States believed that America could *ever* suffer defeat. For generations, Americans had believed that theirs was such a good country, so pure and so right, that it could escape tragedy. Disasters, disappointments, irretrievable failure happened to other countries, they thought, not to America. The need to assist South Vietnam seemed obvious, and an inescapable duty. Through years of Cold War conditioning, Americans assumed that a breakthrough for the Communists anywhere in the world would directly and dangerously threaten the security of the United States and its allies. They believed that the world was a single, unified theatre of events in which everything troublesome was somehow instigated by Moscow. Their task was to repair the dike (by the policy of containment) wherever it was apparently beginning to leak. The possibility that turmoil and civil war might be a purely local event was not seriously considered, save by a tiny group of much-condemned critics.

After all, for many years the West had been fighting to save the world's smaller countries from being conquered by the large, expanding ones. Britain had gone to war in 1914 when the German imperial army invaded and overran Belgium; the invasion of Poland by Hitler's forces in 1939 began the Second World War; and the assault of North Korea upon South Korea had inaugurated a massive United Nations response, led by the United States. A long debate had gone on within the United States from the 1930s onward, in fact, to overcome America's longstanding isolationism and inspire it to take up its international responsibilities. As a result, the conviction that the United States was the Free World's policeman was deeply imbedded in the American mind. To oppose involvement in the Vietnam problem seemed to the nation's foreign policy leadership a deplorable falling backward into isolationism again, which would be irresponsible and an invitation to disaster.

THE END OF AMERICAN INNOCENCE: THE VIETNAM WAR

The conviction that America had an honorable if difficult mission to lead the fight against tyranny wherever it erupted in the world was both admirable and dangerous. It made Americans ready to sacrifice, suffer, and die in the cause of human liberty—tens of thousands of young Americans would go to Vietnam to fight, in the conviction that this was what they were doing—and at the same time it made them heedless and unquestioning. Year after year, American leaders warned that South Vietnam was the point-country "in a series of domino-countries," as Frances Fitzgerald writes in her Pulitzer Prizewinning book, *Fire in the Lake: The Vietnamese and the Americans in Vietnam* (1972), "that in their black-and-white uniformity stood in a row beginning at the Chinese border and ending at the foot of Southeast Asia." If South Vietnam fell, "then it was more than likely that Cambodia, Laos, Thailand, and Malaya (and then, successively, the Philippines, Indonesia, and Australia) would 'fall to the Communists' in their proper order." In addition, Americans believed that South Vietnam was a "small country," endangered by expanding Communist tyranny, which was thirsting to save its freedom. It had been America's duty in the world to save small countries from aggression. In reality, South Vietnam was but half of a country. The United States had blundered into a family feud.

American Confidence

The Second World War, the primary learning experience for all American political leaders from 1940, infused the American people with a soaring confidence that whatever they wanted to do, they could do. Such a notion was not new to them, for occupying a continent and building a great industrial system had long trained them to think in these terms. But the Second World War was such an enormous undertaking that American self-conceit mushroomed (ignoring the immensely important fact that most of Hitler's military might had been chewed up on the plains of the Soviet Union). A nation that could send tens of thousands of aircraft into the enemies' skies, cover the seas with ships, send huge armies of men into battles around the globe, and then top this incredible display by releasing the cosmic power of the atom could only believe that its capabilities were boundless. Assuming that it could "solve" the problem in Vietnam just as it was "solving" a multitude of conflicts elsewhere in the world, the American government entered a crucial stage in its self-education. It was to learn that there are indeed limits to its power. And it was also to learn the ancient lesson taught by Greek drama: no one escapes tragedy, for no one is innocent.

The Two Vietnams

The two Vietnams made a disturbing contrast after 1954. The northern regime had immense advantages. For years on end it had fought bravely to throw off the hated French colonial power, a heroic achievement that had won it the abiding trust and loyalty of its people. Spartan, simple, autocratic, blooded in a long patriotic war, the North Vietnamese government could call endlessly on its citizens for further sacrifice in the holy cause of throwing out the foreigner and unifying all of Vietnam. Leading the North was the venerable Ho Chi Minh, who in North Vietnamese eyes blended the roles of George Washington and Thomas Jefferson: father and chief philosopher of his country. In Hanoi he presided over a clean, quiet, and simple city and a government notably free of corruption. North Vietnam, in short, resembled a well-run military post, unified from top to bottom by strong morale and a belief in its cause.

The South, on the other hand, was confused, spiritless, filled with dissension, and without any sense of national purpose. Its government was run by non-Communist nationalists who for years had been upstaged by the Communists. The southern nationalists were elitists, representatives of traditional Vietnam with a French overlay. Whereas Ho Chi Minh wore a simple peasant outfit, the southern leaders appeared either in mandarin dress or in the snow-white business suits of the French colonial tradition. An upper-class regime through and through, the nationalist government based its power on the small urban population, looked down upon the farming people with contempt, and sided with the landlords. From the beginning, therefore, it was regarded with indifference by ordinary South Vietnamese.

American intelligence persistently warned Washington that the southern regime was unpopular. Ngo Dinh Diem, its president, was a devout and puritanical Roman Catholic who throughout his career as a Vietnamese nationalist had been just as anti-French as Ho Chi Minh. But he was "authoritarian, inflexible, and remote," the CIA observed, and quickly alienated practically everyone by his oppressive rule once he took office (with strong American support) in 1955. In 1956 he made the grave error of ending the ancient system by which villagers elected their own officials and began installing Saigon-appointed functionaries loyal to him. Since these were usually northern refugees and Catholics, they were detested by the villagers and served only to drive further a wedge between the government and the people. Diem's land reform program, much touted in the United States, actually returned to the landowners the property that Communist rebels had distributed to the peasants. The CIA, looking at the work of Diem's men in the countryside, remarked, "Their brutality, petty thievery and disorderliness induced innumerable villagers to join in open revolt against Diem."

Rebellion Begins in the South

When the Geneva Convention divided the country, there existed in the South a tiny Communist cadre of perhaps 5,000 to 10,000 men, whom Ho had instructed to work only peacefully for a changed regime in South Vietnam. They were to wait for the elections that were to be held in 1956, as provided in the Geneva agreement, which the Communists confidently expected to win. Diem, however, refused to hold the elections. Believing, too, that the Communists would win a nationwide election, Washington made no attempt to dissuade Diem from his decision (a policy which is reminiscent of the U.S.S.R.'s refusal to allow elections in Poland).

By 1957 the Communists in the South had decided to take up armed struggle, for peaceful measures appeared useless. Indeed, in that year anti-Diem pressure was building up all over South Vietnam, among non-Communist as well as Communist groups. Massive disaffection was widespread among politicians, intellectuals, military officers, the country people, journalists, government officials, and the Buddhist majority. In 1959 the Hanoi regime responded by authorizing armed struggle in the South and sending a few thousand ex-southerners over the border to help

out. The task of the Vietcong (as Diem labeled all insurrectionary forces composed of South Vietnamese) was to take over the villages. In 1959 the Vietcong felt strong enough to begin attacking large South Vietnamese Army units, and on July 8 of that year the first American died, victim of a terrorist bomb inside a military base in Bienhoa.

John Kennedy Considers Vietnam

When John Kennedy came to the White House, he was trapped by his own rhetoric. He had campaigned on the theme of "getting the country moving again," injecting "vigor" into its operations, and taking quick action to solve the world's problems. It was the Grand Design for Europe, the Alliance for Progress for Latin America. What would it be for Laos and Vietnam? A retreat? It was impossible for the president to contemplate such an action, sure to be thunderously condemned by the Republicans and many Democrats as timid appeasement. The John Kennedy who had written the book *Profiles in Courage* (1956) had to be bold in the face of the enemy or else look like a fool. Furthermore, he and his associates were confident men, proud of their intelligence and "toughness," who believed they could crush Communist uprisings in countries like Vietnam by the use of such counter-guerrilla forces as the army's Green Berets.

This confidence was undergirded by an unquestioned faith in the existing Washington foreign-policy elite. During twenty years of international leadership and the supervision of wide-flung global operations, the American government had built up a gifted corps of men whom the foreign-policy analyst Richard J. Barnet has termed national-security managers. Usually trained in law, engineering, or banking and employed by the State Department, the Pentagon, the National Security Council, or the CIA, these men thought of themselves as hardheaded problem solvers. Having come to power during the Second World War, they had formed the conviction that the basic problem in the world was military aggression, which occurred because of the existence of instability and weakness. Thus, America's fundamental task in the world was to build "situations of strength," which usually ment military as distinct from social strength. Control of the Third World of Africa, Asia, and

President Kennedy decided in 1961 to aid the non-communist regime in Laos. Here, in a televised press conference, he explains his reasons to the nation.

Cornell Capa © 1961, Magnum Photos

Latin America was the new Communist objective. Aggression in these areas, therefore, was to be countered with power. Dean Acheson, Harry Truman's secretary of state and still a major figure in Washington in the 1960s, symbolized in his elegant, brilliant self this breed of national-security managers. His followers were scattered through John Kennedy's government, among them Dean Rusk, secretary of state, Allen Dulles, director of the CIA, W. W. Rostow and McGeorge Bundy, advisers to the president, and Robert McNamara, secretary of defense. Together they formed a compact circle of men whose pride in themselves and in their considerable achievements over the previous twenty years gave them courage and confidence. These honorable and devoted men had also developed the habit of seeing world problems as abstractions, not as human tragedies. As *The Pentagon Papers* reveal, in the thousands of memos, studies, and analyses that these men wrote on the Vietnam problem there was an almost complete absence of soul-searching or moral questioning about their actions. Vietnam was thought of as a practical problem to be solved by well-trained people using statistics and immense physical resources.

Two disenchanted men occupying high positions in government councils during the Johnson and Nixon administrations, Anthony Lake and Roger

Morris, have given us a graphic picture of the atmosphere in which national-security problems were handled at that time. "We remember, more clearly than we care to, the well carpeted stillness and isolation of those government offices where some of the Pentagon Papers were first written. The efficient staccato of the typewriter, the antiseptic whiteness of nicely margined memoranda, the affable, authoritative and always urbane men who wrote them—all of it is a spiritual as well as geographic world apart from piles of decomposing bodies in a ditch outside Hue or a village bombed in Laos, the burn ward of a children's hospital in Saigon, or even a cemetery or veteran's hospital here. It was possible in that isolated atmosphere, and perhaps psychologically necessary, to dull one's awareness of the direct link between those memoranda and the human sufferings with which they were concerned.

"Reasonable, decent men around tables in those quiet, carpeted rooms simply cannot imply that the other fellow, who supports a 'tougher' policy, is a heartless murderer. Subordinates do not wish to tell superiors that they will be acting immorally if they choose the 'tougher' option. Policy—good, steady policy—is made by the 'tough-minded.' To talk of suffering is to lose 'effectiveness,' almost to lose one's grip." (*Foreign Policy* [Fall 1971])

These men gathered reports on the rapidly worsening situation in South Vietnam and warned President Kennedy that Ngo Dinh Diem was on the verge of collapse.

Kennedy Expands the Commitment

In 1961 President Kennedy concluded that the situation in South Vietnam was salvageable, and on this ground he decided to expand considerably America's commitment, though he was determined to keep it limited. He was convinced that in the last analysis, the Communist insurrection could be defeated only by the local people themselves. It was essential, therefore, that President Diem be pressured to make democratic reforms in order to build support among the people. Meanwhile, the American government would help Diem "build a nation" through massive programs of social and economic reform in the countryside. This would involve building schools, distributing land, providing pure water and good roads, fostering elections, and helping farmers apply modern agricultural techniques.

The few hundred American advisers then in

Vietnam were joined by 16,000 more, who worked with the South Vietnam Army and moved into the villages to encourage the formation of anti-guerrilla units. These measures constituted Kennedy's "shot in the arm" for South Vietnam; they were designed to spark a "real transformation" of its government and army. If this did not work, the joint chiefs of staff assured the president it would be necessary only to start bombing North Vietnam and that country would cave in and halt its guerrilla warfare. Thus was President Kennedy given advice that ranks, certainly, with that given King George III by Lord North when he informed his monarch that the American revolutionaries could be quickly put down. In both cases policy was formed on the basis of many years of success, on a habit of authority so bred into the nation that the prospect of its will being frustrated was hardly even considered. In both cases, too, the planners were blind to the power of a revolutionary independence movement supported by the mass of the population.

Optimism and Disaster: 1961–63

Meanwhile, in South Vietnam the Vietcong offensive against Diem's government went on. There were thousands of assassinations of village officials, terror bombings in the larger cities, bridges and roads destroyed, and immense destruction reaching to the gates of each provincial capital. Vast reaches of the South Vietnam countryside were abandoned to the Communists, and thousands of villages came under their control. Since the American generals in South Vietnam strongly supported President Diem and were anxious to prove that they could win, the mounting failure was covered up. Floods of encouraging statistics were sent off to Robert McNamara, the computer-oriented secretary of defense.

Then came crisis. To the world's horror, in June 1963 a Buddhist monk burned himself to death in protest against President Diem's oppressions—and the Diem regime simply scoffed. The American government pleaded with Diem to relent and allow the Buddhists civil and political rights, but his response was to begin attacking the pagodas where young Buddhists were gathering to turn out leaflets, run their radio stations, and demand equality. A strong distaste for Diem began to build up in the United States. In the fall

of 1963, President Kennedy broke relations with the Diem regime and gave tacit support to a plan for overthrowing Diem then brewing among South Vietnamese generals.

Robert Kennedy raised the question within the administration whether the time had come for the United States to get out of Vietnam. President Kennedy, pondering this issue, said in a television interview in September, "I don't think that unless a greater effort is made to win popular support that the war can be won out there. In the final analysis, it is their war. They are the ones who have to win it or lose it. We can help them,

THE VIETNAM WAR

THE END OF AMERICAN INNOCENCE: THE VIETNAM WAR

we can give them equipment, we can send our men out there as advisers, but they have to win it, the people of Vietnam, against the Communists." At the end of October 1963 the pressures in Saigon blew up. The generals gathered together, overthrew Diem, and captured him. While being taken to headquarters, he was shot and killed.

Lyndon Johnson Takes Over

Suddenly, John Kennedy was dead and Lyndon Johnson was president. Kennedy's death brought to the White House a man almost ten years older than Kennedy who had been reared in the simpler days of Franklin Roosevelt, when the issues were clearer and the distinctions sharper. Primarily concerned with domestic issues, Johnson was content with the older Cold War outlook that admired strong anti-Communists and condemned rebels who threatened to upset the Free World. He was not comfortable with Kennedy's warm treatment of reformist Third World politicians from Africa and Asia, and was genuinely worried about the Communists, often saying that their network in the United States was more powerful and effective than the public supposed. In 1961, after visiting Vietnam for Kennedy, Johnson told the president that the American government must "attempt to meet the challenge of Communist expansion now in Southeast Asia by a major effort . . . or . . . pull back [its] defenses to San Francisco and a 'Fortress America' concept. More important," he went on, "we would say to the world . . . that we don't live up to our treaties and don't stand by our friends. This is not my concept."

Lyndon Johnson was motivated also by grander visions. He dreamed of what life might be like for the poor people of the world if their rivers were dammed and prosperous farms spread where now there was the terror of alternating floods and droughts. Sitting on the porch of his ranch, he would rhapsodize about power lines running down the Mekong Valley; about new kinds of crops and the "green revolution" of hybrid rice strains; about clean villages, pure water, and an end to disease. Repeatedly he offered to North Vietnam the gift of immense funds to develop Indochinese TVAs, if they would but end the war. In 1966 he secured the establishment of the Asian Development Bank, headquartered in Manila, whose capital of one billion dollars was designed to underwrite such ventures.

Johnson's "Alamo" Syndrome

Johnson hated the thought of being a war leader. He distrusted the military, at first included no military men in his inner councils, and remarked that "all those generals want to do is bomb and spend." But more than this, he hated the thought that anyone would think him a coward. Observers often remarked on Johnson's "Alamo syndrome," his belief that one must fight to achieve objectives, be tough, be capable of staring an adversary down. In his oversimplified imagery, the Vietcong were wicked gunslingers who had to be put down, after which the simple good folk of the Vietnamese countryside could build abundant lives.

Within days of Kennedy's assassination, President Johnson issued a policy document that stated the goal he would pursue for the next three and a half years: assisting "the people and Government of [South Vietnam] to win their contest against the externally directed and supported Communist conspiracy." More and more he leaned toward the view that since things were going so badly in the South, the next step was to begin a program of gradually escalating pressure on the North. Meanwhile, in Saigon the Americans watched helplessly as a succession of military coups led by South Vietnamese generals paraded one unpopular government after another before the indifferent populace. The Vietcong grew bolder and more powerful, taking over ever larger portions of the countryside.

The Gulf of Tonkin Incident

On July 30, 1964, the American destroyer *Maddox* was approximately twenty miles off the North Vietnamese coast in the Gulf of Tonkin in waters claimed as territorial by North Vietnam. By electronic means it was gathering intelligence to support undercover operations, which included a raid on two North Vietnamese islands then being conducted by South Vietnamese units. Suddenly, three North Vietnamese torpedo boats closed in on the American ship. Brief gunfire ensued, primarily by the Maddox. A few nights later the

Maddox and another destroyer, the *Turner Joy*, mistakenly thought they were being subjected to torpedo attacks (this was later shown to have resulted from misreading of instruments). President Johnson immediately ordered a "reprisal" aerial attack on North Vietnam, using a list of targets already prepared and naval air squadrons that had long since been placed in position near North Vietnam. He went on national television to inform the country of his actions, and then placed before Congress an authorizing resolution (which had also been earlier prepared by his staff and held in readiness). It read:

Resolved by the Senate and the House of Representatives . . . in Congress assembled, that the Congress approve and support the determination of the President, as Commander in Chief, to take all necessary measures to repel any armed attack against the force of the United States *and to prevent further aggression* [emphasis added].

Some senators were worried about the last phrase: might it not be so interpreted, they asked, as to authorize an all-out war? Senator William Fulbright, chairman of the Senate Foreign Relations Committee, remarked, "There is nothing in the resolution, as I read it, that contemplates it. I agree with the Senator that it is the last thing we would want to do. However, the language of the resolution would not prevent it." Senator John Sherman Cooper of Kentucky pushed the matter further: "Are we giving the President advance authority to take whatever action he may deem necessary respecting South Vietnam and its defense?" Senator Fulbright replied, "I think that is correct." Clearly, however, such doubts could not prevent passage of the resolution. The country still trusted the president, and it had become increasingly angry at North Vietnam for "causing" the seemingly endless warfare in the South. The American public was outraged at the North Vietnamese for their "unprovoked" attack. (Not even Congress had been informed of provocative undercover operations the United States had been carrying on for months against North Vietnam.) Johnson's actions, indeed, were immensely popular in the country at large. His "approval" rating in the polls shot from 42 to 72 percent overnight. As always in the past, therefore, Congress swung behind the president and enacted the resolution. It was to be the *only* legal basis, thin as it

was, for everything the American government did thereafter in Indochina.

With the one-time aerial strike over, the president concentrated on his 1964 election campaign. Senator Barry Goldwater, his antagonist, advocated all-out attacks against North Vietnam and massive American involvement, including, perhaps, the use of atomic weapons. The frightened country and world were relieved to hear President Johnson say instead that the American role would remain a limited one, that he would not escalate the war, and that the conflict "is first and foremost a contest to be won by the government and the people of that country for themselves." He thus laid the basis for the subsequent national loss of faith in his honesty that helped destroy his administration.

Massive Aerial Bombing Begins

In February 1965 the Vietcong attacked American installations at Pleiku, killing seven men and wounding many more. The Pleiku attack immediately triggered long-prepared plans, and America's eight-year war in Vietnam suddenly began. Within hours Seventh Fleet aircraft were loosing bombs and rockets upon Dong Hoi, forty miles north of the seventeenth parallel. Operation Rolling Thunder, the systematic air war against

Carrying her belongings in a bundle, a South Vietnamese woman walks around the body of a slain man sprawled on the curb. Her village was one of the many hit by Vietcong terrorists.

United Press International, photo by Dana Stone

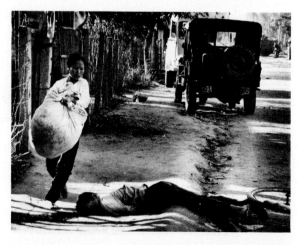

North Vietnam, was under way. Very quickly it was clear that CIA warnings were correct: bombing alone would not halt North Vietnamese support for the warfare in the South. Indeed, at no time did it appreciably reduce Hanoi's ability to send arms and troops southward, even when the ground war had vastly escalated and North Vietnam was maintaining almost 100,000 of its own regular troops in the South. In 1968 the United States dropped 1.2 million tons of bombs a year and flew 400,000 attack sorties (a sortie is one flight made by one aircraft), but with no significant effect on the war. Much of North Vietnam looked like the surface of the moon; tens of thousands of civilians were killed and wounded; and still the North Vietnamese fought on. They developed extremely effective antiaircraft fire. The United States had lost about 3,000 aircraft by 1968. Meanwhile the world had come to look on the United States as it used to look on Nazi Germany: as a nation led by a government of war criminals.

Johnson Sends in Ground Troops

Within two months after beginning Operation Rolling Thunder, President Johnson realized that bombing alone would not win the war. On April 1, 1965, he decided to use American ground troops. The nation-building program begun by the Kennedy administration, which involved working with the villages and stressed the need to avoid the massive destructiveness of all-out conventional military operations, now had few supporters in the government. Lyndon Johnson was faced with the inevitable collapse of the South Vietnamese government; he was determined not to become "the first American president to lose a war"; and he was being advised practically unanimously by his top aides to get American troops in action against the Vietcong. It seemed politically disastrous to do anything less. The American public was in no way prepared to accept defeat.

So, President Johnson vastly changed the character of America's involvement in the war by inundating Vietnam with American troops (from 21,000 at the beginning of 1965 to over 550,000 in 1968), aircraft, immense military installations, and money (by 1969, total expenditures on the Vietnam War exceeded $100 billion). But from the beginning he insisted that this momentous change in policy be kept secret from the public. Troops were to be introduced piecemeal, and with as little public notice as possible. It was all to be made to appear as if it flowed inevitably from decisions made by Eisenhower and Kennedy.

At the same time, by heavy diplomatic pressure the United States had gotten several of its Southeast Asia Treaty Organization (SEATO) allies to send troops. Soldiers came from South Korea, Australia, and Thailand (and a few from New Zealand and the Philippines), totaling 65,000 men. In addition, in 1968 there were almost 800,000 regular South Vietnamese troops under arms, joined by about 180,000 local militia. On the other side there were 35,000 Vietcong (organized units of South Vietnamese), 95,000 North Vietnamese regular troops, and about 100,000 Communist guerrillas in the fighting. The war had become a monstrously swollen holocaust.

"Search-and-Destroy" Tactics

President Johnson put General William C. Westmoreland in command and gave him complete freedom of action. Westmoreland depended on "search-and-destroy" tactics, sending his immense forces ranging about South Vietnam seeking out Vietcong and North Vietnamese units. He was committed to the "body-count" thesis, holding that the Communists could be defeated by killing so many of them that Hanoi would buckle under the pressure. He even stationed American units in exposed locations, hoping for an attack and relying on helicopters and rapid reinforcement to win the battles that resulted. The butchery was sickening: the Communists lost tens of thousands of men, and American losses skyrocketed.

No matter: the North Vietnamese and the Vietcong continued fighting. Having sent relatively few men southward before 1964, Hanoi now simply matched every increase of American troops with more of its own. General Giap commanded the North Vietnamese forces, as he had against the French, and he still relied confidently on his thesis that the domestic pressures within a democratic country faced by a limitless war would eventually force the United States to pull out. The Pentagon, meanwhile, constantly claimed that victory was just around the corner (as had British military leaders during the American Revolution).

The South Vietnamese countryside was devastated. "Nation building" came to an end. American troops bombed and shelled villages at will, on the ground that they contained Vietcong. Vast areas were defoliated by the spraying of plant-killing chemicals so as to uncover jungle trails or deny food to the rebels. Thousands of civilians were killed. By October 1967 almost a million civilians had fled to the cities, thus gigantically enlarging South Vietnam's already grave urban problems. The military now completely dominated all policy arguments.

Johnson and the World

The president was absorbed by Vietnam, but he also had the rest of the world to think about. In April 1965 a revolt erupted in the Dominican Republic. The president had already decided that any chief executive who allowed the appearance of another Communist regime in the Caribbean would be impeached. Worried that the Dominican rebels might be Communist-led, he immediately responded—without the formality of consulting with the Organization of American States or even securing congressional authorization—by sending in the incredible total of 22,000 troops. They remained until 1966, when a man acceptable to the United States was elected to the presidency. This brief intervention was praised in the United States but widely condemned in Latin America. In one swift action Lyndon Johnson had demonstrated how weak was the United States' commitment to its pledges of nonintervention and to the use of the multilateral machinery of the Organization of American States.

President Johnson was too gigantic a personality to get along with France's president, the majestic, anti-American Charles de Gaulle, and relations with him soon deteriorated. In March 1966, de Gaulle capped his drive to break continental Europe away from what he called "Anglo-Saxon dominance" by taking France out of NATO. This action, which required a massive rearrangement of the United States military network in Europe, symbolized the steady drawing

apart of the transatlantic community, a trend that would be capped during Richard Nixon's presidency by Great Britain's entrance into the Common Market.

Johnson's real concern in Europe, however, was with Soviet Russia. In 1966 he began seeking better relations with Russia and eastern Europe by greatly easing trade, liberalizing travel regulations for Americans, and allowing the Export-Import Bank to make loans to eastern European countries in support of trade. Direct air service between Moscow and the United States was established in November 1966. In December of that year a treaty was agreed to that prohibited the placing of nuclear arms or other such weapons in orbit around the earth.

Antiwar Protests

Antiwar protests began as soon as American forces began fighting in Vietnam. Thousands of students attended the first "teach-in," held at the University of Michigan in late March 1965, and the idea swiftly spread across the country, culminating in a two-day gathering at the University of California at Berkeley. Stung, the administration announced publicly that it was ready for "unconditional discussions" with North Vietnam—but adamantly refused to admit the National Liberation Front, the Vietcong's official leadership, to the deliberations.

Protests continued. Peace marches, much condemned by the general public, which was still strongly behind the war, occurred in late 1965 in Oakland, California, only to be attacked by the police. A Quaker, Norman Morrison, burned himself to death on the steps of the Pentagon. Other protestors began burning their draft cards, despite the passage of a federal law threatening five years in prison and heavy fines for doing so.

As 1966 opened, prominent senators, among them William Fulbright of Arkansas, began to be called "doves" for lending their voices to the criticism. In January, Fulbright's Foreign Relations Committee began holding televised hearings on Vietnam. These provided a platform on which Secretary of State Dean Rusk, an unbending "hawk," could be grilled. The nation heard such eminent foreign-policy analysts as the venerable

George Kennan, author under President Truman of the containment policy, state that Vietnam was of little importance to America's security. Now the antiwar movement could no longer be stigmatized as a bunch of radicals and "peacenik" hippies. Stung by the widespread accusation that the president had gone far beyond his powers in launching a full-scale war, the Johnson administration actually claimed that in the shrunken condition of the modern world an attack on any country anywhere by anyone could be a direct threat to the United States, and that therefore, under the Constitution, the president had the power to wage "defensive" war anywhere in the world without congressional consent. According to this astonishing theory, there were literally no bounds to the president's war-making powers. The "imperial presidency," as Arthur M. Schlesinger, Jr., has termed it (in his 1973 book so named) was being boldly proclaimed.

In April 1966 Senator Fulbright spoke at Johns Hopkins University on what he called the arrogance of power: "The causes of the malady are a mystery but its recurrence is one of the uniformities of history: Power tends to confuse itself with virtue and a great nation is peculiarly susceptible to the idea that its power is a sign of God's favor, conferring upon it a special responsibility for other nations—to make them richer and happier and wiser, to remake them, that is, in its own shining image.

"Power also tends to take itself for omnipotence. Once imbued with the idea of a mission, a great nation easily assumes that it has the means as well as the duty to do God's work. The Lord, after all, surely would not choose you as His agent and then deny you the sword with which to work his will. German soldiers in the First World War wore belt buckles imprinted with the words 'Gott mit uns' ["God is with us"]. It was approximately under this kind of infatuation—an exaggerated sense of power and an imaginary sense of mission—that the Athenians attacked Syracuse and Napoleon and then Hitler invaded Russia. In plain words, they overextended their commitments and they came to grief.

"My question is whether America can overcome the fatal arrogance of power. . . . Gradually but unmistakably we are succumbing to [it]. In so doing we are not living up to our capacity and promise; the measure of our falling short is the measure of the patriot's duty of dissent. . . . There is a kind of voodoo about American foreign policy. Certain drums have to be beaten regularly to ward off evil spirits. . . . For example, we will never go back on a commitment no matter how unwise; we regard this

alliance or that as absolutely 'vital' to the free world. . . . I see it as a mark of strength and maturity that an articulate minority have raised their voices against the Vietnamese war. . . ."

In Saigon, meanwhile, there was a merry-go-round of new governments and the reek of corruption. Premier Nguyen Cao Ky, a flashy former fighter pilot, was the dominant figure in 1966, but after the election of a constituent assembly in late 1966 and the adoption by popular vote of the constitution that body formulated, Nguyen Van Thieu emerged dominant. Another former general, he proved amazingly durable as president of South Vietnam, holding that post until North Vietnam's victory, at which point he fled from his country.

Unrestrained Bombing

In 1967, the total number of American casualties passed 100,000 men. Jonathan Schell, a *New Yorker* reporter, observed that "we are destroying, seemingly by inadvertence, the very country we are supposedly protecting." American airplanes bombed villages apparently on the whim of their FAC (forward air controller). A helicopter pilot explained on American television that he had fired on a building simply because he saw footprints heading into it that showed the person making them had been running. Canadian television films showed American pilots cheering as if at a sporting event when they blew up structures whose occupancy could only be guessed at. Henry Cabot Lodge, America's ambassador to Saigon, said, "I expect . . . the war to achieve very sensational results in 1967." Instead, North Vietnam's fighting forces in the South swelled enormously, and American commanders called anxiously for more men. At home, Secretary of Defense Robert McNamara, revolted by the war he was running, fretted for months in silence. In August 1967 he could restrain himself no longer. He publicly informed a Senate committee that the bombing campaign was totally useless. (Within three months he had left his post, at Johnson's request, to become president of the World Bank.)

In April 1967, 125,000 people marched for peace in New York City and 30,000 more did the

American wounded in a military encampment in the Vietnam jungles, which displays the conditions in which much of the fighting took place.

same in San Francisco. Martin Luther King openly condemned the United States as "the greatest purveyor of violence in the world today." Thousands of young men refused to accept induction into the services as draftees, or fled to Canada. In the summer of 1967 thousands more went into the streets to march in protest, surround induction centers, and clamor before war industries. In October a mass of perhaps 70,000 demonstrators picketed the Pentagon and clashed with its guards.

The Beginning of the End

In late 1967 the administration was still pushing the war at full throttle and claiming victory. Nevertheless, debate over the Vietnam War raged on in the public press, on television, and in political life. A Gallup poll in November 1967 showed that 57 percent of the American public disapproved of the president's handling of the war; only 28 percent approved. The Senate seemed to be turning more dovish each day, and even within the bank-

ing and business community important figures began privately communicating their alarm to the president. Everywhere rose a clamor that he end the bombing, for Hanoi had promised that in that event the Communists would be willing to open peace negotiations. *The Saturday Evening Post*, long the voice of WASP America, said, "The war in Vietnam is Johnson's mistake, and through the power of his office, he has made it a national mistake." It was widely pointed out that the enemy forces in South Vietnam were now four times larger than when the bombing and ground fighting began, having reached more than a quarter of a million men.

Then, on January 31, 1968, during the Tet (lunar-new-year) holidays in Vietnam, the Vietcong launched an immense nationwide offensive. They penetrated Saigon, devastating large areas of the city, captured (for a number of weeks) the old imperial capital of Hue, occupied many major towns, drove the South Vietnamese forces out of huge areas of countryside that they had slowly retaken, and killed thousands of Americans and South Vietnamese. Though suffering terrible

796

losses themselves—perhaps 60,000 men—the Communists had demonstrated that even after almost three years of search-and-destroy campaigns they had more power than ever to wreak enormous damage against the South Vietnam regime. The Tet offensive, in short, was a massive political defeat for the United States. It was now clear to all but the most hardheaded hawks that optimism was foolish. Even the *Wall Street Journal* observed in February 1968, "We think the American people should be getting ready to accept, if they haven't already, the prospect that the whole Vietnam effort may be doomed, that it may be falling apart beneath our feet." The last thin shreds of the president's credibility in the country were wearing away.

Days of Crisis

Johnson's war had reached its days of crisis. After the Tet offensive the president asked General Westmoreland what more he needed in Vietnam to win the war. He received a stunning reply: 206,000 more men (in addition to the 500,000 already there). Including the necessary support troops in the United States, this would mean a total of 450,000 more men on active duty. Such an enormous call-up would massively disrupt every aspect of the nation's economic and social life. A shock wave ran through the government, setting off an immediate and drastic reappraisal of the entire Vietnam War policy. In March 1968 the Pentagon, the State Department, and the White House hummed with meetings. The new secretary of defense, Clark Clifford—for many years a powerful figure in Washington and a frequent aide to presidents—instructed his staff to work up fresh analyses of the Vietnam situation. Dean Rusk, W. W. Rostow, and the joint chiefs of staff continued to insist that no change in policy should be made, but a torrent of powerful criticisms poured in from high-ranking civilian officials throughout the government. Secretary Clifford, formerly a hawk, began to turn against the bombing and the unlimited ground war. He could see a fantastic national furor coming when the country learned of Westmoreland's request. *The New York Times* broke the story thereafter, the public was indeed horrified, and new waves of protest erupted.

Then came language that Lyndon Johnson, supreme politician, could understand: Senator Eugene McCarthy of Minnesota, who had been running a lonely race against him in the New Hampshire presidential primary on an anti–Vietnam War platform, swept astonishingly close to victory in the balloting. The president was shocked. When Senator Robert Kennedy entered the presidential race too, enormous crowds turned out to hear his attacks on the war and the polls quickly showed him leading the president. Once more Senator Fulbright began public hearings, skewering Dean Rusk for two full days in the glare of television lights.

Advisers Recommend De-escalation

At this point President Johnson turned to Dean Acheson, the very symbol of the hard-lining Cold Warriors. Always a hawk on Vietnam, a brilliant and gifted public figure, he was held in high regard by the president. Acheson stunned Johnson by telling him that the joint chiefs of staff did not know what they were talking about and were making a fool of the president. No one believed Lyndon Johnson anymore, he said; the war was a failure and could not be won. Johnson reacted almost hysterically by rushing off to the Midwest and, in a widely reported address, publicly appealing for "a total national effort to win the war, win the peace, and complete the job that must be done here at home. Make no mistake about it . . . we are going to win." Once more he called up the image of the Alamo—but as someone remarked, this was an ill-chosen example, for everyone there had died.

The end, indeed, was near. Clark Clifford persuaded the president to convene a meeting of the Senior Advisory Group on Vietnam, a body of distinguished former public servants, many of them men who had helped run the Cold War for twenty years. Every six months it gathered at the White House to counsel with the president on Vietnam. Among its members were Dean Acheson, McGeorge Bundy, Henry Cabot Lodge, General Omar Bradley from the Second World War, General Matthew Ridgway from the Korean War, John J. McCloy, head of the American occupation of Germany, and Cyrus Vance, veteran high government official. After two days of intensive discussions in the White House, the group gave its verdict: military victory was impossible without a total war on the scale of World War II, which the American people would not accept. The president, they said, must make a major change in policy. Johnson was visibly shaken by the news. The men who had all along given him close support were turning against him. The only world that he really knew and understood, that of the ruling elite in the national capital, had told him that the war was hopeless. All those young men had died in pursuit of an impossible objective—and he, who had hoped to be one of America's greatest and most-loved presidents, had become one of its most despised and unsuccessful. The national tragedy had become his own.

On the evening of March 31, 1968, the president revealed his decision to the nation: "Tonight I am taking the first step to de-escalate the conflict. We are reducing . . . the present level of hostilities . . . unilaterally and at once." He went on to say that all aerial bombing attacks north of the twentieth parallel (that is, over some 90 percent of North Vietnam) would be halted. (Just before the November elections the president extended this ban to include the whole of the country.) Johnson asked President Ho Chi Minh to "respond positively and favorably" to his action—that is, to come to the conference table. Then he issued his last bombshell: "I shall not seek, and I will not accept the nomination of my party for another term as your President." Nine months later, Johnson came to the end of his term and left the presidency. With him went, perhaps forever, the notion that there are no limits to what the United States can do. Gone, too, was the myth in which Americans had for so long confidently believed: that whatever their nation did in the world was morally good and proper. The Vietnam War was the true end of American innocence.

The Nixon Revolution

When Richard Nixon took office in January 1969, he profoundly changed American foreign policy. The new theme was withdrawal. Not only in Vietnam but around the world as well. The president pulled back from the old system of rigid and interlocked commitments, shook himself free of entanglements that had existed since the early days of the Cold War, and veered off in new directions almost as if he were a broken-field running back in his favorite game of football. His performance startled a world grown used to living within the crystallized patterns left behind by the Cold War, and it caused seismic tremors of mingled alarm and applause around the globe.

Nixon's performance fell true to type in that these were traditionally Republican tactics. He simply revived the kind of nationalist, unilateral, "going-it-alone" foreign policy his party had always preferred. And he did it with great care and forethought. Few men in American politics knew more about foreign policy than he, had greater experience in international relations, or were as fascinated by foreign affairs. During his long daily periods of seclusion and reflection he and Dr. Henry Kissinger, his foreign-affairs adviser and executive secretary of the National Security Council, discussed the nation's foreign policy, often for hours on end.

The fascinating Dr. Kissinger, who soon became a giant figure in world politics, was a German Jew whose family had fled from Hitler. He was a brilliant Harvard professor and a Republican intellectual of high stature. For years he had been urging presidents to be flexible in the conduct of American foreign relations. Kissinger admired Otto von Bismarck, towering German leader in the nineteenth century, who had helped keep Europe at peace for many years by skillfully shifting around Germany's alignments (and the weight of its powerful armies) in order to keep a balance of power in the world. In contrast with advocates of the William Gladstone–Woodrow Wilson tradition (whom he regarded as utopian idealists), Kissinger had no faith that some form of international government such as the United Nations, would ever be able to provide a stable world order. Instead, like Bismarck and Theodore Roosevelt, Kissinger believed in balance-of-power diplomacy. Since international tensions would never disappear, the proper role for a big power was to stay well armed and keep itself free to move quickly and easily about in the constant flux of world politics—in other words, to speak softly and carry a big stick. The "enemy" in such a system was soon likely to become a "friend," so the Nixon administration no longer talked loudly of the "Free World against totalitarian communism." Indeed, Nixon and Kissinger no longer conceived of the world as bipolar—divided be-

THE END OF AMERICAN INNOCENCE: THE VIETNAM WAR

tween the Free World and the Communist bloc—but as pentagonal, with Europe, the United States, Japan, Russia, and China standing each other off in an equilibrium of power maintained by the skillful movements of Washington, D.C. The Nixon administration did not feel itself irrevocably tied to any former relationship, whether friendly or hostile.

Every nation, according to the Nixon-Kissinger foreign policy, was to be watched carefully, particularly the powerful ones. Caution, a watchful distrust, an avoidance of any kind of deal that might weaken the United States' relative military and economic position—these were the hallmarks of the Nixon-Kissinger negotiating style. Thus, when at the outset of the Nixon administration the Soviets proposed talks on limiting the number of missiles that each nation possessed, Nixon remained unresponsive for many months while building a strong position. He authorized the start of a modified antiballistic-missile system (leading to opposition in Congress) and the development of a frightening weapon, the MIRV (multiple independently targeted reentry vehicle), a kind of missile shotgun in which one rocket would carry many warheads that, at a certain point in flight, would head toward different targets. With these steps Nixon was ready to begin the Strategic Arms Limitation Talks (SALT) with Russia, which eventually produced encouraging but limited results.

Withdrawal From Vietnam

Dr. Kissinger came to his post convinced that the war in Vietnam was a *civil* war: it was not part of a worldwide Communist offensive. The United States should therefore *slowly* withdraw its forces while pouring huge funds into the South Vietnamese army to equip it to fight its own war. This "Vietnamization" policy was announced by the president in June 1969. The fighting died down, and American draft calls were greatly reduced. (A lottery was established in November 1969, and the draft, along with the rest of the Selective Service system, was shut down in 1974. In 1980, in response to the Soviet invasion of Afghanistan, President Carter would reinstitute registration for the draft.) American battle deaths began dropping: to 8,250 in 1969, under 5,000 in 1970, and well under 2,000 in 1971, during which year troop

strength in Vietnam fell under 200,000. In April 1971 the president announced that "American involvement in this war is coming to an end."

The last major burst of American ground fighting took place in April 1970 with a huge invasion of Cambodian territory. The stated objective of this assault was to clear out Communist "sanctuaries" in that country, where massed supplies and large bodies of troops seemed prepared for a renewed campaign against South Vietnam. This action produced the last and most violent of all the campus protest movements in the United States, and rightly so, for Nixon's constitutional authority to invade a neutral bordering state was wholly lacking. Wrapping himself in the mantle of commander in chief, Nixon claimed unlimited powers never advanced by presidents before the 1960s (indeed, specifically rejected by them). Like his predecessor, Nixon had broken loose from all traditional constitutional restraints governing his war-making authority. By the end of June 1970, all American and South Vietnamese troops had been withdrawn from Cambodia, their objectives apparently achieved, though critics worldwide scoffed at this assertion.

Global Withdrawal

American withdrawal continued around the world. As President Nixon said in February 1970 in a formal statement of policy, the United States could not and would not "conceive *all* the plans, design *all* the programs, execute *all* the decisions and undertake *all* the defense of the free nations of the world." He waited for many months after his inauguration to make even a formal statement concerning Latin America, and rarely paid that part of the world much attention. In October 1969 he clearly intimated that the Alliance for Progress was a thing of the past, stating that a "more mature" relationship was needed between the United States and Latin America in which that region's social and economic progress would have to depend largely on its own efforts. As in prior Republican regimes, American business would be relied on to provide the kind of influence that, it was believed, helped the most.

In July 1969, while stopping at Guam on a journey to Southeast Asia, the president stated, in what was quickly called his Guam Doctrine, that there was a need for "Asian solutions to

Asian problems." The free Asian countries would need henceforth to take care of themselves more than they had in the past. The United States intended to maintain forces at key bases, but it would keep an altogether low profile.

The Year of Surprises: 1971

President Nixon began 1971 with a long message to Congress in which he analyzed the state of the world, remarking that "the postwar order of international relations—the configuration of power that emerged from the Second World War—is gone. With it are gone the conditions which have determined the assumptions and practice of United States foreign policy since 1945." The American people, the president observed, were "at the end of an era" in their relations with the other countries of the world.

As if to fulfill his own prophecy, Richard Nixon did indeed fill the year with surprising realignments, so fundamental in character as to change the nature of the world community. Most dramatic, he ended the long quarantine of China, opened the Peking door, and walked in to begin a new era. No development in world affairs was more startling or ironic. Here was an American president who had for years built his career on an almost fanatical anticommunism. In 1950 he had blamed treason in the State Department for the Communist victory in China; had afterward given his support to Senator Joseph McCarthy's carnival of hate and character assassination, which purged the State Department of practically all its trained experts in Far Eastern affairs; and had even talked of dropping atom bombs on Hanoi to halt the outward spread of an allegedly expansionist China. But in his years out of power, Nixon seemed to rethink his ideas and to conclude that it was absurd and dangerous for America, the world's most powerful nation, and China, its most populous one, not to be even on speaking terms. If he ever became president, he once observed, his greatest goal would be to begin a Chinese-American dialogue.

During the first two years of his presidency he gave the Chinese many public and private hints of his intentions. Then, in July 1971, Henry Kissinger suddenly disappeared while on a visit to Pakistan, only to reemerge after a secret trip to Peking with the astonishing news that he had arranged for President Nixon to visit China in February 1972 for general, wide-ranging discussions of all mutual affairs.

Crisis of the Dollar

In August 1971 came a crisis of the American dollar: world traders lost confidence in the sick United States economy and began swiftly exchanging American currency for gold. It was hardly coincidental that Nixon, a Republican president, responded by in effect raising an American tariff against all foreign goods (installing a temporary surcharge of 10 percent) and taking the American dollar off the international gold standard, making its exchange rate with other currencies subject to the American government's own *national* control. It was clearly an age of dying internationalism. The American people, worried about their swiftly rising trade deficit, warmly praised the president, but abroad there was consternation. Euphoria swept the American stock market, but gloom struck America's trading partners, such as Japan, whose overseas sales were hurt by these unilateral actions.

In Europe, Anatole Shub, an American correspondent, wrote that since the mid 1960s, "European leaders have become increasingly dubious about the capacity of the United States either to govern itself or to protect its allies abroad. They have been disturbed by U.S. conduct of the Vietnam war. They are worried by an apparent revival of American isolationism and economic protectionism. They feel threatened by the seemingly insatiable appetites of U.S.-dominated multi-national corporations. . . . Just a decade ago, European leaders envisioned an 'Atlantic Community.' . . . Nowadays the fashionable talk is all about greater European unity. . . . The more the U.S. draws back and turns inward, disregarding European interests, the more the Europeans will be drawn together. . . ." (*Harper's Magazine* [January 1972])

The non-Communist nations of the world had no choice but to submit, and in December 1971 the American dollar was officially devalued (making American goods cheaper abroad, and those of foreign countries more expensive to United States residents) and the gold standard for international commerce was permanently ended. Henceforth, the value of each nation's currency would be established by periodic negotiations between national governments, not set by a free international system of market exchange.

Nixon and Vietnam

By 1971 President Nixon had largely neutralized Vietnam as a political issue. The negotiations begun in Paris in late 1968 ground on without result, for the Communists demanded as a basic condition that all American troops be withdrawn immediately and the government of President Thieu be ended, which the Nixon administration refused to accept. But the continued removal of American troops and the absence of any major battles in South Vietnam drained away the sense of urgency—as did the fact that, because of the draft-lottery system, most American young men no longer had to fear being sent to Vietnam to fight in a hated war. The South Vietnamese army was now in charge of its own war.

Save from the air. United States warplanes had continued thousands of sorties a year to support ground operations. In November 1970 a brief, heavy aerial attack was made on North Vietnam "in response to attacks on our unarmed reconnaissance aircraft" over that country; in December 1971 there was another bombing attack, designed to punish the North Vietnamese for building up large supplies of war matériel north of the seventeenth parallel. In January 1971 Congress had tried to halt the fighting by repealing the Tonkin Gulf Resolution and thereby stripping away the only legal justification for American military operations in Vietnam, but Nixon had brushed aside the action as "without binding force or effect." As commander in chief, he insisted, he had the right to do anything he thought necessary to protect the lives of the American troops already in Vietnam.

A New World Order Takes Form

In the late months of 1971 the shape of the new world order emerged. Only the early years of the Cold War could match this startling year in the magnitude of transformations. Communist China was clearly moving swiftly back into the world community. In October Great Britain ended years of agonized debate by deciding to enter the Common Market, thus opting for inclusion in the "New Europe" and leaving behind its "special relationship" with the United States. In the same year, Great Britain withdrew the last of its troops from Asia; the Asians were indeed being placed on their own. Furthermore, the Soviets, alarmed over the growing friendship between China and the United States and anxious to reduce tension on its western borders, finally came to a formal agreement with West Germany over Berlin, placing the former garrison city on a normalized relationship with the rest of Europe and guaranteeing open access and travel to both east and west.

An English observer, Henry Brandon, wrote of the United States in 1972: "The new generation of Americans is coming to power with a different experience and different outlook [from those of the Cold War generation]. It is hardly aware of the Communist coup in Czechoslovakia in 1947; it has no memory of the Berlin blockade, the invasion of Korea, or the suppression of Hungary. Uppermost in its mind is the catastrophe of Vietnam. The poison from that war will circulate in the American body and the American conscience for some time to come; the war's character and conduct are bound to remain part of the American experience and may leave an imprint as lasting as that of the Civil War. To this new generation it is damning evidence that the far-flung responsibilities of the United States have been executed in a reckless manner, that the limitations of American power have not been correctly assessed, and that American domestic needs have been badly neglected. The aim of this new generation will be to change the priorities of the past. Between those who do not understand the game of world power politics and those who exaggerate the need for overkill capacity, a great political struggle is developing in the seventies. There are many eloquent spokesmen among this new generation for the urgent American domestic needs, but for internationalism there are as yet none who can command the respect of this generation as well as of Congress." (*The Atlantic Monthly* [January 1973])

Richard Nixon's Year of Triumph: 1972

The year 1972 was one of mounting triumph for the president. Inflation slowed as a price-and-wage-control mechanism took hold, the national economy entered a slowly gathering boom that extended well through election day, and the president's political fortunes rose accordingly.

At the same time, a series of dramatic achievements in foreign affairs sent Nixon's prestige soaring, mainly because it appeared he was successfully disengaging the United States from the war in Vietnam and at the same time ending world tensions by bold gestures toward friendship with China and Russia. In February the president made his historic journey to China. The world was treated to a flood of stunning photographs showing Nixon striding along the Chinese Wall and exchanging pleasantries with the Communists. Furthermore, in a milestone event that shocked Taiwan, President Nixon began to phase out America's protection of the Nationalist Chinese regime on that island. The United States would no longer interfere in relations between the Peking government and Taiwan, and would pull out its military forces as soon as tensions in the area ceased.

George Ball, who had been undersecretary of state in the Kennedy and Johnson administrations, keenly summarized the Nixon-Kissinger foreign policy a few weeks after President Nixon's reelection in 1972: The president, he said, had "replaced America's policy of alliance with a policy of maneuver. Instead of continuing to build an expanding circle of like-minded nations that would concert their strategies and combine their resources in seeking a détente with Moscow and Peking, we embarked on an intricate game of check and maneuver with what the President has identified as 'equal' players—the Soviet Union, China, Western Europe, and Japan. The object of this game is to try to maintain a precarious power equilibrium by playing one nation off against the other without distinction between ally and adversary. Essential to success are the exploitation of surprise and the quick reversal of positions—and these, in turn, require the maximum of secrecy and flexibility. . . . [The] hard question remains whether—though productive of successes in the short run—it is a game that can be effectively played by a democracy over the longer pull. Throughout history the best players have been . . . agents of authoritarian governments . . . who felt no obligation to Parliament or public opinion—and for the past year or so this has been the foreign-policy posture of the Nixon Administration. . . . [But] once the country catches on to the implications of the power-juggling act, it is not likely to be comfortable with it. What Americans like is to have a circle of identifiable friends, close allies, companions in a common endeavor—something other than the cold geometry of a shifting balance conducted in secret by alchemists at work somewhere under the stage." (*Newsweek* [November 20, 1972])

Revived Bombing in Vietnam

In April 1972 the war in Vietnam was suddenly ripped wide open as the Communists inexplicably launched a classic conventional invasion across the seventeenth parallel (as well as over the border in other locations), using hundreds of tanks. While the South Vietnamese army slowly fought back this invasion, following initial headlong retreats, President Nixon revived aerial bombing over the North. Only this time the campaign did not cease after the initial crisis was over, but went on month after month. The warplanes used new "smart bombs," which could be guided electronically to bridges and other locations. Using a force of at least 100,000 men, stationed at air bases in Thailand and Guam and on Seventh Fleet ships off the Vietnamese coast, the president devastated huge areas of North Vietnamese countryside.

There was worldwide condemnation of Nixon's bombing, which reached unimaginable

President Nixon shakes hands with Chinese Communist leader Mao Tse-tung during his startling trip to China in 1972. By this act, he reversed decades of American policy toward the Communist world.

Wide World Photos

and terrifying heights. The London *Times* called "the appalling destruction . . . out of all proportion to the end." *The Boston Globe* observed, "The total inhumanity of what Americans are doing on the orders of an American President devastates the spirit. America will be a long time recovering from what it has done not only to a land of peasants but to itself." *The New Yorker* agreed: "This latest form of intervention . . . represents a culmination of our century's tendency toward mechanized killing. The government has made the invaluable discovery that an air force will go on fighting long after ground troops have balked, especially when there is virtually no opposing air force in the sky." But the very abstractness and remoteness of this new assault seemed soon to remove it from public controversy.

Nixon and Russia

In May 1972, Richard Nixon became the first American president to consult with Soviet leaders in Moscow. He left the capital of the U.S.S.R. with a bag crammed full with diplomatic agreements. They concerned a huge expansion in trade overall, until now a field largely untapped by American producers; cooperation in space and technology; and a significant expansion of the cultural exchange program, under way since 1958, to include the mutual exchange of visiting professors under the Fulbright/Hays program (by which, since 1946, hundreds of American scholars, artists, and scientists had been going abroad annually to teach students, and foreign professors had taught in this country). The president's visit to Moscow was soon followed by an enormous purchase of American wheat by the Soviet Union, whose own farming system, based on state-owned and collectivized farms, was so inefficient that it could not adequately feed the Soviet people. Moscow and the United States also agreed, finally, to begin discussions on "mutual balanced force reductions" (troops and aircraft) in Europe in January 1973.

These path-breaking steps aroused serious concern among America's allies. Europe and Japan felt ignored and harmed by this abrupt end to the United States' longstanding policy of close cooperation with its traditional friends. President Nixon was undeterred. He continued to play his lone hand in the classic style of the nineteenth-century Conservative prime minister of Great Britain he so admired, Benjamin Disraeli: nationalist, and unilateral.

The Election of 1972

During these events the Democrats had been slugging through a long series of bruising primary elections, seeking to find a winner among the group of men and women—Hubert Humphrey, Edmund Muskie, George McGovern, Henry Jackson, Shirley Chisholm, and George Wallace—who contended for the party's nomination. Wallace's role was crucial. As the American Independent party candidate in 1968 he had taken 13.5 percent of the popular vote, appealing primarily to those on the right wing of American politics who were most strongly hostile to blacks, intellectuals, and young radicals. Then on May 15, 1972, he was felled by a would-be assassin's bullet and paralyzed from the waist down. By default, his popular following swung behind Richard Nixon. Meanwhile, Senator George McGovern of South Dakota, who since the assassination of Robert Kennedy in 1968 had stood out courageously as an often lonely voice against the Vietnam War, began surging into the lead for the Democratic nomination. By the time of the Democratic National Convention in July—held, like its Republican counterpart, in Miami—he had a commanding margin of delegates and quickly became the party's nominee.

It was a stunningly swift victory for a man who, until these events, had been given little chance. McGovern had long condemned the war with all the genuine moral passion of a Methodist minister's son who had himself briefly considered a career in the pulpit. A professor of history and then an important official in the Kennedy administration, he had emerged as the voice of all those forces that in the late 1960s called for a thoroughgoing transformation of American society, as well as of foreign policy. After the calamitous 1968 convention of the Democratic party, when young protestors had been mercilessly clubbed outside the Chicago convention hall and the old guard of city bosses and union leaders had dominated proceedings, McGovern had chaired the committee that the party then appointed to rewrite its rules. The result was a group of policies that stated that, henceforth, convention delegates were to be selected by proceedings that ensured that youth, women, and minority groups would receive a sizable quota. The discontented, disadvantaged, and alienated were to be given a voice.

Democrats Offend Traditional Support Groups

Thus, the nation that watched the 1972 Democratic National Convention on television was astonished to observe a screen that seemed filled with young people, "women's libbers," and dashiki-clad black Americans. Fuming outside the hall over the seats they had been denied were the labor leaders and city bosses—most notably George Meany, head of the AFL–CIO, and Irish Catholic Richard Daley, mayor of Chicago. They bitterly protested a convention that to them seemed to have forgotten the ancient sources of Democratic voting strength. George McGovern, with his flat South Dakota twang and his preacher's manner, came across as an honest and sincere patriot genuinely determined to aid the nation's poor and end the Vietnam War, but his personal style failed to ignite any mass enthusiasm among the millions of urbanites. As soon as the convention was over, a Gallup poll showed him trailing the president 37 percent to 56 percent, and from then on the margin widened.

Everything went Richard Nixon's way. In late October, indeed, the last shreds of the Vietnam issue that George McGovern had fought for so many years appeared to vanish when Kissinger emerged from long negotiating sessions with the North Vietnamese in Paris and exultantly proclaimed, "Peace is at hand!" McGovern's more radical supporters called loudly for legalized abortion, marijuana, and homosexuality, and for amnesty for the thousands of Americans who had gone to Canada rather than be drafted to fight in Vietnam. These demands simply inflamed mass opinion against the Democratic candidate. At the same time, McGovern's sincere advocacy of women's rights, black equality, and greater

power and influence for the young turned away millions of Americans for whom these causes had become hateful during the volcanic 1960s. In such a setting, President Nixon needed hardly to campaign at all.

Behind the rhetoric and the bombast lay the fact that the United States had finally changed its view of Richard Nixon. Polls revealed that after decades of being called "Tricky Dick," he was now widely respected, though not loved. People regarded him as a principled, thoughtful, forward-looking president who had brought strength and fairness to the chief executive's post. At long last Nixon was admired for himself, and not as a kind of deputy Eisenhower. In every age group, in all parts of the country—especially among white voters in the South—at every level of educational attainment, among both Protestants and Catholics and with women as well as men, Nixon led McGovern in public-opinion polls.

The Nixon Landslide

When the balloting took place, even the young voters on whom McGovern had placed so much of his hope were split evenly, and fewer than half of those newly enfranchised by the Twenty-sixth Amendment actually voted. Black and Latin Catholic voters were the only ethnic groups massively pro-McGovern, but their turnout at the polls was once again gravely disappointing to Democrats. Only 52 percent of eligible black Americans cast a ballot, and only 38 percent of the Latin Catholics. Jews remained two-thirds Democratic in the balloting, but this was a drop of almost twenty percentage points from their performance in 1968. For the first time a Republican candidate won a majority of both the Irish and Italian votes (53 and 58 percent, respectively), which meant that Nixon took the overall Catholic vote (53 percent), an astounding reversal of a pattern as old as the nation itelf. Since a whopping two thirds of the immense Protestant voting group also supported him, Nixon achieved one of the great runaway presidential victories in American history. The president took every electoral vote save those of Massachusetts and the District of Columbia (520 electoral votes to McGovern's 17) and just under 61 percent of the popular vote (4 percent more than the combined Nixon-Wallace vote in 1968). Two of every three white voters had cast their ballot for Nixon.

Although McGovern was massively rejected, the Democratic party itself made a strong showing, capturing 55 percent of the vote for congressional seats. The Democrats actually won two additional seats in the Senate, and lost only about a dozen seats in the House. Thus, they kept firm control of Congress. Nixon's victory, in short, was highly personal. He did very little campaigning to help his party, and this led to bitterness among Republicans in Congress.

The End of the Vietnam War

The postelection days were filled with news. The apparent peace with the Communists in Vietnam broke down over a diplomatic impasse not clearly explained, and the president suddenly and with no prior public statement to the nation ordered massive aerial bombardment of North Vietnam, especially Hanoi. This heaviest concentrated bombing in the history of warfare horrified the nation and the world. The largest weekly publication in France, *L'Express*, observed bitingly, "In this poker game of life, Nixon is a master. By means of this nearly blind monster, the B-52, he has discarded forever an assumption. Mr. Nixon is no longer, and will never again be, a respectable man." *Die Zeit*, a liberal weekly in Hamburg, Germany, deplored the bombing as "nothing but terror and torture; torture with a method in order to make the North Vietnamese pliable. The bombs fall on military targets, but they also hit hospitals and schools, women and children. . . . Even allies must call this a crime against humanity. . . . The American credibility has been shattered." The president halted the bombing after two weeks, and negotiations began again, leading to the announcement in January 1973 of a cease-fire and an exchange of prisoners. There was worldwide relief. However, as Hamilton Fish Armstrong, former editor of the prestigious American publication *Foreign Affairs*, noted, "The President has a second chance now, but nothing will justify the bombing of the North. Millions of Americans are disgusted by it. . . ." And so, within weeks of his immense national victory, Richard Nixon had gravely harmed his moral authority.

At the least, however, the long and wasting American war in Vietnam was over. It had been almost twenty years since the United States had moved in as South Vietnam's protector, following the division of the country in 1954; almost eight years since Lyndon Johnson had decided to make it directly an American war by sending in American troops; and four since Richard Nixon had begun his slow and reluctant withdrawal. And now America had suffered its first military defeat. Little had been proved by the deaths of 56,000 Americans and over a million Vietnamese, and by the expenditure of $150 billion, save that an unpopular government in South Vietnam could be at least temporarily propped up. It was not long before even that shallow achievement was nullified. Fighting within South Vietnam broke out again in 1975, swelling to a savage climax in April, when the Communists won a complete victory. More than 100,000 fled the country, most of them coming to the United States. After the Khmer Rouge —Communist-backed forces—finished taking over Cambodia, southeast Asia quieted. The dominoes did not fall very far.

The Vietnamese Communists were determinedly independent, furthermore, of both Red China and Moscow. The Communist victory that the United States had fought so hard to stave off in Vietnam made little impact, indeed, upon the world balance of forces. A savagely repressive regime took over in Cambodia, one whose subsequent violence against its own people appalled the world. Hanoi's rule over the south in Vietnam was less brutal, but nevertheless harsh. However, in all subsequent discussions of threats to American security, not even Republicans of the most hawkish views ever mentioned the existence of a unified Vietnam under Communist control. Indeed, from any standpoint it was difficult to locate any particular benefit to the United States, or any significant danger warded off, that resulted from this unnecessary war.

The American people had learned great lessons: that their power is not unlimited; that there are "problems" in the world that they cannot solve, even with the lavish use of military power; and that the world is not a single theater of action in which every civil war lost to the "other side" is of vital danger to American security. This was perhaps all that can be said. But that it was in any calculation of human values right that the United States, or any nation, could claim the sacrifice of hundreds of thousands of lives so that it could gain a better understanding of the truths of life was a proposition to which few, certainly among those who suffered or died, would ever agree.

A puritan toughness of spirit, in the mode of the theologian Reinhold Niebuhr, helped set the mood in which, at the beginning of the Cold War, the American people took up the belief that they were guardians of the world's liberties, and that they were empowered by the grandness of this cause to wage war even upon small countries if their perceived enemy were found there. It is fitting, therefore, that the outcome of the Vietnam War inescapably brought to mind for many one of those central human paradoxes that so absorbed Niebuhr: that those who aspire to the noblest motives are in that same impulse made liable through the sin of pride to commit the gravest crimes.

Bibliography

As before observed, concerning such recent history it is difficult to be precise about sources, since on a daily basis so much is read in periodical and other literature. The fundamental work on Vietnam which has to be read by anyone seriously interested in the problem is Bernard B. Fall's *The Two Viet-Nams: A Political and Military Analysis* (1967), written by a brilliant journalist many years in the region who, in 1967, was killed there. The best work now available to Americans on their involvement is Frances Fitzgerald's Pulitzer Prize-winning *Fire in the Lake: The Vietnamese and the Americans in Vietnam** (1972). Then, aside from *The Pentagon Papers** (1971), the spectacular collection of inside documents published by *The New York Times*, I learned a great deal in Roger Hilsman's *To Move a Nation: The Politics of Foreign Policy in the Administration of John F. Kennedy** (1967), written by a man high in the State Department, and Townsend Hoopes's *The Limits of Intervention** (1969), prepared by the man who was undersecretary of the air force under Johnson. Arthur M. Schlesinger, Jr.'s *The Imperial Presidency* (1973), a classic of the period, is of crucial value in gaining a historical perspective on the evolution of the modern presidency.

James William Fulbright, United States Senator from Arkansas and chairman of the Senate's committee on foreign relations, wrote a powerful blast in his *The Arrogance of Power** (1967). David Halberstam's *The Best and the Brightest** (1972) continues to be a brilliant analysis. Robert Manning and Michael Janeway's *Who We Are: An ATLANTIC Chronicle of the United States and Vietnam** (1969) presents a rich collection of contemporary articles. Gabriel Kolko's *The Roots of American Foreign Policy: An Analysis of Power and Purpose** (1969) and Noam Chomsky, *American Power and the New Mandarins** (1969) are sharply critical, rooting the war in the corruptions of American capitalism and intellectuals' arrogance. On the politics of the period, consult books cited for the previous chapter. Henry L. Trewhitt, in *McNamara* (1971), has given us a keen portrait of a major figure. George C. Herring's *America's Longest War: The United States and Vietnam 1950–1975** (1979) is a valuable recent history.

Other perceptive views on Vietnam are advanced in Theodore Draper's *The Abuse of Power** (1967); A. M. Schlesinger, Jr.'s *Bitter Heritage: Vietnam and American Democracy** (1967); R. N. Goodwin's *Triumph or Tragedy: Reflections on Vietnam** (1966); and Chester L. Cooper's *The Lost Crusade: America in Vietnam* (1970), written by a former State Department official.

The theory of counterinsurgency, which was so popular with John Kennedy, is analyzed in *American Strategy: A New Perspective* (1966) by Urs Schwarz. Lyndon B. Johnson's decision to escalate—and the advisers who encouraged him—is discussed in Edward Weintal and Charles Bartlett's *Facing the Brink: An Intimate Study of Crisis Diplomacy* (1967). The progression of the war is followed in a notable work by Dennis Bloodworth, *An Eye for the Dragon: Southeast Asia Observed, 1954–1970* (1970). Jonathan Schell tells a chilling story in *The Military Half: An Account of Destruction in Quang Ngai and Quang Tin* (1968). Jon M. Van Dyke's *North Vietnam's Strategy for Survival* (1972) conveys that nation's determination. Frank Harvey's *Air War–Vietnam* (1967) is a compelling and utterly grim account of massive extermination.

The many abortive peace attempts are described in *The Secret Search for Peace in Vietnam* (1968) by David Kraslow and Stuart H. Loory.

THE END OF AMERICAN INNOCENCE: THE VIETNAM WAR

Teach-ins USA (1967), ed. Louis Menashe and Ronald Radosh, contains early criticism of Johnson's escalation tactics. Kenneth Keniston's *Young Radicals* (1968) explains the important role of New Left activists in Johnson's change of policy. Ken Hurwitz's *Marching Nowhere* (1971) critiques the peace movement. The Vietnam War's impact in the American courts is discussed in Jack Nelson and Ronald J. Ostrow's *The FBI and the Berrigans* (1972).

Lyndon B. Johnson and the World (1966) by P. L. Geyelin is a good study of the president's foreign policy. The Dominican intervention is brilliantly analyzed in Theodore Draper's *The Dominican Revolt: A Case Study in American Policy* (1968) and in John B. Martin's *Overtaken by Events: The Dominican Crisis From the Fall of Trujillo to the Civil War* (1966). Robert Shaplen's *The Road From War: Vietnam, 1965–1971** (1971) provides keen insights into Nixon's policies. A wider perspective, extending from 1957 to 1972, is W. W. Rostow's *The Diffusion of Power* (1972).

* Available in paperback.

38

1975 CIA and FBI investigated; fall of South Vietnam; 44 percent of married women employed; birth rate at 1.8 children per family

1976 Jimmy Carter elected thirty-ninth president of the United States

1977 Carter launches human-rights campaign in world affairs; Department of Energy created; government spending to create jobs expanded; Urban Development Action Grant program (UDAG) initiated

1978 Approval rating for Carter dropping; civil service reorganized; coal strip mining regulated; National Energy Act passed; voluntary wage- and price-control guidelines established; neutron bomb deployment in Europe deferred; Camp David peace accords initiate peace treaty between Egypt and Israel; inflation surging; Panama Canal treaties ratified

1979 SALT II negotiations completed; unemployment and inflation mount; Department of Education created; $100 million authorized for solar-energy research; tight money, high interest, policy adopted to fight inflation; synthetic fuels program enacted; phased ending of price controls on crude oil initiated; windfall oil profits tax enacted; formal recognition of People's Republic of China, treaty ties with Taiwan severed; airlines, trucking, banking deregulated; 84 percent of people dissatisfied with state of the nation; American embassy in Tehran, Iran, occupied, its personnel taken hostage; Afghanistan invaded by U.S.S.R. forces

1980 Carter partially revives Cold War with U.S.S.R.: halts grain shipments, initiates partial international boycott of Summer Olympics in Moscow, initiates major acceleration in defense spending, withdraws SALT II from Senate, declares American security interest in Persian Gulf, begins preparations for deployment of major military force there; recession begins; abortive attempt made to free hostages in Tehran; farm exports reach $40 billion; cruise missile deployment in Europe planned; Ronald Reagan elected fortieth president of the United States

WATERGATE AND THE 1970S

UPI

nois, a classically middle western setting, in comfortable middle-class circumstances. She was daughter to a father who did not like her to read too much, founder of a literary magazine while in high school, and class valedictorian. But Betty Naomi Goldstein was ethnically an outsider. "When you're a Jewish girl who grows up on the right side of the tracks in the Midwest," she later observed, "you're marginal. You're IN, but you're not, and you grow up an observer."

Then came a psychology major at Smith College, graduation summa cum laude and Phi Beta Kappa in 1942, and a graduate-research fellowship at the University of California, Berkeley. But she turned down encouragements to go on to a doctorate, for that was not what women did. It was too competitive with men, and a current boyfriend frowned. Marriage to a successful New York City executive followed, and a large, beautiful suburban home by the Hudson River—and children. These were "schizophrenic years of trying to be the kind of woman I wasn't, of too many lonesome, boring, wasted hours, too many unnecessary arguments, too many days spent with, but not really seeing, my lovely, exciting children, too much cocktail party chit-chat with the same people, because they were the only people there." Friedan came to call her unhappiness the "problem that has no name," for in the 1950s no one publicly talked of it, or seemed even to recognize its existence.

Out of this came *The Feminine Mystique,* which essentially called upon women to enter the mainstream of American life, to realize themselves in the professions, in management, in economic equality. Thousands of miles on the lecture circuit and innumerable conversations with women intensified her conviction that the time for organization had come. In 1966 she founded the National Organization for Women (NOW), which aimed at "a truly equal partnership with men." Through legislation, through changing teaching in the schools and colleges, through court action, NOW labored on a host of specific discriminations against women. By the 1970s NOW was demanding free abortions on demand and free child-care centers, as well as equal opportunity in jobs and education. The Equal Rights Amendment, renewed by congressional passage in 1970, became the rallying cry for "mainstream" feminism. And in every corner of America, women's lives were changing.

It was an instant best seller, like Harriet Beecher Stowe's *Uncle Tom's Cabin* more than a century before. Betty Friedan's *The Feminine Mystique* (1963) eventually sold more than a million copies, in sixteen printings, and was translated into thirteen languages. It seemed to come from nowhere, a book erupting just when the "back-to-the-home" movement for women seemed at its peak. Many thousands of American women, Friedan revealed, were (like her) frustrated by lives in which they were to find their identities, to realize themselves as persons, only through raising families and keeping their husbands happy.

Friedan was born and reared in Peoria, Illi-

Overview

After his triumphant reelection in 1972, President Richard Nixon looked ahead with settled confidence. But before the year 1973 was out, his administration had fallen into the gravest scandal in American history. By March 1974, the stunning events of the Watergate crisis had led to the resignation of more than a dozen men from high national office—including the vice-presidency of the United States—and the indictment or conviction of thirty-five men for criminal acts. In August of that year the president himself, faced by almost certain ejection through impeachment, became America's first chief executive to resign his office.

Gerald Ford assumed the presidency and found himself presiding over the early impact of the nationwide economic crisis that would eventually dominate the 1970s. In the 1976 presidential contest the nation, out of revulsion against the Watergate-stained Republican party, turned to elect from outside of Washington the Georgia Democrat Jimmy Carter, who seemed to bring with him a revival of populist, common-folk, and human rights–oriented Democratic ideology. But the huge Democratic majority in Congress, under recently adopted rules that dissipated authority, was unmanageable; Carter's flood of proposed reforms bogged down; the economic crisis of inflation, energy dependency, and unemployment became ever more severe; and the president himself failed to exert effective leadership. In 1980 he was swept from office in an electoral landslide that returned Republicans to power behind the Californian Ronald Reagan. Meanwhile, the new feminism, which had achieved nationwide momentum in the Nixon years, produced great changes in the lives and status of women.

The gross national product reached $900 billion in 1969, and passed the mind-boggling figure of $1 trillion in 1972. By 1971 the annual median income of American families had passed $10,000, a dollar increase of almost 80 percent since 1960, or a rise of 33 percent in real buying power (allowing, that is, for inflation). The average American, in other words, was one third wealthier than a decade before. The great American surge of affluence came to a startling and dismaying halt, however, in 1974, certainly one of the most important years in modern American history. In that year prices for food and for petroleum produced abroad skyrocketed. Inflation took off in the United States, rising 10 percent. Soon the nation was on a lurching roller coaster of apparently irreversible inflation and growing unemployment, stimulated by recurrent recessions. By the end of the 1970s America's real income per person had sagged, and the future looked, if anything, more disturbing than the past. The era of limits had arrived with a vengeance.

In this setting, millions of Americans lived in poverty. At the opening of the 1970s, when prosperity was the national condition and a fourth of the nation's families had an annual average income above $15,000, another fourth received less than $6,000. The number of families below the government's official poverty line ($4,137 in 1971) had dropped by a third in the 1960s, but at the end of the decade there were still 5.3 million families (a tenth of the total) below that line. Black Americans were much worse off than whites at the opening of the 1970s: though 11 percent of the population, they made up 29 percent of the poor. After that, things got worse.

During the hard-fought presidential campaign of 1976 between Georgian Jimmy Carter and President Gerald Ford, on September 27, 1976, the Chief Executive raises his arms in smiling acknowledgment of the cheers given him by one of his most faithful and enthusiastic support groups, the International Association of Chiefs of Police. He had just pledged spending the first 100 days of his new term, if elected, leading a battle against crime.

United Press International

The Imperial Presidency

The immediate crisis and challenge of the mid 1970s arose from a different source: the swollen powers of the presidency. From the time of Franklin Roosevelt's New Deal, the American presidency had risen in a kind of solitary majesty to become overwhelmingly the most powerful agency of government. Television, and the charismatic personality of John F. Kennedy, introduced the impact of a direct visual presence into every American home. In contrast even political parties seemed shrunken now. The voice and image of the president filled the land.

This was inherently an explosive situation. All that was needed to create a crisis was for a president to appear who would put this "imperial presidency" to its full use. Lyndon Johnson was such a man, for he was driven by gigantic dreams and conceived of the presidency in towering dimensions. The result was America's involvement in the Vietnam War. Richard Nixon also believed that the presidency was an office almost kingly in its occupant's authority to act on his own. In the making of war, as we have seen, he claimed for himself unlimited powers, over which, he insisted, Congress had no control. In domestic affairs he suddenly expanded a little-used and always doubtful presidential tactic—the impoundment of funds voted by Congress—into a major instrument of national government. In effect, he was assuming the right to an "item veto" (the unchecked vetoing of particular items within an appropriation), which the Constitution had not given to the president. Franklin Roosevelt had earlier argued that impoundment "should not be used to set aside or nullify the expressed will of Congress." But Richard Nixon believed he had the power to pick and choose which laws enacted by Congress he would execute, and by 1973 he had impounded some fifteen billion dollars, thus greatly reducing or wholly eliminating over a hundred federal programs concerning health, housing, urban needs, and environmental protection.

Similarly, he made executive privilege a vastly heightened barrier against the acquisition by Congress of any information whatever concerning the actions of various branches of the federal government. At first advancing a vague principle that the president should have the right to confidential conversation with his immediate advisers (as long as criminal activities were not being thereby protected), by April 1973 Nixon had so broadened its outreach as to state that none of the 2.5 million employees of the executive branch could give testimony on any matter to Congress if the president objected. Meanwhile, as if to remind the nation of his imperial powers, in late March 1973 he reinstituted bombing operations in Cambodia, even though the United States was legally at peace with that country and had no right to violate its air space for the purpose of carrying on military operations within its borders. The Tonkin Gulf Resolution had long since been repealed, and American combat troops had departed Vietnam and were no longer in any conceivable danger. Thus were removed the justifications that he had formerly advanced to excuse such actions. And now, as the Watergate investigations soon revealed, he was operating on the belief, as he had at least since 1969, that whenever he judged something to be a national-security matter, at his direction members of the national government could violate the law.

Thus, in an irony of history, the nation witnessed Democrats and liberal intellectuals condemning the strong presidency that they and their forebears had created. In truth, Richard Nixon's version of the strong presidency was not the "tribune of the people" model fashioned by Democratic chief executives—a role that involved working actively with Congress, pouring a long list of reform bills into its hopper, going frequently to the people, being highly visible and accessible, and leading an assault against social ills and the privileged few. Rather, he revived conceptions reaching far back to the Tory governments of traditional Britain: a belief that legislative branches were quarrelsome bodies whose views could be set aside and ignored; a faith in the unchecked "prerogative" of the Crown to do largely what it felt was best for the nation, whatever the laws said; a conviction that criticism is the same as disloyalty; a preference for rulers who were remote, relatively inactive in social affairs, and almost divine; and an instinctive impulse to crush "disorder" and "rebelliousness" with a strong hand. On top of this, in the Watergate affair, he committed a felony.

At that point the republicanism which lies at the root of American institutions and, largely unspoken, resides in the minds of Americans, emerged to shape the national debate. Events that were buried for most Americans in the dust of the past, and the ideas associated with them, became current. The American air was filled with voices crying out the same things that English people had hurled at Charles I 300 years ago in their Civil War, and that Americans had flung at George III 200 years ago in their Revolution. Unchecked power corrupts; it is eternally at war with liberty, cannot ever be trusted: it must be reined in, balanced, disciplined. Congress gathered a corps of American historians to explore examples of past presidential abuses of power, and to explain what has been done before with chief executives accused of such behavior. While nations abroad wondered at the always unpredictable Americans—a head of government had tried to cover up his links to aides caught burglarizing the offices of an opposing political party: what was so extraordinary about that?—the venerable impeachment machinery of the Constitution began to rumble into motion. Richard Nixon had violated republicanism at its core. For millions, therefore, he had become a tyrant who had to be expelled from office.

The Watergate Crisis

As early as 1969 the president illegally authorized the placing of wiretaps on the phones of newspaper reporters (by law he should have secured the approval of the courts in each instance), on the ground that their description of "secret" American bombing raids over Cambodia—secret only to the American people, certainly not to the Communists—endangered national security. Then, when the nation's campuses erupted in massive protest over the invasion of Cambodia that he launched in April 1970, he set off a search for the "foreign agents" who were allegedly behind the turmoil. Indeed, the president was obsessed with "enemies" and constantly engaged in launching petty, concealed campaigns of harassment of political enemies through whatever illegal, undercover means came to hand—such as digging into supposedly confidential Internal Revenue Service files to search out damaging information to use against the targets of his wrath. To read the memoirs of John Dean, the president's counsel (that is, in-house lawyer), *Blind Ambition: The White House Years* (1976) is to be taken behind closed doors into an almost mad-house scene of malicious, revenge-seeking scheming. Intrigue, back-

biting among aides scrambling for advantage in the president's favor, elaborate gestures at being tough and indifferent to the laws: it was a setting of gross public immorality and prostituted ideals.

Then in June 1971 *The New York Times* began publishing *The Pentagon Papers*, which it had received from former Defense Department official Dr. Daniel Ellsberg. This, the president later said, created "a threat so grave as to require extraordinary actions"—though nothing since then has demonstrated that this was so. Nixon established, without any congressional knowledge or authorization, an extralegal Special Investigations Unit within his staff. Headed by a young aide named Egil Krogh, it was to "find out all it could about Mr. Ellsberg's associates and motives." Securing a wig and other preposterous devices from the CIA, members of the unit broke into the offices of Ellsberg's psychiatrist in a vain search for information. There then emerged within the presidential staff a belief that the coming presidential election had to be fought as if against an enemy state. The Gestapolike investigations unit, now apparently financed by the Committee to Re-Elect the President, broadened its activities to include an assault on the nominating processes of the Democratic party. On June 17, 1972, several members of the unit were arrested at the national headquarters of the Democratic party in the Watergate office and apartment complex in Washington while burglarizing its offices and installing bugs on the phones. Among other things, in typical Nixonian fashion the break-in was aimed at trying to uncover political "dirt" which could be used to blackmail Lawrence O'Brien, chairman of the Democratic National Committee and a man particularly hated by the president.

The McCord Revelations

In the ensuing trial, held after the election of 1972, seven men (two from the White House staff) were sentenced to long terms by Judge John Sirica. Convinced that crucial information concerning the involvement of others was being held back, Sirica offered reduced sentences if full confessions were made. In March 1973 one of the burglars, James McCord, made such a declaration, and the whole scandal was ripped wide open. As recounted in the grand-jury indictment issued in March 1974—after a year of national controversy and investigation—what had happened immediately after the Watergate arrests was panic in the White House, and a frantic effort by members of the staff to cover up, by bribes and the subornation of perjury, links between the Watergate burglars and the executive branch. Since this constituted another criminal act—that of obstructing justice—and since the individuals allegedly involved were not simply "overzealous" minor aides (as Nixon euphemistically described them) but such eminent public officials as former Attorney General John Mitchell—and, it was widely alleged, the president himself—the people of the United States found themselves confronted with a stunning national scandal reaching the heart of the constitutional system.

The Senate Watergate Hearings

Millions of Americans watched in fascination and dismay as a special congressional committee under Senator Sam Ervin of North Carolina con-ducted televised hearings from May to August 1973, bringing a steady stream of public officials and undercover men before the cameras to confess grave misdeeds. They learned of millions of dollars jammed into random office safes and sluiced about from hand to hand to finance shady dealings; of idealistic young men deluded into criminal activities to protect a president whom they honored; of elaborate procedures for covering tracks and destroying papers. In July 1973 came the incredible news that for years the president had bugged his own offices, so that all conversations that he had had with aides over the Watergate affair were available. Through the summer months Nixon and the Watergate committee jousted over the possession of these tapes. In September Judge Sirica ordered that they be turned over to him for examination. The president refused, thus becoming the first chief executive ever to defy a formal court order to turn over evidence.

With Watergate eroding Nixon's prestige, Congress finally began lashing back against his regal uses of power. It decreed that no further

The Senate hearings into the Watergate conspiracy fascinated the nation for months on end, revealing sordid, widely illegal maneuverings ordered from the President's oval office.

Wide World Photos

American funds were to be spent for military operations in Southeast Asia after August 15, thus ending the longest war in American history. In November 1973, after extended debate and over the president's veto, Congress passed the War Powers Act, which sharply limited the executive branch's freedom of action. Henceforth the president had to inform Congress forty-eight hours after sending combat troops abroad for action; Congress would have the power to immediately order their return by a majority vote in both houses, not subject to veto; and if that body did not give formal approval for such troops to remain abroad, after sixty days the president would have to withdraw them. Congress also passed a bill requiring that if any government agency involved in international affairs refused to furnish within thirty-five days information it had requested, all funds would be cut off.

Agnew's Resignation

Meanwhile, as a fitting commentary on the diseased state of American government, Vice-President Spiro Agnew pleaded no contest, on October 10, 1973, to one charge of income-tax evasion (for not reporting perhaps $100,000 in graft), was placed on three years' probation, and given a $10,000 fine. He then became the second man ever to resign from the vice-presidency (John C. Calhoun had done so for political reasons in 1832) and the first to leave office because of crimes committed. Almost immediately afterward President Nixon selected Gerald R. Ford, veteran congressman from Michigan and minority leader in the House, as Agnew's successor. A forthright, honest, and thoroughly responsible man, Ford reflected, in his down-the-line conservatism on most social issues, the strong traditional Republicanism of his constituency—heavily Calvinist Dutch in ethnic composition—and was widely respected for his strength of character.

Nixon's Resignation

Ten months later, on August 9, 1974, Richard Nixon was flying home to San Clemente a private citizen and Gerald Ford was taking the oath as the thirty-eighth president of the United States. This unprecedented event was the stunning climax to a series of increasingly spectacular events that utterly destroyed the Nixon presidency. The root of the matter was the disputed presidential tapes, in which lay information so damning to Richard Nixon that he fought doggedly, month after month and through every delaying procedure available to him, to prevent their full disclosure.

The final act began on March 1, 1974, when a grand jury charged H. R. Haldeman, John D. Ehrlichman, John Mitchell, and five other close associates of Nixon with various crimes in connection with the Watergate burglary and cover-up, stated that the president was an unindicted co-conspirator, and delivered a mass of evidence to Judge Sirica. The House Judiciary Committee then subpoenaed a large group of tapes so that it could further its impeachment inquiry. On April 30, 1974, Nixon publicly turned over to the Judiciary Committee some 1,200 transcript pages of taped conversation (but not the actual tapes), insisting that everything now was made public. The transcripts, though severely edited to soften their impact, caused a national sensation. They revealed so sordid a moral atmosphere in the White House that the cry for Nixon's resignation erupted on every hand, even among conservative Republicans.

In July the United States Supreme Court ruled unanimously that Nixon must yield the tapes requested (after screening by Judge Sirica for removal of irrelevant material). Then, in the last few days of that month, the House Judiciary Committee, in a carefully reasoned and widely praised televised debate, voted to recommend three articles of impeachment to the full House: for the president's involvement in the Watergate cover-up; for his abuse of the powers of his office (in the use of such devices as Internal Revenue Service harassment of political enemies); and for his refusal to abide by the committee's subpoenas. The bipartisan majorities behind these actions made it a foregone conclusion that the House of Representatives, for the second time in the nation's history, would vote to begin impeachment proceedings against a sitting president.

On August 5, 1974, President Nixon finally released transcripts of conversations he had had with his aides immediately after the Watergate arrests in June 1972, which proved that he had indeed directly approved the cover-up and had thus obstructed justice and committed a felony. Now his house of cards utterly collapsed. Informed by

Republican congressional leaders that his conviction by the Senate in the coming impeachment proceedings was certain, he resigned, refusing to the end to admit to more than errors of judgment.

Aftermath

"So down he fell," as the poet Edmund Spenser had written centuries before on a similar occasion, "and like a heaped mountain lay." Around the country went a vast sigh of relief, tinged perhaps equally with anger and compassion. The president who was so driven by hatred of his enemies that he would connive to violate the laws of the land to harass them, and to protect his followers guilty of illegal activities in his cause, was gone. A subsequent poll revealed that the American people approved by a four-to-one margin of his resignation.

"The Constitution works," said the new president, Gerald Ford, in his first remarks following the administration of his oath of office, and indeed Americans generally awakened to a growing sense of pleasant surprise that this was so. The Congress had executed its measured proceedings with great credit to the nation; the Supreme Court, with its large component of conservative Nixon appointees, had unanimously struck down his claim to unlimited executive privilege; and even so powerful a man as the President of the United States could be made to depart his great office in scenes not of turmoil and revolution but of quiet orderliness. The air of thoughtful dignity that surrounded these events gave them a majesty few had expected to witness in the affairs of the American republic.

President Ford's obvious goodness and simplicity of character immediately won him wide support. Americans indulged in a hope that the nightmare, as the new president said in his opening remarks, was indeed over, that the future might be a time of healing and quiet.

End of the Honeymoon

Gerald Ford's honeymoon lasted only a month. On the ninth of September, 1974, he startled the nation by issuing an unconditional pardon to Richard Nixon for all federal crimes he may have "committed or taken part in" while in office—before the former president had even been indicted, let alone tried and convicted. This act shattered the nation's trust in Ford's judgment and credibility. The president said that Richard Nixon had already been punished enough by having to give up his great office, and that he wanted to clear the decks, thus saving the nation the ordeal that a trial of the former president would entail. Nonetheless, rumors rushed about that he had made a secret deal with Nixon to pardon him in return for being given the presidency. More than 70 percent of the nation had been positive toward Ford prior to this act. Now his popularity plummeted to below 40 percent, and generally remained there.

Thereafter, his faults were consistently ridiculed: his penchant for fumbling his lines; for saying unfortunate things. He tried a few press conferences and then, like Nixon, largely gave them up. It was widely said that, though a fine and honest man, he was intellectually not up to being president. His conservatism on social and economic policy had critics comparing him to other midwestern Republican presidents, such as Herbert Hoover, Warren Harding, William Howard Taft, and William McKinley. His closest friends were from the corporate community at the highest national levels, and in domestic affairs he gave his strongest support to the two most conservative cabinet members, William Simon of the Treasury and Earl Butz of Agriculture.

Economic Policy

Ford agreed with Simon that the most serious economic problem the nation faced was not unemployment but inflation. This meant maintaining a tight control upon the money supply and keeping interest rates high, so as to cut back on demand. As we have seen, inflation did burst upward in 1974, following major oil price increases by the producing nations, raising the cost of living about 10 percent. At the same time, unemployment mounted rapidly, from about 5 percent to over 8 percent in 1975—a figure thought wholly unacceptable in earlier years. The nation's business began winding down deeper and deeper into a recession, which held through the rest of 1975 and well into 1976.

Secretary Butz's policies, established under Nixon, had a profound impact upon farming, and therefore upon food prices. Former administrations had kept prices relatively low by subsidizing farmers, keeping huge quantities of land in soil banks and maintaining an output keyed primarily to what the nation itself needed. Butz was profoundly opposed to any government intervention in farming. He negotiated huge food sales to foreign countries, chiefly the U.S.S.R., and then urged farmers to turn to "wall-to-wall" agriculture to meet these demands. All available land was put to the plow, production skyrocketed as heavy investments were made in agricultural machinery, and soil banks disappeared. However, since huge amounts of the food thus raised were committed to foreign purchasers, relatively little was left to sell at home. This created a steep rise in food prices to consumers, and an end to most subsidies for farmers. The result was a farming world that could not go backward, for it was too heavily committed to all-out production by large investments in equipment and by a cost of living that could not be pushed downward.

Ford argued constantly with Congress over energy policy. He believed that price controls should be taken off petroleum and natural gas.

Once their prices rose to what the open market would pay, each gallon of gasoline and cubic foot of natural gas would be more expensive to the consumer; people would cut back in their usage, thereby saving energy resources. Also, higher prices would stimulate the oil industry to search at deeper, more costly depths for new pools of petroleum, and to reopen fields then abandoned as insufficiently productive, in order to be profitable. A heavy push to make the nation energy-self-sufficient led to approval of the much-debated Alaska pipeline, which would bring down petroleum from the immense oil fields along the northern shore of that state.

Congressional Elections and Reforms

The Democrats won a large victory in the congressional elections of November 1974, increasing their seats in the House to a two-thirds majority and adding several in the Senate. At the same time, retirement of several older legislators, to-

The incredibly difficult opening of the vast oil resources in the northern Alaska region of Prudhoe Bay showed the desperate straits to which the American national economy, now consuming oceans of oil daily, was reduced in the 1970s.

Alaska Pipeline Service Co.

gether with a marked liberal shift among the newly elected Republicans, made Congress as a whole younger and more reform-oriented.

Reforms pushed through Congress over the previous two years by a group of liberal Democrats had overhauled that body's ancient rules and drastically reduced the power of seniority. The party caucuses (gatherings of party members in the Congress to thrash things out among themselves), whose membership changed in response to each national election, were given effective authority to choose the chairmen of congressional committees. This meant that an inner circle of senior committee chairmen, insulated from the national will by their long tenure in office, would no longer dominate the Congress as formerly. At the same time, many new sub-committees were established, creating a veritable wilderness of such bodies.

Congress also pushed further ahead to recapture the power that had slipped to the presidency. It centralized its procedures in the making up of the national budget, and seized a much larger and more effective role in that process. In addition, it prevented the president from frustrating duly enacted laws by impounding funds. A Freedom of Information Act threw open the files of the federal government to reasonable inquiry, and in fall 1976 a so-called sunshine law was passed requiring more than fifty federal agencies henceforth to conduct their deliberations in sessions open to the public.

The CIA and FBI Investigations

President Ford declared in his first address before Congress that his administration would never engage in the illegal wiretapping and other invasions of privacy that the Watergate crisis had unveiled. Investigations soon revealed that the CIA had for years been directly violating its charter (which specifically forbade it to carry on operations within the United States) by conducting massive, illegal domestic intelligence operations against antiwar and other politically dissident groups during the Johnson and Nixon administrations. Then it was discovered that for thirty years the FBI had gathered political intelligence on journalists, political opponents of sitting presidents, and critics of national policy, and had delivered this information to the White House. Dur-

ing the 1960s the FBI had even tried covertly to discredit Martin Luther King, and had sent him harassing letters. J. Edgar Hoover, in his near half-century as head of the bureau, had become a law to himself long before his death in 1972.

The two agencies plummeted in national standing. Clarence M. Kelley, who became FBI director in 1974, was gravely embarrassed when his flat declarations that these operations had ceased in the early 1960s were shown to be untrue in light of new information, formerly unknown to him. The Socialist Workers party and other political dissidents suffered direct FBI efforts to disrupt their activities; indeed, not until September 1976 did the Attorney General, Edward Levi, announce that surveillance of that party would cease.

Decline in Prestige of Government

Continued inflation, rising unemployment, the impasse in Washington, and the disturbing FBI and CIA revelations all combined to drive national respect for the federal government ever lower. In 1964 polls had shown that 76 percent of the people had a basic confidence in their government; by the early 1970s this had dropped to 52 percent; and after the Watergate crisis, only one out of every three Americans held such sentiments. By the spring of 1976, almost half of those polled said they wished to see someone come in from entirely outside the existing ranks of national politicians to take over the country's leadership. Only 23 percent of them had much trust in President Ford or his cabinet; only 19 percent were positive toward Congress.

The Fall of South Vietnam

The milestone event in 1975 was the final collapse of South Vietnamese government. In March North Vietnamese forces, which had remained deeply implanted in the South after the Americans and North Vietnam signed peace agreements in January 1973, began assaulting Saigon's troops in the central highlands. The South Vietnamese army fell apart, and in a swift few weeks of confusion and bloodshed it was all over. On the twenty-ninth of April, 1975, the last Americans evacuated Saigon by helicopter; a flood of South Vietnamese fled their country (some 130,000 were ultimately given permanent residence in the United States); and peace finally came to Vietnam after thirty years of war.

The Revolution in Women's Lives

In this book we have followed the complex history of women in American life from the colonial period. In the years since 1945, women have gone through a revolution in their ways of living more profound, perhaps, than anything that happened to them earlier. This revolution, furthermore, has moved forward at a pace many thousands of Americans have found almost bewildering, and certainly threatening.

Perhaps the most fundamental change is that by the late 1970s close to half of American women were working—and without massive disapproval, though there is much that people have found to worry about and criticize in this development. In 1935 a Gallup poll found that three fourths of all women disapproved of a married woman having a job. Even after four years of a great war during which millions of such women did go to work, in 1945 a *Fortune* magazine poll found that two thirds of Americans felt a woman should not work if her husband could support her. But despite this sentiment, there was not a great drop-off in the number of working women after the war ended. Where only 15 percent of married women worked in 1940, by 1960 the proportion had almost doubled, and by 1975 it would reach the extraordinary total (when seen against all of former history) of 44 percent! Even among women with children under six years of age, almost 37 percent were working in 1975. In 1973, 65 percent of the respondents to a national poll *favored* wives working, even if their husbands could support them.

During this transformation the kinds of jobs women could take widened enormously. They became accountants, welders, carpenters, electricians, and machinists. Admissions of women to law schools rose from slightly under 5,000 in 1960 to almost 17,000 in 1973; medical-school enrollments doubled in this period; the number of women engineers climbed from 7,000 to almost 20,000; and female real-estate agents rose in number from about 45,000 to almost 85,000. Even

management began to open to women, in some fields. With high public visibility women invaded such earlier male preserves as television announcing and newspaper reporting, and even bus driving and police work. In fact, only in those hazardous, strenuous, and disagreeable jobs that men themselves do not like did the proportion of women at work not rise.

These shifts in place of employment, though striking, were but marginal phenomena. Although far more women were working, in an economy in which service industries were exploding and therefore providing more opportunities, as late as the 1970s they tended still to concentrate overwhelmingly in traditional activities: as typists, maids, teachers, nurses, cashiers, and saleswomen. Relatively few skilled artisans and professionals were women, and in all categories of employment women received less pay. The overall occupational distribution, in fact, was not remarkably different from what it had been in 1940, or even in 1900. If anything, the division of occupations by sexual identity was even more marked in the middle of the twentieth century than it had been at the century's beginning. When women had moved into a major activity, as in banking or shoe manufacturing, men tended to move out—and into higher-paying jobs. In 1960 women received about 83 percent of the salary or wage that black men made, and black men, in their turn, received only 60 percent of that paid to white men. By 1973 the average for women was even lower, and going down.

How Did Women Regard Their Work?

The enormous host of working women who appeared after World War II did not have the same fundamental attitude toward work that men displayed. Most of them thought of themselves as working only for the short term. They were interested primarily in helping their families by bringing in more income for some large expenditure, such as education for the children or a new home. They were not engaged in a career, a life work that gave them their identity as persons. Women clearly shaped their work around their family obligations, whereas for men the priority was reversed. Indeed, a surprisingly large part of the surge in working women comprised women above the age of 35—that is, women whose immediate family responsibilities were beginning to lessen, or whose children were in college and needed help. Here is the probable explanation of the fact that by the 1970s most people favored the idea of wives working: women had demonstrated that by and large they would shape their work patterns to fit their family's needs, that the working-wife phenomenon would not bring disaster to the home.

With this self-image, women were willing to accept jobs in low-paying industries that took temporary or relatively unskilled help. Most people before the rise of feminism in the 1970s believed that men should be paid at a higher rate, on the assumption that they were supporting their families while working women were only helping theirs (an outlook that ignored the large number of working women who, through divorce, widowhood, or the illness of a spouse were the sole support of themselves and their children). The passage in 1963 of the Equal Pay Act, the first piece of federal legislation ever to outlaw discrimination on sexual grounds (and still the only law devoted exclusively to that purpose), began to change all this. Compliance with the law was slow, reluctant, and difficult to enforce, but by the late 1970s equal pay for equal work was much closer to being the norm.

Women Retain Traditional Self-Image

Women were not, therefore, abandoning their self-image as primary custodian of the home and primary rearers of the children when they took on a job. In 1974, 60 percent of all women said being a mother was as challenging as having a high-level job, and only a fifth of them hoped that their daughters would have a career outside the home. In comparison with nineteenth-century women, more of them were married (where in the previous century some ten of every hundred women did not marry, in the 1970s only five women did not do so). Furthermore, only one in twenty women in the 1970s said she did not want to have children. This demonstrated that motherhood itself was probably as strong as ever as a life ideal, though the 1970s woman was waiting longer to start having children, and was having fewer of them.

A century ago a third of all married women had seven or more children; in the 1970s that third had only three or more children.

Since traditional attitudes among women toward their family responsibilities remained strong, American working-class women preferred overwhelmingly to place their children not in child-care centers but rather with relatives or friends. (Conversely, employed middle-class women of feminist persuasion, who tend to favor schooling, peer-group influence, and middle-class teachers, used child-care centers extensively.) Those advocates of radical family change who called for a wholesale use of communal child-care facilities as a means of eliminating the allegedly oppressive family found almost no response among working women. These mothers wanted their children cared for by a female whom they had chosen and trusted, not by an institution. And in the home itself, working women and their husbands continued to think of housework as part of the woman's sphere, the man's role being limited to that of helper. This attitude is reflected, perhaps, in the fact that in the mid 1970s only four of ten working women worked full time and year around, whereas seven of ten men did so. When asked the reason for this, women gave home responsibilities or schooling as answers.

The Nonideological Revolution

Women flooded into work places outside the home waving no banners of ideology. It all happened without fanfare—indeed, with the encouragement of public authorities, since after 1945 manpower experts predicted that the economy would need women at work in order to keep expanding (the generation born in the Great Depression having been so small). This exodus from purely domestic work took place, furthermore, while the ideal of the close and loving family with the wife as companion to the husband reigned supreme in the culture. (Not until the late 1960s would the word *feminism* stop being laughed at and scorned.) Women had the vote now, it was said; what else was needed? They could smoke, they could work outside the home if they wished, and yet they could have recourse also to the role of traditional femininity, which brought lavish praise and admiration. Also, since the Progressive Era, governments at all levels had enacted special protections for women as to hours of work in industry, conditions of work, their claim to their children in divorce, and their claim to property. This, it was presumed, was all that human justice required: a recognition on the part of authority that women had special needs, and special dangers from which they should be protected. President Franklin Roosevelt's secretary of labor, Frances Perkins, and his wife, Eleanor, were the towering women figures of the 1930s and 1940s—indeed, into the 1950s as well. They preached and embodied the concept that women were special people with special qualities to bring to public life, but in that role needed protective legislation. This Progressive Era concept that women needed such protection, like workingmen and working children, like slum dwellers and the poor, was never questioned by the women of their generation.

Feminism A Surprise

So the women's movement that suddenly emerged in the 1960s came as an almost complete surprise to the nation. Were not American women, with their handsome, roomy suburban homes, their station wagons, and their large families and loving husbands, said to be the envy of women the world over? What conceivably could be complained of? President Kennedy had appointed a Presidential Commission on Women, headed by Eleanor Roosevelt herself, which in 1963 issued its report. It focused on discrimination in employment faced by professional women, and upon that which confronted wives in family law and under the Social Security System, while at the same time addressing itself to the question of how to help women perform better in their unique roles in marriage and motherhood. This was the first effort ever made by the federal government to examine the issue of women in American life, and it led to the Equal Pay Act of 1963, a milestone piece of legislation. However, the Commission did not issue a fundamental challenge to the role of women in the family or in American life.

Then came Betty Friedan's book *The Feminine Mystique* (1963) which did indeed issue such a challenge. It was a solitary trumpet, a call to

arms that at first mainly mystified people. But in time the book gave new life to feminism and led to its full-blown re-emergence in American life; that is, to the belief that a basic change should occur in women's role in the family as well as in the economy. Feminism would swiftly expand into a broad movement with its radicals and its moderates, the former insisting upon extreme changes calling for equality between men and women in every imaginable way, the latter focusing upon more limited and, its advocates would say, more justifiable goals, such as equality in employment, or under the law.

Friedan's book had such an impact because it had a large potential constituency: middle-class, usually college-educated women who found their roles as housewives frustrating and constricting. For Friedan and many of her Smith College classmates whom she interviewed there was a distressing gap between the rhetoric of wife-companion and motherhood, and the reality of that life. Since suburban housewives, Friedan said, could realize their own potential only through their children and husbands—that is, through others—they lacked that independent source of selfhood that alone, she wrote, can give a person a sense of competency and freedom. Thus, they could not give their own children a model of the able, successful, independent person. What resulted for too many women, Friedan wrote, was a lack of self-direction, and in its place self-indulgence, neuroticism, and emptiness. They tended to hang too much on their husbands and to make such heavy demands of their sexual lives—since sexual satisfaction was to be the center of everything—that they met only failure and frustration.

It was the psychologists and the Freudian psychoanalysts, Friedan insisted, who were to blame, for they depicted women as happy only when filling their wombs with children, nurturing them, and making successful love with their husbands. In pursuing this ideal, many women became unsuccessful mothers and unsuccessful wives. What was needed instead, Friedan went on, was to recognize that women too needed fulfilling, creative work of their own. This would make them happier and better mothers and wives. Giving birth and making love would come into proper perspective. And work, to Friedan, meant a career, not simply a job; it meant building a new, strong identity around a profession or other demanding task of permanence and primacy in a woman's life. Here lay the answer, Friedan believed, for all women.

Feminism Expands

Out of the royalties from her book, which became a worldwide seller, Friedan in 1966 created the National Organization for Women (NOW). In its Bill of Rights for Women, drawn up in 1967, it called among other things for enactment of the Equal Rights Amendment to the Constitution (strongly opposed by women leaders formerly), on the ground that women did not need protections but rather the removal of all sexual distinctions from all laws. Another important part of the Bill of Rights for Women called for women to have control over their reproductive lives—that is, to be able to have abortions. At that time abortion was illegal in every state in the Union save when the mother's life was endangered. The very word was not spoken easily in polite company, and a woman's having gone to a foreign country to have one was treated as a scandal.

As in the pre–Civil War years, when the rise of abolitionism stimulated an upsurge in the women's-rights movement, in the late 1960s the women's-liberation movement suddenly exploded, catching national attention. This activism reversed quietist, traditional trends that had been dominant for decades.

Wide World Photos

NOW's main campaign under Betty Friedan, however, was to open up the full range of employment outside the home to women; to have women enter completely into the "mainstream" of American life: its economy. Energetically, NOW publicized the extent of discriminations against women: the token appointments, the lack of effort to recruit or promote women, the concentration of their jobs at the bottom of the economic pyramid, the unequal treatment of women in higher education, and their exclusion from professional schools. The media, NOW pointed out, textbooks, the law—every social institution described women in stereotypes that were false. The ultimate goal for NOW was to create for women "an active, self-respecting partnership with men . . . a different concept of marriage, an equitable sharing of the responsibilities of home and children and of the economic burdens of their support."

As yet, the women's movement was not a war of the sexes. NOW was not hostile to men, to sexual relationships with men, to the concept that motherhood was uniquely admirable and female. But by the opening of the 1970s radical feminists were taking over NOW and seizing public attention in groups like the Red Stockings and the Feminists. Leaders like Ti Grace Atkinson, who would have nothing to do with men in her private life, called for an assault on "male chauvinist pigs." From these directions came the assertion that heterosexual sex itself was oppressive, that the dominance of men over women was a conspiracy thousands of years old that must be thrown off, that marriage and the traditional family should be replaced by sisterhood, communal child-care centers, and a forthright declaration of lesbianism. It was "women's liberation" in its most radical sense that was being called for in the early 1970s. Friedan was appalled at its tone. "Ideological tracts on sexual politics," she later wrote, "began to pour out in the name of radical or Amazonian or separatist feminism," and this was leading, she felt, "to a dangerous dead end." Among the elements of that dead end, she pointed out, was a rejection by the mass of American women of such antimale and antifamily radicalism. Indeed, the radical women's liberationists got so much attention from television and print journalism in the early 1970s that for most Americans they gave the very term "women's liberation" a bad name. Others working in the cause stopped using it, preferring the much older and broader concept, feminism.

A New Definition of Womanhood: Woman as Person

In the midst of these increasingly turbulent scenes, a new definition of womanhood was forming in the mind of many thousands of American women: not woman as wife-companion, but woman as person—independent, self-starting and self-directed, vigorous, and able. Special protections were scoffed at. Women were to be thought of as fully capable of deciding what was best for themselves and looking out for their own interests.

This concept was not entirely new, of course; it may be read in the writings of almost every feminist leader since Elizabeth Cady Stanton in the mid-nineteenth century. It had been little spoken of among women leaders since at least the 1920s, however, and as an idea taken on by masses of women in the American population, it was largely unprecedented. It drew its force in part from the rising of black America that was shaking the nation in the latter 1960s. If black Americans could assert that they were equal in dignity to whites and independent as persons, activists said, women of all classes and races should do no less. However, the black movement and women's liberation soon split, for black radicals cared little for the women's objectives and disliked a movement that was so much a product of the white middle class. In a revealing comment, Stokely Carmichael jested that the proper position of women in the black movement was on their backs.

In fact, many women were driven to launch the women's-liberation crusade by their discovery that even in the civil-rights movement (as in the pre–Civil War abolitionist crusade) they were kept in a secondary status. Activist Robin Morgan observed in 1970 that "the current women's movement was begun largely . . . by women who had been active in the civil-rights movement . . . and in the Left generally. . . . Thinking we were involved in the struggle to build a new society, it was a slowly dawning and depressing realization that we were doing the same work and playing the same roles *in* the Movement as out of it: typing the speeches that the men delivered,

making coffee but not policy, being accessories to the men whose politics would supposedly replace the Old Order. But whose New Order? Not ours, certainly."

It was especially notable to women's liberationists that within the radical-hippie world women were routinely cast in a kind of Earth Mother role. In the romantic search for whatever was "natural," there was not only a return to long straight hair, bare feet, and freely swinging breasts but also an almost tribal reversion to a bovine pattern of female submissiveness. Nothing could be further from the woman-as-person concept avowed by NOW and a host of other voices in literature, the film, and popular writing. Opposition was aimed at all policies and practices, wherever located, that "foster in women," as NOW stated the problem, "self-denigration, dependence, and evasion of responsibility."

The Question of Similarities

The national debate in the early 1970s, a crucial period in which key concepts were being argued out, moved into deep and complicated questions. There was much about women's liberation in the broadest sense which argued that men and women should become more like each other, certainly in their places of work and in their public role. In more radical circles among women's liberationists, there were bold assertions that the two sexes were so essentially alike that they should even adopt a new "unisex" style of life involving similar clothing, even common public restrooms.

These views, rejected as absurd by most feminists, touched nonetheless upon real issues. Boys and girls in school, for example, traditionally display contrasting abilities in mathematics. Were boys better at such studies because of something in their genetic makeup, or was it, as many feminists insisted, the product of socializing received from infancy, which induced in girls the feeling that in certain activities they were inferior? In the 1950s, Erik Erikson, the leading child psychologist of that decade, had reported that boys and girls seemed instinctively to exhibit strikingly different play activities. He went on to suggest that the psychology of women was fundamentally shaped around their possession of a productive inner space, their wombs, and the birthing and nurturing of children that this led to. In the late 1960s, this thesis was criticized as fundamentally sexist. Anatomy, it was insisted, was not destiny to the extent that people had long believed. Women were not shaped for particular kinds of lives and particular ways of thinking simply by their bodies, but rather by the sexist organization of society. To radical women's liberationists, the "feminine" image had been thrust upon women by men.

The Framework Is Revolutionized

Far more than just attitudes were being revolutionized. So too was the entire legal framework within which women lived. The Equal Pay Act of 1963 only began the changes that crowded in upon one another. The word *sex* was put into the 1964 Civil Rights bill (whose main concern was to outlaw job discrimination on the basis of race) as a means of making it more "ridiculous" and therefore unlikely of passage. But President Johnson, with strong urging from activist women, insisted not only on the bill's passage but upon keeping its prohibition of sexual discrimination. The result was a historic shift in national policy: from then on, women's equal opportunity in the marketplace had the federal government's authority behind it. The Equal Employment Opportunities Commission, created by the act, at first ignored the act's reference to women. But when it became known that 40 percent of the complaints pouring in about job discrimination came from women, the commission began to take action—if slowly and often ineffectively. In 1967 President Johnson ordered that the thousands of firms doing business with the federal government no longer discriminate against women.

The Abortion Era Begins

On quite another front, the state of California, at the cutting edge in this as in so many other cultural changes, enacted a path-breaking law that allowed women to secure abortions practically on request. In 1973 the Supreme Court upheld this legislation, ruling that in the first trimester of pregnancy a woman had the right, in consultation with her physician, to obtain an abortion. Inter-

ference by a state with that right was unconstitutional, since a citizen's inherent "right to privacy" was involved. "Maternity, or additional offspring, may force upon the woman a distressful life and future," the Court's decision ran. "Psychological harm may be imminent. Mental and physical health may be taxed by child-care. There is also the distress for all concerned, associated with the unwanted child."

Swiftly, America entered upon an astonishingly huge demographic transformation. In 1973 there were 747,000 (known) abortions; in 1975, more than a million—obtained mainly by unmarried young women. Whereas before 1973 the idea of abortion seemed to most people abhorrent, subsequent polls revealed that most people favored it. The question would remain highly controversial, however, as the nationwide "Right to Life" movement of the later 1970s, with strong Catholic and traditionalist Protestant support, demonstrated. Many hospitals resisted strongly, and physicians were ambivalent on the issue. As was so often the case in the feminist movement, this change was primarily to the advantage of those women who were not poverty-stricken. For a time public funds were available to help poor women secure abortions, but by the end of the 1970s this was no longer the case.

In another shift affecting women and the family at the outset of the 1970s, California made divorce much simpler by eliminating the need to demonstrate that one or the other of the persons involved was at "fault." The fact of incompatibility, testified to by one party, became a sufficient ground in this state, and later in most others, for action. This led to a nationwide spurt in the divorce rate, though after a few years it settled down to its former condition—which in truth was alarming to millions of Americans since, even if at a slower pace, it was climbing. (The impact of the divorce rate on marriage and the family will be discussed in the next chapter.)

The National Reaction

Women's liberation attracted a storm of abuse, predictably from men but also from a majority of women, who found its goals—at least as radicals described them—strange if not bizarre. Among women intellectuals there were voices of enthusiastic support and equally enthusiastic dissent after the first surge of radical women's-lib writing had passed. "At the root of liberation's determination to disintegrate the sexes," observed Anne Bernays in *The Atlantic Monthly* in 1970, "is the disabling anxiety that *different* means the same thing as *inferior*. . . . Why is this [differentness] so hard for so many women to swallow? Are we as confused as all that?"

Whatever the reactions, a new life for American women had clearly been inaugurated in the profoundly egalitarian 1960s, just as it had been for blacks and young people. No element of this new life operated more powerfully than the birth-control pill. "The Pill" did not lead to instant promiscuity, as many feared. Studies demonstrated that young women continued overwhelmingly to restrict their sexual activity to men with whom they had a serious relationship. Nevertheless, the pill eliminated the fear of pregnancy (though as the years went by and its physiological impact upon women's bodies became clearer, fears of dangerous side effects arose), and it was widely believed to have a profound impact upon sexual behavior, whatever the reality might have been. At the same time, there flooded in the newer concept that the sexual appetites of men and women were equal, and that women had the same right to sexual experience as men.

This combination of influences inaugurated an era filled with unexplored uncertainties and dilemmas for women. The "real truth about the sexual revolution," wrote the social observer Midge Decter in the August 1972 issue of *The Atlantic Monthly*, "is that it has made of sex an almost chaotically limitless and therefore unmanageable realm in the life of women." Given a sexual freedom undreamed of by their sisters in former generations, Decter went on, the women now pioneering a new way of life were haunted by the question, What shall be done with this freedom? What were its limitations, its prices, its opportunities? No one knew. Old codes of conduct seemed cast aside, and young women were forced to answer for themselves "at a time of life," wrote Decter, "when [they] feel the greatest need for the protection of a fixed set of manners."

A clear result of the pill's advent was to place almost all the burden of preventing pregnancy upon women. Men came to expect their sexual partners to be infertile. This led to an explosion in unwanted pregnancies, and to the surge in abortions obtained by young unmarried

women mentioned above, since forethought appears not to have been universally exercised. Also, venereal diseases, thought since the advent of sulfa drugs and penicillin to be practically non-existent, swept back in near epidemic proportions in the latter 1970s, in good part, authorities held, because the condom, with its protection against disease transmission, was not being relied upon.

Another result of the pill and of changed ideas about childbearing was a sharper drop in the national birth rate. Consternation among demographers—and those who planned the construction of such public facilities as schools—occurred when the "war-baby" crop of young women decided not to have as many children as their mothers when they reached childbearing age in the mid 1960s. Polls showed that women wanted an average of 2.5 children in 1971, as contrasted with 3.03 in 1965 and 3.7 in the era of the baby boom. During the 1960s the number of children born to twenty-four-year-old women just out of college dropped by 55 percent. Furthermore, the number of young women remaining single rose dramatically. Thus, though the number of potential mothers was at an all-time high, the actual number of births dropped sharply, reaching 1.8 per family in the mid 1970s—not enough, in the long run, to keep the national population from declining in numbers.

A New Election Year: 1976

The United States entered 1976 at peace, with a stock market that in December 1975 had begun a long and sustained upward rise that ultimately wiped out its heavy losses of previous years, and with an economy that looked as if it might be recovering from recession. Unemployment remained high—over 8 percent—but in 1975 the consumer price index had risen only 7.6 percent, less than in the year 1974.

President Ford's national standing remained low. The nation was responding to a deep sense that the United States of America was gravely afflicted. This mood had been born in the year 1974, when during the Arab-Israeli war of 1973–74 the Arabs, angered at Western sympathy for Israel, had instituted an oil embargo (and thereafter formed OPEC, an international oil-producers body which kept oil prices high). The embargo triggered an energy crisis in

America that caused hundreds of thousands of workers to lose their jobs, and put an increasingly precarious national economy under tremendous pressure. The skyrocketing high prices for oil that OPEC from that time onward demanded of the world's nations built great and irresistible impetus behind worldwide inflation, which shortly induced a continuing economic crisis.

From the right wing of the Republican party in 1976 came a strong voice that was confident of what was wrong with the country and where it should be heading: that of Ronald Reagan, former governor of California. Deeply respected by conservatives within his party, he announced formally in November 1975 that he was running for the Republican presidential nomination. Repeatedly he called for a greatly reduced role for government and a fiercely aggressive anti-Soviet foreign policy. The Panama Canal, he asserted, was sovereign American territory (which it was not) and should never be relinquished to the Panamanians, whose government for years had been pressing for fundamental changes in this direction. Reagan talked constantly of the classic cultural issues that, in one form or another, have aroused conservative Republicans: abortion, busing to achieve racial balance in public schools, crime in the streets, and alleged abuses in the huge national welfare program. In an emotional national convention Reagan came within 60 votes, out of more than 2,000 cast, of capturing the nomination from Gerald Ford.

Meanwhile, a dozen Democrats clamored for their party's nomination. Among them were Senator Henry Jackson of Washington state, Congressman Morris Udall of Arizona, Governor Jerry Brown of California, and Governor George Wallace of Alabama. However, another candidate, the relatively unknown Jimmy Carter, former governor of Georgia, began to surge. For two years he had been shaking thousands of hands and talking to groups all over the nation. During this startling rise from obscurity he insisted in his speeches that the nation must turn to someone from entirely outside Washington. He called for a politics of love for one another, compassion for the suffering, honesty, and truth. "I will never lie to you," he said, in clear reference to the disgraces of the Vietnam and Watergate years. Like Woodrow Wilson long before, whom among previous Democratic presidents he most resembled in his style and attitudes, he condemned secret government, secret diplomacy, and a government linked to the powerful and wealthy. Government should once more be made open to the people and their ideas, not closed in, arrogant, and elitist, as he described it to be.

What this all meant in terms of specific programs was uncertain, but when Jimmy Carter took the Ohio primary he had enough committed delegates to secure the nomination on the first ballot, and the Democratic race was over. In a peaceful and good-spirited Democratic convention, strikingly unlike those of 1968 and 1972, he was accorded that honor, and he then chose Senator Walter Mondale of Minnesota as his running mate. After more than thirty state primaries, nine more than formerly, and some $70 million spent by the candidates (for the first time, in the form of public funds), the nation had its nominees and its choice to make.

The Campaign

The two men campaigned quite differently. Carter moved constantly about the country, speaking day and night. Ford sought to retain his presidential image by remaining at the White House, holding press conferences in which he took opportunities to condemn big spenders and activist government. Carter's liberal, even populist (the term he used) views turned many voters away from him, for there was a wide impatience with more government-led reformism. President Ford's standing began steadily rising in the polls, and a cliff-hanging race developed.

Carter's support firmed, however, and election night saw the Democratic candidate sweeping the South back into his party's fold, save for Virginia. Ford took all of the West beyond the state of Missouri save for Texas and Hawaii, and the two candidates seesawed until far into the morning hours in the crucial states of the Middle West and the Northeast. When a majority of these states—including the two most populous, New York and Pennsylvania—fell to the Democrat, the White House became Jimmy Carter's. In effect, he had re-created that ancient coalition of the South and the large Middle Atlantic states that since Jefferson's day had delivered the presidency to the Democratic party.

The popular vote stood at 50 percent for Carter and 48 percent for Ford. A difference regarded as narrow, in fact it was wider than the winning margins gained by either Kennedy in

1960 or Nixon in 1968 (the only other nonincumbents to win since Eisenhower's landslide in 1952). Early studies of voting statistics demonstrated that for the first time in many years, cultural issues no longer predominated in shaping the outcome. Jimmy Carter was himself the chief cultural issue, in his Deep South identity and accent, his "born-again" Christianity, and his habit of talking about intimate matters that made many nervous. But much stronger was a deep national sense of alarm over the economy—the classic Democratic issue since the Great Depression. Inflation and high unemployment were burdens Ford could never escape. More than a quarter of the voters described themselves as financially worse off than they had been a year before, and that quarter voted for Carter almost four to one. Millions of Democrats who had supported Nixon in 1972 returned to their party on economic grounds. Manual workers surged behind Carter by about 64 percent, whereas in 1972 only 44 per-

cent of them had supported McGovern. Indeed, Democrats in general voted four to one for their candidate, a return to the levels of support given Kennedy and Johnson.

Cultural Analysis of the Election Results

Among culture groups Catholics turned Democratic again, increasing their 50-percent support of McGovern to almost 60 percent for Carter, despite a widely reported unease among them concerning his openly devout Baptist faith. The most striking voting performance, however, occurred among black Americans, who voted fifteen to one for Jimmy Carter, sensing in him and his past record as governor of Georgia an understanding of and sympathy for their cause. They provided him with his narrow victory in such battlegrounds as New York and Ohio, and it was their huge pro-

THE ELECTION OF 1976

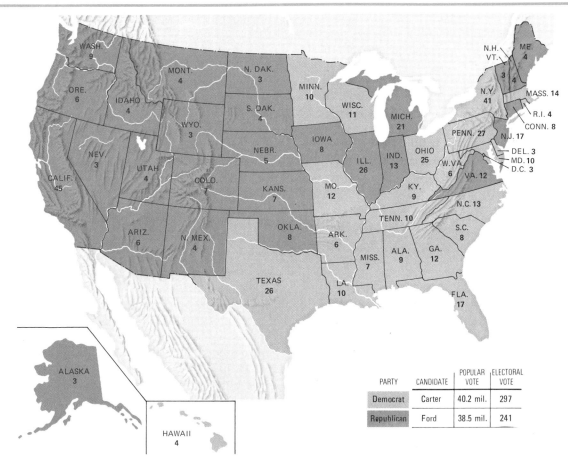

PARTY	CANDIDATE	POPULAR VOTE	ELECTORAL VOTE
Democrat	Carter	40.2 mil.	297
Republican	Ford	38.5 mil.	241

Carter vote in the Southern states that swung that region, aside from Virginia, to the Democrat. (In the South as well as nationally, 51 percent of the whites voted Republican.) The Voting Rights Act of 1965, which effectively enfranchised Southern blacks, won the election for Jimmy Carter by delivering to the Democratic party the last large low-status voting group that, to that point, had remained without political power. As at the nation's beginnings, the Democrats remained distinctively the party of the outgroups.

Carter had appealed to voters to elect him because he had not been part of the Washington Establishment that had got the country into such a mess, but this very lack of experience in the nation's capital almost proved his undoing in the election. In fact, his candidacy revived a traditional national habit. Until Harry Truman, the country had regularly chosen state governors for the White House, men who had not had long experience in Washington. Indeed, Abraham Lincoln himself had been only a one-term congressman and a legislator in Illinois when he became president. Instinctively, the electorate has periodically wished to see fresh men from outside the Washington orbit govern the country.

Gerald Ford came close—but not close enough. Perhaps the crucial factor in his defeat was what he had done within a few weeks of becoming president: his pardon of Richard Nixon. Half of the voters, when asked after the election, said the pardon had been wrong. That half of the electorate voted four to one for Jimmy Carter.

The Carter Administration

On Inauguration Day Jimmy Carter swept into Washington in classic Democratic form. Insisting upon being sworn in as "Jimmy," wearing a business suit bought from the rack instead of the formal attire of tradition, he gave an inaugural address in which he called for a "new spirit." Then he startled and excited the nation by taking his wife Rosalyn by the hand and walking down the middle of Pennsylvania Avenue to the White House, smiling and waving to the hundreds of thousands who lined the route.

His first weeks were devoted to many more such gestures designed to express his view that the government should be brought close to the people again. He began twice-monthly press con-

In a historic event, former Georgia governor Jimmy Carter, though a Deep Southerner and an evangelical Baptist, won both the Democratic nomination to the presidency and the election, and on January 20, 1977, was inaugurated the nation's thirty-ninth president.

Wide World Photos

ferences, took steps to lay to rest the "imperial presidency," at least in its trappings and grandeur. He visited town meetings, encouraged citizens to phone in suggestions for national policies, and made direct contacts with congressional leaders.

His cabinet had relatively few new faces; most of them, such as Cyrus Vance, his secretary of state, were well-known Washington figures. However, among the second-level cabinet positions, where the first-rank leaders of future years are traditionally trained, persons exciting to liberal Democrats took up major posts, including many women, blacks, and young academics. During his presidency Carter would have the rare distinction of not having the opportunity to make any appointments to the United States Supreme Court, but in his term of office he would practically remake the lower courts of the federal system by means of 190 widely praised appointments that brought more women and minorities onto the federal bench than ever before in American history.

The Disappearance of Jimmy Carter

After his first widely publicized gestures to make the presidency close to the people Jimmy Carter seemed suddenly to disappear into the oval office of the White House's west wing. Being a warm, genial, outgoing public figure was simply not natural to him. Carter was a loner who was never comfortable being "one of the boys." Like Herbert Hoover he was an engineer, and he preferred to spend long hours at his desk after an early rising, reading through mountains of paperwork and by himself mastering complex issues. He had campaigned against Washington—against the whole world of bureaucrats, politicians, Washington-obsessed journalists, and lobbyists who ran that town. The new president was a complete newcomer, a former state governor with no experience whatever in the national capital, and yet he reached out very little to Washingtonians for friendship and advice. Rather, he stayed within the small circle of Georgians who came with him to the White House. The result was that he was intensely disliked from the beginning by congressmen, the bureaucracy, and the media.

The president was not only a man of outspoken Southern Baptist piety with a soft Georgia accent, he was also a kind of puritanical Yankee. Austere in his habits, restrained and methodical, he hardly fit the usual image of the Southern politician: gregarious, a "good ol' boy," gracious in hospitality, and flowing in oratory. Clearly one of the more intelligent men to be chief executive, he was logical, concise, exact. The personal touch escaped him even with his own staff, who rarely received a "thank you." Carter wasted no time, recorded and counted everything, and showed an extraordinary talent for mastering details.

The irony was that Carter as a Southerner could never win the affection of the North and West, and as liberal Democrat was rejected by the white South—which, in truth, had not voted for him in 1976. In the 1980 campaign a reporter commented that to New Yorkers, Carter's Southernness was a "cultural albatross. To a New York ear his accent, his piety, his born-again religion, [as well as] his unceasing smile and dial-tone personality come off as, well, *weird*." The first man from the Deep South to lead the nation since before the Civil War, an obvious and classic outsider, he had generations of prejudice against Southerners to work against once the anti-Watergate, anti-Republican mood that had carried him to the White House subsided.

Carter's Lack of Vision

Competent in mastering particulars, Carter failed to acquire a larger vision that could inspire the nation. Washington and the nation at large could not sense where he wanted the country to move, or to what end his many particular proposals were to be molded together. He seemed to move first this way and then that, a pattern produced, perhaps, by too great an analytical turn of mind.

Yet he was an idealistic man, Wilsonian in his obsession with human rights in the world, genuinely compassionate toward minorities, and Trumanesque in his distrust of powerful corporations. (Truman was his idol. A bust of the president from Missouri was prominently displayed before Carter in the oval office.) Americans consistently described him as a good man of high moral principles, a religious person, an intelligent and likable individual, and, like Truman, a person who "says what he believes even if it happens to be unpopular." There was no question, most believed, that he sided with the average person and was sympathetic to the problems of the poor, but the same people were unable to think of him as truly presidential, as a chief executive who was "decisive and sure of himself."

Carter's "Human-Rights" Foreign Policy

For a president who had spent most of his campaign talking about domestic problems, Carter surprised the nation by moving from the outset most boldly in foreign affairs. In his inaugural address he called not simply for control of nuclear weapons but for their elimination. Within weeks of his inauguration he impetuously sought to leap over the tedious delays of the detailed SALT II negotiations with the Soviets, which had been under way since Ford's presidency, by making bold proposals for dramatic slashes of nuclear weapons on both sides. Appalled, the Soviets recoiled from his advances, and in March 1977 formally rejected them.

Perhaps they did so in anger against the

cause Carter was already trumpeting, that of human rights in the world. He openly cast aside Henry Kissinger's theory of "linkage": that criticism of Soviet policies on human rights had to be set aside in order to get Moscow, thus mollified, to negotiate meaningfully on nuclear-arms control and other world problems. "I think we come out better in dealing with the Soviet Union," said Carter, "if I am consistently and completely dedicated to the enhancement of human rights." These words evoked the traditional Democratic urge in foreign policy to improve the world, to follow the "missionary diplomacy" of Woodrow Wilson.

The nation watched with high interest, and western Europe was electrified. The emergence of a Wilsonian world leader in the person of Jimmy Carter stimulated an agitated, Continent-wide outpouring of debate in European countries over human-rights questions that for years had been tacitly ignored. To Moscow's anger, Carter met with Soviet dissident Vladimir Bukovsky, recently expelled from Russia, and sent a personal letter to Andrei Sakharov, Nobel Peace Prize winner and leader of the dissident movement in the Soviet Union (who in 1979 would be stripped of his Soviet honors and placed in internal exile). At the same time, he criticized Czechoslovakia and the bloody dictator of Uganda, Idi Amin, and cut back on foreign aid to Argentina, Ethiopia, and Uruguay on the ground that human rights were being violated in those countries.

Carter quickly ran into the inescapable contradictions and complexities of such a crusade. European leaders grew critical of his conduct of American foreign policy, which seemed to them excessively moralistic, and they worried that Carter's pursuit of human-rights issues would endanger East-West détente. How indeed, they asked, could an America with obvious human-rights failings of its own at home stand in judgment upon foreign countries? Certain realities of Carter's foreign policy seemed also to jar with his cause. In such sensitive locations as South Korea and the Philippines, where autocratic if pro-West governments were in charge and violations of human rights by the authorities were regularly reported, the Carter administration generally felt constrained to hold back. "We must balance," said Secretary of State Cyrus Vance, "a political concern for human rights against economic or security goals."

The Crusade Broadened and Institutionalized

President Carter was not to be quieted, however. The human-rights cause was perhaps the closest of all to his heart—at the end of his administration he would describe it as his greatest contribution to history—and he established a broad and persistent program, backed up by a large State Department staff, to pursue the campaign. At the United Nations in January 1977, Carter asserted that "no member of the United Nations can claim that mistreatment of its citizens is solely its own business. Equally, no member can avoid its responsibilities to review and to speak when torture or unwarranted deprivation occurs in any part of the world."

In its daily conduct of diplomacy the Carter government sought to use the threat of denying military and economic aid, as well as of barring loans granted to particular countries by international development-assistance bodies, to bring pressure upon governments abroad that consistently engaged in gross violations of their citizens' rights. In the more than 130 countries with which the United States had diplomatic relations, a careful monitoring of accusations of violations of human rights was maintained, and where it was felt necessary to do so governments were directly warned of American concern. American diplomats abroad worked for the release of political prisoners, for the reestablishment of constitutional rights where these had been suspended, and for the ending of torture. Repeatedly, aid programs were halted or reduced, or commercial licenses allowing the sale of military equipment were withheld. By the end of 1977, official objections had been entered to the loaning of nearly $500 million to countries guilty of human-rights transgressions.

The Carter administration had consistently prickly relations with the Republic of South Africa as it labored to get that country to moderate its policy of separating the races and keeping blacks in an inferior, powerless position. Throughout black Africa, in fact, in such countries as Rhodesia (later called Zimbabwe), American policy under Carter was to work persistently for majority (i.e., black) rule. Brazil, run by a military regime, angrily canceled its longstanding military-aid treaty with the United States in March 1977 in protest against American pressure on human-rights issues. Working through the Organization of American States, Carter secured in mid 1978 the visit of an investigating commission to Argentina, where government violation of human rights was notorious. In February 1979 he withdrew all support for Nicaraguan dictator Anastazio Somoza because of his refusal to bargain with Sandinista rebels for the creation of a more broadly based government.

The Push Toward Arms Control

Jimmy Carter came to office convinced, in traditional liberal Democratic fashion, that militarism and an obsession with arms, as well as a generally belligerent attitude in diplomacy, leads to world tensions and wars. The president deplored an excessive anticommunism, and he was pledged to slash spending on arms for the American military system. He clamped close controls on arms sales to foreign nations, and terminated plans for building a new manned bomber, the B-1 (which had a price tag of $102 million per airplane). In arms-control negotiations with the Soviets, Carter argued that as long as America had a reserve force sufficiently destructive to punish the Soviets catastrophically if they attacked, the United States could move ahead in an atmosphere of cooperation and enter into agreements to reduce numbers of missiles. Minimal deterrence: this would be the basic principle. Carter believed that one Poseidon submarine armed with atomic-tipped missiles that it could fire at the U.S.S.R. would probably be sufficient protection for the United States. Both superpowers had far more nuclear weapons than they needed to destroy each other many times over, and any further complex calculations about limited exchanges of nuclear strikes and how many missiles would be needed to maintain such a war were to the president meaningless theoretical exercises.

The Strategic Arms Limitation Treaty signed in 1972 by the Nixon administration (SALT I) allowed the Soviets about 2,600 nuclear missiles, on land and in submarines, and the United States more than 1,700. What more, Carter asked, could possibly be needed? In April 1978 Carter moved further to defuse international tensions by deferring the deployment in Europe of what was termed the neutron bomb: a nuclear weapon that relied primarily upon radiation to kill human beings and thereby avoided the devastating physical destruction of existing nuclear explosives. He did so in response to the widely expressed feeling that reliance upon such a "clean" nuclear weapon would make warfare seem once more practicable and enhance the possibility that nations might resort to it.

The SALT negotiations and agreements had consistently been criticized by conservatives in American politics, for whom distrust of the Soviets was a cardinal item of faith, and who believed essentially in ever stronger armaments on the American side. Thus, to the accompaniment of rumblings in Congress, where many thought Carter far too ready to trust Leonid Brezhnev, the president continued his arms-reductions discussions with the Soviets. In May 1979 SALT II negotiations were completed, and in a June ceremony in Vienna that ended in an exultant Carter embracing Brezhnev, formal signatures were affixed to the documents. The goal on both sides seemed to be fully to revive the mood of détente that had come under increasing attack in the United States. An extremely complex agreement that few could genuinely understand, SALT II quickly became a political football.

The Demise of Salt II

The fact was that the nuclear rivalry between the superpowers and indeed the geopolitical setting worldwide had changed drastically from 1972, when SALT I had received practically unanimous approval from the Senate. Recently the Soviets had begun deploying a new generation of missiles close to western Europe that upset the balance of power in that theater, and at the same time they were vastly expanding their naval forces. In countries such as Angola and Ethiopia they had been thrusting Marxist regimes into power, with the aid of thousands of Cuban ground troops. It was known, too, that the Soviets had been making great advances in nuclear-missile accuracy (ironically, with the aid of technology apparently purchased from the West as part of détente), so that America's hundreds of underground silo-located missiles were becoming vulnerable. Under Richard Nixon the United States had vastly multiplied its atomic striking power by developing missiles equipped with multiple warhead tips (MIRVs), which could spray a number of nuclear bombs at selected targets. But it had become clear that the Soviets had by this time matched that capability. Thus, it appeared to Carter's critics that the Soviets might be able to eliminate America's ground-based nuclear force in a "first strike" while perhaps neutralizing American nuclear-armed submarines with its much-expanded undersea submarine-killer fleet. To the Carter administration these seemed absurd and paranoiac delusions, but the political reality was that SALT II was stalled in the Senate committees by these fears. As it turned out, SALT II would never be brought to a vote in the Senate.

The President Declines in the Polls

President Carter had been in office less than a year when his approval rating among the American citizenry began seriously dropping. The uneasiness with Carter that had been building in Washington spread rapidly across the country, and at the same time he made little effort to reach out for support to traditionally Democratic groups such as labor, blacks, and Jews. In traditional Democratic fashion he had poured a long list of reform bills into the congressional hopper—legislation concerning the welfare system, governmental reorganization, energy, taxes, public works, immigration, and other issues—but had failed to follow up by building good relations in Congress and getting his measures through. An aura of ineffectiveness began to surround him.

In truth, it seemed as if nothing Carter could do would be given any praise. In part this came from his own weaknesses: his inability to create affection for himself and to indicate that he was certain of what he was doing. Reflecting these failures, a Gallup poll in the summer of 1978 found that only one of three Americans was ready to say that the President was a man of strong leadership qualities, whereas a year previous two out of three had been ready to make this judgment. This reluctance to give credit to Carter arose also from an unusual readiness among Americans to criticize him simply for his personal style and ethnic origins.

There was more to it, however, than this. Since the rise of the imperial presidency, Americans had built up higher and higher expectations of the man occupying that office. Franklin Roose-velt, who created the powerful presidency, met its incredible challenges with style and amazing effectiveness, considering his extraordinary success in getting legislation through Congress, and this set a standard that few succeeding him seemed able to match. Truman was savaged for incompetence while he was in office, a fact conveniently forgotten by later generations. Dwight Eisenhower was too loved and admired to be subject to more than moderate criticism, and he presided over a relatively contented nation. His successors, however, came in for heavier and heavier condemnation. John Kennedy was facing a mounting chorus of accusations of incompetency at the time of his assassination; after his early successes Lyndon Johnson became a president widely regarded with distaste; and Richard Nixon seemed permanently to sour the national attitude toward presidents with his felonious behavior in the Watergate affair.

Thereafter, an almost morbid fascination with picking out every small fault of the chief executive, in his personal life and his public performance, seized the national mind—and above all, the media, whose tactic of investigative journalism had done so much to expose and topple Richard Nixon. John Osborne of *The New Republic* mused in October 1980 that he had become, "along with the candidates and with everybody else in this country . . . a victim of a media mindset that took hold during the Watergate period and has steadily intensified since then. It is a mindset preoccupied with the personal virtues and flaws—more with the flaws than with the virtues—of Presidents and other newsworthy figures and, in consequence, less and less inclined toward substantive examination of their accomplishments and failures." Ironically, the president who was made by Watergate, Jimmy Carter, seemed ultimately to be its victim.

In the Congress itself a passion for self-reform in the wake of the Watergate scandals, which prompted stern disapproval of any centralization of authority in the hands of a few individuals, created near anarchy. A major piece of legislation, such as a bill on energy, now had to undergo examination and debate by rank upon rank of new committees and new subcommittees before it even came up for a formal decision. In addition, the Watergate era created a national revulsion toward whoever was in office. A great influx of inexperienced and independent-minded legislators, each determined to make his or her mark in Washington, arrived in the capital to turn Congress into a babble of conflicting voices. As the first president to try to get legislation through so disorganized a body, whose behavior exasperated and dismayed even its loyal adherents, Jimmy Carter paid a heavy price in defeat and public disapproval. With some 11,000 staff members at work for individual legislators and 30,000 more employed in the entire congressional establishment (such as in the General Accounting Office), the Congress had ample power to impede presidential leadership; it had no power whatsoever to supply leadership in his place.

Domestic Accomplishments

Nonetheless, as his term proceeded Carter achieved a growing record of legislative successes: more than 60 percent of his proposals, of which in 1978 alone there were some 200, eventually won approval. He had insisted that the national government needed a drastic streamlining, and he got the authority to reorganize it. The results were not very remarkable, but in his first year he pulled together many scattered agencies to create a unified Department of Energy, and in 1979 a separate Department of Education (which resulted in a renaming of Health, Education and Welfare as the Department of Health and Human Services). Carter secured the first major reform of the civil-service system in generations, making that institution more flexible and enhancing the possibility of promotion as a reward for outstanding service. Environmentalists were delighted to see the president succeed at long last in winning stringent controls on strip-mining operations which aimed at restoring the land after mining was completed. At the very end of his administration Carter won another great victory for environmentalists in an enactment that put 100 million acres of public land in Alaska—an area roughly the size of California—under protection against development. Indeed, environmentalists considered Carter as committed a conservationist as the two Roosevelts.

As a farmer, the president was able to construct an agriculture program that was remarkably successful in raising farm prices and promoting sales abroad. During each of his years in office farm exports broke former records. In 1980

the total reached $40 billion, an extremely important fact to every citizen in a country suffering severe balance-of-payment problems due to the high cost of imported petroleum. It was often said that the enormously productive United States farming system was to the world's food needs what the Near East was to its energy demands.

There was more to the record. Convinced that over-regulation in key sectors of the economy had become constrictive and damaging, Carter achieved a historic turnaround for the national economic system by securing from Congress the deregulation of the airlines, of trucking, and of banking institutions. Then, in an achievement surprising in a man of agrarian background, the president actually brought into being what his Democratic forebears, Kennedy and Johnson, could never seem to achieve: a viable, successful urban redevelopment program. So successful was he in this, in fact, that in the presidential election of 1980 most big city mayors were strong Carter supporters.

Urban renewal had been labored at for almost twenty years. At great cost, large downtown areas in declining American cities were slowly cleared—but private investors, who were thereafter expected quickly to fill the vacated space with new buildings, often failed to come forward because the project was not inherently profitable. Urban decline was often accelerated. However in 1977, at the urging of Carter, Congress authorized a new attack on the problem of urban revitalization. Called the Urban Development Action Grant or UDAG program, it scored an impressive record in luring business back into urban centers. By 1981, in fact, more than $8 billion in private downtown investment had been stimulated, a startling six-to-one return on a $1.3-billion federal subsidy—in addition to which, some $2.3 billion in private investment in neighborhood and residential projects had been launched, with a $471-million federal subsidy. In a number of hard-pressed cities in the midwestern and northeastern states, UDAG had helped bring communities to the brink of genuine economic recovery.

How was this achieved? By refusing to spend actual public money on any project unless there were already legally binding commitments from businessmen to build new buildings. Also, by giving local officials great flexibility in using the federal funds so as to enhance profitability, and targeting the funds to cities and urban counties most in need, usually in the Midwest and Northeast.

Failures and Partial Victories

The nation fastened its attentions, however, on Carter's failures. He tried to have a consumer-protection agency established, and failed; was unable to secure approval for new legislation on illegal immigrants; was turned back in an effort to impose controls on rising hospital-care costs; was unsuccessful in obtaining a sweeping reform of the welfare system, proposed within a few months of his inauguration; and could find no agreement on national health insurance. In his 1976 campaign he had called the national taxing system a disgrace to the human race, but the result of his efforts to reform it was an act that benefited mainly middle- and upper-income families, not those below those levels, as he had urged.

Again and again the president sought to get Congress to finally come to grips with the nation's energy crisis, only to meet repeated disappointment. In November 1978 that body finally produced a much-battered National Energy Act. It gave Americans major tax credits if they used solar radiation and wind power in their homes and businesses; encouraged utilities to switch to solar energy where possible; and offered financing and grants to stimulate the use of this energy source elsewhere as well. At the same time, President Carter authorized $100 million for solar-energy research in 1979. In that year he went to Congress again, urging a broad additional energy program that called for federal financing of alternative energy sources (primarily synthetic fuels, derived from coal). Decreasing the United States' reliance upon imports of foreign oil, which were reaching $50 billion a year, was an absolutely crucial national goal, the president said; indeed, it was the "moral equivalent of war." Increasingly he came to the view, much criticized by liberal Democrats as no different from that adopted by Gerald Ford, that the best short-term policy would be to allow America's cheap petroleum (maintained at that level by price controls) to rise in price to the world level. This would induce Americans to finally begin buying less petroleum, adopt rigorous conservation measures, and use petroleum more efficiently.

In late 1979 Congress enacted Carter's synthetic-fuels program (in the process rejecting several of his other proposals). Then the president decided to phase out gradually, over a twenty-eight-month period beginning in August 1979, controls on the price of crude oil. The result by the end of 1980 was not only higher prices but a vast increase in the amount of drilling for oil in the United States (more drilling operations than in all previous American history, it was said) and a sharp decline in the amount of petroleum that Americans used. Together with these measures, in a step Gerald Ford would never have taken and Ronald Reagan condemned, Carter fought for and finally won a "windfall-profits tax" that would siphon off to the national government (and, it was hoped, to the people at large) a major proportion of the huge profits that American oil companies would realize from the advent of decontrolled prices (an estimated $442 billion).

The Economy: Carter's Achilles Heel

Jimmy Carter would be struck down in the election of 1980 as much by his inability to keep the economy healthy as by any other single influence. Worldwide inflation, the falling of the international value of the dollar, the immense bleeding outward of American funds to buy oil, an international boom that intensified demand for all products and raw materials: all of these bore inward upon the American economy with mounting force during the Carter presidency.

He got quickly into the fight to cut back on unemployment, sending to Congress almost immediately upon his inauguration a spending program designed to provide many thousands of jobs to the unemployed and thereby a stimulus to industry. Consequently, the economy brightened and unemployment dropped to a point below 6 percent. However, Carter virtually ignored the inflation problem until late in 1978, at which time he announced voluntary wage-price guidelines designed to keep increases at a modest level. This initiative was not particularly successful, and the president was forced through the rest of his term to make ever more desperate lunges at the problem. Again like his predecessor Gerald Ford and to the outspoken attacks of liberal Democrats, Carter finally swung over to a "tight-money" policy. In 1976 the prime interest rate (the rate of interest at which central banks loan money to other banks) was only 6.84 percent; by late 1979 it was close to 16 percent, a staggering increase; and before Reagan's inauguration it would soar to over 20 percent. On both sides of the Atlantic, worried national governments shifted dramatically to a complete adoption of the theories of the American Nobel Prize–winning economist Milton Friedman, who insisted that the *volume of the money supply* was the principal source of inflation. Cut back on its rise by means of high interest rates, he said, and inflation would cool.

The impact of this policy on the American consumer, however, was appalling. High interest rates made it extremely difficult to borrow, and sales of American autos in the United States, already much damaged by Japanese competition (or so it was believed; there were other influences), sagged drastically. Inflation and a cutback on construction due also to high interest rates had sent the price of homes soaring, and it became almost impossible for young husbands and wives to buy homes. Total employment in the United States surged extraordinarily in the Carter years —from 88.6 million at the president's inauguration to 97.3 million in late 1979—but even so the unemployment rate began creeping upward again, toward 8 percent (the figure was much higher among minority peoples).

Most alarming to many was a continued sag in the rate at which the gross national product was rising. In 1976 the GNP had risen 5.9 percent; in 1978 the rate was down to 4.4 percent; and in 1979 it dropped to 2.5 percent. A recession began in 1980 that moderated briefly as the elec-

tion approached but then became more severe. These influences, combined with a 9-percent inflation rate in 1978, one of 13 percent in 1979, and 12.4 percent in 1980, produced a spreading sense of national alarm over the economy. Not since 1917 and 1918 had there been two years in a row with inflation rates in double digits. In February 1979 the Gallup polling organization found 84 percent of the American people dissatisfied with the state of the nation and expecting worse times ahead—though, paradoxically, three of four said they were satisfied with the way things were going in their personal lives.

A Historic Stroke for Peace in the Middle East

Jimmy Carter's finest hour as president came in September 1978. After two years of painstaking efforts to reconcile Israel and Egypt (and finally, by this means, to remove from the Arab-Israeli conflict the largest of the Arab nations), the president could announce that he had been able to bring President Anwar Sadat of Egypt and Prime Minister Menachem Begin of Israel to an agreement that promised an eventual peace treaty.

This was an event that astonished the world. Its origins lay in a decision by Anwar Sadat, one of the genuinely heroic world figures of the 1970s, to visit the Israeli parliament and personally appeal for peace, despite all the hatred and bloodshed that encumbered the Egyptian-Israeli rela-

In the highpoint of his presidency, on March 26, 1979, President Jimmy Carter joins hands exultantly with Egyptian President Anwar Sadat and Israeli Prime Minister Menachem Begin in celebration of their having successfully negotiated and signed a treaty which for the first time brought peace between the former inveterate enemies, Egypt and Israel.

United Press International

tionship. Announced in November 1977, Sadat's decision had led to involved negotiations. Finally, in an extraordinary last-gasp move, Carter asked Begin and Sadat to come to Camp David, the presidential retreat in the Maryland mountains, and, with himself as mediator, seek a common ground for a peace treaty. The three men met in complete seclusion, and after almost two weeks of negotiations and near breakdowns they achieved "A Framework for Peace in the Middle East," involving complex territorial and other compromises. After thirty years of war and near war, peace was finally established. A major element in the success appears to have been the trust that both Sadat and Begin had developed in the Georgian, Jimmy Carter, whose painstaking achievement won wide praise.

However, much of Jewish America never forgot that the Carter administration had significantly shifted the emphasis in American diplomacy in the Middle East. The president had held out a carefully qualified encouragement to the Palestinians in the Israeli-occupied West Bank of the Jordan River for some form of self-governed homeland. He also took important steps to align the United States with culturally conservative Arab powers in the Near East, in particular Saudi Arabia. The president approved key arms sales to such countries, which were strongly disapproved of by Israel, and was accordingly regarded by thousands of American Jews as not trustworthy on the issue of Israel's independence and security. This distrust was to cost Carter heavily in the election of 1980.

Other Major Foreign-Policy Initiatives

Against often passionate condemnation, Carter insisted upon concluding longstanding and often stalled negotiations begun in the Nixon-Ford years with the Republic of Panama on establishing a phased schedule for placing the Panama Canal under Panamanian control by the year 2000. The basic agreement was made in August 1977, and in March and April 1978 the Senate ratified the two treaties by which the new arrangement was carried out. By this agreement, condemned by many in the United States, the Carter administration had prevented, it was widely believed, an outbreak of guerrilla warfare in the

Panama Canal Zone that would have been impossible to stop—as Vietnam had shown—and catastrophically disruptive to world trade. It had also demonstrated to Latin America, by the most positive step, America's determination to treat with small nations on a basis of respect and equity.

In another bold move (also solidly prepared for by the preceding Republican administrations), the Carter administration, along with the People's Republic of China, announced to a surprised world on the fifteenth of December, 1978, that as of January first of the following year the two countries would establish full diplomatic relations. This step required the formal severing of treaty and defense ties with the government of Taiwan, which to this point the United States had recognized as "The Republic of China." A tacit understanding underlay these measures: the People's Republic of China would not try to take over Taiwan by force. Thus the decades-old controversy over what Americans should do about the two Chinas was resolved. Henceforth, the United States recognized the People's Republic as "the sole legal government of China."

These steps began a dramatic new era not only in Sino-American history, involving extensive trade and cultural relations, but also in world history. The U.S.S.R. fears above all the one billion people of China, with whom it shares a border hundreds of miles long, and thus regards any drawing together of China and the United States—its principal adversaries—with alarm. Under the charismatic Deng Xiaoping, the vast People's Republic had in 1978–79 launched itself on a sharp turn away from extreme Communist ideology and toward what it called the Four Modernizations (agriculture, industry, science and technology, and defense). In this it looked openly toward Japan and the West, especially the United States, for assistance.

Iran and Afghanistan

Two thunderclaps in the Middle East obsessed the United States in the last year of the Carter presidency. On November 4, 1979, radical anti-American Iranian students, angered that the United States should be allowing the deposed shah of Iran to secure medical treatment in New York City, seized the American embassy in Tehran and took its fifty American occupants hostage. Seven weeks later, on the twenty-seventh of December, the U.S.S.R. invaded the Republic of Afghanistan with 85,000 troops, killing that country's president and installing its own regime.

These events dominated all others during the year 1980, save for the steadily worsening inflation and unemployment and the presidential-primary and -election campaigns. Carter's response to the hostage crisis was both cautious and steady, and his national standing soared. There was in fact little anyone could do to extricate the hostages—any military action would doubtless have resulted in their deaths—and this realization both frustrated the nation and stilled criticism. The patriotic surge of approval for the president served to negate the primary campaign of Senator Edward Kennedy, who until then had been thought a two-to-one favorite to take the Democratic nomination. The senator campaigned clumsily at the beginning, and his ill-considered remarks about the hostages and Iran—in which he apparently sided with the radicals by criticizing the shah—renewed the longstanding public uneasiness about his judgment. In May 1980 President Carter, discouraged by the failure of diplomatic measures to free the hostages, authorized a helicopter-borne rescue mission, but it ended in disaster in the Iranian desert.

To the Soviet invasion of Afghanistan the president made far tougher and more spectacular responses. Having so recently signed the SALT II agreement with the Soviets, and having placed his administration at risk throughout his presidency by emphasizing the need to trust the Soviets and to downgrade belligerence, Carter was shocked and angered by the Soviet action. It constituted, indeed, a turning point in recent Soviet-American relations, for the aroused president in effect reversed his course and partially revived the Cold War. Harsh words toward the U.S.S.R., whose leader Leonid Brezhnev the president believed to have personally lied to him, now came from the White House. The Afghanistan invasion, Carter said, was not only a "callous violation of international law and the United Nations Charter," but the gravest threat to world peace since the Second World War, a characterization that puzzlingly ignored such dangerous events as the Berlin Blockade and such outright warfare as that in Korea and Vietnam.

President Carter immediately halted recently negotiated additional grain sales to the So-

viet Union, which totaled seventeen million metric tons. This enormous cutback caused an outcry in American grain-farming regions (until the government made arrangements to buy up the grain), and struck at the Soviet Union's badly strained feed-grain supply. Any further efforts to secure Senate ratification of SALT II were halted; no new cultural exchanges between the two nations were to be negotiated; new sales of high technology were terminated. Soviet fishing rights in American waters were suspended, an action that greatly reduced the crucial annual fish harvest of the U.S.S.R.; and, in a step taken primarily for its high international visibility, Carter initiated a boycott of the Summer Olympics in Moscow in 1980. Scores of Western nations joined in the boycott, and this carefully prepared showpiece for the Soviets lost much of its luster.

In a more direct response, the president immediately warned the world that the invasion of Afghanistan might be the first step in a southward move by the Soviets to seize the immense oil resources of the Persian Gulf region. In his State of the Union address in January 1980, he formally declared that any attempt by an outside force to gain control of the Persian Gulf region "would be regarded as an assault on the vital interests of the United States of America." Following up this important utterance, he began negotiations for bases in the Indian Ocean region, placed a large naval force in that ocean, and initiated a plan to insert American armed might as a standing presence in the Middle East. The president had already secured NATO approval to deploy in Europe more accurate nuclear missiles aimed at the Soviet Union, and he now put much greater stress upon full development of the air-launched cruise missile as the West's new strategic deterrent to the increasingly worrisome buildup of Soviet military strength. Stung by Afghanistan, Carter also authorized a major increase in defense spending in the United States, up to 5 percent above the inflation rate, in each of the succeeding five years. Détente, if not totally destroyed by these grave events, was now a term little used by Americans.

The Rise of Ronald Reagan

The Republicans caught national attention with a hotly contested primary race, in which former CIA director George Bush, Congressman John

Anderson, and a host of other aspirants contended for the party nomination that seemed headed toward Ronald Reagan. By June 1980 it was clear that they were no match for the former governor of California. Both Reagan and Carter, in fact, won enough delegates in the primary elections to claim the nomination without contest in their party conventions, though Edward Kennedy campaigned vigorously to the end, insisting that the Democrats would eventually turn to him. John Anderson took the unusual step of launching an independent candidacy.

Reagan's positions on public issues were classically right-wing conservative. He detested big government, regarded a healthy business world as the source of higher incomes for all Americans, and took a hard line on both the So-

At just under 70 years of age—the oldest man to be elected president—Ronald Reagan in the campaign of 1980 swept up a landslide electoral vote victory over his two opponents, Jimmy Carter and John Anderson, inaugurating a sharp shift rightward in national politics and Washington's policies on spending and social welfare.

United Press International

viets and military defense. As his candidacy became ever more certain, however, he notably tempered his language, reaching for the moderate middle ground that victorious presidential candidates in American politics must always occupy. He insisted that a productive economy depended on sharp slashes (up to 30 percent over three years) in income taxes, which would release buying power. This, Reagan insisted, would reignite the surge in America's standard of living that had reversed itself during the Carter administration, and above all would stimulate industrial productivity. Regulations on business, especially in the form of environmental controls, were to him a major cause of economic stagnation, and he insisted that they be drastically cut back. "Inflation has one cause," he said, "and one cause alone—government. And therefore, less government is the only cure."

The Republican leader wanted to remove Washington from the welfare system and delegate that responsibility to the states and local communities. He had long believed that welfare rolls were swollen by "cheaters," and that this step would meet that problem. Strongly right-wing on the cultural issues that caught wide attention in the 1970s, he opposed busing as a means to effect school desegregation; favored a constitutional amendment to outlaw abortion; was against gun-control legislation; and rejected the Equal Rights Amendment, though favoring the elimination of all statutes oppressive to women. As to the energy crisis, Reagan returned to his favorite principle: let the problem be handled by private enterprise. America had enough petroleum under ground, he insisted, to become energy self-sufficient; all that was needed was to free entrepreneurs from all regulations and let them go after it. Both of Carter's new departments, Energy and Education, he preferred to see dismantled.

The policy of détente had always been condemned by Ronald Reagan, for he greatly distrusted the Soviet Union. The SALT II agreement he roundly criticized as a catering to the U.S.S.R. and a weakening of the United States, and he intended, if elected, to quash it and open a new round of negotiations. Jimmy Carter's foreign policy, Reagan said, was one of "vacillation, appeasement and aimlessness." Above all, huge sums had to be poured into building American military strength far higher. Indeed, Reagan introduced an alarming new note in this area: America should strike not simply for equality in military strength, as appeared to be the existing situation, but for clear military superiority. This position elicited stern warnings from the U.S.S.R. that it would never again allow such a situation to exist, as it had at the time of the Cuban Missile Crisis in 1962, when the Soviets had had to back down in disgrace.

The Election

Jimmy Carter was soon clearly the underdog. National surveys demonstrated that the public regarded Reagan as much more forceful and decisive, as considerably more able to inspire confidence, get the job done, and be consistent on the issues, and as more able to protect American interests abroad. But for a number of weeks in the campaign the question arose, Would the fierce-sounding Reagan be more likely to get the United States into war? The national response was a worried yes, and the Carter campaign hammered on this theme over and over.

On October 28, 1980, the two candidates finally met for a nationally televised debate. The impact of the event was extraordinary. Within a few days the Carter campaign team was plunged

deep in gloom while the Reagan forces, and their candidate, were jubilant. In watching the two men, a decisive part of the American people apparently decided that Ronald Reagan was not the warmonger he had been said to be; that it would be safe to follow their temporarily suspended prior inclination—the "undecided" voter was a large and puzzling phenomenon in all the polls—and vote for the Republican nominee. To the last week the national polls forecast an extremely close election, but on November 4, 1980, Ronald Reagan won an electoral-college landslide of 489 to 49 votes. "Stunning, startling, astounding" were the words *Time* magazine applied to the result. With a popular-vote majority of approximately 51 percent and an astonishing total of forty-four states out of fifty on his side, Reagan had defeated his major rival by 10 percentage points (John Anderson took 7 percent of the vote, but did not affect the outcome in any state). Some 43.9 million votes went to Reagan, 35.5 to Carter, and 5.7 to Anderson. (Only 53.9 percent of the eligible voters cast ballots, the lowest turnout since Truman defeated Dewey in 1948, when 51.1 percent voted.)

Most astonishing was the massiveness of the Republican victory. That party captured the Sen-

THE ELECTION OF 1980

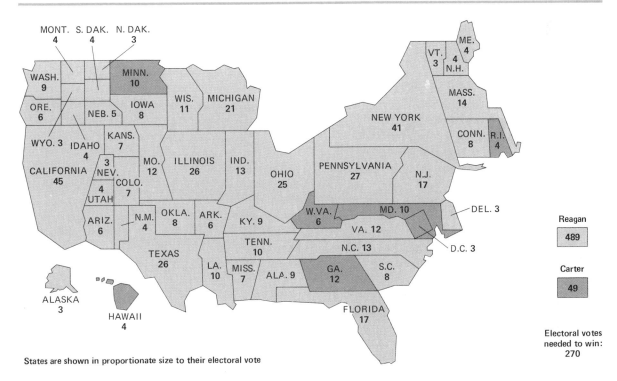

Reagan

489

Carter

49

Electoral votes needed to win: 270

States are shown in proportionate size to their electoral vote

ate for the first time in twenty-six years; made large gains in the House; and acquired hundreds of seats in state legislatures. It was a national tide, not simply a presidential victory. A long list of powerful liberal Democrats in the Senate and House were startlingly defeated; conservatism was clearly in the saddle. Polls taken as voters were leaving the balloting booths revealed that only half of the nation's Jews voted for the Democrat, an unprecedentedly low figure, and that the nation's Catholics voted more heavily for Reagan than Carter (by an estimated 48 to 43 percent—in 1976 Carter had won this crucial group by ten percentage points). That the president could gain only 49 percent of the union voters after having won 62 percent of them four years previously demonstrated the impact of the economic crisis. Only black voters voted overwhelmingly for the Democrat, by a margin of about 72 percent. And the president, as in 1976, lost the white Southern vote—the fifth presidential election in a row in which this occurred.

The Sixth Party System Inaugurated

There is good reason to believe that the election of Jimmy Carter in 1976 was a "blip" in the system, caused by Watergate, and that the election of 1980 confirmed a historic fact: the sixth party system, in the process of being born for a number of years, had arrived.

As we have seen, political history in the United States has gone through roughly thirty-to-forty-year oscillations, or party systems. Each began in a period of national crisis, during which a "critical election" (or a series of them) occurred. The distinguishing feature of these elections is a shifting of the coalitions behind the two parties that makes for a new political order of battle. These changed balances of forces persist until about a generation has passed, when the electorate is composed of people too young to remember at first hand the crisis that, thirty to forty years before, established existing partisan loyalties. In that state of mind they encounter a new national crisis (history produces them regularly), and a new critical election occurs, voters shift sides, and a new party system emerges. We have had five such systems. In the modern era the third party system, inaugurated in the pre–Civil War crisis of the 1850s, lasted until the severe de-

pression of the 1890s, when the Republican-dominated fourth (or Progressive Era) party system began. That system endured until the Great Depression of the 1930s, when the Democratic-dominated fifth (or New Deal) party system arrived.

We have observed that since their emergence in the 1830s the Democrats have been the party of the outsiders: the white South and the non-Yankee, non-WASP minorities, such as the Roman Catholics, Jews, and Irish. In the 1930s that coalition was joined by black Americans shifting away from the party of Abraham Lincoln, the Republicans. In the latter 1960s, however, it was becoming clear that several of those large communities of outgroup peoples were beginning to identify, in life style and ideology, with the WASP core culture in American life, which has traditionally been the heart of the Republican party. Catholics of European origin have recently been shown to have the nation's highest family incomes after the Jews—two groups that were poverty-stricken in earlier times. Moreover, anti-Catholic prejudice, a burning fire in most of American history, has died away since John F. Kennedy's election. His becoming chief executive powerfully enhanced the respectability of Irish Catholics. American culture has in any event become increasingly this-worldly, and religious bigotry is far less powerful now than in the past.

In the 1960s the Democratic party became identified with black America in the way that for many generations it had been identified with Catholic America and the white South. This shift in emphasis soon began draining away Catholic and white Southern support for Democrats. Also shaken loose from their traditional home in the Democratic party were many Jewish voters, perhaps by fears over Israel, by the broad surge of Jewish America into prosperity and cultural leadership, or by distaste for the Democratic party's strong efforts on behalf of black America. The Democrats also became the voice of the new outsiders—Catholics of Latin American background and women's liberationists in the 1960s and homosexual America—in the 1970s. Millions of Americans who had traditionally voted Democratic were repelled by these newly prominent members of their party, and they began turning away from it. Forced busing to achieve racial segregation in the schools corroded white America's efforts to hold onto liberal racial attitudes. Stringent environmental controls on certain kinds of industrial operations, and therefore on jobs; huge welfare rolls reflecting the growing numbers of minority Americans suffering unemployment: these and other powerful forces in national life pushed great numbers of citizens toward the anti-big-government ideology of the Republicans, their emphasis on local control, their friendliness toward big business, and their solid preference for traditional morality and traditional ways of living.

Richard M. Nixon's victory in 1968 was the first indication of the wide impact these shifts in attitude and identification were to have following the cultural revolutions of the 1960s. Nixon won the Catholics of European descent to his side, the first Republican to do so. His immense victory in 1972 showed that these partisan shifts had carried even further. Then came the trauma of Watergate and a national revulsion away from the Republicans. In 1976, therefore, Americans elected a man completely outside of Washington, a man whom they regarded as honest. Jimmy Carter's election, though by a narrow margin, seemed to indicate that the longstanding Democratic majority was once again healthy. In 1980, however, the whole system, and not just the presidency, swung rightward. Republicans regained the White House after their brief ejection, and much else besides.

It appears that a critical series of elections, those from 1968 through 1980, have refashioned the political landscape. What was the crisis underlying these elections? It was threefold: the cultural upheavals of the 1960s, which deeply dismayed most Americans; second, the post-1974 takeoff of inflation and unemployment, which resisted all of Carter's efforts (and may well resist those of Ronald Reagan as well); and the revived Soviet threat, which traditionally produces an eruption of national patriotism and fears over national security, both of which tend to aid the Republicans.

If Catholics and Jews have increasingly lost their "outsider" mentality, the same may be said, apparently, of the white South, now firmly in the Republican camp. How can a region that has produced two of the last five presidents be any longer outside the pale? A vast part of the nation that has been undergoing booming industrialization, urbanization, and modernization, the South, with its swiftly growing Sun Belt states, can no longer feel permanently inferior to the Frost Belt.

The "core culture," long resident in the Republican party, is perhaps best thought of in the 1970s as no longer simply WASP, but as an expanded cultural community of many different kinds of peoples who fit under the name that became current in President Nixon's years, Middle America. It is this community that, with a steady and growing accession of Catholics of European descent, Jews, and the white South, was responsible for the election of Ronald Reagan to the White House. At this time no similar movement toward the Democrats is discernible. Perhaps, though, the "new immigration" from Asia and other non-European parts of the world may, as it builds—clearly the Hispanic portion of the American people will grow very large in future years—do once more for the Democrats what on several occasions in the past such "new" immigrations have accomplished: replenish their ranks and enable them to begin a fresh rise to power.

The sixth party system need not be thought of as one in which a single party, the Republicans, will dominate politics, though such visions are now much current in Washington. In the second and third party systems (from the 1830s to the 1890s), the two parties were essentially equal in power, though Republican dominance in the northern states during the Civil War and Reconstruction, and therefore in Washington, for a time obscured that condition. Among the courses that American politics may take in the 1980s and beyond, a balance of power like that in nineteenth-century politics seems the most likely—a balance that will see first one party and then the other in power. The United States may well be far advanced, in fact, into an era of one-term presidents, as it was in the 1800s. Certainly the problems the country faces now are so complex and resistant to solutions that an exasperated citizenry may regularly dismiss chief executives after their initial four years of authority. The fact that for the second time in a row Americans have chosen a president from outside the world of Washington hints in this direction. Of this, however, we will know more as the coming years unfold.

A Remarkable Day

For fourteen months the United States had watched in total frustration and bitterness as the Iranian government kept fifty-two Americans hostage. Also, during the same period, they had argued out among themselves their presidential choice. The Carter administration labored endlessly, obsessively, to secure the release of the hostages; the president often said that nothing else so occupied his mind. Ultimately the voters, among their other irritations, decided that Carter had mishandled the lengthy crisis, and this feeling told against him in the voting booths. Nonetheless, after the Reagan victory in November, the president continued almost nonstop negotiations, through Algerian diplomatic intermediaries, to win the hostages' freedom.

The Iranian government appeared finally to conclude that it would get better terms from the Carter administration than from the incoming president, Ronald Reagan. At the last possible moment, after all-night vigils, final agreement on release of certain impounded Iranian funds in the United States, in return for the hostages' release, was achieved. On the 444th day of the hostages' captivity, January 20, 1981, Ronald Reagan was sworn in as President of the United States, and—about an hour thereafter—a jet transport lifted from the airport runway at Tehran and, carrying

the hostages, began the long journey home. It was a day of extraordinary drama, one in which the tension building up until the hostages' Tehran departure seemed to draw national attention away from the inaugural ceremonies and the beginnings of the new administration. A rush of joy engulfed the country, during a tumultuous welcoming-home of the hostages. Meanwhile, the oldest man to be elected president—he would be seventy years old within weeks of his inauguration—took office freed of the crisis which had borne down the last year of Jimmy Carter's single term in the White House.

By far the greater burden for the new president, however, was one which would not go away: the gravely afflicted state of the national economy. It was this national ill that was the central concern of his Inaugural Address. President Reagan sought to make of this statement a star-spangled, up-beat, confident proclamation that the spirit of America could once again rise victorious. "We have every right to dream heroic dreams," he said. "Progress may be slow, measured in inches and feet, not miles—but we will progress." The nation was clearly in a mood to give him every benefit of the doubt. The new president took office in an outpouring of warm approval from the media and from millions of American citizens. This same atmosphere, however, had surrounded Jimmy Carter's accession to the presidency four years before. Carter's real testing was yet to come, as this history then observed, and American voters eventually concluded that he had not successfully met that challenge. Another confident man was in the White House at the opening of 1981. What the coming months and years held for him and for the nation was unknowable, but one fact was evident: after four years of a liberal Democrat, the country had returned to the conservative Republican path it had veered strongly toward in 1968. Whatever happened, the directions of national policy henceforth would be strikingly different from those which had pointed the nation's course under Jimmy Carter of Georgia.

A tremendous surge of national relief poured out on January 21, 1981, when after more than 400 days in captivity in Teheran, Iran, freed American hostages arrived at Rhein-Main Air Base in West Germany, after a stop-over at Algiers, to greet cheering crowds of Americans.

United Press International

Bibliography

The narrative this chapter presents has been based primarily upon current sources: newspapers, periodicals, and direct observance. The following comprises a listing of works which were also consulted: Arthur M. Schlesinger, Jr., *The Imperial Presidency* (1973); Carl Bernstein and Bob Woodward, *All The President's Men** (1974); Jerald F. TerHorst, *Gerald Ford and the Future of the Presidency* (1974); Congressional Quarterly, *President Ford: The Man and His Record* (1974); Jimmy Carter, *Why Not the Best?** (1975) and Robert L. Turner, *"I'll Never Lie to You": Jimmy Carter in His Own Words** (1976); John Dean, *Blind Ambition: The White House Years** (1976); David Wise, *The Politics of Lying: Government Deception, Secrecy, and Power** (1973), and *The American Police State: The Government Against the People** (1978).

Carl N. Degler, *At Odds: Women and the Family in America from the Revolution to the Present* (1980); Sheila M. Rothman, *Woman's Proper Place: A History of Changing Ideals and Practices, 1870 to the Present* (1978); William H. Chafe, *The American Woman: Her Changing Social, Economic, and Political Role, 1920–1970** (1972) and *Women and Equality: Changing Patterns in American Culture** (1977); Betty Friedan, *The Feminine Mystique* (1963) and *It Changed My Life: Writings on the Women's Movement* (1976); Robin Morgan, ed., *Sisterhood is Powerful: An Anthology of Writings from the Women's Liberation Movement** (1970). (Other valuable recent works are Barbara Deckard, *The Women's Movement* (1979); Jo Freeman, *The Politics of Women's Liberation* (1975); and Sara Evans, *Personal Politics: The Roots of Women's Liberation in the Civil Rights Movement and the New Left* (1979).)

Michael Novak, *The Rise of the Unmeltable Ethnics: Politics and Culture in the Seventies* (1972); Everett Carll Ladd, Jr., with Charles D. Hadley, *Transformations of the American Party System: Political Coalitions from the New Deal to the 1970s** (1978); Andrew M. Greeley, "The Ethnic Miracle," *The Public Interest,* 45 (1976), 20–36, *That Most Distressful Nation: The Taming of the American Irish* (1972), and *The American Catholic: A Social Portrait* (1977); Richard L. Rubin, *Party Dynamics: The Democratic Coalition and the Politics of Change* (1976); Kirkpatrick Sale, *Power Shift: The Rise of the Southern Rim and Its Challenge to the Eastern Establishment* (1975); Numan V. Bartley and Hugh D. Graham, *Southern Politics and the Second Reconstruction* (1975), and Numan V. Bartley, "Voters and Party Systems: A Review of the Recent Literature," *The History Teacher,* 8 (1975), 452–69. For my own essay on the emergence of the sixth party system, see: "America's Sixth Major Vote Shift," Opinion-Editorial Page, *The New York Times,* November 11, 1980. See also: Norman H. Nie, Sidney Verba, and John R. Petrocik, *The Changing American Voter** (1976); Richard Scammon and Ben J. Wattenberg, *The Real Majority** (1971); and Louise Kapp Howe, ed., *The White Majority: Between Poverty and Affluence** (1970).

* Available in paperback.

39

THE AMERICAN PEOPLE AND NATION: COMPARISONS

It is the year 1867, the Civil War is still red in memory, and an American in his early thirties, a newspaper reporter, is spinning through the countryside of France in a railway carriage and staring in fascination at the scene flying by:

What a bewitching land it is! . . . Surely the leagues of bright green lawns are swept and brushed and watered every day and their grasses trimmed by the barber. . . . Surely the straight, smooth, pure white turnpikes are jack-planed and sand-papered every day. How else are these marvels of symmetry, cleanliness, and order attained? It is wonderful. There are no unsightly stone walls . . . no dirt, no decay, no rubbish anywhere —nothing that even hints at untidiness. . . . All is orderly and beautiful. . . . [We sweep along], always noting the absence of hog-wallows, broken fences, cowlots, unpainted houses, and mud, and always noting . . . the presence of cleanliness, grace . . . the marvel of roads in perfect repair, void of ruts and guiltless of even an inequality of surface. . . .

Samuel Clemens (Mark Twain), who wrote these words, was a Gilded Age American who had suddenly found himself in a highly civilized country, and comparisons thrust themselves at him wherever he went. America in his time, in the era of the Gilded Age and the first centennial (1876), was still crude and unfinished. The Paris toward which his train was heading was still a marvel to people from the United States, who felt themselves rustics and provincials when there. They were, as Twain entitled the book he published in 1869 on these travels, *The Innocents Abroad.*

Gilded Age Americans in 1970s America

How would Americans from the Gilded Age react if they were somehow transported to 1970s America? What comparisons would they find themselves instantly making; how had the American people, and the ways in which they governed themselves, changed? Mark Twain's first responses were to the *appearance* of things in France, as is true even today when travelers from underdeveloped countries visit western Europe and the United States. And so it would be with 1870s Americans visiting 1970s America: they would be struck by the cleanliness, by the neat and precise arrangements of the public scene.

Americans from the Gilded Age, like Twain in France, would exclaim at the lack of dirt and dust, and at much more, which even France in Twain's time could not display: the absence of stinking outhouses set behind homes, standing in multistory columns beside tenement houses, or arranged in great ranks outside of hotels. They would be surprised at the odorless (to them) rest rooms lavishly provided, the refuse cans placed everywhere to receive litter from the streets; the pure water, clean food, hygienic packaging, and meticulous public inspection of restaurant kitchens; the gleaming mounds of washed fruits and vegetables in the stores; the lack of rumpled clothing, tobacco spittle, cigar butts, stains, and patches. Abraham Lincoln and his cabinet, next to the neatly pressed men of modern government, would look like refugees from a rummage sale. Walking about an American city, people from the 1870s would be struck also by the absence in the streets of the thousands of animals used in past times for transportation and labor, and thus the lack of manure and great droning clouds of flies. There are neat roads, painted lines, smoothly riding automobiles, discreet curbs and gutters: the motorcar was approved by most people when it appeared because it thus *cleaned up* the environment. The Gilded Age Americans would observe cars and people waiting quietly at traffic lights, and orderly lines in stores and theaters. The water supplies, heating systems, food markets, flood-control systems, communication networks, and vast departmentalized stores would all seem so logically arranged, measured, and centrally regulated.

Floods of color—kaleidoscopic, rich, and bright—pour from buildings at night and are displayed in everyday clothes, buildings, and advertisements. The world of the 1870s, with its dull black leather, its dirt and smudges, has been replaced by a world of startling oranges, yellows, blues, and reds. And light is everywhere, blurring daytime and evening—light in rooms, streets, buildings, constantly glowing across the countryside, dotting the whole earth with vast spreads of various colors, darting, flashing, steadily burning. People from the 1870s would think the typical home an industry in itself with its array of motorized aids and devices. The terminus of communications systems that pour in floods of information, music, and visual stimulation by the hour, it would seem open, airy, clean.

Range of Life Style

They would note the enormous range in most people's style of life: the distances they travel for enjoyment or for business; the vast array of occupations, most of them unheard of a century ago; the many ways of recreation. They would be surprised by the extraordinary cosmopolitanism of taste in music, books, and art, and by the fact that America is no longer slavishly dependent on Europe for its cultural life; that it has itself become a source of cultural forms and standards, its influence flowing out to all the world. People living in the 1870s would have known a culture determinedly practical and little concerned with aesthetics, but in the 1970s they would see a widespread concern with beauty, styling, and urban beautification. Music is everywhere—in automobiles, offices, supermarkets, and homes. Thousands of local symphonies, play companies, and art programs have sprung to life in the past generation. Allied to this interest in aesthetics is a new attitude toward wilderness, which is considered no longer a howling savageness to be tamed and cut down, but a place of beauty and refuge.

In the midst of an orderly culture that is sensitive to the arts, however, persons from the 1870s would note a contrasting tendency: a disorderly fragmentation of accepted styles. They would be perplexed by the personalization of literature, the uniqueness of each writer's vision expressed in many changing forms; the personalization of dance, people expressing their own feelings in their own patterns; the disappearance of clear social directives on dressing, eating, and behaving. Our society would seem paradoxical to them because in some ways it has become orderly and standardized and in others chaotic and individualized. American city streets, with their sudden anarchic tangles of wires, illuminated signs, and fried-chicken eateries, would seem, in their special squalor, an ironic foil to the remarkable islands of ordered architectural elegance that stand in the midst of most great cities.

Of course the visitors from a century ago would be astonished by America's wealth. Society's capacity to carry through vast projects using immense stores of public and private capital, the enormous social power of government and business corporations—these things would be almost appalling. The sight of soaring buildings and arabesques of concrete freeways circling and swooping through the cities would be breathtaking, quite aside from the endless, roaring streams of automobiles flowing everywhere like metallic rivers. The speed of transport would be a continual wonder to the people of the 1870s—not simply over long distances, for which the railway would have in part prepared them, but over the short distances of everyday life. The ease of going ten miles in one direction, five miles in another, and ten miles in still another, all in the course of a morning; the fact that many people go 500 miles over the course of a weekend to ski, swim, mountain-climb, or carry on business—all this would be amazing.

Would Pollution Surprise?

Produced by this power and affluence, of course, are the polluted skies, lakes, and rivers of present-day America. Would this also astonish Americans from the 1870s? Certainly the cities of their time were massively polluted with human excrement, noisome smells, disease, filthy water, rotten food, choking coal smoke, and the noise of traffic. Urban humanity had to live jammed together, since transportation facilities were meager and jobs had to be nearby. In the 1870s, London had been a polluted city for centuries. In the late nineteenth century, men and women staggered about through blinding fogs in that city because the air was choked with tiny particles of coal ash. Pittsburgh, Chicago, Boston, Philadelphia, and New York were black and grimy as a result of the pervasiveness of coal-fired industries and coal stoves in homes. Humanity has probably never lived in such polluted environments as those of the great cities of Europe and America a century ago.

Then, however, people had a different attitude toward pollution than they do now. The grimy steelworkers of Pittsburgh liked coal smoke, for heavy plumes pouring out of steel-plant chimneys meant jobs. Caught in a nationwide frenzy of development, people were heartened by the sight of factories springing up everywhere and of seemingly limitless mineral resources being mined. Environmental concern is a sophisticated state of mind. Its development depends on mass education, an instantaneous communication system, and the ability to look at the world at arm's length, so to speak, and become conscious of a polluted planet.

It is hard to believe, however, that the massiveness of the problem as it now exists would fail to affect someone from even so environmentally indifferent an era as the 1870s. The incredible rate at which resources are being gobbled up, the fact that 200 miles east—that is, generally downwind—of Los Angeles one can encounter smog so thick that it seems as if a huge forest fire must be nearby—all of this would certainly be alarming to someone from a century ago. The impending death of the biosphere, widely forecast, would be a chilling thought. The loss of blue skies and sparkling rivers outside the cities, as well as the sprawling invasion of streets and homes into vast areas of countryside, would also seem grievous to a visitor from the past.

Wealth and the Masses

It is a safe guess, however, that the people of the 1870s, like anybody from a part of the contemporary world that is markedly less wealthy than the United States, would be more impressed and attracted by the tremendous change in the life style and income of the farming and laboring classes. They would note that farm protest, industrial warfare, and the widespread conviction that bankers and employers are cruelly exploiting the masses have all died down. Protest now comes from culture groups—black Americans, youth, women, Mexican-Americans, and Indians—and not so much from economic classes as formerly. Americans from the 1870s would be surprised at the relative power of workers in relation to their employers, at the much safer working conditions, and at the shorter hours. Instead of the seventy-hour average of the 1870s workweek, the average today is forty hours or less. This decrease has opened up opportunities for leisure and recreation thought only visionary before.

In short, the standard of living soared almost beyond comprehension in the century from the 1870s to the 1970s. Each generation in that period saw its real income double that of the generation before. In the eighty years from 1890 to 1970, the nation's output of goods and services per person—its basic productivity—more than

quadrupled, while working hours were halved. From the 1930s depression to 1980, the average income tripled (after taxes and inflation). Whereas half of Americans owned their homes in 1950, in 1977 about two thirds did so. Advanced technology transformed the home in these same three decades: by the late 1970s almost every home had a television set, more than half had room air conditioners, and almost half had automatic dishwashers. From 1950 to 1980 the number of automobiles owned by Americans tripled, reaching slightly more than one vehicle for every two persons, and from 1960 to 1977 the amount of gasoline consumed doubled. Per capita, Americans used more water each day, had larger homes, required more personal space in which to live, and used increasingly more energy. Real, spendable earnings for the average blue-collar worker (whose numbers accounted for about three fifths of the labor force) rose 23 percent in the 1950s and 13 percent in the 1960s—but then fell off slightly, by 2 percent, in the 1970s, due to rampant inflation. Though the median family income for Americans actually rose by almost 12 percent in 1979, for example—to $19,684—the inflation rate was so high as to practically cancel out this increase.

One major element in the rise in income after 1945 has been discussed earlier: the number of women at work. In reality, American families were working harder in the 1970s than ever before, either to keep up with inflation or to maintain some advance. Two persons were at work in half of the nation's households—husband and wife—and there were also huge numbers of part-time teen-aged workers whose wages added to family income. Thus real, disposable income per person (rather than simply the income of male heads of households) exhibited a continuing, if declining, rise: up 34 percent in the 1960s and 24 percent in the 1970s, but with a sharp falloff in the rate of increase late in the latter decade.

Gilded Age Americans would be startled to see, however, that the kinds of people they thought of instinctively as the poor are no longer in that condition. In their time those of Yankee (and later, WASP) backgrounds monopolized the highest incomes. However, in 1976 a national study made for the Ford Foundation revealed that the family incomes of Jews and European Catholics actually outclassed those of Protestants.

Protestants of British descent, though, still had a higher rate of occupational mobility, securing higher-prestige positions in greater numbers than other groups.

Persistence of Poverty

Therefore, the persistence of widespread poverty would be puzzling to 1870s Americans. They would see millions of people living unskilled and unemployed outside the affluent mainstream of American life. In the South Bronx in New York City, they would observe 40 percent of the 400,000 residents on welfare, 20 percent of the homes without water, drugs and crime so prevalent that fear poisoned the atmosphere, and a tuberculosis rate fifty times higher than the national average—in sum, a degradation probably unparalleled since eighteenth-century London. In this wonderfully abundant country, with its great necklaces of affluent suburbs and countryside estates garlanding its cities, there were in 1978 still twenty-five million Americans in families earning below the government-estimated poverty level of $6,191 a year.

On the other hand, the very fact that the government counted such poor people, gathered immense sums to care for and train them, and mounted years-long campaigns to lift them upward would astonish observers from the laissez-faire era of the 1870s. They would observe a War on Poverty launched in the mid 1960s that in the late 1970s was costing $12 billion annually (compared with its $1-billion expenditure in 1965). In 1978 nearly five million Americans were being directly taught skills that in an earlier era they would have been expected to pick up on their own, or starve. In the program's decade and a half the proportion of Americans living below the poverty line (22.2 percent in 1965) has been halved—primarily, it must be stated, by the vast upward surge in the economy, which provided more jobs.

Though unemployment in 1978 hovered at 6 percent for the entire population, it reached levels of 40 percent for black teen-agers. About three of ten black Americans and other minority-group members lived below the poverty line in 1978 (in the best of circumstances, a dismayingly high figure), while more than half of them (55.9 percent) had been at this level in 1960. Perhaps,

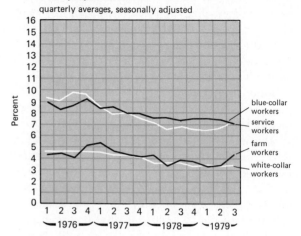

Unemployment Trends
quarterly averages, seasonally adjusted

Source: U.S. Department of Labor, Bureau of Labor Statistics, *Monthly Labor Review.*

however, a rock-bottom figure had been reached: after 1969 the proportion of the poverty-stricken population remained at about 11 percent, despite the billions spent in antipoverty programs. Technological and mechanical changes had eroded the long list of occupations that required almost no skills, from perhaps 9 percent in 1957 to 5 percent in the late 1970s, making it ever more difficult for the genuinely unskilled and undereducated to become self-supporting.

The Variety of Cultures

Gilded Age Americans would be amazed at the enormous population of the United States of America: 226.5 million Americans living in fifty states in 1980, 83.2 percent of them white, as against 38.5 million, 88 percent of them white, living in the 38 states of Centennial (1876) America. Equally astonishing would be the nation's cultural diversity. In the 1870s the American people were simply black or white, with statistically tiny exceptions, and the whites came overwhelmingly from northern Europe and the British Isles. In the 1970s, the United States contained millions of Americans of Asiatic and of Hispanic origin (only 56 percent of the latter in 1980 declared themselves in the census as "white") as well as Afro-Americans, millions of Catholics, Jews, and Orthodox Christian Europeans from the Mediterranean and eastern European countries, and Moslems, Hindus, and Buddhists from that vast arc of countries beginning in the Middle East and sweeping around the earth's bulge to India and Thailand.

Indeed, Census Bureau figures released in early 1981 showed that the 1970s witnessed one of the sharpest and most significant changes in the ethnic and racial makeup of the United States, probably the most marked in any ten-year period. All major racial minorities showed a much sharper rate of growth in numbers than did white Americans, whose numbers in the 1970s grew by 6 percent to 188.3 million (the total population increased from 203.2 million in 1970 to the 226.5 million figure in 1980). Black Americans, still the largest minority in the country, increased by 17 percent from 22.6 to 26.5 million, or a growth from 11.1 to 11.7 percent of the nation's population. However, it was among the Hispanic population that the growth rate was most startling. In 1970 those listing themselves in census returns as of "Spanish origin" were 9.1 million in numbers. By 1980, they had grown to 14.6 million (a 61 percent increase), up from 4.5 to 6.5 percent of the American population. While the actual numbers of "Asian and Pacific Islander" peoples were considerably lower, their rate of increase was even higher (up 128 percent from 1.5 to 3.5 million), making them 1.5 percent of the American population. Clearly, the 1965 immigration reform, stimulated by John Kennedy, was having a continuing and dramatic impact upon the makeup of the American people. In another, much older, category of Americans, there was also marked increase. In those listed as "American Indian, Eskimo and Aleuts," the rise was from 800,000 to 1.4 million, or a 71 percent growth. In fact, the

1980 census was the first to count more than one million American Indians. (Part of these increases, Census officials indicated, was due to improved techniques used to count minority populations.)

Gilded Age Americans would also be astonished at the immense size of the cities of the 1970s. Imagine metropolises of eight million people! The teeming masses in them would seem to visitors from the 1870s to fill city streets like salmon crowding up a river, oceanic in their multitude. And among them there would be, surprisingly, hundreds of thousands of American Indians. No longer at war with the whites or sequestered in remote reservations, a large part of this ancient people in North America would be urban Americans, agitating for their rights from within the body politic, going to work like everyone else in the nation's industries, and struggling to maintain their distinctive identity in the face of overwhelming modernization. Equally striking would be the wide dispersion of black Americans out of the South, where in the 1870s they were concentrated, to the northern and western states, though in these locations like practically all of non-WASP, non-Middle America minorities, they congregated in cities, not in the countryside.

Greatly Increased Life Expectancy

The physical appearance of Americans in the 1970s would fascinate visitors from the 1870s: not simply the rich and colorful clothing worn by ordinary people as well as by the more comfortably situated, but the absence of mutilated people— individuals with open sores, stumps for limbs, ravaged faces, dropsy, filmed eyes, gap-toothed and misshapen mouths—the human wreckage of a premedical society, as the United States had been a century ago. They would note with surprise that most people achieved a healthy adulthood and that chronically ill men and women were seldom seen in private homes. Life expectancy was steadily rising. Where life expectancy for male babies was 56 in the 1870s, they could expect to live 68 years in the 1970s. Taking men and women together, national life expectancy was 73.3 years in 1980, following a notable rise of 2.7 years in the previous decade. In fact, in the mid 1970s, the American death rate declined to its

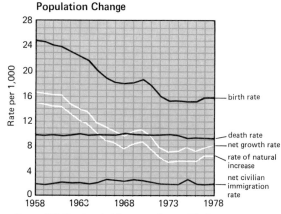

Population Change

Rate per 1,000

birth rate
death rate
net growth rate
rate of natural increase
net civilian immigration rate

1958 1963 1968 1973 1978

Source: U.S. Department of Commerce, Bureau of the Census, *Current Population Reports.*

lowest point in the nation's history—8.9 deaths for every 1,000 Americans each year (in Massachusetts, one of the country's healthier states, the death rate in 1876 was 19.8). Since the proportion of older people in the population was growing (it reached 10.5 percent in 1975), the average age of the American population was steadily rising: in 1980 the Census Bureau could report that the median age was 30 years, up 2.1 years in the previous decade (in 1820 the figure was 16.7). Half a century ago, in the 1930s, there had been 11 working adults for each person 65 and older; in 1980, the ratio was only three to one. Indeed, more than 25 percent of federal spending supported the elderly.

Thus, Americans in the 1970s had not only the gift of long and usually healthy life, they had new problems associated with that phenomenon: the support and care of millions of elderly people by a proportionately smaller population of working people, and the widespread impact of diseases associated with age—cancer, heart disease, and strokes (which, perhaps even more surprising, declined markedly after 1970). Death itself, like birth and wasting disease, had sharply changed its location since the 1870s: from the home to remote, aseptic hospitals, impersonal and bustling, equipped with fantastically sophisticated technology. The wiping away of pain—in much of chronic disease, in surgical operations, in the trauma of physical injuries, and especially in that experience that is everyone's periodic fate, dental care—would be seen as a marvelous, even miraculous, blessing.

Hospitals in Mark Twain's time were dark, dirty, malodorous, and dangerous—places to be avoided. Doctors had very little training, the medicines they prescribed had been in use for centuries, and serious injuries to limbs, which could often lead to gangrene, meant frequent resort to the amputation saw—which, in countryside medicine (experienced by most Americans) would often be applied without anesthesia. Physicians, in fact, were practically helpless against most diseases; their primary function was simply to predict the possible outcome of the disorder from which a patient might be suffering. Louis Pasteur's germ theory of disease, developed in the 1860s, was as yet widely scoffed at, and in any event there was little that could be done if pneumonia, diphtheria, or any other of the great killing diseases struck. Not until about the time of the First World War would medical science have advanced sufficiently for ill people to have better than a fifty-fifty chance that going to a physician would actually help, rather than injure, them.

Gentling of Manners, Improving of Social Justice

The great British political leader William Gladstone said in the 1890s, at the end of his long life, that one of the major changes he had observed since his youth in the 1830s had been a gentling of manners, a reduction in social arrogance on the part of the wealthy, and a mounting sensitivity to the sufferings of the unfortunate. Gilded Age Americans observing life in the 1970s would agree that these trends had continued. Blatant pride of class, haughtiness of manners toward the poor—these were vastly reduced.

It would be clear that in the 1970s ordinary Americans were far more ready to care about others in need, though they would be surprised to be told this. In the 1870s the unemployed, the blind and the crippled, the old, the children without fathers, and the extremely poor were ignored by the taxpayer and by government. There were no schools for the mentally retarded; no public medical care for the needy or the elderly; no old-age pensions; no public fund-raising drives continually in motion to aid victims of various rare diseases, help minority young people get college educations, or pay for the legal costs of people whose rights had been unjustly violated by some local or federal agency in a far distant state. In this history we have seen how in traditional societies the people of each village were hostile to strangers, uninterested in helping people beyond their own community; public executions used to be popular, much attended events. The idea of caring for strangers, of being concerned about suffering and cruel death outside the circle of one's family, is an aspect of modernizing societies.

Police and the courts dealt callously with suspected offenders in the Gilded Age, especially among the poor and the minorities. Quite lacking in most instances was the meticulous concern prominent in 1970s America for insuring elaborate "due process" legal safeguards aimed at protecting the accused and assuring a fair trial. No public defenders, paid for at public expense, were provided. Many "offenses" now regarded as actions protected by the right of privacy were hounded in the 1870s: homosexuality; unusual sexual behavior between consenting adults; men and women living together though unmarried; the sale of birth-control devices and the resort to abortion. Conversely, vast areas of American cities went unpoliced and unregulated a century ago, since few among the comfortable cared about bad housing or violence and death among the poor, whom they commonly spoke of with contempt.

The Revolution of Rising Expectations

One attitude of 1970s Americans that visitors from a century ago would find particularly interesting would be their tendency to react in irritation and even anger at levels of violence and crime formerly ignored, and at a seemingly endless list of social inefficiencies and wastage to which little attention would have been paid in the Gilded Age.

This, the "revolution of rising expectations," was perhaps the most powerful of all the forces that drove Americans to do what they did in the 1970s, from marriage and their personal lives to their opinions about national affairs. This trend, one of very long range, sprang from far back in the eighteenth century, when the conditions of life began slowly to improve. People came to take such improvements for granted and to anticipate more of them. The phenomenon of rising expectations reached an almost breathtaking acceleration after 1945. A century before, in the more clumsily organized and inefficient America of the 1870s, people expected stoically that trains would run erratically and be uncomfortable, drinking water would smell and look impure, streets would be filled with mounds of garbage, politicians would take graft, holdup men would endanger travelers, government would be massively ineffective, and epidemic diseases would arrive annually to sweep off thousands to an early death.

Now, however, that level of stoicism does not exist. Americans expect everything to work well and are upset by levels of performance that would formerly be thought near perfection. For example, people did not in former centuries have high expectations of marriage, though the trend toward the loving marriage may be seen to have begun somewhere in early American history. By the 1970s Americans expected their marriages to be *happy* ones, to be filled with love, understanding, and kindness. Since in reality they often were not, Americans broke them up at a rapid clip. Likewise, Americans appeared to expect to be risk-free in almost every circumstance, and they flocked in waves to the courts to sue each other in consequence of injuries or impaired lives for which the simplest recompense, if any, would have been earlier accepted. Americans expected surgeons to perform open-heart surgery successfully; intricate mechanisms such as their automobiles and their jet airliners always to work; food and water to be pure; government to be financially honest and relatively effective; and the streets to be not only well paved and lighted but also orderly. Social efficiency is a self-feeding mechanism: the more of it there is, the more of it is expected. It is a benign process that generates continual criticism and reform.

The Information Revolution

Although the Americans of the 1870s would be prepared for the telegraph, they would not be ready for the extraordinary instantaneousness and pervasiveness of information from other sources. They would be dazzled by the speed not merely of public information about disasters or great events (in relation to which the nation has become a kind of electronic village, a nonstop town meeting) but of domestic information as well. The husband calling his wife, friends and extended family keeping in touch over long distances, the immense buzzing network of communication lines and radio signals that links business houses and directs government—all this creates far more complex and wider webs of communication than any individual in the 1870s ever maintained. Probably more from the information revolution—from the phenomenon of 350,000 computers at work in American society—than from any other cause, the visitor from the 1870s would feel surrounded by enormous physical power—in armaments, corporations, and technology, and in the extension of people's limbs and agility by electric power and the automobile. Just as Americans in the 1970s move about in a bath of sound, so they are awash in a constant inpouring of information about increasingly complicated national issues.

For this reason, too, visitors from the 1870s would be surprised by the sophistication of ordinary people about matters that few, if any, understood in their day. Many average citizens today know more about the body and its ills and processes, about the natural world and the universe, about psychology, society, politics, world affairs, and economics than even the wisest scholars did a century ago. The knowledge revolution has created an incredible number of intellectuals, whose power and prominence in modern society would stun their counterparts of a century ago. There are scores of learned professions and skilled occupations that did not even exist before. While in the 1870s the average American was either illiterate or had at most three or four years of schooling, now almost everyone is educated at least through high school, and roughly half of the entire population above the age of eighteen will soon have all or part of a college education. The level of technological knowledge alone required to read and understand a modern newspaper is extraordinary when compared with that required in earlier times.

The Revolution Among Women and in the Family

Americans from the 1870s would be astonished at the transformed position and role of women in national life. The spectacle of half of them, including married women, at work outside the home would create consternation. Women voting, wearing (what would seem) shockingly scanty clothes, and being publicly active; the prominence everywhere on paper or in reality of nude or nearly nude female forms—these and so much else about women would come as a shock. The concept of "woman as person" and the women's-liberation movement would seem an almost geological shift from life in the 1870s. Especially arresting to people from the Gilded Age would be the sexual revolution: the explicitness of sexual details in print; the reportedly high rate of intercourse outside of marriage (and outside of prostitution); the ready availability of birth-control aids; the obsession with and explicit description of sexual intercourse in reading material for the

masses; the daily use of what would seem vulgar or at least inadmissible language; the routine use of abortion. To witness a television set would be unsettling enough, but to observe it presenting an unending series of advertisements for devices aimed at tending to the needs of various bodily orifices and recesses would be even more startling.

The family would be seen to be simplified and much changed. It is rarely any longer a place where religious instruction takes place (though in major American subcultures this still occurs), or training in literacy, or medical treatment of serious disorders. It is not as much an economic team as formerly, save on the vastly reduced number of family farms, where parents and children still labor collectively at a common task. Primarily, it would be noted that the modern American family has become fully what people in the 1870s were beginning to see: a place in which to concentrate lovingly on the rearing of children (and not many of them), and provide caring, and emotional sustenance, for one another. Thus, it has been freed to concentrate on what is perhaps its essential function, instead of having to be, as historian Carl Degler writes, "doctor, farmer, manufacturer, food preserver, tailor, baker, and carpenter, as well as a source of affection, spiritual comfort, and teacher of values."

In an intriguing return to older patterns, the flooding of women out of the home to work for income in the past forty years reestablished their role as producers of more than children, and for many Americans made the urban home an economic partnership in something of the fashion of the traditional family farm. In 1950 more than half of American families where both husband and wife were present were supported by the husband; by 1975 this figure had dropped to one third. Since women today work primarily to contribute to the needs of their families, and not in order to have separate careers for themselves (this remains the activity of but a small fraction of women), their pattern of labor is very much that of the American wife of earlier times.

Traditional Family Patterns Persist

American families, therefore, would be seen still to function essentially as they had before. Women continued to rear the children, with modest assistance, if any, from husbands. The care of children remained the focus of family life, in the pattern already emergent in the Gilded Age. The institution of marriage, furthermore, was highly popular. Even in California, thought to be the state of selfish, rootless swingers, an overwhelming majority (70 percent) of people interviewed in the mid 1970s said they were quite satisfied with their marriages, and another 24 percent were reasonably content. Most had been married for many years, and considered divorce highly unlikely. Less than 2 percent reported themselves not at all satisfied with their situation. Nationally, two thirds of all marriages lasted until the death of one spouse; among the failing marriages, two thirds of those who tried again were successful. When asked which aspects of their lives most satisfied them, four of ten Americans replied: their family.

The slogans rampant in the culturally experimental 1960s, which seemed to indicate a new morality in which marriage was being discarded—sex without obligation, cohabitation without marriage, being free to do one's own thing—seemed on balance to create more myth than fundamental change. Although almost a million Americans of opposite sexes were living together in 1977 without benefit of wedding ceremony, they constituted only 2 percent of all married and unmarried couples, and most of them were single persons on their way to marriage. The divorce rate seemed finally be leveling off: in the mid 1970s it was rising at only 2 percent a year, as against a prior annual average of 12 percent. (The most distressing fact, in a generally positive picture, was the high and rising rate of illegitimacy: 15 percent of all births in 1976 were in this category; among black women in 1976 the rate was 50.3 percent, up from 26 percent in 1965.)

The high level of satisfaction with marriage perhaps reflected a deeper historical trend: love between spouses was possibly more central to the average marriage than ever before. Some simple demographic facts are useful here. In the 1800s women spent about twenty years of their lives having and rearing a large brood of children. This left little time for husbands and wives simply to concentrate on loving each other and nourishing their relationship—a fact made even more inescapable by the early-death pattern among men in those times (the life expectancy for men, as we have seen, was fifty-six years). By the 1970s there were fewer children in each family for the mother to care for, they were born closer together, both men and women lived considerably longer, and spouses, as a result, could count on many years that were wholly, or almost wholly, their own. Clearly women were freeing up their lives far more than in the past, perhaps to enjoy their marriages more. In December 1972 American women were found to be bearing children at a rate below the figure of 2.11 per mature woman that is necessary to maintain the population. By the end of the decade the rate was 1.8, and pregnant women were so infrequently observed that it was common for them to be stared at on city streets.

The Question of Divorce

Despite the healthy state of marriage in 1970s America, visitors from a century before would find themselves among people obsessed by the phenomenon of a rising divorce rate and worried that it revealed fundamental moral decay. There was much more to the divorce question, however, than the simple fact of increase in the 1970s. In reality, as we have earlier seen in the social trends of the 1920s, rising divorce rates are a long standing American experience, going back practically to the Gilded Age itself. From before 1900, people had begun increasingly breaking up their marriages because marriage was becoming so im-

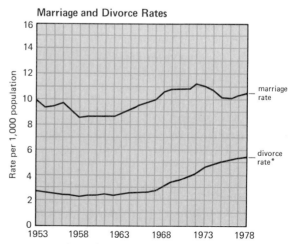

Marriage and Divorce Rates

Source: U.S. Department of Health, Education and Welfare, Public Health Service, *Monthly Vital Statistics Report.*

portant to them. Love was emerging as its fundamental basis, rather the more mundane purposes visible in earlier generations.

In modernizing societies, men and women become less stoical, less ready to put up philosophically with what life gives them. Therefore, if their marriages are not genuinely loving, nothing seems to be left, in people's minds, to justify the continued existence of these unions save the interests of the children, if any. A new concept was emerging in 1970s America: children were regarded as better off if the unhappy couples separated. When this notion joined with the increasing importance that Americans were putting on the quality of the husband-wife relationship, the doors to divorce were swung wide.

However, the important fact remained that the remarriage rate in the 1970s kept pace with the rate of divorce. Americans married at a much greater rate, in fact, than in earlier generations. The number of men remaining single in the 1970s, for example, was only half what it had been in the 1870s. It is a commonplace observation among demographers that Americans are the most married people in the world. Practically 95 percent of all available men and women marry eventually, which is ahead of the marriage rate in the two nearest countries, Germany and Japan, by between 10 and 20 percent. Furthermore, Americans have been marrying at younger ages than elsewhere, though in the 1970s one notable trend reversed this tendency: in 1960 every fourth woman between the ages of twenty and twenty-four was not yet married; in 1980 this proportion had risen to every second woman. In the same two decades the number of unmarried men in that age group rose from half to two thirds. This meant that more and more Americans were waiting until they were better prepared, in terms of education, income, and life situation, before they married, a fact that forecast healthier marriages in the future. It is the very young marriages that are the most unstable, since spouses are less emotionally mature and have greater income and job-stability problems.

Children and Divorce

It was disturbingly true, however, that American children found themselves increasingly in broken families. Traditionally, it has not been unusual for children to be without one parent, but this occurred primarily because of death. In 1965 the number of children without a parent because of divorce finally rose above those in that condition because a parent had died. In 1970 the rising rate of divorce was eloquently clear in one sobering statistic: only seven out of ten children under eighteen were living with two natural parents in their first marriage. (For black children this figure was 45 percent.)

The effect of divorce upon children is not clear. Authorities hold that they are more emotionally resilient than is generally believed, and adjust reasonably well. Nonetheless, almost all children experience a deep and often wounding sense of loss, and many suffer irrational feelings of guilt. In extreme cases these reactions can lead to promiscuity, drug abuse, and suicide. It is clear that children whose divorced mothers do not remarry are much the poorest in the country, have the lowest amount of schooling, get into the most trouble, and have the most distress in launching themselves successfully in life. In 1973 about 45 percent of all families living below the poverty line in the United States were headed only by the mother, and half the children living in poverty were in such families. Since more women with children were securing divorces, the number of mother-headed households was rising: whereas 30 percent of those who got divorces in 1940 were childless, by 1970 this figure had dropped to 18 percent.

Responses to the Broken Home

The broken-home phenomenon would be one of those aspects of American life in the 1970s that people from the 1870s would find most disturbing. It would seem, if nothing else, a disgraceful indication that Americans, in their increasing individualism, were becoming more selfish and irresponsible. This is, in fact, the way modernized societies such as the United States look, in all of their aspects, to people observing them from more traditional settings. The turning away from childbearing by women, one of the towering social facts of twentieth-century America—and especially the recent explosion in abortions—would be seen as a denial of the life force, as a defeminizing trend having profoundly negative implications for the family and society at large. It was commonly said in the 1800s that allowing women to have more freedom to move out in society and to gain an education would ruin them as mothers. Visitors from the 1870s would point to one dramatically evident fact in 1970s America: going to college, and especially taking graduate work and entering a profession, is statistically associated with (which is not the same as saying *causes*) lowered marriage and birth rates. Whereas in 1972 one fifth of the women between the ages of thirty-five and forty-four who had some graduate education, or who made at least $20,000 a year, were not married, barely one out of twenty women in that age bracket who had no college education were single.

Declining birth rates, however, are a worldwide, not just an American, phenomenon. For 200 years the birth rate has in general been dropping in both Europe and the United States, and for shared reasons. In East and West Germany, Austria, and the United Kingdom, birth rates are so low that those countries are already in a "negative-growth" phase. Recent statistics reveal that even in underdeveloped countries the birth rate is dropping. Wherever there exists economic improvement, spreading education, changes in traditional values, and hopes for better lives (which have been seen to be tied to having fewer children), women seem universally determined to break out of their traditional lives and give themselves more personal freedom to work, to consume, and to live differently. It does not require a women's-liberation movement to spread these behaviors. Indeed, as we noted in the previous chapter, the revolutionary movement toward the working wife and mother proceeded in the United States for many years quite without the accompaniment of ideology. Millions of people simply made new choices concerning what to do with their lives.

Youth in Modern America

Young people have experienced more than just the unfavorable effects of the divorce movement. We have seen in this history how each succeeding generation has devoted more love and attention to its children. Since the advent of industrialization gave men enough income to let them be the sole economic support of their families, this trend toward child-centeredness has been the most

powerful of all engines transforming family life. When looking at healthy households, therefore, Americans from the 1870s would be accustomed to the loving-parent and loved-child phenomenon. Only its range, scope, and intensity in the 1970s would suprise them.

There has been another shift as well. Children remain in the home much longer than before, which means deepened parent-child relationships. In 1974 close to nine out of ten young men who were eighteen or nineteen were living at home; for unmarried young women at that age level the proportion was even higher. Keeping the children home until later in life has been a longstanding trend. In the 1870s it was established practice for children to leave home and go to work at around age fourteen or fifteen; in colonial times, perhaps as early as ten.

Clearly young Americans generally prepare for maturity in a vastly improved life situation. Not only are they given much greater care at home over longer periods of their lives, they are freer of cultural restraints to direct their lives as they themselves see fit, there is an elaborate complex of formal educational facilities awaiting them, from kindergarten through graduate and professional training, and a variety of occupations far greater than a century before is available. This means not only more affluence but also a statistically improved chance of finding a life work that suits one's particular abilities and desires. As to the rock-bottom matter of staying alive, simply in the years 1960 to 1980 the mortality rate for young children was cut in half (to 14 per thousand), primarily through the virtual elimination of mass child diseases and the enhanced safety of childbirth. In 1979 four diseases—tuberculosis, diphtheria, poliomyelitis, and gastroenteritis—claimed 10,000 lives. If the death rate from those disorders had been what it was in 1900, the total of such deaths would have stood at 800,000.

The Difficulties and Dangers of Being Young

There is no question, however, that growing up has become in important ways a more difficult and dangerous process for young Americans than it appears to have been in earlier times. Freedom and greater liberty exact many prices. The far greater availability of life choices, in comparison with the Gilded Age—when being a farmer or a housewife was the inescapable future for most young people—means a harrowing struggle with the question What shall I be? This choice, never easy and often painful and filled with doubts, was in earlier eras confined to those few born into affluent households. It is now experienced by millions of young Americans. The identity crisis described by Erik Erikson as characteristic of late adolescence and early adulthood mushroomed in American life as the phenomenon of youth itself, as a stage in life, spread ever wider in the population. No longer going to work at age ten or fourteen but delaying that commitment until much later, perhaps into the middle and late twenties, American young people had long years free from family responsibilities and subsidized by parents in which to agonize through their life decisions; that is, to be in the stage of "youth."

Affluence, too, exacts its prices. As studies of the children of wealthy homes recently concluded by child psychologist Robert Coles demonstrate, the more affluent the young person the more the sense of being "entitled" to good things, to freedom from labor and frustration. This, in turn, can induce self-indulgence, a desire for instant gratification, and aimlessness. Ironically, as millions of black Americans poured out of the South into the northern and western states after 1945, entered urban poverty, and witnessed high rates of unemployment among their young, and as millions from other minority backgrounds experienced the same dismaying disappointments, a parallel sense of aimlessness arose, in this case associated with poverty and anger at discrimination.

Whatever the underlying reasons, which remain complex and elusive, in the 1970s there were clearly some gravely unsettling forces at work in the lives of far too many young Americans. In the United States today, seventy persons commit suicide every day; another thousand or so attempt it. The suicide rate for those aged fifteen to twenty-four tripled between 1960 and 1980. Teen-age suicides now number approximately a dozen a day. Of the 11 to 20 million alcoholics in the country, 1.3 million are teen-agers. Approximately eight out of every ten teen-aged Americans had experience with alcohol in the 1970s, and the percentage of them coming to class intoxicated at least once a month doubled in the years 1965–80, from 10 to 20 out of every 100 students.

Drug use was virtually nonexistent in America in 1950, only 2 percent of the population having had experience with narcotics at that time, but by 1976 six out of ten persons between eighteen and twenty-five had used marijuana and two out of ten were on hard drugs. It was not coincidental that most crime in the 1970s was committed by young men in their teen-age years and early adulthood.

Murder was the leading cause of death among young nonwhite Americans. Among the Americans between fifteen and twenty-four in 1979, the number of homicides was 50,000. Automobiles disabled two million Americans in that year and killed 50,000: more than half of these casualties were persons under the age of twenty-four. Another aspect of the great freedom enjoyed by young people in the 1970s, the sexual revolution, brought with it venereal disease. Syphilis and gonorrhea became the diseases that posed the greatest threat to the young. Twelve million young Americans, it was estimated in 1980, were carrying sexually transmitted disease. For unmarried teen-aged girls, pregnancy became a great risk: a million became pregnant in 1979 (of these pregnancies, three in ten were aborted), of whom 300,000 were under the age of fifteen. The children of such mothers, it must be added, are those with the highest percentages of disabilities of all sorts, whether physical or emotional and whether at birth or later in life.

Intimately linked to the most shocking of these appalling facts—the homicide rate—was the oceanic tide of handguns pouring into American life. Thousands upon thousands of simple arguments, which might otherwise have ended in fisticuffs, escalated into death by shooting. Since 1960, sales of handguns have quadrupled: in 1979, six *million* were sold over the counter and through the mails. In these two decades the murder rate among Americans (primarily males) aged fifteen to twenty-four rose from 5.9 per 100,000 to 14.2. Yet the gun lobby remained so powerful in Congress that despite national polls revealing a dramatically high percentage of Americans favoring gun control, no legislation was enacted.

Rebellious Youth

Visitors from the 1870s would be astonished to learn of the vast rebellion of youth that occurred in the 1960s, though they would expect young people to be bold and reckless. Nineteenth-century Americans took pride in the impatience of youth, accounting it a major reason why progress was inevitable. The whole country was young: millions of young people poured in from abroad as immigrants, built factories, laid out railroad lines, led armies, attacked Indians, rushed westward to plow the Great Plains and mine gold, and founded state after state in the immense continental sweep to the Pacific. Furthermore, college youth (of whom there were few a hundred years ago) were traditionally known to be troublesome and unruly. The colleges then closely controlled their students both outside and inside of class, and violent protest against the strict discipline was frequent. Dormitories were burned down and faculty harassed.

Even so, Americans from the 1870s would be unprepared for the kind of nationwide upheaval against established authority that occurred on hundreds of college and university campuses in the 1960s. They would recognize the anticapitalist, proanarchy cry of the most radical of the protestors, having heard it from young radicals in their own day. What would bewilder them would be the *multitudes* involved, the radicalization, so it seemed, of an entire generation. They would be observing, indeed, the first major rebellion of generation against generation in United States history, though not, of course, the first appearance of a fresh wave of young reformers determined to change things. That had happened almost in waves, as in the Revolution, the Age of Jackson, and in the abolitionist crusade. But mass violence? Student radicals blowing up buildings, storming government offices, skirmishing with police and soldiers? It would seem like the French Revolution.

It has been traditionally true in human history that older generations look upon the younger ones with dismay, believing them decadent in morals and in self-discipline. In the America of the latter 1960s, with its widespread eruptions of drug abuse, violence, and political radicalism among the young, this ancient complaint seemed to be made with more despair than ever, since concrete evidence of alarming changes in behavior was so obvious and indisputable. The rapid rise in illegitimate births, the spread in venereal disease, the dropouts and the hippies, the criminal violence erupting from young men, the regular drug use even in junior high schools: these and other dismaying phenomena among the nation's youth seemed to make of them an almost foreign, and certainly frightening, world to older America.

For this reason, when after 1970 the nation observed college and university students laying aside their radicalism (which in reality but a tiny minority had actually professed) and turning en masse toward academic studies that led toward jobs and not toward social criticism, older Americans felt a vast sense of relief. The "me generation," it was said, had replaced the rebellious generation of the late 1960s. Hard work in college classes and a single-minded drive to gain high grades and thus a coveted place in overcrowded professional schools, or at least a job in a national economy growing ever more difficult to enter, was the 1970s mode. And yet older America was not certain how to take even this more nose-to-the-grindstone youth generation, for its widely described use of drugs, its delaying of marriage and disinterest in having children, carried its own unsettling impact. A brooding uncertainty about young people, therefore, heightened by the epidemic of street crime, persisted.

How Fares the Republic?

In their own time, Gilded Age Americans were sharply conscious that the United States of America was a *republic*. Since the nation's founding, this fact had been trumpeted over and over again to the world and held out in countless orations and sermons as the justification, the glory, of the American adventure at self-government. The Civil War, so recently concluded, had been fought by Abraham Lincoln and the North to prove that a republic, which relied only on the will of the people to hold it together, could survive even the challenge of an attempted (and massive) secession.

Thus, feelings of patriotism and national pride were high—even in the South, which revealed its own deep sense of fundamental loyalty to the Union (in 1860, a majority of Southern voters had actually voted for nonsecessionist candidates) by quietly laying down its arms after Appomattox and once more sending off elected representatives to Washington. Gilded Age Americans unashamedly made almost constant displays of flags. People turned out to march by the thousands in patriotic parades, and when overseas they proclaimed for all who would hear the superiority of their nation and their system of government.

When the Fourth of July arrived on Mark Twain's side-wheel steamship crossing the Atlantic in 1867, an enthusiastic party was arranged, during which the main speaker "rose up and read that same old Declaration of Independence which we have all listened to so often," Twain wrote, "and that same old speech about our national greatness which we so religiously believe and so fervently applaud." Another day a towering clipper ship under a high cloud of sail swept toward the side-wheeler like a great bird. The passengers crowded the rail to watch. "While everybody gazed, she . . . flung the Stars and Stripes to the breeze! Quicker than thought, hats and handkerchiefs flashed in the air, and a cheer went up! She was beautiful before—she was radiant now."

Gilded Age Americans visiting the 1970s, therefore, would be keenly interested to know, How fares the republic? They would be amazed to learn that few would know what was meant by the term. Indeed, they would find that in recent years historians themselves had to laboriously rediscover what republicanism had meant to earlier generations, how powerful an ideology it had been, and how much it had summed up for all Americans the nature and purpose of their country. In the 1870s, almost all the peoples of the world were ruled by unchecked monarchies; feudalism still held fast in most of the societies of Europe; and a nation without a king and a titled aristocracy to govern it, maintain law and order, and uphold an established church was still an unusual spectacle.

Republicanism as an Ideology

Republicanism, in short, had been for centuries the radicalism of what was then called either Christendom or the civilized world. It was a comprehensive theory of human nature, of human society, and of government. Republicans insisted that power corrupts. Monarchists maintained that putting power in the hands of a few individuals at the top was necessary to keep society from tearing itself apart—this would happen, they said, because the common people were ignorant, greedy, and violent. But republicans held that no just society could possibly exist unless the power

of the authorities was under the control of the people it governed. Power, in other words, was a force inherently at war with liberty.

Therefore, sovereignty—that is, *final* authority—had to be taken out of the hands of monarchs and put in the hands of the people at large, who were naturally wise and good because they had never been corrupted by wealth and control over others. They, in turn, had to erect governments with *divided* powers, each of which (legislative, executive, and judicial) would balance and check the others. This called for a written constitution in which the structure and functions of government would be explicitly stated, and the rights of the citizen protected from invasion by that government. By regular elections thereafter, and a wide suffrage, the people would maintain not simply a theoretical but an actual supervision over those in authority. Furthermore, since government was at all times untrustworthy, most of what it did had to be carried out by strictly local governments, in which the people could maintain close control. Thus, a vertical separation of powers would also exist.

All of this was aimed at freeing the (white) individual to live the fullest possible life, to realize most completely his (as yet not her) potential. Alexis de Tocqueville was fascinated by the spectacle of American individualism in the years of President Andrew Jackson. Leaving time behind, and society, family, and all the ancient webs and restraints of history, the American individual, living in his republican society, struck out to enrich himself, improve his condition, conquer his own world. In the 1870s the idea that life in America was open for everyone to make his own way and rise to a comfortable estate was still—whatever the actual social conditions—a faith strongly held and proclaimed. "It's a free country!" No saying was heard more often. The sturdy, self-reliant individual: this was what republicanism in America was all about.

The Four Modes of Republicanism

Republicanism was a national ideology, broad and inclusive. Therefore, Americans disagreed among themselves as to what particular aspects of it they would emphasize. For many Americans, and especially white Southerners, republicanism had above all to protect *liberty;* that is, it had to insure that people were left free to run their lives and use their property (to Southern whites, this had meant their slaves) as they saw fit. For others, particularly minority-group members (Germans, Roman Catholics, and Jews), republicanism's primary emphasis was on *equality:* its real objective was to insure that every (white, male) person was treated equally by government at all levels, had an equal chance to get ahead in life, was given equal respect as a human being, and had an equal right to worship and live according to his own beliefs and morals. From this perspective, no one should receive special privileges, either economic or cultural. The government should keep hands off just about everything; that is, both cultural and economic laissez-faire should rule. Thousands of American farmers, along with urban minority groups (who tended to be the poorer people) felt that the wealthy and powerful were always conspiring to exploit the rest of the people anyway; they needed no help, in the form of protective tariffs or other aids, from government. Thus, libertarian and egalitarian republicans agreed on essentials. As disciples of Thomas Jefferson and Andrew Jackson, they had come together since the 1830s to form the Democratic party, the party of the (white) outgroups.

For many Americans, especially the elite and the moneyed but by no means limited to them, republicanism's true purpose was to create conditions in which imaginative, enterprising individuals could get ahead, free of feudalism's restrictions, and live more abundantly. These people believed in a strong national government that would support the development of the nation's resources and promote a vigorous, enterprising economy. These *nationalist* republicans —Alexander Hamilton's followers, who formed the Federalist party, then the Whig party, and, in the 1850s, the modern Republican party—had their home base among Yankee, New England Americans: busy, hard-working, self-disciplined, efficiency-oriented people. Then there were the *moralistic* republicans—also with strong roots among the pious, puritanical Yankees—who believed the goal of republicanism was to train the people in true religion and true morality. They had a strong sense of team spirit, believing all Americans should live according to commonly shared values (those of Yankeedom). An active government that intervened in private moral behavior (drink, sex, dress, Sunday observance)

was to them an essential instrument of God's work. Pluralism (cultural laissez-faire) was their enemy; homogeneity in life style, according to the true (puritan) faith, their objective. For them, a partnership with nationalist republicans within the Federalist-Whig-Republican party tradition was natural.

Above all, most nineteenth-century Americans believed that a republic was a place of simple, austere, quiet, localized government close to the people. A wealthy and arrogant nation interfering in the affairs of other nations (like Great Britain, that monarchical and domineering nation against which Americans had rebelled) was exactly what they wished not to be. However, some nationalist republicans, inheriting Alexander Hamilton's outlook, rather liked Britain's way of doing things and sought to model America after that fashion.

The Republic in the 1970s

In the Gilded Age, Americans still lived in a republic that bore most of these characteristics, though Revolutionary republicans would have found it surprisingly active, centralized, and costly. In the bicentennial year of 1976, the external form of the American republic would still be essentially as set down in the constitution of 1789, but Gilded Age visitors would be overwhelmed by how immense the operations of the government of the United States of America had become by the 1970s. It was certainly wealthy and arrogant, and until the disaster in Vietnam it regularly interfered in the affairs of other nations, performing essentially the role that Great Britain played in the nineteenth century: self-professed leader of freedom, keeper of the peace, guardian of the seas (and skies) and of the rights of small nations.

Few things would so astonish visitors from the 1870s as the huge size and everyday *presentness* of government. They would see that almost nothing occurs in city, county, state, or nation that was not in some way linked to an agency of government. From decisions on how people are to build structures, pay employees, advertise goods, plant crops, minister to patients, set aside funds for retirement, wire a house, or cohabit with an unemployed husband, to negotiations between labor unions and employers, modes of electric-power distribution, and the intricate mechanisms of international finance, government was involved.

To carry out its tasks, the United States government in the 1970s employed more people than any other country outside of the Communist bloc (where practically everyone is a government employee): some 2.9 million civilians, together with 2.3 million in the armed forces and 3 million employed in companies that engage exclusively in supplying the federal government. Altogether, such people constituted 10 percent of Americans at work. When the roughly 12 million who worked for state and local governments and the 4 million supplying their operations were brought into the computation, about one quarter of the working population in the United States in the 1970s was in some way laboring for government.

People from the Gilded Age would marvel to learn that there were no fewer than 23,000 distinct "special-district" governments in operation in the United States (for fire, recreation, water, sanitation, and a host of other functions), in addition to the regular hierarchy of federal, state, and local governmental agencies—and that these special districts were growing at the rate of 12 percent a year. Simply to record the federal laws and regulations in effect in 1975 required a multi-volume *Federal Register* comprising more than 60,000 pages and covering a shelf more than fifteen feet long. In any given year in the 1970s the United States Congress added about 200 new laws to that compendium, and federal agencies about 7,000 regulations that had the force of law. In fact, legislative bodies in various American jurisdictions enacted about 600 new laws every day in the 1970s, or about 10 million during the course of an ordinary person's life. Between 1960 and 1977 alone, the federal government swelled by 3 new cabinet-level departments (a fourth came in 1979), 14 new independent agencies, 50 new regulatory bodies, and more than 200 new advisory agencies. In one typical small city in Pennsylvania of 16,500 citizens, *seventeen* different layers of government influenced daily life.

The small and limited government of a century before quite disappeared, along with the passenger pigeon, the dime novel, and the dictatorial employer who ran his factory out of his back pocket. The search for order, which originated in the late nineteenth century, and the drive to build a more egalitarian nation by exerting supervision over private business, taking care of the unfortunate, and working toward racial and sexual equality, produced an immense machinery of centralized regulation. Bureaucracy, a new and pervasive force, flourished in American business life in the 1970s as well as in public affairs. Born in the Gilded Age in the effort to make the railroad system efficient, it proliferated like a gigantic plant, sending its tendrils throughout the social system.

Vague and remote but nonetheless everywhere, it presented contradictory aspects. Rigid, impersonal, self-serving, and self-perpetuated, the bureaucracies were also responsible for the creation of a society in which there was regularity of operation, predictability, orderliness, even-handed treatment, carefully made decisions, a diffusion of power, and a concern for the public interest. Capable of generating an irreversible momentum in one direction—as, for example, in the Vietnam War—and resistant to change in ways that frustrated congressmen and presidents alike, the bureaucracies also provided a steady accumulation of knowledge and management by experts who were not subject to public whims.

In this, as in so much of 1970s American life, visitors from the 1870s would be forced to reflect on a paradox: the creation of great power, traditionally the bane of republicans, together with an ever wider spread of justice, or at least the possibility of achieving it. Who in the 1870s would have dreamed that governments would try, even fitfully, to regulate how foods are produced, how products are advertised, and how employees are treated by their employers?

The Democratic Outlook

In the midst of this vastly changed setting, so different from the republic of the 1870s, Gilded Age visitors would be surprised to learn that the basic ideological positions of the two major parties persist in roughly the same form as two centuries before. If Thomas Jefferson were alive in the 1970s, he would have little difficulty seeing which party was his. His ideology of equality and personal liberty attracted the minority groups of his own day to his political following, and the outsiders—those made to feel excluded by the host culture, the WASP community—still cluster in the Democratic party today. Jefferson and his followers hotly condemned the efforts of the (Yankee, puritan) pious to impose their moral beliefs on the behavior of others, and Democrats in the 1970s were still the party that resisted campaigns to use government to supervise private moral behavior.

With its voting base in the minorities, which have historically tended to be lower in income, the Democrats in the 1970s continued, as in Jeffersonian and Jacksonian times, to conceive of themselves as the party of the poor and of those of middling incomes, while being the opponent of the rich and powerful. That is, Democrats leaned toward helping the *consumer*, as against the merchant, the producer, and the financier. (Jimmy Carter's effort to create a consumer-protection agency, much condemned by 1970s Republicans, was a classic Democratic gesture, as was the fight of liberal Democrats in Congress to keep price controls on petroleum.)

Though clearly not a radical, anticapitalist organization, the Democrats in the 1970s distrusted organized capital, as in Jefferson's time, and instinctively seemed to believe that businessmen and bankers conspired to exploit the public. Andrew Jackson and the stern Democratic president of the Gilded Age, Grover Cleveland, deplored the power of great corporations and brooded about the harm done to the country by unrestrained "development." In the 1970s the Democrats were preeminently the party of environmentalists, who sought to put controls on developers, and of those who distrusted powerful corporations and clapped a windfall-profits tax on the huge oil firms when prices were decontrolled. Thus, although still Jeffersonian and Jacksonian in its aims and fears, the Democratic party in its drive to control powerful business enterprise has left far behind Jefferson's laissez-faire methods, save in cultural issues. From Franklin Roosevelt's time its commitment has been to build a more egalitarian country by means of a (Democratically controlled) system of strong centralized authority.

The Republican Outlook

The Republicans in the 1970s, as they had been for generations, were the voice of the entrepreneur, the helpmeet of the aggressive and self-reliant individual who labored to enrich himself—and therefore, without necessarily intending it, society. Until the 1930s Republicans were the advocate of strong, interventionist government.

They liked the ancient Yankee and puritan notion of a vigorous, elitist central authority that looked out for the common welfare and struggled to make a cohesive community out of a huge country by encouraging economic development (through the use of protective tariffs, centralized banking systems, bounties, and the like) and cultural uniformity (principally through temperance and other crusades at the state and local level).

The New Deal killed the idea of a strong central government for Republicans, for it was taken over by the Democrats for social-welfare and regulatory purposes. But this simply encouraged Republicans to place even greater emphasis on building and maintaining a complex of centralized *private* institutions that directed the economy from behind closed doors: Wall Street banks and investment firms, the great corporations (increasingly multinational in outreach), and agribusiness. Ronald Reagan acted directly in the Republican tradition when he insisted that the oil shortage be solved by throwing the entire task, without strings, into the hands of the oil firms, and called for dispensing with Jimmy Carter's Energy Department. Republican economic ideology in the 1970s, in short, remained that of Alexander Hamilton in the 1790s, Henry Clay in the 1830s, and James G. Blaine in the 1870s. That is, if government does anything at all with regard to the economy, it should be to help the businessman, to encourage and unleash him, for he creates jobs and opportunities, and develops the country. The first item on the agenda of any Republican regime taking over the executive branch was to put people friendly to unrestrained freedom of enterprise in charge of the complex of independent regulatory commissions and powerful government departments that the Democrats had built in Washington.

A government sympathetic to entrepreneurs, therefore, was inclined to grant them the railroad rate increase, the liberalization of regulations, or the license to drill for oil that they requested. In this way the bureaucratic system built in the twentieth century did not function, as Democrats would have had it, in a spirit of critical watchfulness over businessmen, but instead provided the aids to business efficiency that can flow from centralized decisions and common regulations. *Producers*, not consumers, were fostered by the Republican-controlled White Houses of the 1970s, as they had been in the 1870s. As Richard Nixon said, there would be no damned trust busting in his administration! Defining the boundaries of free enterprise much more widely than Democrats, Republicans held fast to the ancient faith that left to itself, the business system and freedom of enterprise would do far more to solve the nation's social problems, by creating jobs and widely shared affluence, than government ever could.

Cultural Alignments in Politics

Republicans instinctively held to another venerable conviction: that they were the host culture, the home base of true Americanism. From the beginning of the American nation the Federalist-Whig-Republican political parties were preeminently the parties of those who had founded the country, shaped its culture, established its language, and provided its central institutions: the English—or, in American terms, the Yankees. Eventually, as this core community expanded to take in peoples who were formerly its enemies (the Scotch-Irish, Germans, Dutch, and Scandinavians), it became simply white, Anglo-Saxon, Protestant—i.e., WASP—America. Being the self-appointed custodians of the truest Americanism, Republicans tended also to think of themselves as the special guardians of true patriotism. As they would say in the Gilded Age, were not Democrats disloyal white Southerners, who in 1860 had tried to break the nation apart? or Rome-leaning Catholics and other aliens of strange ways and languages? How could such people possibly know what true Americanism was? Was it not the Republican party that had saved the Union in the Civil War?

The characteristic paranoia of Democrats has been to believe that wealthy capitalists are plotting to exploit the people. That of the Republican tradition has been to suspect that radicals and immoral people, sheltered by the Democrats —in the presidential campaign of 1968 Spiro Agnew called Hubert Humphrey "squishy soft" on communism—are conspiring to subvert the government by selling it out to the Communists, and to debase the morals of the young by spreading permissiveness, pornography, and drugs. Thus, the government should not only root out security risks, it must also supervise the private moral lives of individuals. It was the Republican convention in 1976 that busied itelf with resolutions on abortion and drugs; it was the Democratic candidate who refused to support a constitutional limit on abortion, and who even talked about his sexual lusts in *Playboy* magazine—to the disgust of Middle America.

Shifts Take Place

Gilded Age Americans would notice a dramatic change in the cast of characters, however, on both sides of the partisan line. There would be so many minority groups! And the Democrats, who in the 1870s had been the racist, antiblack party, had by the 1970s fully absorbed black Americans into their ranks. In the 1960s they had even pushed through bold national reforms to carry through the Second Reconstruction and give a strong impetus to the cause of black equality— thus giving expression once more to the egalitarian thrust that since Thomas Jefferson had traditionally been theirs. This, in turn, produced another historic event: a massive decamping to the Republicans of the minorities who had formerly claimed the Democrats' attentions, the Catholics of European lineage, the white Southerners, and to a lesser extent the Jews. Out of this tidal movement among voters came the election of Richard Nixon in 1968, his popular-vote and electoral-college landslide in 1972, and the sweeping nationwide victory of Ronald Reagan in 1980.

The Catholics, Jews, and white Southerners making this political transition did so, as we have seen in the preceding chapter, not only in reaction to the swelling of black America within Democratic ranks and the reforms made to aid it, but because they were feeling increasingly less like outsiders. To vote Republican in American politics has always been a cultural statement as well as a gesture of support for a candidate or a set of proposals. It has been a declaration that one is a member of the club—the well-educated, the established, the respected, the able, and the managerial: the *American*. The Watergate crisis temporarily halted this transition by putting the Republicans in a bad light, but the fading of that event in national memory, the rise of a renewed Communist threat abroad, and the advent of an intractable economic crisis set it in motion again in 1980.

Party Differences in Foreign Policy Persist

The deep involvement of the United States in global politics would at first surprise the people of the 1870s, for in their day the United States had practically no foreign policy. But if they had lived into the 1890s, they would recognize present patterns. They would see the Republicans, as in the 1890s, leaning toward the nationalist side and the Democrats toward the internationalist side. While Republican administrations tended to go it alone in world affairs, pulling back from multilateralism, Democrats stressed the building of an ever widening circle of friends with whom they maintained a joint policy toward world events. Among the Republicans in the 1890s were most of the strong voices that insisted that the world is a place of constant threat requiring the protection of strong military forces, a pattern that remained largely true in the 1970s. Among the Democrats in the Gilded Age, as in the Nixon-Ford-Carter years, were to be found most of those urging cooperation, coexistence, and the reduction of arms. Indeed, this cause undid the Carter administration, which was much condemned nationally for arms cutbacks and the proposed SALT II agreement, as much as anything else.

In the 1870s, as now, there was a foreign-policy elite—composed of newspaper editors, magazine publishers, scholars, bankers, and corporation presidents—that was seized with the notion that the United States must be a power in world affairs. This elite played a leading role in taking the United States to war with Spain in 1898, and strongly advocated the country's subsequent acquisition of an empire. In the 1960s this same confident group of men helped take the nation into the Vietnam disaster on the ground that America was the high guardian of liberty around the globe. In this destructive experience, which could only appall Americans from the 1870s, both Democrats and Republicans were implicated. It was, however, within the former party that the strongest chorus arose condemning the involvement and calling for disengagement; among the latter, with their greater inherent trust in military responses to world challenges, the disengagement was assented to most reluctantly. Visitors from the 1870s would recognize the isolationism that in the 1970s gathered momentum and ended America's thirty-year adventure with international crusades.

What of Liberty?

Of the four principal emphases in American republicanism, we have seen that egalitarianism, moralism, and nationalism (with its corollary of a booming economy assisted by the government and built on freedom of enterprise) were alive and at work in 1970s America. What of liberty?

To millions of Americans, it was this venerable lodestone in American republicanism that was most embattled in post–New Deal America. The thousands of laws and regulations pouring forth from thousands of government units; the host of regulatory agencies and departmental bureaus; the controls of environmental protectionism; the spying upon ordinary citizens not engaged in criminal activity by the FBI and a CIA apparently pliant in presidential hands: what of this immense apparatus, the very existence of which would dismay the republicans of earlier generations?

Clearly Americans have built in the twentieth century a huge and powerful government whose operations are inescapably subject to the ancient republican criticism: power corrupts. Clearly, too, Americans over several twentieth-century generations have redefined "liberty." It was recast to mean not simply freedom from governmental interference in private affairs, but freedom from person-to-person oppression, from exploitation by the wealthy and powerful. It meant being freed from ignorance, prejudice, poverty, fraud in the marketplace, high-handedness by great corporations, bad water, unchecked taking of profits by monopolies (as, for example, in the provision of electric power), unsafe products, and polluted air. Indeed, the very concept of what is "private" has been changed in an almost infinite variety of situations. Parents are no longer free to abuse their children, people may no longer refuse on racial grounds to serve customers in their places of business, manufacturers are no longer allowed to stuff any substance they wish into sausages, and entrepreneurs cannot sell stocks that falsify their descriptions of company assets. In a modernizing, increasingly complex economy and society, the meaning of liberty has necessarily grown more complicated, and its protection more difficult.

Distrust of Power Endures

Also, as 1870s Americans would see, the ancient republican distrust of power is actually flourishing. The Watergate crisis, which much of the outside world saw as a puzzling national uproar over trifles (and therefore as simply an anti-Nixon conspiracy rather than a sincere effort to protect the constitution and the laws), revealed that Americans continue to be extraordinarily prickly at usurpations of power. Nowhere else in the world are heads of government and state badgered so regularly by the newspapers. Nowhere else do chief executives have to make such elaborate gestures to prove that they are of "the people," and want continually to stay in touch with them.

The unending presidential campaigns in the United States, which send the men who seek the nation's most eminent position into hundreds of local communities to shake hands and show themselves closely tied to the citizenry, puzzle the world. In the late 1970s the prime ministers of Canada's provinces bitterly protested a plan to establish an American-style bill of rights and constitution for that country, because they feared what they saw in the United States: government agencies almost constantly in court, forced to defend their powers and actions against citizen lawsuits based in constitutional guarantees of personal rights. The idea that all government records must be thrown open to every citizen, as they are in the United States under the Freedom of Information Act, unless an agency can prove a special exclusion in court, astonishes (and appalls) European politicians and officials.

The antipower, antigovernment populism that flared so strongly in eighteenth- and nineteenth-century America was mirrored in post–1960 events by a continental resurgence of direct citizen-governance and citizen-action politics. The New Deal ethos, which regarded strong government as trustworthy and inherently goodspirited, faded dramatically once the war in Vietnam began and once problack reforms began to impinge upon the freedom of white America to live in its old ways. National polls revealed that public confidence in the presidency and in Congress dropped from 41 to 23 percent and from 42 to 17 percent, respectively, from 1966 to 1977.

This new national mood stimulated an almost bewildering proliferation of citizen-action groups desiring to monitor government and force it to cease what many saw as misuses of its powers. Rushing into national prominence were White Citizens' Councils, parents organized against busing implemented to achieve integration, initiative campaigns to overturn laws mandating racially integrated housing, Common Cause, Friends of the Earth, the National Organization for Women, Ralph Nader's Public Citizen and local Public Interest Research Groups, the National Association of Neighborhoods, and vastly revived older organizations: the Sierra Club, the American Civil Liberties Union, and the National Urban League. In addition, there were hundreds of smaller bodies focusing on consumer protection, utility regulation, taxation, and other causes. Twice as many people contributed money to these citizen-action groups (1.4 million) as to the Democratic and Republican parties. Taken together, these grass-roots movements gave testimony to the sturdy persistence of the tradition of voluntary, organized citizen action that Alexis de Tocqueville had noted in the years of President Andrew Jackson. Indeed, the phenomenon reached levels in the 1970s not matched at any other time since the Progressive Era.

Direct Citizen Governance

Paralleling this upwelling of citizen action was an ambitious assumption of legislative power by organized citizens. The initiative process, which came into existence in the Progressive Era but had long been little used, suddenly became a weapon in many states for aroused citizens directly to assault what they took to be oppressive, swollen government. Of these efforts, one of the more dramatic in its nationwide impact occurred in 1978 in the passage of California's Proposition 13. This step drastically slashed the property tax levied in that state, and sent massive repercussions not simply through California's government but into many other states and even into Washington, D.C. It would be a spectacle surprising to Gilded Age Americans, one that would make it seem absurd to say that 1970s citizens had less control over government than earlier generations.

Accompanying this invasion of legislative power by the citizenry was a seizing of the power to nominate presidential candidates. Here, too, a reform with Progressive Era roots, the direct presidential primary, finally reached its full development. The presidential primary system spread to many more states in the years after 1960, eventually reaching the point of critical mass—that is, the point at which there were enough primaries to allow the citizens at large to nominate presidential candidates. Those campaigning for president could win enough delegates in the primaries to make the voting in subsequent national party conventions a foregone conclusion.

The Question of National Virtue

One especially nagging question presented itself to American republicans as they established their nation two centuries ago. American republicanism released people to enrich themselves largely without restraint, and this, more than anything else, made ex-president John Adams worry about the future of the United States of America. How could people lose themselves in riches and materialism and yet retain the simple virtues of self-denial and community spirit upon which the principle of government by the people depended?

A century after the Revolution, so determined a republican as the Democratic president Grover Cleveland continued to contemplate the question of American virtue. In his Fourth Annual Message to Congress (1888), Cleveland somberly described a nation that in its race for riches was losing its moral health. Great and wealthy cities filled with luxury; immense factories; a mad race for profit; massive concentrations of capital in few hands: these were what met his eye, and he was alarmed. "Communism," he said, "is a hateful thing and a menace to peace and organized government, but the communism of combined wealth and capital, the outgrowth of overweening cupidity and selfishness . . . is not less dangerous than the communism of oppressed poverty and toil, which, exasperated by injustice and dis-

content, attacks with wild disorder the citadel of rule." The boast of free institutions, Cleveland went on, was that they served the humblest. Giving into wealthy hands the control of society, however, would make free institutions "a glittering delusion and the pretended boon of American citizenship a shameless imposition."

The question of national virtue remained as fresh and as pressing in the 1970s as it had been in the 1880s, and in the generations before. It was, of course, this spectacle of a lavish, wealthy, and profiteering America that made the United States in the 1970s seem to foreign peoples a fascinating but ultimately sick society. It is this race for material possessions and profit, Soviet newspapers daily insist, that makes the United States a racist, crime-ridden, drug-cursed, unhappy country exploited by its powerful capitalists. Drugged by their affluence, American workers allow themselves to be made slaves by employers.

Visitors from the Gilded Age would unquestionably see that republican institutions in the 1970s were still no guarantee of a virtuous nation. They needed to be worked with attentively, in a labor without end, to make them produce the good society. Gilded Age visitors would recognize the stink of old-style corruption in the Washington atmosphere of the 1970s. The national government was simply too huge, its expenditures too enormous, to escape any longer—as for many years, after the anticorruption reforms of the Progressive Era, it seemed to do—from the impulse to reach into the till and take public funds. The civil-service revolution, called for and carried through generations before to fight this tendency, had in general been successful. The many millions of government servants in the 1970s customarily cared honestly for the funds in their charge, since they were not as beholden for their jobs to political manipulators as their predecessors were a century before. However, studies by the Justice Department led to the estimate (thought by many to be much too high) that in the 1970s perhaps $25 billion in federal funds were being annually diverted to private use by fraud and theft.

In the late 1970s corrupt behavior was uncovered at the nation's highest levels as the result of a law-enforcement campaign initiated by President Jimmy Carter to search out "white-collar crime." Public officials all over the nation, and even in the Congress of the United States, were found to have sold their services to wealthy interests. For the first time since the Civil War, in 1979 congressmen were expelled from that body for taking graft; others were simply sent down to defeat by the voters. All of this called to mind the fear of corruption constantly felt by American republicans in earlier generations. Corruption was to them perhaps the most powerful antidemocratic, antirepublican force. Selling influence, buying votes, handing out special favors to insiders: these were the qualities of eighteenth-century British government that Revolutionary-era republicans were convinced made it possible for royal dominance to grow and for individual liberties to be endangered. In the Gilded Age too, the specter of corruption, growing out of illicit partnerships between capitalists and the government, came to dominate the public mind. Democrats warned continually that the idea of a cooperative partnership between business and government, in the Republican mode, led inevitably to corruption; that this was, in reality, the principal means by which the wealthy were able through protective tariffs and other special privileges to exploit the people at large.

Most disturbing to Americans from the 1870s, however, would be the *constitutional* corruption displayed in the Watergate scandal. It had been common a hundred years ago for Americans to warn themselves that some day, if they were not vigilant, they might build a national government like those then existing in continental Europe: so strong and militarized that they depended on secret police, spies, and undercover operations against their political critics to stay in power. Powerful government agencies and a mighty presidency were warned against precisely because they were potential enemies of civil liberties. So, indeed, did it turn out in the mid 1970s. Watergate was not a simple affair, like the timeless search for money and contracts; it was, rather, a corruption of the heart of the American system of government itself, ideally a free and uncontrolled political process presided over by a national government that does not arrogantly regard itself as above the law.

The Fear of Size

For many Americans, nothing else as effectively and alarmingly explained the corruptions seeping into the nation's life as the immense size of all its institutions. "Our crises," wrote Kirkpatrick Sale in 1980 in his book *Human Scale,* "are not only different in degree, they are also, *because of that,* different in kind. Never before have nations grown so large, never have corporations become so powerful, never have governments swollen to such sizes, never have the instruments, the factories, the farms, the technologies been so huge —hence, never before have the crises been so acute." Certainly this immensity of the republic and its institutions would astonish Americans from the Gilded Age. (In Chapter 35, we learned of the complexity and powerful role of the great corporations.)

In a spontaneous revolt against bigness, tens of thousands of Americans were engaged in the 1970s in what *The New York Times* called "a full-scale back-to-the-land movement": a campaign to find ways of living simply, outside the system. In their new life style they demanded "less machinery, less technology, less everything that comes from and depends on big business." The movement's adherents saw the nation "as controlled by unbridled corporate power, corrupted with surfeit and crazed by an impulse to consume and throw away more and more faster and faster." In the 1970s more Americans moved out of the big cities than into them; small-town America became, after decades of losing population to the metropolises, the most rapidly growing unit of population in the society. (For every 100 persons moving into metropolitan areas in the years 1970–75, the Rand Corporation found, 131 moved out.) Patrick Caddell, Jimmy Carter's pollster and adviser, remarked in 1977 that "the idea that big is bad and that there is something good to smallness . . . has been one of the biggest changes in America over the past decade."

The prominence of giant corporations in American life is the feature that Soviet scholars point to as proof to them that the United States is moving inevitably toward communism. This apparently ever increasing centralization of economic affairs in fewer and fewer hands, and the growing intimacy between big government and big business, means to Soviet scholars that "state capitalism" has emerged, the last stage before government simply takes over the entire economy so that it will be run by central public authority. The corruption inherent in American republican institutions, they believe, will inescapably produce a collapse: oversize institutions will be seen by the people to be ultimately exploitive, and will be seized and operated for them.

Counter-Trends

As the shift away from big cities reveals, however, American life is constantly exhibiting tendencies that are more complex than they seem. Individualism seems perennially heading in contrary directions and breaking out in new forms. In the 1970s it pushed away from depersonalizing influences to assert self-identity and self-worth in seemingly hundreds of ways: new marriage and family styles; new fashions; "self-assertiveness" training for women: the do-it-yourself movement (an explosion in the economy); the feminist insistence upon women controlling their own bodies; individualistic, almost anarchic, dance and music; "flextime" in work schedules; the growing trend toward more worker participation in factory decision making; the assertion of individual rights above those of the military in cases involving female pregnancy and the treatment of recruits; and the enhanced rights of individuals in judicial proceedings. "The self," observed the Harvard sociologist Daniel Bell, "is taken as the touchstone of cultural judgments."

Even in the big American corporation, thought by the Soviets to be massively centralized, the reality was significantly different from the common stereotype: great localization of authority allowed plant managers to follow the market and make a profit, which was certainly flatly contrary to Soviet-style industrial management. In that system, which is an "administered" rather than a "market" economy (that is, not "this is what is selling—make more of it," but "this is what we decide is needed") every production decision affecting any one of the U.S.S.R.'s 160,000 industrial enterprises is made at the center, in Moscow. The result is a lack of initiative, gross and multiplying errors, rigidity, low productivity, and constant shortages. By contrast, even the largest American corporations, relatively speaking, are models of dispersed authority, localism, and flexible response to demand (though as we have earlier seen in Chapter 35 the more complex and expensive the product, the more lead time in making new products is needed, the more investment is required, and the more rigid the system

is). Indeed, it is this localism, scattering of authority, and individualism that the Soviets find hardest to understand in the American system. Individualism not only seems to them destructive, selfish, and disorderly, it raises puzzling problems. How does the American system stay afloat? Surely there must be some hidden central agency which directs it all? Learning that in so basic a matter as water-resource management the United States works through thousands of locally-controlled and poorly-coordinated agencies, Soviet students and scholars shake their heads in disbelief. How strange a system! How does the American economy not fall into total disorder? (How indeed?)

How can it be right, the Soviets ask, to stand aside and let individuals enrich themselves and grow powerful? Free enterprise is rooted in the notion that the urge to self-improvement, to profit, is ultimately a dynamic, creative, and never failing source of innovative energy that should be released, so that society may benefit. To the Russian mind, this simply means letting some individuals grab profit out of others' labor. Their literature, and their common memory of serfdom, and of immense wealth and landholdings concentrated in the hands of a tiny class of aristocrats who exploited the labor of the masses, makes it impossible for them genuinely to understand how individual initiative cannot be ultimately destructive to the community. Adam Smith's theories of the free market and rising productivity can be carefully explained to them but they remain mystified. The idea sounds not only exploitive, but risky, uncertain. The riskiness of American life in general, everyone being on their own, having to find their own jobs, facing unemployment and possible bankruptcy; the mobility; the sink-or-swim atmosphere; it is an alarming spectacle to the Russian person.

It is important to observe, in short, that in 1970s America there was immensely more individualism, localism, and smallness than stereotypes of American life usually allow. Certainly, by comparison with the Russians, the American people were almost wildly individualistic, verging on (what the Russians would term) anarchy, the social condition they fear the most. Small business in the American economy remains surprisingly alive and vital. Just as two out of three Americans actually lived in small cities or in villages in the 1970s (the Census Bureau obscures this fact by reporting every community of over 2,500 people as a "city"), so all but 2 percent of American businesses operated with less than a hundred employees. Even in the manufacturing part of the economy, where huge assembly lines and immense, smoking steel plants seem the rule, two out of three businesses employed less than 20 persons in 1967; in all of manufacturing, the average number of workers in each unit was slightly under 45. There were 1.6 *million* corporations in the United States in the 1970s. About 165,000 of them did over a million dollars in business annually, but 843,000 took in no more than $100,000, a modest sum in any business setting. In the plastics industry alone there were 4,500 separate companies; in the manufacturing of machines, about 15,000. In the automobile industry, traditionally the seat of great producers, such as Ford and General Motors, 4 corporations put out 60 percent of all parts, but close to 1,500 more were involved in the making of the remaining 40 percent.

The True Test of Republican Virtue: The Treatment of Minorities

The fundamental test of republicanism has always been: how does the majority treat the minorities? This, said critics of republicanism in the eighteenth and nineteenth centuries, was the weakest point in any system built upon letting the majority rule. Prejudice, jealousy, greed, envy of the wealthy, the urge to dominate, and the other human failings warned of for millennia would lead to oppression. The Founding Fathers put numerous safeguards in the Constitution, notably the checks and balances of power, so that majorities could not work their will easily. But it has remained true nonetheless that in the American republic, as in any society, the position of minorities has always been difficult and, in the cases of greatest weakness, cruel and discouraging. Visitors from the Gilded Age would find the situation of American minorities vastly changed in the 1970s, and in most respects for the better, but the egalitarian promise of American republicanism was still a long distance from full realization.

Racial discrimination would be a familiar sight to Americans from a century ago. The Civil War and the first Reconstruction would certainly prepare them for the Second Reconstruction of

the 1950s and 1960s, when the turmoil over Afro-Americans and their status in national life renewed itself. It is not too much to say that in American history black-white relations have been the most crucial and telling of all American problems, and the most faithful indication of the true state of American republicanism.

Gilded Age Americans would observe that in the past twenty years the United States has been going through a transformation from a caste society, in which black Americans were by law and practice kept in a separate and depressed status, to one of legal equality. Of the four aspects of equality—civil, political, economic, and social—the Radical Republicans of their day had been concerned with only the first two, working (in the long run unsuccessfully) to guarantee fair trials and the vote to the black community. Since these had been lost in later years in the Southern states, the Second Reconstruction had to labor all over again to achieve them once more. Furthermore, strong efforts were made in the 1960s to extend the concept of equality into economic and social spheres.

Americans from the 1870s would be surprised to see how markedly, in the face of great odds (and with the occasional and crucially important aid of government), black Americans have improved their life. They would be surprised, indeed, to see how strikingly the situation of all ethnic groups has changed. The fact that Irish Catholics are no longer reviled and segregated would be especially notable. They would see that the spread of black Americans across the continent has made what their generation thought of as a Southern problem a national one. They would, in fact, observe with a certain wry detachment that northern whites are drawing back from northern blacks like their white countrymen in the South did over many generations, a phenomenon that is leading to a Southernization of politics throughout the country. Black Americans have participated in all the sweeping changes described earlier in this chapter, but to what degree?

On August 28, 1963, 200,000 white and black Americans gathered in the shadow of the Lincoln Memorial, around its long reflecting pool, and listened with lifting hearts to Dr. Martin Luther King, Jr.'s great oration "I have a dream!"

I have a dream that my own little children will one day live in a nation where they will not be judged by the color of their skin, but by the content of their character.

Then came the historic Civil Rights acts of 1964 and 1968 and the Voting Rights Act of 1965, reiterating the constitutional rights of black Americans and mandating equal voting rights for them and equal access to public accommodations, jobs, and housing. The Economic Opportunity Act of 1964 aimed to parallel these civil and political rights by throwing open economic advancement to black Americans. Billions of dollars in social-welfare programs followed.

The 1970s

As the years of the 1960s were a time of vast changes in race relations in the United States, the 1970s began as a time of consolidation. No more reform proposals emerged from a White House now ruled by Richard Nixon. In thousands of local situations, however, the drive was still under way to integrate black Americans into all phases of life. There had apparently emerged a new consensus among white Americans, who, at least in good part, accepted the notion that it was right for blacks to become first-class citizens. Entrance requirements for schools and colleges were changed; hundreds of communities tried hard to work out equitable arrangements to end de facto segregation in the schools (usually with limited success); graduate programs searched for black applicants; and integration in jobs and in the professions continued to expand. The influence of radical black movements waned, and the voting-rights acts of the 1960s transformed national politics. Blacks now moved into the mainstream of the party system. Thurgood Marshall had been appointed the nation's first black Supreme Court justice by President Johnson, and in the nation at large black elected officials increased rapidly in numbers. In 1967 there were 475; in 1971, 1,860; and in 1979, 4,767 (this figure still represented less than 1 percent of all elected officials). The daily impact of television, where black Americans appeared regularly in shows and commercial advertisements, made them seem more an accepted part of a pluralistic nation.

White resistance to mixed schooling and mixed neighborhoods continued, however, fueled by a widespread conviction that blacks were violent and crime-prone. Though desegregation was

reasonably smooth in most communities, thousands of white parents placed their children in white schools or moved to the suburbs. In Atlanta, where in the years 1970–73 segregation was reduced by almost half, 51 percent of the white schoolchildren disappeared from the public schools; in Dallas, where segregation was cut by a quarter in these years, 26 percent of the white children shifted out of the school system. Boston, Detroit, and Los Angeles were in turmoil over court-ordered busing.

There was an ever more powerful ground swell of opinion in the 1970s that the courts should concern themselves only with de jure discrimination (segregation in schooling brought about by the specific and conscious acts of public authorities), and not with de facto segregation (which was caused by patterns of residence by different ethnic groups). The Supreme Court, increasingly dominated by a conservative group of justices appointed to that body by President Nixon, appeared to be swinging in this direction.

What were the results of the affirmative-action policy mandated in the 1960s by federal law —the requirement that all public agencies move positively to assure equal access to black Americans? "It doesn't take a statistician to perceive the shifting racial and ethnic makeup of the American social and economic structure," said Jack Greenberg of the NAACP Legal Defense and Educational Fund in January 1981. "Anyone who walks down the corridors of a major corporation or looks into a university classroom can readily observe the difference between today and a decade ago. There are conspicuously more blacks, Latinos and women everywhere." Rarely were "quotas" actually resorted to in order to make these changes. Establishing goals, timetables, and recruitment programs usually sufficed. In 1964 one out of a hundred American law-school students were minority persons; in 1980 that figure had risen to ten out of a hundred. In 1969 three of every hundred medical-school students were of minority origin; here again, by 1980 the figure had risen to 10 percent. Proportionately as many black young people were receiving higher education as whites in 1980 (following a 100-percent increase by blacks in the 1970s).

Even after the election of Ronald Reagan, whose victory sprang in part from antiblack sentiment, a Louis Harris national poll found that whites favored continuing affirmative-action programs by more than two to one (this ratio held among Reagan voters as well). The percentage of black homeowners increased, if only slightly, from 41.6 to 43.3. However, members of the minority groups were still concentrated in the lower levels of management; their economic toehold in the middle class and higher was as yet small. Although the proportion of black Americans in the middle class was solidly and distinctly established at about 10 percent (the number of blacks living in the suburbs increased by 34 percent from 1970 to 1977), the overall economic situation of black Americans was much below that of whites, and at the end of the 1970s was deteriorating. Three of four black families lived in America's metropolitan areas, and most of these congregated in the inner city, with its searing problems of drugs, crime, bad housing, and high unemployment. Indeed, this concentration of the black poor in the 1970s was so great that one study remarked that the "cities have been cast as reservations for the poor and despised minorities of our society." The levels of crime and death in the inner cities were such that a black male child in urban America at the end of the 1970s had only a 60-percent chance of reaching the age of twenty-five. The mortality rate of black babies in their first year held at almost double that of whites.

In 1974 black families still made 40 percent of the food-stamp purchases. The black jobless rate that year was 13.7 percent, as against 7.6 percent for whites, and among black teen-agers it often reached as high as 50 percent. Many of these young Americans were so discouraged that it appeared they were becoming a permanent underclass in the economic system: undereducated, idle, and adrift, with few if any marketable skills or job prospects. The alarming surge in violent crime at the end of the 1970s seemed directly associated with this grave situation. Of the nation's entire prison population in 1972, which traditionally consists overwhelmingly of young, single males, approximately 42 percent was black—almost four times the percentage of blacks in the nation's population. Actual purchasing power for black families, adjusting for inflation, declined 3.2 percent in 1974, and their median income that year was $7,808 (that of white families was $13,356). At the end of the decade the National Urban League, one of black America's longstanding voices, said that blacks were worse off than ten years before. In 1970 the average income of black families had been 60 percent that of white families; by 1979 it had dropped to 57 percent.

Among black heads of households, the League reported, the unemployment rate was 24 percent, as against 8 percent among all Americans. Understandably, three out of four black heads of household queried by the League felt that progress toward racial equality was too slow.

The Era of Limits

In the bicentennial year of the American nation, 1976, its people shared a pervasive sense of subdued concern. The two hundredth birthday itself passed as a warming, folkish observance, but once it was over a brooding conviction settled in again that the picnic was over. The American dream was in the process of being slimmed down. The country's affluence was staggering, by comparison with practically all of the rest of the world (some countries in western Europe were richer per-capita). Yet the quantum jump upward in energy and raw-material costs was widely believed inevitably to cause a downward spiral in consumption: less automobile driving, everything more costly and fewer things bought, less lavish use of resources. Owning a home was becoming a luxury that fewer and fewer could afford as land and construction costs rose breathtakingly. Economic progress could no longer be taken for granted, certainly in the sense that each generation would get richer and live more bountifully.

Even the steady rise in the height and weight of young people that had persisted for generations came to an end in the 1960s, hinting at the reaching of some natural limitation. One of the brightest flares in the politics of 1976 was the campaign of young Governor Jerry Brown, Jr., of California, who based his appeal to the electorate during the presidential primaries on the assertion that the country had reached an "era of limits," and must begin making painful adjustments to that fact. Ominous warnings were being issued by leading scholars that the American economy was indeed in grave, long-range trouble because of the ending of cheap raw materials and energy. The consensus of economists was that growth in productivity had been slowing substantially for a decade; that full employment would be impossible to reach again; and that the heavily urbanized and industrial regions of the Northeast and upper Middle West had entered a long stagnation and decline in which new jobs would be ever harder to generate. Joining these gloomy prognoses was the continuing loss of confidence by Americans in their government.

The First Centennial's Mood

This national state of mind would be familiar to those living a century ago. The nation's first centennial, 1876, was hardly a time of unmixed and gladsome self-pride. The economy was still suffering from the depression that had begun in 1873, and industrial warfare was beginning to rage between labor and capital, fatally sapping the long-held myth that America was the land of classless equality. The most violent labor outbreak in American history, the railway strike of 1877, was soon to devastate national morale; it was becoming ever more clear that the long and bloody effort to create racial justice in the South was failing; and at every level of government and in every state, corruption in politics made it almost impossible to move toward the solution of any social problem. Government had practically broken down; the whole democratic experiment seemed to be failing miserably.

Those devoted to the democratic experiment felt it all as a deep wound upon the spirit. "It is not necessary for me to attempt to paint the state of political corruption to which we have been reduced," said the reformer Henry George during the presidential-election campaign of 1876. Corruption, he went on, "is the dark background to our national rejoicing, the skeleton which has stood by us at the feast. Our Fourth of July orators do not proclaim it; our newspapers do not announce it; we hardly whisper it to one another, but we all know, for we all feel, that beneath all our centennial rejoicing there exists in the public mind to-day a greater doubt of the success of Republican institutions than has existed within the memory of our oldest man."

A Crisis of the National Spirit

In the middle of the year 1979 the accumulated disappointments and frustrations of 1970s America produced an even more somber warning, only in this case from the president of the United States, Jimmy Carter. In July the president, deeply discouraged at the nation's refusal to believe his repeated insistence that there was an en-

ergy crisis, and dismayed at Congress's repeated failure to pass his many proposals concerning it, withdrew to his favorite resting place, the presidential retreat Camp David in Maryland's Catoctin mountains. To this spot he brought more than 130 national leaders to talk with him about the state of the nation. In relays they arrived daily by helicopter, descending into the woodsy silence of the Catoctins, while a storm of national alarm raged, including even rumors that the president had suffered a mental breakdown. For two weeks the discussions went on, during which Jimmy Carter's national approval rating, long slumping, reached an almost record low: 25 percent, close to that of Harry Truman in 1951 and Richard Nixon in 1974.

He emerged to go on national television on July 15, partially to announce a new energy program (a segment of which Congress later enacted), but primarily to communicate to the country the message brought to him again and again by his many visitors: that there was "a crisis of the American spirit," as the president phrased it, abroad in the nation.

"The threat [to the nation] is nearly invisible in ordinary ways," the president said. "It is a crisis of confidence. . . . We can see this crisis in the growing doubt about the meaning of our own lives and in the loss of a unity of purpose for our nation. . . . [In the past] confidence in the future has supported everything else—public institutions and private enterprise, our own families and the very Constitution of the United States. Confidence has defined our course and has served as a link between generations. We've always believed in something called progress. We've always had a faith that the days of our children would be better than our own. Our people are losing that faith. Not only in Government itself, but in their ability as citizens to serve as the ultimate rulers and shapers of our democracy. . . . We always believed that we were part of a great movement of humanity itself called democracy, involved in the search for freedom. . . . But just as we are losing our confidence in the future, we are also beginning to close the door on our past. In a nation that was proud of hard work, strong families, close-knit communities and our faith in God, too many of us now tend to worship self-indulgence and consumption. Human identity is no longer defined by what one does but by what one owns. But we've discovered that owning things and consuming things does not satisfy our longing for meaning. . . .

"For the first time in the history of our country a majority of our people believe that the next five years will be worse than the past five years. Two-thirds of our people do not even vote. The productivity of

American workers is actually dropping and the will-ingness of Americans to save for the future has fallen below that of all other people in the Western world.. . . We were sure that ours was a nation of the ballot, not of the bullet, until the murders of John Kennedy and Robert Kennedy and Martin Luther King, Jr. We were taught that our armies were always invincible and our causes were always just only to suffer the agony of Vietnam. We re-spected the Presidency as a place of honor until the shock of Watergate. We remember when the phrase 'sound as a dollar' was an expression of absolute dependability until ten years of inflation began to shrink our dollar and our savings. We believed that our nation's resources were limitless until 1973, when we had to face a growing dependence on for-eign oil. These wounds are still very deep. They have never been healed."

The United States of America in 1980

By the 1970s the United States of America had re-alized so many of its dreams that it had lost count. Evils that had caused decades of bitter contro-versy seemed largely to have disappeared, or at least to have lost almost entirely their former viru-lence. Perhaps more striking than anything else to a group of Americans from the 1870s, as they observed the America of the 1970s and reflected on the enormous changes it had undergone since their time, would be the fact that few people seemed aware of these vast improvements. The "world-taken-for-granted" attitude would mystify them. Especially arresting would be the common tendency among 1970s Americans to idealize the past. They would find such misplaced nostalgia to be, at the least, amusing. Things that had seemed like fantasies in their own day were common-places in the 1970s. For most Americans, life was much easier, more bountiful, and potentially more various and interesting than it ever was in earlier times. It was richer in its forms, more open, less vexed by the limitations of ignorance, poverty, and social weakness.

The possibility of experiencing life itself in health was incomparably greater. The opportuni-ties for finding the particular way in which an in-dividual might best express himself or herself were far greater in the pluralistic, many-doored society of the 1970s. The prospects of a lifetime of labor in brutalized conditions, of injury and death in factories built without concern for human safety, of deadening work for long hours and star-

vation wages, of having one's dignity violated by the arrogance and exploitation of superiors—these, for most Americans, had been vastly re-duced. This fundamental fact of improved life, one of the highest outcomes of the two-century experiment in American republicanism, was re-flected in a national survey among thirty-year-olds in the bicentennial year of 1976. Despite the widely current anxiety over the state of the na-tion, three out of four Americans queried thought the quality of their own life "quite good," consid-ering their health, love lives, and jobs (though al-most half were not happy with their intellectual development, that is, their understanding of life). Indeed, since the 1950s the proportion of Ameri-cans describing themselves as "very happy" has declined but marginally (from 35 to 30 percent).

The Persistence of Social Sickness

Yet the United States still struggles with social sickness, sometimes in gargantuan forms un-known a century ago. Having realized so many of their dreams, the American people have in truth found that this is not enough, as President Carter said. American society is so opulent that it is choking on its wastes; such intricate mechanisms are so widely in use that only huge and virtually uncontrollable corporations can produce them. There is the constant presence of a military estab-lishment bristling with doomsday weapons, and a presidency so powerful and unregulated that its occupant can rain millions of tons of bombs on an-other country apparently at will. America is still soured and twisted by social prejudice and un-equal treatment. Millions live in wretched pov-erty, subsisting on welfare checks, frightened by inner-city crime, and surrounded by the wasting social disease of drug addiction. The country clubs and the comfortable suburbs are still over-whelmingly WASP; the slums are still predomi-nantly black or brown. The inescapable question remains before us: how can all Americans, what-ever their sex, ethnic membership, or class posi-tion, find an equal opportunity for self-fulfillment in this country?

The most appealing quality in the older American scene—the optimistic belief that life could be beautiful in the here and now if only cer-tain problems were solved—seems vanished. As we lay each problem down, another, more subtle and elusive, rises in its place. Americans have always been a happiness-oriented people, the innocents in a grieving world, but now, in the latter decades of the twentieth century, they are coming ever more to the seasoned and rueful understanding that the ancient societies of Europe have long possessed: life can never be made serene; unease lies in the human condition itself. And yet each generation cannot feel its humanity, cannot fulfill its own inner nature, unless it continues this unequal struggle, hoping somehow to leave its mark and make the world better than it has been.

This book has been written in part to show that American cultural history is a record of oscillations in temper, characterized by broad swings from relative confidence to alarm and back again, not of movement in but one direction. By looking backward a century we see that feelings of stagnation and dismay have not just arrived for the first time in the American experience. As the psychologist Erik Erikson observed, mood swings from carnival to atonement seem to be our basic emotional rhythm. Human society is enormously volatile, able with startling suddenness to break from gloom into periods of astonishing intellectual excitement and creative response, especially in so open and libertarian a country as this one.

Perhaps Americans are to be denied any such revivals of spirit; perhaps a gray sterility is what lies ahead. But it would be, at the least, unhistorical to regard such forecasts as irresistibly persuasive to the reasonable mind. Life grows more complex and puzzling in good part because our understanding of it grows more sophisticated and our knowledge of its difficulties more exact. Innocence lost is irretrievable. It is not likely that the nation's earlier buoyant optimism will ever return. This is not, however, the same as saying that Americans are fated henceforth to suffer despair as an unrelieved state of mind, or that they are to be denied those tidal upwellings of fresh vision and renewed vigor that have recurred so persistently in their public life and consciousness.

Bibliography

This chapter has been derived from a retrospective view of the preceding chapters in the book, from a wide variety of contemporary periodical and newspaper articles, and from my own observations. The following is intended to provide a brief guide to some published works of value: W. Elliot Brownlee, *Dynamics of Ascent: A History of the American Economy* (1978); the works cited on women's history for the previous chapter, as well as Elaine Tyler May, *Great Expectations: Marriage and Divorce in Post-Victorian America* (1980), and three articles in the Summer, 1980, issue of *The Wilson Quarterly*, vol. IV: Arlene Skolnick, "The Paradox of Perfection," Graham B. Spanier, "Outsiders Looking In," and Mary Jo Bane, Lee Rainwater, and Martin Rein, "Filling the Cracks," pp. 112–146; Kirkpatrick Sale, *Human Scale* (1980); Gabriel Kolko, *Main Currents in Modern American History** (1976); Ben J. Wattenberg, *In Search of the Real America: A Challenge to the Chaos of Failure and Guilt** (1976); Sar A. Levitan, William B. Johnston, and Robert Taggart, *Still A Dream: The Changing Status of Blacks Since 1960** (1975); Landon Y. Jones, *Great Expectations: America and the Baby Boom Generation* (1980); Christopher Lasch, *The Culture of Narcissism: American Life in an Age of Diminishing Expectations** (1979); Faustine Childress Jones, *The Changing Mood in America: Eroding Commitment?** (1977); Richard Lemon, *The Troubled American** (1970); a series of three articles in the Spring, 1980, issue of *The Wilson Quarterly*, vol. IV: Cary Kimble, "In Pursuit of Well-Being," Charles L. Bosk, "The Doctors," and Lewis Thomas, "The Right Track," pp. 61–98; Andrew M. Greeley, *The American Catholic: A Social Portrait* (1977); Richard Polenberg, *One Nation Divisible: Class, Race, and Ethnicity in the United States Since 1938* (1980); E. J. Kahn, *The American People** (1974); William H. Masters and Virginia E. Johnson, *The Pleasure Bond: A New Look at Sexuality and Commitment** (1976); Hugh Davis Graham and Ted Robert Gurr, *The History of Violence in America** (1969). For books on changing American voting patterns, ethnicity, and related trends, see the bibliography at the end of the preceding chapter. On elites, and their role in public policy, see Leonard Silk and Mark Silk, *The American Establishment* (1980). Concerning Russian perspectives on America, I have relied upon my own observations while in that country, and upon the works cited at the end of Chapter 33, on the Cold War.

* Available in paperback.

TIME LINE OF WOMEN'S HISTORY

Colonial Period

Isabella of Spain supports discovery voyages of Christopher Columbus.

Elizabeth I of England generates vigor and outward adventurousness in that country, supports round-the-world exploring, the founding of Virginia.

Pocahontas is pivotal figure in early history of Virginia, representing failing effort to build biracial society.

Colonial white women mainly on farms, serving in "Adam's Rib" relationship with husbands; closely interdependent relationship in work, family support; colonial black women overwhelmingly slaves, worked in fields, subject to savage punishments, loss of family through sale of its members, sexual domination by white males.

Home the center of everything: white women the principal manufacturers of most objects in colonial life.

Puritans and Quakers treat women as persons of substance and value: marriages "arranged," but expected to be loving.

Average of about eight births per wife: in every thirty births, one woman dies: delivery by midwives.

National Period (to Civil War)

In cities, sharp separation between men and women's "spheres" appearing. However, women beginning to work in certain industries, as textiles.

Men and women start choosing marriage partners for love; arranged marriages disappearing; patriarchalism slowly beginning to lessen; more egalitarian, sharing, "modern" marriage starting to appear.

Women imaged as morally superior to males, "Cult of True Womanhood" emerges. Extreme modesty of women demanded; kept out of public affairs; but education for girls and young women beginning: by mid-century, high schools opening to them.

Birth rate begins long decline: children valued more, more attention and investment of time and effort put into their rearing: women beginning to move toward lives freer of constant childbirth.

Women's rights to property, children after divorce, entering business, are improved in Age of Jackson reforms, responding to rising ideology of liberation and equality in America.

Lucretia Mott, active from 1820s to 1870s in social reform and slavery issues, helps slowly open right to public agitation for women, against massive condemnation. Harriet Tubman leads hundreds of slaves to the free states.

Elizabeth Cady Stanton and Mott lead Seneca Falls, N.Y., women's rights convention, issue *Declaration of Sentiments*, modeled on *Declaration of Independence*, 1848. Annual women's rights conventions held thereafter. Demand for women's vote ridiculed.

Harriet Beecher Stowe, highly popular writer, publishes *Uncle Tom's Cabin* (1852), becomes worldwide best seller, great impact upon North-South feelings.

Growing women's employment in industries, especially textiles, outside the home, but usually young unmarried women.

Post Civil War America

Birth rate continues dropping, and trend toward single women working outside the home persists, but range of employments restricted.

Frances Willard, head of Women's Christian Temperance Union, 1870s–1890s, becomes dramatic national leader of women, working for Social Purity cause (against drinking, prostitution, to save family), and for suffrage, labor rights.

Social revolution underway among middle class white women, whose lives were being freed of drudgery by technological revolution at home and in cities: many enter social reform causes, woman's club movement expands.

Black women, freed from slavery, turn away from working in the fields, begin building strong family life, form the legal marriages slavery had prohibited, serve in "Adam's Rib" role in tenant farmsteads with husbands, complementing their labors in the fields by work in the home, and with the children.

Women's colleges (Vassar, Barnard, et cetera) are formed: women being allowed to enroll in the new state universities.

Liberation of sexual attitudes and repressions begins in late nineteenth century, after the prudery and repression of the mid-nineteenth century.

Divorce rates begin to rise slowly in the 1880s, as modern marriage model of love and mutual support creates rising expectations, and therefore disappointments, of marriage.

Helen Hunt Jackson, in *Century of Dishonor* (1881), focuses national attention on the cause of the Indian.

Progressive Era

Jane Addams leads settlement house movement, progressive education, becomes model for "new woman" activism, 1880s–1930s.

Ida Tarbell, historian of Standard Oil, becomes leading "muckraker" of the new reforming journalism.

Concept of "Educated Motherhood" emerges, to train mothers how to rear better-equipped children for an increasingly complex society.

Carrie Chapman Catt elected president of National American Suffrage Association, 1900; with Alice Paul and Anna Howard Shaw, leads national crusade for women's voting.

By 1910, 4 of 5 single women work outside the home; 1 of 20 married women do so; 8 million women employed outside the home in 1910.

In 1900, 17 per cent of college alumni were women; by 1920, 40 per cent. Child study and home making courses introduced, as well as curricula looking toward social reform. Women active in the political parties.

Reforms to protect working women enacted: working conditions, hours of labor. Also mother's pensions established for women without husbands and with children to raise. Average family size at 5 by 1900.

Women's suffrage crusade grows nationally prominent; opposition to vote among women themselves (fearing loss of "woman's sphere") fades as they see government emerging as a social welfare agency helping women, families, children.

Jeanette Rankin, first woman to be elected to Congress, takes her seat in the House in 1917. Serves until 1940s.

Huge numbers of women at work in industry during the First World War; Nineteenth Amendment, giving vote to women, ratified 1920.

America Between the World Wars

Divorce statistics rising rapidly, creating national concern, as women's rising expectations of what a marriage should be leads them increasingly to set aside stoicism and passivity. Every sixth marriage ending in divorce in 1930.

Ideal of woman as wife, homemaker, and mother continues preeminent for practically all women, despite availability of vote, freedom in dress styles, social behavior. Careers regarded as secondary. Feminism fading.

A new equality in sexual experience between men and women being demanded; sexual behavior between young women and men, in the new automobiles, becomes considerably freer, though intercourse morally condemned by young unless married.

Urban, middle class WASP homes put child ever more at their center; tremendous concentration of attention and concern upon child rearing, families much smaller. Rise of "peer group" influence as children remain longer in school. Middle class families down to one or two children. More democratic family style.

Eleanor Roosevelt, the first activist First Lady, sets high example of social awareness and strong public role for women; Frances Perkins becomes first woman member of the president's cabinet (Labor); anthropologist Ruth Benedict, in her *Patterns of Culture* (1934), has great impact upon national thinking about values, family, young people, and society; sociologist Helen Lynd, with her husband Robert, makes major contributions to thought about American values in their *Middletown* studies; Mary Beard, in her own writings and with husband Charles, writes powerful new histories of American life and women.

Post Second World War America

In 1940s and 1950s, birth rate soars spectacularly, dream of large, healthy family and of woman as "wife-companion" to husbands becomes predominant. Huge numbers of women work in war industries, 1940–45, and though reassertion of traditional family role strong thereafter, the drop-off in outside-of-the-home employment is not great: 31 per cent of all women worked in 1950, as against 27 per cent in 1940. Still working at restricted list of occupations, much sexual division in occupations.

Great surge to more spacious, private suburban living, ideal number of children desired by women approaches 4. Intense stress upon warmth, intimacy, and trust between mothers and children.

Helene Deutsch, in widely authoritative work, *The Psychology of Women* (1945), stresses that only in motherhood do women achieve true happiness.

Black America fleeing from rural South by millions, and into urban centers, South and North. Black women follow earlier movement of white women into working outside the home, but at much lower incomes and in highly restricted occupations. Rosa Parks in 1954 initiates massive civil rights drive for black people.

Trend toward women working outside the home accelerates. By 1975, 44 per cent so employed; among women with children under six, almost 37 per cent. In 1973, 65 per cent of Americans favor wives working, even if their husbands could support them. Going into many new occupations, although general picture remains the same for most women: typists, maids, teachers, nurses, cashiers, saleswomen, little invasion of management. In 1960, women receive 83 per cent of salary made by black men, who receive only 60 per cent of that made by white men.

However, women continue in general to regard "career" as secondary; rather, think of working as supplementary to family income, or temporary; big surge in employment among older women whose children were reared.

First law the sole purpose of which is to outlaw sexual discrimination: Equal Pay Act, 1963. Compliance slow, resisted.

More women married in 1970s than ever before (some 10 per cent of women in 1800s did not marry; now only 5 per cent not married).

Feminism makes surprising re-emergence in 1960s, in instant best-selling book, *The Feminine Mystique* (1963), written by Betty Friedan. Calls for women to find self-realization not only through family, but in a career. Swiftly expands into spectacular national movement, "women's liberation," featuring at its most radical boundaries crusaders like Kate Millett, who in *Sexual Politics* (1970) condemns men as exploiters, condemns male sexual domination, patriarchal family.

National Organization for Women (1966) created by Betty Friedan, issues 1967 Bill of Rights for Women, demanding all sexual distinctions in laws be rendered invalid by passage of Equal Rights Amendment; calls for legalization of abortions; for opening up the full range of employment, outside the home, to women.

New model of "Women as Person" emerges, calling for complete independence and equality, elimination of special laws protecting women at work, in family relations. Great influence upon white women of rising movement of black demands for rights and equality.

1964 Civil Rights Act outlaws discrimination in employment on grounds of sex; Equal Employment Opportunities Commission to enforce.

1973 Supreme Court decision approves abortion, effectively, on request, through first trimester of pregnancy. Tremendous rise in abortions begins. "No fault" divorce laws initiated in California, spreads widely. The "Pill" available to damp down female fertility, new sexual era filled with uncertainties for women emerges. Average of 2.5 children wanted by women in 1971, as compared with 3.7 in era of baby boom. Percentage of young women remaining single rises dramatically; having children put off past mid-twenties. Actual birth rate down to 1.8 per woman in mid-1970s.

By 1975, only one-third of families with husband and wife present are supported only by the husband (down from one-half in 1950).

Yet older family patterns remain, with women continuing to be the primary child-rearers, with modest assistance, if any, from husbands. Thus most women work only part time. Care of children remains focus of family life. Two thirds of all marriages remain together until death of one spouse; among second marriages, two thirds successful. A million Americans living together without marriage, but this constitutes only 2 per cent of total of all couples. Divorce rate high, but levelling off in latter 1970s; remarriage rate keeps pace. But among those families below poverty line, in 1973 some 45 per cent were headed only by a woman.

Equal Rights Amendment enacted by Congress, but stalled several states short of ratification in 1981, national opinion swinging against it.

THE DECLARATION OF INDEPENDENCE

When in the Course of human events, it becomes necessary for one people to dissolve the political bands which have connected them with another, and to assume among the Powers of the earth, the separate and equal station to which the Laws of Nature and of Nature's God entitle them, a decent respect to the opinions of mankind requires that they should declare the causes which impel them to the separation.

We hold these truths to be self-evident, that all men are created equal, that they are endowed by their Creator with certain unalienable Rights, that among these are Life, Liberty and the pursuit of Happiness. That to secure these rights, Governments are instituted among Men, deriving their just powers from the consent of the governed, That whenever any Form of Government becomes destructive of these ends, it is the Right of the people to alter or to abolish it, and to institute new Government, laying its foundation on such principles and organizing its powers in such form, as to them shall seem most likely to effect their Safety and Happiness. Prudence, indeed, will dictate that Governments long established should not be changed for light and transient causes: and accordingly all experience hath shown, that mankind are more disposed to suffer, while evils are sufferable, than to right themselves by abolishing the forms to which they are accustomed. But when a long train of abuses and usurpations, pursuing invariably the same Object evinces a design to reduce them under absolute Despotism, it is their right, it is their duty, to throw off such Government, and to provide new Guards for their future security. — Such has been the patient sufferance of these Colonies; and such is now the necessity which constrains them to alter their former Systems of Government. The history of the present King of Great Britain is a history of repeated injuries and usurpations, all having in direct object the establishment of an absolute Tyranny over these States. To prove this, let Facts be summitted to a candid world.

He has refused his Assent to Laws, the most wholesome and necessary for the public good.

He has forbidden his Governors to pass Laws of immediate and pressing importance, unless suspended in their operation till his Assent should be obtained: and when so suspended, he has utterly neglected to attend to them.

He has refused to pass other Laws for the accommodation of large districts of people, unless those people would relinquish the right of Representation in the Legislature, a right inestimable to them and formidable to tyrants only.

He has called together legislative bodies at places unusual, uncomfortable, and distant from the depository of their public Records, for the sole purpose of fatiguing them into compliance with his measures.

He has dissolved Representative Houses repeatedly, for opposing with manly firmness his invasions on the rights of the people.

He has refused for a long time, after such dissolutions, to cause others to be elected: whereby the Legislative Powers, incapable of Annihilation, have returned to the People at large for their exercise; the State remaining in the mean time exposed to all the dangers of invasion from without, and convulsions within.

He has endeavoured to prevent the population of these States; for that purpose obstructing the Laws of Naturalization of Foreigners: refusing to pass others to encourage their migration hither, and raising the conditions of new Appropriations of Lands.

He has obstructed the Administration of Justice, by refusing his Assent to Laws for establishing Judiciary powers.

He has made Judges dependent on his Will alone, for the tenure of their offices, and the amount and payment of their salaries.

He has erected a multitude of New Offices, and sent hither swarms of Officers to harass our People, and eat out their substance.

He has kept among us in times of peace, Standing Armies without the Consent of our legislature.

He has affected to render the Military independent of and superior to the Civil power.

He has combined with others to subject us to a jurisdiction foreign to our constitution, and unacknowledged by our laws: giving his Assent to their acts of pretended Legislation:

For quartering large bodies of armed troops among us:

For protecting them, by a mock Trial, from punishment for any Murders which they should commit on the Inhabitants of these States:

For cutting off our Trade with all parts of the world:

For imposing taxes on us without our Consent:

For depriving us in many

cases, of the benefits of Trial by Jury:

For transporting us beyond Seas to be tried for pretended offences:

For abolishing the free System of English Laws in a neighbouring Province, establishing therein an Arbitrary government, and enlarging its Boundaries so as to render it at once an example and fit instrument for introducing the same absolute rule into these Colonies:

For taking away our Charters, abolishing our most valuable Laws, and altering fundamentally the Forms of our Governments:

For suspending our own Legislature, and declaring themselves invested with Power to legislate for us in all cases whatsoever.

He has abdicated Government here, by declaring us out of his Protection and waging War against us.

He has plundered our seas, ravaged our Coasts, burnt our towns, and destroyed the lives of our people.

He is at this time transporting large Armies of foreign Mercenaries to compleat the works of death, desolation and tyranny, already begun with circumstances of Cruelty & perfidy scarcely paralleled in the most barbarous ages, and totally unworthy the Head of a civilized nation.

He has constrained our fellow Citizens taken Captive on the high Seas to bear Arms against their Country, to become the executioners of their friends and Brethren, or to fall themselves by their Hands.

He has excited domestic insurrections amongst us, and has endeavoured to bring on the inhabitants of our frontiers, the merciless Indian Savages, whose known rule of warfare, is an undistinguished destruction of all ages, sexes and conditions.

In every stage of these Oppressions We have Petitioned for Redress in the most humble terms: Our repeated Petitions have been answered only by repeated injury. A Prince, whose character is thus marked by every act which may define a Tyrant, is unfit to be the ruler of a free People.

Nor have We been wanting in attention to our British brethren. We have warned them from time to time of attempts by their legislature to extend an unwarrantable jurisdiction over us. We have reminded them of the circumstances of our emigration and settlement here. We have appealed to their native justice and magnanimity, and we have conjured them by the ties of our common kindred to disavow these usurpations, which, would inevitably interrupt our connections and correspondence. They too have been deaf to the voice of justice and of consanguinity. We must, therefore, acquiesce in the necessity, which denounces our Separation, and hold them, as we hold the rest of mankind, Enemies in War, in Peace Friends.

We, therefore, the Representatives of the United States of America, in General Congress, Assembled, appealing to the Supreme Judge of the world for the rectitude of our intentions, do, in the Name, and by Authority of the good People of these Colonies, solemnly publish and declare, That these United Colonies are, and of Right ought to be Free and Independent States; that they are Absolved from all Allegiance to the British Crown, and that all political connection between them and the State of Great Britain, is and ought to be totally dissolved; and that as Free and Independent States, they have full Power to levy War, conclude Peace, contract Alliances, establish Commerce, and to do all other Acts and Things which Independent States may of right do. And for the support of this Declaration, with a firm reliance on the protection of divine Providence, we mutually pledge to each other our Lives, our Fortunes and our sacred Honor.

THE CONSTITUTION OF THE UNITED STATES

We the people of the United States, in Order to form a more perfect Union, establish Justice, insure domestic Tranquility, provide for the common defense, promote the general Welfare, and secure the Blessings of Liberty to ourselves and our Posterity, do ordain and establish this CONSTITUTION for the United States of America.

Article I

Section 1. All legislative powers herein granted shall be vested in a Congress of the United States, which shall consist of a Senate and House of Representatives.

Section 2. The House of Representatives shall be composed of Members chosen every second Year by the People of the several States, and the Electors in each State shall have the Qualifications requisite for Electors of the most numerous Branch of the State Legislature.

No Person shall be a Representative who shall not have attained to the Age of twenty-five Years, and been seven Years a Citizen of the United States, and who shall not, when elected, be an Inhabitant of that State in which he shall be chosen.

Representatives and direct Taxes shall be apportioned among the several States which may be included within this Union, according to their respective Numbers, which shall be determined by adding to the whole Number of Free Persons, including those bound to Service for a Term of Years, and excluding Indians not taxed, three fifths of all other Persons. The actual Enumeration shall be made within three Years after the first Meeting of the Congress of the United States, and within every subsequent Term of ten Years, in such Manner as they shall by Law direct. The number of Representatives shall not exceed one for every thirty Thousand, but each State shall have at Least one Representative; and until such enumeration shall be made, the State of New Hampshire shall be entitled to chuse three, Massachusetts eight, Rhode Island and Providence Plantations one, Connecticut five, New York six, New Jersey four, Pennsylvania eight, Delaware one, Maryland six, Virginia ten, North Carolina five, South Carolina five, and Georgia three.

When vacancies happen in the Representation from any State, the Executive Authority thereof shall issue Writs of Election to fill such Vacancies.

The House of Representatives shall chuse their Speaker and other Officers; and shall have the sole Power of Impeachment.

Section 3. The Senate of the United States shall be composed of two Senators from each State, chosen by the Legislature thereof, for six Years; and each Senator shall have one Vote.

Immediately after they shall be assembled in Consequence of the first Election, they shall be divided as equally as may be into three Classes. The Seats of the Senators of the first Class shall be vacated at the Expiration of the second Year, of the second Class at the Expiration of the fourth Year, and of the third Class at the Expiration of the sixth Year, so that one-third may be chosen every second Year; and if Vacancies happen by Resignation, or otherwise during the Recess of the Legislature of any State, the Executive thereof may make temporary Appointments until the next Meeting of the Legislature, which shall then fill such Vacancies.

No Person shall be a Senator who shall not have attained to the Age of thirty Years, and been nine Years a Citizen of the United States, and who shall not, when elected, be an Inhabitant of that State in which he shall be chosen.

The Vice President of the United States shall be President of the Senate, but shall have no vote, unless they be equally divided.

The Senate shall choose their Officers, and also a President pro tempore, in the absence of the Vice President, or when he shall exercise the Office of the President of the United States.

The Senate shall have the sole Power to try all Impeachments. When sitting for that purpose, they shall be on Oath or Affirmation. When the President of the United States is tried, the Chief Justice shall preside: And no person shall be convicted without the Concurrence of two thirds of the Members present.

Judgment in Cases of Impeachment shall not extend further than to removal from Office, and disqualification to hold and enjoy any Office of honor, Trust, or Profit under the United States: but the Party convicted shall nevertheless be liable and subject to Indictment, Trial, Judgment, and Punishment, according to Law.

Section 4. The Times, Places and Manner of holding Elections for Senators and Representatives, shall be prescribed in each state by the Legislature thereof: but the Congress may at any time by Law make or alter such Regulations, except as to the Places of Chusing Senators.

The Congress shall assemble at least once in every Year, and such Meeting shall be on the first Monday in December, unless they shall by Law appoint a different Day.

Section 5. Each House shall be the Judge of the Elections, Returns and Qualifications of its own Members, and a Majority of each shall constitute a Quorum to do Business: but a smaller number may adjourn from day to day, and may be authorized to compel the Attendance of absent Members, in such Manner, and under such Penalties, as each House may provide.

Each House may determine the Rules of its Proceedings, punish its Members for disorderly Behaviour, and, with the Concurrence of two thirds, expel a Member.

Each House shall keep a Journal of its Proceedings, and from time to time publish the same, excepting such Parts as may in their Judgment require Secrecy; and the Yeas and Nays of the Members of either House on any question shall, at the Desire of one fifth of those Present, be entered on the Journal.

Neither House, during the Session of Congress, shall, without the Consent of the other, adjourn for more than three days, nor to any other Place than that in which the two Houses shall be sitting.

Section 6. The Senators and Representatives shall receive a Compensation for their Services, to be ascertained by Law, and paid out of the Treasury of the United States. They shall in all Cases, except Treason, Felony, and Breach of the Peace, be privileged from Arrest during their Attendance at the Session of their respective Houses, and in going to and return-

ing from the same: and for any Speech or Debate in either House, they shall not be questioned in any other Place.

No Senator or Representative shall, during the Time for which he was elected, be appointed to any civil Office under the Authority of the United States, which shall have been created, or the Emoluments whereof shall have been increased, during such time: and no Person holding any Office under the United States shall be a Member of either House during his continuance in Office.

Section 7. All Bills for raising Revenue shall originate in the House of Representatives: but the Senate may propose or concur with Amendments as on other Bills.

Every Bill which shall have passed the House of Representatives and the Senate, shall, before it become a Law, be presented to the President of the United States: If he approve he shall sign it, but if not he shall return it, with his Objections, to that House in which it shall have originated, who shall enter the Objections at large on their Journal, and proceed to reconsider it. If after such Reconsideration two thirds of that House shall agree to pass the Bill, it shall be sent, together with the Objections, to the other House, by which it shall likewise be reconsidered, and if approved by two thirds of that House, it shall become a Law. But in all such Cases the Votes of both Houses shall be determined by Yeas and Nays, and the Names of the Persons voting for and against the Bill shall be entered on the Journal of each House respectively. If any Bill shall not be returned by the President within ten Days (Sundays excepted) after it shall have been represented to him, the Same shall be a Law, in like Manner as if he had signed it, unless the Congress by their Adjournment prevent its Return, in which Case it shall not be a Law.

Every Order, Resolution, or Vote to which the Concurrence of the Senate and House of Representatives may be necessary (except on a question of Adjournment) shall be presented to the President of the United States: and before the Same shall take Effect, shall be approved by him, or being disapproved by him, shall be re-

passed by two thirds of the Senate and House of Representatives, according to the Rules and Limitations prescribed in the Case of a Bill.

Section 8. The Congress shall have Power To lay and collect Taxes, Duties, Imposts and Excises, to pay the Debts and provide for the common Defense and general Welfare of the United States: but all Duties, Imposts and Excises shall be uniform throughout the United States;

To borrow money on the credit of the United States;

To regulate Commerce with foreign Nations, and among the several States, and with the Indian Tribes;

To establish an uniform Rule of Naturalization, and uniform Laws on the subject of Bankruptcies throughout the United States;

To coin Money, regulate the Value thereof, and of foreign Coin, and fix the Standard of Weights and Measures;

To provide for the Punishment of counterfeiting the Securities and current Coin of the United States;

To establish Post Offices and post Roads;

To promote the Progress of Science and useful Arts, by securing for limited Times to Authors and Inventors the exclusive Right to their respective Writings and Discoveries;

To constitute Tribunals inferior to the Supreme Court;

To define and punish Piracies and Felonies committed on the high Seas, and Offenses against the Law of Nations;

To declare War, grant Letters of Marque and Reprisal, and make Rules concerning Captures on Land and Water;

To raise and support Armies, but no Appropriation of Money to that Use shall be for a longer Term than two Years;

To provide and maintain a Navy;

To make Rules for the Government and Regulation of the land and naval forces;

To provide for calling forth the Militia to execute the Laws of the Union, suppress Insurrections and repel Invasions;

To provide for organizing, arming, and disciplining the Militia, and for governing such Part of them as may be employed in the Service of the United States, reserving to the States respectively, the Appointment of the Officers, and the Authority of training the Militia according to the discipline prescribed by Congress:

To exercise exclusive Legislation in all Cases whatsoever, over such District (not exceeding ten Miles square) as may, by Cession of particular States, and the acceptance of Congress, become the Seat of Government of the United States, and to exercise like Authority over all Places purchased by the Consent of the Legislature of the State in which the Same shall be, for the Erection of Forts, Magazines, Arsenals, dock-Yards, and other needful Buildings:— And

To make all Laws which shall be necessary and proper for carrying into Execution the foregoing Powers, and all other Powers vested by this Constitution in the Government of the United States, or in any Department or Officer thereof.

Section 9. The Migration or Importation of such Persons as any of the States now existing shall think proper to admit, shall not be prohibited by the Congress prior to the Year one thousand eight hundred and eight, but a tax or duty may be imposed on such Importation, not exceeding ten dollars for each Person.

The privilege of the Writ of Habeas Corpus shall not be suspended, unless when in Cases of Rebellion or Invasion the public Safety may require it.

No Bill of Attainder or ex post facto Law shall be passed.

No Capitation, or other direct, Tax shall be laid unless in Proportion to the Census or Enumeration herein before directed to be taken.

No Tax or Duty shall be laid on Articles exported from any State.

No Preference shall be given by any Regulation of Revenue to the Ports of one State over those of another: nor shall Vessels bound to, or from, one State, be obliged to enter, clear, or pay Duties in another.

No Money shall be drawn from the Treasury, but in Conse-

quence of Appropriations made by Law; and a regular Statement and Account of the Receipts and Expenditures of all public Money shall be published from time to time.

No title of Nobility shall be granted by the United States: And no Person holding any Office of Profit or Trust under them, shall, without the Consent of the Congress, accept of any present, Emolument, Office, or Title, of any kind whatever, from any King, Prince, or foreign State.

Section 10. No State shall enter into any Treaty Alliance, or Confederation; grant Letters of Marque and Reprisal: coin Money: emit Bills of Credit: make any Thing but gold and silver Coin a Tender in Payment of Debts: pass any Bill of Attainder, ex post facto Law, or Law impairing the Obligation of Contracts, or grant any Title of Nobility.

No State shall, without the Consent of the Congress, lay any Imposts or Duties on Imports or Exports, except what may be absolutely necessary for exercising its inspection Laws: and the net Produce of all Duties and Imposts, laid by any State on Imports or Exports, shall be for the Use of the Treasury of the United States: and all such Laws shall be subject to the Revision and Control of the Congress.

No State shall, without the Consent of Congress, lay any duty of Tonnage, keep Troops, or Ships of War in time of Peace, enter into any Agreement or Compact with another State, or with a foreign Power, or engage in War, unless actually invaded, or in such imminent Danger as will not admit of delay.

Article II

Section 1. The executive Power shall be vested in a President of the United States of America. He shall hold his Office during the Term of four Years, and, together with the Vice President, chosen for the same term, be elected, as follows:

Each State shall appoint, in such Manner as the Legislature thereof may direct, a Number of Electors, equal to the whole Number of Senators and Representa-

tives to which the State may be entitled in the Congress: but no Senator or Representative, or Person holding an Office of Trust or Profit under the United States, shall be appointed an Elector.

The Electors shall meet in their respective States, and vote by Ballot for two Persons, of whom one at least shall not be an Inhabitant of the same State with themselves. And they shall make a list of all the Persons voted for, and of the Number of Votes for each; which List they shall sign and certify, and transmit sealed to the Seat of the Government of the United States, directed to the President of the Senate. The President of the Senate shall, in the Presence of the Senate and House of Representatives, open all the Certificates, and the Votes shall then be counted. The Person having the greatest Number of Votes shall be the President, if such Number be a Majority of the whole Number of Electors appointed: and if there be more than one who have such Majority, and have an equal Number of Votes, then the House of Representatives shall immediately chuse by Ballot one of them for President; and if no Person have a Majority, then from the five highest on the List the said House shall in like Manner chuse the President. But in chusing the President, the Votes shall be taken by States, the Representation from each State having one Vote; a quorum for this Purpose shall consist of a Member or Members from two-thirds of the States, and a Majority of all the States shall be necessary to a Choice. In every Case, after the Choice of the President, the Person having the greatest Number of Votes of the Electors shall be the Vice President. But if there should remain two or more who have equal votes, the Senate shall chuse from them by Ballot the Vice President.

The Congress may determine the Time of chusing the Electors, and the Day on which they shall give their Votes; which Day shall be the same throughout the United States.

No person except a natural-born citizen, or a Citizen of the United States, at the time of the adoption of this Constitution, shall be eligible to the Office of President; neither shall any Person be eligible to that Office who shall not have attained to the Age of thirty-five Years, and been fourteen Years a Resident within the United States.

In case of the Removal of the President from Office, or of his Death, Resignation, or Inability to discharge the Powers and Duties of the said Office, the same shall devolve on the Vice President, and the Congress may by Law provide for the Case of Removal, Death, Resignation, or Inability, both of the President and Vice President, declaring what Officer shall then act as President, and such Officer shall act accordingly, until the Disability be removed, or a President shall be elected.

The President shall, at stated Times, receive for his Services a Compensation, which shall neither be increased nor diminished during the Period for which he shall have been elected, and he shall not receive within that Period any other Emolument from the United States, or any of them.

Before he enters on the Execution of his Office, he shall take the following Oath or Affirmation:
—"I do solemnly swear (or affirm) that I will faithfully execute the Office of President of the United States, and will, to the best of my Ability, preserve, protect, and defend the Constitution of the United States."

Section 2. The President shall be Commander in Chief of the Army and Navy of the United States, and of the Militia of the several States, when called into the actual Service of the United States; he may require the Opinion, in writing, of the principal Officer in each of the executive Departments, upon any subject relating to the Duties of their respective Offices, and he shall have Power to Grant Reprieves and Pardons for Offenses against the United States, except in Cases of Impeachment.

He shall have Power, by and with the Advice and Consent of the Senate, to make Treaties, provided two thirds of the Senators present concur; and he shall nominate, and by and with the Advice and Consent of the Senate, shall appoint Ambassadors, other public Ministers and Consuls, Judges of the su-

preme Court, and all other Officers of the United States, whose Appointments are not herein otherwise provided for, and which shall be established by Law: but the Congress may by Law vest the Appointment of such inferior Officers, as they think proper, in the President alone, in the Courts of Law, or in the Heads of Departments.

The President shall have Power to fill up all Vacancies that may happen during the Recess of the Senate, by granting Commissions which shall expire at the end of their next Session.

Section 3. He shall from time to time give to the Congress Information of the State of the Union, and recommend to their Consideration such Measures as he shall judge necessary and expedient; he may, on extraordinary occasions, convene both Houses, or either of them, and in Case of Disagreement between them, with respect to the Time of Adjournment, he may adjourn them to such Time as he shall think proper; he shall receive Ambassadors and other public Ministers; he shall take Care that the Laws be faithfully executed, and shall Commission all the Officers of the United States.

Section 4. The President, Vice President and all civil Officers of the United States, shall be removed from Office on Impeachment for, and Conviction of, Treason, Bribery, or other high Crimes and Misdemeanors.

Article III

Section 1. The judicial Power of the United States, shall be vested in one supreme Court, and in such inferior Courts as the Congress may from time to time ordain and establish. The Judges, both of the supreme and inferior Courts shall hold their Offices during good Behaviour, and shall, at stated Times, receive for their Services, a Compensation, which shall not be diminished during their Continuance in Office.

Section 2. The judicial Power shall extend to all Cases, in Law and Equity, arising under this Constitution, the Laws of the United States, and Treaties made, or which shall be made, under

their Authority;—to all Cases affecting Ambassadors, other public Ministers and Consuls;—to all Cases of admiralty and maritime Jurisdiction;—to Controversies to which the United States shall be a Party;—to Controversies between two or more States;—between a State and Citizens of another State;—between Citizens of the same State claiming Lands under Grants of different States, and between a State, or the Citizens thereof, and foreign States, Citizens or Subjects.

In all Cases affecting Ambassadors, other public Ministers and Consuls, and those in which a State shall be Party, the supreme Court shall have original Jurisdiction. In all the other Cases before mentioned, the supreme Court shall have appellate Jurisdiction, both as to Law and Fact, with such Exceptions, and under such Regulations as the Congress shall make.

The trial of all Crimes, except in Cases of Impeachment, shall be by Jury; and such Trial shall be held in the State where the said Crimes shall have been committed; but when not committed within any State, the Trial shall be at such Place or Places as the Congress may by Law have directed.

Section 3. Treason against the United States, shall consist only in levying War against them, or in adhering to their Enemies, giving them Aid and Comfort. No Person shall be convicted of Treason unless on the Testimony of two Witnesses to the same overt Act, or on Confession in open Court.

The Congress shall have power to declare the Punishment of Treason, but no Attainder of Treason shall work Corruption of Blood, or Forfeiture except during the Life of the Person attainted.

Article IV

Section 1. Full Faith and Credit shall be given in each State to the public Acts, Records, and judicial Proceedings of every other State. And the Congress may by general Laws prescribe the Manner in which such Acts, Records and Proceedings shall be proved, and the Effect thereof.

Section 2. The Citizens of each State shall be entitled to all

Privileges and Immunities of Citizens in the several States.

A Person charged in any State with Treason, Felony, or other Crime, who shall flee from Justice, and be found in another State, shall on demand of the executive Authority of the State from which he fled, be delivered up, to be removed to the State having Jurisdiction of the crime.

No Person held to Service or Labour in one State, under the Laws thereof, escaping into another, shall, in Consequence of any Law or Regulation therein, be discharged from such Service or Labour, but shall be delivered up on Claim of the Party to whom such Service or Labour may be due.

Section 3. New States may be admitted by the Congress into this Union; but no new State shall be formed or erected within the Jurisdiction of any other State; nor any State be formed by the Junction of two or more States, or parts of States, without the Consent of the Legislatures of the States concerned as well as of the Congress.

The Congress shall have Power to dispose of and make all needful Rules and Regulations respecting the Territory or other Property belonging to the United States; and nothing in this Constitution shall be so construed as to Prejudice any Claims of the United States, or of any particular State.

Section 4. The United States shall guarantee to every State in this Union a Republican Form of Government, and shall protect each of them against Invasion; and on Application of the Legislature, or of the Executive (when the Legislature cannot be convened) against domestic Violence.

Article V

The Congress, whenever two thirds of both Houses shall deem it necessary, shall propose Amendments to this Constitution, or, on the Application of the Legislatures of two thirds of the several States, shall call a Convention for proposing Amendments, which, in either Case, shall be valid to all Intents and Purposes, as part of this Constitution, when ratified by the Legislatures of three fourths of the several States, or by Conventions in three fourths thereof, as the one or the other Mode of Ratification may be proposed by the Congress; Provided that no Amendment which may be made prior to the Year One thousand eight hundred and eight shall in any Manner affect the first and fourth Clauses in the Ninth Section of the first Article; and that no State, without its Consent, shall be deprived of its equal Suffrage in the Senate.

Article VI

All Debts contracted and Engagements entered into, before the Adoption of this Constitution, shall be as valid against the United States under this Constitution, as under the Confederation.

This Constitution, and the Laws of the United States which shall be made in Pursuance thereof; and all Treaties made, or which shall be made, under the Authority of the United States, shall be the supreme Law of the Land; and the Judges in every State shall be bound thereby, any Thing in the Constitution or laws of any State to the Contrary notwithstanding.

The Senators and Representatives before mentioned, and the Members of the several State Legislatures, and all executive and judicial Officers, both of the United States and of the several States, shall be bound by Oath or Affirmation to support this Constitution; but no religious Test shall ever be required as a qualification to any Office or public Trust under the United States.

Article VII

The Ratification of the Conventions of nine States shall be sufficient for the Establishment of this Constitution between the States so ratifying the same.

Done in Convention by the Unanimous Consent of the States present the Seventeenth Day of September in the Year of our Lord one thousand seven hundred and Eighty seven and of the Independence of the United States of America the Twelfth. In Witness whereof We have hereunto subscribed our Names.

Articles in Addition to, and Amendment of, the Constitution of the United States of America, Proposed by Congress, and Ratified by the Legislatures of the Several States, Pursuant to the Fifth Article of the Original Constitution.

Amendment I [1791]

Congress shall make no law respecting an establishment of religion, or prohibiting the free exercise thereof; or abridging the freedom of speech, or of the press; or the right of the people peaceably to assemble, and to petition the Government for a redress of grievances.

Amendment II [1791]

A well regulated Militia, being necessary to the security of a free State, the right of the people to keep and bear Arms, shall not be infringed.

Amendment III [1791]

No Soldier shall, in time of peace, be quartered in any house, without the consent of the Owner, nor in time of war, but in a manner to be prescribed by law.

Amendment IV [1791]

The right of the people to be secure in their persons, houses, papers, and effects, against unreasonable searches and seizures, shall not be violated, and no Warrants shall issue, but upon probable cause, supported by Oath or affirmation, and particularly describing the place to be searched, and the persons or things to be seized.

Amendment V [1791]

No person shall be held to answer for a capital or otherwise infamous crime, unless on a presentment or indictment of a Grand Jury, except in cases arising in the land or naval forces, or in the Militia, when in actual service in time of War or public danger; nor shall any person be subject for the same offence to be twice put in jeopardy of life or limb; nor shall be compelled in any criminal case to be a witness against himself, nor be deprived of life, liberty, or property, without due process of law; nor shall private property be taken for public use, without just compensation.

Amendment VI [1791]

In all criminal prosecutions, the accused shall enjoy the right to a speedy and public trial, by an impartial jury of the State and district wherein the crime shall have been committed, which district shall have been previously ascertained by law, and to be informed of the nature and cause of the accusation, to be confronted with the witnesses against him; to have compulsory process for obtaining witnesses in his favor, and to have the Assistance of Counsel for his defence.

Amendment VII [1791]

In Suits at common law, where the value in controversy shall exceed twenty dollars, the right of trial by jury shall be preserved, and no fact tried by a jury, shall be otherwise re-examined in any Court of the United States, than according to the rules of the common law.

Amendment VIII [1791]

Excessive bail shall not be required, nor excessive fines imposed, nor cruel and unusual punishments inflicted.

Amendment IX [1791]

The enumeration in the Constitution, of certain rights, shall not be construed to deny or disparage others retained by the people.

Amendment X [1791]

The powers not delegated to the United States by the Constitution, nor prohibited by it to the States, are reserved to the States respectively, or to the people.

Amendment XI [1798]

The Judicial power of the United States shall not be construed to extend to any suit in law or equity, commenced or prosecuted against one of the United States by Citizens of another State, or by citizens or Subjects of any Foreign State.

Amendment XII [1804]

The Electors shall meet in their respective States and vote by ballot for President and Vice President, one of whom, at least, shall not be an inhabitant of the same State with themselves; they shall name in their ballots the person voted for as President, and in distinct ballots the person voted for as Vice-President, and they shall make distinct lists of all persons voted for as President, and of all persons voted for as Vice-President, and of the number of votes for each, which lists they shall sign and certify, and transmit sealed to the seat of the government of the United States, directed to the President of the Senate;—The President of the Senate shall, in the presence of the Senate and House of Representatives, open all the certificates and the votes shall then be counted;—The person having the greatest number of votes for President, shall be the President, if such number be a majority of the whole number of Electors appointed; and if no person have such majority, then from the persons having the highest numbers not exceeding three on the list of those voted for as President, the House of Representatives shall choose immediately, by ballot, the President. But in choosing the President, the votes shall be taken by states, the representation from each state having one vote; a quorum for this purpose shall consist of a member or members from two-thirds of the states, and a majority of all the states shall be necessary to a choice. And if the House of Representatives shall not choose a President whenever the right of choice shall devolve upon them, before the fourth day of March next following, then the Vice-President shall act as President, as in the case of the death or other constitutional disability of the President.—The person having the greatest number of votes as Vice-President, shall be the Vice-President, if such number be a majority of the whole number of Electors appointed, and if no person have a majority, then from the two highest numbers on the list, the Senate shall choose the Vice-President; a quorum for the purpose shall consist of two-thirds of the whole number of Senators, and a majority of the whole number shall be necessary to a choice. But no person constitutionally ineligible to the office of the President shall be eligible to that of Vice-President of the United States.

Amendment XIII [1865]

Section 1. Neither slavery nor involuntary servitude, except as a punishment for crime wherof the party shall have been duly convicted, shall exist within the United States, or any place subject to their jurisdiction.
Section 2. Congress shall have the power to enforce this article by appropriate legislation.

Amendment XIV [1868]

Section 1. All persons born or naturalized in the United States, and subject to the jurisdiction thereof, are citizens of the United States and of the State wherein they reside. No state shall make or enforce any law which shall abridge the privileges or immunities of citizens of the United States; nor shall any State deprive any person of life, liberty, or property, without due process of law; nor deny to any person within its jurisdiction the equal protection of the laws.
Section 2. Representatives shall be apportioned among the several States according to their respective numbers, counting the whole number of persons in each State, excluding Indians not taxed. But when the right to vote at any election for the choice of electors for President and Vice President of the United States, Representatives in Congress, the Executive and Judicial officers of a State, or the members of the Legislature thereof, is denied to any of the male inhabitants of such State, being twenty-one years of age, and citizens of the United States, or in any way abridged, except for participation in rebellion, or other crime, the basis of representation therein shall be reduced in the proportion which the number of such male citizens shall bear to the

whole number of male citizens twenty-one years of age in such State.

Section 3. No person shall be a Senator or Representative in Congress, or elector of President and Vice President, or hold any office, civil or military, under the United States, or under any State, who, having previously taken an oath, as a member of Congress, or as an officer of the United States, or as a member of any State legislature, or as an executive or judicial officer of any State, to support the Constitution of the United States, shall have engaged in insurrection or rebellion against the same, or given aid or comfort to the enemies thereof. But Congress may by a vote of two-thirds of each House, remove such disability.

Section 4. The validity of the public debt of the United States, authorized by law, including debts incurred for payment of pensions and bounties for services in suppressing insurrection or rebellion, shall not be questioned. But neither the United States nor any State shall assume or pay any debt or obligation incurred in aid of insurrection or rebellion against the United States, or any claim for the loss or emancipation of any slave: but all such debts, obligations, and claims shall be held illegal and void.

Section 5. The Congress shall have the power to enforce, by appropriate legislation, the provisions of this article.

Amendment XV [1870]

Section 1. The right of citizens of the United States to vote shall not be denied or abridged by the United States or by any State on account of race, color, or previous condition of servitude—

Section 2. The Congress shall have the power to enforce this article by appropriate legislation.

Amendment XVI [1913]

The Congress shall have power to lay and collect taxes on incomes, from whatever source derived, without apportionment among the several States, and without regard to any census or enumeration.

Amendment XVII [1913]

The Senate of the United States shall be composed of two Senators from each State, elected by the people thereof, for six years: and each Senator shall have one vote. The electors in each State shall have the qualifications requisite for electors of the most numerous branch of the State legislatures.

When vacancies happen in the representation of any State in the Senate, the executive authority of such State shall issue writs of election to fill such vacancies: *Provided*, That the legislature of any State may empower the executive thereof to make temporary appointments until the people fill the vacancies by election as the legislature may direct.

This amendment shall not be so construed as to affect the election or term of any Senator chosen before it becomes valid as part of the Constitution.

Amendment XVIII [1919]

Section 1. After one year from the ratification of this article the manufacture, sale, or transportation of intoxicating liquors within, the importation thereof into, or the exportation thereof from the United States and all territory subject to the jurisdiction thereof for beverage purposes is hereby prohibited.

Section 2. The Congress and the several States shall have concurrent power to enforce this article by appropriate legislation.

Section 3. This article shall be inoperative unless it shall have been ratified as an amendment to the Constitution by the legislatures of the several States, as provided in the Constitution, within seven years from the date of the submission hereof to the States by the Congress.

Amendment XIX [1920]

The right of citizens of the United States to vote shall not be denied or abridged by the United States or by any State on account of sex.

Congress shall have power to enforce this article by appropriate legislation.

Amendment XX [1933]

Section 1. The terms of the President and Vice President shall end at noon on the 20th day of January, and the terms of Senators and Representatives at noon on the 3rd day of January, of the years in which such terms would have ended if this article had not been ratified: and the terms of their successors shall then begin.

Section 2. The Congress shall assemble at least once in every year, and such meeting shall begin at noon on the 3d day of January, unless they shall by law appoint a different day.

Section 3. If, at the time fixed for the beginning of the term of the President, the President elect shall have died, the Vice President elect shall become President. If a President shall not have been chosen before the time fixed for the beginning of his term, or if the President elect shall have failed to qualify, then the Vice President elect shall act as President until a President shall have qualified; and the Congress may by law provide for the case wherein neither a President elect nor a Vice President elect shall have qualified, declaring who shall then act as President, or the manner in which one who is to act shall be selected, and such person shall act accordingly until a President or Vice President shall have qualified.

Section 4. The Congress may by law provide for the case of the death of any of the persons from whom the House of Representatives may choose a President whenever the right of choice shall have devolved upon them, and for the case of the death of any of the persons from whom the Senate may choose a Vice President whenever the right of choice shall have devolved upon them.

Section 5. Sections 1 and 2 shall take effect on the 15th day of October following the ratification of this article.

Section 6. The article shall be inoperative unless it shall have been ratified as an amendment to the Constitution by the legislatures of three-fourths of the several States within seven years from the date of its submission.

Amendment XXI [1933]

Section 1. The eighteenth article of amendment to the Constitution of the United States is hereby repealed.

Section 2. The transportation or importation into any State, Territory, or possession of the United States for delivery or use therein of intoxicating liquors, in violation of the laws thereof, is hereby prohibited.

Section 3. This article shall be inoperative unless it shall have been ratified as an amendment to the Constitution by conventions in the several States, as provided in the Constitution, within seven years from the date of the submission hereof to the States by the Congress.

Amendment XXII [1951]

No person shall be elected to the office of the President more than twice, and no person who has held the office of President, or acted as President, for more than two years of a term to which some other person was elected President shall be elected to the office of the President more than once.

But this Article shall not apply to any person holding the office of President when this Article was proposed by the Congress, and shall not prevent any person who may be holding the office of President, or acting as President, during the term within which this Article becomes operative from holding the office of President or acting as President during the remainder of such term.

Amendment XXIII [1961]

Section 1. The District constituting the seat of Government of the United States shall appoint in such manner as the Congress may direct:

A number of electors of President and Vice President equal to the whole number of Senators and Representatives in Congress to which the District would be entitled if it were a State, but in no event more than the least populous State: they shall be in addition to those appointed by the States, but they shall be considered, for the purposes of the election of President and Vice President, to be electors appointed by a State: and they shall meet in the District and perform such duties as provided by the twelfth article of amendment.

Section 2. The Congress shall have the power to enforce this article by appropriate legislation.

Amendment XXIV [1964]

Section 1. The right of citizens of the United States to vote in any primary or other election for President or Vice President, for electors for President or Vice President, or for Senator or Representative in Congress, shall not be denied or abridged by the United States or any State by reason of failure to pay any poll tax or other tax.

Section 2. The Congress shall have the power to enforce this article by appropriate legislation.

Amendment XXV [1967]

Section 1. In case of the removal of the President from office or his death or resignation, the Vice President shall become President.

Section 2. Whenever there is a vacancy in the office of the Vice President, the President shall nominate a Vice President who shall take the office upon confirmation by a majority vote of both houses of Congress.

Section 3. Whenever the President transmits to the President pro tempore of the Senate and the Speaker of the House of Representatives his written declaration that he is unable to discharge the powers and duties of his office, and until he transmits to them a written declaration to the contrary, such powers and duties shall be discharged by the Vice President as Acting President.

Section 4. Whenever the Vice President and a majority of either the principal officers of the executive departments, or of such other body as Congress may by law provide, transmit to the President pro tempore of the Senate and the Speaker of the House of Representatives their written declaration that the President is unable to discharge the powers and duties of his office, the Vice President shall immediately assume the powers and duties of the office as Acting President.

Thereafter, when the President transmits to the President pro tempore of the Senate and the Speaker of the House of Representatives his written declaration that no inability exists, he shall resume the powers and duties of his office unless the Vice President and a majority of either the principal officers of the executive departments, or of such other body as Congress may by law provide, transmit within four days to the President pro tempore of the Senate and the speaker of the House of Representatives their written declaration that the President is unable to discharge the powers and duties of his office. Thereupon Congress shall decide the issue, assembling within 48 hours for that purpose if not in session. If the Congress, within 21 days after receipt of the latter written declaration, or, if Congress is not in session, within 21 days after Congress is required to assemble, determines by two-thirds vote of both houses that the President is unable to discharge the powers and duties of his office, the Vice President shall continue to discharge the same as Acting President: otherwise, the President shall resume the powers and duties of his office.

Amendment XXVI [1971]

Section 1. The rights of citizens of the United States, who are 18 years of age or older, to vote shall not be denied or abridged by the United States or any state on account of age.

Section 2. The Congress shall have the power to enforce this article by appropriate legislation.

PRESIDENTIAL ELECTIONS

Year	Candidates	Party	Popular vote	Electoral vote
1789	**George Washington**			69
	John Adams			34
	Others			35
1792	**George Washington**			132
	John Adams			77
	George Clinton			50
	Others			5
1796	**John Adams**	Federalist		71
	Thomas Jefferson	Republican		68
	Thomas Pinckney	Federalist		59
	Aaron Burr	Republican		30
	Others			48
1800	**Thomas Jefferson**	Republican		73
	Aaron Burr	Republican		73
	John Adams	Federalist		65
	Charles C. Pinckney	Federalist		64
1804	**Thomas Jefferson**	Republican		162
	Charles C. Pinckney	Federalist		14
1808	**James Madison**	Republican		122
	Charles C. Pinckney	Federalist		47
	George Clinton	Independent-Republican		6
1812	**James Madison**	Republican		128
	DeWitt Clinton	Federalist		89
1816	**James Monroe**	Republican		183
	Rufus King	Federalist		34
1820	**James Monroe**	Democratic-Republican		231
	John Quincy Adams	Independent-Republican		1
1824	**John Quincy Adams**	Republican	108,740	84 (elected by the House of Representatives)
	Andrew Jackson	Republican	153,544	99
	Henry Clay	Republican	47,136	37
	William H. Crawford	Republican	46,618	41
1828	**Andrew Jackson**	Democratic	647,286	178
	John Quincy Adams	National Republican	508,064	83
1832	**Andrew Jackson**	Democratic	688,000	219
	Henry Clay	National Republican	530,000	49
	William Wirt	Anti-Masonic	255,000	7
	John Floyd	National Republican		11
1836	**Martin Van Buren**	Democratic	762,678	170
	William H. Harrison	Whig	549,000	73
	Hugh L. White	Whig	146,000	26
	Daniel Webster	Whig	41,000	14
1840	**William H. Harrison**	Whig	1,275,017	234
	Martin Van Buren	Democratic	1,128,702	60
1844	**James K. Polk**	Democratic	1,337,243	170
	Henry Clay	Whig	1,299,068	105
	James G. Birney	Liberty	62,300	
1848	**Zachary Taylor**	Whig	1,360,101	163
	Lewis Cass	Democratic	1,220,544	127
	Martin Van Buren	Free-Soil	291,263	

Year	Candidates	Party	Popular vote	Electoral vote
1852	**Franklin Pierce**	Democratic	1,601,274	254
	Winfield Scott	Whig	1,386,580	42
1856	**James Buchanan**	Democratic	1,838,169	174
	John C. Frémont	Republican	1,335,264	114
	Millard Fillmore	American	874,534	8
1860	**Abraham Lincoln**	Republican	1,866,452	180
	Stephen A. Douglas	Democratic	1,375,157	12
	John C. Breckinridge	Democratic	847,953	72
	John Bell	Constitutional Union	592,631	39
1864	**Abraham Lincoln**	Republican	2,213,665	212
	George B. McClellan	Democratic	1,805,237	21
1868	**Ulysses S. Grant**	Republican	3,012,833	214
	Horatio Seymour	Democratic	2,703,249	80
1872	**Ulysses S. Grant**	Republican	3,596,745	286
	Horace Greeley	Democratic	2,843,446	66
1876	**Rutherford B. Hayes**	Republican	4,036,572	185
	Samuel J. Tilden	Democratic	4,284,020	184
1880	**James A. Garfield**	Republican	4,449,053	214
	Winfield S. Hancock	Democratic	4,442,032	155
	James B. Weaver	Greenback-Labor	308,578	
1884	**Grover Cleveland**	Democratic	4,874,986	219
	James G. Blaine	Republican	4,851,981	182
	Benjamin F. Butler	Greenback-Labor	175,370	
1888	**Benjamin Harrison**	Republican	5,444,337	233
	Grover Cleveland	Democratic	5,540,050	168
1892	**Grover Cleveland**	Democratic	5,554,414	277
	Benjamin Harrison	Republican	5,190,802	145
	James B. Weaver	People's	1,027,329	22
1896	**William McKinley**	Republican	7,104,779	271
	William J. Bryan	Democratic; Populist	6,502,925	176
1900	**William McKinley**	Republican	7,219,530	292
	William J. Bryan	Democratic; Populist	6,356,734	155
1904	**Theodore Roosevelt**	Republican	7,628,834	336
	Alton B. Parker	Democratic	5,084,401	140
	Eugene V. Debs	Socialist	402,460	
1908	**William H. Taft**	Republican	7,679,006	321
	William J. Bryan	Democratic	6,409,106	162
	Eugene V. Debs	Socialist	420,820	
1912	**Woodrow Wilson**	Democratic	6,293,454	435
	Theodore Roosevelt	Progressive	4,119,538	88
	William H. Taft	Republican	3,484,980	8
	Eugene V. Debs	Socialist	897,011	
1916	**Woodrow Wilson**	Democratic	9,129,606	277
	Charles E. Hughes	Republican	8,538,221	254
1920	**Warren G. Harding**	Republican	16,152,200	404
	James M. Cox	Democratic	9,147,353	127
	Eugene V. Debs	Socialist	919,799	
1924	**Calvin Coolidge**	Republican	15,725,016	382
	John W. Davis	Democratic	8,385,586	136
	Robert M. LaFollette	Progressive	4,822,856	13
1928	**Herbert C. Hoover**	Republican	21,392,190	444
	Alfred E. Smith	Democratic	15,016,443	87
1932	**Franklin D. Roosevelt**	Democratic	22,809,638	472
	Herbert C. Hoover	Republican	15,758,901	59
	Norman Thomas	Socialist	881,951	
1936	**Franklin D. Roosevelt**	Democratic	27,751,612	523
	Alfred M. Landon	Republican	16,618,913	8
	William Lemke	Union	891,858	
1940	**Franklin D. Roosevelt**	Democratic	27,243,466	449
	Wendell L. Willkie	Republican	22,304,755	82

Year	Candidates	Party	Popular vote	Electoral vote
1944	**Franklin D. Roosevelt**	Democratic	25,602,505	432
	Thomas E. Dewey	Republican	22,006,278	99
1948	**Harry S. Truman**	Democratic	24,105,812	303
	Thomas E. Dewey	Republican	21,970,065	189
	J. Strom Thurmond	States' Rights	1,169,063	39
	Henry A. Wallace	Progressive	1,157,172	
1952	**Dwight D. Eisenhower**	Republican	33,936,234	442
	Adlai E. Stevenson	Democratic	27,314,992	89
1956	**Dwight D. Eisenhower**	Republican	35,590,472	457
	Adlai E. Stevenson	Democratic	26,022,752	73
1960	**John F. Kennedy**	Democratic	34,227,096	303
	Richard M. Nixon	Republican	34,108,546	219
1964	**Lyndon B. Johnson**	Democratic	43,126,233	486
	Barry M. Goldwater	Republican	27,174,989	53
1968	**Richard M. Nixon**	Republican	31,783,783	301
	Hubert H. Humphrey	Democratic	31,271,839	191
	George C. Wallace	Amer. Independent	9,899,557	46
1972	**Richard M. Nixon**	Republican	47,168,963	520
	George S. McGovern	Democratic	29,169,615	17
	John Hospers	Republican (noncandidate)		1
1976	**Jimmy Carter**	Democratic	40,827,292	297
	Gerald R. Ford	Republican	39,146,157	240
	Ronald Reagan	Republican (noncandidate)		1
1980	**Ronald Reagan**	Republican	43,899,248	489
	Jimmy Carter	Democratic	35,481,435	49
	John Anderson	Independent	5,719,437	

DATE OF STATEHOOD

Delaware	December 7, 1787	Michigan	January 16, 1837
Pennsylvania	December 12, 1787	Florida	March 3, 1845
New Jersey	December 18, 1787	Texas	December 29, 1845
Georgia	January 2, 1788	Iowa	December 28, 1846
Connecticut	January 9, 1788	Wisconsin	May 29, 1848
Massachusetts	February 6, 1788	California	September 9, 1850
Maryland	April 28, 1788	Minnesota	May 11, 1858
South Carolina	May 23, 1788	Oregon	February 14, 1859
New Hampshire	June 21, 1788	Kansas	January 29, 1861
Virginia	June 25, 1788	West Virginia	June 19, 1863
New York	July 26, 1788	Nevada	October 31, 1864
North Carolina	November 21, 1789	Nebraska	March 1, 1867
Rhode Island	May 29, 1790	Colorado	August 1, 1876
Vermont	March 4, 1791	North Dakota	November 2, 1889
Kentucky	June 1, 1792	South Dakota	November 2, 1889
Tennessee	June 1, 1796	Montana	November 8, 1889
Ohio	March 1, 1803	Washington	November 11, 1889
Louisiana	April 30, 1812	Idaho	July 3, 1890
Indiana	December 11, 1816	Wyoming	July 10, 1890
Mississippi	December 10, 1817	Utah	January 4, 1896
Illinois	December 3, 1818	Oklahoma	November 16, 1907
Alabama	December 14, 1819	New Mexico	January 6, 1912
Maine	March 15, 1820	Arizona	February 14, 1912
Missouri	August 10, 1821	Alaska	January 3, 1959
Arkansas	June 15, 1836	Hawaii	August 21, 1959

POPULATION OF THE UNITED STATES

1790	3,929,214	1890	62,947,714
1800	5,308,483	1900	75,994,575
1810	7,239,881	1910	91,972,266
1820	9,638,453	1920	105,710,620
1830	12,860,692	1930	122,775,046
1840	17,063,353	1940	131,669,275
1850	23,191,876	1950	150,697,361
1860	31,443,321	1960	179,323,175
1870	38,558,371	1970	204,765,770
1880	50,155,783	1980	226,504,825

TERRITORIAL EXPANSION

Louisiana Purchase	1803	Gadsden Purchase	1853	Guam	1899
Florida	1819	Alaska	1867	Amer. Samoa	1900
Texas	1845	Hawaii	1898	Canal Zone	1904
Oregon	1846	The Philippines	1898–1946	U.S. Virgin Islands	1917
Mexican Cession	1848	Puerto Rico	1899	Pacific Islands Trust Terr.	1947

900

903